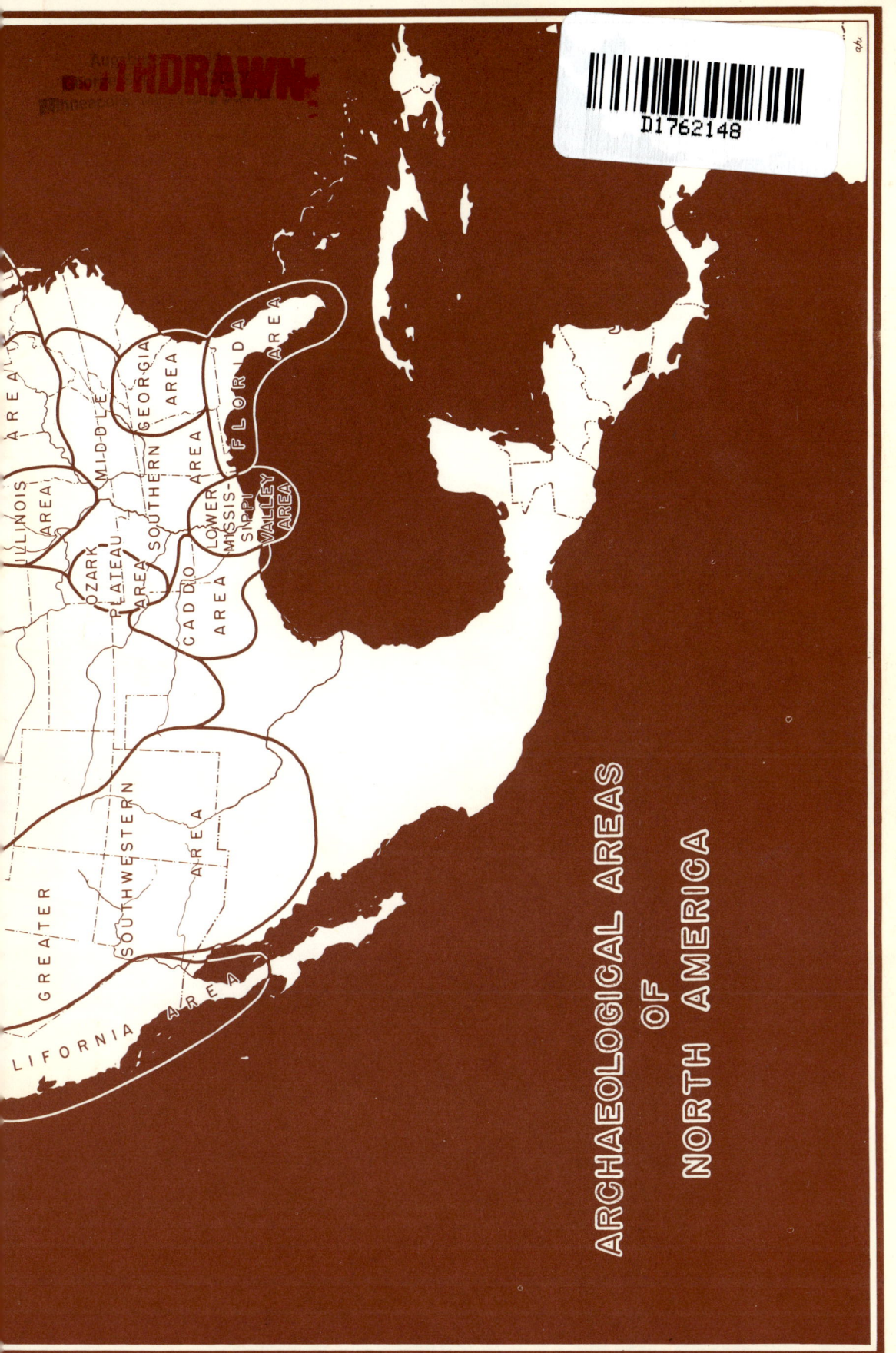

HEW Grant Purchase
CLIC 1973

Indians before Columbus

Cliff Palace, Mesa Verde National Park, Colorado
A village of the Pueblo III period, built A.D. 1175–1273, Anasazi culture. (Courtesy National Park Service.)

PAUL S. MARTIN · GEORGE I. QUIMBY · DONALD COLLIER

Indians before Columbus

Twenty Thousand Years of North American History Revealed by Archeology

THE UNIVERSITY OF CHICAGO PRESS
CHICAGO AND LONDON

*A CONTRIBUTION OF THE
CHICAGO NATURAL HISTORY MUSEUM*

The University of Chicago Press, Chicago & London
The University of Toronto Press, Toronto 5, Canada

© 1947 by The University of Chicago. All rights reserved
Published 1947. Ninth Impression 1967. Printed in the
United States of America

E
61
M36

PREFACE

THIS book has been written for the interested layman and for students taking introductory courses in anthropology. It is not intended as a general reference book for professional anthropologists.

We have been compelled to omit certain facets of culture and certain geographical areas because of lack of space or poverty of data. For example, a great stretch of Canada from the St. Lawrence to the Yukon River, much of Alaska, and the Middle Atlantic Seaboard have not been included for the reasons just given.

Some readers may object because we have simplified; because we have sometimes used the terms "culture" and "civilization" interchangeably; because of our arbitrary treatment of classificatory schemes; or because we have condensed our data and have also fitted them to a chronology. Others may object to the interpretations and conjectures that we have freely presented. Some of these interpretations differ from those of other anthropologists. This does not mean that we are right and that they are wrong. We think that the reconstructions which we have presented are justified by the data we possess; we have tried to tell the story of the Indians by piecing together the bits of available information. We make no apology for our particular treatment of these matters or for the chance we have taken in making reconstructions. Whenever we depart from facts, we freely say so by using such words as "probably," "guesses," and "conjectures." The data we have presented are accurate, and we have tried to set forth the facts as interestingly as possible.

From our contacts with interested laymen and with beginning students, we believe that we have learned what they want to know about archeology. This desire for knowledge may be divided up into four inquiries:

1. How long have the Indians been in the New World?
2. Who built the mounds, shell middens, cliff dwellings, etc.?
3. How long ago were they built?
4. What became of the builders?

v

117351

We do not know the answers to all these questions; but we have tried to answer some of them. In addition, we have attempted to go deeper into the subject by pointing out the purposes of archeology and, indirectly, what lessons may be learned from the trials and errors, accomplishments and failures, of the Indians.

For errors in this book we assume collective responsibility. But, without the aid of friends, it would never have come to fruition. Miss Lillian Ross, associate editor of scientific publications, Chicago Natural History Museum, has edited and styled much of the manuscript. Mrs. Donald Collier, anthropologist in her own right, has also read much of the manuscript for factual errors, inconsistencies, and style. Miss Agnes McNary, secretary to the Department of Anthropology at the Museum, added portions to, and helped recast parts of, chapter 10. Mrs. J. N. Emerson, assistant secretary, made available to us her editorial experience and revised many portions of the manuscript. Mr. Gustaf Dalstrom, staff artist in the Department of Anthropology at the Museum, executed the drawings which are scattered throughout the text.

To Dr. Fay-Cooper Cole, chairman of the Department of Anthropology, University of Chicago, we owe a debt of gratitude for permitting Mr. Alfred Harris, cartographer of the Department, to compose the maps and the charts used herein; and to Mr. Harris, our thanks for undertaking a difficult job.

For their generosity in allowing us access to their unpublished data and ideas we are indebted to Philip Drucker, of the Smithsonian Institution; Charles Fairbanks, of the Ocmulgee National Monument, Macon, Georgia; James A. Ford, of Louisiana State University; James B. Griffin, of the University of Michigan; Robert F. Heizer, of the University of California at Los Angeles; Richard MacNeish, of the University of Chicago; and W. C. McKern, of the Milwaukee Public Museum.

We are especially happy that this work is one of the first fruits of the new co-operative relationship between the Chicago Natural History Museum and the University of Chicago. Director Clifford C. Gregg and President Stanley Field of the Museum made it possible to write during Museum time; and the Press of the University of Chicago undertook to publish our manuscript.

Unless otherwise noted, all illustrations are published by the courtesy of the Chicago Natural History Museum.

Chicago Natural History Museum

Paul S. Martin
Chief Curator, Department of Anthropology

George I. Quimby
*Curator of Exhibits, Department
of Anthropology*

Donald Collier
*Curator of South American Archeology and
Ethnology, Department of Anthropology*

TABLE OF CONTENTS

LIST OF ILLUSTRATIONS xvii
GLOSSARY xxi

PART I. BACKGROUND

1. WHAT IS ARCHEOLOGY? 3
    How the Archeologist Works 5
    Methods of Dating 9
    Summary 13
2. ORIGIN OF THE AMERICAN INDIANS 15
    Who Discovered America? 15
    Speculations concerning the Origin of the Indians 15
    The Origin of the Indians 16
    Summary 22
3. FALLACIES CONCERNING THE AMERICAN INDIAN 23

PART II. ARTS AND INDUSTRIES

4. OBJECTS OF STONE 29
    Kinds of Stone 29
    Processes of Manufacture 29
    Kinds of Stone Objects Manufactured and Their Uses . . 34
5. OBJECTS OF COPPER 40
    Mining 40
    Manufacture of Copper Tools and Ornaments 42
6. OBJECTS OF BONE AND OF SHELL 47
    Bone Work 47
    Shell Work 48
7. POTTERY 50
    Distribution 50
    Importance of Pottery to the Archeologist 50
    Manufacture 51
    Prehistoric Mending 60
8. THE TEXTILE ARTS—BASKETRY AND CLOTH 61
9. TRADE AND COMMERCE 66
    General Discussion 66
    The Southwest 69
    Eastern United States 72
    The Plains 73

TABLE OF CONTENTS

    California 73
    Northwest Coast and Plateau 74
    The Arctic 75

PART III. THE EARLIEST INDIANS

10. ANTIQUITY OF THE AMERICAN INDIANS AND THE FIRST AMERICAN CULTURES 79
    Evidence of Antiquity and Routes of Migration 79
    The Folsom Culture 83
    The Cochise Culture 85
        The Sulphur Spring Period 87
        The Chiricahua Period 88
        The San Pedro Period 89
        Conjectures 90
    Summary 91
    What Happened Next? 92

PART IV. THE SOUTHWEST

11. GENERAL REMARKS ON THE SOUTHWESTERN AREA 97
    Geography 97
    Race 97
    Language 99

12. THE ANASAZI CULTURE 101
    Introduction 101
    The Basket Maker Period 103
    The Modified Basket Maker Period 111
    Pueblo I 120
    Pueblo II 124
    Pueblo III 129
    Pueblo IV 149
    End of Pueblo IV and First Contact with Europeans . . . 156
    The Navaho Indians 157
    Pueblo V 159

13. THE HOHOKAM CULTURE 168
    Area and General Remarks 168
    The Pioneer Period 169
    The Colonial Period 174
    The Sedentary Period 182
    The Classic Period 188
    Conjectures 195

14. THE MOGOLLON-MIMBRES CULTURE 198
    Area and General Remarks 198
    The Pine Lawn Period 200
    The Georgetown Period 206

TABLE OF CONTENTS

The San Francisco Period	206
The Three Circle Period	207
The Mimbres Period	210
The Chihuahua Periods	214

15. AREAS PERIPHERAL TO THE SOUTHWEST 218
- General Remarks 218
- Southwestern Texas 218
- The Maravillas Culture 219
- The Big Bend Cave Culture 219
- The Bravo Valley Culture 221
- Northern Utah 223
- The Black Rock Cave Culture 223
- The Puebloid Culture 224
- The Promontory Culture 226
- Southeastern Nevada 227
- Southeastern Oregon 228

PART V. EASTERN NORTH AMERICA

16. SUMMARY OF THE ARCHEOLOGICAL AREAS OF EASTERN NORTH AMERICA 231
- People 231
- Language 232
- Chronological Stages 232
- Dating Method 238

17. THE NORTHEASTERN AREA 239
- Introduction 239
- The Lamoka Culture 240
- The Frontenac Culture 241
- The Laurentian I Culture 243
- The Laurentian II Culture 246
- The Early Coastal Culture 247
- The Orient Culture 248
- The Middlesex Culture 248
- The New York Hopewell Culture 250
- The Point Peninsula Culture 251
- The Owasco Culture 254
- The Old Iroquois Culture 255
- Summary 258

18. THE OHIO AREA 259
- Introduction 259
- The Indian Knoll Culture 259
- The Glacial Kame Culture 262
- The Adena Culture 263
- The Hopewell Culture 267
- The Intrusive Mound Culture 278
- The Younge Culture 280
- The Whittlesey Culture 281

TABLE OF CONTENTS

The Middle Mississippi Culture in the Ohio Area	283
The Fort Ancient Culture	284
Summary	287

19. THE ILLINOIS AREA — 289
- Introduction — 289
- The Faulkner Culture — 289
- The Baumer Culture — 290
- The Red Ocher Culture — 291
- The Morton Culture — 292
- The Hopewell Culture of Illinois — 293
- The Lewis Culture — 294
- The Middle Mississippi Culture in Illinois — 294
- The Tampico Culture — 295
- The Fisher Culture — 295
- Summary — 295

20. THE WISCONSIN-MINNESOTA AREA — 297
- Introduction — 297
- The Browns Valley Find — 298
- The Old Copper Culture — 299
- The Effigy Mound Culture — 303
- The Wisconsin Hopewell Culture — 305
- The Laurel Culture — 307
- The Mille Lacs Culture — 309
- The Keshena Culture — 310
- The Clam River Culture — 312
- The Aztalan Culture — 313
- The Oneota Culture — 315
- Summary — 317

21. THE PLAINS AREA — 319
- Introduction — 319
- The Old Signal Butte Culture — 320
- The Sterns Creek Culture — 322
- The Mira Creek Culture — 323
- The Kansas Hopewell Culture — 325
- The Upper Republican Culture — 326
- The Nebraska Culture — 328
- The Dismal River Culture — 331
- Other Cultures of the Plains Area — 333
- The Plains and the Southwest — 333
- Summary — 334

22. THE OZARK PLATEAU AREA — 337
- Introduction — 337
- The Proto–Bluff Dweller Culture — 338
- The Ozark Bluff Dweller Culture — 339
- The Top-Layer Culture — 342
- Summary — 343

23. The Middle Southern Area ... 344
Introduction ... 344
The Lauderdale Culture ... 345
The Alexander Culture ... 347
The Candy Creek Culture ... 348
The Hamilton Culture ... 350
The Copena Culture ... 351
The Middle Mississippi Culture ... 353
The Southern Death Cult ... 361
Summary ... 366

24. Georgia ... 369
Introduction ... 369
The Early Macon Culture ... 369
The Savannah River Culture ... 371
The Deptford Culture ... 374
The Wilmington Culture ... 375
The Swift Creek Culture ... 376
The Savannah Culture ... 378
The Irene Culture ... 380
The Macon Plateau Culture ... 382
The Lamar Culture ... 385
The Etowah Culture ... 386
The Ocmulgee Fields Culture ... 387
Summary ... 388

25. The Florida Area ... 390
Introduction ... 390
The Tick Island Culture ... 391
The Deptford Culture ... 391
The Santa Rosa–Swift Creek Culture ... 392
The Crystal River Culture ... 392
The Weeden Island Culture ... 393
The Fort Walton Culture ... 394
The Key Marco Culture ... 395
Summary ... 398

26. The Lower Mississippi Valley ... 399
Introduction ... 399
The Copell Culture ... 400
The Tchefuncte Culture ... 401
The Poverty Point Culture ... 404
The Marksville Culture ... 406
The Troyville Culture ... 409
The Coles Creek Culture ... 411
The Plaquemine Culture ... 415
The Natchezan Culture ... 417
Summary ... 419

27. THE CADDO AREA	421
Introduction	421
The Caddo Culture	421

PART VI. THE PACIFIC SLOPE

28. CALIFORNIA	427
Introduction	427
Northern California	428
Central California	428
Southern California	436
Conjectures	438
29. THE PLATEAU AREA	442
Introduction	442
The Upper Columbia Region	444
The Thompson River Region	452
The Middle Columbia Region	455
The Snake-Clearwater Region	459
Conjectures	460
30. THE NORTHWEST COAST	462
Introduction	462
The Prehistoric Culture	463
Conjectures	469

PART VII. THE FAR NORTH

31. THE NORTHWESTERN ESKIMO AREA	473
Introduction	473
The Original Eskimo Culture	473
The Okvik Culture	474
The Old Bering Sea Culture	477
The Ipiutak Culture	481
The Punuk Culture	484
The Birnirk Culture	486
The Post-Punuk Culture	487
Summary	489
32. THE SOUTHWESTERN ESKIMO AREA	490
Introduction	490
The Early Aleut Culture	490
The Middle Aleut Culture	493
The Late Aleut Culture	495
The Pre-Koniag Culture	496
The Koniag Culture	498
The Early Kachemak Bay Culture	499
The Middle Kachemak Bay Culture	500
The Late Kachemak Bay Culture	501
Summary	502

TABLE OF CONTENTS

33. THE EASTERN ESKIMO AREA 503
    Introduction 503
    The Dorset Culture 503
    The Thule Culture 505
    The Inugsuk Culture 508
    Summary 509

PART VIII. CONCLUSION

34. CHRONOLOGY AND CORRELATION OF SEQUENCES OF CULTURES . . . 513

BIBLIOGRAPHY

BIBLIOGRAPHY 523

INDEX

INDEX 547

LIST OF ILLUSTRATIONS

Cliff Palace, Built a.d. 1175-1273. Mesa Verde National Park, Colorado. Anasazi Culture . . . . *Frontispiece*
1. Stripping the Layers of Dirt from an Ancient Anasazi Village, Colorado 6
2. Model of an Indian Mound in Illinois 7
3. Dating a Prehistoric Beam 12
4. Navaho Man 18
5. Manufacture of Stone Artifacts 30
6. Methods of Drilling 32
7. Types of Projectile Points of Stone 35
8. Types of Pecked and Ground Tools of Stone 36
9. Hopi Woman Making Pottery 52
10. Principal North American Pottery Shapes 55
11. Weaving Techniques 64
12. Stone Tools, Cochise Culture 88
13. Longheaded and Roundheaded Skulls, Anasazi Culture . . 98
14. Grave-Offerings, Anasazi Culture 107
15. Anasazi Sandal Types 109
16. Restoration of a Modified Basket Maker Village, Anasazi Culture 112
17. Cooking Pottery, Anasazi Culture 114
18. Lino Black-on-Gray Pottery Bowl and Notched Pebble-Axes, Anasazi Culture 115
19. Abajo Red-on-Orange Bowls, Anasazi Culture 116
20. Anasazi Metates 118
21. Kana-a Black-on-White Pottery, Anasazi Culture . . . 122
22. Red Mesa Black-on-White Pottery, Anasazi Culture . . 126
23. Black Mesa Black-on-White Pottery, Anasazi Culture . . 127
24. Mancos Black-on-White Pottery, Anasazi Culture . . . 128
25. Reconstruction of a Pueblo III Village, Anasazi Culture . . 131
26. Anasazi Masonry 132
27. Restoration of Room in Chaco-like Village, Anasazi Culture . 133
28. Restoration of a Kiva, Anasazi Culture 134
29. Cross-Section and Ground Plan of a Kiva of Mesa Verde Type, Anasazi Culture 135
30. A Great Kiva, Anasazi Culture 136
31. Chaco Black-on-White Pottery, Anasazi Culture . . . 138
32. Mesa Verde Black-on-White Pottery, Anasazi Culture . . 138
33. Sagi Black-on-White Pottery, Anasazi Culture 139
34. Bone Tools, Anasazi Culture 141
35. Jeddito Black-on-Yellow Pottery, Anasazi Culture . . . 152

36. Sikyatki Polychrome Pottery, Anasazi Culture	152
37. Salado Polychrome Pottery, Anasazi Culture	153
38. Four-Mile Polychrome Pottery, Anasazi Culture	153
39. Heshotauthla Polychrome Pottery, Anasazi Culture	154
40. Oraibi, Arizona, Anasazi Culture	163
41. Sweetwater Red-on-Gray Pottery, Hohokam Culture	171
42. Pottery Figurines, Hohokam Culture	173
43. Gila Butte Red-on-Buff Pottery, Hohokam Culture	176
44. Santa Cruz Red-on-Buff Pottery, Hohokam Culture	176
45. Santa Cruz Red-on-Buff Pottery, Hohokam Culture	177
46. Santa Cruz Red-on-Buff Pottery, Hohokam Culture	177
47. Bowl of Polished Quartzite, Hohokam Culture	180
48. Bowl of Carved Stone, Hohokam Culture	180
49. Palettes of Carved Stone, Hohokam Culture	181
50. Sacaton Red-on-Buff Pottery and Remains of Cremation, Hohokam Culture	183
51. Sacaton Red-on-Buff Pottery, Hohokam Culture	183
52. Gila Plain Pottery, Hohokam Culture	184
53. Pottery Figurines, Hohokam Culture	185
54. Stone Bowls, Hohokam Culture	186
55. Effigy Vessels of Stone, Hohokam Culture	186
56. Effigy Vessel of Stone, Hohokam Culture	187
57. Shell Ornaments, Hohokam Culture	188
58. Cotton Poncho, Hohokam Culture	195
59. Shell Ornaments, Hohokam Culture	196
60. Charts Comparing Various Elements of Mogollon, Anasazi, and Hohokam Cultures	199
61. Mogollon Pit-House	201
62. Cross-Section and Ground Plan of Mogollon Pit-House	202
63. Mogollon Undecorated Pottery	203
64. Mogollon Stone Tools	204
65. Mogollon Choppers of Stone	204
66. A Mogollon Burial	205
67. Mimbres Black-on-White Pottery, Mogollon-Mimbres Culture	212
68. Chihuahua Pottery, Mogollon-Mimbres Culture	216
69. Laurentian Types of Tools and Weapons of Stone	245
70. Clay Tobacco Pipes and Pottery of the Iroquois Culture	257
71. Construction of Adena House	264
72. Effigy Tobacco Pipe of Stone, Adena Culture	266
73. Hopewell Pottery	269
74. Tools and Weapons of the Hopewell Indians of Ohio	270
75. Effigy Tobacco Pipe of Stone	271
76. Hopewell Ornaments	272
77. Hopewell Man	273
78. Ornaments of Sheet Copper for Attachment to Robes of the Hopewell Indians of Ohio	274
79. Ornaments of Sheet Mica Made by the Hopewell Indians of Ohio	275

LIST OF ILLUSTRATIONS

80. Ornament of Sheet Copper, Probably Representing the Head of a Serpent	276
81. Hopewell Ornaments of Sheet Copper	276
82. Hopewell Panpipes of Bone and Copper	277
83. Copper Weapons and Tools of the Old Copper Culture	301
84. Stone Axes and Cord-marked Pottery Jar from Wisconsin	304
85. Construction of Middle Mississippi House	355
86. Middle Mississippi Pottery	357
87. Middle Mississippi Pottery	358
88. Painted and Effigy Pottery of the Middle Mississippi Culture	359
89. Shell Gorgets of the Southern Death Cult	364
90. Pottery of the Southern Death Cult	365
91. Sacred Paraphernalia of the Southern Death Cult	365
92. Stone Idol of the Southern Death Cult	366
93. Pottery of the Savannah River Culture	372
94. Tools, Utensils, and Weapons of the Key Marco Culture	396
95. Key Marco Art	397
96. Tchefuncte Pottery	402
97. Tchefuncte Tools, Utensils, and Weapons	403
98. Pottery of the Marksville Culture	407
99. Marksville Tools and Ornaments	408
100. Reconstruction of a Coles Creek Village	412
101. Coles Creek Pottery	413
102. Caddo Pottery	423
103. Implements from Humboldt Bay, California	429
104. Succession of Implement Types in Central California	431
105. Steatite Objects from the Santa Barbara Region and San Nicolas Island	435
106. Stone Projectile Points, Tools, and Pipes from the Upper Columbia Region	447
107. Tools, Projectile Points, and Ornament from the Upper Columbia Region	448
108. Fish Spears from the Plateau	449
109. Pit-House of Thompson River Type	453
110. Carved Bone Implement from the Dalles, Columbia River	458
111. Northwest Coast House Forms	465
112. Canoes of the Northwest Coast Indians	466
113. Tools and Weapons of the Northwest Coast	467
114. Decorated Objects of the Okvik Eskimo	476
115. Art of the Old Bering Sea Eskimo	479
116. Ipiutak Weapons and Ornaments	482
117. Art of the Punuk Eskimo	485
118. Tools and Weapons of the Early Aleut	492
119. Middle Aleut Pottery Bowl	493
120. Middle Aleut Stone Lamps	494
121. Koniag Hat of Wood with Ivory Ornaments	498
122. Chronological Chart of North America	514

GLOSSARY

Any technical term which is completely described in the text is not included herein but may be found by consulting the Index.

Adz.—A cutting tool with the plane of the blade set at right angles to the handle, thus differing from an ax.

Annealing copper.—The process of heating copper and then plunging it into cold water in order to make it tougher, more elastic, and less brittle.

Arrowhead.—A small projectile point often arbitrarily defined as a point less than $2\frac{1}{2}$ inches long. Specimens longer than this may have served as knives or spearheads. *See* Projectile point; Spearhead.

Artifact.—Any object manufactured by human beings, applied especially to distinguish between natural objects and those of human workmanship.

Atlatl, or spear-thrower.—A device or implement that makes it possible to hurl a spear or lance farther and with greater speed than with the arm only. The spear lies on the atlatl, which functions as a mechanical extension of the arm and acts as an extra joint.

Ax, fluted stone.—A sharp-edged cutting implement with one or more parallel grooves or flutings, which may be longitudinal or diagonal. These flutings served no practical purpose so far as is known and may have been ornamental.

Ax, stone.—A sharp-edged cutting implement made from some hard, resistant stone and provided with a groove for hafting.

Bannerstone.—A perforated object of polished stone of any of a variety of forms. Some were weights for spear-throwers; others had some ceremonial function the exact nature of which is unknown.

Bar-shaped stone.—A stone probably used as a spear-thrower weight.

Birdstone.—A bannerstone shaped like a bird or an animal.

Boatstone.—A boat-shaped stone probably used as a spear-thrower weight.

Bolas.—A hunting weapon consisting of two or more balls of stone, bone, or ivory attached to the end of a cord by means of shorter cords. It was used to entangle the legs of animals or the wings of birds.

Broadheaded.—*See* Roundheaded.

Celt.—An ungrooved ax of stone or metal.

Chert.—A kind of flint.

Chunkeystone.—A circular stone ranging in size from 1 to 8 inches in diameter and from 1 to 6 inches in thickness, with flat, convex, or concave faces. It was used in a game called *chungke, chenco,* or *chunkey.*

Conchoidal.—Having shell-shaped depressions and elevations.

Core-implement.—A tool made by striking flakes from a piece of rock by the percussion method. The remaining core was the implement.

Discoidal stone.—*See* Chunkeystone.

Draw knife.—A blade with a handle at each end.

Ear-spool.—A spool-shaped ornament worn in the ear.

Extended burial.—A mode of burial in which the body is stretched out flat.

Fishgig.—A fish spear with two or more barbed prongs.

Flake-tool.—A flake struck from a rock core and used as a tool.

Flexed burial.—A method of burial in which the body is placed in the grave with knees drawn up to the chin.

Flint.—An opaque, indistinctly crystalline quartz, dark gray or black in color.

Full-grooved ax or maul.—An ax or maul with a groove completely encircling it.

Gorget.—An ornament of stone usually worn over the chest.

Guilloche.—A pattern made by interlacing curved lines.

Haft.—A handle; to supply with a handle.

Handstone.—A stone used with a milling-stone for crushing and grinding wild seeds. The action of the handstone is not so rigidly confined as that of a mano because it may be moved round and round as well as forward and backward on the milling-stone.

Hardness of minerals.—See Scale of hardness.

Hemiconical.—In the shape of a half-cone.

"Killed" pottery.—Pottery with a hole punched in it to release the spirit of the vessel.

Lanceolate.—Rather narrow, tapering to a point at the apex and sometimes at the base also.

Longheaded (dolichocranic) skull.—A skull having a cranial index of 74.9 or less. The formula for obtaining this index is Breadth of skull/Length of skull $\times$ 100.

Mano.—The upper part of an Indian mill, generally used to grind grains. *See also* Handstone.

Metate.—The bottom part of an Indian mill, generally used to grind grains and usually associated with agriculture.

Midden.—A collection of refuse such as ashes, shells, garbage, potsherds, or corncobs around a dwelling-place. Middens vary in thickness from a few inches to many feet.

Milling-stone.—A general term applied to all types of artifacts which were used as the lower part of a grinding mill. They may be flat, slightly hollowed out (basin type), or deeply hollowed out (mortar type). They are usually not associated with agriculture and were used for crushing and grinding wild seeds.

Muller.—A stone used as a pestle for grinding seeds, grains, or paint.

Native copper.—An almost pure copper found in nature, in many cases containing traces of silver and other minerals.

Ovoid; ovoidal.—Egg-shaped; ovate.

Patina.—Any compact, adhesive coating covering objects. This crust is formed by surface alteration due to aging. Patina does not necessarily imply great antiquity.

Potsherd.—Any broken piece of pottery or earthenware.

Projectile point.—A point used on an arrow, spear, or lance, usually referred to as an arrowhead or a spearhead. The point may be made of stone, copper, bone, wood, or shell. *See also* Arrowhead; Spearhead.

Rectanguloid.—Roughly rectangular in shape.

Repoussé.—A pattern in relief raised by hammering or pressing on the reverse side.

GLOSSARY

Roundheaded (brachycranic) skull.—A skull having a cranial index of 80 or more. The formula for obtaining this index is Breadth of skull/Length of skull × 100.

Rubbing-stone.—See Handstone.

Scale of hardness.—Used to test the hardness of a substance by comparing it with a standard series of minerals of different grades of hardness. Herewith are given ten minerals arranged according to their increasing hardness (after Moh): (1) talc (softest in scale); (2) gypsum; (3) calcite; (4) fluorite; (5) apatite; (6) feldspar; (7) quartz; (8) topaz; (9) corundum; (10) diamond (hardest in scale).

Sherd.—See Potsherd.

Slip.—A thin wash of fine, liquid clay applied to the surface of a vessel to give a colored coating (often whitish, red, or orange). Colored designs are painted on the slip when it is dry.

Spearhead.—A large projectile point often arbitrarily defined as a point over $2\frac{1}{2}$ or 3 inches long. *See also* Arrowhead; Projectile point.

Spear-thrower.—See Atlatl.

Spheroidal.—Nearly but not perfectly spherical.

Tabular.—Tablet-shaped; having a flat surface.

Temper.—A substance such as sand or pulverized rock, shell, or pottery, which is added to the clay used in making pottery. Pure clay, when baked, tends to crack. The tempering material checks the progress of flaws or breaks and prevents them from running in ruinous straight lines.

Three-quarter-grooved ax or maul.—An ax or maul with a groove running around three sides.

Throwing-stick.—See Atlatl.

Trait, cultural.—Any single element or any individual part of human behavior or activities. For example, pottery-making is a cultural trait; likewise the use of bone wedges, of the throwing-stick, or of stone gouges may be termed "cultural traits."

Trianguloid.—Roughly triangular in shape.

PART I

BACKGROUND

CHAPTER 1

WHAT IS ARCHEOLOGY?

MANY people think that archeology is a treasure hunt. Digging is really hard labor done under adverse conditions—excessive heat or cold, dust, bugs, drought, tropical dampness, and disease. The popular belief is that archeologists unfold the past of strange people—giants, pigmies, and the like. Actually we find that the ancient peoples were basically human beings, much like ourselves, with the same kinds of loves, hates, and quarrels.

What, then, is archeology?

Before we can answer that question, we must define the science of anthropology, because archeology is part of that science. Anthropology is the science that treats of mankind and his behavior. Since the field is broad, it is divided into a number of branches: archeology, ethnology, linguistics, physical anthropology, social anthropology, and applied anthropology.

Archeology reconstructs human history from earliest times to the present. It deals, too, with man's rise from earlier forms. It utilizes the buried and fragmentary remains of civilizations (houses, pottery, tools, etc.) to formulate the histories of peoples for whom no written records exist. It is concerned with the beginnings of cultures and also with cultures and civilizations that are now extinct.

Archeologists seek to gather from ruined buildings and potsherds the same sort of knowledge that historians derive from books and manuscripts. Both archeologists and historians strive to recover and to interpret the story of man's past. Years ago archeologists collected antiquities more for their rarity or their beauty than for what they might tell of the doings and thoughts of the men who made them. However, in recent years emphasis in archeology has shifted from mere things to the meaning of things.

Since we are attempting to reconstruct the history of the Indians, who left no written records, we are forced to deal exclusively with material remains—houses, pottery, bone and stone tools—and our first task is to build up histories of material culture that will serve as the basis for deductions as to the daily life and the events in the career of the peoples under investigation. In order to work out the complete history of the Indians, it is necessary to excavate not only in places where rich and spectacular finds are to be expected but also in regions where less showy materials but more important historical information may be obtained.

But many readers will wonder why we are eager to investigate the life of the ancient Indians. In short, why dig up dead Indians?

We are living today in a very sick world. If civilization is to endure, we must push forward the study of man in every way possible. We must understand man in order to understand the culture which he has evolved. In our particular culture science has permitted man to bring some of the physical world under control. This knowledge may be used for good as well as for evil. At present much of our scientific knowledge is being used for destructive purposes. Many people blame science for this state of affairs.

Actually this is an uninformed point of view. The present chaotic condition of the world is not new; it is only worse than ever before. Every major invention, from the time of the first use of fire down to the airplane, though capable of bringing benefit and comfort, has sooner or later been abused and misused. Fire is useful for warmth and cooking, but it may be used for destructive purposes. What the atomic bomb will do to us, no one knows; but everyone is agreed that the study of nuclear physics, if man chooses to make it so, may be beneficial to him.

If through anthropology we can understand all the facets of life in a relatively simple culture, if we can discover the whys and wherefores of such a culture, then we are better able to understand and attack the greater and more complex problems that must be solved if we are to attain real knowledge of man in the modern world. In other words, archeology contributes to the understanding of the factors that cause civilizations to come into being, to flourish, and then to collapse.

Although we cannot prophesy about the future, we can build upon a solid foundation composed of lessons learned from past experiences of mankind. Progress is made only by trial and error. But we do not have to repeat the same trials and make the same errors.

Thus, digging up dead Indians has a very real significance and holds possibilities that stagger the imagination.

Furthermore, the study of the history of the Indians is important because they have made contributions to our own history and civilization. Few people realize that the following items in our culture have been borrowed directly from the Indians: corn, pumpkins, maple syrup, tobacco, pipe- and cigarette-smoking, succotash, beans, moccasins, toboggans, snowshoes, corncribs, and canoes.

Throughout this book we have used the terms "culture" and "civilization." In some places we have used the two words synonymously. Defining these two words is difficult, and the definitions given here are arbitrary and brief.

The word "culture" as used by anthropologists does not mean the improvement and refinement of the mind, an action which implies a conscious, voluntary effort. Culture in an anthropological sense embraces the sum total of human behavior and activities which are handed on by precept, imitation, and social heritage. This includes all customs, habits, usages, attitudes, beliefs, religious and political ideas, and material products, such as methods of building houses, of manufacturing all kinds of artifacts (weapons, pottery, ornaments, baskets, cloth), of planting and harvesting.

When a culture becomes complex and advanced, especially in a material way, it is customary to refer to it as a "civilization" (e.g., the Maya civilization); but, in reality, culture covers all the elements of civilization and does not necessarily connote any degree unless the term "high" or "advanced" is used.

HOW THE ARCHEOLOGIST WORKS

The archeologist is often asked, "How do you know where to dig?" In choosing a site to excavate, the archeologist is guided by his past experience and his knowledge of the problems for a given area. Usually no excavation is undertaken until an archeological survey has been made.

During a survey an archeologist searches out evidence of ancient houses, graves, village sites, mounds, etc. This usually entails much walking over a specified region and a careful scrutiny of the ground. A record is kept of all the graves, middens, mounds, and house ruins which are observed. Collections of potsherds and stone tools are made at each site and later studied and compared with similar collections from other areas. Then, with all this information provided by the survey, the archeologist can intelligently select a site for excavation.

Another question frequently asked the archeologist is, "How do you dig these ruins after you find them?"

After a site has been chosen, it is usually mapped with surveying

FIG. 1.—Stripping or peeling the layers of dirt from an ancient Indian village in Colorado

instruments. This is done before digging starts. The actual excavation depends in part upon the type of site that is to be investigated. In general, excavation consists of peeling or stripping down the site, layer by layer. In a mound, a refuse heap, a midden, or a town the top layer would be completely removed, then the next layer, and so on, down to the bottom. Ideally, it would be like removing the layers

FIG. 2.—Model of an Indian mound in Illinois, showing vertical face of exploratory trench

of a cake. Actually, the removal of the strata is not that simple, for the reason that they were not laid down in a clear-cut fashion. Usually, the archeologist arbitrarily decides that each layer shall be, for example, six inches thick. Then the site is stripped down in six-inch levels or steps (Fig. 1). By means of the surveying instrument, some stakes, and string, this can easily be done.

Sometimes the archeologist first cuts a trench through a mound or a refuse heap (Fig. 2). By examining the vertical face of the cut or trench, he can many times distinguish the "natural" layers—that is, the strata of dirt deposited by man—and can remove them one by one.

In order to locate pit-house depressions, old camp sites, house floors, and other archeological "features," the archeologist often sinks a trench (perhaps three feet wide). This may vary in depth from a few inches to several feet and may be hundreds of feet long. In this way, he can "pick up" or "run across" features that otherwise are hidden by the topsoil. But after the "feature" has been found, he may resort to the stripping technique. If a house floor or some other obvious level of occupancy is found, digging proceeds along that level.

Although much digging is done with shovels and picks, they are not the only tools employed. When skeletons, pottery, postholes, implements, etc., are encountered, the digger then resorts to a trowel, a grapefruit knife, brushes, and perhaps even a bellows!

There are no set rules for digging a site. It is only after years of training and actual digging experience that a man becomes a good "dirt" archeologist.

Often the objects found are so fragile that they must be strengthened before removal. In cases in which the earth is moist, pottery, bone, and shell objects are allowed to dry slowly and are then treated with a thin solution of celluloid and acetone. There are numerous methods for the preservation of all kinds of materials.

During the excavations the archeologist maintains a careful record showing the find-spot of every object, the construction features, and all other details. Theoretically, then, it would be possible to replace each object in its original position. Because interpretations are based on the sum total of information extracted from the excavation, meticulous note-taking is of paramount importance. Digging a site usually entails the reading and understanding of the unintentional record left by people who possessed no system of writing.

The complete interpretation of an excavation cannot be made until much laboratory work has been completed. The proportion of digging time to laboratory work is about one to three—that is, three months of digging to nine months of laboratory work.

In the laboratory all the excavated materials are cleaned, mended, and restored, when necessary. After this has been done, classifying begins. The archeologist sorts his materials, placing like with like, and then makes comparisons with other similar or identical materials from near-by sites. The only way one can learn to classify this material is by doing it under the supervision of a competent archeologist.

When all the materials have been classified, the archeologist can then determine whether one or more cultures are represented at his site and whether some materials are older than others. He can also determine the relationship of his site to other sites in the neighborhood. In this way, the excavations yield a historical record. True, it is not the kind of document or history book to which we are accustomed. It is an unwritten story, and it takes an archeologist to read and translate or interpret it.

METHODS OF DATING

In order to convert the archeological records of a particular region or of a wider area into cultural history, it is necessary to develop a time perspective that tells us which prehistoric ruins or cultural periods are oldest and which are youngest. Such a temporal sequence is called a *chronology*. A chronology may be relative or absolute. A relative chronology tells us the age of a particular culture relative to the other cultures in a sequence, whereas an absolute chronology gives us dates in years.

The most common and soundest method of establishing relative chronology is by means of stratigraphy, or the study of the position and order of sequence of the layers in which prehistoric remains are found. These layers or strata may be composed of rubbish, ashes, broken tools and pottery, and remains of buildings; or they may consist largely of natural soil deposits with a few artifacts scattered through them. Generally, the lowest or bottom layer of a deposit is the oldest and the top layer the most recent. It follows that the tools and other remains found in the bottom layer are older than those from the middle layer and that the latter are older than objects from the top layer. If the remnants of cultures of different types are found in each of the three layers, it is then possible to establish a relative chronology or sequence for the three cultures. Minor variations through time within a single culture can be placed in a sequence by the same method.

The investigations at the ancient Hohokam village of Snaketown in southern Arizona (chap. 13) are a good example of the application of the stratigraphic method. The careful excavation of this site, layer by layer, furnished evidence of the three earliest Hohokam periods, lying one above the other and embracing a time span of more than a thousand years.

The chronological correlation of several prehistoric sites or of two or more stratigraphic sequences in different regions is called *cross-*

dating. The least satisfactory method of cross-dating is by means of typological comparison. In this comparison it is assumed that if two prehistoric peoples within a given area shared a number of highly distinctive traits, such as forms of tools and styles of decoration, they lived at about the same period. More satisfactory cross-dating is achieved when tools or ornaments from a site or group of sites of known relative or absolute age are found in a site of unknown age. These objects are usually called *trade pieces*, on the assumption that they reached the foreign site as a result of trade. This method of cross-dating was used successfully at Snaketown (chap. 13), where the finding of fragments of types of Anasazi and Mogollon trade pottery of known dates in the remains of the Colonial and Sedentary periods made it possible to assign dates to these periods.

Two stratigraphic sequences may be tied together if a single cultural period or phase is found to be common to both. For example, if Period A, the youngest in a sequence of four periods, is found at the bottom of another sequence of three periods, then the two sequences may be combined to give a complete sequence of six periods.

In the absence of documentary evidence and of calendrical inscriptions, such as those of the Mayas, dating of prehistoric sites in terms of years can be obtained only from geological and related evidence or by the tree-ring method. Geological evidence and evidence of climatic changes yield only approximate dates and, in general, are useful only in the dating of sites having an antiquity of two thousand years or more. Geological processes and changes in climate are too gradual to be very useful as indices of age in more recent times.

The oldest Indian sites in North America have been dated by means of their association with old lake beaches, alluvial fans, and other deposits formed during or shortly after the last glacial period. In the nonglaciated regions of the Southwest and adjacent areas there prevailed during the time of the last glaciation a cool and wet, or pluvial, period lasting from about 35,000 to 10,000 years ago. The subsequent warmer and drier postpluvial period lasted from 10,000 to about 4,000 years ago. There followed a minor wet period of about 1,000 years' duration, and, finally, modern climatic conditions prevailed from some time after 1000 B.C. until the present.

This history of climatic changes, as yet far from complete, has been worked out by geologists, paleontologists, and paleobotanists. It is based on evidence concerning the formation and disappearance of ancient lakes and streams, the variable conditions of deposition and erosion of soil, and the changing forms of plant and animal life.

The early Indian cultures, such as Folsom and Cochise (chap. 10), have been dated by relating the strata in which they were found to periods in this climatic sequence. These dates are given in terms of millenniums rather than centuries. The associations of early Indian remains with extinct forms of Pleistocene mammals, such as the horse, camel, ground sloth, mammoth, and fossil bison, are spectacular although uncertain indications of antiquity, since we do not yet know how long after the glaciers these animals survived.

The method of absolute dating by means of tree rings is one of the most astounding and valuable contributions ever made to American archeology. It has made possible the exact dating of many of the major prehistoric ruins in the Southwest and has contributed greatly to our understanding of the culture history of the whole continent.

Tree-ring dating was developed by Dr. A. E. Douglass, an astronomer engaged in the study of sunspots. His conclusion that disturbances in the sun affect weather led him to seek a way of obtaining long-range records of weather fluctuations which would enable him to study sunspot cycles. From his observations of pine trees in the Southwest he determined that variations in rainfall are reflected in the width of the annual growth rings of trees; that wet years produce broad rings and dry years produce narrow rings. As a result of his further discovery that all or nearly all of the trees in a region will register the same pattern of narrow and broad rings during a given period of time, he concluded that tree-ring records would furnish the desired long-range weather records.

By careful study of hundreds of trees from various localities in the Southwest, Dr. Douglass was able to obtain an unbroken succession of tree-ring patterns reaching backward in time nearly two thousand years. This was done by overlapping (cross-dating) the ring patterns of old living trees with those of still older logs found as beams in old houses and mission churches, and these in turn with the ring patterns of beams and charred posts from prehistoric Indian ruins. For example, a large pine tree cut in 1920 had 300 annual rings; therefore, it had begun to grow in the year 1620. The pattern of wide and narrow rings yielded a record of wet and dry years during this period of 300 years. In an old church was found a large beam with 150 rings. The pattern of the 30 outermost rings of this beam matched perfectly that of the 30 innermost rings of the tree that had begun to grow in 1620. Therefore, the church beam had been cut in 1650 and had begun to grow in the year 1500. By finding still older timbers, the ring patterns of which successively matched and overlapped backward in time, the chronology was carried still further back. In this illustration the process seems simple, but actually large numbers of beams had to

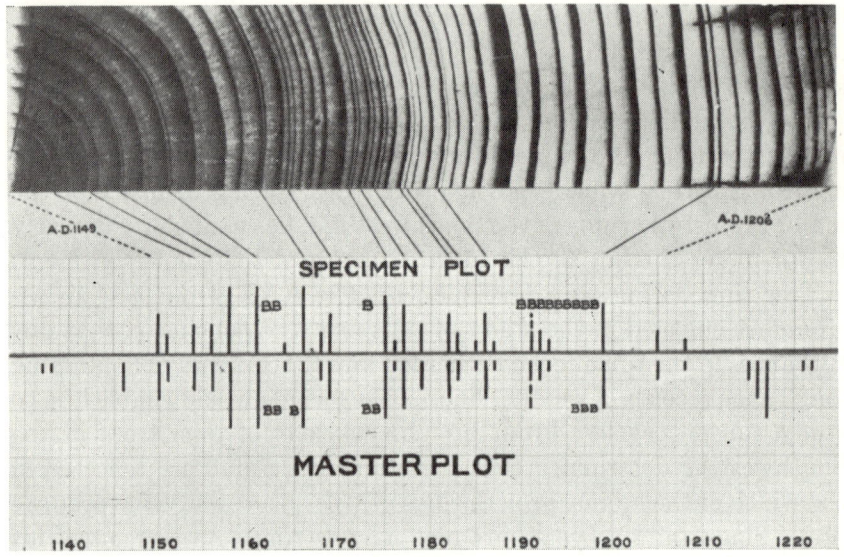

Fig. 3.—Dating a prehistoric beam cut in A.D. 1206. *Top:* section of beam (center ring at left) from Balcony House, Mesa Verde. *Center:* specimen plot. *Bottom:* master-plot. Long vertical lines represent drought years (narrow rings), and shorter lines moderately dry years. The letter *B* indicates an unusually wet season (very broad ring).

be matched against one another and against the critical places of overlap in order to establish a sound chronology.

By the application of this method Dr. Douglass was able to build a continuous weather record or tree-ring calendar extending from A.D. 11 to the present. This tree-ring calendar has been recorded on cross-section paper, and the resulting chart is called the "master-plot." The fact that the pattern in one section of the plot is never duplicated in another section makes it possible to date a log of unknown age by fitting its pattern of rings to the corresponding pattern on the master-plot.

In actual practice, when a beam is to be dated, the very broad and narrow rings, representing wet and dry years, respectively, are plotted by means of vertical lines on cross-section paper. Long lines represent drought years and shorter ones represent moderately dry years; an unusually wet season is indicated by the letter B. Then, by sliding this specimen graph or plot along the master-plot until the pattern sequences of the principal dry and wet years coincide, the date on which the beam was cut is obtained.

This process is illustrated in Figure 3. At the top is a section of a beam from Balcony House, Mesa Verde National Park, Colorado. The center ring is at the left, and at the right is the last ring to grow before the beam was cut. Below the beam section is the specimen plot showing the wet and dry years that prevailed during the growth of this tree. At the bottom is a section of the master-plot extending from A.D. 1135 to 1225. The specimen plot has been matched to the master-plot, giving the date 1149 for the beginning of the growth of the beam and 1206 as the year in which the beam was cut. The room from which this beam came was therefore built in 1206 or soon after.

A beginning has been made in applying the tree-ring method to eastern United States and to Alaska, and the preliminary results are promising. Eventually it may be possible to date many ancient sites in these areas. The possibilities in other parts of the continent have not yet been explored.

SUMMARY

From studies of past or extinct culture the archeologist paints a picture of what has gone before. Such a picture enables us to orient our own culture with reference to all others, past and present, and gives us a complete temporal and spatial perspective. Many of the ingredients of our industrial civilization have been handed down to us from earlier cultures—for example, the wheel, the alphabet, accounting systems, and parliamentary government. We learn that the world was not created in 4004 B.C. Rather, man has been on this planet about a million years. Laboriously and slowly, he has unconsciously created cultures and civilizations which have been handed on by precept, imitation, and social heritage. New methods of obtaining food, new systems of social organization, conflicts between technology and the social controls, migrations, cultural mixing, new and elaborate ways of living—all these are indicated in the temporal and spatial perspective of archeology.

In the chapters dealing with the archeological areas (chaps. 10–33), we have described the cultures according to the following outline:

Area	Travel and transportation
People	Costume
Language	Cradles
Houses and/or villages	Weaving, bags, and textiles
Livelihood	Ornaments
Pottery	Musical instruments
Metals	Games
Basketry	Art
Wood-working	Burials
Tools, utensils, and weapons	Conjectures and/or comments
Pipes	

Wherever a category is omitted from the text, the reader is to understand that we have no information on that subject.

SOURCES

ANTEVS, 1945; DIXON, 1928; DOUGLASS, 1935; KROEBER, 1923; ROBERTS, 1940; SAPIR, 1916; SAYLES and ANTEVS, 1941; STALLINGS, 1939.

CHAPTER 2

ORIGIN OF THE AMERICAN INDIANS

WHO DISCOVERED AMERICA?

SCHOOL children are usually taught that Columbus discovered America. Actually, as will be shown later in this chapter, people from northeastern Asia discovered this continent some twenty thousand years ago. These Asiatics are called American Indians.

It is possible also that a small outrigger canoe, sailing from one of the Pacific islands, was now and then blown off its course and landed by chance on the western shores of the New World. The number of people who came ashore here in this way must have been small.

Columbus cannot really be given credit for being the first European to discover America, because the Norsemen beat him to it. They discovered Greenland as early as A.D. 985, establishing colonies there by 1350. They also reached "Vinland" (the coast of North America somewhere north of Cape Cod, Massachusetts) about A.D. 1000. It is most probable that exploring parties of Norsemen reached the regions of the upper Great Lakes and the Hudson's Bay areas, for several Norse axes (dating from about A.D. 1350) and one or two runic inscriptions on stone have been excavated in those areas.

The number of men in these exploring bands could not have been large, as no Norse influences can be recognized in Indian cultures. Norse settlements in Greenland and their explorations in North America died out about A.D. 1400. Knowledge of America was then forgotten in Europe.

SPECULATIONS CONCERNING THE ORIGIN OF THE INDIANS

Ever since Columbus discovered America and misnamed the New World aborigines "Indians," the question as to when America was first peopled has been of great interest to both students and laymen who have been and are studying the history of the American Indian. The term "Indian," although patently a misnomer, is still so commonly used and popularly understood that it seems preferable to continue its use rather than to substitute "Amerind" or any other term.

Naturally, a subject which cannot be verified by documentary evidence has produced many theories, wild guesses, and endless speculations. One of the first explanations of the origin of the American aborigine was that the Indians were the direct descendants of the Ten Lost Tribes of Israel. In some unexplained manner, it is stated, some of the tribes became lost and eventually turned up in North America.

No account of the legends concerning the origin of the Indians would be complete without mention of the story of the so-called "lost continent" of Atlantis. The proponents of this fable saw a fancied resemblance between the civilization of the Egyptians and that of the Maya Indians of Central America. To explain this imagined similarity and the peopling of the New World, they revived the legend of the lost continent of Atlantis, which had been described by Plato, who probably had the island of Crete in mind.

Not to be outdone, the Pan-Pacific enthusiasts concocted the unfounded story of the hypothetical continent of "Mu," which was supposed to have existed in the Pacific Ocean. Just prior to the "catastrophe" that caused Mu to sink, the "highly intelligent natives" had a premonition concerning their impending doom and were wise enough to take to boats that finally drifted to the New World.

Still other professional guessers, seeking for a logical source for the Indians, have derived them to their own satisfaction from the Egyptians, Greeks, Romans, Aryans, Japanese, Polynesians, Phoenicians, and Irish. Most of these hypotheses are based on flimsy and chance analogies in languages, arts, customs, elements of culture, and myths. Needless to state, all these ideas are pure fiction, founded not on provable observations but on superficial resemblances, worthless opinions, and arbitrary fancies.

THE ORIGIN OF THE INDIANS

Before any theory can be advanced concerning the origin of the American Indian, it is necessary to gather some facts, the first of which should be concerned with the question as to whether or not the Indians represent one or more racial stocks. The best available evidence comes from a detailed study of the identities and similarities of the body and skeleton.

It is not possible here to enter into a detailed, technical discussion of this subject, but this much may be said: The American Indians probably represent several different racial types. It is not surprising, therefore, to learn that the Indians are similar in some physical characteristics and dissimilar in others. There is no racial unity among them, and they vary considerably.

We present here a list of the physical traits that are similar and stable in many American Indian groups (Hooton, 1933):

1. The hair tends to be blue-black, straight, and coarse. (Hair samples of "mummies" from Peru and the Southwest are often reddish-brown, probably because of post-mortem changes.) Although hair on the head is thick, hair on the body and face is scant.
2. Skin color ranges from light yellow-brown through darker yellow-brown to red-brown.
3. Eyes are nearly always dark.
4. Cheekbones are usually prominent, causing the face to appear broad in respect to the width of the head.
5. Prognathism (projecting jaws) is present to a moderate degree.
6. Chins are not very prominent.
7. The face size is generally large.

The following features vary greatly from one Indian group to another:

1. Head shapes range from extreme longheads to extreme roundheads. The longheads seem to have been the earliest migrants from Asia to the New World.
2. The nose form varies greatly.
3. The so-called slanting or "almond-shaped" eye (caused by the epicanthic fold) is frequent among the Eskimos but is lacking in most Indians.
4. The mouth opening is generally wide, but the lips vary from very thin to more than average thickness.
5. Height ranges from about five feet to five feet eight inches.

It should be apparent that, while the American Indians have several physical or anatomical traits in common, there are some features which show great diversity. But if the American Indians represent several diverse physical types, with which of the primary groups—White, Negroid, and Mongoloid—are they most closely allied? Do the Indians represent a composite group derived from intermixtures of the primary stocks?

In skin, eye, and hair color, Indians are most like the Mongoloids. Hair form and scant bodily and facial hair also align them with the Mongoloids. Large faces and cheekbone projections are typical of both American Indians and Mongoloids (Fig. 4). Some features on the skull—such as horizontal axes of the eye sockets, projection of the upper jaw (prognathism), spacious palates, and shovel-shaped incisor teeth—are fairly typical of American Indians and Mongoloids. Thus these features, which are the most stable and the most characteristic

Fig. 4.—Navaho man. Note large face and prominent cheekbones, features typical of American Indian and Mongoloid peoples.

physical traits of the American Indians, are likewise the most characteristic of the Mongoloids.

There seems to be little doubt, then, that the American Indians, physically at least, present more fundamental parallels and marked affinities with the Mongoloid division of mankind than with the Negroid or the White divisions. This does not mean that the Indian is Chinese; it implies that there was, long ago, a proto-Mongoloid stem and that from it branched on the one side the Mongoloids (to which division belong the Chinese) and on the other the American Indians.

Although most or all Indians have Mongoloid features, some of them show some strains that are non-Mongoloid. The non-Mongoloid strains may represent some Mediterranean (a branch of the White group) and some Oceanic Negroid elements. In the South American forests one sometimes finds Indians with coarse noses, thick lips, and some prognathism (projection of upper jaws), which hint at Oceanic Negroid elements.

The possibility that there are some non-Mongoloid traits in American Indians explains an earlier statement of ours, namely, that the American Indians represent several different physical types and that they do not all show uniform physical characteristics by any means. There is great variability among the Indians; so much, in fact, that it is impossible to characterize an "Indian" in any brief, general manner. The Indian as we know him today is not pure Mongoloid or pure anything else. He represents a fusion of several strains. And it is not surprising to discover in the South American forests, for example, some Indians possessing traits that are rather more Negroid than Mongoloid. If the New World was peopled by successive waves of immigrants from Asia, one would expect to find that the most "primitive" or the earliest comers were pushed into remote areas by later immigrants and that these earliest comers would persist longest in isolated areas. The Oceanic Negroid elements, hinted at before, were probably brought in by some of the earliest invaders who may have been Asiatics with some Negroid characteristics.

Thus the diversity or lack of homogeneity of American Indians may be due to the fact that the American continent (via Bering Strait) was invaded many times by successive waves of Asiatic migrants. These represented a composite of several racial strains, some bearing Mediterranean strains, some bearing Oceanic Negroid strains, and most of them bearing Mongoloid strains. In other words, the primary divergences of physical types, now observable in the American Indians, first appeared in Asia and then were perpetuated in the New World.

Since there is not a shred of evidence for supposing that the American Indian originated in the New World (no modern or fossil forms of anthropoid apes have ever been found in the New World) and inasmuch as he belongs to the Mongoloid branch that originated in Asia, the questions arise as to how and why he emigrated from Asia to the American continent.

Prehistoric man had such limited and primitive methods of transportation at his disposal that he must have entered by the easiest and shortest route. The only region in the New World which lies in close proximity to the Old is that which is adjacent to Bering Strait, for the least distance between South America and Africa is about fourteen hundred miles, and the distance between the closest Pacific islands and the west coast of South America is more than two thousand miles. These great distances would have made it practically impossible for wanderers to emigrate to the New World unless by chance or unless they were well equipped for a long voyage. Moreover, all the evidence at hand seems to indicate that the Pacific islands were settled only in comparatively recent times, perhaps a few thousand years ago. Therefore, it is necessary to suppose that the peopling of the New World took place by way of Bering Strait, a channel of water about sixty miles wide which separates Alaska from Siberia. This channel is narrow enough so that on clear days the shores of Alaska are visible from the Siberian side. It is possible that the original groups of settlers (without realizing that they were settling new territory) came across to the new land by boat or even on foot, because the strait freezes over a few months each year, at which time crossing on foot would be feasible. It is possible that the strait was narrower in those days or that a land bridge existed.

In connection with this question of the peopling of the New World it is interesting to point out that many students of zoögeography believe that, during the periods of glaciation in Europe, part of the animal population retreated to southern Europe and part, by way of a route south of the Ural Mountains, to northern Asia, which was probably not glaciated. This wholesale migration to northern Asia was easily possible because of the east-west trends of the Eurasian mountain systems. It is probable that nomadic groups of Asiatic peoples were attracted to northern Asia because of the existence of a superabundance of game, which insured a steadier supply of food. After the ice sheets receded, and the animals began to move north, west, and east, man probably followed the chase, as many nomadic peoples do, and some groups may have surged up into northeastern Siberia and spilled over into North America. The reasons for emigrating were probably those that have reacted on man and beast alike in all times: pressure by other stocks, dissatisfaction, wandering propensities, or need for new hunting and fishing grounds. Once in the New World, where food was more plentiful and climate more inviting, man stayed.

It should be understood that the Americas were not settled within a short time or by one group of people. This immigration was a slow, prolonged dribbling and spread of successive waves of peoples. There was no mass migration.

We must not believe that after the New World was populated it marched along in splendid isolation without receiving certain Asiatic traits from time to time through the agency of diffusion. It seems certain that the following traits found in portions of the New World are directly due to Asiatic influences: cord-marked pottery (see chap. 7), the composite bow, the moccasin, tailored clothing, ivory carving, and many folk tales.

Practically all the other cultural traits, such as agriculture, architecture, pottery-making, and writing, which the Spaniards found when they first entered and explored America, were invented, discovered, or developed in the New World.

As the people multiplied, they spread ever east and south, and, when Columbus arrived, the greater part of both the Americas was well settled. The population of North America alone (north of Mexico) is estimated to have been about a million or a million and a half.

We do not know how long it took these invading bands to spread over two continents. At first, it may have been a slow process; but, as more arrivals drifted in, the tendency was to push southward, since there was little resistance from established camps either at the gateway to the New World or to the south. It has been estimated that if a tribe of people moved camp but three miles each week, the southernmost tip of South America could be reached in about seventy years. Although such an event probably never took place, it is unnecessary to postulate thousands of years of moving and multiplying to account for the peopling of the New World.

SUMMARY

There are many fairy tales, speculations without foundations, and yarns concerning the origin of the American Indian and the peopling of the New World. A few of the worst of these theories—the Ten Lost Tribes of Israel, the mythical continents of Atlantis and Mu (which never existed)—have been briefly alluded to. None of these guesses has any foundation in reality and fact; they are all figments of the imagination. Some of them still make good "copy" for newspaper stories, but they are, nevertheless, rubbish. No reputable anthropologist accepts them.

Racially the American Indians do not manifest uniform physical characteristics. They represent several different physical types, which originated, probably, in northern, central, and eastern Asia. Since they show great physical variability, it is impossible to characterize them briefly. Many of us think of the "buffalo-nickel" Indian as typical, which he certainly is not. This diversity of types is explained by assuming that the Indians came to the New World from Asia via the Bering Strait. These migrants represented a composite of several strains, the most important of which is Mongoloid. Therefore, we may speak of the Indians as being related to the Mongoloid division of the human race.

The American Indian did not originate in the New World. Since he is most closely related to Asiatic peoples, it is logical to assume that he came from Asia. The easiest route for entry to the New World would have been by Bering Strait. These explanations are now generally accepted.

SOURCES

ANTEVS, 1935; HOLAND, 1940; HOOTON, 1930, 1933; HOWELLS, 1944; KROEBER, 1923; LAUFER, 1929, 1931; MOONEY, 1928; SCHMIDT, 1931; SPINDEN, 1939.

CHAPTER 3

FALLACIES CONCERNING THE AMERICAN INDIAN

THE North American Indian has played an important role in the conquest, history, and expansion of the United States. He has become a legendary person, cursed and denounced as being cruel, bloodthirsty, dirty, and lazy, or defended and extolled as being chivalrous, kindly, and noble. Needless to state, neither conception is correct or fair. Indians are human beings with all their faults and virtues. Some were undoubtedly dishonest, cruel, and warlike; but in many instances the Indians were forced to resort to cruel, retaliatory raids in order to defend themselves, their families, and their lands from an ever increasing flood of White settlers who were determined to grab what lands they could and to push the Indian off the continent.

It may be interesting, therefore, as well as profitable, to examine a few of the popular but incorrect ideas concerning the American Indian, his way of living, his philosophy, and the implements he has made.

Some Indian tribes deformed their heads by artificial means. Very often such deformation was unintentional and was caused by a hard cradleboard that pressed against the skull of the infant. In other instances the forehead was intentionally flattened by means of pressure from a board or by means of bandages or wrappings. Intentional head-flattening was probably practiced because the result was considered smart, fashionable, or becoming. However, it has been stated that this custom was practiced so that the Indians could spy from behind trees or peek over logs without displaying their heads as a target for the enemy to shoot at. Such a notion is manifestly absurd.

Stone drill points are sometimes called hairpins. It is extremely unlikely that the drills which are to be seen in many private and public collections were ever used in that manner. The Indians bored holes with them.

One often hears that arrowheads and spearheads were chipped by means of fire and water. As stated on page 30, such a method would have been positively disastrous and would not have produced any sort of implement.

The Indians possessed no secret for tempering copper to make it as hard as steel. They did harden it somewhat by beating and pounding it.

Legend has it that the American Indian was taciturn. Doubtless some Indians were reserved, but, on the other hand, many of them were gay, friendly, fond of jokes, and talkative.

It is sometimes stated that an Indian suffered less from torture than would a White man. Such an idea arose from the accounts of early travelers who related bloodcurdling tales of the various torments that Indian braves underwent in ceremonies. Many of the ordeals required by tribal custom were painful. They were borne uncomplainingly, not because the victims enjoyed being tortured or because they were incapable of feeling pain, but because they were proud to exhibit self-command and personal strength in this manner. It is to be remembered that certain religious fanatics in the Old World customarily exhibited fortitude and contempt for pain by various sorts of self-torture. Therefore, such stoicism was a matter of training, pride, and philosophy rather than liking for torture.

Indians were supposed to possess extraordinarily keen senses which enabled them to see farther, and hear and smell better, than could Whites. Such differences are probably more imaginary than real. Tests have shown that keen vision is largely due to practice in interpreting familiar objects. The same may be said of hearing and smelling. Special interests and training would account for many of the feats of the Indians in hearing and smelling. White people who have lived with the Indians for many years have developed as keen senses of vision, hearing, and smelling as the Indian was supposed to enjoy.

It has often been stated that Indian men allowed the women to do all the hard work. Among most tribes the division of labor was strict and fair. To the women fell the duties of caring for the children, tending the crops (in a sedentary economy), cooking, erecting the habitation, preparing skins, and making basketry and pottery (in an economy that included pottery). To the men were allotted the tasks of hunting, fishing, trapping, defending the camp, and making war, all of which were dangerous, exhausting, and time-consuming duties. To us, hunting and fishing are pleasurable pastimes; to them, these occupations were extremely important as a means of obtaining food.

All sedentary groups of Indians were supposed to have been agriculturists. However, the sedentary tribes that inhabited the Pacific Coast region did not practice agriculture but subsisted on roots, berries, acorns, fish, and game.

In addition to these more common fallacies concerning the American Indian, a few more have been pointed out by Charles Amsden:

A mysterious race lived in America before the Indians came. Races of giants and pigmies once lived in North America. Disease and illness were almost unknown in ancient times. Every scratch made by primitive man has a meaning; every figure or design created by him, a symbolic meaning. Indian pictographs are a system of writing that will one day be deciphered and tell wonderful tales. All Indians understand and frequently use the expressions "How!" "Ugh!" "papoose," and "squaw."

Most of these ideas have sprung from ignorance, garbled stories, or misunderstanding and misinterpretation of Indian customs and manners. Needless to state, they are incorrect. However, because many of the ideas given here are embodied in novels, poems, and essays about the American Indian, and, because it is often difficult to know which is fact and which fancy, these fallacies and erroneous impressions are submitted. It is hoped that these explanations will aid in branding these legends as false and in erasing them from people's minds.

SOURCES

AMSDEN, 1932.

PART II
ARTS AND INDUSTRIES

CHAPTER 4

OBJECTS OF STONE

KINDS OF STONE

IN THE manufacture of artifacts the North American Indians used stones of different kinds chosen for the qualities best suited to the use to which the finished product would be put. For the larger implements that would be given rough usage (axes, hammerstones, mauls, etc.) the following stones were chosen, depending, of course, on which could be easily obtained: diorite, which is almost as hard as quartz, syenite, granite, and other rocks of approximately the same hardness and compactness of texture. Sometimes axes, hammers, and celts are found to have been manufactured from softer stones; in those instances, one must conclude that better grades were lacking or that the articles were made in haste to meet an emergency.

For smaller objects that required a cutting edge (arrowheads, spearheads, drills, and knives) quartz, flint, chert, quartzite ("sugar stone"), argillite, chalcedony, obsidian, jasper, and slate were employed. There is considerable confusion between the terms "flint" and "chert," and actually only a mineralogist can tell the difference. We define flint as an opaque, indistinctly crystalline quartz. The term is generic and includes chert, hornstone, jasper, chalcedony, and other similar stones.

Spear-thrower weights were usually manufactured from slate, but quartz, sandstone, granite, diorite, mica-schist, soapstone, and serpentine were likewise utilized.

Large quantities of partly worked stone were often carried from the quarries to the camps and then buried in caches to keep the stone fresh or "green," since fresh stone is more easily worked than that which has been exposed to the air. These caches served as reserve supplies and were drawn on from time to time.

PROCESSES OF MANUFACTURE

The stone was shaped by various processes that may be divided into four groups: (1) fracturing, breaking, chipping, and flaking; (2) pecking, grinding, and polishing; (3) drilling; and (4) sawing.

1. *Fracturing, breaking, chipping, and flaking.*—There have been many misconceptions about the method of chipping stone implements (such as arrowheads, spearheads, drills, knives, scrapers, hoes). One of the commonest errors in regard to this subject finds expression in the idea that, when an Indian wanted to chip an arrowhead, he heated the material to be worked and then dashed cold water on it! This treatment would result only in some fractured or shattered pieces of rock and would not produce even an incipient arrowhead. However, it is possible that large pieces of rock were broken into smaller ones by this fire-and-water method.

The process of fracturing is commonly employed in the manufacture of arrowheads and spearheads, knives, drills, and scrapers.

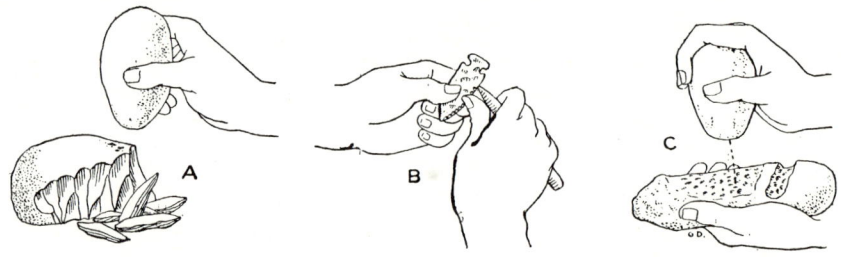

Fig. 5.—Manufacture of stone artifacts: *a*, fracturing process; *b*, secondary flaking or pressure chipping; *c*, pecking process.

There are many variations of this fracturing process, but only the common ones will be described.

The first step in the making of an arrowhead is the use of the percussion fracture process, by which small pieces or flakes are chipped from large stones (Fig. 5, *a*). In knocking off such chips, the hammerstone is most frequently employed. A hammerstone might be simply an unshaped river boulder, which for all intents and purposes would serve very well.

After several chips of suitable size and thickness for arrowheads have been split off with a hammerstone, the next process consists in secondary flaking by means of pressure fracture or pressure chipping. Many kinds of stone can be shaped by means of pressure with a small tool of bone, horn, or ivory. A small, unshaped thin blank can be converted with ease and dispatch into a well-shaped, sharp-edged arrowhead. This process of fracturing by pressure, which is particularly well adapted to the specialization and finishing of arrowheads and spearheads, knives, and scrapers, is that method which is used for chipping small, delicate flakes from thin-edged blanks by applying abrupt pressure with a bone or antler tool (Fig. 5, b).

One way of chipping by pressure may be described as follows: The blank to be chipped, resting on a bit of leather, is placed in the left hand and firmly held there by the fingertips. The point of the bone or antler chipping tool, guided by the right hand, is placed on the upper side of the blank very near the edge, and by an abrupt downward pressure a chip is removed from the underside of the blank. This process is continued until the arrowhead has been shaped and provided with more or less sharp, delicate edges.

A well-made projectile point, knife, or scraper can be completely made from quartzite in about five minutes and from obsidian in two or three minutes. A very long blade or agricultural implement might require as much as thirty minutes for completion.

2. *Pecking, grinding, and polishing.*—Axes, adzes, chisels, mauls, hammerstones, ulus, atlatl weights, and pipes were generally made by what is called the pecking (Fig. 5, c) and grinding processes. The pecking process may be defined as an operation in which a hard, tough hammerstone is used to peck, batter, or crumble minute portions from the surface of a stone that is sufficiently tough and compact to resist fracture from an ordinary blow. The crumbling process was often preceded by the percussion fracture process and was followed by polishing, grinding, or sharpening, or by all three of these treatments.

Experiments have been made by the late J. O. McGuire in the United States National Museum to determine the length of time needed to produce a stone implement, such as an ax. He used tools similar to those of the North American Indians, and all objects that he made were fashioned entirely with the tools that he produced from raw materials. He succeeded in pecking or crumbling stone with the stone hammer and in carving, polishing, rubbing, and boring stone with the crudest of tools. He concluded that the time required for manufacture of stone implements was very short, especially if done by a skilled workman, which he was not.

McGuire made a grooved ax by primitive methods from a rough block of New Zealand nephrite, a very tough mineral having a hardness of 6 (see Glossary). In the process of pecking or crumbling, about 140 blows a minute were struck. The hammerstones which he first used were quartzite pebbles found near Washington, D.C. Most of these pebbles lasted no more than ten minutes before becoming useless. He then tried hammerstones made from gabbro and gneiss; but these, too, crumbled to pieces and were worthless. Finally, a piece of compact yellow jasper from the Yosemite Valley was produced, and about forty hours of work were performed with it.

After the specimen had been roughly shaped, the pits were removed by grinding for about five hours on a block of disintegrated or rotten granite, which was kept wet. After a polish was attained by rubbing the ax for six hours with a quartzite pebble, further polishing was attempted by rubbing with wood and buckskin, but without any effect. Thus, the manufacture of this ax from a rock which was harder than those usually employed by the Indians and which in the beginning bore not even a rough semblance to the de-

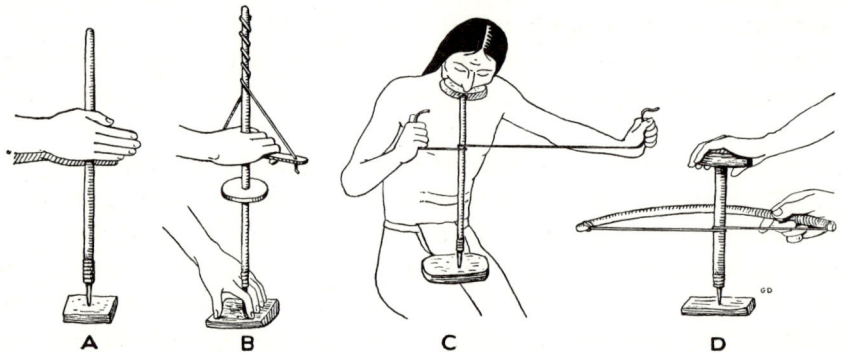

FIG. 6.—Methods of drilling: *a*, hand drill; *b*, pump drill; *c*, strap drill; *d*, bow drill

sired shape, required a total of sixty-six hours, including pecking, grooving, grinding, and polishing.

A second ax was made from a mineral called kersantite, which has a hardness of 3 or 4. It took McGuire less than two hours to turn out an ax. The pecking in this instance was done with a quartzite hammerstone, and the polishing with a smooth quartzite pebble plus sand and water.

It seems obvious, then, that if an inexperienced person could turn out axes in a comparatively short time, an experienced person could produce a creditable, serviceable, grooved ax in from one to three hours.

3. *Drilling.*—Holes were drilled in a variety of materials, such as stone, bone, shell, copper, or pottery (Fig. 6). Drilling can be accomplished in two ways. If a drill point of reed or tubular copper is employed, the entire drilling operation may be done from one side,

and the resultant hole will be of uniform diameter throughout. If a conical drill (drill with edges flaring outward) is used, be it copper, stone, shell, bone, or wood, the hole must be bored from both sides (perforation made half from either side). This method prevents binding, and the resultant hole will be shaped like an hourglass.

The drill point was probably fastened to a simple shaft or hand drill. This type of tool is merely a straight shaft of wood, about one-half inch in diameter and varying in length from ten inches to two feet. It may be provided with a drill point of copper, stone, or bone. The shaft is revolved in alternate directions by rolling it between the palms of the hands (Fig. 6, a). This mode of drilling seems to have been widespread in North America.

Among the Eskimo and some northern Algonkin tribes two other modes obtained—the strap drill (Fig. 6, c) and its close relative, the bow drill (Fig. 6, d). The strap drill is operated by twirling it in alternate directions by means of a strap or cord which is wound once around the shaft and pulled first to the right and then to the left. The shaft is kept in position by means of a mouthpiece or with the aid of a helper. The bow drill is operated in almost the same manner, except that the shaft may be steadied by the left hand, while the right saws a bow back and forth, thus causing the shaft to revolve in alternate directions. These two methods are vastly superior to the simple shaft drill, because the number of revolutions may be increased and greater pressure may be imparted to the shaft.

The pump drill (Fig. 6, b) is a mechanical device that is much more efficient than the types of drill described above. There is some doubt as to whether or not it was ever used in North America before European colonists arrived. A pump drill consists of a thin, wooden shaft about two feet long. A disk (of wood, stone, pottery, or bone) is fastened near the lower end of the shaft; to the end of the shaft is affixed a drill point. A bow or crosspiece, which is perforated in the center and to the ends of which are attached a bowstring tied to the upper end of the shaft, is lowered and raised on the shaft, which runs through the perforation of the bow. As this bow is quickly lowered, the shaft revolves, unwinding the bowstring. The downward pressure is then relaxed; the impetus of the disk, which functions as a flywheel, is sufficient to wind the string up on the shaft in the reverse direction. Then the whole operation is repeated. With a bit of practice, the pump drill can be operated so quickly that the shaft hums as it revolves in alternate directions.

4. *Sawing.*—Raw materials such as stone, copper, bone, and pottery are sawed in two ways. In the first, a thin, hard stone, which has been pecked and ground down to a suitable edge, is used. Teeth or notches in the cutting edge are produced by chipping or grinding. Frequently, instead of a toothed blade, a sharpened beaver tooth or a thin, unnotched piece of quartz or sandstone is used for sawing. In some tough rocks the groove is started by means of a horsetail rush. In the second way, sand is placed in a groove, already started, and a thin piece of rawhide is pulled back and forth over the sand, the latter acts as an abrading agent.

KINDS OF STONE OBJECTS MANUFACTURED AND THEIR USES

1. *Fracturing, breaking, chipping, and flaking.*—The objects which were produced by means of fracturing, breaking, chipping, and flaking include projectile points (Fig. 7), knives, scrapers, drill points, blanks, and choppers.

The term "projectile points" includes both arrowheads and spearheads, which were used in hunting and in warfare.

Many projectile points that are to be seen in private and museum collections are beveled on one edge, generally on the left. It is commonly supposed that the beveling was intended to impart a rotary motion to the arrow when in flight, but tests have shown that this belief is unfounded.

It should be noted that the feathering of an arrow keeps the rear end of the shaft in the line of progress of the arrowhead and produces rotation while in flight. If the feathering is too heavy, the air friction is increased, and the loss of penetration due to the diminished velocity is very appreciable. The arrow-shaft need not be feathered if the foreshaft or head is heavy enough. The rotation of an arrow does not increase the violence of the wound; it merely assists in delivering the greatest possible blow, which is accomplished only when the long axis of the arrow is in the line of direct motion. An arrow that weaves or wobbles is inefficient.

Most of the beveled projectile points are much too long and heavy to have served as arrowheads. Such implements were probably hafted and used as skinning knives, since the bevel on the left side would be pointed downward when the tool was grasped by the right hand. Such a tool would have been most useful for loosening the hide of an animal.

The functions and uses of knives, scrapers, and drill points should be clear from the names applied to them; that is, knives were used for cutting; scrapers, for scraping and dressing hides and for working bone, shell, and wood; and drill points, for making perforations in stone, wood, bone, shell, skin, and metal.

Blanks or blades or disks were probably roughed out at the quarry and carried back to the camp. Here they were turned into projectile points, knives, scrapers, and drills or cached in lots ranging from four or five to eight thousand. Since weathered flint is more difficult to work, the Indians may have buried the blanks in order to keep them "green" and fresh.

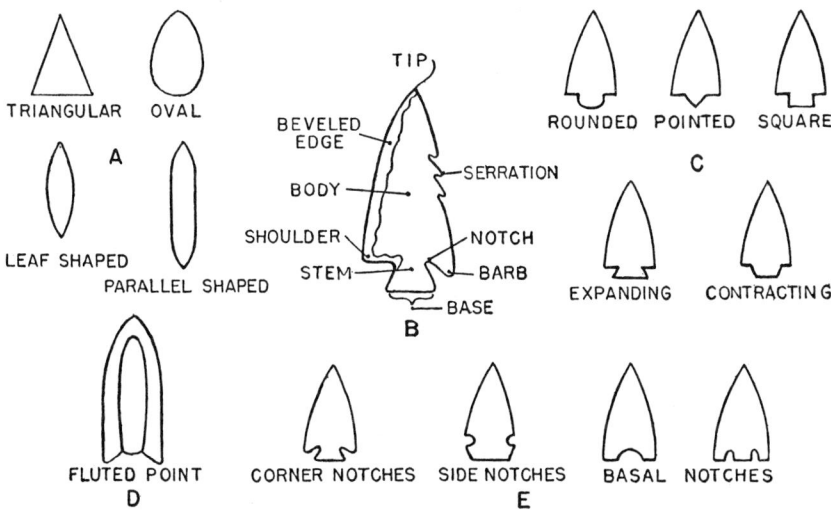

Fig. 7.—Types of projectile points of stone: a, shapes; b, parts; c, stems; d, fluted or Folsom point; e, notches.

The average chipped object may have been utilized in a number of different ways. Just as we may use a screwdriver as a chisel, a jimmy, an ice pick, or a hammer, so the Indians may have used and misused their tools. It is sometimes very difficult to distinguish a knife from a projectile point or a scraper from a knife. Our classifications and names must, therefore, be used with caution and only in a general fashion.

2. *Pecking, grinding, and polishing.*—A complete list of stone objects produced by pecking, grinding, and polishing would be out of place in this handbook. Only the most important and the commonest ones will be mentioned and briefly described.

Stone axes were used primarily for chopping. Axes were often provided with a groove or notches to which the handle was attached. If the groove completely encircles the ax, the tool is described as a "full-grooved ax" (Fig. 8, *d*); if it extends only part way around the ax, the tool is called "a three-quarter-grooved ax" (Fig. 8, *f*). Some full-grooved or "fluted" axes are decorated with one or more parallel flutings or shallow grooves that run the long way of the ax. These flutings serve no known purpose and were probably ornamental.

A celt is merely an ungrooved ax and is often shaped somewhat like a chisel (Fig. 8, *b*).

In order to answer the question as to whether one could really cut anything with a stone ax, some practical tests were undertaken by

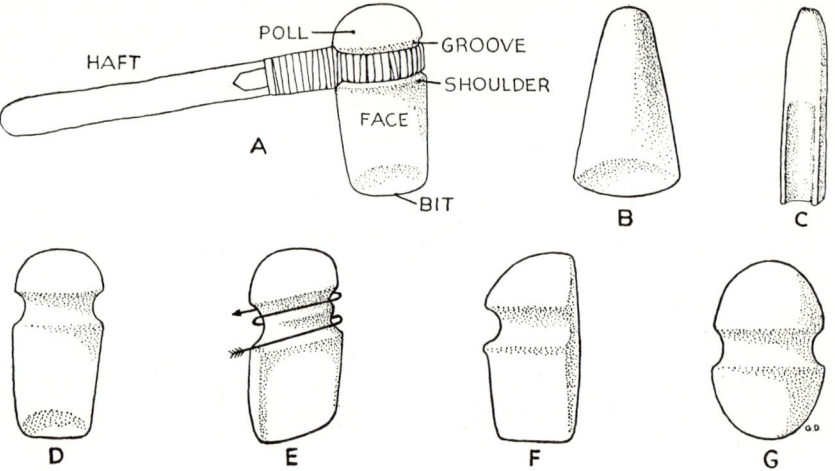

Fig. 8.—Types of pecked and ground tools of stone: *a*, parts of ax; *b*, ungrooved ax; *c*, gouge; *d*, full-grooved ax; *e*, spiral-grooved ax; *f*, three-quarter-grooved ax; *g*, grooved maul.

G. V. Smith, of Copenhagen, Denmark, and H. L. Skavlem, of Kale Koshkonong, Wisconsin. With a stone blade fastened to a wooden handle in primitive fashion, Smith was able (1) to cut in two in 45 seconds a stick of fresh pine wood—fixed perpendicularly to a workbench—measuring $2\frac{1}{4}$ inches in diameter; (2) to cut in two in 10 minutes, under the same conditions, a stick of pine measuring $4\frac{3}{4}$ inches in diameter; (3) to cut in two in 8 minutes a pine log measuring 5 inches in diameter; and (4) to mortise and tenon two bark-covered logs.

Smith concluded that it would be much easier to fell standing trees than to chop them as he did at a workbench, that not too complicated carpentry can likewise be easily accomplished, and that a stone blade may be used for several cuttings without damaging the cutting edge to any noticeable extent.

Skavlem pecked, grooved, and polished an ax in four and one-half hours, made a crude handle in a short time, and cut down in ten minutes a water elm tree whose trunk measured three inches in diameter. The ax manufactured for this purpose was a more elaborate specimen than really was necessary and probably cut no better than one that might have been made in two hours or less.

Thus it should be clear that an ax can be produced in a few hours and that, as a cutting instrument, it is serviceable and fairly efficient.

Mauls (Fig. 8, *g*) and hammerstones, grooved and ungrooved, were used for shaping and breaking stone, for driving pegs and stakes, for killing game and enemies, for breaking up animal bones, and for pounding pemmican and seeds. Unhafted mauls and hammerstones (without grooves) were generally employed for lighter tasks, such as pecking and flaking operations and pounding pemmican and seeds.

The mill used for grinding corn and other seeds consists of two parts: the metate, the lower part of the mill; and the mano or muller, the upper part of the mill (see Fig. 20). The word "metate" comes from the Aztec word *metlatl;* "mano," from the Spanish word for "hand." Metates and manos are very common in the Southwest (Arizona, Utah, Colorado, New Mexico) and became very specialized. Some of them are provided with rather deep troughs (from ten to fourteen inches wide and several inches deep), and most of them are concave. In many parts of the southeastern United States, flat, unshaped stones were also used for crushing and grinding corn and other seeds.

Mortars and pestles were also used for grinding purposes. In some instances it is possible to trace the development of mortars and pestles through intermediate stages from metates and manos. Paint cups, so called, although the use to which they were actually put is unknown, are only miniature mortars.

Arrow-shaft straighteners are stones pierced at one end with a small hole. Through this hole the arrow-shaft was pulled in order to remove bends from the shaft.

Arrow-shaft rubbers are grooved pieces of stone (generally sandstone) used for smoothing and polishing arrow-shafts.

Ulus or semilunar blades are knives made of polished slate and used mostly by Eskimos and neighboring tribes (see Fig. 69, *c*).

Bannerstones, boatstones, butterfly-stones, pick-shaped objects, and so-called "problematical" objects are now called spear-thrower or throwing-stick weights (see Fig. 69, *g*). They are therefore no longer a mystery, thanks to recent archeological evidence obtained from Indian graves in Kentucky and Alabama. Bannerstones were found there near spear-thrower hooks or sockets of antler. These hooks or sockets correspond in function to the hooks or spurs found on modern Eskimo throwing-sticks. The holes of both the bannerstone and the hook were, when unearthed, in perfect alignment, and it is therefore reasonable to assume that a wooden shaft or a throwing-stick—long since completely decomposed—connected the stone and the antler hook. In other words, such stones were atlatl weights which were probably attached to a throwing-stick.

Since atlatl weights are often so well made and since they illustrate refinements of the pecking, grinding, and polishing techniques as well as methods of sawing and drilling, it might be well to examine the details of their manufacture. From a great many series found principally in prehistoric quarries and on camp sites it is possible to reconstruct the methods, as well as the successive stages, in the manufacture of problematical objects.

The first step in the manufacture of an atlatl weight was to quarry and shape with a hammerstone a rough, rectangular slab of stone, the length, breadth, and thickness of which corresponded approximately to the size of the finished product which the lapidary had in mind. The edges of this slab were first shaped with a hammerstone until the blank began to take on the appearance of an atlatl weight. Then the sides were gradually pecked down to the desired thinness, and a centrum, through which the perforation was to go, was marked off and permitted to maintain its original thickness. Sometimes the holes were drilled through the centrum after the hole was merely indicated and the centrum shaped around it. After pecking had reduced the edges to the proper shape and the faces or sides to the correct thinness, the traces of the pecking hammer were removed by stone scrapers. Scraping was followed by polishing, which was probably accomplished with sandstone or wood and sand. Finally, a hole was drilled through the centrum or short axis.

Discoidals, sometimes called "chunkeystones," are circular disks of stone, ranging in size from one to eight inches in diameter and from one to six inches in thickness. The faces or sides may be flat, concave, or convex. A few of the discoidals having concave sides may have served as paint mortars, while others may have been used in a game called *chungke, chenco,* or *chunkey* (the traders' name for this game). Chunkey was a man's game played with a stone disk and a long-forked pole. One of the players, who played in pairs, would roll the stone ahead; then both players would charge after the disk and at the proper time would try to slide their poles after the disk in such a way that it would come to rest in the fork of one of the poles.

Plummets—so called because of their resemblance to a builder's plumb bob—were probably used as fishnet or fishline sinkers (see Fig. 69, *d* and *e*).

"Pulley-stones" and "spools" may have served as ear or lip ornaments.

Cones, spatulate-shaped objects, gorgets, tablets, and birdstones are objects the uses of which are not known. We can only conjecture that they were probably worn as ornaments.

In addition to the objects described in the sections of this chapter, there are scores which, because of limitations of space, we have necessarily omitted. For further information the reader is referred to the bibliography which follows this chapter and to the *Handbook of the American Indians* (Bureau of American Ethnology, Bulletin 30 [Washington, D.C., 1910]).

SOURCES

BAER, 1921; CUSHING, 1895; ELLIS, 1940; FOWKE, 1894, 1896, 1913; HOLMES, 1919; KROEBER, 1927; McGUIRE, 1892, 1896, 1899; MASON, 1891, 1894; MOOREHEAD, 1910, 1917; PATTERSON, 1937; POND, 1930; POPE, 1922; SMITH, G. V., 1893; WEBB and DE JARNETTE, 1942; WEBB and HAAG, 1939, 1940; WILSON, 1899.

CHAPTER 5

OBJECTS OF COPPER

MINING

WHEN Europeans first explored and settled the St. Lawrence River and Great Lakes regions, they observed that copper implements were used, and they heard of great copper deposits which were to be found "to the west." It is evident from the earliest accounts of French and English explorers that the Indians were at that time (*ca.* 1650) still mining copper from the Lake Superior region, although in limited quantities; but after the advent of the Whites it was far easier for the Indians to obtain iron and brass implements and utensils and guns by trade than it was to mine and manufacture copper objects.

Native copper (i.e., almost pure copper found in nature) occurs in small quantities in many places in North America, but the largest deposit and the one which probably furnished most of the copper used in prehistoric times is that located on the Keweenaw peninsula of northern Michigan and on Isle Royale. The Indians knew of this immense deposit as well as of a smaller one near the Coppermine River in northwestern Canada, and both were worked to a considerable extent.

The term "mining" is used with a special significance, for the Indian never mined in our sense of the word, that is, with tunnels, shafts, explosives, and powerful cutting tools. An aboriginal copper mine was a shallow trench which was dug into the side of a hill with the floor at the entrance or beginning of the cut low enough to provide natural drainage. These trenches were rarely, if ever, more than twenty-four feet deep and might be two hundred feet long. Sometimes the excavation was merely a pit seven or eight feet deep.

With only the crudest methods of mining at their disposal and with no knowledge of smelting or of stamping (a process that crushes copper-bearing rocks into tiny particles so that the grains of copper can be separated from the rock by washing), the Indians were interested only in pieces or veins of copper large enough to be easily detached from the matrix. Mass copper was frequently encountered. There is a record of one such mass weighing 5,720 pounds which had been detached from the rock by the Indians but which had to be abandoned in the bottom of the pit because there was no way of cutting such a huge piece into smaller ones. Before abandonment, however, all projecting pieces and irregularities had been removed with stone hammers.

The mining operations may be fairly accurately reconstructed from a thorough knowledge of the appearance of the ancient mines and the tools and other evidences of work that remain. In the old workings were found marks of fire on the walls of the pits, masses of wood ashes and charcoal, countless grooved and ungrooved stone mauls and hammers weighing from five to twenty-five pounds, and a few copper implements, wooden bowls, and wooden paddles. The latter would have been unhesitatingly called canoe paddles if found near water, but they were probably used as shovels for moving back the rock refuse. The wooden bowls may have been used for bailing out the mine, but in all likelihood they were utilized in the actual mining process.

The method of mining was probably as follows: The rock around the copper was heated by building fires on the outcrops, and the hot rock was then cracked and partially disintegrated by suddenly dashing water on it. Any bits of rock adhering to the copper were knocked off with stone mauls and hammerstones. This procedure would account for the quantities of ash and charcoal found within the ancient mines and for the fire-marks on the walls and on the wooden bowls.

Not all the copper used in the central, eastern, and southern parts of North America was mined. Some was picked up in the regions that had been covered at one time by glacial drift. These pieces, ranging in size from small nuggets to large masses of fifteen hundred pounds or more, had been torn by glacial action from the parent-veins of the Lake Superior region, transported great distances, and deposited on the surface when the snow and ice melted. Such pieces are commonly called "float" or "drift" copper and are still reported from Iowa, Minnesota, Illinois, Indiana, Ohio, Michigan, Wisconsin, and Pennsylvania. Many copper implements and ornaments were doubtless manufactured from float copper. Lake Superior unworked copper must have been traded great distances, for ornaments found in Florida, Alabama, and Louisiana were probably made from copper from the Lake Superior region, although there is a possibility that some native copper was obtained from the Appalachian Mountains or from Cuba.

MANUFACTURE OF COPPER TOOLS AND ORNAMENTS

If one were to plot a map of North America to show the distribution of types of copper objects made by the Indians, one would see that in the East and South copper was principally utilized for ornaments, while in Wisconsin, Illinois, Michigan, and adjacent areas it was employed almost exclusively for utilitarian implements such as celts, picks, gouges, wedges, awls, fishhooks, knives, drills, and arrow-, spear-, and harpoonheads (see Fig. 83). In the Hohokam culture of southern Arizona, bells were produced by casting molten copper in molds.

There exists a fallacious idea that the Indians possessed a secret process for so hardening or tempering copper that their knives, axes, chisels, and wedges were as hard and sharp as steel. Such a belief is unfounded. Considerable research has been done in recent years by specially trained persons who were interested in discovering how the Indians made their copper objects. With the aid of the microscope, ancient copper implements have been carefully studied and subjected to laboratory tests. No copper object of Indian handiwork has yet been found that has a greater hardness than can be imparted by cold hammering or by working when hot. Metallurgists know of no process which will temper copper, nor were the Indians aware of any. Many pieces of copper obtained from burial mounds and from aboriginal camp sites have been chemically analyzed, with no trace of any tempering agent ever reported. In fact, the analyses prove conclusively that the copper in all the specimens examined is native copper, such as is obtainable without smelting at certain places in North America today, and that the aboriginal inhabitants were ignorant of the process of recovering copper from copper ores or of tempering or hardening by alloying copper with other metals.

Careful microscopic observation has determined that certain tools were fashioned from unheated copper and that most ornaments and many tools were hot-worked at temperatures varying from about $500°$ to $800°$ C. Fortunately for the Indians copper is very malleable and ductile and therefore yields easily to manipulation.

A number of the ornaments recovered from mounds in Ohio, Georgia, Florida, and elsewhere exhibit a surprising neatness of finish and amazingly intricate, regular, and artistic designs (see Figs.

78 and 81). It was formerly believed that, lacking knowledge of casting and steel tools, the Indians could not have manufactured such beautiful copper ornaments. Several experiments were therefore made in order to ascertain whether or not these ornaments could have been made from native copper with nothing but tools of a primitive nature such as stone hammers, bone chisels, and an open fire.

The late Frank Hamilton Cushing of the Bureau of Ethnology was intensely interested in primitive processes and methods of manufacture and developed a remarkable skill in primitive practices. Cushing started his experimental studies in primitive copper craft with the assumption that the first work in copper was influenced directly by other antecedent arts such as bark, skin, and horn work.

The process of annealing (making metal tougher, less brittle, and more elastic by heating it and then plunging it into cold water) was apparently generally known among the Indians. Even the northern Athapascans, a people of low cultural status, were reported as understanding this procedure. Cushing believed that this process, so important in beating the copper into thin sheets, was undoubtedly suggested to the Indian coppersmiths by the fact that heat was used in working hides and horn, as well as in straightening arrow-shafts, in mining copper, and in disintegrating portions of rock which adhered to drift copper.

In attempting to make sheet copper with primitive tools, Cushing found that, when it is hammered on a slant, copper spreads out as rawhide does. He discovered also that a rough stone maul of granite or quartzite aided him in thinning and spreading the copper by displacing the surface molecules at many points. This treatment pitted the face of the metal, thereby toughening it so that it did not scale or crack so easily as it did when a smooth-faced iron or steel hammer was used. When Cushing had reduced the metal to the desired thinness, he found that he could remove the irregularities with a smoother stone and then grind and scour the surface to a finish with a flat piece of sandstone.

To reproduce the figure of an eagle in this sheet of copper, Cushing first softened it by annealing. He then lightly traced the eagle pattern on one face of the plate and placed it on a buckskin mat on a level, hard piece of ground. Using a long, pointed tool made of buckhorn, he graved or etched the design into the plate, butting the tool against his chest and applying sufficient pressure to make the point sink deeply into the soft metal. This simple treatment produced sharp, smooth grooves wherever the horn point had been applied. When the plate was reversed, the design stood out clearly in raised outline or embossment. Cushing then ground off the tips of the ridges which formed the outline of the eagle pattern with a flat piece of sandstone, thus entirely severing the outlined eagle from the rest of the plate. The place from which the design had been cut resembled the open spaces of a stencil and could have been used for drawing the eagle pattern on another plate.

From this and other experiments Cushing concluded that he had never seen or heard of an Indian object in copper which he could not reproduce from native copper with primitive tools and methods.

C. C. Willoughby, director emeritus of the Peabody Museum, Harvard University, likewise performed experiments in working native copper with nothing but primitive tools. He made two trials, both successful, at forming sheets from native copper. In the first, a sheet was hammered from a copper nugget from an Indian mound in Ohio; in the second, he used a piece of native copper obtained from the Lake Superior region.

Because the process involved all the steps the Indians used in making primitive copper objects—hammering, annealing, grinding, cutting, embossing, perforating, and polishing—it was decided to reproduce an ear ornament. A sea beach strewn with waterworn stones was chosen for the experiment.

The piece of native copper was placed upon a smooth stone which served as an anvil and was beaten with a stone hammer. After a few blows the copper began to crack at the edges. This difficulty was overcome by annealing. Careful hammering and repeated annealing finally produced a thin sheet which was then ground down between two flat stones to a uniform thickness. This sheet was made circular by cutting it part way through with sharp flints and breaking off the undesired pieces. The rough edges were filed down with grindingstones.

Willoughby had assumed for his experiment that the ear ornament which served as his model had been made over a mold, because the disks in it were practically alike in size and contour. He therefore made a mold by charring a piece of driftwood and scraping and cutting it with sharp flints until it was the desired size and shape. The copper was then laid over this form and molded into shape by light hammering and pressure from a tool made from a splinter of bone found on the beach. During this process it was again necessary to resort to annealing several times. The perforations in the ornament were made with a rude flint used both as a drill and as a reamer. A final polishing was administered with fine sand and wood ashes. Aside from the fact that the ornament which Willoughby made is uncorroded and so shows no age, there is no difference between his product and the original that he so carefully copied.

The results of these experimental efforts proved that the primitive methods and tools used by the Indians were quite adequate to produce elaborate and well-executed work.

Some of the copper ornaments found in eastern and southern United States are so well made that investigators have thought that they had perhaps been made in Europe and traded to the Indians. Others who did not doubt that the ornaments were of Indian handiwork believed that the copper plates from which they were made had been produced in Europe. There are now little if any grounds for holding either of these views.

Several years ago Clarence B. Moore solved the problem by submitting a number of genuine copper artifacts to competent chemists for analyses. The results of the study show that the objects in question were made from native copper, which is much purer than any copper of Europe smelted by the processes known in the sixteenth and seventeenth centuries.

Since copper which is only 99 per cent pure is considered a very poor quality, a variation of 0.2 or 0.4 per cent makes all the difference between good and bad grade. For example, a native sheet contained 99.913 per cent copper, whereas a piece of European manufacture known to have been traded to the Huron Indians yielded only 98.97 showing the large difference of 0.943 per cent between the native American and the European smelted copper.

European smelted copper of that era always contains a comparatively large amount of impurities such as lead, iron, nickel, arsenic, silver, antimony, and bismuth, whereas native copper from North America never shows a trace of lead and contains but minute traces of silver, arsenic, nickel, and cobalt.

From these findings Moore concluded that the ornaments and tools obtained from the Indian mounds had been made by the Indians from native copper.

Old copper objects are green in color when found. Many collectors attempt to distinguish between very ancient copper tools and those of more recent origin by the amount of this green corrosion. Such a criterion for estimating age is useless, because the amount of corrosion varies according to the soil conditions in which the objects were found and depends upon exposure and other factors which are not yet fully understood.

SOURCES

Cushing, 1894a; Gladwin, Haury, Sayles, and Gladwin, 1937; Holmes, 1901; Houghton, 1879; McCleod, 1937; Mason, 1895; Moore, 1894, 1903; Packard, 1892, 1893; Phillips, G. B., 1925; Putnam, 1881; West, 1929, 1932; Whittlesey, 1863; Willoughby, 1903; Wilson and Sayre, 1935.

CHAPTER 6

OBJECTS OF BONE AND OF SHELL

BONE WORK

BONE and similar materials, such as horn, ivory, whalebone, turtle shell, teeth, beaks, and claws, served an infinite variety of uses and were commonly employed all over North America in the production of both utilitarian and ornamental objects. Bone tools and ornaments were easily and quickly manufactured with the aid of such stone tools as knives, drills, scrapers, saws, and grinders. Bone was used in the manufacture of awls, needles, fishhooks, pins, arrow points, harpoons, cutting and scraping tools, tool handles, chipping implements, and spear-thrower hooks. Flutes, whistles, and instruments for imitating animal calls were also made of bone. The shoulder blades of large animals, such as the elk, buffalo, and deer, were sometimes employed as digging-tools or scrapers. Dippers, cups, and ceremonial headdresses were frequently prepared from horn and shell.

Probably it was because polished bone is pleasing to look at and agreeable to the touch that it was employed to such an extraordinary extent in the manufacture of pendants, gorgets, hairpins, wristlets, necklaces, and bracelets. Teeth, claws, and small bones were likewise utilized as ornaments.

Dice, gaming-sticks, and other game paraphernalia were fashioned from the teeth, the large bones, and the many small foot and hand bones of animals.

In northern North America, where wood is scarce or absent, bone was used as a substitute. In this remarkable adaptation, bone became very important and was put to many and extraordinary uses. Whale ribs served as the framework for houses, caches, and shelters, as the ribs of boats, and as the runners for sleds. Bone, ivory, and antlers were invaluable for making clubs, boxes, picks, scrapers, knives, harpoons and harpoon shafts, spears, bows and arrows, smoking-pipes, toys, dolls, amulets, beads, pendants, hairpins, and combs, and for tools used in weaving, netting, and sewing.

Although wood was plentiful on the Northwest Coast (British Columbia and Vancouver Island) and was used extensively by the tribes of that region, bone likewise was employed for many objects, such as cups, ladles, spoons, clubs, awls, ornaments, and charms. In southern California, especially on the Channel Islands, where stone axes and celts were never manufactured or used, clubs and chisels were fashioned from whalebone. Needless to state, bones, claws, skulls, and teeth were often employed in making up "medicines" and in warding off disease, trouble, and danger.

SHELL WORK

Rocks and minerals were commonly used by all North American aborigines, and copper was utilized by many tribes; but considerable effort had to be expended to obtain these natural materials. Shell, on the other hand, abounds in regions near oceans, lakes, and streams. Being easily obtained and lending itself to an almost endless variety of uses, it was eagerly sought in trade by groups of Indians living at a distance from the natural supplies. It is not surprising, therefore, that shell objects of one kind or another are commonly recovered from ancient house sites and graves.

Shell was used in the production of both utilitarian and ornamental objects. Unworked clam, scallop, and mussel shells served as cups, dippers, and vessels. Large conchs were cut up and made into adzes, gouges, scrapers, and celts. Some cultures possessed conch-shell vessels or containers. In the regions near the Atlantic seaboard large clam shells served as agricultural implements. Along the Pacific Coast fishhooks made from abalone shells are frequently recovered from ancient graves and shell heaps.

Shell ornaments (see Fig. 89) were widely used and are frequently encountered in archeological investigations. Shell pins are often found in many places in the southern, eastern, and western portions of North America. This class of ornaments was manufactured by dint of much exertion and skill from the rod or central pillar of conch shells. Although their use is unknown, they were probably highly valued and may have served as hair ornaments, awls, bottle stoppers, gaming pieces, or ear ornaments.

By far the most common type of shell ornament was made of beads, which were fashioned from almost every kind of shell. Some beads were made from small, whole shells, pierced for suspension; others from small pieces cut from the most easily worked portions of abalone, clam, scallop, and mussel shells. Shell beads may be divided into three types: discoidal or flat, spherical, and tubular or cylindrical. Their functions may be classed as necklaces, hair ornaments, neckbands, ear pendants, and bracelets; as ornaments for decorating baskets, bags, and clothes; etc.

Another ornament utilized by the prehistoric Indian consisted of pearl beads. These were most common to the Hopewell cultures (see chap. 18), which employed river pearls both as beads and as materials for inlay work.

SOURCES

HOLMES, 1883; PUTNAM, 1887.

CHAPTER 7

POTTERY

DISTRIBUTION

POTTERY-MAKING was an art that flourished over the greater part of North America, but to the first Indians who migrated to North America from Asia it was an unknown art. After they had lived in the New World for many thousands of years, the Indians hit upon the idea of creating from clay a container which, if fired, could be used for a variety of domestic purposes.

Apparently, then, pottery-making developed independently in several places in the world: in the Near East about seven thousand years ago, perhaps in China about four thousand years ago, and in the New World about twenty-five hundred years ago.

Long after pottery had been independently developed in the New World, later waves of Indian migrants to North America may have brought pottery with them from Asia. This deduction is made because some pottery types found in northern North America seem to have been derived from Asiatic types. Any types brought over from Asia would probably have been considerably modified by local practices.

IMPORTANCE OF POTTERY TO THE ARCHEOLOGIST

Of all the various items in the unintentional records left by aboriginal peoples, pottery is the most useful to the archeologist. Pottery is relatively indestructible. Pottery vessels may break into hundreds of pieces, but each fragment retains its identity, and the archeologist can recognize it for what it is with a minimum of effort. On the other hand, a stone ax when broken into many pieces loses its identity more readily. A fragment of a stone ax can scarcely be differentiated from any given piece of stone. Then, too, pottery vessels and sherds are not subject to the destruction of erosional and chemical forces within the ground. They long outlast such perishable objects as those made of wood, bark, fiber, and animal skin.

Pottery is a very sensitive indicator of changes within a civilization or of the mixing of influences from other civilizations. Since it is made of plastic clay and decorated freehand, it registers changes and reflects trends of style from century to century and from region to region; for example, the Anasazi pottery of the Southwest (see chap. 12) shows definite variations from period to period, thus registering the changes within that civilization; furthermore, the designs and general style of the Chihuahua pottery (northern Mexico) indicate that some designs, elements, and colors were borrowed from the Mimbres culture (southwestern New Mexico), thus showing the influence of one region on another. In this way the archeologist is able to use whole pots or sherds to study the improvement or decline in techniques, to observe the changes through time, and to note the influence of one civilization on another.

In classifying pottery into types, the archeologist usually employs the binomial or two-name system. The first part of the term is the name of a place or other geographical feature; the second part is descriptive of the pottery decoration, for example: Mesa Verde (name of national park) Black-on-White (descriptive of pottery decoration); Marksville (name of town) Stamped (descriptive of pottery decoration).

The study of pottery, then, along with other specimens, enables us to reconstruct the history of a people who left no written records.

MANUFACTURE

Ingredients.—The potter is usually careful to choose the clay best suited to his purpose. Through trial and error he quickly learns which clays are best adapted to pottery-making. Before the clay is mixed and kneaded, it has to be cleaned to remove gravel, twigs, and small pebbles.

Preparation consists of mixing and kneading. The mixing combines the dry, clean clay and the "temper." "Temper" or "grog" includes such materials as sand, crushed rocks, crushed shell, fired clay, and vegetal fibers. It is mixed with the pure clay to counteract excessive cracking or shrinking that takes place in sun-drying and in firing. After the correct amount of water has been added to the clay and temper, the paste is kneaded until it has a uniform consistency. Clay that is ready to be molded and shaped has the consistency of putty.

Molding and shaping.—The methods of making pottery varied somewhat in different localities. The first and most important thing to note is that in North America, so far as is known, the potter's wheel was never used for the manufacture of pottery. Sometimes a shallow basket may have been used as a base in which the growing pot rested.

There are five methods of making pottery: (1) the coil method (Fig. 9); (2) the coil method used in conjunction with the paddle and anvil; (3) the paddle-and-anvil method; (4) the modeling method; and (5) the method whereby pottery is molded in baskets.

Fig. 9.—Hopi woman making pottery by the coil method

The coil method was practiced among many tribes of North America; for example, some Eskimos, the Mono, the Hopi and Rio Grande Pueblo Indians, the Navaho, the Caddo, the Natchez, the Catawba, and the Cherokee. The coil method of making pottery, as its name implies, makes use of long strips or coils of clay. The potter first forms the base of the future pot by pressing it out of a lump of properly tempered paste or clay or by using the end of a roll of clay that has coiled on itself and worked into the proper shape; the base thus formed is then generally placed in a shallow basket or pottery dish in which the growing vessel rests. Then the potter builds up the walls of the pot by the addition of strips or rolls or ropes of clay, which are often long enough so that they will extend around the top more than once, thus producing a spiral effect Fig. (9). Sometimes, a pot is ring- or band-built, that is, the walls of the vessel are built up by adding successive rings of clay, one on top of another. The obliteration of these coils and of fingerprints is generally done with a piece of gourd, a shell, or a smooth stone. To make the whole mass complete, to weld together the coils, and to eliminate any air bubbles that may have formed, the potter pinches the rolls at every possible point.

The coil method used in conjunction with a paddle and an anvil is essentially the same process except that the coils are rarely applied spirally and that a paddle and an anvil are employed to thin, compress, and weld them. The paddle is of wood and usually consists of a short handle and a blade about four or five inches square. The anvil may be merely a smooth stone or a mushroom-shaped, convex-faced piece of baked clay usually provided with a short stem or handle. (Sometimes the hand served as an anvil.) The face of the anvil is pressed against the inside of the vessel's walls to resist the blows administered with the paddle on the outside of the pot. It is reported that pottery made by this method was found, for example, among the Cocopa, Mohave, Cahuilla, Luiseno, Pima, Papago, Diegueno, Havasupai, and Ute and was made by the prehistoric peoples of the Middle and Lower Gila River districts of Arizona.

The paddle-and-anvil method is essentially different from the first two methods in that no coils or sausage-like ropes of clay are used. This method as practiced among the Arikara Indians of North Dakota is best described by M. R. Gilmore as follows:

> The potter took a quantity of the clay, sufficient for a pot of the size she had in mind. She placed a flat boulder for use as a working table on a hide spread on the ground, the hide being for the purpose of catching any of the loose crushed stone that might fall from the stone working table, so that it might be gathered again for

use. She took the lump of clay on the stone table, thoroughly kneaded it with her hands, and mixed with it what she judged to be a proper amount of the crushed stone for tempering. Now she shaped the tempered clay, working it out from the bottom upward to the top. When she had approximated the shape of the pot, she took in her left hand a smooth, round cobblestone, which she inserted in the pot. In her right hand she took a wooden tool like a flat club, eight or nine inches long, with which she beat the clay against the shaping stone held in the other hand. When she had drawn up the clay to the proper shape and sufficiently thin, she applied the desired pattern of decoration by incision with a small pointed and edged wooden tool, or by pinching and crimping the edge of the pot with thumb and finger.

Beating pottery from masses of clay by this method was practiced by the Mandan, Hidatsa, and Yankton Dakota Indians of the Plains area and by many other groups in the northern part of North America.

The modeling method of making pottery consists of taking a mass of plastic clay and modeling it into the desired shape without the aid of coils, rings, or paddle and anvil. School children in our civilization often make crude vessels by this method. Certain Eskimo pots were probably modeled in this way.

The fifth method, whereby woven baskets were utilized for making pottery, is reported; but the exact distribution of such a method or the extent to which it was employed is, like the preceding one, unknown at present. The inner surface of a basket was coated with a proper thickness of clay. When the clay was dry, the clay-lined basket was fired, a process which destroyed the basket-form but baked the pot. A pot made in this manner would bear the impression of the basket weave on its exterior.

Shapes and forms.—The prehistoric Indians of North America made their pottery vessels in a variety of shapes: bottles, bowls, effigy vessels, jars, ladles, mugs, pitchers, and plates. Some of these forms are illustrated in Figure 10.

Finishing, surface treatment, and decoration.—After the vessel is dried in the air to a leathery consistency, it may be scraped to improve the symmetry or to thin the walls. Scraping was probably done with a piece of stone, a shell, a rind of a gourd, a potsherd, a piece of wood, or a wad of grass.

Various means were used to give the whole exterior of a vessel its finished appearance. These include paddle malleations, smoothing, slipping, and brushing. The paddle treatment took place while the clay was still somewhat plastic. The entire exterior surface of the vessel was patted or lightly pounded with a paddle or similar instrument wrapped with cord or fabric, so that the impressions of this instrument covered the vessel. A variation of this technique was the dragging of the paddle, so that the impressions were partly obliterated. In other cases a paddle or perhaps a pottery stamp was used, leaving checked or complicated stamped impressions upon the vessel's exterior surface.

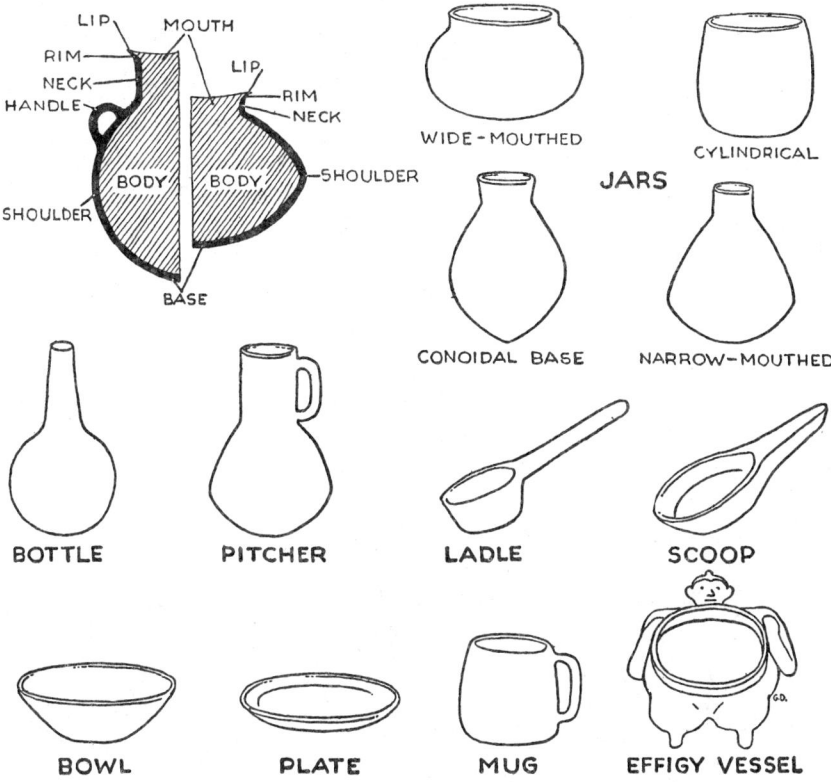

Fig. 10.—Principal North American pottery shapes and the anatomy of a vessel

In some instances it is difficult for the archeologist to distinguish between surface finish and decoration. For instance, the over-all stamping of a pottery vessel with a checked stamp or a cord-wrapped paddle would be both surface treatment and decoration. The stamping would help weld the coils together, or, in the case of the paddle-and-anvil method of construction, the stamping would assist in the shaping of the vessel. At the same time the stamp impressions would decorate the pottery. Therefore, in these instances, the distinction between surface treatment and decoration is quite arbitrary. For the sake of convenience, we shall treat cord-wrapped paddle malleations as surface finish and other types of over-all stamping as both surface finish and decoration.

The various techniques of decoration used in North America fall under the headings of incising, engraving or etching, stamping or impressing, punctating, sculpturing, and painting.

Incising consists of making incisions in the finished vessel while it is plastic. The incised lines may be narrow, broad, shallow, deep, U-shaped, V-shaped, or square in cross-section. The technique of making broad incised lines is sometimes called *trailing*.

Engraving or *etching* consists of cutting lines into a vessel that has been well dried or fired. Because of the hardness of the clay, a sharp instrument must be used, and the line widths are usually narrower than most incised lines.

Stamping or *impressing* consists of pressing any object into the plastic clay of the vessel so that it leaves an impression of that object. Some of the objects used for stamping were cord-wrapped shell (sometimes called pseudo-cord-wrapped stock), plain stocks, various kinds of cord, various kinds of dentate stamps such as a comb or the notched edge of a shell or some similar instrument, and the edges of shells such as the periwinkle.

Rocked dentate stamping, sometimes called *rouletting*, can be duplicated with the slightly curved edge of a notched mussel or marine shell. By rocking the shell and slightly offsetting the free end before the start of the next stroke, one can produce the curved or straight zigzag denticulated impressions. Plain rocker stamping can be done in the same way by using the plain edge of a shell which has not been notched.

Checked-stamp impressions can be produced by means of a wood or pottery paddle with the checked die carved or incised into the stamp. The various forms of complicated and grooved stamps are similarly constructed.

Punctating is akin to stamping in that the instrument is pressed into the plastic clay. However, the term implies the use of a more or less pointed and rather small instrument such as a hollow reed or the end of a stick. When the instrument is pushed through the clay sufficiently to raise a bump on the opposite side, the technique is called *noding* or *embossing*. Usually this is done from the inside of the vessel so that the nodes or bosses appear upon the exterior surface. The various shapes of punctate impressions are hemiconical, hemicircular, trianguloid, square, circular, rectanguloid, circular with a raised center such as might be produced by a hollow reed, and many others.

Sculpturing consists of making from plastic clay decorative appendages of various shapes and sizes. There is considerable variation in modeling, which ranges from the production of a zoömorphic or anthropomorphic vessel to small heads of humans or animals appended to portions of the vessel.

Painting, which is done before firing, requires great skill, an innate feeling for colors, designs, and design layouts, and a steady hand.

Before a pot is painted it is sometimes slipped. A slip is a fine wash of clay that is applied to the surface of the vessel (before firing) to produce a smooth texture, a uniform color, a pleasing appearance, and a background upon which designs may be painted. Some pots are merely slipped and bear no other decoration. Others bear painted designs and are not slipped; instead, they are polished by compacting the surface with a smooth, hard tool. In other words, the terms "self-slip" or "pseudo-slip" or "floated surface" give a false impression and should not be used. What is really meant is that the surface of the pot is well smoothed, polished, or compacted.

Paints are derived from a variety of organic and inorganic substances such as (organic) Rocky Mountain bee plant or guaco, which probably produced the black colors on Anasazi wares; and (inorganic) ferruginous clays (red or yellow ochers), manganese, lead, and copper.

The glaze paint used on late Anasazi vessels was composed of lead oxide combined with silica. Pottery bearing glaze-paint designs was fired at a temperature somewhat higher than that used for unglazed vessels. In this way the lead and silica were vitrified. Various colors were imparted to the glaze by the oxides of manganese, iron, and copper.

Glaze paint and slip may appear on the same vessel. Both the glaze paint and the slip are applied before firing. Some people have thought that a vessel was slipped, then fired, then decorated with glaze paint, and then refired, but this was not the method used by the American Indians. The colors were applied with brushes made from plant stems, chewed twigs, slivers of yucca, or possibly bird feathers.

Designs were produced either by direct or by negative (reverse) painting. In negative painting the design appears in the basic color of the pottery and is outlined or surrounded by a different color. Some negative painting was achieved by means of the "lost color," "lost wax," "resist," or "batik" method, which may be described as follows: Wax was applied to those portions of the vessel that were to remain uncolored or unpainted. The vessel was then dipped in paint of the desired color, after which the wax and the paint covering it were melted off. This left the color unimpaired on the rest of the vessel. A more tedious method of negative painting consisted of painting all the background except the design areas, which were in the basic color of the vessel. Both methods of negative painting were used in southeastern United States. Although negative painting occurred in the Southwest, the method employed is not known.

Designs, layouts, and color schemes are treated in the various sections in which pottery types are described.

Firing.—Baking or firing was resorted to by all North American pottery-makers with the exception of the early Basket Makers, some Eskimos, and perhaps some others. This is a process that hardens the vessels so that they may be more easily handled and may be used for holding or carrying water. Without such treatment the clay would quickly disintegrate.

The process of firing generally took place after the pottery had been dried in the air for several hours; the method used varied from place to place. The following account of two principal methods is based on observations of modern Pueblo firing:

1. By means of a *reducing* atmosphere. A reducing atmosphere is one in which the circulation of the air is restricted, and thus the oxygen is prevented from reaching the pottery; in other words, one would have a smothered fire. Pottery which is to be all-over black or black-and-white is fired in a reducing atmosphere.

A preliminary fire is first started (outdoors) to dry the ground on which the "oven" is to be built. Over the heated area a grate of stones (nowadays, of iron rods, tin cans, or bricks) is set up. The vessels to be fired are placed upon the grate in an inverted position. Kindling is placed under the grate, and corncobs and wood are heaped around and over the pottery, inclosing it in a dome-shaped "oven." The Indians of the Hopi area may have used local soft coal for firing pottery (*ca.* A.D. 1400–1600). (Today dung cakes are used for fuel, but, of course, this material was not available in prehistoric days, because there were no domestic sheep or cows to furnish it.) The fire is started and is allowed to burn freely and fiercely for a while and then is smothered by wet wood (?), grass, or earth. (Today powdered dung is used.) Dumping this material breaks the arch of the "oven," but this does no harm. The smoke thus created deposits its carbon in the pores of the vessel and produces a black surface.

If a black-on-white type is desired, the pot is made as described above, painted, and fired in a somewhat reduced atmosphere. If it were subjected to an oxidizing atmosphere, the black paint would burn out completely, if organic, or turn red, if mineral.

2. By means of an *oxidizing* atmosphere. An oxidizing atmosphere is one in which an excess of oxygen is present, that is, a good strong draft. Pleasing and varying shades of creams, buffs, browns, and reds are obtained by firing with a good draft. The method of firing and the oven used are the same as described above, except that the fire is never smothered. A free circulation of air is permitted all through the oven, thus preventing the formation of reducing gases which will produce grays or whites.

When the potter thinks that the burning has been completed, the fire is pushed away, and the vessels are exposed.

Firing temperatures vary from about 650° C. for black ware to 900° C. for other wares.

Time needed for making pottery.—From studies in modern pueblos in New Mexico, we know something about the amount of time necessary for making, decorating, and firing a vessel. This does not include the time spent in gathering or preparing the clay or paints.

A bowl can be coiled, scraped, and set out to dry in from 8 to 14 minutes; a jar (14 inches in diameter), in about 5 hours.

Air-drying depends on the weather and the time of year. The amount of time varies from 12 hours to 3 days.

Scraping and thinning (done after air-drying and before firing) requires from 8 to 35 minutes.

Slipping and polishing (done after air-drying and before firing) may be done in 25 minutes for a small bowl; in 2 hours for a large jar (14 inches in diameter).

Painting the design on a bowl (done before firing) would require about 35 minutes; on a jar, $2\frac{1}{2}$ hours.

Firing in a reducing (smothered) atmosphere takes about 80 minutes; in an oxidizing atmosphere (with good draft) only 36–55 minutes.

Thus, a skilful potter could make a small bowl from start to finish in approximately 2 hours plus 12 hours for drying.

PREHISTORIC MENDING

It might be of general interest to note that the ancient Indians rarely threw away a pot until it was broken into many pieces. Even then, the pieces were used as scrapers, mortuary offerings, and, when ground up, as temper for new pots. If a jar or bowl was merely cracked, its life was lengthened by ingenious mending. A small hole was bored (with a stone drill) on each side of the crack. These holes were more or less in line. A piece of fiber string or sinew was used to lace up the break, and the crack sometimes sealed with pitch. If the crack was long, several pairs of holes were drilled at various places along the split. These are sometimes called "crack-lacing holes."

SOURCES

CUSHING, 1894b; GIFFORD, 1928; GILMORE, 1925; GUTHE, 1925; HARRINGTON, 1908; HAWLEY, 1929.

CHAPTER 8

THE TEXTILE ARTS—BASKETRY AND CLOTH

THE term "basketry" includes matting, bags, and receptacles commonly called baskets, no matter what shape or size. In North America basketry is at least twenty-five hundred years old and probably much older and may be one of the oldest traits in the New World. By means of tight weaving or by coating the basket with pitch, baskets could be used for cooking by peoples who did not know pottery-making. (Cooking in baskets was accomplished by dropping hot stones in the basket receptacle containing the food to be boiled.) Baskets were also used for storage, for carrying, for gathering, and for parching seeds and nuts.

The materials from which baskets were woven varied from place to place, the commonest being roots, willow branches, shredded fibers, grass, cane, the inner bark of many trees, ferns, hemp, rushes, cattails, and yucca.

Baskets were decorated with beads, porcupine quills, and feathers, by using materials of different colors, by false embroidery, and by means of a technique called "imbrication" (see below).

Weaving cloth is the other textile art in which the Indians were proficient. The art of weaving in the New World may date back twenty-five hundred or more years.

Weaving may be defined as interlacing yarns or other similar strands so as to form a textile or fabric. Animal fibers (hair) or vegetable fibers, such as cotton and yucca, were most commonly used. Spinning was accomplished by employing a slender rod with a circular block for a flywheel.

There are two types of weaving: finger and loom.

Finger-weaving, such as plaiting, braiding, knitting, tatting, or twining, may be done without a device of any kind except possibly a needle or a bodkin. This simple type of weaving may also be accomplished by fixing the warp to a stake, by suspending one end of the warp from a horizontal pole, or by fastening both ends of the warp to opposite ends of a frame (sometimes called an "incomplete loom").

Warp is defined as the fibers or yarns the upper ends of which are tied to a horizontal bar and the lower ends of which hang loose (suspended warp); or fibers or yarns which are stretched on the loom preparatory to weaving.

Weft is defined as the fiber or yarn carried by hand, bobbin, or shuttle from side to side across and in and out of the warp in weaving.

Cloth woven on a *true* loom represents several kinds of weaves, such as plaiting or plain weave (sometimes called "homespun" or "basket weave"), twilled weave (producing a fabric of diagonal ribs), two-faced weave, double cloth, and variations of these techniques.

A true loom differs from a suspended warp or a fixed warp setup in that it has a heddle or a heald. A heddle is a device for shifting the whole set of alternate warp strands by one movement so as to avoid the labor of lifting each strand separately. This device (the heddle) consists of a rod provided with string loops that encircle the alternate warps. When the heddle is pulled toward the weaver, one set of warp strands (either the odd or the even ones) is separated from the other. The opening thus produced is called a "shed."

Therefore, a true loom includes (1) a frame (either horizontal or vertical) for stretching the warp and holding it rigid and (2) a heddle.

Often accompanying the true loom is a batten or a sword. A batten is a flat, smooth, pointed stick (about two feet long, three inches wide, and one-fourth inch thick) which is inserted in the shed or opening made when the heddle is pulled toward the weaver. Then, when it is turned through a right angle, the width of the batten is employed either to create a shed or to enlarge the shed or opening and to hold it open. The enlarged opening facilitates passing the weft strands through by hand or by shuttle. After the weft strand has been passed through, the batten is turned back through a right angle and is used to beat or batter down the weft so that the fabric may be firm and tightly woven.

In addition to the batten, the weaver sometimes makes use of a comb. The comb presses home the weft much as the batten does, but not so effectively or so quickly. But it is necessary in weaving the last few inches of the fabric, because at this point there is not sufficient space to move the batten up and down. The comb is helpful in finger-weaving or in weaving on a fixed warp (without heddle rig), because probably no batten is employed in the simpler setups.

Thus, a true loom (fixed warp, heddle, and batten) is an ingenious machine that speeds up weaving enormously. Larger widths of cloth and greater quantities of it can thus be quickly and efficiently produced.

As far as we know, there is no positive evidence of the true loom north of Mexico until after the arrival of the White men. This conclusion contradicts the opinions of many archeologists. The only possible archeological evidence of a true loom would be the finding of a heddle or some other mechanical device that would lift a number of warp threads at one time. Thus far, no such evidence has been unearthed. Furthermore, from examining a fabric it is impossible to tell whether or not it was woven on a loom, because some weaves can be produced either by looms or by any one of several finger techniques.

The articles woven by means of the finger techniques or on the true loom are blankets of fur or fibers, garters, belts, sashes, and dresses.

Usually the cloth was not cut up but was woven in a web which was the correct length or width. Sometimes several webs of cloth were sewn together to produce a larger piece of goods.

In this chapter, as well as in some of the others, the reader will encounter technical terms with which he may not be familiar. All the important words which are used in connection with the textile arts are listed here.

Braiding.—The process of intertwining or weaving together three or more strands or elements.

Checkerwork.—*See* Plain weave.

Coiled basketry.—A type of basketwork in which a foundation of rigid or semirigid circular rods, arranged in a spiral, is held in shape by sewing or looping pliable strands over the rods. The foundation, bundle, or rod consists of loose fibers, grass, stems, or twigs used singly or in various combinations.

Coiled baskets may also be made without foundation, using a soft, pliable material in a looped or overcast stitch. The basket would grow like a crocheted cap, the entire fabric being formed by the continuous stitches.

Coiling.—A basket or textile achieved by utilizing a series of interlocking loops with or without a foundation (Fig. 11, *d*).

Embroidery.—An ornamentation added after the fabric (basket or textile) has been completed.

False embroidery.—A technique of covering the outer surface of twined cloth or basketry with designs that do not show on the other surface. A colored element is wrapped around the twined element or weft that is on the outside of the warp element. The colored element always remains on the outside of the warp elements.

Imbrication.—A decorative technique in which a colored element is laid over the stitches of coiled basketry. This is done by bringing the colored element over the outside of the last stitch and forward, then doubling it back and catching the double end with the next stitch. The whole outer surface of the basket may be covered in this manner,

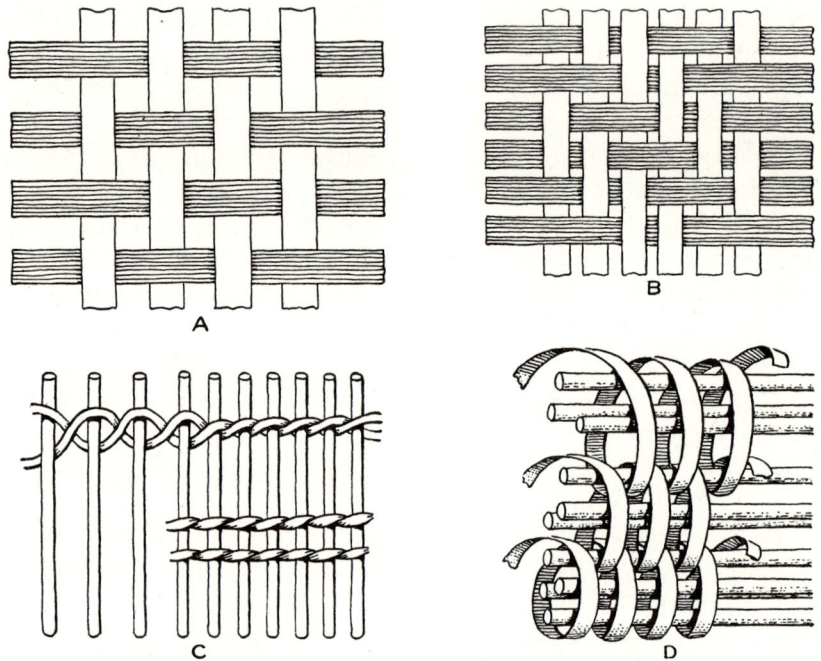

Fig. 11.—Weaving techniques: *a*, plain weave or checkerwork; *b*, twilled plaiting; *c*, twining; *d*, coiling.

the sewing being entirely concealed, or only a portion of the surface may be so treated in order to carry out a design.

Knitting.—A form of looping.

Looping.—A technique for producing a fabric that is bonded by a continuous series of interlocking loops. No foundation is required.

Netting.—A form of looping.

Plain weave.—The simplest kind of weave in which the materials interlace alternately with each other so that a checker pattern results. This is often called "over-one-and-under-one weave" (Fig. 11, *a*).

Plaiting.—Same as plain weave.

Twilled plaiting.—A technique of producing a fabric in which the elements are woven under-two-over-two, or under-one-over-two, or under-three-over-three, or in any combination of these in such a way as to produce a diagonal pattern (Fig. 11, *b*).

Twining.—A method of making baskets and cloth in which weft elements are applied in pairs to a set of warp elements. In passing a pair of weft elements from warp to warp, the weft elements are twisted in a half-turn on each other so as to form a two-strand twine inclosing the warp elements (Fig. 11, *c*).

Warp is defined as the elements on which the fabric is built up. It is the foundation of all weaving.

Weft is defined as the element that crosses the warp.

Wickerwork.—A type of basketry in which the warp is rigid and the weft is flexible.

Except in unusual circumstances—such as preservation in dry caves or by contact with copper salts—basketry and cloth rot and are therefore not found.

SOURCES

AMSDEN, 1934; MASON, O. T., 1904; MORRIS, 1941; O'NEALE, 1937; WELTFISH, 1930.

CHAPTER 9

TRADE AND COMMERCE

GENERAL DISCUSSION

THE prehistoric Indians of North America possessed no wheeled vehicles and no beast of burden save the dog. Yet from early times in all parts of the continent raw materials and manufactured articles were transported and exchanged. The study of Indian trade and commerce is interesting and important because customs and ways of doing things were transmitted from one Indian group to another in the course of trading activities. A knowledge of trade helps to reveal the character and direction of contact and cultural influence among Indian tribes, as well as the nature of handicraft specializations in different Indian groups and something of the way in which natural resources were exploited.

In order to obtain information about the trading activities of a particular group of prehistoric Indians, the archeologist must first establish the foreign origin of manufactured objects or raw materials that have been excavated from the houses, refuse heaps, or graves of this group. Next, he must discover the place of origin of these objects and, if possible, the route that they followed in reaching the group. The study of Indian commerce is highly technical, involving not only exact knowledge of art styles and methods of manufacture but also the precise identification of animal, vegetal, and mineral materials. This work requires the services of trained specialists in such fields as petrography, mineralogy, metallurgy, geology, zoölogy, and botany. With the aid of this technical analysis it is possible to show, for example, that a type of pottery excavated at Village A was actually made in Village B, because the mineral temper or the clay used in manufacture is found only in the neighborhood of the latter; that a species of marine shell used for ornaments by an inland group was gathered in a restricted area on a particular coast and traded inland, and that the copper of a prehistoric ornament found in Georgia was mined on the shore of Lake Superior. Many examples of such conclusions will be given presently.

Although the advent of the White man intensified Indian trade in many regions of North America, we know that extensive commerce reaches back at least two thousand years. Shells from Gulf of Mexico or Florida waters are found in villages of the Archaic period in Kentucky and New York, and Pacific Coast shells occur in the earliest Hohokam and Anasazi periods in the Southwest. Trading activities are undoubtedly as old in other regions.

The extent and complexity of Indian trade varied in different times and places, for it depended on the natural distribution of raw materials, the tastes and wants of particular Indian groups, and the degree of specialization in manufacture within these groups. As will be shown, sometimes the transportation of materials did not involve an actual exchange of goods.

Of basic importance in trade was the gathering, transporting, and exchange of raw materials. Certain materials, because of their high quality for manufacturing purposes or because they were of intrinsic beauty, were in great demand and were traded over wide areas. Obsidian, fine flint, jadeite, and pipestone (catlinite) were in demand for the manufacture of tools and implements; and marine shells, quartz crystals, copper, mica, mineral paints, turquoise, and feathers were wanted for ornaments and ceremonial objects. Salt was an important item of trade, as were wild and cultivated food products and furs and hides.

Probably the most frequent way of obtaining a raw material not locally available was by trading with a neighboring tribe in whose territory the material occurred. Or if the material came from a great distance, it was traded from one tribe to the next and in this way was transported for hundreds of miles. But sometimes trading expeditions traveled long distances to the sources of the desired materials, which were obtained by trading with the local inhabitants or less often were gathered directly. Thus the Mohave of northwestern Arizona, who were great traders in early historic times, traveled to the Pacific Coast to obtain shells from the coastal tribes, and in turn exchanged the shells with Hopi traders (Pueblo Indians of Arizona) for textiles. On the other hand, the Hopi journeyed to the Colorado River to gather salt, and it is thought that the Hopewell people of Ohio sent expeditions to Lake Superior to mine copper and to the Rocky Mountains for obsidian and grizzly-bear teeth.

Manufactured goods were also important in trade. They were exchanged for raw materials and for other manufactured goods. Shells made into beads, pendants, and other ornaments were widely exchanged. Pottery, baskets and textiles, stone pipes, and canoes were other goods often traded.

Generally, Indian trade was carried on by barter without the aid of any medium of exchange, but in a few regions standards of value were developed which facilitated the exchange of goods. Along the Atlantic Coast strings of shell beads called "wampum" had a more or less fixed value in terms of goods and were an important feature of commerce among Indians and between Indians and Whites. During the seventeenth century the use of wampum as money was so common that in several of the colonies its value in terms of European currencies was fixed by law. Although shells and shell beads were important items of prehistoric Indian trade in this region, probably the use of wampum as currency developed largely if not entirely after the first contacts of the eastern Indians with Europeans. The introduction of iron tools, which greatly increased the ease and rapidity of the manufacture of wampum, was an important factor in this development.

There is some evidence for the prehistoric use of strings of dentalium shells for currency along the Pacific Coast from northern California to Alaska, although here also trade with White men stimulated the use of shell money and brought about standardized values. In central and southern California strings of disk-shaped beads of shell were used in the same way. In other parts of the continent furs and hides, particularly the pelt of the beaver, served as measures of value in trade, although the standardization of the values of these commodities was brought about by the White fur trade.

Before the coming of the Whites, trading languages which facilitated commerce over wide areas existed in three regions of the continent. In the Southeast a Choctaw jargon called "Mobilian" was spoken from Florida to Louisiana and up the Mississippi River as far north as the Ohio. On the Northwest Coast another trading language called "Chinook jargon" was spoken from Alaska to northern California. It was composed of Chinook, Nootka, and Salish words. And on the Plains from the Rockies to the Missouri and from Saskatchewan and Alberta to Texas the Indians of different tribes could talk together by means of a highly developed gesture or sign language which was fully as adequate for communication as Mobilian and Chinook jargon.

In the following sections the trading activities in the Southwest, the eastern United States, the Plains, the Pacific Coast, and the Far North will be described in greater detail.

THE SOUTHWEST

In the Southwest marine shells, used largely for ornaments such as beads and pendants, were the most important trade material in terms both of their wide distribution and of their antiquity as trade items. They came principally from the California coast and the Gulf of California (sixty-four species), a few shells reaching the Southwest from the Gulf of Mexico (nine species). Pacific Coast shells were traded as far north as southwestern Colorado and as far east as the Texas Panhandle.

A few shells from the California coast were used by the Basket Maker people (see chap. 12). In the succeeding Anasazi periods an increasing quantity of shells and number of shell species were secured, of which about one-third were from the California coast and two-thirds from the Gulf of California. The culmination of shell trade in the Anasazi area was reached in the Pueblo III and IV periods. The Hokoham people to the south secured most of their shells from the Gulf of California and only a few from the California coast. In the earliest phase of the Pioneer period, probably dating from before Christ, two species of Gulf of California shell were found, and thereafter the quantity and number of species of marine shells used by the Hohokam people steadily increased to a maximum in the Sedentary period (A.D. 900–1100).

Shells from the Gulf of Mexico did not reach the Southwest until after A.D. 900, and never in any quantity until the Pueblo IV period (1300–1700). They were rarely traded westward of the continental divide and were most common in eastern sites like Pecos, where eight species of shell from the Gulf of Mexico were found.

Pacific Coast shells reached the Southwest over three main trade routes: (1) a southern route from the Gulf of California to the middle Gila and thence northward and eastward; (2) a middle route from the vicinity of San Diego to the Gila; and (3) a northern route from the Los Angeles region across the Mohave Desert to northern Arizona.

The Hohokam people acted as middlemen in passing on to the Anasazi and Mogollon peoples to the north and east of them the shells from the Gulf of California and the San Diego coast. It is clear that the Hohokam traders manufactured shell ornaments for trade as well as dealing in unworked shells, for shell ornaments carved in Hohokam style have been found in many places to the north and east. Fine cotton textiles and cast copper bells also reached the Anasazi peoples from the Hohokam area. A small amount of Anasazi pottery went southward in return, but it is not known what other goods the Hohokam traders received for their wares—perhaps baskets, mineral paints, and turquoise.

In early historic times the Mohave were the middlemen for the northern trade route across the Mohave Desert, and no doubt in earlier times their ancestors served a similar function. They journeyed to the coast to secure shells, shell beads, and fishhook blanks of abalone shell manufactured by the coastal Indians, and in turn they traded these objects to the Anasazi Indians for pottery and textiles. The fishhook blanks were used by the Indians around Flagstaff for earrings.

Shells from the Gulf of Mexico came to the Southwest across Texas and probably through the Plains to the north also. In historic times as early as 1540, and probably in prehistoric times also, Plains Indians came to the eastern Rio Grande pueblos to trade buffalo hides and meat for farm products, and eastern shells may have been brought to the Southwest in this way.

Pottery was extensively traded in the Southwest from very early to late times, a practice which not only throws much light on prehistoric trade but also makes possible the cross-dating or chronological correlation of prehistoric sites. A few examples will suffice to indicate how widely pottery was exchanged. Our earliest knowledge of pottery trading comes from the oldest Hohokam phases at Snaketown, in which were found remains of a polished red pottery (San Francisco Red) from the Mogollon area. Anasazi pottery began to reach the Hohokam area about A.D. 700. Surprisingly little Hohokam pottery was traded northward.

A type of prehistoric Hopi pottery called Jeddito Black-on-Yellow, made during the Pueblo IV period, was traded as far as the Verde and Gila valleys to the southwest, the Mohave Desert to the west, and Zuñi and Pecos to the east. Similarly, pottery from the Kayenta region in northeastern Arizona was transported to the Salt River Valley and to Chaco Canyon.

In the above examples the amount of pottery traded was extremely small, but we know that sometimes a prehistoric group secured substantial amounts of pottery from near-by villages. This was the case at Pecos, a large town southeast of Santa Fe occupied from about A.D. 1300 until 1838. For a period of some fifty years beginning in 1375 the inhabitants of Pecos imported large quantities of Glaze ware made by villagers in the Galisteo Basin to the west, and Biscuit ware from pueblos to the north beyond Santa Fe. This trade decreased as the Pecos people produced more and more of their own pottery.

During the five hundred years that Pecos was occupied, pottery reached it by trade from many other parts of the Southwest also: from the Acoma and Zuñi regions in western New Mexico, from the Hopi and St. Johns regions in Arizona, and even from Casas Grandes in Chihuahua.

Many raw materials such as obsidian for arrow points and knives, diorite for axes, mineral paints (hematite, cinnebar, and malachite), and red argillite, lignite, steatite (soapstone) and turquoise for ornaments, were widely traded in the Southwest. The exact sources of many of these are not known, but a few examples can be given.

In the seventeenth century the Havasupai mined a superior grade of red ocher in the Grand Canyon and traded it to the Hopi, whence it was transported as far east as Santa Fe. Probably this source of red paint was exploited in earlier times also.

Steatite used for carved ornaments in the Flagstaff area came from the mountains flanking the Gila Valley to the south.

An important source of turquoise was the Cerrillos Mountain near Santa Fe. Other turquoise workings were located in the Turquoise Mountains in southeastern Arizona and in Mohave County in extreme western Arizona. And Anasazi people journeyed to the Mohave Desert in California to work the turquoise mines there.

There were numerous sources of salt in the Southwest, such as the Manzano Salines in central New Mexico and a salt lake in the Zuñi region. Salt was secured by trade and by expeditions to the sources of supply. The Hopi salt expeditions to the Grand Canyon are an example of the latter.

A final example of trade is the transporting of macaws some twelve hundred miles from Mexico to northern Arizona and New Mexico. These birds have been found in prehistoric sites in the upper Verde Valley and in the Flagstaff region and at Pueblo Bonito in Chaco Canyon, New Mexico. Apparently they were traded alive and evidently were highly valued and may have had ceremonial significance, for at death they were carefully buried.

EASTERN UNITED STATES

In eastern United States, as in the Southwest, there was extensive trade in shells and other raw materials used for tools and ornaments and in manufactured goods. Exchange of pottery in prehistoric times seems to have been much less frequent than in the Southwest. The waterways of the Mississippi drainage, the Great Lakes, and the St. Lawrence were extensively used for travel by canoe, and there were many well-worn overland trails. In general, trading was between the interior and the Atlantic and Gulf coasts and from the Great Lakes southward and eastward.

Although the occurrence of shells from the Gulf of Mexico or the Florida coast in the Archaic villages of Kentucky and New York and of copper from Lake Superior in the latter indicates the existence of trading over considerable distances at an early period, not until Hopewell times (A.D. 900–1300) is there evidence of the exchange of a great variety and quantity of goods. The Hopewell artisans sought many kinds of exotic materials for ornaments and ceremonial objects, and this demand stimulated a widespread trade which reached from the Rockies to the Atlantic and from Lake Superior to the Gulf of Mexico. Grizzly-bear teeth, mountain-goat horn, and obsidian were obtained from the Rockies, the latter possibly from the Yellowstone Park region. From the Dakotas came a special flint and from the south shore of Lake Superior raw copper. Rock crystal was secured from Arkansas, mica from North Carolina and New England, fossil shark teeth for beads from Chesapeake Bay, and galena from southern Illinois or Missouri. The Gulf Coast furnished many varieties of conch shell used for ornaments and receptacles; shark and alligator teeth and barracuda jaws were also used for ornaments. For these marine products the Hopewell people exchanged copper and probably copper ornaments of their own manufacture. They traded copper and Ohio flint to New York State.

Although trading from tribe to tribe was no doubt a part of this extensive commerce, it is thought that Hopewell trading expeditions traveled long distances to secure raw materials and to exchange goods. The supply of copper of the Hopewell people was so great that they probably mined at least some of it themselves, and it is not improbable that they secured obsidian at its source. And trading trips to the Gulf Coast were probably frequent.

During the Middle Mississippi period following Hopewell, there was a continuation of extensive commerce, although there was a decline in the variety of shells traded and in the amount of copper that reached the South. No longer were copper ornaments traded southward but only the raw metal, and imports from the Rocky Mountains ceased.

In early historic times there was a lively trade in furs, agricultural products, baskets, textiles, nets, canoes, and birchbark, as well as in the nonperishable raw materials previously mentioned. No doubt many of these were important in prehistoric commerce also, but the evidence has not been preserved.

THE PLAINS

Not a great deal is known about prehistoric trade in the Plains. No doubt flint and other stones for tools and mineral paints were widely traded. In late prehistoric times obsidian, probably mostly from Wyoming, was also exchanged extensively, and Gulf of Mexico shells and Lake Superior copper reached the Plains. Catlinite from Minnesota, raw and in the form of pipes, was widely distributed in late prehistoric and historic times.

There were evidently prehistoric trading contacts with the eastern Pueblo peoples, and these contacts were intensified upon the introduction of the horse to the southern Plains in the seventeenth century. With the arrival of the horse simultaneously in the Plateau and the northwest Plains about 1730, there was a stimulation of trade there also, the Plains Indians exchanging such goods as hides and catlinite pipes for Pacific Coast shells and shell ornaments.

CALIFORNIA

Knowledge of Indian trade in California, as on the Northwest Coast and in the Arctic, is based to a great extent on conditions in the early historic period; but there is ample reason to believe that the trading activities described below were substantially similar in prehistoric times.

In general, trade in California was between coast and interior and between the interior valleys and the higher regions of the Sierras. Certain raw materials and manufactured goods were also traded from one interior valley to another.

The most important items carried inland were marine shells. In northern California these consisted mainly of dentalium shells which came ultimately from Vancouver Island and locally gathered haliotis (abalone) and olivella shells. Along with these went seafoods such as dried haliotis, mussels, and seaweed and seal furs. From the interior came furs, deerskins, baskets, and such inland foods as acorns and pine nuts.

Dentalium shells did not reach central and southern California. In their place strings of disk-shaped beads made from clam shells were used. Haliotis shells were also important in commerce. These shells were traded inland along with other coastal products such as dried fish and sea-otter furs. The manner in which shells reached the Southwest from southern California has already been described.

The best deposit of steatite (soapstone) in California is located on Santa Catalina Island. The inhabitants of the island and the adjacent mainland mined the material and traded it, as well as steatite cooking pots, beads, and ornaments, to the people of the interior and the inhabitants of the Channel Islands off Santa Barbara in exchange for basket materials, skins, nuts, acorns, and meat.

NORTHWEST COAST AND PLATEAU

Along the Northwest Coast, owing to the sheltered inland passages and the high development of navigation, travel was extensive and easy. Contact with the interior was made through the many deeply indented tidal inlets and up the Columbia, Fraser, Skeena, and Stikine rivers.

The marine shells most important in commerce were dentalia, olivella, and haliotis. Dentalium shells were gathered largely in Nootka territory on the west coast of Vancouver Island and from there were traded northward to southern Alaska and southward as far as northern California. They reached the interior Plateau up the great rivers and also across the Bella Coola Mountains, being exchanged for nephrite (jadeite), furs and skins, and the horns of mountain sheep and goats.

Copper was another important trade material. It came from the Copper River in Alaska via the Tlingit and was carried as far south as the Columbia River. Some copper may have come from the interior of British Columbia also. Thus there was a steady flow of copper southward from Alaska which was exchanged for shells, shell ornaments, and shark teeth. Other commodities widely traded on the coast were eulachon (candle fish) oil, baskets, canoes, and Chilkat blankets.

Nephrite occurring along the Thompson and Fraser rivers was traded northward and southward in the Plateau, as well as to the coast. The Plateau people secured their obsidian from the interior of British Columbia and from southeastern Oregon.

THE ARCTIC

In the Eskimo area there was extensive trade in steatite, stone for tools, copper, wood, and ivory. Steatite was used to make lamps and cooking vessels and was traded from district to district. Eskimo families traveled hundreds of miles to a source of steatite and manufactured vessels on the spot. They carried home with them a surplus of the raw material to exchange with their neighbors.

Nephrite from the Kobuk River in northern Alaska was traded as far as the Mackenzie Delta. The Eskimos of Coronation Gulf secured copper from the Coppermine River and from Victoria Island and bartered it with the Eskimos to the east and west of them. In parts of the Arctic far beyond the limits of trees wood was an important article of trade, and journeys southward to the nearest forests were made to secure it. It has been said that in these areas a plank large enough to make a sled runner was worth several times its weight in ivory.

SOURCES

BRAND, 1938; CHAMBERLAIN, 1907; COLLIER, HUDSON, and FORD, 1942; COLTON, 1941, 1945; GATSCHET and THOMAS, 1907; GLADWIN, HAURY, SAYLES, and GLADWIN, 1937; HARGRAVE, 1932a; HAURY, 1945b; HEWITT, 1910; JENNESS, 1932; KIDDER and SHEPPARD, 1936; KROEBER, 1925; MASON, O. T., 1907; ROGERS, M. J., 1929a, 1941, 1945; SHETRONE, 1930; STEARNS, 1889; SWANTON, 1907.

PART III

THE EARLIEST INDIANS

CHAPTER 10

ANTIQUITY OF THE AMERICAN INDIANS AND THE FIRST AMERICAN CULTURES

EVIDENCE OF ANTIQUITY AND ROUTES OF MIGRATION

THE history of man in Europe and Asia goes back approximately a million years to early Pleistocene times, but the available evidence indicates that he has lived in North America probably no more than twenty thousand years. Geological and tree-ring evidence offers the most reliable proof of man's antiquity in North America, but speculations also have been advanced in an effort to determine the length of time he has been on this continent. Let us look at some speculative arguments first.

It has been argued that the development of the high degree of civilization attained by the Peruvians, the Mayas, and the Aztecs must have required a very long period of time—perhaps fifty or a hundred thousand years. However, it is known from recorded dates that some of the most advanced civilizations in Mesopotamia, starting from a fairly primitive agricultural level, waxed and waned within a maximum period of three or four thousand years. The Egyptian Empire rose from a primitive agricultural status, flourished, and declined within the comparatively short period of some three thousand years.

The earliest culture in Peru—the Chavin—dates from about A.D. 1. Even if we were to grant a thousand years for the development of Chavin culture, the total duration of Peruvian civilization would still not be very great—perhaps twenty-five hundred years in all.

The oldest Maya city, dated by means of the hieroglyphic inscriptions on its monuments, is Uaxactun, Guatemala. The date of its founding, according to the Thompson-Martinez-Goodman system, corresponds to A.D. 328 in our chronology. It must have taken the Maya Indians several centuries to develop their system of writing and their intricate calendar, yet a thousand years, more or less, prior to 328 would probably have been sufficient time for the growth and development of Maya culture.

A second speculative argument put forward by some students is that the development of corn from its wild ancestral form to the cultivated plant found by the Spaniards must have taken many thousands of years. Recent studies on the origin of Indian corn or maize indicate that the wild ancestor of corn—known as pod corn—grew in favorable sites scattered through the tropical forests of the Amazonian region of South America. (Some botanists believe that corn may possibly have originated in southeastern Asia and may have been transferred to the New World long before 1492.) When man penetrated into this Amazonian region, he came up against circumstances that forced him to change his way of life. Here were very few game animals; but edible wild plants such as manioc, sweet potatoes, and pod corn were abundant. Existence for a nomadic and nonagricultural people would have been difficult or impossible had these wild plants not flourished in that region.

It is assumed that man's first attempts at agriculture were confined to root crops such as manioc and sweet potatoes. Gradually, he hit upon the idea of planting seeds, and perhaps the seeds of wild pod corn were among the first to be planted. At any rate, it seems reasonably certain that a wild pod corn was the first maize to be domesticated, since corn as we know it today (i.e., a naked-seeded corn) cannot and will not survive unless tended and replanted by man. Therefore, after pod corn became domesticated, it began to vary. But the most important variation came when the mutation from pod corn to naked-seeded corn occurred. Man must have recognized how much easier it was to use a naked-seeded corn than a primitive pod corn, each seed of which was entirely inclosed in husks. It seems probable, then, that he propagated this new and more useful form. From South America, maize spread northward through Central America, where some new types probably arose—pop, dent, flint, and flour corns—and thence to North America.

Did the evolution of our modern corn varieties require a long time? No, it did not. If man has been in the New World fifteen or twenty thousand years, more than ample time has elapsed, according to botanists, to account for the domestication of pod corn, the development of modern types of corn, and their spread over the two continents.

Some very interesting nonspeculative information on late prehistoric times has been furnished by the study of tree rings (see chap. 1). The earliest date established by tree-ring methods is A.D. 217, a date that was recovered from a roof pole of a storage pit in a Utah cave. In the thirteen hundred years that elapsed between 217 and the coming of the Spaniards in 1540, Southwestern culture evolved from a fairly simple state to a sophisticated one. We can trace the growth of pottery, agriculture, weaving, towns, and ceremonialism from crude beginnings to an advanced stage of development. And yet all this took place in a comparatively short span of time—a mere thousand years. In other words, this continuous archeological sequence carried us back only two thousand years from the present.

What conclusion can be reached on the basis of an examination of these theories and the tree-ring evidence so far? Only that man has lived in the Western Hemisphere at least three or four thousand years. This conclusion does not preclude the possibility of a much longer period of habitation.

Longer-range evidence that man came to America twenty thousand years ago has been supplied by archeology with the help of geology, paleontology, and paleobotany

Geologists agree that the time of the migrations to America by way of Bering Strait must have depended largely on the advances and retreats of the continental glaciers. Unless corridors or passages existed through the glaciers, man could not have crossed them. Travel would have been very hazardous because of the crevasses and the lack of vegetation and animal life. Therefore, the migrations must have been limited to periods when the glaciers had retreated north, opening up corridors in which vegetation and animal life could exist. Geologists estimate that the present period of mild climate goes back ten or twenty thousand years. Between that time and about thirty thousand years ago all possible routes of migration were blocked by the glaciers. However, there is evidence that approximately twenty thousand years ago the climate in North America became sufficiently mild to permit vegetation characteristic of present-day Minnesota and southern Manitoba to grow in what is now the state of Wisconsin. So far, the archeological excavations in North America giving evidence of moderate antiquity fall within the Recent period or at the end of the Pleistocene; they are not much more than fifteen thousand years old.

The route by which the first immigrants came to this hemisphere is believed to have been across Bering Strait, east to the Mackenzie River, and down the Mackenzie Valley to the Plains region. Another route which opened up later lies between the Rocky Mountains and the Coast Range, leading into the Great Basin.

What, now, is the actual evidence we have of the presence of man on this continent in those early times?

Tools (arrowheads or spearheads) obviously made by man have been found imbedded in or closely associated with bones of extinct animals—the camel, an early type of bison, the giant ground sloth, and the original American horse (for horses originated in the Americas, spread to the Old World, and were later reintroduced into the New World by the Spaniards). In considering this evidence, however, two obstacles must be taken into account: (1) We do not know just when these various animals became extinct. We can be sure they were living here in early postglacial times and probably earlier; but they may have continued to survive long enough to vitiate any claim to great antiquity. (2) The possibility of fortuitous association must be carefully studied and eliminated. Floods might have shifted material in such a way that ancient and modern bones and tools were deposited together in the same stratum; or windstorms might have blown away surface soil and laid bare really ancient bones. In times to come, modern material could easily be deposited thereon with no intervening layers to indicate the real lapse of time; or it could even be fused with the older layers so that many years hence an incautious archeologist might find evidence of the coexistence of extinct animals and twentieth-century gadgets.

On the other hand, tools have also been found in locations that lend themselves to geologic dating. To fulfil requirements for such dating, the material must be found in undisturbed ground, so that the possibility of recent deposition or tampering is ruled out. Then, the objects must be associated with a bed or beds related to some geologic event of wide geographic extent, and this event must, in turn, be related to some known geologic chronology. It is small wonder that comparatively few archeological excavations fulfil these requirements!

Many sites have been excavated in an attempt to determine how long the New World has been inhabited by man. Since the Great Plains area and the Southwest in general are the most logical regions in which to expect the earliest finds, that is where most of the work has been done. These sites include the Folsom culture (Colorado and New Mexico), from 10,000 to 13,000 years old (Figgins, 1927; Roberts, 1939); the Sandia culture (New Mexico), probably 15,000 years old (Hibben, 1941); the Gypsum Cave culture (Nevada), probably from 5,000 to 8,000 years old (Harrington, 1933); the Cochise culture (Arizona), which lasted from 15,000 to 2,500 years ago (Sayles and Antevs, 1941); the lowest layer in Ventana Cave, Arizona, 12,000 years old (Haury, 1943); the Lake Mohave culture (California), from 3,000 to 10,000 years old (Campbell and others, 1937); the Pinto Basin culture (California), from 2,000 to 9,000 years old (Campbell, 1935); and the George Lake Industry (Ontario, Canada), perhaps 10,000 years old (Greenman, 1943; Greenman and Stanley, 1943).

From this list we have chosen two for brief description: Folsom and Cochise.

THE FOLSOM CULTURE[1]

From 10,000 to 13,000 years ago

Area.—Folsom material has been found on the east side of the Rockies from Alberta, Canada, to southern New Mexico. Folsom-like materials have been found scattered throughout most of North America east of the Rocky Mountains; except for a few examples of this culture found in California, none has been located west of the Rockies.

The most important sites include the type site near Folsom, New Mexico; a site near Clovis and Portales in central-eastern New Mexico; and the Lindenmeier site, north of Fort Collins, Colorado.

Evidence of antiquity.—Archeologists have worked closely with geologists in determining the approximate antiquity of these sites. Such factors as stratified layers of undisturbed earth, terraces correlated with local and continental glaciers, changes of climate, relation to ancient lake beds, and association with bones of extinct animals have entered into their calculations. The extinct animals whose bones were found in close association with Folsom tools include bison, a large deerlike mammal, mammoth, and a large American camel.

On the basis of such evidence, the Lindenmeier site in northern Colorado is believed to be between 10,000 and 25,000 years old, probably nearer 10,000; and the Clovis-Portales site is also thought to be about 12,000 years old.

People.—No human skeletal material was found.

Villages.—No evidence of shelters (either permanent or temporary) was found. The sites were probably hunting camps. Charcoal has been found, indicating the use of fire for heating and probably for cooking. Hearths were either in slight depressions or on the surface.

[1] Name derived from Folsom, New Mexico, near which original discovery was made.

Livelihood.—These Indians were nomads who lived chiefly on game, but they probably supplemented their diet with seeds and roots. In other words, theirs was primarily a hunting economy.

Tools, utensils, and weapons.—The principal and most characteristic tool found was the "Folsom-fluted" point of stone with a lengthwise fluting or groove on one or both faces (see Fig. 7, *d*). This groove frequently extends to the tip but leaves room at the sides and around the tip for secondary chipping, which gives a sharp, fine cutting edge. It is assumed that these grooves were made to permit secure fastening of the point to the shaft of the arrow or spear and to facilitate penetration. The base is characterized by "rabbit-ear" downward projections.

The only other typically Folsom tools are two kinds of knives—one characterized by longitudinal fluting and secondary chipping around the edges, and the other consisting of channel flakes removed from fluted points and knives.

Two other types of points, together with Folsom-fluted, were found to represent sequent stages. Folsom-fluted was earliest, followed by a point with no central groove but having a thinned base, and that in turn was followed by a triangular-bladed point with a long, broad stem. This sequence furnishes something more than guesswork on which to depend for the time relationship of various Folsom-like points.

A very small percentage of the points found were typical oblique Yuma points—long and narrow, with sides parallel most of the way, and with parallel flaking extending across the blade at a slight angle and no fluting. It is believed that these points were later than the Folsom points, or perhaps contemporaneous with the latter part of the Folsom period. Yuma points had a wider distribution than Folsom points and probably survived them.

Other stone implements have been found in Folsom sites: scrapers of various kinds, including several forms of "draw knives"; several kinds of knives, including some made from channel and other flakes; flakes with small, sharp, graver points; large blades; rough choppers; hand hammers; drills; rubbing-stones; shaft-smoothers of sandstone; and small sandstone palettes for mixing paint. (Also found were pigments consisting of hematite and red and yellow ocher.) The larger scrapers, hammers, and choppers are core-implements; the others were made from flakes. Percussion or percussion-and-pressure chipping and flaking techniques were used exclusively. None of the stone tools showed evidence of polishing.

Bone tools found are punches and awls, fine bone needles with eyes, pointed fragments (possibly spearheads?), bones with spatulate ends, and bits of polished bone.

Ornaments.—Tubular bone beads were found, as well as game-counter-type tabular pieces of bone with simple incised decorations, and ornamented fragments of bone from larger objects of unknown use. The decorated fragments show the use of a simple geometric art form.

Materials not found.—Pottery and pipes were lacking, and there is no information concerning clothing, textiles, basketry, cradles, houses, or burial customs.

Conjectures.—Folsom man was probably a nomadic hunter, moving with the changes in season and the migration of game. The absence of food-grinding tools indicates a different economy from that of the Cochise, who depended primarily on the gathering of wild, edible foods such as nuts, berries, roots, and bulbs.

THE COCHISE CULTURE[2]

From 15,000 to 2,500 years ago

Area.—The southeastern corner of Arizona and adjacent New Mexico. This region extends from the Santa Cruz River on the west to Playas Lake on the east, and from Mexico on the south to Safford on the Gila River to the north. Most of the sites are along Whitewater Creek near Double Adobe; others are in the vicinity of Fairbank and Portal.

Evidence of antiquity.—Cochise materials were found in river-deposited sands and gravels covered by clay and silts. Recent channel erosion of Whitewater Creek exposed this material and thus fortuitously aided in its discovery.

How do we know that these sites have not been disturbed by floods and that the tools and bones found here have not been brought from some later site and redeposited by flood waters? In other words, are we sure that the deposits and sites are really old and that the tools and refuse piles remain exactly where they were left by the Cochise?

---

[2] Named for Cochise County, which in turn was named for Chief Cochise of the Chiricahua Apache Indians.

How do we know that these strata were not deposited by floods that occurred in the last two or three hundred years?

Hearths, hearthstones, and charcoal have been uncovered on camp sites. We speak of these as being "in place." If floods had washed over these ancient middens and camp sites, everything would have been scattered and redeposited with a hearthstone here and a piece of charcoal hundreds of feet away. Since no such scattering took place, the possibility of redeposition is precluded.

Furthermore, if stone tools had been subjected to floods and had been washed and rolled about, they would have become smooth and rounded and waterworn. The Cochise tools were not waterworn. In other words, they have not been washed about.

CHART I

Cochise Culture

Estimated Dates	Period
13000–8000 B.C.	Sulphur Spring
8000–3000 B.C.	Chiricahua
3000– 500 B.C.	San Pedro

Another bit of evidence consists of finding articulated animal bones along with tools; that is, the joint connecting the leg bones, for example, was still unbroken. If these articulated bones had been subjected to floods and redeposition, they would have been torn one from another and would have been found yards or miles apart.

Therefore, it is safe to assume that these deposits in ancient camp sites are more or less where they were laid down thousands of years ago by the Cochise Indians.

The culture is divided into three periods as shown in Chart I.

The Sulphur Spring period occurs below and deeply imbedded in deposits of the last Pluvial period (35,000[?]–10,000 years ago). The cool, moist climate prevailing at that time in this region permitted the growth of cottonwood and hickory trees—plants that are found in relatively moist woods, on the banks of permanent streams, and about the edges of swamps. At the present time they do not grow within seven hundred miles of this area. In association with tools of the Sulphur Spring period were found bones of various animals, in-

THE FIRST AMERICAN CULTURES

cluding the dire wolf, camel, mammoth, and early forms of the bison and American horse, all of which are now extinct.

Some Chiricahua material was found in layers superimposed on the Sulphur Spring deposits, establishing clearly the time sequence of these two periods. While no San Pedro material has been found directly above the Chiricahua deposits, the layers containing San Pedro deposits are geologically younger than those of Chiricahua, and typological comparisons confirm this evidence.

THE SULPHUR SPRING PERIOD[3] OF THE COCHISE CULTURE

Probably from 15,000 to 10,000 years ago

People.—Probably small, longheaded Indians.

Livelihood.—The Cochise Indians gathered seeds, berries, nuts, and other wild edible foods, some of which they ground with milling-stones. They also used wild animals for food, since charred and split bones have been found associated with their tools.

Tools, utensils, and weapons.—The workmanship of Sulphur Spring tools is so very crude that they are often identified only by their shapes and the evidence of use (Fig. 12, *a* and *c*). The principal tools found were thin, flat milling-stones and small handstones of the one-hand type with a flat grinding surface. Both were made of sandstone. Most of these have weathered and disintegrated into small fragments. There was a much smaller representation of plano-convex, percussion-flaked stone tools for cutting, scraping, and pounding. The edges of some knives and scrapers show evidence of retouching, but this may sometimes be the result of use. These chipped tools were made of local igneous rock (porphyry) and of limestone. A battered pebble and several handstones apparently served as hammerstones.

No projectile points were found, but the Cochise possibly may have made theirs of a perishable material such as wood or bone.

Other early cultures of the Great Basin and Plains areas are characterized by chipped tools with projectile points (marks of a nomadic hunting economy), whereas in the Sulphur Spring culture (a semi-sedentary economy) grinding tools took precedence, and chipped tools were secondary in importance. This fact is important in con-

---

[3] Named for Sulphur Spring Valley, which includes Whitewater Creek but extends farther north.

sidering the development of the sedentary agricultural cultures of later groups such as the Basket Maker Indians.

Burials.—Although parts of one skeleton were found, we know nothing of the burial customs of the Cochise Indians.

Materials not found.—Nothing is known concerning the clothing or houses used by these people, and there is no evidence of pottery, basketry, pipes, or ornaments.

FIG. 12.—Stone tools, Cochise culture, Arizona: *a*, metate or milling-stone, Sulphur Spring period; *b*, handstone or one-handed mano, Chiricahua period; *c*, handstone or milling-stone, Sulphur Spring period; *d*, scraper, San Pedro period; *e*, hand-ax or cleaver, Chiricahua period; *f*, scraper, Chiricahua period; *g*, pestle, San Pedro period.

THE CHIRICAHUA PERIOD[4] OF THE COCHISE CULTURE

Probably from 10,000 to 5,000 years ago

Livelihood.—Food-gathering and some hunting furnished subsistence.

Tools, utensils, and weapons.—A greatly increased variety of tool forms was produced in this period (Fig. 12, *b, e, f*). Milling-stones were larger, and each usually had a shallow basin hollowed out either by the action of handstones or by intentional shaping. Many of the

[4] Named for the near-by Chiricahua Mountains.

handstones were so weathered that it was difficult to be sure that they were tools. One mortar was found and some multifaced handstones, which had been used as pestles. One grooved, crudely shaped stone was probably used as a maul.

Practically all chipped implements were percussion-flaked from porphyry, limestone, and coarse-grained quartzite. Many of these specimens have become so oxidized that it is hard to determine the kind of stones from which they were made. These tools included hand-axes, blades of the plano-convex and biface types, knives, scrapers, hammerstones, and draw knives.

The few pressure-flaked tools present (fluted points highly suggestive of Folsom) were made of an alien material (fine-grained quartzite) and apparently were brought in from some outside, contemporary culture.

Antler fragments and bone splints found at the type site near Portal indicate that bone tools doubtless were made. However, only one complete bone awl has been found, and that was recovered from a site in the Sulphur Spring Valley.

Both grinding tools and chipped implements show an evolution from Sulphur Spring types and fit in as prototypes of the later tools of the San Pedro period. The extent of development and the variety of forms suggest a considerable lapse of time between the Sulphur Spring and Chiricahua materials.

Materials not found.—Nothing is known concerning the physical appearance, clothing, houses, or burial customs of these people; and there is no evidence of pottery, basketry, pipes, or ornaments.

THE SAN PEDRO PERIOD[5] OF THE COCHISE CULTURE

Probably from 5,000 to 2,500 years ago

Livelihood.—Food-gathering was still an important part of the food economy, but there was greater emphasis on hunting than in the preceding periods.

Tools, utensils, and weapons.—This period produced a much greater percentage of chipped implements in relation to grinding tools, indicating greater reliance on hunting as a source of food; and pressure-flaking became part of the stone-working pattern (Fig. 12, *d* and *g*). The typical milling-stone was large, with a deep, oval basin.

[5] Named for the near-by San Pedro River.

Handstones, too, were larger than in the earlier periods, and their grinding surfaces were convex. Mortars and pestles emerged as fully developed tools. Grinding tools were made mainly of igneous stone.

Chipped implements were made of fine-grained igneous stone, quartz, and some chert and obsidian. They include plano-convex and biface axes, biface blades (both thick and with fine pressure-flaking along the cutting edges), knives (both heavy and thin with minute retouching), and various kinds of scrapers. Some hammerstones were large and were probably used for pressure-flaking or for sharpening grinding tools. There were also small disks and projectile points with a broad lateral notch, both pressure-flaked.

The wide distribution of San Pedro sites indicates that this culture was well established.

Ornaments.—Fragments of shell and mica were present and may have been used for ornaments; however, they could not be identified as such.

Materials not found.—Nothing is known concerning the physical appearance, clothing, houses, or burial customs of these people; and there is no evidence of pottery, basketry, or pipes.

CONJECTURES ABOUT THE COCHISE CULTURE

The earliest Cochise culture is at least as old as that of Folsom man. It differs from the culture of Folsom man in that grinding tools were its predominant feature, with chipped implements decidedly secondary in importance, while in the Folsom type chipped tools were of primary importance. There is no evidence to indicate that either culture is the outgrowth of the other. It seems safe to assume that the two cultures had independent origins and that a gradual merging or borrowing took place later on.

Before the Cochise material was found, we thought of the earliest Indians as hunters, and there was nothing to show how the later agricultural cultures developed from such a nonagricultural beginning. Since we now know that some of the earliest inhabitants of North America were gatherers and grinders of natural wild foods, the later developments are more easily understood.

There is a sequence unbroken from the earliest to the latest Cochise periods—a sequence extending to the time just preceding the introduction of pottery and agriculture. This sequence is important because it probably bridges the gap previously existing between the culture of the earliest Indians in southeastern Arizona and that of later ones.

Grinding tools (mortars, handstones, pestles, flat grinding-stones) and evidence of Cochise-like food-collecting habits are characteristic of the earliest known cultures of eastern North America. There may be a connection between some Cochise period and the early periods (before Christ) of the eastern Archaic cultures.

SUMMARY

From the evidence derived from the Folsom and Cochise sites, it seems probable that man entered the New World about fifteen or twenty thousand years ago. The evidence consists of camp sites, hearths, bone and stone tools, and bones of extinct species of mammals which man hunted and ate. This material has been dated by means of geological evidence, such as dried-up lakes, cave deposits, and glacial deposits.

Few human skeletal remains from these early finds have yet turned up. But we are sure that man was here in early times because we have found his tools and the places where he camped.

Although man has been in the New World some fifteen or twenty thousand years, we feel fairly certain that the higher civilizations that developed in Peru, Central America, and the southwestern United States are not very old. Many people believe that it takes from five to ten thousand years or more for a civilization to mature. We now know this is an erroneous belief. From all the available evidence yielded by the study of Maya inscriptions and the Maya chronology, by the study of tree rings in the Southwest and the dates derived from them, and by the archeological data from Peru, we can state that none of the highest civilizations in the New World could be dated much earlier than A.D. 1. Even if we grant another thousand years or so for the development of the Peruvian and Maya civilizations, we cannot claim any great antiquity for them, certainly not more than three thousand years from the present. Furthermore, botanists, who have worked on the problem of the origin of Indian corn, tell us that the development and spread of corn could easily have taken place within a comparatively short time.

If the Indians came here—say about twenty thousand years ago—and if none of the Indian high civilizations did evolve, as we know them, until about the year A.D. 1, what were the Indians doing in the New World during these thousands of years?

WHAT HAPPENED NEXT?

Archeologists have been able to work out a continuous sequence of civilizations in the Southwest—a sequence that carries us back about two thousand years. In other words, the year A.D. 1 is the starting-point for the known developments of southwestern cultures.

East of the Mississippi the story is about the same. The estimated terminal date for the Archaic cultures is about A.D. 500–700. It is estimated that these cultures had their beginnings several thousand years earlier. Parenthetically, the higher civilizations of Central America (Maya) and Peru also began their sequential developments about the beginning of the Christian Era.

Two thousand years, then, will account for all known developments of Indian cultures.

We have suggested that the Indians arrived in North America about twenty thousand years ago, and it was stated above that the Cochise, Sandia, and Folsom cultures were at least twelve thousand years old. What, then, were the Indians doing between 10,000 B.C. and the year A.D. 1? This hiatus between the very early cultures (Cochise, Sandia, and Folsom) and the later cultures (Hohokam, Mogollon, and Anasazi for the Southwest and the Archaic for the eastern United States) is an embarrassingly real one. Fortunately, we have some information that fills this gap.

We should point out that the dating on some of the early finds (Pinto Basin, Gypsum Cave) is perhaps extreme. Archeologists are like other people. The earlier the date, the more attractive it is to them. The association of man-made tools with bones of extinct animals does not necessarily indicate great antiquity, as some of those animals may have died off just a few thousand years ago. We have attempted in this book to give conservative dates that are supported by the best evidence we could collect.

However, we have two excellent records of what the Indians were doing between 10,000 B.C. and the year A.D. 1.

One record is that afforded us by the Cochise culture. In this developmental sequence we have a continuous history of Indian life for ten thousand years. The Cochise Indians camped along streams and lakes; they hunted; they gathered seeds and nuts which they ground up on milling-stones (metates); they probably made wooden and bone objects; and they got along without farming, pottery, and permanent houses. They evolved some new types of tools from time to time, but their culture remained basically the same from beginning to end.

Probably some centuries before Christ, pottery, permanent houses, and agriculture were introduced into the area and were added to the San Pedro culture elements, thus ushering in the Mogollon culture.

Therefore, we have here in a capsule what the Indians were doing for ten thousand years in southern Arizona.

In Ventana Cave, in southern Arizona, we have a similar historical sequence. The earliest and lowest layer of cave debris contained tools suggesting a Folsom-like culture. On top of that were two layers containing stone tools similar to those found in the Chiricahua and San Pedro periods of the Cochise culture and also similar to stone tools found in the Mohave and Pinto basins of California. On top of these three pre-pottery and pre-agricultural layers was found a fourth layer containing Hohokam pottery (dating from about the year A.D. 1 to A.D. 1400). The topmost layer (the fifth) contained modern Indian debris dating from about 1500 on down to the 1800's.

These Ventana Cave finds have not yet been definitely dated, but from the evidence at hand it seems safe to conclude that Indians used this cave more or less continuously for about twelve thousand years.

It is highly probable that the history of the Cochise culture and of Ventana Cave was the history of the Indians of all of North America. Their cultures were founded on gathering and collecting seeds and nuts (the Cochise type) or on hunting (the Folsom type), or on hunting, fishing, and food-gathering.

It is barely possible that Burnet Cave in New Mexico represents a recent period in the history of the Indians (maybe three or four thousand years old). Other sites which may be only a few thousands of years old might include the caves near Salt Lake City, the Oregon caves, the Big Bend sites, and the Boylston fish-weir site (Boston).

This last-named "site" was actually an ancient structure of about 65,000 wooden stakes, which had been interlaced with brush. The arrangement and placement of the stakes suggested that this structure was used to catch fish. This weir is probably about four or five thousand years old and is one of the best pieces of evidence concerning man's presence in early times in eastern United States.

From about 6000 B.C. to 2000 B.C. a warm and dry period occurred in the Great Plains. It has been suggested that the Folsom Indians moved eastward from the Great Plains to regions with heavier rainfall. Since fluted (Folsom-like) projectile points have been found in the earliest stages of the eastern Archaic period, and since that period may extend from A.D. 500 back to about 2000 B.C., an eastward migration of the Folsom Indians seems plausible.

At any rate, it should be clear that there is no real hiatus between the early cultures, such as Cochise and Folsom, and the later-dated cultures of the Southwest and the eastern Archaic. The Indians continued to live by means of hunting or food-gathering, and their culture remained more or less unchanged for thousands of years. With the introduction of agriculture and pottery, the process of becoming more sophisticated was greatly accelerated.

SOURCES

Antevs, 1935, 1937; Bryan, Kirk, 1929, 1937; Bryan and Ray, 1940; Bryan, W. A., 1929; Campbell, E. W., et al., 1937; Campbell, W. H. and Elizabeth W., 1935; Cook, 1903; Dixon, 1913; Figgins, 1927; Greenman, 1943; Greenman and Stanley, 1943; Harrington, 1933, 1934; Haury, 1943; Hibben, 1941; Howard, 1935; Johnson, 1942; Laufer, 1929; MacCurdy, 1937; Mangelsdorf and Reeves, 1939; Roberts, 1939b, 1940b, 1941; Sayles and Antevs, 1941; Stallings, 1941.

PART IV
THE SOUTHWEST

CHAPTER 11

GENERAL REMARKS ON THE SOUTHWESTERN AREA

GEOGRAPHY

THE Southwest area—in approximate terms—includes the southern portions of Colorado and Utah, most of Arizona and New Mexico, and part of northern Mexico. Many people think of the Southwest as a desert area. While it is true that much of it is dry, with a rainfall of only 10–15 inches per year, yet some of the higher plateaus, the mountains, and the Alpine valleys receive abundant rainfall (22–40 inches per year) and are covered with grass and forests of pines and aspens. It is therefore impossible to characterize the Southwest in any general way. Some of it is high, moist, and cool; some of it is high, dry, and cool; and some of it is low, arid, and hot.

The Indians of the region lived at elevations varying from about 1,100 feet (southern Arizona) to about 8,000 feet (northern Arizona).

The specific environments for the three separate Southwestern civilizations or cultures—Anasazi (Basket Maker–Pueblo), Mogollon, and Hohokam—will be included with the discussions of these three civilizations.

RACE

All peoples who inhabited North, Central, and South America before the coming of Columbus (1492) were Indians and were most closely related to the Mongoloid division of the human race. As explained in chapter 2, it is believed that the Indians migrated to America from Asia via Bering Strait.

All the prehistoric inhabitants of the Southwest were, therefore, Indians. It seems probable that the Basket Maker and Pueblo Indians were derived from a single racial stock or that they belong to intimately related strains. These Indians are now referred to as the "Southwest Plateau" Indian stock. It is evident that this stock has been continuous from Basket Maker times right up to the present day.

There were, however, minor physical differences among some of the Southwestern Indians. These differences will be briefly described.

The skulls of the Basket Maker Indians, the earliest representatives of the Anasazi culture (the newer inclusive term for the Basket Maker and Pueblo cultures), were predominantly longheaded; but some medium longheaded and some roundheaded types were present in this early population (Fig. 13). A "long" skull indicates a skull which is long in relation to its width. The stature of these Indians was short, being possibly about five feet eight inches.

Most of the Pueblo Indians were medium longheaded or roundheaded people, with almost all the skulls flattened in the rear. It is likely that these Indians looked very much like the present-day

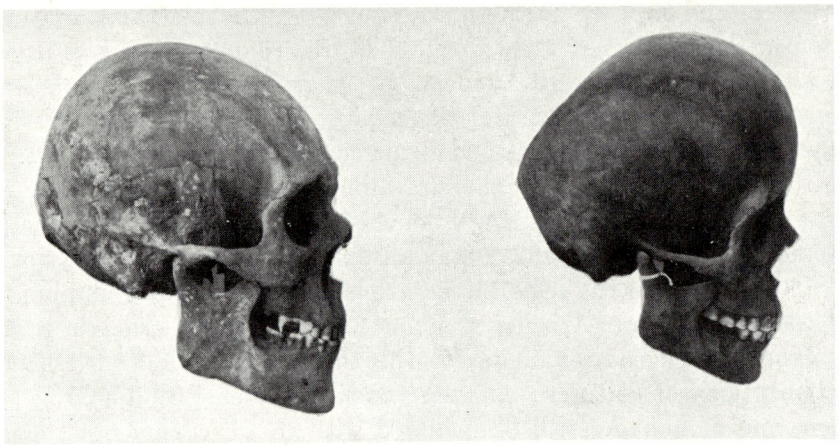

Fig. 13.—Longheaded and roundheaded skulls. Southeastern Utah, Anasazi culture. (Skull on right also shows posterior deformation.)

Hopis of northern Arizona or the Zuñis of western New Mexico. It is also very likely that the Hopis, Zuñis, and the Indians living near Santa Fe, New Mexico, are the descendants of the ancient Pueblo Indians, some of whom built cliff-houses.

Very little is known about the physical appearance of the Indians who were responsible for the Mogollon culture or civilization, because only a few of their skeletons have been found. In general, however, it may be stated that the Mogollon Indians resembled the Pueblo Indians.

Because the Indians of the Hohokam culture cremated their dead, it is not possible to make any statement about their physical characteristics. Only two male skulls have yet been discovered. These are round and are not flattened or deformed in any way. Nothing further can be said at this time about the Hohokam physical type.

THE SOUTHWESTERN AREA

LANGUAGE

We do not have the remotest idea what language or languages were spoken by the ancient Indians of the Southwest. It is probable that the Basket Maker, Pueblo, Mogollon, and Hohokam Indians all spoke different languages; but we have no way of proving this. In fact, nothing that has been dug up or that will be dug up will help solve this mystery. This is one question which can never be answered. Guesses on this subject have been and will be made, but they are, after all, only guesses.

What is the relationship among language, race, and culture? Is it like an algebraic equation, which can be solved if two of the unknowns are given? That is, if one finds (from archeological work) two of these unknowns—race and culture—can he solve for the third unknown—language? If, for example, we determine that some houses, tools, and pottery which were excavated in New Mexico belong to the Mogollon culture (civilization) and that the accompanying skeletons belong to the Pueblo subrace of the American Indians, can we then state what language was spoken by the people of this culture?

The answer is "No." One cannot reduce these three complex factors—language, race, and culture—to an equation. The language spoken by the people of an ancient culture (civilization) cannot be determined from an examination of skeletons, pottery, houses, or tools.

There is, then, no connection between race, language, and culture. This should be obvious, for all who speak English are not of the White stock. The racial subdivision to which a man belongs depends upon his mother, father, and progenitors. One does not *choose* his race; he is, rather, born into it. The individual has nothing to do with it.

A man's language depends upon the speech or language which he was taught when he was a child. A Chinese born in America will speak English; yet he belongs to the East Asiatic or Mongoloid division of the human race. This same Chinese born in America would be an "American" in the sense that he would think, act, and talk like any of us.

As further examples of what we mean, we shall cite two more instances. The Aztec Indians spoke the Aztec language, which is a dialect related to the language spoken by the Hopi, Ute, Shoshoni, and other Indians. And the Aztecs, Hopis, Utes, and Shoshonis are all racially the same—that is, they are all Indians and are classed as a branch of the Mongoloid (Asiatic) stem of the human family. But certainly the Aztec civilization, as we know it, differed greatly from the civilizations of the Hopis or the Utes or the Shoshonis.

The Indians who in the early 1700's, founded the town of Hano, in the Hopi country of northeastern Arizona, formerly lived in central New Mexico. They fled from their original home to escape the vengeance of the Spaniards. Today they have completely assimilated Hopi ways and make typical Hopi pottery; yet they still speak their own Tewa language, which is quite different from the Hopi tongue.

Because we know of these complicated relationships and changes in historic times, it would be unwise to make any assumptions about languages spoken by the prehistoric peoples. The Hopi Indians for instance are related by race and civilization (culture) to the Indians who built towns in caves—the so-called cliff-dwellers. But we do not know whether the Hopis took over the language spoken by the cliff-dwellers when they moved into the Hopi country, whether the cliff-dwellers took over the Hopi language, or whether any language shift took place.

Thus, we see that language, race, and culture (civilization) are not related. Man's behavior, language, and civilization (culture) may and do change, but his race does not. Race is hereditary; language and culture are social ways that are acquired and learned.

We shall now describe the three principal prehistoric civilizations (cultures) of the Southwest. The Anasazi culture will be treated first, following which will come résumés of the Hohokam and the Mogollon cultures.

SOURCES

COLTON, 1945; GLADWIN, W. and H. S., 1934; KROEBER, 1928.

CHAPTER 12

THE ANASAZI CULTURE

INTRODUCTION

THE Anasazi or Basket Maker–Pueblo civilization flourished from about A.D. 200 down to the present time in what is known today as the "four corners" region. This region may be roughly described as northeastern Arizona, northwestern New Mexico, southeastern Utah, and southwestern Colorado.

A brief explanation of the terms "Anasazi," "Basket Maker," and "Pueblo" should first be made.

"Anasazi" is the anglicized form of a Navaho Indian word which is supposed to mean the "old peoples" who formerly inhabited the houses which are now ruins. It is customary now to use this newer, more inclusive term "Anasazi" for the older divisions, which were Basket Maker culture and Pueblo culture, or Basket Maker and Modified Basket Maker periods, and Pueblo periods I, II, III, IV, and V.

Basket Maker Indians were early dwellers in the northern portion of the Southwest (*ca.* A.D. 200). At first, they did not know the art of making pottery, although they wove excellent baskets, hence the name "Basket Makers." Later on (*ca.* A.D. 500), the idea of making pottery spread from southern New Mexico, Arizona, or Mexico to the Basket Makers, who then adopted it. The Basket Maker culture is usually broken down into two periods called "Basket Maker" and "Modified Basket Maker." These periods will be briefly described later.

The classification of the Anasazi—that is, the Basket Maker–Pueblo groups—into periods as listed above is not entirely satisfactory.

In the first place, the divisions would lead one to think that it is possible to draw a sharp line, for example, between Pueblo I period and Pueblo II period. As a matter of fact, it is very difficult to make such a distinction because some elements of Pueblo I culture persisted into and through the Pueblo II period. It would be just as difficult for us to draw a line between the Victorian and Edwardian eras in English history. It is only when we see that several new elements have merged with older features of the Pueblo I culture and then are able to recognize a marked change in the total civilization that we can label the culture "Pueblo II."

Another objection to the Pueblo I, II, III, etc., classification is that it implies a simultaneous development. That is, one might logically infer that the Pueblo I period, whether in Utah or in Colorado, would always date from about 700–900. It is quite possible, however, to find a Pueblo I village which was in existence after 900; while at the same time another village, two hundred miles away, was enjoying the advances represented by the Pueblo II culture. In other words, there were communities in which culture stood still or lagged. One may observe the same phenomenon of cultural lag today in our own culture. A village in the Kentucky hills or in the Ozarks is less likely to be up to date than one which is closer to the swift current of progress and change and near a large metropolitan area such as New York or Chicago.

The point to be stressed, then, is that historical periods may overlap. Village A might have been carrying on its same old ways long after Village B had adopted new ideas and inventions.

A third objection to this convenient I, II, III, etc., classification is that one might think that a single village would have been occupied continuously from Basket Maker to Pueblo V—a period of about two thousand years. Actually, this was never the case. Archeologists have discovered a few large pueblos whose activity spanned two periods or occasionally three. Or again the Basket Maker stage of culture continued at a particular village until Pueblo II styles came along. This village, never adopting the Pueblo I fashions, would not show a continuous development from Basket Maker to Pueblo II because Pueblo I styles would be lacking. Very often a village was inhabited for a few years only—perhaps twenty—and thus partook of only a portion of any one culture period.

Thus, any system of classifying the various stages of human history has disadvantages. Keeping in mind these drawbacks, however, one will find that this systematic classification of history and civilizations is useful for reducing to a common denominator a great mass of indigestible information and for interpreting the significance and interrelationship of disconnected facts. It is especially convenient for general readers because it introduces some logic into what otherwise would be a bewildering set of facts.

We are now going to sketch the history of the Anasazi (Basket Maker–Pueblo) culture (civilization) in the following order: the Basket Maker and Modified Basket Maker periods and Pueblo periods I, II, III, IV, and V (see Chart II). The Anasazi culture is also sometimes referred to as the "Plateau culture" in contradistinction to "Mountain culture" for the Mogollon, and "Desert culture" for the Hohokam. The terms are descriptive and fitting.

CHART II

DEVELOPMENT OF THE ANASAZI CIVILIZATION

Estimated Date	Period
A.D. 1700 to date	Pueblo V
A.D. 1300–1700	Pueblo IV
A.D. 1050–1300	Pueblo III
A.D. 900–1050	Pueblo II
A.D. 700– 900	Pueblo I
A.D. 500– 700	Modified Basket Maker
A.D. 100– 500	Basket Maker

THE BASKET MAKER PERIOD

Ca. A.D. 100–500

Area.—The Basket Maker Indians were concentrated in the so-called "four corners" region, or in that region where the states of Utah, Colorado, Arizona, and New Mexico have a common meeting-point. But they also occupied much of what is now Utah, northern Arizona, southern New Mexico, and possibly western Oklahoma. The elevations for the inhabited portions of the Basket Maker area range from about 4,000 to 7,000 feet. The climate is semidesert, as the average annual precipitation is less than 15 inches. The vegetation consists of sagebrush and piñon and juniper trees.

People.—The people of this period belonged to the "Southwest Plateau" stock and were basically the same as the Pueblo Indians of all later periods up to and including present-day Pueblo Indians. The skulls of the Basket Makers were predominantly long; but some were medium long and some short and round. The rear portion of the skulls was not flattened or deformed.

Language.—We do not know what language the Basket Makers spoke.

Houses.—The Basket Maker Indians constructed shelters in caves and in the open.

In the caves the dwellings were single-roomed houses with saucer-shaped floors, each containing a firepit and a storage bin. The manner in which walls and roofs were constructed is unknown, although we know that poles, twigs, and mud were used in some combination.

Houses built in the open were similar to those of the cave. They ranged from ten to thirty feet in diameter; the floors were saucer-shaped with firepits in the center. Metates (corn-grinding mills) were set up near storage bins. The walls consisted of wood-and-mud masonry, that is, logs, poles, and twigs laid horizontally. Mud was used for chinking as in our log cabins. The roof was of timbers and probably hemispherical in shape.

For storage of food the Basket Maker Indians dug pits in the floors of caves and of the houses. The cave pits were two to four feet in diameter and two to three feet deep and varied somewhat in shape. Some of them were walled with flat stone slabs set on edge and some were roofed with poles covered with mud. When these pits were no longer needed for storage of food, they were secondarily used as graves. The so-called "mummies" (which are really just well-dried bodies) come from these pits.

Livelihood.—Judging from the evidence obtained from pits and graves, we may infer that the Basket Maker Indians were hunters, farmers, and gatherers of wild seeds.

In the storage pits many important articles are often found. It is from such finds that we obtain our information about the daily life of the ancient Indians. Some of these pits contained nets, snares, hunting implements, and agricultural products and tools.

Snares, nets (one of which measures 240 feet in length), wooden hunting clubs (?), and spears and spear-throwers (no bow and arrow) were extensively employed for securing such animals as deer, mountain sheep, elk, badgers, rabbits, squirrels, and prairie dogs. The flesh of all these animals was eaten, and the skins were used for making bags, pouches, and robes of fur string.

The two principal food crops grown by the Basket Maker Indians were maize (corn) and pumpkin. It is possible that beans were grown later in the Basket Maker period, although this is not yet certain. The only agricultural tool was the wooden digging-stick. This implement is usually about three or four feet long and was beveled at the lower end to a broad, thin blade or sharpened to a point. Such a tool was used generally for turning the soil, for making small holes in which the seeds were placed, and possibly for weeding.

In addition to meat and corn and squash, these Indians also depended on wild vegetable foods to a large extent. Sunflower seeds, yucca pods, Indian mountain rice, pinon nuts, acorns, seeds of a plant related to Spanish needles, pigweed seeds, and seeds of Brigham tea were gathered and stored in dry, rodent-proof pits.

Dogs were kept by the Basket Makers (mummies of two types of domesticated dogs were found buried with human bodies in an Arizona cave); but whether they were used for food is not known. These dogs were derived from Old World ancestors and accompanied man to America.

Turkeys may have been kept also, since turkey-feather blankets have been found in Basket Maker graves; but possibly these turkey feathers were secured by hunting the wild turkey. Certainly no turkey pens or droppings have been found in Basket Maker sites.

Pottery.—Pottery was unknown to the Basket Maker Indians.

Basketry.—In a group that was handicapped by the lack of clay vessels, baskets became an important and acceptable substitute. It is not surprising, then, to find that the Basket Maker Indians cooked in baskets, stored food, water, and clothing in baskets, and transported burdens in specially constructed baskets. Basketry, in short, was an important and well-developed art.

Baskets were constructed by means of two different techniques or weaves: coiling and twill plaiting.

Basket shapes consisted of trays, bowls, large, deep carrying or transport containers, and water bottles.

The designs, which were always in black, were produced by weaving black-dyed splints into the uncolored body of the basket. These were composed of spiral or straight radii, small triangles, zigzags, or diamonds. These patterns were, of course, limited by the basket-weaving technique and were symmetrical.

Tools, utensils, and weapons.—The bow and arrow was entirely absent from the Basket Maker culture (civilization). Instead, the spear-thrower (or atlatl) was used for hunting and defense (Fig. 14). A curved wooden club was also utilized by the Basket Maker Indians. The exact use of this club is not known, but it may have served as a defensive weapon to fend off the spears thrown from the spear-thrower. Such clubs may also have been used at close quarters as cudgels.

The only agricultural tool was the wooden digging-stick. This implement was three or four feet long and was used for turning the soil or for making small holes in which seeds were planted.

Wooden scoops were used for digging storage pits in the caves and may also have been used as food trays, as paint palettes, as grass shredders, and (in pairs) for lifting hot stones from the fire to cooking-baskets.

Corn, seeds, nuts, and berries were ground or reduced to flour by means of stone grinders or millstones, operated by hand. The upper part of the mill consisted of an oval-shaped stone of such size that it could easily be held in the hand. This stone is sometimes called a "rubbing-stone" or a "handstone" or "mano," which is Spanish for "hand." The lower part of the mill consisted of a large flat stone about twenty inches long, having on its top surface an oval or saucer-shaped hollow into which the mano fitted. This lower part is sometimes called a "milling-stone" or a "metate," which is derived from the Aztec word *metlatl*, meaning "corn-grinder." The material to be ground was laid in the hollow of the large flat stone. The handstone was then placed on the grains or nuts and rubbed back and forth and in a rotating motion until the latter were pulverized.

Stone knives made from chert or chalcedony were large, well-chipped blades with side or diagonal notches. The sharp cutting edges were produced by fine secondary chipping.

Spear or lance points of stone were stemmed, notched at the sides, fairly uniform in shape and size, and well flaked and shaped.

Spear-thrower weights or charms occur with some frequency. These are small loaf-shaped stones which were lashed to the underside of the spear-throwers. Bone was utilized for making awls, beads, and whistles.

No stone axes or mauls, grooved or ungrooved, occur in this period.

Pipes.—Cylindrical pipes of stone and clay are frequently found (Fig. 14). Some of the pipes are long and slender; others are short and squat. The bowl was relatively large, while the stem hole was very small. It is possible that a mouthpiece of bird bone (which is hollow) was sometimes inserted in the stem hole. These pipes do not resemble those which Europeans and Americans smoke but look something like a short cigar.

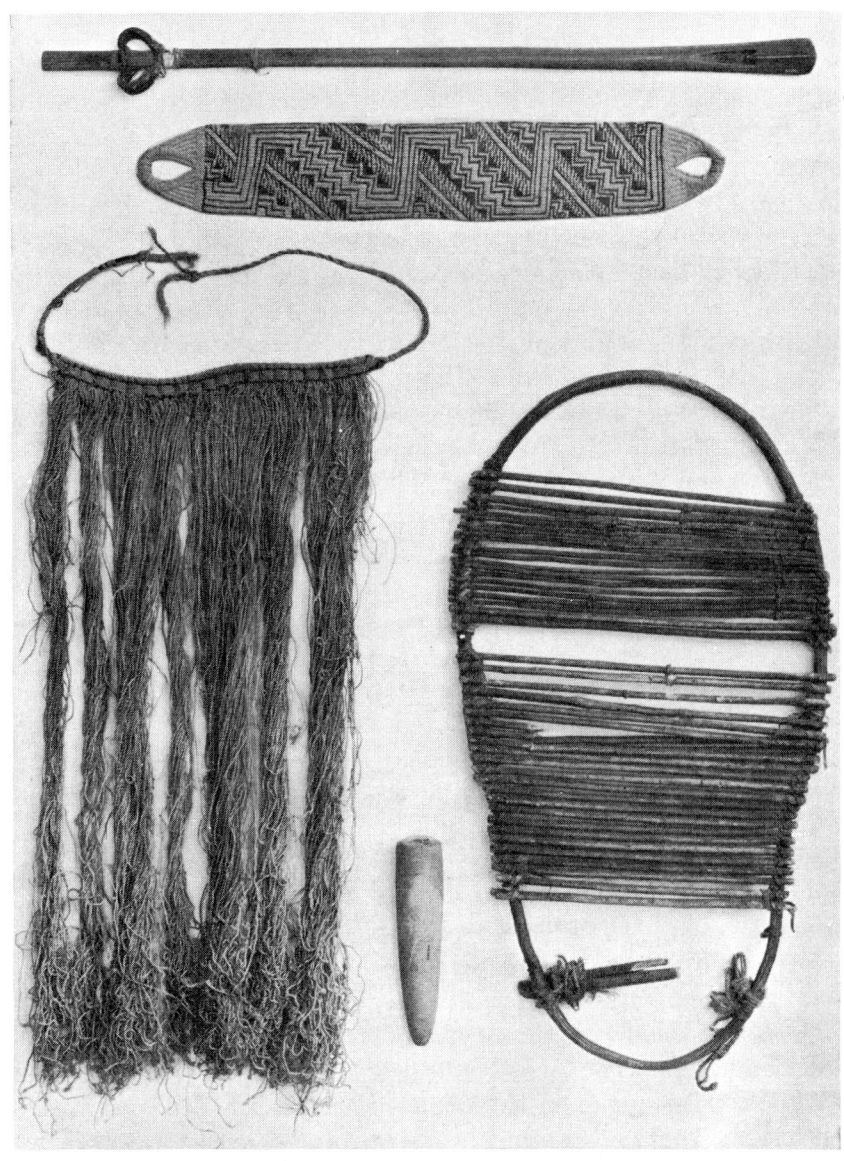

Fig. 14.—Typical grave-offerings. *Top row:* throwing-stick of wood; woven, pointed carrying-band. *Bottom row:* string apron; tobacco pipe of stone; oval-shaped rigid cradle of hardwood sticks. Basket Maker period, Anasazi culture.

Costume.—From all the available evidence, it seems apparent that the Basket Maker Indians wore only sandals in the summertime and no loincloth or gee-string. The women probably wore aprons only during menstruation periods. One apron was made of a hank of woody fiber (cedar bast or yucca fiber) which was passed through the crotch and fastened in the front and in the back to a string belt. Another type consisted of strings dangling from a band (Fig. 14). One skirt or apron of woven human hair has been reported. In the wintertime a small fur blanket was thrown about the shoulders. The blanket was made of cords wrapped with strips of fur woven into an open meshwork fabric. Skins were sometimes used as garments and blankets. No other clothing has yet been found.

Sandals are typically rectangular and square-toed with reinforced soles (Fig. 15a). There are four types, all cross-woven (not plaited): (1) whole or crushed yucca leaf; (2) cedar bark; (3) yucca cord; and (4) hide.

The Type 3 sandals, woven from yucca cord, have square heels and square toes. Sometimes the toes are fringed with bunches of fiber or deerskin strips. Some of the sandals are also provided with reinforced soles.

The men dressed their hair in a rather elaborate manner. The hair was parted in the center from forehead to crown and fell loose on either side or was bound into tresses, while the hair on the back of the head was gathered into a queue, the end of which was turned back on itself and wrapped with a fine string. Occasionally, a lock of hair on the back of the head hung from the crown and was wound with string and bound up with the end of the queue. Frequently, some of the hair from the forehead to the crown was shaved off. The women wore their hair cropped short; and it is possible that it was cut off to provide material for making cordage and belts, which are found in graves.

Cradles.—There were three types of cradles: rigid, flexible, and the cedar-bark type. The rigid cradle was oval-shaped (Fig. 14). The outer rim was made up of two trimmed and peeled hardwood sticks. The body of the cradle was made of series of slim, peeled willow twigs, some of which ran crosswise and some up and down. A soft padding of bark or skin was placed on top of these twigs. Across the bottom of the frame was a roll of cedar bark which formed a rest for the baby's feet. At both ends of the cradle were string loops (made from human hair) which served to suspend the cradle in a horizontal position.

The flexible cradle of yucca was provided with a rim of tightly rolled grass bent in the form of an oval hoop. The body of the cradle was made up of a mesh of yucca leaves fastened to this rim.

The cedar-bark cradle consists of a mat of long strips of cedar bark held together by rows of woven yucca leaves. The edges of the mat were turned up and fastened together by yucca to form the rim.

Weaving, bags, and textiles.—Since the Basket Maker Indians did not know the true loom, all their weaving was finger-weaving done either by warps fastened to a stake (fixed warps) or by suspending the warp from a horizontal pole (suspended warp). Since cotton was also unknown to the Basket Maker Indians, their fabrics were woven from other vegetal fibers, usually yucca or apocynum.

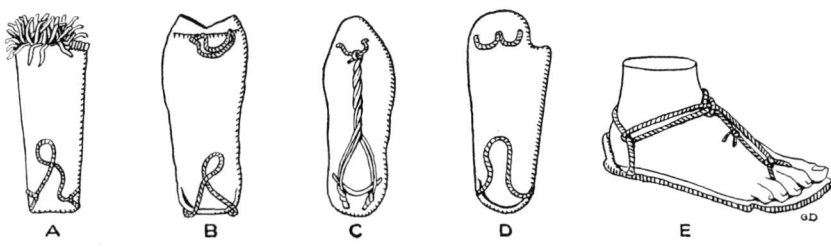

FIG. 15.—Sandal types: *a*, square-toed, fringed sandal, Basket Maker period; *b*, V-notch sandal, Modified Basket Maker period; *c*, pointed-toe sandal, Pueblo I; *d*, jog-toed sandal, Pueblo III; *e*, jog-toed sandal on foot. Anasazi culture.

The weaves used were plain (over and under weave), twining (wrapping the weft around the warp as in our surgical bandages), and coiling.

One piece of Basket Maker material made from yucca fibers measures about twenty-seven inches square. It is an example of plain over-and-under weave and was used as a burial wrapping for an infant. This fabric bore a design of red and black rectangles.

Plain weaving was employed likewise for producing narrow fabrics such as carrying-bands which were attached to pannier baskets (Fig. 14).

Twined weaving, with warp and weft of vegetal fibers, was commonly used for making bags. Such bags ranged in length from an inch and a half to two feet and were decorated with geometric designs in red and black colors. Twining was also used for manufacturing fur cloth.

Coiling or looping or knitting was also used for making sacks and nets.

Ornaments.—Necklaces were the commonest kind of personal adornment. They were composed of beads made from many kinds of materials: shell, lignite (soft coal), colored stones, wood, bone, and seeds. No turquoise has ever been found in Basket Maker graves or houses. The shapes of the beads were cylindrical, spherical, or discoidal.

Pendants or short strands of beads were suspended from small perforations in the lobe of the ear.

Hair ornaments consisted of three or four long bone pins lashed together with feathers attached.

Burials.—So far as is known at present, all Basket Maker burials were in caves, either in suitable crevices or in pits. These pits had been dug for storing food and were used secondarily for burial purposes. (See description of pits under section on "Houses.")

The bodies of the Basket Maker Indians were not treated with preservatives; they were merely buried. However, since moisture rarely penetrated caves, the bodies became thoroughly desiccated and thus were preserved. Thanks to the extreme dryness of the caves, not only bodies but also cloth, fur, baskets, corn and other perishable foods, wooden implements, leather, and wood survived the passage of time.

The body was flexed (i.e., knees drawn up toward the chin) and was usually wrapped in a fur-cloth blanket or in a tanned deerskin mantle. Sometimes a large bag was split open and used as a body wrapping. The body was placed in the grave in any convenient position and without regard to orientation.

Much of our knowledge of the Basket Maker civilization comes from the presents placed in the graves, and, owing to the complete dryness of the graves, the bodies, the wrappings, and the grave-offerings or presents are perfectly preserved. The grave-offerings would include articles of daily life, such as pipes, baskets, beads and ornaments, sandals, aprons, food, weapons (the atlatl or throwing-stick), stone and bone tools, and cradles (Fig. 14).

The presence of grave-offerings with the dead may indicate that these Indians believed in future life.

Summary and conjectures.—The typical features which set Basket Maker culture off from other periods are: half-nomadic and half-farmer economy, corn, definite burial practices, excellent coiled basketry, well-woven sandals, twined bags, and the spear-thrower in place of the bow. Completely lacking are axes of any kind, permanent houses, the bow and arrow, and fired pottery.

This early culture, which was the foundation of the later Pueblo civilization, was rich and varied. Although it sired the later and more highly developed Pueblo culture, it was, itself, the result of many centuries of growth. More information about the Basket Maker culture and its antecedents is needed, and this can and will be obtained by carrying on further archeological investigations in the Southwest.

SOURCES

GUERNSEY, 1931; GUERNSEY and KIDDER, 1921; HAURY, 1945a; McGREGOR, 1941; MORRIS, 1939, 1941; MORRIS and BURGH, 1941; NUSBAUM, 1922; RINALDO, 1941; STALLINGS, 1941.

THE MODIFIED BASKET MAKER PERIOD
Ca. A.D. 500–700

The name of this period indicates that its culture is similar to the preceding one (Basket Maker) except that many of the cultural items have been modified somewhat.

Area.—This culture is found in northeastern Arizona, northwestern New Mexico, extending possibly as far east as Santa Fe, southeastern Utah, and southwestern Colorado. In general, the area covered is the same as for the preceding period.

People.—The Indians of this period belong to the Southwest Plateau stock and represent the same basic physical type as those who preceded and followed them. The skulls are long or medium long and some are round. All of them are high, and the face was medium broad. The skulls were not deformed.

Villages.—Villages were located either in caves or out in the open. Villages in caves consisted of from ten to twenty separate pit-houses and some small storage bins. Villages built in the open were of similar form or consisted of above-ground contiguous rooms arranged in a straight line or in the form of an arc or a crescent (Fig. 16). In front of these or between the horns of the crescent were the pit-houses.

Pit-houses were more or less round with floors sunk below ground level. The roof was a mud-covered platform made up of horizontal poles and supported by four or five wooden uprights. There were two entrances: one, through smoke hole or hatchway; the other, through an entry-way at the south side of the house. A low bench encircling the wall is found in some houses. The southern portion of the house was separated from the rest of the chamber by means of a low ridge and, in the later part of the period, by a low partition wall. Metates are often found in this southern portion of the house. The southern entryway-ventilator was provided with a vestibule or antechamber in later houses of this period. Pit-houses were erected as separate units, each one being placed a few feet from the others.

Fig. 16.—Restoration of Modified Basket Maker village. *Left:* great kiva (unroofed). *Center right:* smaller great kiva (unroofed). Pit-houses (low, dome-shaped structures). Surface rooms arranged in a straight line or in the form of a crescent. Southwestern Colorado, Anasazi culture. (Painting by Arthur G. Rueckert.)

Cave storage bins were built near the houses or between the back wall of the house and the cliff wall. The shape and size of bins varied; some were jug-shaped holes; others were small, room-sized structures, with walls of stone slabs and mud and roofs of mud-covered timbers.

The above-ground houses consisted of a double row of contiguous rooms arranged in a straight line or in the form of a crescent or an arc. In front of these houses or between the horns of the crescent were from five to fifteen pit-houses. The walls of the above-ground rooms were of upright poles set close together; the spaces between the poles were plugged with mud, which was strengthened with reed or grass binder. The walls of the rear line of storage rooms were constructed of rubble (i.e., of small stones and mud). The roofs were probably flat and were constructed of horizontal poles covered with bark, brush, and earth.

These larger pit-house villages usually date later than the cave villages, but they are an outgrowth of earlier cave hamlets in form, function, and general plan (pit-houses and storage rooms).

Undoubtedly, such agglomerations of dwellings produced many social activities. The pit-house in this period probably served as a place for domiciliary and ceremonial activities. Although the above-ground rooms served mostly as storage places, they were sometimes used for living quarters. The social organization which came into being at about this time probably remained practically unchanged for a thousand years or more. It is possible that the persistence of this social organization—which was well adapted to *small* communities— eventually brought about the collapse and desertion of many of the large towns (such as Cliff Palace at Mesa Verde National Park). This point will be discussed in the section on Pueblo III.

Later, in Pueblo periods, we shall see that the pit-house evolved into a special and sacred chamber called the *kiva*, set away from the living quarters and used only for ceremonies but still retaining many of its early features such as the firepit, partition wall, bench, ventilator, and smoke-hole hatchway. The above-ground storage rooms developed into quarters used only for domiciliary purposes.

In addition to the surface rooms and pit-houses, there is another important building to describe—the great kiva.

A kiva, as we have said, is a ceremonial chamber, usually round and often below ground. A great kiva is simply a large kiva. Ordinary kivas range from ten to twenty feet in diameter, whereas a great kiva ranges from forty to eighty feet in diameter. It is possible that these large early structures were used for public ceremonies and communal religious dances. Great kivas probably were built during the next two periods (i.e., Pueblo I and II) and were certainly present in highly specialized form in Pueblo III.

Livelihood.—The Modified Basket Maker Indians paid more attention to farming than did Indians of the preceding period. Game was also hunted and wild seeds were gathered; but the emphasis on agriculture was greater.

Maize (corn) and pumpkins continued to be important, and beans were now added to the list of crops.

The agricultural implement (wooden digging-stick) and hunting tools (snares, nets, wooden hunting clubs) were the same as in the preceding period plus one new weapon—the bow and arrow. This weapon came into use during the latter part of this period and entirely supplanted the spear and spear-thrower.

Turkeys were kept in captivity and possibly domesticated. They were used either for ceremonial purposes or as food. Dogs were a part of every household.

Pottery.—The earliest pottery was sun-dried, unfired, and made of mud. As time went on, the mud pots were made more resistant to moisture by being fired; and the mud walls were reinforced or tempered by sand and, later, by crushed rock.

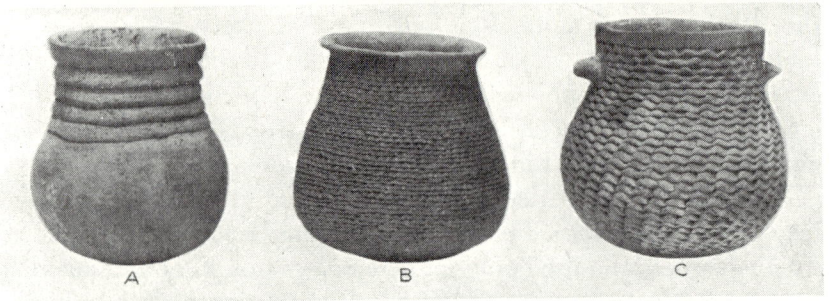

FIG. 17.—Cooking pottery: *a*, banded-neck pot, Modified Basket Maker period; *b*, indented corrugated pottery, Pueblo III period; *c*, "exuberant," wavy indented pottery, Pueblo II period. Anasazi culture.

The first pots were constructed in basket molds, but later they were modeled freehand. The walls of each pot, whether constructed in basket molds or shaped freehand, were always ring- or band-built; that is, the walls were built up by adding successive rings of clay. These rings were similar to varying-sized hoops. This method of pottery manufacture is not to be confused with the later method, called spiral coiling, in which vessel walls are constructed of a continuous thin strand of clay applied spirally from base to mouth.

Three pottery types prevailed: (1) Lino Gray; (2) Lino Black-on-Gray and La Plata Black-on-White; and (3) Abajo Red-on-Orange.

1. *Lino Gray* is a hard, undecorated, thin gray ware, the surfaces of which are usually coarse and grainy-pebbled. Occasionally, some vessels are provided with banded necks (called Kana-a Gray). These show a series of unobliterated bands or rings, built up by adding successive rings of clay. The bands were confined to the neck, the rest of

THE ANASAZI CULTURE

the pot being smooth (Fig. 17, *a*). Lino Gray and Kana-a Gray pottery was made in various shapes: squash pots (form possibly suggested by squash shell and thus without neck); jars with necks; pitchers; slender bottles with and without necks; effigy pots; large water and storage jars with necks and handles; and vessels with lateral spouts. They were used probably for cooking and storage purposes.

2. *Lino Black-on-Gray* and *La Plata Black-on-White* are unslipped, hard, gray-to-white ware, the surfaces of which are finely pebbled and relatively smooth. They bear simple, geometric, rectilinear designs in black-to-brown colors (Fig. 18) and were painted

FIG. 18.—Lino Black-on-Gray pottery bowl and notched pebble-axes. Modified Basket Maker period, Anasazi culture. (Courtesy Earl H. Morris.)

with vegetal coloring (for Lino) and iron oxide (for La Plata). The earliest decorations were probably taken over from basketry designs. The walls were built up by adding successive rings of clay. Lino Black-on-Gray pottery was shaped into squash pots, dippers, submarine-shaped vessels, and bowls and were used for nonculinary purposes.

3. *Abajo Red-on-Orange* is a fine-textured, smooth, well-rubbed type, unslipped, which bears designs in red (to black) on an orange background (Fig. 19). Iron manganese was used as paint, the orange color being produced by using clay different from that employed for Lino types and by firing in oxidizing (excess of oxygen) atmosphere, opposed to reducing (smothered fire and supply of oxygen cut off) atmosphere, which latter produced gray, white, and black-on-white pottery. Broad lines and heavy black lines predominate, and the

designs usually cover nearly all of the bowl interiors. Elements consist of broad parallel wavy lines, strings of triangles, and checkerboards. Abajo Red-on-Orange is shaped into dippers, jars, bird effigies, bottles, squash pots, gourds, and bowls. They were used for nonculinary purposes.

The question of origin of Abajo Red-on-Orange is not settled. Competent students such as Morris (1939) and Brew (in Martin, 1939) believe that this excellent pottery was a product of the Basket Maker Indians; while Haury (verbally), McGregor (1941), and Martin are of the opinion that it lacks the Basket Maker "flavor" and

Fig. 19.—Abajo Red-on-Orange pottery bowls. Mesa Verde Area, Modified Basket Maker period, Anasazi culture.

that, therefore, it may have been introduced to the Basket Makers from some other area.

Occasionally, three other types of pottery turn up in Basket Maker III sites: a black shiny ware, called Forestdale Smudged; a highly burnished plain red ware, called San Francisco Red; and a mustard-brown, fine-grained ware, called Alma Plain. These three wares are typical of the Mogollon area, which lies to the south of the Anasazi locale (see Mogollon chapter), and were possibly traded to the Basket Maker Indians. Alma Plain and San Francisco Red probably date from about the time of Christ. Mogollon-like pottery has been found with Lino Gray and unfired, sun-dried mud vessels in Obelisk Cave, Arizona, which was inhabited about A.D. 500.

The fact that well-made Mogollon (?) pottery was found associated with the cruder Lino Gray and even with Basket Maker *unfired* mud vessels may be one more bit of evidence for helping to establish the priority of Mogollon over Basket Maker pottery.

Basketry.—Baskets are of finer texture than in the previous period because of more closely spaced stitches and narrower rods. The same weaving techniques prevailed: coiled and twilled. In the previous period black was the only color used; but now red is used with black for ornamentation. Designs were usually produced by weaving in dyed splints; occasionally, the designs were painted on after completion of weaving. The shapes are the same as in the preceding period (trays, bowls, water bottles, and large, deep transport containers) plus one new form: a globular carrying-basket. The designs become progressively elaborate, more involved, with black balanced against red elements, and a larger part of each basket is covered by designs. The efflorescence in designs parallels vigorousness in bags, sandals, and pottery forms.

Tools, utensils, and weapons.—The bow and arrow now supplanted the spear-thrower; but we do not know how or why this change was made. It is not known whether the wooden club continued in use or not.

The digging-stick was the same as in the preceding period and was the only agricultural tool. It was also used for digging excavations for pit-houses.

The metate forms changed from those with an oval depression to the long open-end trough-type (flat slab usually unmodified except for the trough on one surface; trough open at one end only) (Fig. 20, *a*). The manos were relatively short and broad; some were provided with single grinding surfaces; others, with two grinding surfaces. Manos were probably operated by one hand only.

This type of millstone differs considerably from the ovoid type of the Basket Maker period.

Metates and manos were used for reducing corn and seeds to flour and were made of stone. Metates ranged in length from sixteen to twenty-five inches.

Stone projectile (arrowheads and spear points) points and knives were well flaked and shaped; secondary chipping is present on edges and faces.

The following types are characteristic of Modified Basket Maker:

    A. Projectile points and knives without stems.
        1. Leaf-shaped, pointed at one end, square at the other.

B. Projectile points and knives with stems.
 1. Leaf-shaped, broad; expanding stems, narrower than shoulder.
 2. Triangular; straight stem, symmetrical and asymmetrical blades.

Stone drills are scarce and apparently were not frequently used.

Stone choppers and side-scrapers are not abundant. They consist of blades, roughly rectangular, with secondary chipping along the edges and crude chipping on all other surfaces.

Axes consist of flat pebbles with a notch ground in each side and sometimes one ground in the center of the poll end; surfaces may be

Fig. 20.—Trough-type metates or millstones: *a*, Modified Basket Maker period; *b*, Pueblo I period. Anasazi culture.

smooth and polished, or pecked and crudely chipped; cutting edge is usually polished and medium sharp (Fig. 18).

Grooved axes (three-quarter or full-grooved) are rarely, if ever, found. Arrow-shaft smoothers were developed with the introduction and use of the bow and arrow. Mauls were oblong pebbles with a full groove around the middle; ends were flat and usually battered.

Miscellaneous stone tools, such as floor-polishers, pot-polishers, pecking-stones or hammerstones, and notched hoes are found in abundance. For descriptions consult Martin (1939), Morris (1939), Rinaldo (1941), and Roberts (1929, 1930, 1931).

Bone tools are very abundant in this period. The most common types are fleshers or end-scrapers, needles, awls, punches, and flakers.

These tools were usually made from the bones of deer, rabbit, fox, and birds.

Pipes.—Pipes were made of baked clay, slate, sandstone, and limestone. The characteristic form is conical, resembling a cigar-holder. The bowl is relatively large and the mouthpiece end is small. Some pipes were used with mouthpieces of bone or wood.

Costume.—Apparently little or no clothing was worn in warm weather, and what there was may have consisted only of an apron of yucca string or a gee-string. In cold weather, blankets of fur cloth, feather cloth, and occasionally dressed skins were used. A feather-cloth blanket was made by splitting soft feathers down the vane and winding them around fiber cords to be used in weaving.

The art of sandal-weaving reached its zenith during the Basket Maker III period. The weaving technique was usually cross-weaving, although some sandals may have been plaited. Yucca and other plant fibers constituted the raw materials. Sandal toes were scalloped, notched, and round; sometimes the scallop is so deep that it resembles a V-shaped notch (Fig. 14, *b*). The V-notch and the scalloped toe were distinguishing marks for sandals of this period. Woven and colored patterns were common.

The men wore their hair long as in the previous period; the women bobbed theirs. The cut hair was used for strings and cordage.

Aprons of yucca string were worn by women.

Cradles.—Probably the same as those of the preceding period.

Weaving, bags, and textiles.—The true loom probably was not known to these people. Twined woven bags with colored patterns, beautifully decorated carrying-bands (or tumplines)—all made from plant fibers—and sashes have been reported.

Ornaments.—Ornaments were more abundant and varied than in Basket Maker II period. Beads of wood, shells, seeds, turquoise, and lignite were common. Beads were massive, saucer-shaped and disk-shaped. Pendants of turquoise, stone, lignite, and shell were worn. Some delicate mosaic ornaments of shell and turquoise have been found. Shell bracelets and necklaces of crystals, bones, and animal claws were great favorites. Hair ornaments consisted of feathers and bone pins. A few bird effigies of stone and lignite have been recovered from burials.

Burials.—Burial practices were more or less the same as in the preceding period. Since some caves were not large enough to provide space for both houses and burials, the dead were placed in the debris in front of the caves. The burial grounds for many villages in the open have not been found, although house burial was not usually practiced. Graves belonging to sites in the open sometimes contain several skeletons, the latter usually flexed and often laid on the back with the knees upward.

Graves in the open were subjected to moisture, and perishable objects (wood, cloth, feathers, baskets) have long since turned to dust. One usually finds only pottery and objects of bone and stone in these graves. Cave burials, which are usually dry, yield many finds, however, such as fur and feather mantles, hair ornaments, necklaces, baskets of corn and smoking materials, games, flutes, implements of war, sandals, stone and bone implements, and pottery. Such graves, of course, yield more information concerning the daily life of these people.

Summary and conjectures.—The features which are typical of Modified Basket Maker period are fired pottery, permanent houses of a definite type, grooved mauls and notched axes, bow and arrow replacing the spear-thrower, beans and several varieties of corn, and domesticated turkeys.

It is difficult to draw a definite line between the end of the Basket Maker and the beginning of the Modified Basket Maker periods, because the latter period carried on the same general manner of life of the preceding period. Gradually, changes crept in, notably those named in the preceding paragraph. Morris (1939) names the following conspicuous modifications: dropping of the toe fringe on sandals; change of sandal form from square to scalloped toe and an increase in improved weaving techniques; and the use of more red in conjunction with black patterns in basketry. Thus, the progression from Basket Maker to Modified Basket Maker was a continuous development without any sharp break between the two periods.

SOURCES

COLTON and HARGRAVE, 1937; GUERNSEY, 1931; GUERNSEY and KIDDER, 1921; HARGRAVE, 1932a; HAWLEY, 1936; KIDDER, 1924; KIDDER and GUERNSEY, 1919; MCGREGOR, 1941; MARTIN, PAUL S., 1939; MORRIS, 1939; MORRIS and BURGH, 1941; RINALDO, 1941; ROBERTS, 1929; SELTZER, 1944.

PUEBLO I
Ca. A.D. 700–900

Information concerning this and the next period is scarce. It is impossible, therefore, to characterize it as fully as was done for the Basket Maker periods.

Area.—The civilization of Pueblo I covered slightly more territory than did the Basket Maker civilizations. The spread of Pueblo I was (broadly speaking) from the "four corners" region westward and southward. Some sites have been reported from the vicinity of Santa Fe.

People.—Most of the skulls of the Indians of this period were medium long, although some long and round ones occur. Many were flattened in the occipital (back of the skull) region. This deformation, presumably practiced because the fashions of the time demanded it, did not in any way affect the brain size of the individual or his intelligence. There is no evidence that a new group of Indians entered this region at this time in significant numbers. The Indians of this period are basically the same type as those of the preceding one.

Villages.—The earlier Modified Basket Maker crescentic house type two rooms wide, all rooms contiguous and above ground, with pit-houses in front of the crescent or arc, was still built and used in Pueblo I. The outer file of rooms was mostly used for storage, with the inner rooms being used for storage and as living quarters. The pit-houses were used both for living quarters and for ceremonies. The Pueblo I above-ground rooms and pit-houses contained more stone masonry (walls built of horizontally laid stones) and were better and more massively constructed than were those of the preceding period.

The general arrangement of a Pueblo I village (i.e., a compact mass of above-ground rooms with subterranean chambers near by and to the south or southeast) is similar to the village layout for the later Pueblo periods.

Livelihood.—The agricultural products were the same as in the Modified Basket Maker period (several varieties of corn, pumpkins, and beans). Cotton was also probably now grown. Dogs and turkeys were still domesticated.

In all other respects means of livelihood were the same as those of the preceding period.

Pottery.—The pottery of this period is related to that of the preceding period. It is, however, more varied as to form and decoration. Types increased, but we mention only five here.

1. *Lino and Kana-a Gray*, which were described in the preceding section, are classed as culinary or cooking types.

2. *Kana-a Black-on-White* is a smooth, white to slate-gray pottery, usually slipped, decorated with a vegetal paint, and fired in an oven

from which excess oxygen was excluded ("reducing atmosphere"). The patterns consist of geometric designs made up of fine lines, solid triangles, attached dots, and stepped elements (Fig. 21). Kana-a Black-on-White pottery was shaped into squash pots, pitchers, slender-necked bottles, gourd-shaped pots, bird forms, scoops, ladles, and bowls (usually decorated on interiors only).

3. *La Plata Black-on-Red* is a pottery similar to Abajo Red-on-Orange except that designs were usually executed in dense black paint on an orange background.

4. *Kiatuthlanna Black-on-White* pottery shows affiliations with pottery of the preceding period, many of the designs being carried over from La Plata Black-on-Gray. It was used for nonculinary pur-

FIG. 21.—Kana-a Black-on-White jars and bowl. Kayenta Area, Pueblo I period, Anasazi culture.

Basketry.—Very few baskets from Pueblo I period have been found. We know that coiled bowls and carrying-baskets and ring baskets of standard twill were also made, as a few of these have been recovered. Designs were done in black on red.

Tools, utensils, and weapons.—The bow and arrow and the wooden planting-stick were still in use.

Two metate types have been reported. One is similar to the Modified Basket Maker type—that is, it is troughed with the trough open at one end only (Fig. 20, b). The other type is made from a thin slab of stone and is also troughed, with the trough open at both ends. Both types range in length from fourteen to twenty inches.

The manos are rectangular stones wedge-shaped in cross-section. They generally show wear on one surface only, although some of them are worn on both surfaces.

Mortars for grinding paint and seeds are large roundish pebbles or

THE ANASAZI CULTURE

rough, irregularly shaped blocks of stone with a large cup-shaped depression in one face. Pestles are cylindrical stones, battered at the ends, and are rare.

Information about projectile points (arrowheads) of stone, drills of stone, and stone knives is scarce. The most characteristic type of point is the triangular, with straight stem or corner notches. Leaf-shaped spear points and knives are also reported. Most of the blades are well made, and secondary chipping is present on all edges and faces. Knives with diagonal notches are broad, pointed at the tip, and bear secondary chipping on all surfaces. Leaf-shaped knives also occur.

Stone scrapers, drills, and gravers occur.

Stone axes with three notches (side and poll) and with two notches (side-notched) are common, and full-grooved axes occur for the first time in this period.

Mauls were roundish or oval pebbles, with a groove pecked around the middle, or were flat tablet-shaped stones, grooved or provided with side notches.

Other miscellaneous stone tools—chipped hoes, hammerstones, and floor-polishing stones—also occur.

Bone tools consist of flaking implements (used for chipping stone), weaving tools, needles, bodkins, end-scrapers, side-scrapers, awls, and chisels. These were made from bones of deer, rabbits, birds, and deer and mountain-sheep horn.

The uses to which these tools were put may be briefly mentioned. The bow and arrow was used for hunting and warfare; the digging-stick for planting corn, beans, and squash and for digging excavations for pit-houses; the metate and mano for grinding corn into flour; the stone projectile points for hunting and warfare; the knives for cutting, whittling, and scraping; the scrapers for dressing skins; the drills for drilling holes; the gravers for carving and incising; the stone axes for cutting logs for walls and roofs of houses and pit-houses; the mauls for shaping stones and for driving stakes; the hoes for agriculture; the flaking tools for chipping stone; the needles for sewing; the awls for making holes and weaving baskets; and the chisels for finishing wooden implements and door lintels.

Pipes.—Pipes of this period were usually conical—that is, the bowl end is much larger than the stem end, the pipe tapering down to the stem end. The bowl portion is usually shallow. Pipes were made of baked clay and of slate, sandstone, limestone, and soapstone.

Costume.—Very little information concerning this subject is available.

Sandals were provided with a pointed toe and were cross-woven of fine string, with a design in color on the upper side and woven pattern on the under (Fig. 14, *c*).

Fur-cloth and feather-cloth robes, dressed skins, and leggings (netted of yucca string and feathers) were worn in cold weather.

Women's hair was worn long and was gathered into a heavy knot bound with cord on each side of the head.

Weaving, bags, and textiles.—Cloth of plain checkerboard weave was made, probably without the use of the true loom. Twined woven bags went out of style about A.D. 750. Carrying-bands or tumplines were probably used.

Ornaments.—Beads of shell, walnuts, seeds, lignite, and stone are common. Long rectangular pendants of lignite, pendants of shell, and thin shell bracelets were made.

Burials.—The dead were buried in refuse mounds, located in the open. Graves usually contain only one flexed burial and sometimes a mortuary offering of pottery. It is possible that clothing and other perishable articles were buried with the individual, but moisture has completely disintegrated them, if they existed. The burials were placed without regard to the cardinal points.

SOURCES

COLTON and HARGRAVE, 1937; GUERNSEY, 1931; HARGRAVE, 1932*a*; HAWLEY 1936; KIDDER, 1924; MCGREGOR, 1941; MARTIN, PAUL S., 1938; MARTIN and WILLIS, 1940; MORRIS, 1939; MORRIS and BURGH, 1941; RINALDO, 1941; ROBERTS, 1930, 1931, 1939–40; SELTZER, 1944.

PUEBLO II
Ca. A.D. 900–1050

Area.—The area covered by Pueblo II culture was much larger than that of any preceding period. In addition to occupying the original area around the "four corners" region, the civilization spread north and west into Utah, farther north in Colorado, and farther east in New Mexico.

People.—We know very little about the people of this period because few skeletons have been found. It seems fairly certain that the "Southwest Plateau" stock still flourished because (1) the few available skeletons are of the "Plateau" pattern and (2) that stock existed in Basket Maker times and persisted in all later periods. Most of the skulls were medium long, with their backs flattened. Changing the

THE ANASAZI CULTURE

shape of the skull was probably done in order to be stylish and did not in any way affect the intelligence of these Indians.

Villages.—Although the ground plan of Pueblo II villages is essentially the same as or similar to those of earlier periods, a slight architectural change had taken place. The houses of this period are called "unit houses"; they consist of a single or double row of surface rooms, the principal axis being east to west. Sometimes, there are two or three rooms forming a southward extension at one or both ends of the main block of rooms (like the arms of an **E**). The rooms were usually only one story high. An underground ceremonial room (kiva) and a refuse heap lay south of the surface rooms.

The kivas were round (ten to fourteen feet in diameter), were underground (the roof being flush with the ground), were usually provided with a bench, and were often walled in part or completely with stone masonry. The roof of wooden beams was supported by stone pillars built on top of the bench. A fireplace was always present. Entrance to the kiva was through the smoke-hole hatchway (which was located in the middle of the roof). A ladder (either the notched-log type or the rung type) was used for descent or ascent (see Fig. 29).

The southern antechamber or vestibule and the partition wall of Modified Basket Maker and Pueblo I pit-houses shrank in size and changed somewhat in function. In these two periods the vestibule served both as an entryway and as a ventilator shaft for introducing air currents into what would otherwise have been a smoky house. The partition wall in these periods not only divided the house into two parts but functioned also as a deflector or baffle to check the air currents from blowing directly upon the fire.

In the kivas of Pueblo II period, however (and in all kivas of the next two periods), the vestibule is no longer an entryway. It is greatly reduced in size (about a foot square), is vertical rather than horizontal, resembles a flue, and serves only to introduce fresh air into the chamber. The partition wall is also greatly reduced in size; instead of running across the kiva from wall to wall, as it did in previous periods, it is now only two or three feet long and about eighteen inches high. It functions only as a deflector.

By Pueblo II times the domiciliary functions were divorced entirely from the underground rooms and transferred to the above-ground rooms. The underground room, formerly referred to as a pit-house and now as a kiva, was by this time a separate and distinct chamber set aside primarily for ceremonial purposes and secondarily as a lounging place for males. The etymology of "kiva" (a Hopi word meaning "old house") suggests also that kivas were the original houses of Indians of the Southwest. The kiva of the present-day pueblos is a necessary adjunct and is the source of most of our information concerning these ceremonial structures.

Thus in Pueblo II villages we have two separate units of architecture, the above-ground rooms, which were used for all ordinary household purposes, and the near-by kivas, which were underground and were used primarily for ceremonies performed by males and secondarily as a kind of clubhouse for men. The kiva is roughly similar to the ceremonial or chapter room of a modern college fraternity.

Fig. 22.—Red Mesa Black-on-White jar, pitcher, and bowl. Chaco Canyon District, Pueblo II period, Anasazi culture.

Livelihood.—Same as preceding period.

Pottery.—The variety of designs became greater as the potters began to understand the manifold possibilities inherent in ceramics. Archeologists sometimes refer to pottery of this period as "exuberant." Since it is not possible here to list the scores of pottery types for the Pueblo periods, we shall list a few of the most characteristic. For complete details the reader is referred to the bibliography for the Southwest.

Of the nonculinary ware, the most important painted types were: Reserve Black-on-White, Red Mesa Black-on-White (Fig. 22), Black Mesa Black-on-White (Fig. 23), and Mancos Black-on-White (Fig. 24). Decorations consisted of scrolls, stepped terraces, checkerboards, and hatchings. Shapes were about the same as those of the preceding period.

The cooking pottery is distinct from that of the preceding periods. The broad, unobliterated bands on the necks of vessels of earlier times disappeared. Instead, a narrow rope of clay was applied in successive whorls to form a continuous spiral. Each coil was pressed with the fingers so that it would adhere to the coil beneath. Such finger pressure produced indentations which were controlled so as to form patterns. At first, the indentations were applied to the neck only but later were applied to the whole surface of the vessel. This pottery is called *Indented Corrugated* (see Fig. 17, c).

Shapes are intermediate between those of Pueblo I and Pueblo III, with globular jars the most common forms.

Basketry.—Little is known concerning the baskets of this period, since only fragments have been recovered. It is assumed, by infer-

Fig. 23.—Black Mesa Black-on-White jars. Kayenta District, Pueblo II period, Anasazi culture.

ence, that baskets were manufactured, because they occur abundantly in the following period.

Tools, utensils, and weapons.—The bow and arrow and the planting-stick were probably used.

The metate or milling-stone types were the same as those of the preceding period: the scoop type (a troughed metate with the trough open at one end only) and the troughed type with trough open at both ends. These ranged in length from sixteen to twenty inches.

The manos and mortars are the same as those of Pueblo I.

Stone projectile points (arrowheads and spear points) were mostly side-notched triangular points and triangular points without any notches. Spear points of stone were long slender blades notched at right angles to the long axis of the blade. Knives were the same as in Pueblo I.

Stone scrapers, hammerstones, drills of stone, mauls, chipped hoes, and floor-polishing stones occur in abundance. Some of these types remained unchanged for many centuries; some changed from one period to the next. It is not possible in this handbook to list the many distinguishing characteristics, and the reader interested in more detail should consult Martin (1938), Morris (1939), Rinaldo (1941), and Roberts (1930).

Stone axes were mostly full-grooved; that is, a groove was ground around the full circumference of the ax about halfway between the cutting edge and the head. The groove was used for fastening the handle to the ax.

Bone tools were made and used and were the same as those of Pueblo I.

Fig. 24.—Mancos Black-on-White bowls and mugs. Mesa Verde District, Pueblo II period, Anasazi culture.

The uses for these various tools is explained in the section on Pueblo I.

Pipes.—Three types of pipes, made of stone or baked clay, were used: the conical type (bowl end larger than stem end); the tubular type (hollow cylinders, with bowl and stem ends about the same size), with a bone tube for the stem; and the elbow type (with bowl at right angle to stem). The elbow type looks very similar to the pipes we smoke.

Ornaments.—Same as in Pueblo I.

Burials.—The dead were usually buried in refuse mounds which, as a rule, were located a few feet south of the kivas. The majority of burials were placed in a flexed (knees drawn up toward chest) or a semiflexed position.

Some graves contain whole or broken pots or merely portions of a pot, shell bracelets, stone ornaments, and stone or bone tools. Some graves contain nothing. It is possible that clothing, food, and other perishable articles were buried with the dead and have long since rotted away.

SOURCES

Beals, Brainard, and Smith, 1945; Colton and Hargrave, 1933, 1937; Guernsey, 1931; Hargrave, 1932a; Hawley, 1936; Kidder, 1924; McGregor, 1941; Martin, Paul S., 1938; Martin and Willis, 1940; Morris, 1939; Morris and Burgh, 1941; Rinaldo, 1941; Roberts, 1939–40; Seltzer, 1944.

PUEBLO III
Ca. a.d. 1050–1300

Area.—The Pueblo III period is often referred to as the "Great period," the "Classic period," or the "Golden Age" of the Pueblo Indians. More is known about the civilization of this period than about any other because pot-hunters and amateur and professional archeologists have done much digging in Pueblo III towns. One can understand this readily enough when it is realized that ruins of this period are large and impressive and thus easily found. Then, too, digging in a large ruin yields abundant specimens and has a romantic appeal. Moreover, the ruins in caves are usually protected from snow and rain; therefore, perishable objects, such as basketry, wooden objects, clothes, "mummies," etc., are well preserved.

The large and famous cliff-houses (towns built in caves) and the large towns built in the open on the mesa tops belong to this "Great period." During this time architecture and pottery rapidly developed and became stylized and specialized in three localities of the San Juan River basin: Mesa Verde (in southwestern Colorado), Chaco Canyon (in northwestern New Mexico), and Kayenta (in northeastern Arizona). The Mimbres area, on the periphery of the Anasazi area, will be treated under the section on the Mogollon culture. The district names are also used as tags which are attached to the locally specialized civilization or culture of an area; for example, one may speak of the Mesa Verde culture or variant. This term means any part or all of the archeological complex of materials found in or around the type area—Mesa Verde National Park—regardless of time. Of course, one can also speak of the Mesa Verde cliff-house type and thus distinguish it from any other.

In other words, local and divergent tendencies in pottery and architecture and in the other arts and crafts generated a blend or a combination (or a "complex," "assemblage," or "association," as archeologists would say) of traits that make it possible to set any one of these districts apart from the other two. The Pueblo III houses and pottery of the Mesa Verde district possess definite and unique characters that distinguish Mesa Verde Pueblo III from any other Pueblo III; and yet Mesa Verde Pueblo III belongs to the Anasazi family just as much as Chaco Pueblo III does, and both are typically Anasazi.

It should be noted, however, that house and pottery types from a given area may be found in another district. Chaco houses and pottery have been found in the Mesa Verde district; Mesa Verde materials have been found in the Kayenta area. But, by and large, the cultural assemblages tended to remain in the home locality.

The extent of area covered by the civilization of Pueblo III was considerably smaller than that of any previous period. Fewer but larger sites were characteristic of this period. The area of greatest concentration again seems to have centered in the "four corners" region.

Thus, from Basket Maker times down to Pueblo III, we have witnessed expansion and shrinkage of territory occupied by Indians of the various periods. The Basket Maker Indians probably occupied the greatest extent of territory. After that, through Modified Basket Maker to and including Pueblo I, the amount of territory occupied by Pueblo culture shrank somewhat; in Pueblo II it greatly expanded; and in Pueblo III it shrank drastically. In Pueblo IV and Pueblo V it shrank even more.

There is such a wealth of knowledge about Pueblo III that we cannot include in this brief sketch all the remarkable and interesting details that are now available. For more information the reader is referred to Fewkes (1911), Kidder (1924), McGregor (1941), Morris (1939), and to the host of references included in these publications.

People.—The Pueblo III people belonged to the "Southwest Plateau" stock; they were similar to the Indians of the Basket Maker, Pueblo I and II periods, and to the modern Pueblo Indians. The skulls were medium longheaded and roundheaded. The rear portion was usually deformed or flattened to conform with the style of the time.

Villages.—This is the period of large towns, although it is probable that there were "rural" or "suburban" Pueblo III villages also. About half of the large towns of this period were built in caves (cliff-houses) and about half in the open, on mesa tops (Fig. 25) or in river valleys.

The general plan for both types of village was similar. It consisted of a compact mass of contiguous rooms (from twenty to about a thousand), from one to four stories high, often terraced (i.e., with setbacks as in a skyscraper) and built in the form of a rectangle, an oval, or a D. Kivas of the rectanguloid pueblos were often included within the building mass. In large oval or D-shaped pueblos, the living-rooms faced a court in which great and small kivas were placed. In cliff-houses the living-rooms faced the cave openings and the kivas were located along the front of the cave.

The masonry of pueblos in the Chaco area consisted of thin tabular stones carefully laid in horizontal bands of varying thickness (Fig. 26). In the Mesa Verde area loaf-shaped blocks were laid in

FIG. 25.—Reconstruction of a Pueblo III village built in the open. Great kiva in foreground. Lowry Ruin, Colorado, Anasazi culture. (Painting by Anne Harding Spoehr.)

horizontal courses (sometimes with wall surfaces brought to an even facing by a pecking process). In the Kayenta area irregularly shaped stones were carelessly laid in crude courses by means of abundant mud mortar. The Kayenta masonry is inferior to either the Chaco or the Mesa Verde types. There are many variations of these masonry types.

The size of the rooms varied from place to place, but in general the largest were those in Chaco ruins. Many of these were about 10 by 16 feet, and a few larger ones measured 10 by 25 feet. Ceilings ranged in height from about 6 to 8 feet. Doorways were likewise relatively large; 5 feet high by 2 feet wide is not an unusual size (Fig. 27).

The rooms in villages of the Mesa Verde variety were smaller; 6 by 8 feet with a 4-foot ceiling is a common size. Doorways averaged about 16 inches wide and 2 feet high.

The rooms and doorways of Kayenta villages were somewhat larger than those of the Mesa Verde district.

Roofs were constructed more or less in the same fashion: from 3 to 10 heavy poles were laid across the walls as main roof supports. Over these was spread a thatch of smaller poles, brush, and sticks, and the thatch was then covered with a layer of adobe mud from 4 to 8 inches thick.

Fig. 26.—Section of wall showing excellence of masonry. Pueblo Bonito, Chaco Canyon, New Mexico, Pueblo III period, Anasazi culture.

Kivas were an important part of every town, whether built in a cave or in the open (Fig. 28). A brief description of the functions of a kiva is given in the chapter on Pueblo II. The kivas of the three districts (Mesa Verde, Chaco Canyon, and Kayenta) varied somewhat.

Mesa Verde kivas (Fig. 29) averaged about 12 or 14 feet in diameter and 7 or 8 feet in depth. Each kiva usually contained a bench or ledge on which rested six masonry pillars. These supported the cribbed-log roof, which was flush with the court yard and was used as a plaza. The kiva was entered by means of a ladder that rested

Fig. 27.—Restoration of room in Chaco-like village. *Left corner:* Wife grinding corn on metate. *Right:* Husband returning from hunt. Pots on floor; bag, corn, basket, and gourds hanging on walls. Lowry Pueblo, Colorado, Pueblo III period, Anasazi culture. (Painting by Anne Harding Spoehr.)

on the kiva floor and extended through the smoke hole. Fresh air was introduced by way of the ventilator shaft (Fig. 29, *a* and *b*). In the floor of the kiva was a small round hole called *sipapu*, the symbolical entrance to the underworld.

Chaco kivas consisted of two types: the small kiva, which was generally larger and deeper than the Mesa Verde type, and the great

FIG. 28.—Restoration of a kiva. Symbolic decoration on bench face; ceremonial masks on bench. *Center:* firepit, kiva jar, and prayer plumes. *Back of firepit:* deflector. Lowry Pueblo, Colorado, Pueblo III period, Anasazi culture. (Painting by Anne Harding Spoehr.)

kiva. The small, distinctive Chaco kiva ranged from 18 to 25 feet in diameter and from 12 to 16 feet in depth. A bench (2 or 3 feet high and about a foot wide) usually encircled the wall. The manner in which the roof was supported is not clear, since pillars or roof supports have not been found in most Chaco kivas. It is possible that beams long enough to reach across the kiva were laid on top of the walls. A firepit was located in the center of the floor.

Ten great kivas of Pueblo III period (not counting those of the Basket Maker period) have been reported from the Mesa Verde and

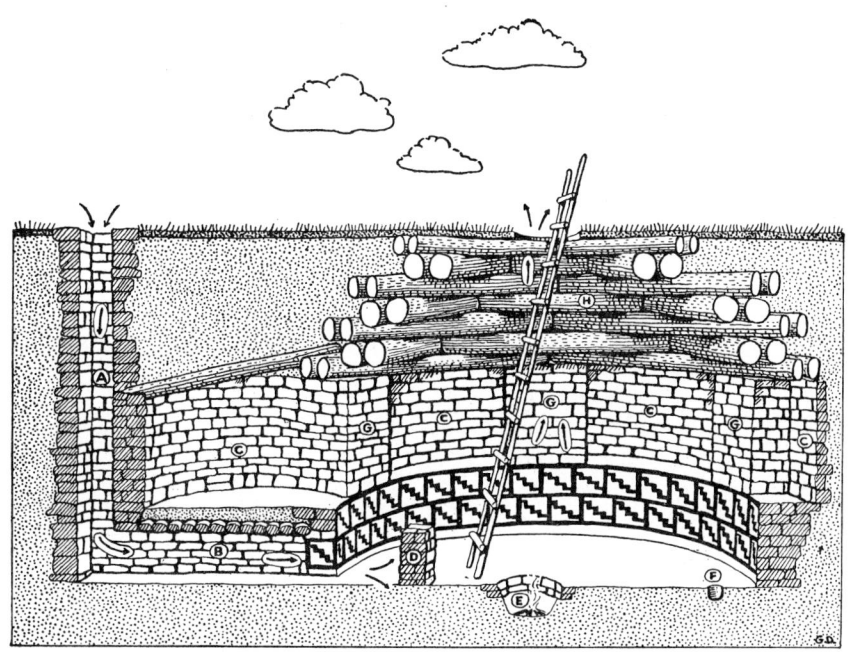

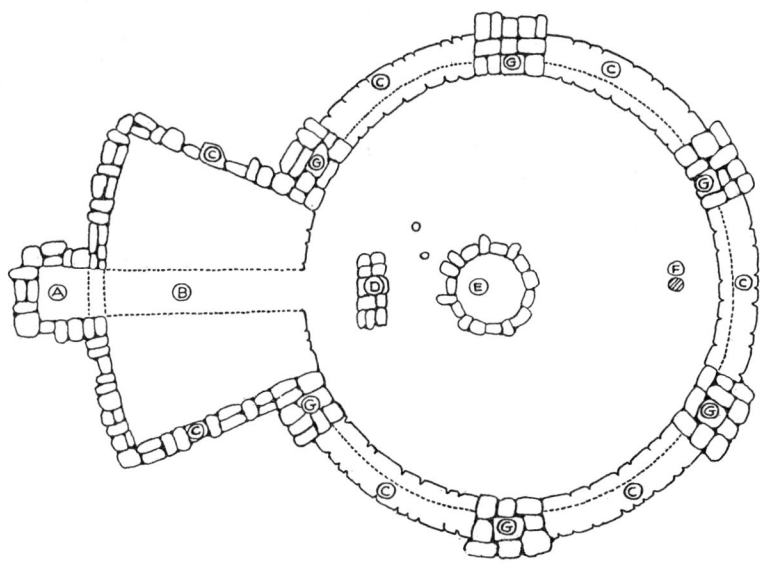

Fig. 29.—Cross-section and ground plan of kiva of Mesa Verde type: *a* and *b*, fresh-air duct (shaft and tunnel); *c*, kiva wall; *d*, deflector or baffle; *e*, firepit; *f*, *sipapu* or symbolic entrance to Spirit World; *g*, masonry pillars for supporting roof; *h*, cribwork roof. Arrows in upper drawing indicate direction of fresh-air currents. The kiva is about 14 feet in diameter. Lowry Pueblo, Colorado, Pueblo III period, Anasazi culture.

Chaco regions; none has yet been reported for the Kayenta area. These range in diameter from 47 feet (Lowry Ruin) (Fig. 30) to 78 feet (Village of the Great Kivas), and in depth from 6 to 8 feet.

A great kiva may be described as a large, round, subterranean chamber surrounded by small above-ground rooms that may have been dressing-rooms for the priests. Entrance to the kiva was by means of a stairway. Near the middle of the floor was a large firebox,

FIG. 30.—Great kiva. *Center:* firepit. *Left and right of firepit:* masonry pillars for supporting roof and masonry-lined vaults. *Top:* entrance (with stairs). Diameter 47 feet. Lowry Pueblo, Colorado, Pueblo III period, Anasazi culture.

on either side of which was a masonry-lined vault about 8 feet long, 4 feet wide, and 3 feet deep. The exact use of these vaults is unknown. One clue as to their function comes from recent information concerning kiva ceremonies at the modern pueblo of Acoma, New Mexico. One of the Acoma kivas is provided with a vault roughly similar to those found in ancient great kivas. This vault is covered with planks on which, during ceremonies, the priests dance in order to produce a deep, booming sound, the vault thus acting as a resonance chamber or a large built-in drum. The roof of a great kiva was supported by four wooden or stone pillars set well out from the wall.

Kivas of the Kayenta district were both round and rectangular but were less specialized than those of the Chaco or the Mesa Verde districts. So few of these kivas have been excavated and described that it is impossible to characterize them further.

In the chapter on Pueblo II, it was suggested that (small) kivas grew out of pit-houses. The origin of great kivas is not known. They have been reported from the Modified Basket Maker and Pueblo III periods but not from Pueblo I and II. The villages of Pueblo I and II may have been too small and scattered to warrant the building of such a large ceremonial chamber; or possibly the religious ideas of the times were not the same as those of Basket Maker or Pueblo III, and a large, supersized kiva was frowned upon. At any rate, great kivas (so far as we now know) did not prosper in Pueblo I and II times but again became popular in Pueblo III.

The exact use of the great kiva is likewise unknown. It may have been reserved for rituals in which the whole village took part, or a few priests representing many different religious societies (fraternities) from near-by towns may have gathered in the great kiva at intervals to perform special ceremonies.

Many people wonder why whole towns were built in caves. There are several possible reasons: (1) custom or fashion; (2) convenience of constant and close water supply furnished by springs; (3) easy defense from attack by enemies; and (4) the natural attraction of such a site. The caves selected by the Indians faced south and were therefore warm and sunny in the winter and cool in the summer; they were also well protected from rains and snows.

Livelihood.—The Pueblo III Indians followed the custom of their forefathers and continued to raise several varieties of corn, pumpkins, beans, and cotton. Planting was done, as in earlier times, by means of a planting-stick. Fields were probably larger in order to support greater populations. Sunflower and other seeds were eaten; dogs and turkeys were kept. Meat was obtained from turkeys, deer, rabbits, mountain sheep, bears, squirrels, and foxes.

Pottery.—In this period certain ornaments, styles, and forms were carried to a high degree of specialization and variety. Each area—Chaco, Mesa Verde, and Kayenta—produced a specialized type which can easily be distinguished from the others.

The most important and better-known types were:

1. *Chaco area:*
    a) Chaco Black-on-White (Fig. 31) decorated with mineral (iron) paint; designs are made up of fine-lined hatching (fine lines close together), triangles, inter-

locking rectangular scrolls. Shapes: bowls with sloping sides and pointed rims, pitchers with small bodies and high necks, jars, and ladles.
   b) St. John's Polychrome.
   c) Indented Corrugated cooking ware. The indented corrugations cover the entire outer surface of the vessel.
2. *Mesa Verde area:*
   a) Mesa Verde Black-on-White (Fig. 32) decorated with vegetal (organic) paint; designs are geometric and occur in bands or zones with parallel framing lines

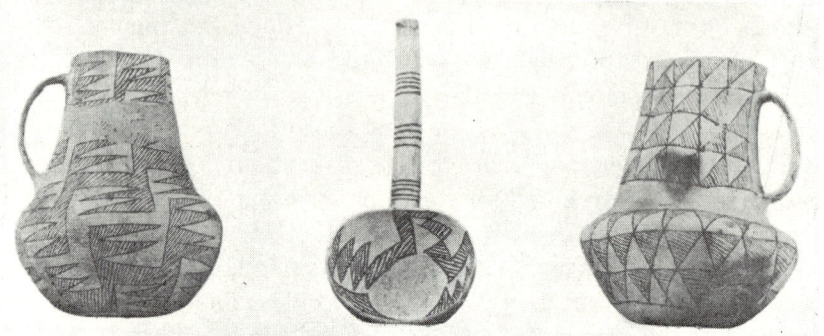

Fig. 31.—Chaco Black-on-White pitchers and ladle. Pueblo III period, Anasazi culture

Fig. 32.—Mesa Verde Black-on-White bowls and mug. Pueblo III period, Anasazi culture

above and below, hatching (much coarser than in Chaco Black-on-White) and half-key meanders (terraces) are common. Shapes: jars, bowls, mugs, ladles, and canteens.
   b) Indented Corrugated cooking ware. The indented corrugations cover the entire outer surface of the vessel (see Fig. 17, *b*).
3. *Kayenta area:*
   a) Tusayan Black-on-White decorated with vegetal (organic) paint; designs are negative zigzag lines set in rectangular blocks, and large hatched (fine lines set close together) scrolls are typical. Shapes: bowls (sometimes with single horizontal handle), jars, pitchers, ladles.
   b) Sagi Black-on-White (Fig. 33) (often referred to as Kayenta Black-on-White) decorated with vegetal (organic) paint; designs are interlocking scrolls, "mosquito bar" (very fine) cross-hatching with little of white background showing,

interlocking terraces, and stepped lines. Shapes: bowls, ladles, jars, and colanders.
  c) In addition to the Black-on-White wares, there were several colored wares: Jeddito Black-on-Orange, Tusayan Black-on-Red, Tusayan Polychrome, and Kayenta Polychrome. (Polychrome pottery is pottery decorated with more than two colors; e.g., Tusayan Polychrome bears three colors: red, black, and orange.)
  d) Indented Corrugated cooking ware. The indented corrugations cover the entire outer surface of the vessel.

In addition to the types here briefly described, there are many others: Kiet Siel Polychrome, Tularosa Black-on-White, St. John's Polychrome, Pinedale Polychrome, Zuñi glazes, Roosevelt Black-on-White, Pinto Polychrome.

Fig. 33.—Sagi Black-on-White bowls. Kayenta Area, Pueblo III period, Anasazi culture

For more detailed information on pottery of this or any period consult Colton and Hargrave (1937), Hawley (1936), McGregor (1941), Mera (1935), and Martin and Willis (1940).

Basketry.—Coiled and twilled basketry were the two types of construction (see chap. 8). Coiled basketry was about twice as plentiful as was twilled. The coiled specimens were of closer, finer weave than were those from other, earlier periods. Colored ornamentation was rare, however.

The basket shapes were trays, bowls, miniature carrying-baskets, globular baskets, shields, and rectangular baskets.

Tools, utensils, and weapons.—The bow and arrow was the weapon of the period. The planting-stick was characteristically a curved, swordlike stick with a thin, flat blade at one end and a distinct knob at the other. In addition to this tool, the Pueblo III Indians also used a *tchamahia* (stone hoe) lashed to the long axis of the digging-stick. As stated before, digging-sticks were employed for making the hole in the ground into which seeds were dropped, for cultivating, and for digging pits and kivas. The stone hoe was probably used for cultivating, for mounding the earth over the seeds, for hoeing and weeding, and for digging up roots for food.

The characteristic metate was a flat slab of sandstone. This type was often set in a stone box, and box and metate became part of the permanent house fixtures. Metates were most often made of sandstone, but conglomerate, lava, and granite were also used. The manos were tabular, or were wedge- or triangular-shaped in cross-section. The tabular type was the most common. Manos were usually made of sandstone, conglomerate, granite, or limestone.

Spear points and arrowheads were the same as those in Pueblo II period. Axes were full-grooved and three-quarter-grooved. The latter type, as the name indicates, is provided with a groove around only three sides of the ax. The knife of the period was made of flint and the blade was sometimes provided with side notches for hafting. The more common form was leaf-shaped without side notches. The blade was usually broader and heavier than spear points. Grinding-stones, rubbing-stones, hammerstones, mortars, pestles, mauls, and drills were in common use.

Bone needles, awls, rubbers and polishers, and end-scrapers differed little from those of preceding periods (Fig. 34).

Pipes.—The tobacco-pipe types are the same as those of Pueblo II.

Costume.—Two types of sandals were worn: (1) the wickerwork type, with squarish toes and heels, and (2) the jog-toed type, a sandal with an offset at the toe and on the little-toe side (see Fig. 14, *d* and *e*). Sizes of the latter type ran from about 6 to 11. This sandal may have been patterned after the so-called "sandal-last stone," a smooth, flat, thin stone which has been found in various sizes and which was provided with an offset in the little-toe position. Such a stone may have furnished a smooth place on which to work and a pattern to which the finished sandal could conform.

Feather-cloth robes were an important article of clothing and were probably worn in cold weather. Aprons with long fringes of string were worn by women. Men wore breechclouts made of yucca fibers. Leggings of feather cord were also worn, probably only in cold weather.

We do not know just how men wore their hair in this period, but they may have used a style similar to that of today; that is, brow and cheek bangs and long hair in back. Women wore their hair bound in two knots, one at either side of the head (the "squash-blossom" style).

Cradles.—There were three cradle types: (1) the "snowshoe" type, an oval loop of bent withe, with a filling of yucca strip network; (2) the rigid type, a loop-shaped frame with a filling of reeds or peeled sticks running horizontally and longitudinally; and (3) the "slab" type, a rectangular slab of wood 8 by 15 inches to which were hinged narrow sideboards which would fold over an infant's arms.

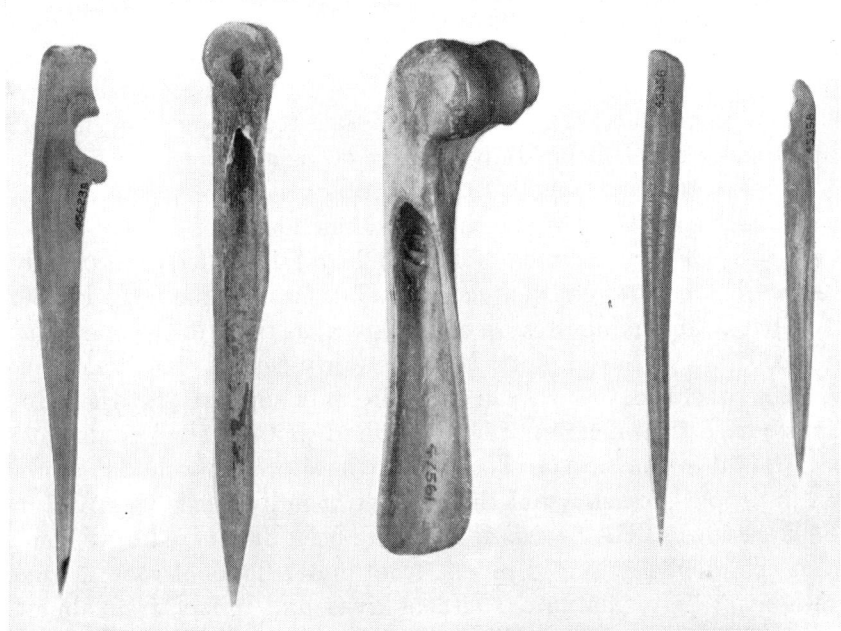

Fig. 34.—Bone awls and end-scraper (*center*). Pueblo III period, Anasazi culture

Weaving, bags, and textiles.—Cotton cloth was used for ponchos, blankets, and bags. The commonest weaves were checkerboard or plain, twining, and twill. It is quite possible that even in this period the true loom was not known.

Strung willow mats or willow screens were often used for burial purposes, for giving a beautiful finish to the ceilings of rooms, and possibly as door coverings. These screens were made of peeled or unpeeled willow stubs and resemble the slatted curtains which we use at windows and which can be rolled up or down. Such mats were used for covering the dead and were possibly hung in doorways.

Matting of yucca or rushes was very common and was used for burial purposes, for covering the floor, and possibly as sleeping mats. It was twilled plaited.

Carrying-bands or headbands (long woven straps with loop ends to which a carrying line was fastened) were woven of yucca fiber or animal hair in plain and twined weaves.

The cloth bags of yucca or other fibers were twined, woven, seamless sacks with full round bodies and unconstricted necks. Bags were usually from 5 to 8 inches long.

Ornaments.—The most common ornaments were beads of bone, shell, and stone; pendants of shell and stone; shell bracelets; feather tassels; rings of bone and shell; pendants and bracelets encrusted with small, cut pieces of turquoise (mosaic technique); and labrets (lip ornaments) of shell. Many of these occur also in earlier periods. Ornaments that were typical only of this period were thunderbird pendants, pendants of whole shell, and thick shell bracelets.

Burials.—Burial mounds of Pueblo I and II periods are usually easy to locate, but persistent search in and around the large Pueblo III villages (including those in caves as well as those in the open) has yielded no large burial plots. It seems fairly certain that cremation was not practiced, and we can therefore only suppose that these Indians buried their dead in widely scattered spots. A few burials have been found in Pueblo III villages, but these probably do not represent a proper percentage of the number of individuals who lived in the large towns. The burials which have been discovered have come from abandoned or sealed rooms, from under floors of rooms, from trash heaps, from ventilator shafts of kivas, and, in fact, from almost any easily dug, likely or unlikely spot.

The majority of burials were placed in a flexed or semiflexed position, although some of them are extended. There seems to have been no fixed rule about burial position or orientation of the body. Sometimes the head of the grave was toward the south and often it was toward the east, but exceptions to this statement can be cited.

Usually some ornaments were placed on the body, which was wrapped in a feather-cloth robe and placed on a willow or plaited yucca mat, or covered with a willow screen. Sometimes bows and arrows, awls, pottery, or baskets were buried with the dead.

Burials made in caves are usually well preserved, the skin and other soft parts being completely dehydrated. Such desiccated bodies are often called "mummies."

Miscellany.—Many other articles have been found in Pueblo III dwellings. A few of the more interesting ones are arrow-shaft straighteners, "wrenches," punches of bone, whistles, mortars and pestles, wooden vessels, pot lids of stone, pot rests of woven cedar bark, fire drills and hearths (equipment for making fire by friction), buttons of bone and stone, lapstones or paint palettes, weaving tools of bone, weaving battens of oak, needles and bodkins of bone, combs of wood and horn, small copper bells, hairbrushes of stiff plant fibers, choppers, mauls, floor-polishing stones, chisels, walking canes, crutches, rattles of deer hoofs, bone rasps, and "dice."

Conjectures.—It will be seen from Table 1 that the Basket Maker and the Pueblo civilizations, although separated by a span of five centuries, are basically the same. Almost all the traits present in Pueblo III time (except massive, storied dwellings and cotton) were present in the Basket Maker civilization. In other words, the Pueblo III Indians merely developed and improved some of the traits and skills that had been handed down to them.

Several years ago archeologists believed that a sharp break existed between the Basket Maker and the Pueblo I civilizations. The Pueblo I Indians were supposed to represent a new race of "round-heads" who came from the north, conquered and swamped out the Basket Makers, and introduced into the area all the more specialized and highly developed traits, which are called "Puebloan."

The Basket Maker Indians, on the other hand, were depicted as a longheaded race which had existed for a long time in the Southwest and had never made much progress. They were regarded as being on the fringe, so to speak, and were thought of as "poor relations" as far as the development of culture was concerned.

We now know that this picture is false. There was no sharp break between the civilization of the Modified Basket Maker Indians and that of the Pueblo I Indians. In fact, from the preceding comparative table, one can see that there is very little difference between the Modified Basket Maker culture and the Pueblo III culture, which came into being at least five hundred years later. Almost all the items which make up any of the Pueblo periods may be traced back to the Basket Maker period, in which these items were originated and first used. Take architecture, for example. Pueblo III villages were made up of large masses of contiguous rooms with walls of coursed masonry and kivas near by. Basket Maker villages were also units of many contiguous rooms with walls of crude coursed masonry and

TABLE 1

Comparisons between Modified Basket Maker and Pueblo III Civilizations

	Modified Basket Maker Period	Pueblo III Period
PEOPLE	Undeformed long, medium-long, and round (a few) skulls; "Southwest Plateau" stock	Deformed medium-long and round skulls; "Southwest Plateau" stock
VILLAGES	Located either in caves or out in open. Isolated semisubterranean pit-houses; or above-ground, one-story, contiguous rooms arranged in form of arc or crescent, built of crude, coursed masonry. Between horns of crescent were pithouses (subterranean), used for domiciliary and/or ceremonial purposes. Great kiva present, but not specialized	Compact mass of contiguous rooms (20 to about 1,000); built of coursed masonry in form of rectangle, oval, or D; several stories (two to four) high. Many small kivas and, in Chaco-type villages, a large, highly specialized great kiva
LIVELIHOOD	Holes for seeds made with planting-stick. Corn (possibly several varieties), pumpkin, beans cultivated. Dogs and turkeys kept. Seeds and roots eaten as well as game. In early part of this period, spear and spear-thrower used; in latter part, bow and arrow	Holes for seeds made with planting-stick. Several varieties of corn beans, pumpkin, and cotton cultivated. Sunflower seeds eaten as well as game. Dogs and turkeys kept. Bow and arrow only weapon
POTTERY	Constructed by series of bands or rings, often called concentric coil technique. At first, sun-dried; later fired. Types: Lino Gray and Kana-a Gray; Lino Black-on-White and La Plata Black-on-White; White Mound Black-on-White; Abajo Red-on-Orange. Trade wares: Forestdale Smudged and San Francisco Red	Constructed by spiral coil technique. All intentionally fired. Types: Chaco, Mesa Verde, Tusayan, and Sagi Black-on-White; Jeddito Black-on-Orange; St. Johns, Tusayan, and Kayenta Polychromes; Indented Corrugated culinary vessels
BASKETRY	Coiled and twilled techniques; patterns in color; well woven. Carrying-basket common	Coiled and twilled techniques, although coiled was about twice as plentiful. Fine, close weave; colored ornamentation, rare. Carrying-basket not made. Varied shapes
TOOLS	Bow and arrow (late), spear-thrower (early). Digging-stick. Metate long, trough-shaped stone, trough open at one end only. Chipped projectile points and knives, mauls, hammerstones, notched hoes. Axes with side notches; grooved axes very rare. Bone fleshers, scrapers, needles, awls, punches, and flakers	Bow and arrow. Digging- and planting-stick. Metate usually flat slab of stone. Projectile points, knives, grinding-stones, hammerstones, mortars, pestles, mauls, drills. Axes full- and three-quarter-grooved. Bone needles, awls, rubbers, scrapers
PIPES	Conical, with relatively large bowl and smaller mouthpiece (resembling our cigar-holders), made of stone or pottery	Three types: conical, tubular (hollow cylinders), and elbow (similar in shape to our pipes), made of stone or pottery

TABLE 1—*Continued*

	Modified Basket Maker Period	Pueblo III Period
COSTUME	Fur-cloth and feather-cloth blankets, dressed skins, and sashes, aprons, and gee-strings. Leggings. Sandals of vegetable fibers; toes typically notched and scalloped. Long hair worn by men; bobbed, by women	Feather-cloth robes for cold weather; otherwise women wore fringed aprons and men breechclouts. Leggings of feather-cord. Sandals of vegetable fibers; two types: square toes and heels and jog-toed. Hair probably worn long by men; "squash-blossom" style by women
CRADLES	Three types: flexible with a grass-stem hoop, rigid, and cedar-bark	Three types: "snowshoe," rigid, and "slab"
WEAVING	Bags, headbands, sashes, and nets woven from plant fibers	Cotton cloth woven for ponchos, blankets, sashes, and bags. Strung willow mats used for burials, for ceiling finish, and for door coverings. Rush matting very common. Carrying or headbands
ORNAMENTS	Beads of wood, bone, shell, turquoise; pendants of stone, shell, lignite, turquoise; necklaces of animal claws, crystals; shell bracelets; hair ornaments of feathers	Beads of shell, bone, turquoise, stone; pendants of stone, shell, lignite, and turquoise; shell bracelets; zoömorphic images of stone; mosaics of turquoise, shell
BURIALS	Body usually flexed and laid on back. Few cemeteries found for cave villages, but often not located for villages in open. Cremation not practiced. Burials in caves become "mummified" through desiccation	Cemeteries for large pueblos not located. Cremation not practiced. A few burials have been located in trash heaps and sealed rooms. Most of these have been flexed; a few were extended. Burials in caves become "mummified" through desiccation

pit-houses (which are related to kivas) near by. The fundamental arrangement and plan are the same in both periods. The Pueblo III Indians improved the houses by adding several stories and improving the masonry; but the general ideas were present in Basket Maker times.

Furthermore, there was no change in physical type (race) at the beginning of Pueblo I. Recent research by Seltzer has shown that there was no "tidal wave of new peoples resulting in submergence of the old and original stock," nor any invasion of "roundheads." Dr. Seltzer believes that his "study of the time relationships of the units forming the 'Southwest Plateau' stock strongly suggested the existence of a continuity of 'Southwest Plateau' stock from the Basket Maker period clear up to recent times." In other words, the Basket Maker and Pueblo Indians belong to the same stock. Minor modifications of that stock may have taken place from time to time and would have been due to tribal adoption of occasional "hobo" Indians who drifted into the area and whose blood was easily absorbed through marriage.

Thus the Basket Maker and Pueblo physical types are essentially the same. And, likewise, the Basket Maker and Pueblo civilizations are merely different facets (at different time levels) of one civilization or culture—the Anasazi. The Basket Maker and Pueblo civilizations are not two separate and distinct units.

The beginning of the Anasazi cycle took place about the time of Christ. Slowly, it has developed, borrowed new ideas occasionally from Mexico, expanded and receded geographically, and maintained its individuality and distinctiveness for over a millennium. It is still flourishing today. When one visits modern Anasazi towns in New Mexico (Zuñi, Acoma, Jemez, etc.) or Arizona (Walpi, Mishongnovi, etc.), it might be stimulating to realize that here is a hardy culture, the seeds of which sprouted about two thousand years ago, and which, in spite of various social upheavals, droughts, Spanish and American conquests, continues to prosper.

It was noted above that in late Pueblo III times (*ca.* 1300) the Anasazi civilization declined somewhat and that no other great villages in southeastern Utah, southwestern Colorado, and northeastern Arizona came into existence. In fact, all the large towns in the areas just mentioned were abandoned, the people moving southward. What caused this great exodus and the abandonment of the comfortable, large, well-built cave and open villages where the people had lived for some years?

No one knows the precise answer to this question, but there are several guesses.

1. *Pressure from nomadic enemies or from unfriendly neighbors.*—It is possible that the Navaho Indians had begun to wander into the Southwest at about this time (A.D. 1300). Recent archeological work makes this date seem reasonable. Furthermore, in the "Origin Legend of the Navaho Flintway," mention is made of Sun Temple—a building in Mesa Verde National Park—which was probably abandoned about 1300. If the legendary evidence can be trusted, the Navaho must have been in the Mesa Verde district while this Anasazi building was in use—and that would mean about 1250–1325.

There is practically no evidence, however, of any great amount of warfare during or at the end of Pueblo III. Quarrels between individuals or towns probably occurred; but certainly there was no widespread strife. Now and then, one finds a burned room or even several; but usually one does not find charred skeletons or mashed skulls or even the burned furnishings of a room. The great towns, many of which were built with an eye to defense, therefore were not sacked and destroyed, nor did any catastrophic calamity descend upon them. It seems evident that the owners of the dwellings packed up their belongings and voluntarily left. We cannot hold nomadic enemies or unfriendly neighbors entirely responsible for this wholesale exodus.

2. *A great epidemic of some virulent but unknown disease.*—But there is no evidence for this theory. Furthermore, we know from studies of present-day Hopi (Anasazi) Indians that they would not budge from their towns even if an epidemic were threatening them with extinction. Therefore, pestilence cannot be counted as a factor in causing the Indians to move out.

3. *Drought.*—Dr. A. E. Douglass of the University of Arizona has published a number of studies dealing with climatic cycles (rain and drought) in the Southwest. Dr. Douglass has found that a severe drought existed from A.D. 1276 to 1299. A drought of this length would certainly have disturbed the equilibrium of the Pueblo peoples. Crops would not have flourished, animals would have abandoned the area, and drinking water might even have become scarce. Certainly, during such a period of stress, living would have been difficult and the population may have faced starvation. If there were unfriendly peoples about, such a time would have been propitious for making trouble. The Pueblo peoples may have decided, then, to pack their possessions and to move south to join their kinfolk.

However, drought was probably not *the* major cause for the scattering of the Pueblo peoples.

4. Recent research has shown that the answer to the problem may be better found in *a study of Pueblo social organization*. In other words, is there some aspect of Pueblo social organization that would have caused the Indians to abandon their comfortable, well-built villages?

From early times (Basket Maker to Pueblo II) the Pueblo Indians lived in small, independent villages that were dominated by social units (the clan) containing from thirty to sixty persons, all blood relatives. At the beginning of Pueblo III these small communities may have found it to their advantage to band together and to found larger towns. It seems likely that the material aspects of Pueblo culture became adjusted to large-town existence, but the social and religious organizations were unchanged and continued to function in terms of small (clan) town units.

In other words, Towns A, B, C, and D, each consisting of forty or fifty people, all related to one another, gathered together and built a big cliff-house, "X." These four groups were then amalgamated and helped one another in various ways: defense, preparation of fields, use of a common water supply, manufacture of one style of pottery and basketry, etc. But each group insisted on maintaining the social and ceremonial structures which were well adapted to a small town but not to a large one. In other words, each town (clan) unit in Town X preserved its own social organization (affairs pertaining to marriage and method of reckoning blood descent) and its own ceremonial life. The marriage and blood ties prevented the development of a strong central administration that would have acted for the whole group.

Suppose you gather together four different families, each of which has been accustomed for generations to living its own separate existence and each of which has its own religion. Suppose the families to be made up of relatives (in-laws, nephews, aunts, uncles, grandparents and grandchildren). One family is Catholic; one, Lutheran; one, Episcopalian; and one, Methodist. Then suppose you plant these four families in one town unit, permitting each to maintain its own family and religious life with no town administration to bind it together. This is similar to the situation in Town X, and it can easily be imagined that there would have been internal feuds and dissensions.

Therefore, this large Town, X, could not endure because it really consisted of four independent towns, each functioning separately from the others. These four towns (clans) were never welded into one larger unit, because each town (clan) insisted on maintaining its own wholeness. Town X was constantly faced with internal quarrels and divisions. Then, when a **serious** crisis appeared (such as a long drought), X collapsed, and each unit (clan) packed up its belongings and went away to found another small town which was more to its liking.

Thus Town X is abandoned because of "internal disintegration arising from a weakly-knit social structure" (Titiev, **1944**).

This, then, is probably the reason why the large Pueblo III towns were all abandoned. In the next sections we shall see what happened after this major exodus.

SOURCES

COLTON and HARGRAVE, 1937; COLTON and McGREGOR, 1941; FEWKES, 1911; GUERNSEY, 1931; HARGRAVE, 1932a; HAURY, 1945a; HAWLEY, 1936; KIDDER, 1924; KIDDER and GUERNSEY, 1919; McGREGOR, 1941; MARTIN and WILLIS, 1940; MORRIS, 1928, 1939; MORRIS and BURGH, 1941; NORDENSKÏOLD, 1893; PEPPER, 1920; RINALDO, 1941; ROBERTS, 1931, 1932, 1939–40; SELTZER, 1944; SPIER, 1917, 1918, 1919; TITIEV, 1944; WATSON, 1940; WEST, 1927.

PUEBLO IV
Ca. A.D. 1300–1700

Area.—Pueblo IV period is sometimes known as the "Renaissance." The name is fitting because many techniques were improved or new ones borrowed during this time.

The area covered was probably greater than that of the preceding period, Pueblo III. Pueblo IV sites have been found in the Hopi country (northeastern Arizona) and in the areas bordering on the Little Colorado, the Puerco, the Verde, the San Francisco, the Rio Grande, the Pecos, the Upper Gila, and the Salt rivers.

Some of the people from the Mesa Verde region moved south into the Rio Grande area and exerted some influence on the development of pottery and architecture of that area in Pueblo IV. Others moved south toward Gallup, while others probably moved into the Hopi country. This pressure of peoples from the north caused dislocations of other peoples all through the Southwest and perhaps also brought about an amalgamation of the Salado Pueblo Indians with the Hohokam Indians of southern Arizona. This will be discussed in the chapter on the Hohokam culture.

In Pueblo IV times, as in Pueblo III, several subareas developed: (1) the Hopi area of northeastern Arizona (the Lower Little Colorado drainage); (2) the Salado area of central Arizona (the Upper Gila and the Upper Salt River districts); (3) the Zuñi area of eastern Arizona and western New Mexico (sometimes called the Cibola area); (4) the Rio Grande area of central New Mexico; and (5) the Chihuahua area of northern Mexico. This last-named area will be discussed in the section on the Mogollon culture.

People.—With the exception of the people in the Rio Grande area, all the other Indians of Pueblo IV period probably belonged to the Southwest Plateau type, described in the preceding pages.

The Rio Grande Indians of Pueblo IV times were physically slightly different from the Indians of western New Mexico and eastern Arizona. Possibly this change was due to mixture with groups that had recently moved into the Southwest. The Rio Grande skulls are somewhat more roundheaded, are lower relative to the breadth and higher relative to the length, and are shorter and broader in the total facial proportions.

Skulls from all areas were usually deformed.

Villages.—Many of the settlements of this period were huge, and some were larger than those of Pueblo III.

Some of the towns were built in caves, but most of the villages and "cities" were built out in the open. The largest towns covered as much as ten or twelve acres, while the smaller ones covered an acre or less.

The cliff-house villages were similar to those of Pueblo III period but were fewer in number and inferior in construction.

The towns built in the open usually consisted of a square, rectangular, or oval mass of contiguous rooms, arranged in tiers, grouped about one or more plazas or patios. The rooms were generally only one story high. In some towns one finds buildings of two or three stories in height. The kivas, or ceremonial chambers, were located in the plazas.

The "cities" of late Pueblo IV consisted of straight rows of rooms (one to three stories high) separated by "streets" or plazas in which the kivas were located. The masonry was generally inferior, crude, and often not coursed, although in some towns it was good. Frequently, it consisted of large boulders set in mud mortar—an inferior construction. Occasionally, walls were built entirely of adobe mud.

Kivas were both round and rectangular. Some of them were built below ground and some above ground. There were no great kivas.

In the Hopi country local soft coal was apparently used for heating some houses, and small chimneys were sometimes constructed to carry off the fumes. In all North America the Hopi were the only prehistoric Indians to use chimneys and coal.

Detailed information concerning many of the excavated Pueblo IV villages is lacking because full reports on these researches are not yet available.

Some of the better-known "cities" are Awatobi, Kokopnyama, Chucovi, Oraibi, Homolobi, Cottonwood Ruin, Chevlon, Pecos, and

Tyuonyi (located in the canyon of Rito de los Frijoles, now called Bandelier National Monument).

Livelihood.—Probably the same as in Pueblo III.

Pottery.—The character of the pottery of this period changed as to design, color, placement of designs on vessels, and painting technique. It is possible that some of these changes were due to influences from Mexico.

Simple and geometric designs of the former periods were replaced by dynamic representations of birds, animals, and insects. Human figures wearing ceremonial masks were portrayed. The older geometric designs were retained, though sometimes modified, and were used as fillers on the wings and bodies of birds and in other places on vessels.

New decorative techniques were introduced, such as stippling, spattered backgrounds, and incising. Glazing became frequent, and the amount of unpainted, open spaces between designs was greater.

The pottery of this period, then, represents very marked and even surprising developments and changes.

Each area—the Hopi, the Salado, the Zuñi, and the Rio Grande—produced a characteristic kind of pottery. Only the most important and better-known types are listed. For further and detailed information on pottery types consult Colton and Hargrave (1937), Fewkes (1919), Gladwin (1930), Haury and Hargrave (1931), Hawley (1936), Hodge (1923), Kidder (1931), Kidder and Shepard (1936), McGregor (1941), Martin and Willis (illus., 1940), Mera (1933, 1935, 1939, 1940), and Spier (1917, 1918, 1919).

1. *Hopi area (northeastern Arizona).*—

a) Jeddito Black-on-Yellow: Decorated with black (mineral) paint on yellow surface; yellow color the result of making pot of iron-bearing clay and baking pot in fire with ample draft. Designs are geometric and realistic (animals, people, insects). Shapes: bowls, jars, and ladles (Fig. 35).

b) Sikyatki Polychrome (Fig. 36): Decorated with black and red (mineral) paint on yellow background; yellow produced as in Jeddito Black-on-Yellow. Designs are geometric and realistic (insects, animals, and people). Shapes: jars, bowls, and ladles.

c) Utility pottery: Yellow or brown in color; undecorated; Jeddito Plain, Jeddito Corrugated, and Jeddito Tooled.

2. *Salado area (Upper Gila and Salt River drainages) (Fig. 37).—*

a) Gila Polychrome pottery: Bears three colors—red, black, and white. Designs are massed black elements such as triangles, scrolls, steps, and hatching. Shapes: bowls and jars.

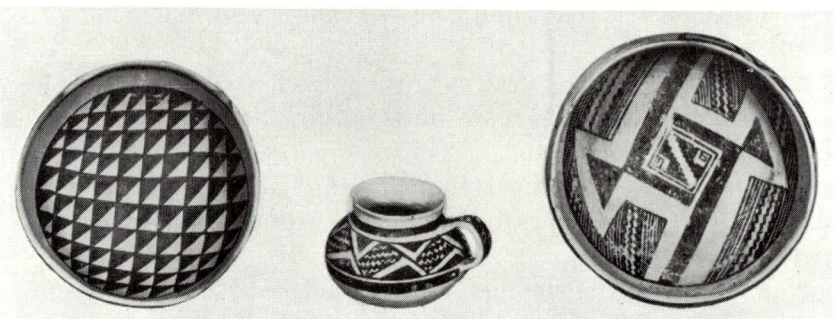

Fig. 35.—Jeddito Black-on-Yellow bowls and mug. Hopi area, Pueblo IV period, Anasazi culture.

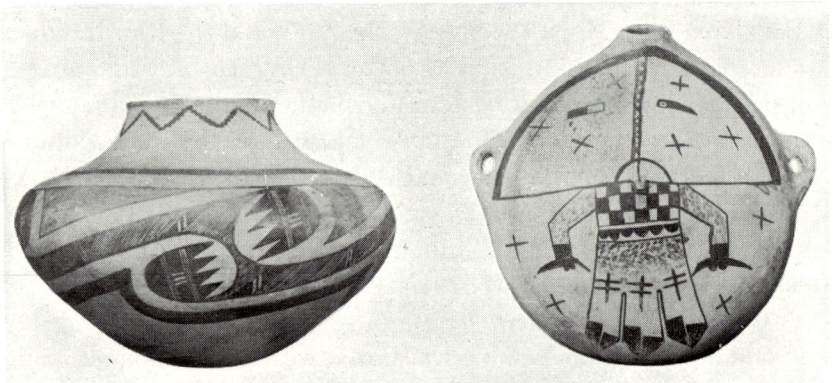

Fig. 36.—Sikyatki Polychrome jar and canteen. *Colors:* black and red on yellow background. Hopi area, Pueblo IV period, Anasazi culture.

b) Tonto Polychrome pottery: Bears three colors—black, white, and red. Designs are similar to those on Gila Polychrome. Shapes: bowls and jars.

c) Four-Mile Polychrome pottery: Black and white on red background. Shapes: bowls, jars, and animal effigies (Fig. 38).

d) Utility pottery: Indented Corrugated cooking ware.

3. *The Zuñi or Cibola area (eastern Arizona and western New Mexico) (Fig. 39).—*

a) Heshotauthla Polychrome: Bears three colors—black or greenish glaze and white on orange-red background; basic red color due to firing with ample draft. Designs are geometric. Shapes: bowls and jars.

FIG. 37.—Polychrome pottery. *Left:* Tonto Polychrome (black and white on red) jar. *Center:* Gila Polychrome (black, white, and red) bowl. *Right:* Tonto Polychrome bowl. Salado area, Pueblo IV period, Anasazi culture.

FIG. 38.—Four-Mile Polychrome pottery bowls. *Colors:* black and white on red. Salado area, Pueblo IV period, Anasazi culture.

b) Hawikuh Glaze on White: Bears two colors: purplish-black or dark-green glaze paint on white background. Designs are geometric. Shapes: bowls and jars.

c) Utility pottery: Indented Corrugated cooking ware.

In addition, there are several other important pottery types from the Zuñi area: Wallace Polychrome, Pinnawa Polychrome, Pinnawa Red-on-White, and Arauca Polychrome.

4. *The Rio Grande area (central New Mexico).*—There are some twenty-odd pottery types present in the Rio Grande area during the

Pueblo IV period. Mere description, without colored plates, and the naming of these types would make for arid reading and would add little, if anything, to the reader's general knowledge. Our remarks, then, will be confined to a few brief generalizations.

The Rio Grande pottery of Pueblo IV period consisted for the most part of vessels decorated in two or three colors (polychrome), one of which is a glaze paint. Such pottery is called "Glazed Ware." This really means glaze decorated, because glaze was never applied to the entire surface of any vessel.

Glazed decorated pottery occurs sporadically in modified Basket Maker, Pueblo I, and Pueblo III periods. The use of a paint which

Fig. 39.—Heshotauthla Polychrome pottery bowls. *Colors:* Greenish glaze and white on orange-red base. Zuñi (Cibola) area, Pueblo IV period, Anasazi culture.

would glaze or vitrify may have been accidental in these early, rare instances. At any rate, glazed paint decoration was not adopted as a new method of decoration until about 1290.

At about the date just mentioned, glazed paint as a new method of decoration came into vogue in the drainage of the Upper Little Colorado region (e.g., near Showlow and Pinedale, Arizona).

Thus by the year 1300 glazing was well established in the Upper Little Colorado area. From there, this new method of decoration spread eastward toward Zuñi and thence to the Rio Grande Valley. The glazed decorated wares of the latter valley, then, are the outgrowth of a new style, which probably originated in the Little Colorado drainage.

The chemical composition of the glaze paint was mostly lead.

Glazed ware types are distinguished one from another on the basis of (*a*) rim forms of bowls and (*b*) features of color and decoration. The various glazed ware types are useful in dating sites in this area (e.g., Largo Glaze Polychrome = A.D. 1425–75).

The shapes of glazed wares are bowls and jars.

Decorations consist mainly of geometric designs; occasionally, birds or human heads were employed as design motifs.

In addition to the glazed wares, there were three types of black-on-gray pottery and some plain red-and-black wares.

The utility or culinary ware was Indented Corrugated.

Tools, utensils, and weapons.—Some tools were the same as those used in Pueblo III period: bow and arrow, the planting-stick, slab metates and tabular manos (wedge- and triangular-shaped in cross-section), knives, and full-grooved mauls.

Arrowheads of stone were mostly side-notched triangular points and triangular points without any notches. Spear points of stone were long, slender blades and were notched at right angles to the long axis of the blade.

Several types of stone axes were made in this period: (1) full-grooved; (2) spiral grooved (groove placed well toward poll and set obliquely and fashioned to accommodate a haft which was wrapped twice about the ax); (3) double-grooved; (4) three-quarter grooved; and (5) double-bitted.

Several new tools appeared in this period: arrow-shaft straighteners, bone hooks, pemmican pounders (resembles a miniature maul), and loom weights (shaped stones for holding lower yarn beam in place).

Rubbing-stones, hammerstones, mortars, pestles, and drills of stone were in common use.

Bone awls, fleshing tools, needles, rubbers, polishers, scrapers, and flakers were important tools used in daily tasks.

The uses to which these tools were put are explained in the section on Pueblo I.

Pipes.—Four types of tobacco pipes were used: (1) the conical (straight, with bowl end larger than stem end); (2) the tubular (hollow cylinders, with both ends the same size); (3) the elbow (same shape as our common pipe); and (4) the straight, elaborately decorated, with raised or incised designs. This last type appears for the first time in this period.

With the exception of the elaborately decorated pipes which were made only of pottery, the other three types (conical, tubular, and elbow) were made either of baked clay or of stone.

Costume.—Little information is available, but probably the clothes of this period were very similar to what the Spaniards saw (in the Zuñi region) and described in 1540. According to their account, both men and women wore kilts or loincloths of cotton, long robes of rabbit fur or of feathers, and mantles of cotton or of deerskin. The women wore a sleeveless dress fastened over the right shoulder, leaving the left one exposed. Embroidered sashes were worn by women and sometimes by men also. Sandals of yucca leaf were the usual footgear. The men bobbed their hair; and some of the women (unmarried?) wore their hair in whorls, one over each ear.

Weaving, bags, and textiles.—Same as preceding period.

Ornaments.—Ornaments consisted of beads of various shapes made from shell, bone, and stone; pendants of shell and stone (including a "thunderbird" effigy type); and pendants of animal teeth and claws.

Burials.—Bodies of the dead were buried in abandoned rooms or in trash heaps. Most of the bodies were placed in a flexed or semiflexed position, although some of them were laid out flat. Orientation of the body (fixing with respect to the cardinal points) was not important.

Sometimes, some of the possessions—pottery, bow and arrow, awls, pipes, corn-grinding stones—of the dead person were placed in the grave with him.

END OF PUEBLO IV AND FIRST CONTACT WITH EUROPEANS

In the year 1540 the Spaniards under the leadership of Coronado entered what is now New Mexico and conquered the Zuñi towns—often referred to as the Seven Cities of Cibola. The word "Cibola" is probably a corrupted form of the Zuñi tribal name Ashiwi or Shiwi.

Why did the Spaniards want to conquer these and other pueblos (towns)? Mostly because they hoped to find treasure which they could plunder. One must remember that the tales about the great treasures found by Pizarro in Peru and by Cortes in Mexico were widely circulated and were incentive enough to spur many to look for new lands to conquer. Actually, of course, the Pueblo Indians were relatively poor in comparison with the Aztecs or the Incas. They possessed no gold or silver of any kind, or any other metal, except an occasional copper object brought in by trade with the Mexicans. One can judge from the information given in this and preceding sections how little "wealth" they had.

Nevertheless, the Spaniards had heard accounts of large cities inhabited by people who wore cotton garments and had vessels, nose and ear ornaments, and meat scrapers of gold.

Because no treasure was found and because the Indians were so hostile, Coronado withdrew from the Pueblo country and returned to Mexico City in 1542. For some years no further attempt was made to explore or to settle the country.

In 1598 permanent occupancy of New Mexico was effected by Juan de Oñate. In 1609 Santa Fe was founded and became the capital of "New Spain." Since no wealth had been discovered in New Mexico, the province remained chiefly a rich field for the missionaries who had accompanied Oñate.

The Spaniards attempted to stamp out the religious beliefs of the Indians, made many of them servants or slaves, and exacted tribute in the form of cloth and corn. This caused discontent and hostility, and general restlessness increased year by year. In 1680, therefore, the Pueblo Indians revolted, killed many of the priests and colonists, and drove the rest of them back to El Paso. In 1692 Diego de Vargas led an expedition against the Pueblo Indians and after many battles finally reconquered the territory in 1694. The Spanish regime was thus restored, although there were minor revolts up to 1697.

We have arbitrarily placed the ending of the Pueblo IV period at 1700, because from this time on the Indian cultures were subjected to strong and continuous European influences.

During this revolt period (1680–97) there were many shifts of the population. Whole towns were abandoned forever, and new ones were founded in isolated localities or in more easily defended places. The number of towns declined greatly in number. There were perhaps seventy or eighty in existence in 1540; but, by 1700, there were only about twenty-five or thirty.

Although the Spanish influences on the native cultures have been very great, surprisingly enough much of the Pueblo civilization still remains.

THE NAVAHO INDIANS

Living in the Pueblo or Anasazi area during Pueblo IV was a large group of non-Puebloan Indians—the Navahos. Both the Navahos and the Apaches belong to what is called the Athabascan language group. (Navahos and Apaches are, of course, still present in the area.)

The Athabascans for the most part live in northwestern Canada. Since the Navahos and Apaches both speak the Athabascan language, it is assumed that they migrated from their home in the northland to the Southwest. No one knows exactly when this migration took place; but, from the scanty evidence at hand, it seems fairly certain that the Navahos were living in northern New Mexico as early as 1550 and possibly several centuries earlier. They are, therefore, part of the Pueblo IV picture.

Some students of the Anasazi civilization believe that the Navahos frequently raided and harassed the Pueblo towns and, perhaps, were even responsible for the abandonment of some of them (e.g., Cliff Palace at Mesa Verde). This belief is not confirmed, although there may have been occasional struggles between the Navahos and some of the Pueblo towns. On the other hand, there is reason to believe that the Pueblos and Navahos joined forces at the time of the Pueblo revolt (1680-97), and both groups even fled to northern New Mexico into remote canyons. There, it would seem, these two groups of Indians, each possessing different civilizations or cultures, lived amicably side by side for a dozen or so years.

We have spoken of the difference between the Navaho and Pueblo cultures. Wherein did they differ?

The Navaho Indians, as stated above, came from northwestern Canada and brought with them the culture of that area. Briefly, that culture may be described as "nomadic" or "food-gathering," that is, the Navahos were not farmers and did not plant crops, their economy consisting of hunting, fishing, and gathering of seeds, nuts, berries, and roots.

We actually know nothing in detail of the various facets of Navaho culture of the early sixteenth century (see Keur, 1944), but from later reports of Spanish conquerors we learn that the culture was simple in contrast to the Anasazi (Pueblo).

One of the earliest house types, influenced possibly by contacts with the Pueblo Indians, was of stone. (The Navaho word for house is *hogan*.) These early houses were round, with walls of coursed or uncoursed stones, and roofed over with cedar or piñon timbers. Entrances usually faced the east. It is probable that earth-covered houses built of logs were also in existence then.

The Navaho made pottery, some painted and some plain—the latter being conical-bottomed and scored (by the use of corncob scraping tools). This plain pottery may have been brought into the Southwest by the Navaho.

Weaving, altars (consisting of colored sands and earths strewn on the ground in patterns and often called "sand-paintings"), agriculture, possibly some ceremonies, and perhaps other traits were also borrowed from their Anasazi neighbors.

Today, the Navaho Indians display a remarkable virility and ability to accommodate themselves to changing cultural conditions. They have become famous for their blanket-weaving and silver-making occupations. The former was borrowed from the Pueblo Indians and the latter from Mexican silversmiths about 1870.

SOURCES

COLTON and HARGRAVE, 1937; FEWKES, 1919; HACK, 1942; HAILE, 1943; HALL, 1944a, 1944b; HARGRAVE, 1932a; HAURY, 1934; HAURY and HARGRAVE, 1931; HAWLEY, 1936; HENDRON, 1940; HODGE, 1923, 1937; HOOTON, 1930; JEANÇON, 1923; KEUR, 1941, 1944; KIDDER, 1924, 1931, 1932; KIDDER and SHEPARD, 1936; MCGREGOR, 1941; MALCOLM, 1939; MARTIN and WILLIS, 1940; MERA, 1933, 1935, 1939, 1940; REITER, 1938; RINALDO, 1941; SELTZER, 1944; SPIER, 1917, 1918, 1919; WINSHIP, 1896.

PUEBLO V
A.D. 1700 to date

Pueblo V is simply another term for the historic period—the period in which the Indian civilizations have been subjected to European influences and political domination. Although our government grants considerable autonomy to the various pueblos (towns), the Indians are not free to move their villages from place to place (as of old) and must respect our laws as well as their own. Furthermore, there are clashes between the Indians and the Whites over water rights and boundaries. These new conditions, so vastly different from those of pre-White days, have produced marked changes and adaptations in the Indian civilizations. This process of change and accommodation to different cultures is sometimes called "acculturation." In spite of these profound modifications, the Pueblo Indians have maintained a remarkable portion of their own way of life, unaltered by Spanish or American customs. Archeologists have been better able to understand the tools, pottery, houses, and kivas which they have excavated because they are similar to those used today by modern Pueblo Indians. And from the study of modern Pueblo customs and ceremonies, we can infer something about the ancient way of life. The fact that many of the groups are living more or less as did their ancestors makes it possible, as Lummis said, to "catch our archeology alive." Many modern Pueblo Indians (e.g., Acoma, Jemez, Taos, Oraibi) still build terraced houses several stories high, similar to the ancient houses, and all modern pueblos are provided with kivas.

In other words, the modern Pueblo civilization, in spite of contacts with foreign cultures, has come through pretty much unaltered. This civilization, originating some two thousand years ago, has passed through many stages (which have been briefly described here) and has weathered many a storm and drought.

We have followed the vicissitudes of the Pueblo cultures from Basket Maker times down to the present. We have observed the growth of towns and villages from small hamlets of two or three houses; we have noted the abandonment of a large part of the northern Pueblo area; we have witnessed the displacement of the Salado people and their subsequent junction with the Hohokam people (chap. 13, p. 188); and we have further observed a renaissance of Pueblo culture during Pueblo IV times—a renaissance which was smashed by the advent of the Spanish conquerors. This invasion was almost as devastating to the simple Pueblo culture as the atomic bomb may be to our own culture.

And then what?

As stated earlier, the upheavals of early Spanish towns brought about shifts and reductions in populations and abandonment of towns. In many instances we do not know what became of the towns or of the townspeople. Undoubtedly they either formed new settlements or amalgamated with other already existing towns. But since adequate historical records are lacking, we cannot always demonstrate the fate of many of the towns which existed at about 1680 and which afterward were abandoned. Certainly the people did not disappear into thin air, unless most or all of them perished from one cause or another. We can in a few cases give some clue as to what happened to the ancient towns and are able in this way to trace the origin of some of the modern Pueblo towns. Accordingly, it has seemed desirable to list the present Pueblo towns and, wherever possible, to state their history. These towns are listed alphabetically.

Acoma (about sixty miles west of the Rio Grande River, New Mexico), reached by means of steep trails partly cut in solid rock, is perched on top of a large mesa, from which it looks down four hundred feet over the surrounding valley. The present site of Acoma has been continuously occupied since the Spaniards entered the Southwest in 1540. How much older the village is than this or what its origins are, no one knows. The Acoma people may have come from the cliff-dwellings at Mesa Verde which were deserted about 1300.

The population in 1944 was 1,355; and the people speak Keres.

Cochiti is a Keresan pueblo located about twenty-seven miles southwest of Santa Fe, New Mexico, on the west bank of the Rio Grande. The inhabitants of this village claim that they originally lived at Tyuonyi in the canyon of Rito do los Frijoles. After leaving the cliff-dwellings there (see Pueblo IV), they settled several places before founding their present village. These movements all occurred before the Spaniards discovered them in their present location. The town of Cochiti may have been founded, then, about 1500.

The population in 1944 numbered 353.

The Hopi pueblos, of which there are seven principal ones, are perched atop three mesas in northeastern Arizona. These mesas, which jut southward into the desert like fingers of a giant hand, are part of Black Mesa, a dissected (eroded) highland about sixty miles in diameter. The mesas are separated by broad, steep-walled valleys through which ephemeral streams flow. The southern portion of the Hopi country is relatively flat.

The Hopi pueblos have been occupied from Modified Basket Maker times right on up to the present time, but no one site, of course, has been continuously occupied for that span of time (about fifteen hundred years).

A recent study on the changing physical environment of the Hopi Indians shows how closely dependent they are on their environment. Their agricultural produce is directly associated with climatic and other physical conditions. It has been assumed that the introduction of livestock by Americans was the sole cause for the ruination of the Hopi country. It is now known that there have been minor climatic changes during the last two thousand years and that they have also been responsible for erosion and the ruination of fertile land. Major droughts in this area occurred near 715, 1100, 1290, 1585, and 1800.

With the exception of the people of Hano, all the other Indians occupying the Hopi mesas speak a Shoshonean dialect.

The famous Snake Dance is held in the Hopi province.

The population in 1944 of all the Hopi towns was 3,558.

On top of the first or easternmost mesa are the towns of Walpi, Sichomovi, and Hano.

Walpi, located on the southern tip of the first mesa, was founded about 1700. The older Walpi, which came into existence around 1300, was built on a lower terrace below the present town.

Sichomovi, a kind of suburb of Walpi, was first settled about 1700 or 1750.

Hano was established around 1700 by some Tewa Indians from near Abiquiu or Santa Clara, New Mexico, who came on the invitation of the Walpi Indians. The Tewa had probably fled from the vengeance of the Spaniards after the revolt of 1680 or were invited by the Walpi to help them against the Ute Indians. The people of Hano still speak their own language (Tewa), but in most other ways they have adopted Hopi customs.

These three towns are so close together that it is difficult to tell where one begins and the other ends.

On top of the second or middle mesa lie the towns of Shungopovi, Shipaulovi, and Mishongnovi.

Shungopovi was first located about 1250 in the foothills at the base of the mesa. In the early part of the fifteenth century the population moved a few yards away. After 1700 the people moved to the top of the mesa and founded the present village.

Shipaulovi was settled about 1700 by some of the inhabitants from old Shungopovi.

Mishongnovi was first located (*ca.* 1250) on the terrace below the present pueblo, which was established about 1700.

On the third or westernmost mesa is the oldest Hopi town, *Oraibi*, which has been continuously occupied since about 1150 (Fig. 40). Oraibi may be, then, the oldest continuously occupied town in the United States, although Acoma may be as old, or it may be a runner-up. Oraibi was visited by some of Coronado's men in 1540.

Until 1906, Oraibi was the largest Hopi pueblo. In that year the "liberals" and the "conservatives" quarreled over many pueblo issues. The matter was settled by means of a "push-of-war" (like a tug-of-war, except that each group shoved forward against the other and no rope was used). This ended in the defeat of the conservatives, who were then compelled to leave Oraibi that evening. They were permitted to take food, bedding, and whatever personal belongings they could carry. The defeated people, about three hundred in number, made camp at Hotevilla near an excellent spring, seven miles from Oraibi. The settlement became permanent, and now Hotevilla overshadows the parent-pueblo.

It is important to pause here a moment to examine this incident. The causes of the quarrels were numerous: whether the people should be friendly and conciliatory toward the Whites, some of whom had treated the Indians barbarously; whether the Indian agent should be allowed to take a census; whether the children should be sent to government schools; whether certain ceremonial attributes should be shared in the town; etc. The important thing is that, as a result of these issues, about half the townspeople were ejected from the parent-town and had to establish new homes elsewhere.

This illustrates perfectly what probably happened many times in the past, especially at the end of Pueblo III times. The sociological

Fig. 40.—Oraibi, Arizona, a present-day village of the Hopi Indians. Smoke-hole entrance to underground kivas in foreground. Style of building parallels that of Pueblo III periods (Photograph taken in 1900.)

factors of Pueblo organization prevented the formation of strong, central village administrations. As a result the pueblos were never welded into a homogeneous unit. The centrifugal quality of the pueblo social organization provided a constant threat of ultimate collapse. Towns were ever faced with the possibility of internal rows and divisions. And then, when a very powerful disintegrating force was exerted on a village, the village would collapse. Oraibi, as a result of such internal feuds and disruptive forces, eventually split up into four new settlements: Hotevilla, Bakavi, Moenkopi, and New Oraibi.

In the same manner the large villages of Pueblo III and IV times must have been cleaved by internal disintegration arising from a weakly knit social structure. This would explain both the quick termination of the Pueblo III period and the abandonment of sites for no apparent reason. It may explain the breakup of the Salado-Hohokam combination described in chapter 13 and the sudden desertion of Mimbres villages.

By studying the breakup at Oraibi, we can make certain deductions about the past. That is what is meant, in part, by the phrase "catching our archeology alive."

It will be noted from the dates given for the Hopi towns that the oldest continuously occupied one is Oraibi and that its date goes back only to about 1150.

Where were the Hopi, then, prior to this date?

The answer seems to be that they were in that immediate neighborhood, for early sites, containing pottery ancestral to later Hopi wares, have been discovered throughout the Hopi province. These early sites may have been occupied around A.D. 500.

Probably the Hopi country became a haven for refugees who streamed in from the north (Kayenta and Mesa Verde areas) about 1300. As a result of the increase in population and the assimilation of new ideas from the migrants, the Hopi civilization expanded and flowered as never before. Thus was ushered in the great Pueblo IV age.

The pueblo of *Isleta*, the most southerly of the Rio Grande pueblos, is situated about twelve miles south of Albuquerque, New Mexico. The inhabitants speak Tigua, a branch of the Tanoan linguistic stock. It probably stands on or near the site it occupied when the Spaniards passed a winter near by in 1540–41. Where the Isletans lived before or the age of their present village is not known.

The population in 1944 was 1,336.

Jemez is a pueblo on the west bank of the Jemez River, about twenty miles northwest of Bernalillo, New Mexico. These Indians speak Jemez. The present pueblo was founded about 1700, but the Jemez people had already lived in that general vicinity for at least three hundred years. Their pre-Spanish pottery was remotely related to Chaco pottery and was also greatly modified by admixture with Mesa Verde styles. We know that the Mesa Verde people left their homeland about 1300 and that some of them probably strayed into the Jemez area, because Mesa Verde pottery is found in near-by sites. Some of the earlier Jemez people may have come originally from the large pueblos in Chaco Canyon.

In 1838 seventeen people from the pueblo of Pecos, New Mexico, abandoned their pueblo and moved to Jemez. The language spoken at Pecos and Jemez was akin. Thus ended the great city of Pecos, mentioned under Pueblo IV.

In 1944 the population consisted of 792 people.

Laguna, a pueblo located about forty-five miles west of Albuquerque, was established in 1699 by Keresan-speaking people, some of whom probably came from Acoma, Santo Domingo, and Cochiti.

The population in 1944 was 2,712.

Nambé is sixteen miles north of Santa Fe. Its history is unknown. The 1944 population was 147.

Picuris is about forty miles north of Santa Fe. The present village was built about 1692 near its former location. The older, now abandoned, village was probably settled by people from Taos.

The inhabitants speak Tigua and in 1944 numbered 117.

Sandia, a Tigua-speaking village, is situated about twelve miles north of Albuquerque. In 1680, after the bloody Indian revolt, the Sandians moved to the Hopi country and built a village on the second Hopi mesa called Payupki. About 1740 the people moved back to the Rio Grande Valley and founded the present village, which probably is not on the original site.

In 1944 the population numbered 136.

The present pueblo of *San Felipe* was built about 1700 and is about twelve miles north of Bernalillo, New Mexico. Originally, the people of San Felipe claimed, as do the Cochiti, to have come from Tyuonyi, the ancient pueblo in Frijoles Canyon. After leaving Tyuonyi, they lived in several places, all of which were fairly near the present town. The people speak Keres.

In 1944 the population was 700.

San Ildefonso lies about eighteen miles northwest of Santa Fe. The present town was probably founded about 1700. The older and perhaps original village was seven or eight miles west of the present one. The language spoken is Tewa.

The pueblo in 1944 numbered 151 inhabitants.

San Juan today stands about twenty-five miles northwest of Santa Fe at the junction of the Chamita and the Rio Grande rivers. Before the present town was established (prior to 1598), the San

Juan people had occupied three other villages, all of which were near the present town. The people speak Tewa.

The population was 713 in 1944.

Santa Ana, whose inhabitants speak Keres, stands on the north bank of the Jemez River about ten miles northwest of Bernalillo, New Mexico, and was founded about 1700. The former pueblo of Santa Ana was located on a mesa some few miles to the east. The earlier history of these people is not known. There is some archeological evidence for supporting the idea that their former home may have been in or near Mesa Verde in southwestern Colorado.

The population in 1944 was 274.

The present pueblo of *Santa Clara*, about thirty miles north of Santa Fe, was established probably after the Indian uprisings, that is, about 1700. Before that time, the ancestors of these people had probably occupied several other near-by sites. The Santa Clarans claim that they had at one time dwelt in the cave village now called Puyé, a well-known archeological site in New Mexico. The language spoken at this village is Tewa.

In 1944 the population consisted of 547 inhabitants.

Santo Domingo pueblo has been moved several times because of flooding from the Rio Grande River. The present village was founded about 1700 and stands about eighteen miles north of Bernalillo, New Mexico. The older, ancestral towns of the Santo Domingo Indians were within a radius of twenty miles of the present town. The ancestors of the Indians of Santo Domingo may originally have come from the pueblos located near or in Mesa Verde National Park in southwestern Colorado. The Domingo people also claim to have lived in the pueblos in Frijoles Canyon. The people speak Keres.

The population numbered 1,020 in 1944.

Sia, whose inhabitants speak Keres, is a pueblo located on the north bank of the Jemez River, about sixteen miles northwest of Bernalillo. The Indians claim that the present village occupies the same site as it did in 1540. If this is true, Sia would perhaps be as old as Acoma and, possibly, Oraibi. The ancestors of the Sia Indians, like all other Keresan-speaking peoples, may have once lived in the cave pueblos at Mesa Verde, Colorado, and may have split from their relatives, the Zuñi.

The population in 1944 was 237.

Taos is a Tigua-speaking village consisting of two house groups, one on each side of the Taos River. The town is located about fifty-two miles northeast of Santa Fe in mountainous country. The houses are terraced and reach four or five stories in height. In fact, Taos pueblo represents one of the best examples extant of the ancient Pueblo III style of architecture. The old Taos, which was sacked and destroyed during the Spanish-Indian struggle, was located a few hundred yards upstream. The present town was founded about 1700. The origin of the Taos Indians is not known; but the earlier Taos black-on-white pottery bears resemblances to some Chaco black-on-white pottery. What this apparent relationship means is not clear. Possibly the Taos region was peopled (*ca.* 1100) by Indians acquainted with the Chaco type of Anasazi culture. The people may have come from or near Chaco Canyon, New Mexico.

The population in 1944 was 840 inhabitants.

Tesuque is situated about eight miles north of Santa Fe. The town formerly stood some three miles east of the present pueblo and was abandoned during the Pueblo revolt of 1680–96. The modern town was founded probably about 1700. The origin of the Tesuque people, who speak Tewa, is not known.

The population of the village as of 1944 was 147.

Zuñi is a large pueblo located about thirty miles south of Gallup, New Mexico. In 1540, when the Spaniards first entered the country, there were six or seven Zuñi towns—sometimes called the Seven Cities of Cibola. The present town was built about 1695 after the Indian revolts near or on the site of one of the old Zuñi towns, Halona. There the remnants of the tribe concentrated and have lived ever since.

The origin of the Zuñi tribe, who speak Zuñi, is not surely known. Some of the people may have come from Chaco Canyon and some from farther south and west (from the Hohokam area?). Chaco-like ruins and pottery occur in the area adjacent to the town of Zuñi.

The population of the Zuñi in 1944 was 2,406 inhabitants.

SOURCES

BANDELIER, 1892; COLTON and BAXTER, 1932; CURTIS, 1926; DONALDSON, 1893; FORREST, 1929; HACKETT, 1942; HARGRAVE, 1932*b;* KIDDER, 1924; MERA, 1939; PARSONS, 1939; STIRLING, 1942; TITIEV, 1944; UNDERHILL, 1945; WHITE, 1932*a,* 1932*b,* 1935, 1942.

CHAPTER 13

THE HOHOKAM CULTURE

AREA AND GENERAL REMARKS

THE Hohokam[1] Indians occupied central and southern Arizona. The center of the area was, roughly, the junction of the Gila and Salt rivers, west and south of the present city of Phoenix. Hohokam influences and traits are found, however, at some distance (e.g., at Flagstaff) from the central part of the area.

Central and southern Arizona was and is a desert. There is no evidence of any significant or marked climatic changes during the last fifteen hundred or two thousand years.

The elevation of the area is approximately 3,500 feet. Snaketown, the largest Hohokam site yet excavated, is about 1,200 feet above sea-level. Salt bush, mesquite, and various kinds of cacti are the typical plant life. The average annual precipitation is 10 inches. In summer the temperatures run over 100° F.; in winter, they rarely fall to 32°. The climate of the area is more arid than that occupied by either Anasazi or Mogollon peoples. The Hohokam people could have farmed only by means of intensive irrigation (flood or ditch). This is the only known instance of canal irrigation in pre-Columbian North America.

At the time that this area was occupied by the Hohokam, the Gila River was a permanent stream. A dam has recently been erected at Coolidge, and the bed is now usually dry. Hohokam villages were built on the highest terrace above the river in order to avoid danger from floods, but crops were grown on both the highest and the middle terraces.

The Hohokam culture, then, can be roughly described as a desert culture, in contrast to the Anasazi, which thrived mainly on a plateau and to the Mogollon, which flourished in a mountainous area.

The Hohokam culture has been divided into five main periods, each of which is subdivided into smaller units, called *phases*. A phase is a unit composed of one or more sites (ruins), all of which are in the same general geographical area and are of the same culture and the same time period (see Chart III).

[1] Pima Indian word meaning "those who have gone."

The evidence for establishing the first three periods—Pioneer, Colonial, and Sedentary—was obtained from stratified refuse at the ancient village of Snaketown, Arizona.

The dates given in Chart III were obtained by examination of Anasazi and Mogollon pottery found associated with Hohokam "domestic" pottery in Colonial and Sedentary periods. All the Anasazi and some of the Mogollon types have been dated on the basis of tree-ring evidence. In this way a correlation has been worked out between the pottery from the Colonial and Sedentary periods of the

CHART III

DEVELOPMENT OF THE HOHOKAM CIVILIZATION

Estimated Dates	Period	Phase
A.D. 1400 to date	Historic	Present-day Pimo and Papago Indians of southern Arizona and northern Mexico(?)
A.D. 1100–1400	Classic	Civano Soho
A.D. 900–1100	Sedentary	Santan Sacaton
A.D. 500–900	Colonial	Santa Cruz Gila Butte
300 B.C.(?)– A.D. 500	Pioneer	Snaketown Sweetwater Estrella Vahki

Hohokam culture and that from dated Anasazi villages. The dates for the Pioneer and Classic periods are inferential but are relatively correct.

The origin of the Hohokam culture is still unknown. Its roots may penetrate the pre-agricultural, pre-pottery horizons of the San Pedro stage of the Cochise culture (see chap. 10).

THE PIONEER PERIOD
Ca. 300 B.C.(?)–A.D. 500

People.—The physical type of this period is unknown because the Hohokam practiced cremation. It is assumed, however, that the Pioneer people were Indians.

Villages.—Hohokam villages were similar to those of the Basket Maker periods in that the dwellings were pit-houses set apart one from another. The Hohokam Indians built contiguous rows of rooms only in the Classic period, and they never constructed compact villages of many-storied houses such as the cliff-houses described for the Anasazi. The large, four-storied, adobe-walled, many-roomed house, to be described later for the Classic period, was the result of Anasazi influences brought in from the north by the Salado Indians. The Hohokam rarely built walls of stone and never located their villages in caves. Because of the absence of sites in dry caves, we have little or no information on perishable materials and on certain details, such as costume and methods of hairdressing.

The typical Pioneer pit-house was square or rectangular. The house was erected in a pit and was independent of the pit in that its earthen sides did not really serve as walls. The houses ranged in size from about 32 feet square to about 17 feet long and 7 feet wide. The floor, of prepared earth or gypsum, ranged from 18 to 36 inches below the surface of the ground.

Near the middle of one side of each pit-house was a covered entrance passage or vestibule that sloped upward to the outside ground level.

The roofs and walls were composed of cottonwood or mesquite rafters and a matting made up of twigs, reeds, grass, and earth. The roof was supported by four or more upright cottonwood or mesquite timbers. These woods (the only woods available) cannot be dated by the tree-ring method.

In each house, near the passageway, was a basin-shaped firepit.

The Hohokam houses of the Pioneer period were considerably larger than those of the Anasazi or Mogollon peoples.

No kivas (ceremonial chambers) were ever built by the Hohokam Indians. Nothing concerning the ceremonial life of this period is known.

Livelihood.—The Hohokam people depended mainly on agriculture for subsistence. Corn was probably the staple food. No evidence of squash or beans has been found. To supplement corn, mesquite beans, screw beans, and the fruits of the sahuaro cactus were gathered and eaten. The Hohokam probably planted corn by means of a planting-stick.

In the arid climate of southern Arizona, crops could not have been grown without some form of irrigation. Irrigation canals have been identified for all later periods (Colonial, Sedentary, and Classic), but not for the Pioneer period. How was agriculture practiced then?

Probably by means of flood-water irrigation. The Hohokam people lived near streams, and, knowing the habits of the rivers, the Indians could have selected spots where, in times of flood, the ground is well moistened; in those places, corn could have been grown.

Hunting was done with the bow and arrow but was unimportant, apparently, because few hunting implements or animal bones have been found in the trash mounds. The animals most commonly hunted were the jackrabbit, the cottontail, and the deer. The bones of sturgeon are found in some of the trash. It is possible that the Gila River may have been deep enough for this fish to have been in the vicinity.

The dog was apparently present during all Hohokam periods. Turkeys were not domesticated in any period of Hohokam culture.

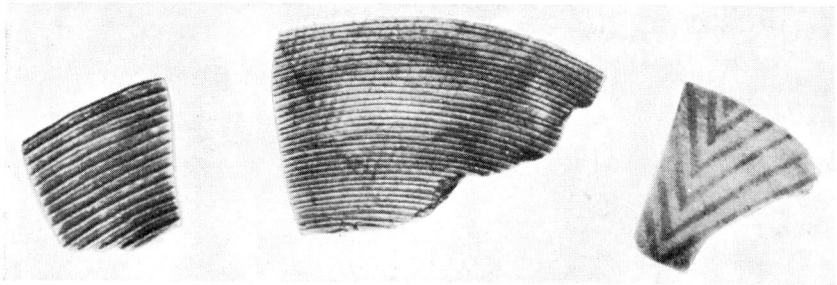

FIG. 41.—Sweetwater Red-on-Gray incised and painted pottery fragments. Pioneer period, Hohokam culture. (Courtesy Gila Pueblo.)

Pottery.—There were seven types of pottery found in the Pioneer period. The earliest types, called Vahki Plain, Vahki Red, and Gila Plain, were unpainted. Vahki Plain and Gila Plain wares were light brown or gray in color. These three types were used for cooking and storage purposes.

The decorated or painted pottery falls into four types: Estrella Red-on-Gray (the earliest), Sweetwater Red-on-Gray (Fig. 41), Sweetwater Polychrome, and Snaketown Red-on-Buff.

The designs on Estrella Red-on-Gray pottery consist of lines, hatching, scrolls, and small elements in red paint on a gray background. Sometimes the designs are polished. This pottery was made in two shapes: bowls and jars.

The designs on Sweetwater Red-on-Gray pottery consist of hatching, scrolls, and small elements in red paint on a gray background. Shapes were varied: bowls, jars, dippers, beakers, effigy vessels, and heavy-walled vessels.

Sweetwater Polychrome was the same as Sweetwater Red-on-Gray, except that two colors (red and yellow) were used for decoration.

Snaketown Red-on-Buff was made in a variety of shapes: bowls, jars, scoops, and effigy vessels. Decoration in the form of line work, hatching, bull's-eyes, scrolls, keys, and life-forms was painted in red on a buff background.

An imported ware—San Francisco Red—found in this period came from the Mogollon country and will be treated in the section on that culture. We mention its presence with these early Hohokam wares to show that Mogollon pottery is at least as old as Hohokam ceramics. Since early Mogollon sites, yielding San Francisco Red, have not been dated by means of the tree-ring method, this imported pottery does not help us to date early Hohokam wares.

Hohokam pottery was finished by means of the paddle-and-anvil method. It may be recalled that the Anasazi made their pottery by loops or bands laid on top of one another like barrel hoops or coiled in a spiral. The bands or coils were then scraped until the desired thinness was obtained. The Hohokam process was somewhat different. Broad coils were used, each as a unit addition to the vessel. Shaping the vessel and thinning the vessel walls were done by means of a wooden paddle and a mushroom-shaped anvil of pottery or clay. The anvil was placed inside the vessel, and the paddle was pounded on or scraped over the outer surface of the coil. Anvil marks may often be seen on the inner surfaces of Hohokam pottery.

The Hohokam usually did not permit the coils or grooves to remain on the finished pot, as did the Anasazi from Pueblo I times on to Pueblo III (the Anasazi Indented Corrugated culinary ware). The Vahki Red of the Pioneer period is the only Hohokam grooved pottery. In later types the visible evidence of grooving disappeared, and the grooving became incising—a very different technique.

Clay human figurines were modeled and then fired or baked (Fig. 42). These figurines are crude and unpainted, with the heads generally flat on top and concave in the rear and the faces primitive and stylized. Slits or dots represent the eyes. It is not known whether these human effigies were used as toys, as representations of gods, or for some other purpose.

Tools, utensils, and weapons.—Metates were trough-shaped, open at both ends, and rectangular in shape. They were made of lava.

Manos were rectangular slabs of lava or quartzite, nearly flat on the grinding surface.

Three-quarter-grooved axes of diorite, slate, or sandstone were characteristic of the Hohokam culture.

Vessels (or bowls) and dippers were also made of stone, and stone palettes were one of the most distinctive traits of the Hohokam culture. Their use is not actually known, although they may have been employed for compounding pigments, since traces of paint are found on some of them. In later periods they became elaborate and well sculptured, but in the Pioneer period they were merely flat slabs of abrasive stone. Palettes occurred most abundantly with cremations.

FIG. 42.—Pottery figurines. Pioneer period, Hohokam culture. (Courtesy Gila Pueblo.)

Drills, scrapers, and arrowheads were rare. The arrowheads were of two types: triangular blades with lateral notches or with narrow stems.

Other stone objects occurring were reamers, whetstones, anvils, ungrooved hammerstones, polishing stones (for pottery), mortars, and long rodlike pestles. These objects were made of slate, sandstone, pumice, schist, or lava.

No bone tools have been found.

Ornaments.—Ornaments were scarce and plain. They consisted of flat disklike beads of stone and shell, pendants of turquoise and shell, small bits of cut turquoise and shell used for mosaic work, plain shell bracelets, and bone tubes bearing incised designs.

The shells used for ornaments came from the Pacific Ocean and were probably obtained by barter. Turquoise occurs abundantly in southern Arizona.

Burials.—Cremation was the usual way of disposing of the dead. The bodies, along with offerings of stone and bone ornaments and intentionally broken pots, were placed in special crematory pits and thoroughly burned. After the burning, the ashes, unconsumed bits of human bones, pottery ornaments, and other objects were transferred to a special trench or pit, where they finally rested.

THE COLONIAL PERIOD[2]
Ca. A.D. 500–900

All features found in the previous period were present here, but new influences were beginning to bring about changes.

Area.—The villages of the Colonial period were located mainly in the middle Gila River and lower Salt River drainages. However, the influence of the Colonial period extended over almost all the southern half of what is now Arizona. Hohokam culture expanded more during this time than during any other period.

Villages.—Separate pit-houses were still in fashion and resembled those of the Pioneer period. They were usually oblong, with rounded ends, and measured about 9 by 19 feet. The floor consisted of native earth or of earth plastered with gypsum and was usually from 18 to 22 inches below the surface of the ground.

Each house was provided with a roofed entrance-passage (about 5 feet long) that faced east. The earthen floor sloped upward from the interior to the outside ground level.

The firepit was located on the east side of the house near the inner end of the entryway.

The main supports for the roof consisted of two or more upright posts set in the floor without fixed pattern. Smaller, secondary upright roof supports were set about the outer edges of the room. Rafters rested on these posts, and across the rafters were laid smaller timbers. On top of the timbers was placed a matting of twigs, reeds, and grass, and this matting was covered with a layer of dirt.

The presence of "ball courts" in this period marks an architectural innovation. Ball courts were common in the Mayan area of Central America. The Mayan ball courts were rectangular in plan and were unroofed. Stone walls, in which stone rings were set vertically, constituted the sides of the court. In such a court a ceremonial ball game was played, of which good accounts have been left us by Spanish writers. The Mayan game was played with a solid ball of native rubber, and points were scored by passing the ball through the vertical

[2] Assumed to be a time when the Hohokam people were establishing their colonies in the Gila and Salt River basins.

rings. Any part of the body except the hands and feet could be used for moving the ball about.

The Hohokam ball courts were similar in plan and size to the Mayan courts. The playing floor of the largest Hohokam ball court measured about 180 by 61 feet. The walls of the Hohokam courts were adobe. No rings have been found in the walls of the Hohokam courts, but it is possible that the rings were made of perishable materials. Since the Hohokam courts resemble those of the Maya Indians, they were probably used for a similar game. A rubber ball was found in a later Hohokam site in Arizona. Hohokam courts have been reported from many sites in central and southern Arizona and even as far north as Flagstaff.

The ball courts may have originated in the Maya area and spread northward; or they may have originated with the Hohokam and spread southward; or the Hohokam and Central American ball courts may have been derived from a common source.

Such large projects as the ball courts and canals could have been planned and directed only by an exceptional social organization. What that organization was, we do not know.

Livelihood.—Corn and cotton were grown in this period. Charred corn and cotton seeds have been found in Colonial houses. No squash seeds or beans have been found. Wild foods, such as mesquite beans, screw beans, and the fruit of the sahuaro cactus were probably also utilized as food.

In the latter part of the Colonial period, an irrigation canal was constructed at Snaketown, and surveyors have been able to trace this ancient ditch for a distance of about three miles, though its original length may have been ten miles. The canal which furnished water to a later village, Casa Grande, may have been sixteen miles long. The direction of the canal was governed by "the lay of the land." The average drop in grade was about eight feet per mile, and such a gradient would produce little current in the stream. Excavation of the ditch at Snaketown clearly showed that the Indians contended with the same difficulty as do modern irrigators, namely, the problem of silting-up. Maintaining the canal must have required much labor. The Colonial ditch was about five feet wide and probably about five feet deep; the water was about three feet in depth.

Pottery.—Four Hohokam pottery types, three Anasazi "trade" or "imported" types, and several Mogollon trade types have been reported for this period.

The Hohokam types are Gila Plain, Gila Butte Red-on-Buff, Santa Cruz Buff, and Santa Cruz Red-on-Buff. These were all made by the paddle-and-anvil method (see chap. 7).

Gila Plain has already been described in the section on the Pioneer period.

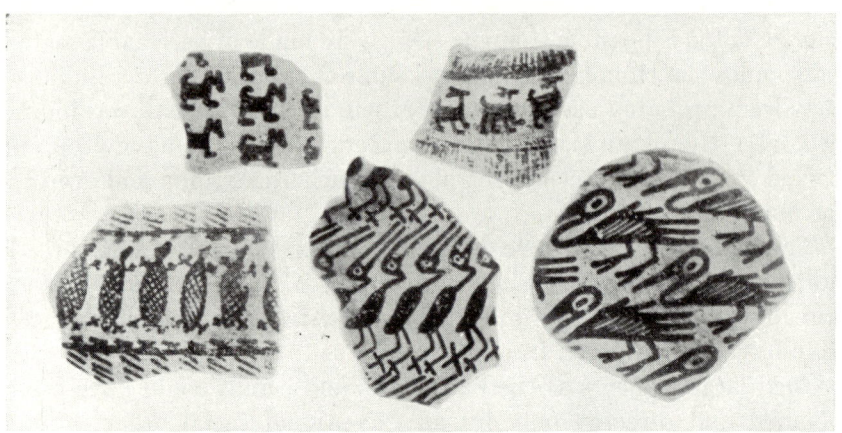

Fig. 43.—Gila Butte Red-on-Buff pottery fragments. Colonial period, Hohokam culture. (Courtesy Gila Pueblo.)

Fig. 44.—Santa Cruz Red-on-Buff pottery jar and bowls. Colonial period, Hohokam culture. (Courtesy Gila Pueblo.)

Gila Butte Red-on-Buff pottery (Fig. 43) is decorated with conventionalized scrolls, hatching, repetition of elements, and life-forms in red paint on a buff background. The usual forms are bowls, jars, scoops, and plates.

Santa Cruz Buff is notable for its thinness and was probably a culinary ware. It is undecorated and occurs in jar forms only.

THE HOHOKAM CULTURE

Santa Cruz Red-on-Buff pottery (Figs. 44–46) is decorated with red paint on a pinkish-buff background. Decorations consist of "fringe," massed line work, hatching, bull's-eyes, scrolls, and life-forms such as birds, snakes, human beings, animals, and insects. This

FIG. 45.—Santa Cruz Red-on-Buff pottery jars and bowls. Colonial period, Hohokam culture. (Courtesy Gila Pueblo.)

FIG. 46.—Santa Cruz Red-on-Buff pottery fragments. Colonial period, Hohokam culture (Courtesy Gila Pueblo.)

pottery occurs in bowls of various kinds, jars, vases, plates, scoops, ladles, and beakers.

The Anasazi "trade" wares are stressed here because they have been dated by means of tree-ring evidence. Thus, we can assign dates to particular Hohokam pottery and houses with which the Anasazi pottery is associated.

The Anasazi trade wares are Lino Black-on-Gray, Kana-a Black-on-White, and Deadman's Black-on-Red. The dates assigned to the first two (from tree-ring evidence) are A.D. 500–700 and A.D. 700–900, respectively.

Lino Black-on-Gray sherds were found associated with Gila Butte Red-on-Buff pottery. Since Lino Black-on-Gray has been dated at A.D. 500–700, we can safely assign the same date to Gila Butte Red-on-Buff.

Kana-a Black-on-White pottery was found in association with Santa Cruz Buff and Santa Cruz Red-on-Buff. The date of 700–900 already assigned to Kana-a Black-on-White can thus be given to the Hohokam types—Santa Cruz Buff and Santa Cruz Red-on-Buff. A check on these dates has been obtained through excavations at Flagstaff. Colonial Red-on-Buff pottery has been found there in sites that date from 700 to 900.

The Mogollon pottery found in Colonial rubbish mounds and houses was Mogollon Red-on-Brown, San Francisco Red, Forestdale Smudged, and some plain, culinary pottery. Two of these types—Mogollon Red-on-Brown, dated at about 900, and Forestdale Smudged, dated at 600–800—are of assistance in verifying the dates assigned to the Colonial period.

Gila Butte Red-on-Buff pottery has been found at a village (Forestdale) bearing both Mogollon and Anasazi characteristics. This village has been dated at 600–800.

Thus the dates for the Colonial period have been established in three ways:

1. Anasazi trade pottery dated at A.D. 500–900 has been found associated with materials of the Colonial period.

2. Hohokam trade pottery of the Colonial period has been discovered near Flagstaff in Anasazi villages that have been dated by tree-ring evidence at A.D. 700–900.

3. Mogollon trade pottery dated at A.D. 500–900 occurred with materials of the Colonial Hohokam period.

4. Hohokam trade pottery of the Colonial period was found at a Mogollon-Anasazi village dated at A.D. 600–800.

This kind of dating or fixing chronological limits for a particular period is called *cross-dating*. Thus we feel fairly certain that the Colonial period of the Hohokam culture fell within the limits of 500–900.

A few pottery (fired clay) figurines have been found in Colonial trash and cremations. These figurines are all modeled, and both heads and torsos were made. The heads were modeled in the round and were more realistic than those of the preceding period. Eyes were sometimes indicated by a short, incised slit. More often small, bean-shaped blobs of clay were added to the face, and eyelids were indicated by means of an incised slit. The added incised pellets of clay form what is called the "coffee-bean" eye. These figurines are unpainted, and their meaning is unknown.

Basketry.—No baskets have been found, but the impression of a coiled basket was found on the bottom of a flat, rectangular Santa Cruz Red-on-Buff bowl.

Tools, utensils, and weapons.—Metates were long, rectangular, and open at both ends. They were made of lava. Manos were long slabs of lava or quartzite, with parallel sides. The grinding surface is nearly flat and is polished from use.

Three-quarter-grooved axes continued to be the only type of ax made.

Stone bowls were better made than those of the previous period (Figs. 47 and 48). Some were highly polished; some, incised. These bowls were circular-shaped or globular-shaped with straight sides. Some of them are carved on the exterior to represent frogs, snakes, birds, mountain sheep, and human beings. Other effigy vessels of stone apparently represent human beings, bears, ducks, turtles, mountain sheep, frogs, and snakes. In the center of the back of each effigy is a rounded basin. The carving is realistic, well done, and sometimes elaborate. The largest vessel measures about $5\frac{1}{2}$ inches in diameter.

Palettes of stone were produced in greater abundance (Fig. 49). Typically, they were thin and rectangular with raised and ornamented borders or with carved effigies decorating the borders. The lengths varied from 8 to 12 inches.

Arrowheads were rare. Those found are long and slender and are provided with saw-toothed, serrated edges. They were fashioned from chert and obsidian. A highly specialized form with multiple barbs, long, narrow blades, and needle-like points occurred in quantity.

Drills and scrapers were lacking.

Stone reamers, whetstones, and knives, all of which may have been used for working shell, were more common than in the previous period.

Fig. 47.—Bowl of polished quartzite. About 6¾ inches high. Colonial period, Hohokam culture. (Courtesy Gila Pueblo.)

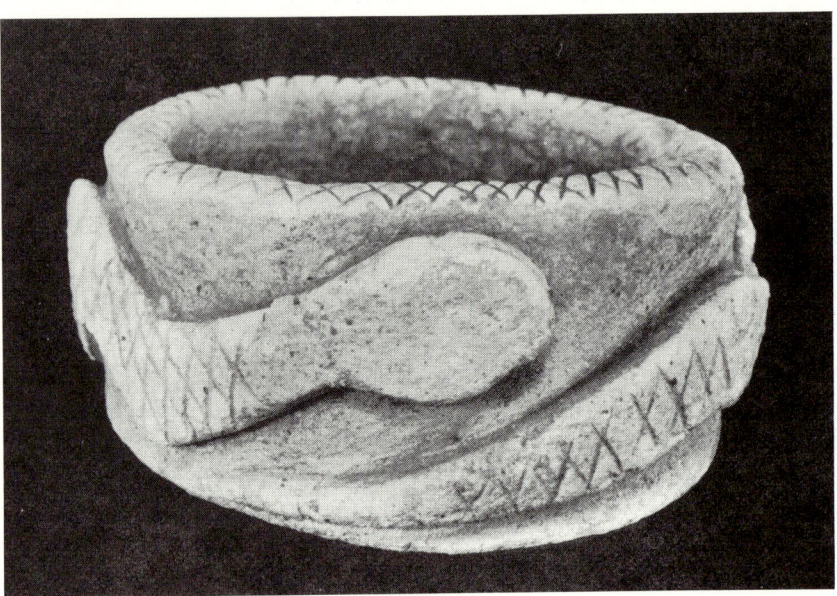

Fig. 48.—Bowl of carved stone, snake motif. Colonial period, Hohokam culture. (Courtesy Arizona State Museum.)

THE HOHOKAM CULTURE

Polishing stones and hoes of stone were absent.

Bone implements were rare. Only a few awls of bone have been reported.

The bow and arrow continued to be used.

Pipes.—Pipes are lacking. Cane cigarettes may have been smoked in ceremonies.

Costume.—Fragments of what appeared to be charred textiles or sandals have been found in cremations. No other information is available.

FIG. 49.—Palettes of carved stone. Colonial period, Hohokam culture. (Courtesy Gila Pueblo.)

Ornaments.—Beads of shell and of stone (turquoise, steatite, argillite) were more numerous in this period than in the Pioneer. Other ornaments were better made and include shell overlay used in mosaic work; finger rings of shell and stone; mosaic plaques (often called "mirrors"); well-carved shell bracelets bearing decorations portraying frogs, snakes, and birds; and shell pendants.

A mosaic plaque consisted of a round, precisely shaped base of sandstone (about 5 inches or less in diameter) and thin pieces of pyrites. The pyrite plates were affixed to the base and held in place with an organic adhesive.

Burials.—The dead were disposed of by cremation. After the body had been burned, the ashes, unconsumed bits of bones, pottery, ornaments, and other offerings were gathered and buried in a pit.

Rubbish was piled in mounds (some of which were large) instead of being scattered indiscriminately.

THE SEDENTARY PERIOD[3]
A.D. 900–1100

Many of the features found in the previous period were present in this stage, although some of them were considerably altered. The crest of Hohokam civilization was reached in the early part of this period and in late Colonial times.

Area.—The area occupied by the Hohokam during the Sedentary period was perhaps somewhat smaller than that of the Colonial period. Most of the villages were concentrated near the Gila and Salt rivers.

Villages.—There was no particular plan to the villages of this period. Separate houses were erected wherever convenience dictated. The usual type was a pit-house, but in this period it was more carefully built; for example, a rim about 5 or 6 inches high was added to the pit to prevent moisture from seeping in. The entryway was furnished with a step instead of a ramp.

The house was oblong, with rounded corners. The typical house was about 27 feet long and about 15 feet wide, exclusive of the vestibule.

The other features—roof, firepit, floor—were the same as those described in the previous period.

Sometimes the houses were set within a rectangular inclosing wall. The resultant inclosure, house, and walls are sometimes called a "compound."

Ball courts, though present, were much smaller (about 74 feet long) than the one described for the Colonial period. This smaller, later type, called the "Casa Grande," varied in other minor details.

Livelihood.—Corn and cotton were still grown, and some animals were hunted with the bow and arrow. Irrigation canals were more extensive.

Pottery.—There were five types of pottery made during the Sedentary period: Sacaton Red-on-Buff, Santan Red, Sacaton Buff, Sacaton Red, and Gila Plain. Only one—Sacaton Red-on-Buff—bore painted decorations.

The Sacaton Red-on-Buff shows a marked change (Figs. 50 and 51). Large jars, holding as much as thirty gallons, were made instead of small ones. Rims were smaller. A shoulder, called the Gila shoulder, was added as a sharp angle at the greatest diameter, and this imparts

[3] So called because it is believed that the people deserted the submarginal areas and settled in favorable places along the Gila and Salt rivers.

to these jars a strange, almost awkward appearance. This pottery is decorated with designs representing complex woven fabric patterns (embracing fringes, hatching, triangles, scrolls, birds, snakes, lizards, and mammals). The decorations are painted in red on a buff back-

Fig. 50.—Sacaton Red-on-Buff pottery jar and charred human bones remaining from cremation. Sedentary period, Hohokam culture. (Courtesy Arizona State Museum).

Fig. 51.—Sacaton Red-on-Buff pottery bowls. Sedentary period, Hohokam culture. (Courtesy Gila Pueblo.)

ground. Some authorities feel that the style of decoration on Sacaton Red-on-Buff is better than any other in the Southwest.

There was a marked increase in the variety of vessel shapes for Sacaton Red-on-Buff. The list includes about twenty different bowl forms; ten different jar shapes, including some with the Gila shoulder; plates; three- and four-legged vessels; scoops, ladles, beakers, and effigy vessels.

Sacaton Buff, Sacaton Red, and Gila Plain (Fig. 52), as noted above, are plain, undecorated pottery types. Their colors are respectively buff and red. The forms represented in these types are bowls, scoops, and jars.

In addition to these "homemade" types, several imported kinds of pottery have been found associated with the Hohokam wares. The Anasazi imported types are Black Mesa Black-on-White, Kana-a Black-on-White, and Deadman's Black-on-Red. The Mogollon traded types are Mimbres Boldface Black-on-White, San Francisco Red, and Forestdale Smudged.

The Anasazi trade pottery, found in association with Hohokam pottery of this period, came from sites near Flagstaff dated by tree rings from 900 to 1100.

FIG. 52.—Gila Plain heavy-walled pottery jars. Sedentary period, Hohokam culture. (Courtesy Gila Pueblo.)

The Mogollon trade pottery—Mimbres Boldface Black-on-White—is dated at about 950–1050. San Francisco Red was made for so many centuries that it is useless for cross-dating purposes.

Sacaton Red-on-Buff has been found in Pueblo II villages (near Flagstaff, Arizona) dated from 900 to 1100.

Thus by a three-way cross-check (Anasazi pottery at Hohokam villages, Mogollon pottery at Hohokam villages, and Hohokam pottery at an Anasazi village and at Forestdale, a Mogollon-Anasazi village) a satisfactory dating of the Sedentary period has been obtained.

Figurines of baked clay were well modeled and were realistic (Fig. 53). In fact, some of them suggest protraiture.

There were two types of figurines: (1) pottery heads and (2) full-figure pottery effigies modeled in a seated position. The latter were painted.

Metals.—Copper bells, similar in size and type to our sleigh bells, occur in this period. These bells were cast by the "lost wax" method.

THE HOHOKAM CULTURE

(This is the same method used by dentists in casting gold inlays.) It is fairly certain that these copper bells were not cast in the Hohokam area. The source of the copper cannot be traced with certainty by analysis as there is too much variability in the copper of any one region. However, general archeological evidence points to Mexico as the source of these bells.

Basketry.—A decayed fragment of a coiled basket (see description of coiled basketry, p. 63) was found in a house of the Sedentary period.

Tools, utensils, and weapons.—Metates, made of lava, were troughed with both ends open and were 18 or 19 inches long and 11

Fig. 53.—Pottery figurines. Sedentary period, Hohokam culture. (Courtesy Gila Pueblo.)

or 12 inches wide. Manos were brick-shaped slabs of lava or quartzite.

The three-quarter-grooved ax was the only kind of ax used.

Stone bowls were still made, but most of them were decorated with incised lines instead of with realistic carving in relief (Figs. 54–56). Steatite (soapstone) was more frequently used than were harder rocks, such as quartzite. Palettes were still manufactured but were inferior to those of the previous period.

Both side-notched and unnotched arrowheads were used and were well made.

In addition to these important tools, the Sedentary people produced and used whetstones, reamers, knives, hammerstones, and mortars and pestles. Bone was not highly prized as a medium for tools. Only a few bone awls have been recovered from this period.

Pipes.—Pipes were not used by the Hohokam, but cane cigarettes may have been smoked.

Weaving, bags, and textiles.—Impressions on burned clay of twilled matting is the only available evidence that matting existed. Judging from other impressions on burned clay, double warp fabrics (sandals?) were woven. A charred piece of cotton cloth was found in a burned house of this period (Sedentary). Across this textile was a

Fig. 54.—Stone bowls with incised decoration. Colonial and Sedentary periods, Hohokam culture. (Courtesy Gila Pueblo.)

Fig. 55.—Effigy vessels of stone. Colonial and Sedentary periods, Hohokam culture. (Courtesy Gila Pueblo.)

row of round open spaces which were produced by a weave called "weft-wrap openwork technique."

Ornaments.—Beads and pendants of shell and stone, turquoise and shell mosaic or inlay work, finger rings of stone and shell, carved and plain bracelets of shell, mosaic plaques (mirrors) incrusted with thin plates of iron pyrites, carved shell hair ornaments, pieces of painted shell, and etched shell were the important items used for adornment (Fig. 57). The shells on which designs and figures had been etched with acid were not numerous but are unique specimens in North America. It is not known exactly how this etching was done, but it

Fig. 56.—Stone vessel carved to represent horned toad. Sedentary period (or later), Hohokam culture. (Courtesy Arizona State Museum.)

seems evident that the Hohokam Indians of this period were familiar with liquids that would attack the shell and with a resist which would protect the portions of the surfaces that were not to be etched. Raw materials for the etching were at hand: gum and pitch for the resist; saguaro fruit juice, which was allowed to ferment, for an acid (weak and impure acetic acid).

Burials.—Disposal of the dead was usually by means of cremation (see Fig. 50). Toward the latter part of the period the remains of burned bones and ash were collected and placed in a small pottery

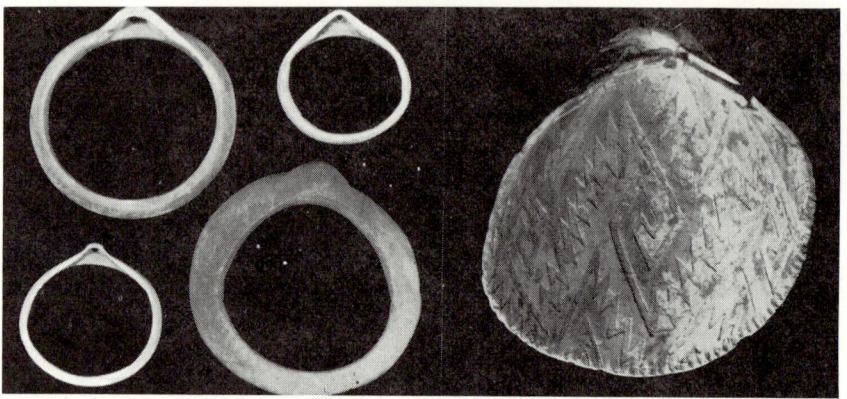

FIG. 57.—Shell bracelets and etched shell ornament. Sedentary period, Hohokam culture (Courtesy Arizona State Museum.)

jar or urn which was then buried. Inhumation (placing of uncremated body in a grave) was occasionally practiced.

THE CLASSIC PERIOD[4]
A.D. 1100–1400

Area and general remarks.—During this period the Salado (Spanish for "salty"; from Salt River Valley) tribes moved into the Hohokam area from east-central Arizona, and the two peoples lived peacefully together. The area they occupied was much smaller than that of the preceding period. The greatest concentration of villages was at the junction of the Gila and Salt rivers.

The Salado people were close cousins of the Pueblo (Anasazi) Indians. They made polychrome pottery (black-and-white on red background) which is different from the Hohokam red-on-buff. Their

[4] So named because it was formerly thought that the civilization of the Hohokam Indian had reached its peak at this time. Actually, the crest of their civilization was reached in the Sedentary period.

towns were built within walls, each town consisting of many contiguous, several-storied rooms of stone construction, as contrasted to the Hohokam villages composed of separate house units, each house being only one story high. The Salado buried their dead instead of cremating them.

The Salado civilization, a blend of Mogollon and Anasazi ingredients, probably developed in east-central Arizona. The Salado branch was already well developed by the year 700, as shown by recent excavations at the Bear Ruin in the Forestdale Valley, northern Fort Apache Reservation, Arizona. After that date, it assumed greater individuality, and by 1200 it had taken on a distinctively southern Anasazi character—villages of contiguous, multi-storied rooms with walls of stone; each village surrounded by a stone wall forming a compound; polychrome pottery; and inhumation of the dead as opposed to cremation. From the year 700 and on, the center of the Salado culture moved southward and westward. About the year 1300, the Salado and Hohokam cultures overlapped, and the two groups lived amicably together for several decades.

Why did the Salado people move south and west to live with the Hohokam people? No one knows precisely, but some speculations have been advanced by competent students.

What started the movement of the Salado Indians is not known, but their later drift was probably accelerated by events occurring to the north. It may be remembered that at the end of the section on Pueblo III we stated that the Pueblo Indians abandoned their well-built towns in the San Juan River drainage and moved southward. Such a movement of people would naturally cause an unbalance in populations throughout the Southwest. The Indians of the Little Colorado River area undoubtedly felt this pressure and were also forced to move; and they, too, moved south. Thus, the Salado Indians gradually established themselves in existing Hohokam villages, built their own style of houses, threw their refuse on the Hohokam trash dumps, and co-operated with the Hohokam in maintaining irrigation canals and in using the land. Each group was thus given ample opportunity to study the customs and technical processes of the other; but a blended, hybrid civilization did not emerge. Instead, while living together, each group conserved its own way of life, each adopting little from the other.

This is truly astonishing. Usually, when two cultures meet in intimate contact, a hybrid pattern is produced or one culture destroys the other. In the United States we have a hybrid culture, one made up of patterns of culture from many countries in Europe, Africa, and Asia. Most of the North American Indian civilizations have been stamped out to such an extent that most of these Indians now live in our types of houses and wear our style of clothing. But not the Hohokam and Salado. Each group maintained its own traditions and customs and yet lived peacefully with the other. Furthermore, there is no evidence that one group dominated the other.

People.—Since cremations destroyed most of the skeletons, it is impossible to state with certainty what physical type or types were present. The Hohokam may have been longheaded, but this guess has not been confirmed; and the Salado Indians were probably similar in physical type to the Indians of Pueblo III period.

Villages.—The villages of this period were utterly different from those of the preceding periods and were unlike any other in the entire Southwest. In the first place, two peoples, with differing customs, traditions, and backgrounds, met and lived peacefully together. There is ample evidence for believing that the greatness of the Classic period was achieved by the pooling of the efforts of both peoples. It was a co-existence that produced results unique in Indian America.

There were several types of villages and houses during this period.

1. Some houses were built over shallow pits and were probably inhabited by the more conservative people. They were roughly similar to the earlier pit-houses and were situated outside the compound wall. A group of such houses constituted a village.

2. In the early part of the period, just before the Saladoans moved in, the Hohokam villages assumed a radically different form. An adobe wall (perhaps 4 or 5 feet high and 7 or 8 inches thick) inclosing a rectangular space was erected. Inside this inclosure, a number (twelve to fifteen) of contiguous, one-storied rooms or houses were built. The inclosing or compound wall served as one wall for the outer tiers of rooms. The compound wall, as well as the interhouse walls, was composed of mud partly supported and strengthened by posts set vertically.

3. Another type of village in vogue during the early part of the Classic period consisted of a rectangular unit bounded by a massive compound wall built of adobe mud. These compound walls varied in size and height. At a ruin now called Los Muertos, near Phoenix, Arizona, the compound wall was 7 feet thick and perhaps 10 or 12 feet high. The compound inclosed by the wall measured 200 by 320

feet. Part of the inclosure or compound was divided into small plazas and room clusters. The room clusters were made up of small, one-storied, contiguous rooms, with thin walls made of poles and adobe.

The greater part of the compound was occupied by what may be called a "walled-house mound." This architectural curiosity may be described as follows: massive retaining walls (from 4 to 7 feet thick and from 7 to 10 feet high?) were erected inclosing a rectangular space of, say, 80 by 120 feet. Earth was packed into this area and was held in place by the heavy retaining walls. Thus a flat-topped walled mound or platform was produced, on top of which flimsy brush houses were constructed.

4. The villages of the late Classic period, when Salado influence was at its height, were similar to the walled inclosures described above; in fact, the compound wall of early Classic times was probably borrowed from the Salado civilization, before the Saladoans merged with the Hohokam.

The distinguishing characteristic of the late Classic compounds was the presence of great houses—that is, multiple-storied houses with massive walls of adobe mud. These walls were sometimes 4 feet thick at the base and were built without the use of forms. The dirt of which they were made was mixed with water until a stiff mud was produced. This was then laid course by course and layer by layer.

The "Great House" at Casa Grande, Arizona, a site of late Classic times, is 40 feet wide and 60 feet long; the walls stand 40 feet high. This house was four stories in height and contained sixteen rooms; but since the lowest floor was intentionally filled in, only three stories and eleven rooms were occupied. Doors and windows were small, not because the Indians were short, but because small openings help keep out rain and snow and make ingress more difficult for enemies.

The "Great House," along with smaller, one-storied, thin-walled houses, was set within a compound wall (perhaps 7 feet high and from 2 to 4 feet thick), thus making a walled village.

Probably, even in late Classic times, there were individual flimsy houses outside the compound.

The multiple-storied or "Great" houses were built by the Salado Indians and clearly show Anasazi influence. As the reader may remember, the houses of Pueblo III times were several stories high and contained many rooms. The "Great House" of Colonial times in the Hohokam area is in essence the same type of architecture. The one big difference is that the Saladoans in the Hohokam area used mud for walls, whereas the Pueblo III Indians used cut stone laid in courses.

The Salado Indians used mud because there was no building stone. Indeed, one admires the tenacity with which they adhered to their traditional house type, in spite of the fact that building stone was not available and a different medium had to be sought.

Sites which show joint occupation are Casa Grande, Adamsville, Casa Blanca, Los Muertos, La Ciudad, and Pueblo Grande. All these are located in southern Arizona.

Ball courts may have persisted into the early part of this period but probably went out of style before the Salado people moved in. None has been found in late Classic sites.

Livelihood.—Corn was still the main staple crop, but beans and squash were also grown. It may be remembered that beans and squash were not reported for any of the earlier Classic periods. Meat was obtained by hunting, and some wild seeds and roots were eaten. Irrigation canals were larger and watered more acreage than in any previous period. One of the main ditches near the ancient site of Los Muertos was 30 feet wide and 7 feet deep. Some of the ancient Hohokam ditches have been cleaned out within the last forty years and incorporated in present-day irrigation systems.

Dogs were present as in all previous periods. Turkeys may have been kept but probably not in great numbers.

Pottery.—Four principal Hohokam types of pottery were manufactured: Gila Plain, Gila Red, Gila Smudged, and Casa Grande Red-on-Buff. These types were made by coiling with paddle and anvil.

Two Salado types prevailed: Gila Polychrome and Tonto Polychrome.

Gila Plain, used for cooking purposes, has been described in the section on the Pioneer period.

Gila Red and Gila Smudged are very similar; both types have polished red exteriors, but the Gila Smudged is smudged black on the interior. The chief characteristics of the two types are conspicuous mica particles, porosity, and polishing striations, often arranged in patterns. The vessel forms for Gila Red and Gila Smudged are bowls, jars, pitchers, and scoops. These receptables served as food containers.

Casa Grande Red-on-Buff, made with paddle and anvil, is a light-buff pottery decorated with rectilinear designs in red paint. This pottery type is not so abundant in this period as are the plain wares. The most common shapes were jars and pitchers.

Gila Polychrome, a later southern Anasazi type of pottery, was decorated with black-and-white patterns, while red was used for covering the unornamented areas. Tonto Polychrome pottery was decorated with designs in red, black, and white. Both these pottery types were made in the typical Anasazi fashion—that is, by coiling and scraping. Bowls, jars, vases, and some eccentric forms were the common shapes. Gila Polychrome is dated at about 1300, and Tonto Polychrome at about 1400.

Trade pottery found in Classic sites includes Four-Mile Polychrome and Jeddito Black-on-Yellow. Both types come from the Little Colorado area and have been dated approximately at 1300.

Thus, the latter part of the Classic period is fairly well established by these dated pottery types as occurring at 1300–1400.

Only a few poorly made figurines of baked clay have been recovered from this period. Apparently the urge to create them was dying out.

Metals.—One cast copper bell has been found. No other metal objects have been reported.

Basketry.—Coiled basketry was certainly woven, for several fragments were, fortunately, preserved. Hohokam villages were located in the open, never in caves, and, unfortunately, perishable materials such as basketry, textiles, wooden objects, and the like, are rarely preserved. It seems likely that the Hohokam Indians, who achieved greatness in many ways, were also skilful weavers, woodworkers, and makers of baskets. The absence of good specimens, then, does not mean that these people were not conversant with many of the arts and crafts.

Tools, utensils, and weapons.—Manos and metates were essentially the same as those of the preceding period.

Single-bitted and double-bitted three-quarter-grooved axes were plentiful and were better made than in any preceding period.

In this period several new stone tools appeared, the presence of which can be attributed to the Salado people. The more important of these new implements were the adz, a polished, wedge-shaped implement, with a three-quarter groove; the pick, a cylindrical, axlike implement with a point in place of a cutting edge; the saw, a flake with a serrated edge; and the arrow-shaft straightener, a grooved stone for straightening and smoothing arrow-shafts.

Hoes have been occasionally found in sites belonging to the Colonial period, but they were rare. In Classic times, however, they became very important and, along with the palette and the three-quarter-grooved ax, are typical of the Gila-Salt region. The name "hoe" is applied to thin stone blades, one edge of which is sharpened. Some of them are notched or "eared." They were not hafted as our garden hoes are; indeed, it is doubtful if they were hafted at all. Most of them were hand tools used in cultivating fields and in digging irrigation canals. They range in length from about four to ten inches.

Several types of stone implements found in the Sedentary period were found also in Classic times. These are polishing- or rubbing stones, reamers for boring holes in shells, and hammerstones.

Knives of stone are merely bulky flakes and are crude. Projectile points (arrowheads and spearheads) were well made. Blades were thin and carefully retouched. Most of these points are triangular in outline, long in proportion to the width, with a very thin blade which is widest near the base. About 50 per cent of the blades have stems.

Drills of stone occurred in this period but are comparatively rare.

Bone tools were exceedingly scarce. Tools made from hard woods may have been used, but, of course, wooden objects disintegrate in the ground more quickly than bone and, therefore, are rarely found. The most important bone-tool type was an awl made from deer bone.

Palettes of stone were no longer made.

Pipes.—Pipes were not manufactured.

Costume.—Cotton garments and sandals were worn, as fragments of these two items have been recovered (Fig. 58). No other information is available.

Weaving, bags, and textiles.—Twilled matting was woven from vegetal materials; but the size of the mats or the purpose for which they were used is not known. Only the impressions in clay of matwork remain.

Semidecayed fragments of a coiled-work basket have been found. This specimen bears traces of a painted decoration. Cotton and fiber textile remains have also been found. If bags existed, none has been found.

Ornaments.—The only ornaments in this period were beads of shell and stone (Fig. 59); pendants of stone and shell and inlaid turquoise; and shell bracelets. No mirrors have been reported.

Games.—Some balls of stone (1¾–3 inches in diameter) have been reported. These may have been used in a kick-ball game.

Burials.—Both inhumation and cremation were practiced. The Salado people adhered to inhumation, which is traditionally an Anasazi custom. Salado graves are further identified by means of skull type and Salado pottery—Tonto and Gila polychromes. These burials were found under the floors of rooms or under the court yards. The Hohokam continued to practice cremation, a custom which dated back many centuries. After the individual and his possessions

Fig. 58.—Child's poncho of cotton. Woven by means of weft-wrap and openwork techniques. Classic period, Hohokam culture. From Ventana Cave, Arizona. (Courtesy Arizona State Museum.)

had been burned, the ashes, bits of unburned bone, and the remnants of grave-offerings (jewelry, pottery, stone tools) were raked together and placed in an urn. Each house unit contained a plot in which burial urns were placed. In one Classic Hohokam site (Los Muertos) there were three times as many cremations as inhumations.

Thus, in the Classic period, we have two distinct burial patterns. This is another bit of evidence that the Hohokam and Saladoans lived together in the same village and that each group was able to retain its own traditions.

CONJECTURES

We have now traced Hohokam history from about 300 B.C. to A.D. 1400. We have noted the peaceful penetration of the Salado people into the Hohokam territory, where they lived side by side for over one hundred years.

What, then, became of these peoples? What caused them to separate? The answer to these and a host of other questions is not known.

There are several possible reasons for the breakup of the thriving Hohokam-Salado communities: internal friction and bickering; exhaustion of the soil; failure of the canal system; clogging of the arable land by silt-laden, alkaline irrigation water; or the advent of the Apache Indians. Any or all of these factors might have operated to bring about drastic changes, or there might have been some other, and as yet undiscovered, reason for the exodus of the Salado Indians

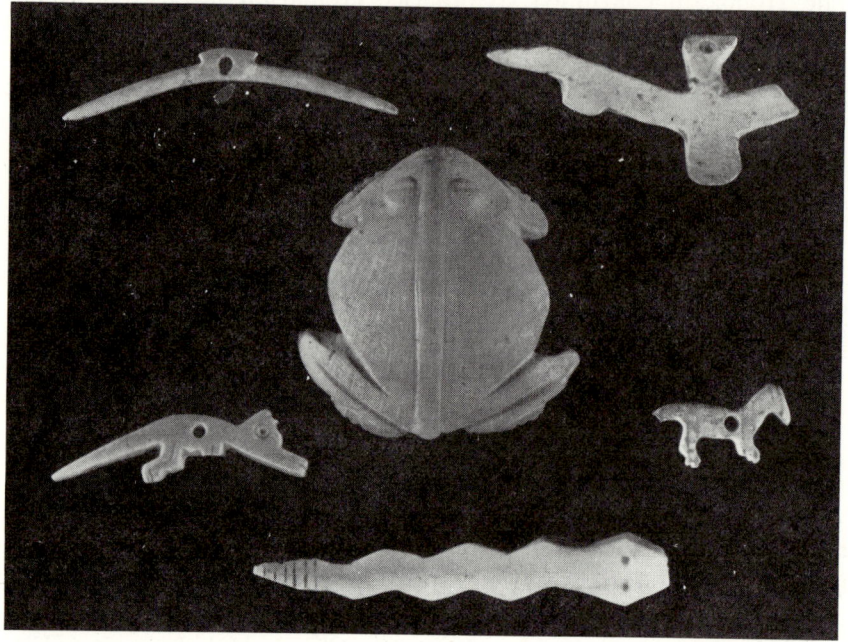

Fig. 59.—Shell ornaments. Sedentary and Classic periods, Hohokam culture. (Courtesy Arizona State Museum.)

and the decline of the great Hohokam-Salado merger. Whatever the cause or causes, disintegration took place about 1400 or 1450.

What became of the Hohokam Indians? Did they disappear into thin air? No. The Hohokam people probably stayed right where they were. They had lived there for centuries, were adjusted to the environment, and had created many miles of irrigation ditches. These considerations and investments would tend to make them cling to their domain. Instead of living in large towns, they reverted to the house type used by their forefathers—a simple brush superstructure set over a pit. These shelters were scattered here and there, some of them being, quite probably, near the large towns, now deserted.

The basic pattern of Classic Hohokam civilization—scattered houses, pit-house style; canal irrigation; pottery made by paddle and anvil; red-on-buff painted pottery; effigy vessels; cultivation of cotton—is similar to that of the Pima Indians when first seen by European explorers (about four hundred years ago). It seems fair, then, to infer that the Pima Indians who live today in southern Arizona in the same area that was occupied by the Hohokam peoples are the cultural descendants of the Hohokam Indians.

What became of the Salado people? Where they went is as mysterious as why they went. It is fairly certain that they did not move northward or westward. They probably moved eastward. One author believes that they moved into Chihuahua and amalgamated with the Indians of that region. Another thinks that they may have moved northeast to the Zuñi area.

When the Spaniards entered the Hohokam area in 1540, the great, thriving Hohokam-Salado towns had been abandoned and were falling into decay. The Hohokam—or the Pima Indians, shall we say?—deserted by the Saladoans, had returned to a simple culture reminiscent of that of the Pioneer period. The Gila Basin of southern Arizona had witnessed the rise and fall of a great culture, one which endured for over a thousand years.

Why do societies develop along certain lines, accept or reject innovations, become advanced, and then collapse? These are a few of the questions anthropologists are wrestling with and attempting to answer. When these and other more complicated questions are answered, the science of human behavior will have a wider scope and a greater accuracy.

SOURCES

CHARD, 1940; GLADWIN, 1928; GLADWIN, H. S. and W., 1930; GLADWIN, HAURY, SAYLES, and GLADWIN, 1937; HAURY, 1932, 1934, 1943, 1945b; HAWLEY, 1936; MCGREGOR, 1941; MCLEOD, 1937; WOODWARD, 1931.

CHAPTER 14

THE MOGOLLON-MIMBRES CULTURE[1]

AREA AND GENERAL REMARKS

THE Mogollon civilization is frequently designated as one characteristic of mountainous, forested, or brushy country in contrast to the Hohokam, which was essentially a desert culture; and to the Anasazi, a plateau culture. Actually, many Mogollon sites are in arid as well as in mountainous country.

The area occupied by the Mogollon Indians lies in southeastern Arizona and southwestern New Mexico. The origins of this civilization are not yet surely known. On the basis of present evidence it seems safe to guess that there is a close relationship between early Mogollon and late Cochise (see chap. 10). One author (Haury) feels that the addition of pottery, agriculture, and a few other traits to the San Pedro stage of the Cochise culture ushered in the earliest Mogollon period, or, in other words, the earliest Mogollon period grew out of Cochise. This opinion agrees with our experience and field work.

Many types of stone tools seem to have been inherited from the Cochise culture. If one compares some early Mogollon stone tools with similar types from the late Cochise period, one cannot tell which is Mogollon and which is Cochise. Out of thirty-four stone traits occurring in the Cochise culture, thirty-three were found at one of the earlier Mogollon sites (the "SU" site).

From recent evidence obtained in Ventana Cave in southern Arizona, it seems probable that the Hohokam culture also sprang from the San Pedro stage of the Cochise culture. The Cochise culture, then, is credited with being the parent of both the Mogollon and the Hohokam cultures.

It is important to note that about A.D. 500–700 Mogollon civilization probably somewhat influenced the Anasazi civilization. After 700 or 800, Anasazi characteristics seeped into the Mogollon area and eventually dominated the Mogollon civilization (see Fig. 60 for chart which shows Mogollon, Anasazi, and Hohokam traits at about

[1] The name Mogollon is derived from the near-by Mogollon Mountains; Mimbres, from the Mimbres River in southwestern New Mexico.

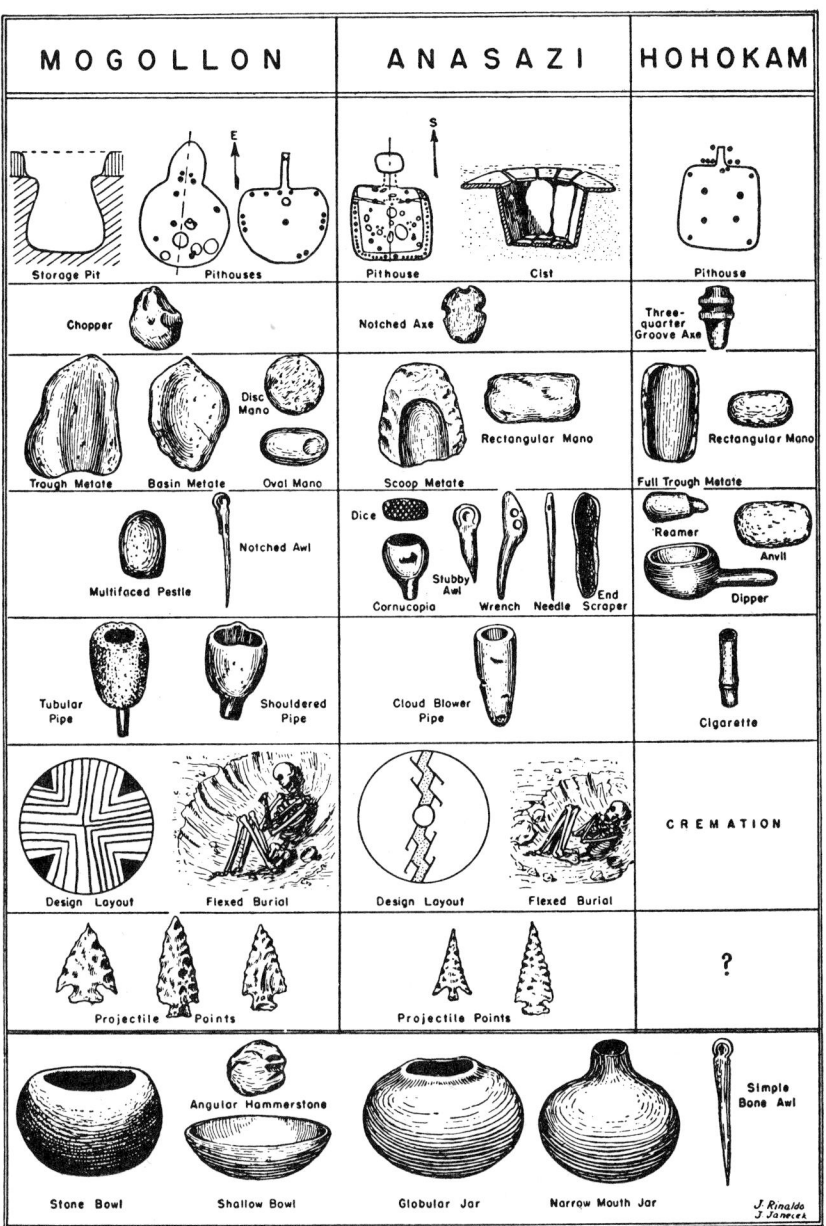

FIG. 60.—Comparison of Mogollon, Anasazi, and Hohokam culture elements before A.D. 700. *Bottom panel:* traits shared in common. *Above:* analogous and distinctive traits.

the period of 500–700). Thus came into being the Mimbres phase, which was more Anasazi than Mogollon.

The Mogollon culture has only recently been delineated; therefore, our knowledge about it is scanty. Within the next few years we may expect to accumulate more data by means of excavations.

On the basis of our present admittedly incomplete knowledge, the Mogollon civilization has been subdivided into a number of phases or periods. Chart IV will make clear the order of these various pe-

CHART IV

DEVELOPMENT OF THE MOGOLLON-MIMBRES CIVILIZATION

Estimated Date	Phase or Period
A.D. 1200–1450	Babicora* Ramos* Animas*
A.D. 1050–1200	Mimbres
A.D. 900–1050	Three Circle
A.D. 700–900 (tree-ring dates)	San Francisco
A.D. 500–700	Georgetown
A.D. 400–500	Pine Lawn
500 B.C.–A.D. 400	Bluff Site phase and probably two or three others, but field work is not yet reported on
3000–500 B.C.	San Pedro (Cochise culture)

* Found only in Chihuahua, Mexico.

riods. The San Pedro phase is included in the chart because the Mogollon civilization probably grew out of the Cochise culture, but some archeologists are not yet convinced of this connection (for details of the San Pedro see chap. 10).

THE PINE LAWN PERIOD[2]
Ca. A.D. 400–500

People.—Skeletal material is scarce, but the physical type appears to conform to the Southwest Plateau type. The skulls are mostly roundheaded; a few are deformed slightly at the rear.

Villages.—A Mogollon village of this period consisted of ten or more unconnected pit-houses separated by 3–10 feet and situated on

[2] Named after a small community near Reserve, New Mexico.

a terrace easily approachable from all directions. It is probable that the occupants considered themselves quite secure and did not feel that they needed an easily defended site. The houses were more or less round, varying in diameter from 13 to 28 feet (Fig. 61). Floors were from 10 to 40 inches below the ground. Most houses had tunnel entrances on the east. Their roofs were usually supported by one central post or by several large ones and several secondary posts placed

Fig. 61.—Pit-house, partially excavated. On floor are mortars, metates, and stones. The purpose of the stones is unknown. At left is the entrance to house. Pine Lawn period, Mogollon culture.

without any apparent plan. Firepits or hearths are lacking for the most part except outside the houses, and from this we infer that cooking was done mostly out of doors. Pits of varying depths (6 inches to 4 feet) were found in the floors of most of the houses and may have been used for food storage (Fig. 62). These pits were covered with branches or poles.

No ball courts have been found in any Mogollon period.

Livelihood.—Agriculture was apparently unimportant because only a few kernels of charred corn have been recovered from one burned house and because the milling-stones used were not the type characteristic of agricultural peoples. In the Anasazi area, where corn was an important foodstuff, we usually find quantities in burned houses.) It seems probable that these Indians lived mostly on seeds, roots, bulbs, berries, nuts, and insects. Hunting was probably likewise unimportant, since arrowheads and spearheads are scarce and since few animal bones were found. Because fish bones have not been recovered from any of the sites, we may judge that fishing was probably not carried on.

The domestic dog was present. Turkey bones have been identified, but it is not known whether turkeys were domesticated or not.

No evidence of cotton or of irrigation has come to light.

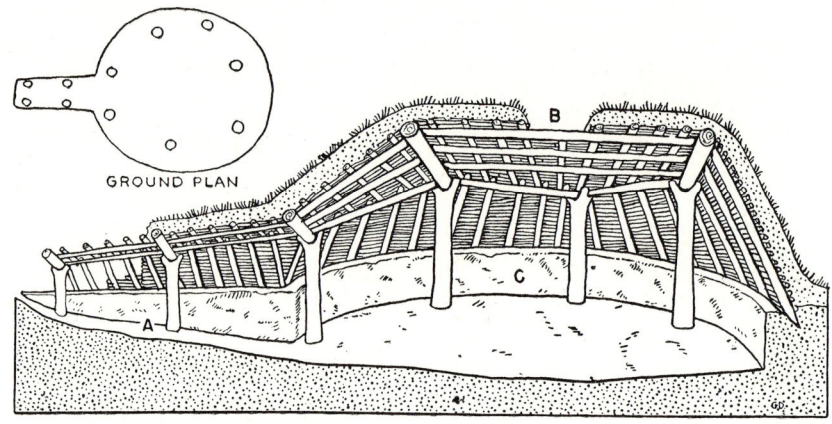

FIG. 62.—Cross-section and ground plan of pit-house with some features theoretically restored: *a*, eastern tunnel entrance; *b*, smoke hole; *c*, native soil forming walls of pit-house. Pine Lawn period, Mogollon culture.

Pottery.—Mogollon pottery of this period is distinctly different from either Anasazi or Hohokam of any period. It is plain brown (polished or unpolished) or plain, polished red, and was probably fired in a kiln supplied with ample air (an oxidizing atmosphere).

There were three plain, undecorated pottery types in this period: (1) Alma Plain, an undecorated, *polished* brown ware in bowl and jar shapes (Fig. 63, *a*); (2) Alma Rough (Fig. 63, *c*), an undecorated, *unpolished* brown ware in bowl, jar, and ladle shapes; and (3) San Francisco Red (Fig. 63, *b*), an undecorated, *polished* red ware produced by adding a thin surface coating or "wash" of red clay to a brown core. This is the ware that was referred to under the Hohokam trade types (chap. 13).

All Mogollon pottery, including Mimbres, was made by the coiling method.

THE MOGOLLON-MIMBRES CULTURE

Tools, utensils, and weapons.—Most of the stone-tool types of this period had their counterparts in the Cochise culture, and that is why we assume that the Mogollon civilization grew out of the Cochise. Many of the stone tools were "primitive" or crude, consisting mostly of random, unworked flakes or nodules of stone chosen because they were suitable for cutting and scraping. The natural surfaces of these random flakes were unmodified except for some chipping along the cutting edges.

Stones for milling or grinding seeds and nuts were a slab type (Fig. 64, *a*), a basin type, and a modified basin type with one end open. A suitable-sized handstone formed the upper part of the mill.

FIG. 63.—Undecorated pottery: *a*, Alma Plain jar; *b*, San Francisco Red bowl; *c*, Alma Rough jar. Pine Lawn period, Mogollon culture.

Mortars (usually large, round pebbles with unworked exteriors and deep, cup-shaped depressions pecked in the center of one face) and pestles (long, unworked, or natural stones) were plentiful and were perhaps used for crushing food (Fig. 64, *b* and *d*).

Mauls with a full groove around the middle, hammerstones, polishing-stones, and rubbing-stones were numerous.

No axes of any kind have been found in the Pine Lawn or in any of the Cochise periods.

Chipped stone implements show scarcely more than preliminary shaping, and the majority of knives and scrapers are merely random flakes of stone used for cutting and scraping usually with only secondary chipping to sharpen the edges or a little chipping that resulted from use.

Other implements show more chipping. Choppers, used in place of a grooved ax, were sharpened to an edge by heavy percussion blows from a hammerstone, but frequently they have a portion of the "crust" of the original core left intact to grasp in the hand (Fig. 65).

All major surfaces of arrowheads and spearheads, knife blades, and drills show secondary chipping (pressure flaking with a bone tool in contrast to percussion flaking with a hammerstone).

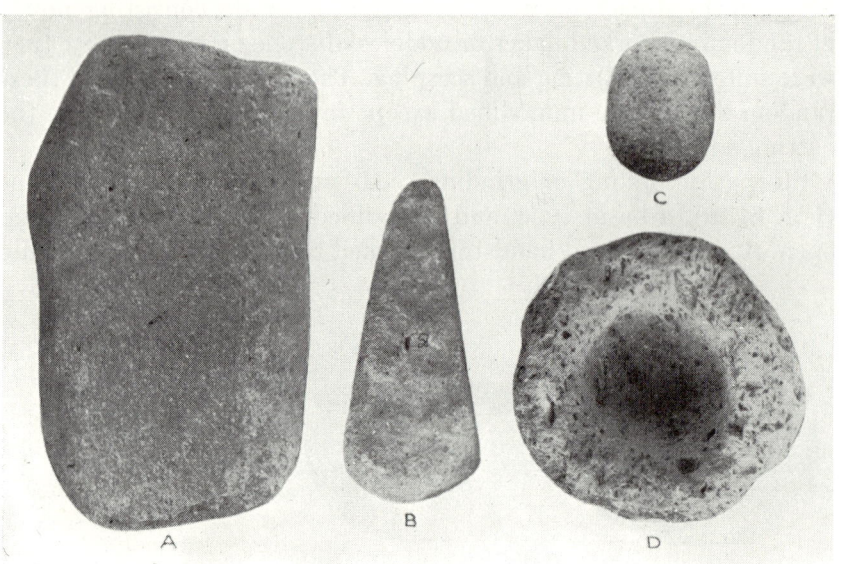

FIG. 64.—Stone tools: *a*, slab metate; *b*, pestle; *c*, multifaced pestle; *d*, mortar. Pine Lawn period, Mogollon culture.

FIG. 65.—Choppers of stone. Pine Lawn period, Mogollon culture

Chipped implements include arrowheads and spearheads, knives, scrapers, choppers, drills, and hoes. The hoes differ from those found in the San Francisco period.

Very few bone tools occur. Flakers (used for chipping or flaking stone), needles, and especially awls have been reported.

Pipes.—Tobacco pipes were funnel-shaped and made of pottery, the greatest diameter being at the bowl end; or they were cylindrical or tubular and made of stone, sometimes with a hollow bone mouthpiece.

Fig. 66.—A burial. *Left:* shell bracelet and arm bones. *Center:* tubular tobacco pipe of stone. *Right:* remains of skull. Arrow, 30 cm. long, points north. Pine Lawn period, Mogollon culture.

Ornaments.—Simple stone and shell beads, carved pendants, and shell bracelets were worn.

Burials.—Inhumation, and not cremation, was practised. Apparently no special place was reserved for burials, as skeletons have been found on the floor of houses (presumably placed there after the house was abandoned), in pits in the floors of houses, or outside in shallow graves. The body was interred in a flexed position without any mortuary offering except in a few instances where bracelets, a pipe, and a bone awl were found (Fig. 66).

THE GEORGETOWN PERIOD[3]
Ca. A.D. 500–700

Area.—Same as in preceding (Pine Lawn) period.

People.—Same as in previous period.

Villages.—Houses were similar to those of the preceding periods except that all of them were provided with firepits. The villages lay in easily accessible spots, making it evident that the occupants had no fear of invaders. Houses were set several feet apart.

Livelihood.—The economy was similar to that of the preceding period, except that more remains of corn and more animal bones have been found, from which we assume that game and agriculture were important and that less dependence was placed on wild foods and seeds.

Pottery.—Two types, San Francisco Red and Alma Plain, continued to be utilized right up to and through the Mimbres period. Alma Rough became extinct. Two new types, Alma Neck-banded and Alma Scored, put in an appearance.

Alma Neck-banded pottery consisted of jars of Alma Plain ware with flat coils at the neck. Alma Scored pottery is Alma Plain ware plus scratches or scoring applied to a limited surface of the vessel.

Tools, utensils, and weapons.—Only one type of metate was used in this period. It was an unshaped block of stone with a grinding surface that was oblong and somewhat basin-shaped. The mano was an unshaped, oval stone. The grinding motion of this stone followed several directions—i.e., back and forth, side to side, and round and round.

The other stone and bone tools were similar to those described under the Pine Lawn period.

Pipes.—Same as in preceding period.

Ornaments.—Same as in preceding period.

Burials.—Same as in preceding period.

THE SAN FRANCISCO PERIOD[4]
Ca. A.D. 700–900

Area.—Same as in Pine Lawn period.

People.—Same as in Pine Lawn period.

Villages.—The houses of this period were rectangular rather than circular pit-houses, each with a long entrance passageway which

---

[3] Named after a town located northwest of Silver City, New Mexico.

[4] Named after the San Francisco River, which flows through western New Mexico and is a tributary of the Gila River.

sloped up from the floor to the outer ground level. The vestibule-entrance usually faced east. The roof was supported by a central post and auxiliary posts placed near the side walls. Houses were about 10 by 12 feet, were 5 or 6 feet deep, and were set several feet or yards apart. There were usually from five to twenty houses to a village. Apparently there were few enemies, as most of the villages lay on open terraces.

Livelihood.—Same as in the preceding (Georgetown) period.

Pottery.—Four pottery types from the preceding period persisted into this one: San Francisco Red, Alma Plain, Alma Neck-banded, and Alma Scored. In addition, three new ones appeared: Mogollon Red-on-Brown (named after the near-by Mogollon Mountains), Three Circle Red-on-White (named for the ruin "Three Circle" in southwestern New Mexico), and Alma Punched (Alma Plain pottery with tool or punch marks on the necks of jars and pitchers). These are the first pottery types with painted designs to occur in some quantity.

Tools, utensils, and weapons.—Two types of metates occurred in this period, one exactly like that described for the Georgetown period, and the other a type with a trough-shaped grinding surface, one end open. The grinding stroke of the mano was confined to one axis by the more or less parallel sides of the metate.

A crude stone hoe fashioned from a broad flake of stone with one end sharpened was used for cultivating maize (see discussion of hoes under Hohokam).

The mauls, choppers, arrowheads and spearheads, knives, scrapers, drills, mortars, pestles, hammerstones, and bone awls were about the same as in the Pine Lawn period.

Pipes.—Both short and long tobacco pipes were made of stone and were tubular in shape.

Ornaments.—Same as in the Pine Lawn period.

Burials.—Same as in the Pine Lawn period.

THE THREE CIRCLE PERIOD[5]
Ca. A.D. 900–1050

Area.—Same as described in the Pine Lawn period.

People.—Same as in previous periods.

Villages.—Pit-houses were scattered about on open terraces with no consideration given to defense. Two types existed during this

[5] Named for a ranch-ruin on the Mimbres River in southwestern New Mexico.

period. The first type was rectangular, with mud-plastered walls and with an eastern vestibule-entrance that sloped up from the floor to the outside ground level. The firepit was near the entryway. The roof was supported by four posts set in the corners of the room. There was no central support. The average house size was about 8 by 12 feet, and the floor was about 40 inches below the ground level. The second type was really a rectangular, masonry-lined pit-house with square corners and walls of stone masonry. It should be noted that this is the first time that masonry appears in the Mogollon civilization. The roof was supported by four wooden posts incorporated into the walls. The vestibule-entryway was very short, and the fire-pit was just inside the doorway. These houses averaged about 14 by 16 feet, with the floors about 30 inches below ground level.

This latter type of house represents an advance in the art of house-building.

Both architecture and pottery show some significant changes at this point, and it is probable that these events were due to stimulation from the north—the Anasazi area. In the next period the change in architecture was more pronounced.

Ceremonial pit-houses were present during the Three Circle period, and some authorities believe that they existed in previous periods also. The ceremonial structures of Three Circle times were large (about 35 by 39 feet and about 6 feet deep), with some masonry along the pit walls, and with a vestibule passage, the floor sloping upward to the level of the outside ground. The roof was supported by massive posts, some imbedded in the walls, and some placed in the floor. There were three firepits instead of one, as in domestic houses.

In some ways this structure probably corresponds to the kivas of the Anasazi civilization and may have been inspired by Anasazi influences which were beginning to seep into the Mogollon area.

Livelihood.—Same as in preceding periods.

Pottery.—Four pottery types which survived from the previous period were Three Circle Red-on-White, San Francisco Red, Alma Plain, and Alma Punched. Two new types which appeared were Mimbres Boldface Black-on-White (which grew out of Mogollon Red-on-Brown and replaced it) and Three Circle Neck Corrugated.

Mimbres Boldface was made in three forms: bowls, jars, and pitchers. Some of the design elements, such as scrolls, wavy hachure, and life-figures, were probably borrowed from Hohokam potters.

Three Circle Neck Corrugated is a pottery which developed out of Alma Neck-banded. The upper portion of jars and pitchers (the only known forms) is covered with coils laid on obliquely like clapboards on a house.

Basketry.—Only small, burned fragments of basketry have been discovered for this period.

Tools, utensils, and weapons.—Metates were made from crude blocks of lava or sandstone and were provided with a trough-shaped grinding area at one end. A small mano of stone was used back and forth in one axis.

Mauls with three-quarter and full grooves were present. Crude axes appear for the first time in the history of the Mogollon Indians. These axes are pieces of tough rock sharpened along the edges by percussion flaking. Near the broad end, a notch and a groove were pecked for hafting. Mortars (some with scratched patterns on the sides) and pestles were still useful. Arrowheads and spearheads were long and narrow, with a stem for hafting, and serrated edges. Stone paint palettes with incised borders and grooves about the edges are reminiscent of Hohokam palettes. Stone knives, drills, scrapers, and hoes are similar to those of previous Mogollon periods.

The awl was the only bone tool.

Pipes.—Three types of pipes have been found, two similar to those of the previous period. The third was short, made of pottery, and fitted with a bone stem.

Weaving, bags, and textiles.—Some fragments of matting have been recovered, but they are so poorly preserved that weave and material cannot be determined.

Ornaments.—Same as those of preceding periods.

Burials.—Same as in previous periods.

General remarks.—The reader will note that few changes were manifested from the Pine Lawn to the Three Circle periods. House types changed slowly, and pottery types became slightly more sophisticated; but many other items remained more or less static.

This apparently changeless condition may have several causes: (1) lack of information on hand; (2) isolation, voluntary or involuntary (the Mogollon people may have been mild, timid, retiring, homogeneous, and rigid, and therefore would probably have had few contacts with other near-by civilizations); and (3) the possible crystallization of the general Mogollon way of life in early times into simple and undramatic patterns, which drifted along, resisting innovations.

Whatever the reason or reasons, the Mogollon reserve was finally overcome by successive waves of influences from the Anasazi area. Some of the Anasazi people may have moved into the area at about this time. But whether the Anasazi actually advanced into the Mogollon stronghold or not, it is certain that Anasazi ideas and the Anasazi way of life finally dominated the Mogollon civilization.

After the Three Circle period came the Mimbres and the Chihuahua periods, both hybrids (that is, Mogollon and Anasazi traits plus some ideas from the Hohokam culture). From then on, the presence of Anasazi and Hohokam ideas was apparent, and we will note only the more obvious ones throughout this section.

THE MIMBRES PERIOD[6]
Ca. A.D. 1050–1200

People.—From the small amount of available evidence, it seems probable that the Mimbreños were physically much the same as the Anasazi Indians (deformed roundheads). Thus we may say for the present that the Mimbreños belonged in physical type to the Southwest Plateau stock (see chap. 12).

Villages.—Houses and room arrangements are considerably different from previous Mogollon periods. The people lived in pueblos with masonry walls, each room (and therefore the whole pueblo) being one story high. By "pueblo" we mean a group of adjoining or contiguous rooms built *on top of the ground*. This arrangement is similar to Anasazi villages and probably represents one of the Anasazi traits which drifted into the Mogollon area. Pit-houses with floors below the surface of the ground went out of style.

The masonry of these pueblos was crude, since the walls were built of unshaped river boulders. The average wall was 8–10 inches thick and may have stood 5 or 6 feet high. Inner walls were plastered with mud. Roofs were made by laying brush, grass, branches, and mud over roof beams which spanned the rooms. These beams measured 6–8 inches in diameter and lay on top of the masonry; in some cases they were also supported by posts. Floors were at ground level and consisted mostly of pecked dirt, although occasionally they were paved with stones on which mud plaster was laid.

The villages of this period sometimes contained forty to fifty rooms, which were often arranged about a court or plaza. (Again

---

[6] Named for the Mimbres River of southwestern New Mexico.

Anasazi influence.) At the Swarts village in southwestern New Mexico there were two such groups of rooms, one possessing two inner courts, and the other none. In general, the villages of the Mimbres period did not manifest the same orderly arrangement of rooms as did the later Anasazi towns.

Rooms were rectangular (6 by 8 feet to 12 by 16 feet) or square (9 to 12 feet).

No outer doorways existed; the rooms were normally entered through the roofs. (Anasazi influence?) The roof opening or hatchway was covered by a trap door made of a thin slab of rock. Doorways between rooms were usual, and it has been assumed that a family occupied three or four rooms. Most of these rooms were provided with firepits, each of which was sunk into the floor. Fires were used for heat and light as well as for cooking purposes in the living quarters, which were otherwise fairly dark.

Kiva-like rooms are sometimes found in villages of this period. They were large (11 by 16 feet) rectangular, and semisubterranean. They were entered by means of a long, inclined passageway and had a ventilator shaft and firepit. The ventilator shaft, firepit, and semisubterranean floor were similar to those of an Anasazi kiva of Pueblo III times.

No proof exists that such kiva-like rooms were used for ceremonies, but these rooms are different from the living-rooms, and therefore a different usage is probable.

Livelihood.—Corn must have been the major food crop as so much of it (charred) has been found—both shelled and on the cob. No beans or squash seeds have been discovered, and this negative evidence is interpreted as meaning that these were unknown to the people of this period. It seems odd that beans and squash seeds were not imported into the area along with the other Anasazi traits and ideas; but the fact remains that these foods were lacking. Nor is there evidence that cotton was grown.

Wild foods such as mesquite beans, grass seeds, sweet acorns, black walnuts, and the roots and leaves of century plants were doubtless gathered and eaten.

Meat was obtained by hunting mule deer, pronghorn antelope, rabbits, gophers, prairie dogs, squirrels, and birds. Bones of these animals were very numerous in the village dumps. Fish and turkey, often depicted on the pottery, were probably eaten also, although no fish or turkey bones have been found.

The domesticated dog was undoubtedly part of the village life, since dog bones occur in the house and village ruins.

No evidence of irrigation has yet been discovered in this area.

Pottery.—Two new types of pottery appeared and two old types survived in this period. The old types were San Francisco Red and Alma Plain, both with a history of about a thousand years in span. The new types were Mimbres Black-on-White and Mimbres Corrugated.

Mimbres Black-on-White is justly famous because it is unrivaled in the Southwest for excellent brushwork and for variety in decoration (Fig. 67). The most interesting aspect of Mimbres decoration is

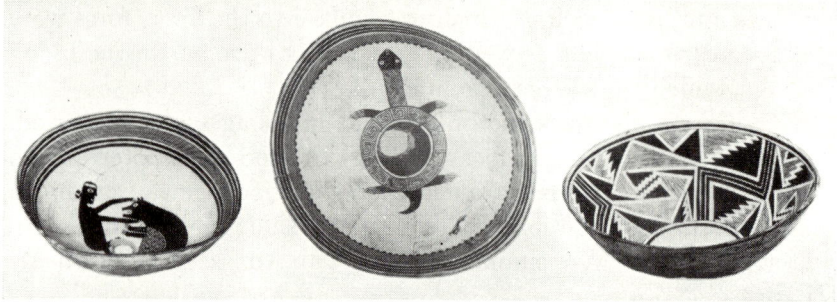

Fig. 67.—Mimbres Black-on-White pottery bowls. Mimbres period, Mogollon-Mimbres culture. (Courtesy Peabody Museum of Harvard University.)

the frequent use of naturalistic or life-figures on the interiors of about one-third of the bowls depicting animals, human forms, and insects. It is probable that this idea of pottery decoration was borrowed from the Hohokam Indians.

The majority of bowl forms were decorated with geometric designs which are unexcelled anywhere for technical perfection of brushwork. Bowls were the principal forms in Mimbres Black-on-White pottery, but a few jars have turned up.

The corrugated pottery reminds one of Anasazi pottery and occurs in the forms of bowls, jars, and jugs.

Tools, utensils, and weapons.—Metates were formed by pecking a flat depression into one face of a stone leaving a ridge on either side and a trough running through from end to end. The manos were flat and oblong.

Stone bowls, mortars and pestles, paint cups, rubbing-stones, three-quarter and full-grooved mauls, and hammerstones occur in quantities and are much better fashioned than those of previous periods. The stone palettes are similar to those of the Hohokam people. (Hohokam influence?)

For the first time in Mogollon history three-quarter-grooved axes of stone appeared and were abundant. (Again Hohokam influence?)

Stone hoes are fairly common throughout the Mimbres region but are not the same shape as those of the Classic Hohokam period, although their function was probably similar. The Mimbres hoe is a long, narrow tool with a rounded base and a pointed top. (Anasazi influence?)

Arrowheads and spearheads, scrapers, knives, and drills were similar to those of the preceding period.

Two bone tools occurred, as did bone awls (very numerous) and flaking tools (used for chipping flakes from stone). The heads of some awls were carved.

Pipes.—Long, slender, conical stone pipes and short, conical pottery (baked clay) pipes were common. In general, they resembled those of earlier Mogollon periods, although some pipes of the Mimbres period were very well made, and occasionally one was painted with colored stripes.

Costume.—There is no information on this subject, since all perishable materials quickly rot in graves and in houses located in the open. One small item was recovered—a fragment of a yucca sandal.

Cradles.—No information is available, but probably a hard type was used in order to produce deformed skulls.

Weaving, bags, and textiles.—Only a small piece of coiled basketry was preserved. The impression of coarse cloth was observed in a grave.

Ornaments.—The types found (mostly in graves) are markedly similar to those of previous Mogollon periods and consist of stone, shell, and turquoise beads, shell bracelets, shell tinklers used on necklaces, and stone and turquoise pendants and finger rings.

Burials.—Apparently house burials were the normal custom for the Mimbreños, although some interments have been found outside buildings. Since grave-offerings occurred with bodies buried both inside and outside the houses, it would seem probable that each was held in the same esteem.

Usually bodies were buried in a semiflexed or a flexed position. Occasionally, cremations occurred. House burials were placed in graves under the floor, and it is probable that the houses continued to be occupied after the interments. Some rooms had no burials; others contained one or two; and still others had as many as ten to thirty placed well below the floor levels and sealed in by the heavy adobe coating with which the floor was covered. Apparently there was no fear of the dead. Although burying the dead in the house may seem strange to us, perhaps these people felt the same as the young cowboy who pleaded:

> Oh, bury me not on the lone prairie,
> Where the wild coyotes will howl o'er me. . . . .

Grave-offerings consisted of metates, manos, rubbing-stones, hammerstones, pottery, beads, ear pendants, and shell bracelets. No implements of war or pipes were found with any of the burials. It is interesting to note that the pottery bowls which were placed with the dead were always "killed." By "killed" we mean that a hole was knocked in the bottom. The pieces which were broken out were usually in the grave. In the case of an infant burial, a large sherd was used instead of a whole bowl (economy?), but the sherd was also "killed," or punctured.

THE CHIHUAHUA PERIODS: BABICORA, RAMOS, AND ANIMAS PHASES
Ca. A.D. 1200–1450

General remarks.—The Chihuahua periods are included in order to complete the story of the Mogollon culture. Actually little is known about these phases because detailed investigations have never been carried on in the Chihuahua area. We shall therefore make no distinction between these three phases but shall lump them together as a single unit covering about two centuries. This treatment is arbitrary, but no other is possible at this time; and, since there is such a dearth of details, we shall treat these phases briefly.

On the basis of an excellent archeological survey of the area, Sayles was able to set up five prehistoric phases. We mention only three— the Babicora (earliest), the Ramos, and the Animas (latest). These names are derived from local geographical terms.

Many Chihuahua traits seem to have been derived from the Mimbres phase of the Mogollon and many from the Salado people, some of whom may have moved here from the Hohokam area.

Area.—Chihuahua is a state of Mexico which adjoins Arizona, New Mexico, and Texas on the south. The Chihuahua civilization treated here flourished in the northern part of the state, which is a hilly plateau about three to five thousand feet high, and mostly desert covered with creosote bush, scrub mesquite, yucca, and cactus. Willow and cottonwood trees grow along the streams, and pine trees grow in the higher, mountainous parts. The rainfall is only four to six inches a year. Summers are fairly warm and the winters are long and severe. In many ways, the area resembles those inhabited by the Anasazi, Hohokam, and Mogollon peoples.

Villages.—(1) Houses were individual, usually but one story high, and built of adobe mud reinforced with stone. Occasionally one finds remains of houses with walls of unshaped rock, covered with plaster. (2) Multistoried houses of many rooms and walls of puddled adobe mud were fairly common. These appear to resemble the "Great Houses" at Casa Grande and at Los Muertos described under the Classic phase of the Hohokam civilization (see chap. 13). The pottery associated with some of these houses is local polychromes and also Gila and Tonto polychromes, the same as those found with the "Great House" period (Classic) of the Hohokam. (3) Community cliff-houses were built in caves. The walls of these were of adobe mud and stone and stood three stories high. T-shaped doorways (broader at the top than at the bottom) were often present. Pottery associated with these dwellings consisted of local polychromes and Salado pottery—Gila and Tonto polychromes. These cliff-dwellings remind one of those found in the Roosevelt Lake area of Arizona—the so-called Tonto cliff-dwellings.

Livelihood.—Corn was certainly grown in large quantities, but whether other crops were raised is not now known. The domesticated dog was present.

Pottery.—In addition to the Salado pottery types from north-central Arizona mentioned above (Gila and Tonto polychromes), an abundance of excellent pottery was produced locally. Some of this shows definite influences from the Mogollon Red-on-Brown and from Mimbres Black-on-White. Most Chihuahua pottery techniques originated from the Mogollon-Mimbres traditions of rectilinear designs, decoration in red-on-brown, red wares, polishing, and texturing (like Alma Incised). A few of the better Chihuahua painted pottery types are Dublan, Babicora, Villa Ahumada, and Ramos polychromes and Madera Black-on-Red (Fig. 68).

Basketry and weaving.—Twilled yucca-leaf trays and baskets were common, and textiles of fiber and cotton were produced.

Tools, utensils, and weapons.—Troughed metates with one end open were the usual type. Arrow-shaft smoothers; three-quarter-grooved axes; scrapers; small, triangular projectile points with deep side and base notches; knives; pestles; and square and oval vessels occur—all made of stone.

Awls were the only bone tools.

Pipes.—The only type reported is tubular and made of stone.

Costume.—Sandals with square, round, and pointed toes were worn. These were woven from corn husks or yucca leaves. The texture is not so fine as in sandals of the earlier Anasazi.

Fig. 68.—Chihuahua pottery. Dublan Polychrome effigy jar; Madera Black-on-Red basket-handle jar; Ramos Polychrome jar. Mogollon-Mimbres culture.

Ornaments.—Abundant ornaments manufactured from shell, stone, clay, copper, turquoise, and jadeite included plain and inlaid pendants, copper bells, copper rings and cones, beads, bracelets, and well-made animal effigies polished and perforated for suspension.

Burials.—The dead were usually buried in a flexed position under the floors of the rooms (as in Mimbres). They were usually provided with pottery, ornaments, and various tools for use in the afterworld. Occasionally a burial is found in the village refuse, but this does not seem to mean any defilement or lack of esteem. Just as now, people at that time had various ideas about such things. Some people today prefer simple interments; others, cremation. There is no accounting for tastes in cultural matters.

Conjectures.—Because of the presence of Gila and Tonto polychrome pottery types, cliff-houses, "Great Houses," three-quarter-grooved axes, T-doorways, pottery effigies, and other traits in Chihuahua, it seems a logical assumption that some of the Salado people moved into Chihuahua when they parted company with the Hohokam (*ca.* 1350 or 1400).

Similarly, it seems probable that influences from the Mogollon-Mimbres region had also penetrated the Chihuahua area, because the Chihuahua people buried their dead under the floors of rooms and made beautiful and highly distinctive polished pottery with rectilinear decorations in red-on-brown in which one can observe the same evolution of designs which took place farther north in New Mexico. It is even possible that the Mimbres people themselves migrated to Chihuahua, for we know that they abandoned their own home area about 1200, the very time when Mimbres influences were really arriving in Chihuahua in some force.

Thus two streams of culture—Salado and Mogollon-Mimbres—met in Chihuahua, far from their native soil, and merged with a local and less advanced culture to form the Chihuahua civilizations. By the time the Spaniards arrived in the northern part of Mexico (in the 1500's) the "Great Houses" with adobe walls and the impressive cliff-dwellings were deserted.

Again we are confronted with the mystery of why these people renounced a way of life which, from our point of view, seems desirable. We do not know just why this happened, or what became of the Indians themselves. The most likely, and certainly the simplest, guess about what became of them is that the present-day Tarahumara Indians who live near by are the descendants of the ancient Chihuahuans. Certainly, present-day Tarahumara civilization has definite Puebloid rather than Mexican affinities.

SOURCES

BRADFIELD, 1931; COSGROVE, H. S. and C. B., 1932; DOUGLASS, 1942; HAURY, 1936a, 1936b, 1940, 1942, 1943; HAWLEY, 1936; McGREGOR, 1941; MARTIN, PAUL S., 1940, 1942; NESBITT, 1931, 1938; SAYLES, 1936a, 1936b.

CHAPTER 15

AREAS PERIPHERAL TO THE SOUTHWEST

GENERAL REMARKS

THE areas peripheral to the Southwest constitute a baffling problem for the culture historian. In the Anasazi culture of the Southwest, for example, we have a clear-cut, observable civilization, the development of which can be investigated, dissected, and synthesized with comparative ease. It is an area in which a strong culture flourished, furnishing the archeologist something that he can "get his teeth into."

But the areas peripheral to the Anasazi, Mogollon, and Hohokam cultures do not manifest such cultural distinctiveness. In them we can see influences from the Southwest, Mexico (?), the Columbia Plateau, and California. In fact, the peripheral cultures are the products of many borrowings from different places at different times. Take all these borrowed ingredients, mix well, and add some internal original development, and you have the cultures of the areas peripheral to the Southwest.

In this chapter we shall deal with these complex yet nebulous cultural manifestations by area and, wherever possible, by time period. There will be no orderly sequential development to present as there was, for example, for the Anasazi or Hohokam or Mogollon. Since in most cases the available information is scanty, the presentation will necessarily be brief.

SOUTHWESTERN TEXAS

Area.—The area lies west of the Pecos River and within the "Big Bend" region of the Rio Grande River. It includes Jeff Davis, Presidio, and Brewster counties. The country within this area contains three major subdivisions: (1) the high mountains and associated canyons; (2) the high interior basins, valleys, and plains; and (3) the Rio Grande Valley, which has a relatively low elevation. Annual rainfall varies from 18 inches in the mountains to 9 inches in the Rio Grande Valley. The vegetation in the mountains is pine, piñon, and oak and, in the lower valleys, mesquite and greasewood. The area in which we are most interested at the moment is the mountainous country where the walls of the canyons and gorges are honeycombed with rock shelters and caves.

There are three "civilizations" or developments to be mentioned. These are the Maravillas civilization or complex, the Big Bend Cave civilization, and the Bravo Valley civilization.

THE MARAVILLAS CULTURE
Ca. 3,000 years ago

The Maravillas civilization is probably the oldest in the West Texas area. It appeared there several thousand years ago during a period of drought. The movement of people into this area during a dry period may reflect widespread movements stimulated by climatic changes.

The camp refuse consists of hearthstones, charcoal, projectile points, knives, scrapers, choppers, metates, and manos. Nothing is known about the houses of this culture. We assume from the tools that the people were not agriculturists but were food-gatherers (i.e., collected and ate nuts, roots, and berries) and hunters.

The Maravillan types of tools are similar to types found in the Chiricahua period of the Cochise culture.

THE BIG BEND CAVE CULTURE
Ca. A.D. 300–900

People.—Indians, with long, high-vaulted heads and broad faces. No skull deformation.

Villages.—The camps were built in rock shelters, in the mouths of caves, or out in the open.

Livelihood.—Hunting, fishing, and food-gathering furnished subsistence. Toward the latter part of the period, corn, beans, and squash were grown.

The presence of the dog and of cotton has not been reported.

Pottery.—None.

Basketry.—Basketry was coiled, twined, or plaited. Most of the coiled basketry techniques are not similar to those used by the Basket Maker Indians; and one type (wrapped twined or horizontal and vertical single-rod foundation) is similar to a fragment found in Gypsum Cave, Nevada.

Tools, utensils, and weapons.—Both the atlatl and the bow and arrow were used as weapons for hunting and warfare (?). A flat, curved, fending or "rabbit" stick decorated with groups of parallel lines was also a common "weapon." This rabbit stick is similar to that of the Basket Makers. Its use is unknown. With agriculture came wooden digging-sticks, used for making the holes in the soil into which the seeds were dropped.

There were two types of metates: the oval bowl type and a flat, thin stone slab type. Manos were flat or wedge-shaped. Deep, circular bowl mortars formed in bedrock are numerous. No grooved axes have been reported, but small hand-axes were made by chipping the end of a flat pebble to a rounded cutting edge. Knives, scrapers, projectile points, hammerstones, drills, and pestles were also made of stone.

Painted waterworn pebbles are numerous. The meaning or use of these is unknown.

Bone tools consist of awls, spatulas, needles, gouges, scrapers, and flaking tools (for removing flakes from stone implements).

Pipes.—A tubular stone pipe has been excavated from one site.

Costume.—Rabbit-skin blankets similar to those found in Basket Maker sites were common. These fur robes were made by twisting narrow strips of fur around a hide or a fiber foundation. Fur and rawhide gee-strings and shirts of fiber cordage were worn.

Sandals were made from woven fiber or from dressed skins. One type of sandal woven from coarse yucca or sotol leaves is known as the "fishtail" type because both toe and heel are pointed.

Cradles.—A few cradles have been reported, but these are not the same as those found in Anasazi ruins. This type of cradle consists of a V-shaped frame, to which were lashed two crosspieces and on them were tied slats or twigs.

Weaving, bags, and textiles.—Netting was woven of yucca or sotol by means of loops or series of slipknot loops. Matting also was woven of the same fibers, the weaves being checkered and twilled. Some mats bear painted designs. Cordage was made of fiber in one, two, and four strands and of human hair in two strands. Bags were woven of cords made from plant fibers.

Ornaments.—Beads were made of bone and shell, and pendants, sometimes engraved, of shell.

Burials.—Inhumation and cremation were practiced. Bodies were flexed and were usually wrapped in matting and accompanied by manos, metates, projectile points, and ornaments. Burials were placed in refuse and sometimes were covered by stone slabs. Cremated bones were placed in woven fiber-cord bags and buried in the rock shelters.

After A.D. 900 some Southwestern (Anasazi?) traits seeped into the Big Bend Cave civilization. These items are small, fine arrowpoints; El Paso Polychrome and Chupadero Black-on-White pottery (both dated at about 1100–1400); crude masonry house structures; and unfired clay figurines.

The civilization of the Big Bend Cave Indians is sometimes called "Basket Maker." This is an unfortunate term to apply to the Big Bend culture, because its basketry, sandal types, and almost all other objects are entirely different from anything Basket Maker. There are four classes of objects that are roughly similar to Basket Maker materials: the atlatl, fending sticks, twined woven bags, and rabbit-fur robes. It is probable that all Indians of early times possessed articles more or less like those found in the Big Bend caves, for materials from the caves in the Ozark Mountains, in Tennessee, in northern Mexico, and in Oregon are roughly or actually similar. In other words, the civilizations of early times were basically alike, and the variations found from place to place merely represent special local developments. For the present, then, it is better to regard the Big Bend Cave articles as being a part of a larger prehistoric basic culture.

THE BRAVO VALLEY CULTURE
Ca. A.D. 900–1400

A third civilization, the Bravo Valley, appeared in the West Texas area about a thousand years ago, during a period of aridity. (And it was during a dry period that the Maravillas civilization appeared there, too.) One may wonder how we know that droughts existed so long ago. By studying the earth's layers as exposed in river valleys and ravines, geologists can detect a dry period by the heavy erosion that took place and by the thick layers of dust that were laid down in caves and on the earth's strata. Conversely, wet periods can be determined by the sedimentation that was laid down on the eroded formations and layers of dust. In Pueblo III times, it will be remembered, a prolonged drought disrupted the social organization of the Indians and led them to abandon their superbly built cliff-houses.

We all know that a long drought causes people to alter their way of life, to move, to take any drastic action to get away from a thirsty land. We can all remember the tragedy of the "Oakies" who fled from a "dust bowl." And so it was in ancient times. Droughts forced the Indians to seek out greener pastures. The West Texas area may have been chosen for the new home because it was less dry than the neighboring country. The civilization of the invading group evolved and expanded during subsequent humid periods.

Villages.—Some Bravo people lived in rock shelters and some in the open. Those who preferred rock shelters camped there without building a superstructure. Those who preferred the open built several kinds of houses: (1) small, shallow, circular pit-houses; (2) deep, rectangular pit-houses, with a low, mud curb around the edge of the pit (to keep water from running in?); and (3) houses with rectangular rooms, built in long rows, with walls of adobe mud and T-shaped doorways. The superstructure of the first two types of houses was made of poles, branches, and mud.

Livelihood.—Corn, beans, and squash were grown, and this diet was supplemented by hunting, fishing, and food-gathering. There is no evidence of cotton or of the dog.

Pottery.—Some Southwestern pottery types were traded to the Bravo Valley people for El Paso Polychrome, and Chihuahua pottery and pottery from the Kayenta region (in Arizona) have been found. These types can be dated as occurring between 1150 and 1400. In addition to the trade wares, some polished and semipolished brown and red wares were locally manufactured.

Tools, utensils, and weapons.—The stone tools were, on the whole, better made than those of the Big Bend Cave period. The most important stone tools were large basin-shaped oval metates; carefully shaped small manos or handstones that were used with the metate; rodlike pestles; paint mortars; polishing-stones; crudely chipped hand-axes; drills, knives, and well-made finely chipped projectile points.

Bone awls, needles, spatulas, and flaking tools (for removing chips from arrowheads) were numerous and well made.

No grooved ax has been reported.

Ornaments.—Articles of adornment consisted of tubular bone beads, shell beads, shell pendants, and shell disks.

Burials.—The bodies of the dead were generally flexed and buried below house floors. Sometimes offerings of weapons, tools, and pottery were placed in the graves.

Conjectures.—We have briefly surveyed a bit of the history of southwestern Texas and have discussed three civilizations: (1) the

Maravillas, which is probably several thousand years old; (2) the Big Bend Cave; and (3) the Bravo Valley.

The Maravillas Indians and the Big Bend Cave Indians probably moved into the southwestern Texas area during drought, which was responsible for widespread movements of people. Southwest Texas may have been less dry than other neighboring areas.

From the evidence at hand, it would seem that the Bravo Valley civilization grew out of the Big Bend Cave civilization and that it, in turn, was the descendant of the Maravillas civilization.

NORTHERN UTAH

Area.—Inhabitable areas were limited, because of marked aridity, restricted amounts of wild plant and animal foods, and limited tillable land. The inhabited portions range from three to five thousand feet above sea-level. The plateaus are dissected with canyons and valleys, some of which are so alkaline that vegetation is virtually lacking. The mountains are high, rugged, and cold in winter. This particularly unfavorable topography made living difficult and restricted communication with neighboring areas.

In and around Salt Lake, Utah, evidence of four civilizations has been found. These are, in chronological order: (1) the Black Rock Cave; (2) the Puebloid; (3) the Promontory; and (4) Shoshoni and Ute. The Black Rock Cave is the earliest and the Shoshoni-Ute Indian civilization is the latest, extending into the twentieth century. The Shoshoni-Ute complex will not be treated here.

THE BLACK ROCK CAVE CULTURE
Tentatively dated *ca.* 2,000–3,000 years ago(?)

Evidence of the Black Rock Cave civilization, as the name implies, has thus far been found in caves. The civilization lacked the richness of the Puebloid and Promontory cultures. Only stone and bone artifacts have been recovered. No basketry, woven materials, or garments have been found; and, since such materials usually are well preserved in dry caves, we can assume that vegetable fibers, hide, and fur were not extensively used.

The only evidence of this civilization consists of small projectile points, distinctive corner-notched projectile points of gray or reddish quartzite; leaflike flint knives; flint scrapers; shale sinkers; flat, untroughed milling-stones; grinding-stones; bone awls; and bone needles. The milling-stones were probably used to grind up nuts and seeds.

These materials have been found in stratified deposits underlying Puebloid and Promontory articles. The dating of the Black Rock Cave finds is tentative and was done by studying the geology of the Great Salt Lake region in relation to other postglacial lakes in the Great Basin area.

THE PUEBLOID CULTURE
Ca. A.D. 500–1300

The term "Puebloid" is used because the stimulus for many phases of the Puebloid civilization came from the Anasazi (Basket Maker–Pueblo) area; hence the name. The Anasazi traits that penetrated into northern Utah probably originated in northeastern Arizona. Two phases of Puebloid development are evident: Phase I, which is a blend of Modified Basket Maker and Pueblo I traits; and Phase II, which is an attenuated manifestation of Pueblo II elements.

Phase I.—The principal means of subsistence were corn, beans, squash, seeds, nuts, and game. The villages consisted of square pit-houses, similar to those described under Pueblo I, and slab-lined square or circular pit-houses. These pit-houses were grouped in communities, from ten to twenty to a village. No specialized ceremonial rooms or kivas have been noted with these villages.

Since hunting, as indicated above, was important, many arrowheads and grooved arrowshaft smoothers were found. The bow and arrow, nooses, and nets were used for hunting deer, rabbits, muskrats, squirrels, sage hens, and mallard ducks. The throwing-stick and the curved rabbit club, both characteristic of the Basket Maker culture, have not been reported.

Corn and seeds were ground to flour on a large, heavy metate, somewhat similar to the Basket Maker type; that is, the metate was troughed, with the trough open at one end only. At the closed end there was a flat shelf or ledge in which there was a slight depression. In eastern Utah a thick, ungrooved stone was used for a metate.

Like the Basket Makers, the Utah Indians of this period gathered wild seeds, berries, and nuts for food. Coiled basketry bowls and sifters and flat, circular baskets which may have been used for parching and winnowing seeds and nuts are found in Utah sites. Conical seed baskets and pitch-coated basketry jars (for carrying water over the deserts) have also been reported.

The pottery is for the most part Basket Maker–like in being plain gray (probably like Kana-a Gray). Some black-on-gray painted pottery, corrugated, and special local forms and wares were also manufactured. Unbaked clay figurines, tubular stone pipes, fur and feather cloth, and twined-rod cradles also were derived from the Arizona area.

Other traits common to the Utah and Basket Maker cultures are twined bags, mats and blankets of coarse bark, fiber shirts, tubular bone beads, stone and bone pendants, and hafted knives made of flint.

Some characteristic Basket Maker traits did not penetrate to the Utah area: certain pottery forms and decorations, twined string bags, and woven fiber sandals. The Utah Indians preferred hide to vegetable fibers (even hide moccasins) for making various articles, and, as a result, bone awls are numerous.

No evidence of the dog has been found.

Phase II.—In this period the villages became larger as a result of greater dependency on agriculture and less on hunting, fishing, and seed-gathering. There were several types of houses: (1) clusters of rectangular surface houses with masonry walls; (2) shallow pithouses with slab and rubble walls or with walls of poles, brush, and mud; and (3) clusters of rectangular surface houses with walls made of adobe mud. In the villages one finds also square, semisubterranean kivas, possessing many of the details of the kivas of the Mesa Verde area. Added to these items was Pueblo-like pottery—i.e., corrugated, black-on-white, black-on-red, and black-on-orange—which resembles Kayenta and Mesa Verde pottery of Pueblo II and Pueblo III periods. Plain gray pottery (like Kana-a Gray of Modified Basket Maker period) also occurs. In other words, one finds in Phase II of the Puebloid manifestation in Utah a mixture of both early and late Anasazi (Pueblo) traits. The early traits (especially pithouses and plain gray pottery) seem to have lingered on to and through the latest occupation. The chronologically distinct periods of the Kayenta (Arizona) and Mesa Verde (Colorado) areas blended and formed a complex that was typical of central and northern Utah. Thus the Puebloid culture of Utah is a jumble of traits. In the instances just cited, one can recognize Modified Basket Maker traits at villages that also yield Pueblo I, II, and III traits!

Minor artifacts of Phase II include stone projectile points; flint drills, knives, and scrapers; bone awls; tubular pipes; crude clay figurines; and shell beads.

Curiously enough, the Indians who possessed the Utah Puebloid culture and who borrowed some traits from Arizona and southwestern Colorado, did not accept other Anasazi (Pueblo) characteristics, such as cotton, the loom, twilled baskets, fiber sandals, the dog, the domesticated turkey, grooved stone axes and mauls, and thin slab metates. None of these traits occurs in northern or central Utah.

However, the Indians of the Utah Puebloid culture did develop some distinctive traits: a preference for hide garments and moccasins, rectangular dice or gaming pieces of bone, anthropomorphic pictographs (which were painted or pecked on rock walls), the "Utah metate" (shovel-shaped or grooved, one end of the groove closed, and at the closed end a shelf in which was a small basin), and false corrugated pottery.

THE PROMONTORY CULTURE
Ca. A.D. 1200–1300 or 1400(?)

The Promontory Indians were hunters and food-gatherers who elected to live in caves. Their culture lacks nearly all the distinguishing Puebloid traits. It seems to have appeared abruptly in the area and probably was brought in by Indians coming from the north. Although several cave shelters have been dug, no trace of agriculture has yet turned up.

A type of moccasin like that found only in northeastern and northwestern Canada, fur mittens, a pottery type utterly unlike Southwestern pottery but similar to some northern Plains types, gaming bones like those found in the Plains, beaver-teeth dice like those of the Northwest Coast, and the sinew-backed bow (which is a northern type) are other distinctive Promontory characteristics.

Other traits, probably borrowed from the local and contemporary Puebloid people, include twined mats and bags, cane arrows, grooved arrow-shaft smoothers, triangular arrowheads with side notches, hafted knives of flint, stone scrapers, digging-sticks, bone awls, fire drills, skin and fur bags, fur and birdskin twined cloth, coiled, basketry, and tubular stone pipes.

There is no evidence of the dog, of houses, of agriculture, or of metates.

A unique characteristic of Promontory culture is the small stone or bone slab delicately etched or painted.

AREAS PERIPHERAL TO THE SOUTHWEST

The bearers of the Promontory culture arrived while the Puebloid Indians were still occupying central and northern Utah and remained for some time after the latter had moved elsewhere.

From the meager data at hand, it has been suggested that the Promontory Indians were Athabascans—that is, ancestors of the Navaho Indians. Certainly they were not the ancestors of the modern Shoshoni.

SOUTHEASTERN NEVADA

Area.—Southeastern Nevada is an arid plateau with sparse vegetation consisting of sagebrush, cresote brush, and cactus plants. The desert is broken here and there by medium to high mountain ranges. The elevation of the plateau ranges from 1,500 to 2,500 feet above sea-level. The annual rainfall is scanty—from 6 to 9 inches.

The earliest remains of man in this area were found at Gypsum Cave, Nevada. These early finds are probably several thousands of years old, although dating them is difficult. The oldest tools were undoubtedly pre–Basket Maker and were found associated with several extinct species of animals, such as the ground sloth, the American camel, the horse, and the dire wolf.

The next Indian civilization to appear in the area is one with both Modified Basket Maker and Pueblo I characteristics. In other words, the situation in Nevada is similar to the one that was described for the Puebloid culture of Utah. The Anasazi civilization was a virile one, and its influences emanated in all directions. Naturally, the farther one gets from the heart of the Anasazi stronghold, the weaker are the influences.

The early Anasazi characteristics that reached Nevada were agriculture, baskets, pit-houses, and pottery.

Later Anasazi impulses and traits (Pueblo III?) which spread to Nevada were large villages of many rooms, which were arranged about a courtyard so as to form a defensive inclosure; masonry; black-on-white, black-on-red, and corrugated pottery resembling wares from the Kayenta region; flat metates; chipped-stone arrowheads, knives, and scrapers; bone awls; and tubular pipes of stone.

The dates for these Puebloid manifestations in Nevada can be determined only by the pottery. Since some of it resembles Modified Basket Maker wares, and some, Pueblo III wares, we can infer that Pueblo influences reached Nevada about the year 800 and persisted until about 1200 or 1300.

SOUTHEASTERN OREGON

Area.—The area under consideration is at present a desert about 5,000 feet above sea-level, with the usual accompanying extremes of temperature. Sage and rabbit brush are the dominant plants, and the higher plateaus and mountains are covered with juniper or pine trees. This desert country was formerly (about ten thousand years ago) a lake basin. Along the tops of the terraces the waves of the lake cut caves, which became inhabitable as the lakes dried up.

The oldest culture of this region was found in a cave. The only articles thus far reported consist of matting, knives, scrapers, drills— all of stone—and probably the throwing-stick. The dog was not known. This culture is probably not more than two thousand years old.

A later culture is also found in the Oregon caves. It was based on hunting and food-gathering (nuts, seeds, roots). Agriculture was not practiced. The chief elements of this culture were the atlatl, the bow and arrow, both coiled and twined basketry, fiber sandals, metates, and L-shaped bone awls. Other traits such as the dog, flint knives, drills, scrapers, matting, twined bags, fire drills, bone awls, and projectile points were shared by neighboring peoples and are, therefore, not useful as diagnostic criteria. We know nothing more about the civilization of these cave-dwellers.

Probably the coiled basketry, metates, fiber sandals, and the peculiar L-shaped awls are of Anasazi origin.

The dating of these late materials in Oregon is still uncertain. At present it is safest to assume that the late cave materials from Oregon date from about A.D. 1000 or later.

SOURCES

COFFIN, 1932; CRESSMAN, 1942, 1943; GARDNER and MARTIN, G.C., 1933; GILLIN, 1938, 1941; HAYDEN, 1930; KELLEY, CAMPBELL, and LEHMER, 1940; MARTIN, G. C., 1933; MORSS, 1931; SAYLES, 1935; SETZLER, 1935; SMITH, E. R., 1941; STEWARD, 1933, 1936, 1937, 1940.

PART V
EASTERN NORTH AMERICA

CHAPTER 16

SUMMARY OF THE ARCHEOLOGICAL AREAS OF EASTERN NORTH AMERICA

EASTERN North America is a vast region that stretches from the Atlantic Ocean to the Rocky Mountains and from the Arctic to the Gulf of Mexico. Quite arbitrarily we have divided this region into eleven areas. The archeology of each of the eleven areas will be described in the following chapters, but in this chapter we shall attempt to describe briefly the archeology of the region as a whole. Naturally, such a description will be too general and simplified to allow for the areal variations of cultures, periods, and environment.

PEOPLE

The people in our story were American Indians of several types. Knowledge of these types is based upon studies of skeletal remains, particularly the skull. The major types of Indians with whom we are concerned are called Sylvids, Centralids, Pacifids, and Prairids.

The Sylvids were longheaded, high-vaulted, and relatively narrow-faced. There were, of course, varieties of Sylvids which could be further differentiated within the basic type, but they need not concern us here.

The Centralids were roundheaded (head broad in proportion to length), medium high-vaulted, and relatively broad-faced. There were also different varieties of Centralids, but a knowledge of these is not necessary for our purposes.

The Pacifids were roundheaded, low-vaulted Indians with large, flat faces.

The Prairids were a hybrid type resulting from the intermixture of either Centralid and Pacifid or of Sylvid and Pacifid. The Prairids produced by the Pacifid-Centralid admixture were generally round-headed and high-vaulted with broad, flat faces; whereas the Prairids resulting from the Pacifid-Sylvid intermixture were characterized by relatively long but also broad heads, low vaults, and high, broad, flat faces.

The Sylvids and Centralids probably were the oldest Indians in North America, the Pacifids were the most recent immigrants from Asia, and the hybrid Prairids were the latest type to appear. Since Sylvids and Centralids play the most important roles in our story, they will appear many times in the following chapters.

LANGUAGE

At the time of their discovery by White men, the different groups of Indians spoke languages belonging to many different linguistic families. In some instances groups of Indians with the same language had different cultures, or groups of Indians with the same culture spoke different languages.

We, of course, cannot tell what languages were spoken by groups of prehistoric Indians, but we suspect that the situation was essentially similar to that of historic times. We therefore caution the reader to remember that almost any one of the cultures we describe could have belonged to a number of different groups of Indians who spoke different languages.

CHRONOLOGICAL STAGES

The prehistory of eastern North America may be viewed in terms of four chronological stages. The periods and cultures of each stage vary somewhat from one area to another within the region, but the stages remain relatively constant.

THE FIRST STAGE

The first stage probably lasted from early postglacial times to about A.D. 500–700. What little evidence there is suggests that the Indians who lived in the earliest part of this stage had a Folsom-Yuma-Cochise–like culture.

We can more easily characterize the Indians who lived in the latter part of this stage. They were variants of the Sylvid physical type and obtained their food by hunting and fishing and by gathering nuts, seeds, roots, berries, and shellfish. They had no agriculture, pottery, or mounds. For the most part, they lived a seminomadic existence, wandering about in search of food and living in temporary dwellings or rock shelters; but in certain favorable localities where there was an abundance of shellfish or other collectible foods some had permanent settlements.

In contrast to those of later stages, these early cultures were relatively homogeneous. This homogeneity is probably a reflection of the simplicity and of the stable and integrated nature of these early cultures which were adapted to their environment and to a hunting economy and which had probably had little opportunity or reason to change radically for hundreds of years.

THE SECOND STAGE

This stage probably lasted from about A.D. 500 to A.D. 900. During this time some Indian groups developed or adopted new customs and ways of living such as pipe-smoking, the manufacture and use of pottery, the building of burial mounds, and agriculture. It is improbable that all these new things appeared at exactly the same time or in the same places. This stage shows a marked tendency toward increasing differentiation of cultures despite a persistence of many older traits.

The beginnings of pottery.—The earliest pottery in the southern part of eastern North America consisted of plain and decorated bowls made of clay tempered with fiber. In certain stratified sites in Florida, Georgia, and Alabama this pottery suddenly appeared in a cultural setting which in other respects was the same as that of the first stage. Where this first pottery came from we do not know. It might have been developed independently in the South, or it might have been introduced from Central or South America.

The earliest pottery in the northern part of eastern North America consisted of granular tempered jars with rounded, conoidal, or flattened bottoms; smoothed, stamped, or cord-malleated surfaces; and (when present) simple geometric decorations produced by stamping techniques.

This northern pottery probably was introduced from northeastern Asia, where similar pottery was in use. We do not know how the introduction was accomplished. But, whatever the origin, this pottery was at first distinct from that of the South, though both appeared at about the same time. Within a very short period the northern and southern pottery traditions became intermixed, and many different styles were developed, especially in the southern areas.

Certain groups had pottery before they had agriculture, and others seem to have had agriculture before they had pottery.

Beginnings of agriculture.—When first encountered by White men, the Indian farmers of eastern North America were raising such crops as corn, beans, squash, gourds, pumpkins, and melons. We are certain, however, that these food plants were not domesticated in eastern North America. All these crops are known to have been grown by Central and South American Indians at a much earlier time, and it is generally believed that the first cultivation of these plants in the New World took place in Central and South America rather than in North America. Consequently, it is reasonable to assume that the Indians of eastern North America obtained their agricultural information either directly or indirectly from Mexican or South American Indians.

In addition to this tropical agricultural complex of corn, beans, and squash, there was a local complex of domesticated plants such as sunflowers, giant ragweed, pigweed, marsh elder, canary grass, and gourds. This local complex seems to have been coeval with the tropical complex, although possibly it was slightly earlier.

At present it is not known whether the tropical agricultural complex of corn, squash, and beans reached eastern North America as a unit, but there is some reason to suspect that each of these items had its own history. Different kinds of corn, for example, probably reached the eastern part of the United States at various times and from various places. Some of the earliest corn may have come into the area from Mexico by way of the Southwest. Some of the latest corn in the region may have come from Guatemala via the east coast of Mexico.

Whatever the history of agriculture in eastern North America, the archeological evidence indicates that it is not very ancient and that it makes its first appearance in the second stage (500–900). The early Indians of the South, who would have been most receptive to agriculture, were the shell-mound-dwelling peoples who already had established a pattern for sedentary living necessary for farmers.

Advantages of agriculture.—Agriculture offered many opportunities which were generally lacking to hunters, fishers, and food-gatherers. It permitted higher concentrations of people in a restricted area, provided a stable food supply which could be stored against time of want, and permitted greater leisure, which in turn made possible the greater specialization of skills and talents, as well as pursuits not directly concerned with the getting of food.

Changes brought about by agriculture.—Naturally, all these changes required additional ones in the social lives of the new farmers. The social organization of the group had to be adapted to sedentary village life, special occupations, and the like. The political organization had to be modified in harmony with the new economy. The old gods of hunting and fishing had to be replaced by new gods who specialized in agriculture, etc.

Burial mounds.—Burial mounds of earth appeared in the Mississippi Valley early in the second stage. Such mounds were evidence of changes in religion and ideas regarding the dead. Instead of merely burying the deceased in pits, as was the custom formerly, some of the Indians now erected mounds of earth over the more important of their dead. All groups, however, did not build burial mounds. Some continued their ancient forms of burial.

We do not know whether the custom of mound-building was earlier in the South or in the North, nor do we know the source of the custom. It could have been brought from Asia; it may have diffused from the South; or it might have developed independently.

First pipe-smokers.—Another innovation of the second stage was the custom of smoking. The earliest pipes were tubular in form and made either of clay or of stone, and there may possibly have been an early prototype made of reed. Many types of cane or reed have a segmented structure, with interior constrictions at the junction of each segment. Reed pipes found in some of the Big Bend Basket Maker sites of southwestern Texas showed that the interior constriction of the reed was used to provide a separation between the mouthpiece and the tobacco chamber, a feature found also in tubular pipes of clay and stone. All later pipe forms (platform, elbow, etc.) can be typologically derived from the tubular type. With the invention of later forms, however, the tubular pipe did not always disappear from use. Some Indians had tubular pipes in historic times.

An early American revolution.—Although we possess no definite information, it seems reasonable to assume that the addition of pottery, agriculture, burial mounds, and pipe-smoking made considerable impact upon the cultures of the Indians of the first stage. The old ways of life were not immediately abandoned but persisted side by side with the new customs. At first, the culture change was slow. Probably the Indian elders longed for "the good old days," and the young people were impatient because their elders were so "old-fashioned." In certain backward areas the new and radical ideas were not accepted at all, probably either because the environment made acceptance difficult or because the Indians were too reactionary. In general, these must have been uneasy times for everybody. Probably there was a lack of cultural integration. There were movements of people into areas more suited to agriculture, and conflicts between the argicultural way of life and the old hunting economy resulted.

THE THIRD STAGE

The third stage probably lasted from about A.D. 900 to A.D. 1300. In this stage some groups of Indians had achieved a spectacular and well-integrated civilization based upon an agricultural economy, although hunting, fishing, and gathering wild foods were still valuable adjuncts, perhaps even more important than farming. The largest burial mounds and earthworks were constructed, and work in copper and in polished stone reached its apogee. Religion and art flourished as never before, and trade and commerce were established among distant peoples.

The archeological evidence leads us to suspect that important social changes were in the making or had already taken place. Some groups were politically organized in such a way that they were capable of undertaking large public projects, such as building mounds and earthen walls, which must have required co-operative labor on a large scale.

The wealth and diversity of some of the cultures of this stage suggest social elaborations such as class systems, religious societies, and specialization of labor. Burial customs indicate a preoccupation with death.

We would guess that the third stage was a period of expansion and development. Broadly speaking, a part of the civilization of this period was comparable to that of the Mayas of Central America. It had a dignity and formality which was lacking in earlier times or in later stages.

Some of the Indians of this period probably knew more about the geography of their world than any of their predecessors had known. Their trade routes led all over eastern North America, and it is not impossible that some kind of contact was established with South America, Mexico, and Central America.

Many groups, however, perhaps because of conservatism, lack of stimulation, or unsuitable environment, continued to live largely as they had in previous times. There was, therefore, greater differentiation among cultures, as well as an increasing elaboration of function within cultures.

THE FOURTH STAGE

This stage is estimated to have lasted from about A.D. 1300 to A.D. 1700, the time of settlement by White men. More advanced groups of this stage made their living by intensive agriculture, supplemented by hunting, fishing, and the gathering of wild foods. Hoes, made of stone, bone, or shell and hafted to short wooden handles, were used extensively in cultivation. Principal crops were corn, squashes, and beans.

Not all groups were farmers, however. Some were hunters, fishers, and food-gatherers who lived in much the same manner as their ancestors in the first stage. Others practiced a little agriculture, but these too, were dependent upon hunting, fishing, and food-gathering.

It was during these times that some of the southern Indians made polychrome pottery. Although certain pottery prior to this time had been painted with one color, some of the new was painted with three. There were, of course, many other kinds of pottery made during this stage. Some of it was rather crude and similar to the earliest known, but some of it was exceptionally fine. Taken as a whole, the pottery of this stage was the best produced in eastern North America.

One of the most spectacular developments of the fourth stage was the appearance of flat-topped mounds of earth in the Mississippi Valley and its tributaries and in the South in general. These mounds, usually square or rectangular truncated pyramids but sometimes truncated cones, were used as substructures for temples or chief's houses. Access to the mound summits was by means of ramps or stairways. Toward the latter part of this period some Indians built tremendous mounds sixty to one hundred feet high, generally within a plaza or grouped at the ends of a plaza or central square.

Another innovation of this stage was the palisaded village comparable to a fortified village-state. The larger villages were probably ceremonial centers for smaller communities surrounding them.

In the northern areas the Indians did not build temple mounds, but in some places they continued to build burial mounds. Most of the Plains area and the Northeast did not have painted pottery generally, nor did they possess certain of the other characteristics of the high-culture southerners. Taken as a whole, the fourth stage was a time of intensive hoe agriculture, sedentary village life, fortified towns, and the use of the bow and arrow. We do not know when the bow and arrow first appeared in eastern North America, but it definitely was present in this fourth stage.

In the latter part of the period there occurred the religious phenomenon called the Southern Death Cult, which, in a very diluted form, is found even in some of the northern areas.

DATING METHOD

Although the relative succession of cultures and periods in eastern North America is fairly clear, the dates assigned to these cultures and periods are merely surmises. These guesses, however, are conditioned by some knowledge of the rates of culture change, known duration in comparable cultures and periods elsewhere, some vague cross-dating with cultures of known date, and other tenuous criteria. We believe that our dates have a large degree of probability, and we should be surprised if, when tree-ring dating (dendrochronology) is generally applied to the region and more objective dating is obtained, there will be any great discrepancy.

The chapters which follow give more details of the periods and cultures of these various stages in the archeological areas of eastern North America.

SOURCES

FORD and WILLEY, 1941; GRIFFIN, 1946; KROEBER, 1939; McKERN, 1937; NEUMANN, 1943.

CHAPTER 17

THE NORTHEASTERN AREA

INTRODUCTION

THE Northeastern area included the state of New York and all of the New England states. Most of this area is part of the Appalachian Highlands, but the area bordering the lower Great Lakes is part of the central lowlands, and there is a narrow strip of coastal plain along the Atlantic Ocean. The native vegetation consisted of southern hardwoods (chestnut, chestnut-oak, yellow poplar, and oak-pine), northeastern hardwoods (birch, beech, maple, and hemlock), and northern conifers (spruce and fir).

CHART V

Probable Date	Period	Culture
A.D. 1300–1600	Late Prehistoric	Owasco, Iroquois
A.D. 900–1300	Intermediate	Early Coastal, Orient, Middlesex, New York Hopewell, Point Peninsula
? B.C.–A.D. 900	Archaic	Lamoka, Frontenac, Laurentian I and II

The annual precipitation ranged from 30 to 60 inches, and the frostless season lasted from 90 to 180 days. Winters were severe. The soils, rainfall, and growing season combined to make conditions favorable for the introduction of agriculture, and the fauna and flora of the area supplied food to wandering hunters and food-collectors.

The periods and cultures of the Northeastern area with which we deal are outlined in Chart V.

The Indians of the early Archaic period were hunters and food-collectors who made their tools, weapons, and utensils of bone, stone, and wood and who probably used the spear and spear-thrower. The late Archaic period saw the use of copper tools, the introduction of an Eskimo-like complex of ground-slate tools and weapons, and the beginning of pottery.

The cultures of the Intermediate period saw the disappearance of copper tools and the appearance of copper ornaments and clay or stone pipes; the florescence of problematical forms, such as birdstones, plummets, boatstones, and gorgets; a moderate development of pottery; and the beginning of agriculture.

In the Late Prehistoric period problematical forms such as birdstones, bannerstones, and boatstones disappeared. The triangular projectile point of chipped stone supplanted the many styles of points that had characterized the earlier periods. Copper articles disappeared, and implements and weapons of bone became more numerous. In this period agriculture became the main source of food supply.

The Historic period, essentially a continuum of the Late Prehistoric, was a time of intensive agriculture, extensive commercial and political relations, and, finally, disintegration caused by conquests of the White man. This was the age of the great Iroquois confederacy.

THE LAMOKA CULTURE
(Archaic Period)
Probably before A.D. 500

Area.—New York State.

People.—The Lamoka Indians were tall, slender Sylvids, with long heads, high, narrow faces, and narrow noses.

Villages.—Each village probably consisted of a group of rectangular bark houses. Hearth and refuse pits were scattered throughout the houses.

Livelihood.—Subsistence was provided by hunting, fishing, and gathering such wild foods as berries, nuts, roots, and clams. Animal bones were cracked to obtain the marrow.

Pottery.—None.

Tools, utensils, and weapons.—The spear-thrower and spear was the chief hunting weapon. The spear was made of wood, to which was hafted a rather crude notched point of chipped stone. Some points were long and narrow; others were short and broad. Other utensils made of chipped flint were drills and large triangular and ovate knives, the former notched and the latter plain.

Mortars, several styles of grinding-stones, long cylindrical pestles, and mullers were probably used for grinding acorns. Crudely chipped choppers (celtlike tools) may have been used for digging roots.

Fish were caught with bone hooks or bone gorges or in nets weighted down with notched stone netsinkers.

The beveled stone adz, a characteristic tool of the Lamoka Indians, probably was used in wood-working. Other stone tools were plano-convex adzes, whetstones, hammerstones, and crude celts.

Tools made of bone were various types of awls, scrapers, and flakers. Some awls were decorated with simple designs engraved or painted upon them.

Pipes.—None.

Ornaments.—Antler sections and antler-tine pendants striped with red paint were characteristic ornaments of the culture. Some bone awls and bone objects of unknown use were similarly decorated with red stripes or **were** engraved. Necklaces were composed of shell beads and animal canine teeth.

Musical instruments.—Bone flutes and probably drums.

Burials.—The deceased were interred in pits in the villages and were not accompanied by burial offerings. The bodies were flexed.

Conjecture.—The later stages of the Lamoka culture were coeval with the Frontenac and Laurentian I cultures, and there were cultural connections among the three.

SOURCES

RITCHIE, 1944.

THE FRONTENAC CULTURE
(ARCHAIC PERIOD)
Ca. A.D. 300–500

Area.—Central New York State.

People.—Some were longheaded, some had skulls of medium length, and others were broadheaded.

Villages.—A village probably consisted of huts made of saplings and covered with skin, bark, or mats. Such a village is characterized by refuse, hearths, and refuse pits. Villages may have been occupied seasonally.

Livelihood.—Food was obtained by hunting, fishing, and collecting. The dog was the only domesticated animal.

Pottery.—None.

Tools, utensils, and weapons.—Probably the spear and spear-thrower was used in hunting. Stemmed or notched points of chipped stone were attached to spears or other projectiles. Crescentic bannerstones were probably used as weights for the spear-thrower. In addition to the stone projectile points, there were conical points of antler and flat, leaf-shaped points of bone.

Projectile shaft straighteners (wrenchlike objects with one or two perforations) were made of deer antler. There were several styles of harpoon heads made of bone or antler, and these presumably were fastened to wooden shafts.

Fish were caught with hooks of bone or with gorges (small bone splinters pointed at each end and fastened to a line). Fish were also caught in nets weighted with notched, flat pebbles.

Daggers were made of mammal long bones; the handle of one dagger was decorated with stripes of red paint.

Knives were manufactured of bone, chipped stone, or ground stone. The bone knives had rounded, sharpened ends. Some flint knives were made of flakes, others were ovate or trianguloid, and still others were ovate, with side or corner notches.

Blades of ground slate were either broad with straight stems or narrow with serrated stem. There were many different styles of chipped-stone scrapers and drills.

Ungrooved axes, plano-convex adzes, beveled adzes, and plummets were made of polished stone.

Stone mortars and pestles probably were used for grinding nuts and other collected foods. Stone choppers of many different shapes may have been used as digging tools. Hammerstones, abrading stones probably used for sharpening bone implements, and pyrites for making fire complete our inventory of stone tools.

Conch-shell bowls were used occasionally. Awls, needles, flakers, punches, chisels, gouges, spoons, and cups were made of bone or antler. Chisel-like tools or gravers were manufactured from the incisor teeth of porcupines and beavers.

The Frontenac Indians made comparatively little use of copper, although some copper awls have been found.

Pipes.—None.

Musical instruments.—Turtle-shell rattles, flutes, and whistles of bone, and probably drums.

Ornaments.—Necklaces were made of Marginella shells, animal teeth, and possibly bone tubes. Pendants were made of antler or conch shell, and gorgets were made of conch shell. Some utilitarian objects were decorated with stripes of red paint or with engraved, triangular designs. Worked jaws and teeth of wolves may also have been ornaments. Combs were made of antler.

Burials.—The deceased were buried in pits dug into the village refuse midden. The bodies were flexed, semisitting, or extended.

Cremations and bundle burials were rare. Grave-offerings were not uncommon. In a few instances the dead were covered with powdered red ocher or accompanied by an extra skull. Some burials were partly outlined or covered with stones.

Dogs seem to have been revered, for in a number of instances they were found interred with human bodies or in separate graves.

Conjectures.—The Frontenac Indians seem to bridge the cultural gap between Lamoka and the Laurentian. But although the Frontenac Indians partake of each of these cultures, Lamoka and Laurentian, they also have a separate and distinct cultural core.

In the following description of the Laurentian culture we have separated it into an early and a late stage: Laurentian I and Laurentian II.

SOURCES

RITCHIE, 1944.

THE LAURENTIAN I CULTURE
(ARCHAIC PERIOD)
Ca. A.D. 300–500

Area.—Our characterization of the Laurentian I Indians is based upon this culture as it was found in the lowest levels of two sites in New York. Other sites have been discovered in lower Ontario, Quebec, and in upper New England.

Villages.—The villages were located along rivers. The houses were probably skin- or bark-covered shelters. The villages may have been occupied only in summer, when bands of Indians who had spent the winter ranging over scattered hunting territories would return to visit with friends and relatives and perhaps to bury their dead.

Livelihood.—These Indians made their living by hunting, fishing, and food-gathering. They did no farming, and the dog was their only domesticated animal. A knowledge of modern Indians with a similar economy and culture suggests that groups of these ancient Indians may have roamed distant hunting territories during the winter months when they were dependent upon animal life for food. With the return of summer they congregated in villages for a more communal life sustained by food-gathering, fishing, and hunting.

Pottery.—None.

Tools, utensils, and weapons.—We suspect that the hunting weapon was the spear and atlatl. The wooden atlatl was provided with a handle, at the other end of which was a carved projection for engaging the butt of the spear. Stone weights (Fig. 69, *g*) were attached to the shaft. These weights were prism-shaped and winged bannerstones.

The wooden spears thrown with the atlatls were tipped with large, or stemmed or side-notched, points made of chipped flint. There were a few small, chipped flint triangular points and some small notched and stemmed points that may indicate the use of the bow and arrow.

Fish were caught with a line and a baited bone or copper gorge— a short pin pointed at each end and tied to a line at the middle. Such a gorge, when swallowed by a fish, would pierce its sides, holding the fish securely, Fish were also taken in nets weighted with notched pebbles or with plummets of stone (Fig. 69, *d* and *e*).

Shallow mortars, grinding-stones, mullers, and cylindrical pestles were probably used for grinding acorns, nuts, roots, and wild seeds. It is likely that the pestles were used with wooden mortars.

Rough stone choppers must have served a variety of purposes.

Wood-working tools were copper or polished stone gouges (Fig. 69, *a*); rectangular, plano-convex adzes (Fig. 69, *b*); copper axes and awls; chipped-flint drills; end- and side-scrapers; and ovate or triangular knives. Of course, these tools could have been used with materials other than wood.

There were various styles of bone awls, bone needles, antler flakers, bone spatulate implements of unknown use, and chisels made of beaver teeth. Whetstones were probably used for pointing awls and needles and for shaping bone tools.

Pipes.—None.

Ornaments.—These early Laurentian Indians probably were too busy getting food to spend much time in aesthetic pursuits. Red-ocher paint may have been used.

Burials.—Some of the deceased were buried in pits in the village, but so few of them have been found that it seems likely that most were buried elsewhere. Some of the bodies were cremated or arranged in disarticulated bundles; others were flexed or extended. Most burials were without grave-offerings, but a few were accompanied by small amounts of burial goods and powdered red ocher.

Conjectures.—The Laurentian I culture seems to have been truly Archaic, whereas its continuum, the Laurentian II culture, was probably transitional between the Archaic and the Intermediate periods.

SOURCES

RITCHIE, 1944.

Fig. 69.—Laurentian types of tools and weapons of stone: *a*, gouges; *b*, adzes; *c*, crescent-shaped knife; *d, e*, plummet-shaped stones, perhaps fishline sinkers; *f, h*, slate knives or spear points; *g*, bannerstone weight for spear-thrower.

THE LAURENTIAN II CULTURE
(Archaic Period)
Ca. A.D. 500–900

Area.—Manifestations of the Laurentian II culture are spread over Quebec and Ontario, upper New England, and New York State. In some instances the same villages were occupied by both the Laurentian I and the Laurentian II Indians. Remains of the former are found in the lowest levels of these sites.

Villages.—Same as Laurentian I. Coastal shell middens and rock shelters have also been found in some places.

Livelihood.—Same as Laurentian I.

Pottery.—Crude, unpainted pottery kettles or jars have been found, and these probably were used in cooking. Such vessels were straight-sided, with direct, straight rims and conoidal bottoms. Particles of grit were used for tempering the clay, which had a brown, buff, or gray color when fired. Vessel surfaces were crudely smoothed or covered with impressions of fabric or cord-wrapped paddles.

Pottery decorations consisted of simple, geometric patterns produced by punctating, impressing with a cord-wrapped stick, crude incising, and dentate stamping. The vessel interiors were marked by channels or grooves, probably the result of scraping.

Tools, utensils, and weapons.—Most of these were the types in use during the Laurentian I period. Projectile points (spearheads or arrowheads), both stemmed and notched, were generally smaller, although the large types were also used. An important new addition to Laurentian II tools consisted of long, ground-slate knives (Fig. 69, *f* and *h*) (similar to the "men's knives" of the Eskimo) and semi-lunar blades or "ulus" of ground slate (Fig. 69, *c*) (similar to the Eskimo woman's knife).

Pipes.—None.

Ornaments.—Same as Laurentian I.

Burials.—Same as Laurentian I.

Conjectures.—The culture change between Laurentian I and II may have been caused in part by the arrival of new Indians in the area, who brought with them a knowledge of pottery and the custom of using ground-slate tools.

SOURCES

RITCHIE, 1944.

THE EARLY COASTAL CULTURE
(INTERMEDIATE PERIOD)
Ca. A.D. 700–1100

Area.—Tidewater New York, New Jersey, and Pennsylvania.

People.—Longheaded Sylvids.

Villages.—These Indians lived in small villages or camp sites that may indicate seasonal occupancy rather than year-round habitation. Probably skin- or bark-covered wigwams were constructed.

Livelihood.—Food was obtained by hunting, fishing, and gathering, and, possibly, there were some simple agricultural activities.

Pottery.—Crude, straight-sided jars with conoidal bottoms were the only pottery made. The clay paste was grit-tempered, and vessel surfaces were covered with the impressions of fabric or a cord-wrapped paddle. Decoration, when present, consisted of a simple design made by punctating or incising.

Tools, utensils, and weapons.—Stone was the principal material used by the Early Coastal Indians in making tools. By the grinding, pecking, and polishing processes they manufactured grooved axes and clubs; celts; adzes; sinew stones; shallow mortars; cylindrical pestles; grooved, notched, and perforated bannerstones that probably were atlatl weights; and plummets that may have been net or fishline sinkers or bolas stones.

Chipped-flint implements were diamond-shaped and semidiamond-shaped projectile points; stemmed and notched projectile points, all with narrow blades; drills; and ovoid end-scrapers.

Characteristic tools made of animal bone were splinter awls; flat needles; antler flakers, wedges, or chisels; and conical projectile points.

Pipes.—Pipes were made in two styles of clay or stone. One of these was tubular; the other, an obtuse-angled elbow type.

Ornaments.—Polished stone gorgets.

Burials.—The dead were usually interred in pits, with the flexed body position preferred.

Conjecture.—The Early Coastal culture had its roots in the Archaic period, reached its climax in the Intermediate period, and persisted into the Late Prehistoric period. It finally developed into the Late Coastal culture.

SOURCES
RITCHIE, 1944.

THE ORIENT CULTURE
(Late Archaic and Early Intermediate Periods)
Ca. a.d. 800–1000

Area.—The east end of Long Island in New York State.

Villages.—The camp sites or villages were probably occupied throughout the year, although it is possible that the occupancy was seasonal. If the latter alternative is true, then it seems probable that the villagers spent part of the year in nomadic hunting.

Livelihood.—The Orient Indians were primarily hunters, fishers, and food-gatherers.

Pottery.—Pottery has been found only in one site, where it was probably intrusive. These vessels were grit-tempered, with cord-marked surfaces.

Tools, utensils, and weapons.—Characteristic tools were made of stone. Tools manufactured by grinding, pecking, and polishing were soapstone bowls; rectangular celts; plano-convex adzes, some of which were grooved; short gouges; and grooved axes. Chipped-flint knives, spears, and projectile points (arrowheads or spearheads) were narrow and were side-notched or had flaring concave bases (fishtail type).

Burials.—The dead were placed in deep pits in cemeteries. The bodies were cremated or disarticulated and arranged in bundles. Grave-offerings were placed with the burials, and many of the objects were ceremonially "killed" by breaking them. The graves were also liberally sprinkled with powdered red ocher.

Conjectures.—The Orient culture was apparently influenced by Laurentian and Early Coastal, but it seems to have remained a relatively isolated and independent entity.

SOURCES
Ritchie, 1944.

THE MIDDLESEX CULTURE
(Intermediate Period)
Ca. a.d. 800–1100

Area.—Archeological remains of the Middlesex culture have been found in Maine, Vermont, and central and east-central New York. Surface finds indicate that the range of distribution may have included the Upper St. Lawrence Valley.

People.—The Middlesex Indians were Sylvids with heads of medium length.

Villages.—The camp sites or villages were generally located near streams or rivers. Probably skin- or bark-covered wigwams were used as dwellings.

Livelihood.—These Indians made their living by farming, hunting, and food-collecting. Corn was the principal crop.

Pottery.—The pottery consisted of rather crude, grit-tempered jars with conoidal bottoms. Vessel surfaces were covered with fabric impressions or with the impressions made by a cord-wrapped paddle. Decoration, when present, was confined to the rim and consisted of simple patterns achieved by punctating or stamping with a cord-wrapped tool.

Tools, utensils, and weapons.—Tools were made of stone, copper, and bone. Boatstones, bars, and birdstones were probably atlatl weights. Plummets may have been used as net or fishline sinkers or perhaps as bolas stones. They also had chipped-stone knives which were leaf-shaped or triangular, and side- and corner-notched projectile points, drills, and scrapers. Ungrooved axes and awls were made of copper.

Animal bone was used for the manufacture of awls, projectile points, and gouges.

Pipes.—Pipes were made of clay, in two styles; one was a tubular pipe, the other was an elbow pipe of the obtuse-angled variety. The latter may have developed from the tubular types, since such development could have been achieved merely by bending the tube into an obtuse angle.

Ornaments.—Ornaments consisted of copper tubular and spheroidal beads, perforated elk teeth, marine shell beads, stone pendants, and stone gorgets.

Burials.—The dead were buried in grave pits. Usually they were accompanied by burial offerings and sprinkled with powdered red ocher. The bodies were flexed, extended, or bundled. In some instances the deceased were cremated.

Conjectures.—Toward the end of the period of Middlesex culture it seems likely that some Hopewell Indians from Ohio arrived in New York State. The resulting or following New York Hopewell culture is a mixture of Hopewell and Middlesex.

SOURCES

RITCHIE, 1944.

THE NEW YORK HOPEWELL CULTURE
(Intermediate Period)
Ca. A.D. 1100–1250

During the Intermediate period the native cultures of New York were probably influenced by the arrival of bands of Hopewell Indians from Ohio. These invaders seem to have received cultural elements from the Middlesex and, later, the Point Peninsula cultures. The New York Hopewell culture appears to be a combination of Ohio Hopewell ceremonial concepts and the village culture of Middlesex.

Area.—Central and western New York.

People.—Probably longheaded or medium longheaded Sylvids.

Livelihood.—These Indians probably obtained their food by farming, hunting, fishing, and the gathering of wild plants, berries, and the like.

Pottery.—Of all Hopewellian potters, those in New York State were the poorest. The jars were coarse and grit-tempered, with elongated bodies and conoidal bottoms. Such jars had either straight sides and direct, vertical rims or constricted necks and slightly outcurved rims. Vessel surfaces were impressed with fabric stamp, malleated with a cord-wrapped paddle, or coarsely smoothed.

One vessel was decorated with impressions made with a cord-wound stick and placed vertically in a band around the upper portion of the jar; the lower part bore an over-all pattern of the same impressions placed obliquely or horizontally. This decoration appears to be a crude imitation of Hopewellian pottery decorated with a dentate stamp.

Tools, utensils, and weapons.—Points for arrows or spears were made of chipped stone and usually notched or stemmed. There were flake knives and thin, leaf-shaped and triangular knives of chipped stone. Rude, thick, ovate, or triangular knives were placed in caches for unknown reasons. Grooved stones probably were used as bolas.

Fish were caught with lines and hooks of bone. Probably nets were also used.

Tools of general utility were chipped-stone drills, scrapers, rectanguloid celts (ungrooved axes), rectanguloid or trianguloid adzes, hammerstones, abrading stones, copper axes, and copper awls.

In addition to pottery vessels, there were containers of conch shell and of steatite.

Pipes.—Like many other Hopewellian Indians, those of New York smoked with the aid of curved or straight-based platform pipes of polished stone. They also used slightly bent elbow pipes of clay.

Ornaments.—Ellipsoidal or rectangular gorgets were made of polished stone and probably were suspended by cords over the chest. An especially elaborate breast ornament, rectangular in shape, was made of wood covered with sheet silver over sheet copper. Necklaces were composed of pearls or of disklike beads of shell. Ear ornaments of copper were the familiar double-cymbal type of ear-spool. Other possible ornaments were unworked quartz crystals, small uncut pieces of mica, and red ocher.

Burials.—The dead were placed beneath mounds of earth. Some burials were in stone slab-lined and covered cists partly beneath the mound floor. Other bodies were laid to rest under heaps of stone slabs, pebbles, and boulders on the floor of the mound.

The bodies of the deceased were sometimes cremated, but more often they were buried in a flexed or in an extended position. Bundle burials (disarticulated body in a bundle) also occurred. Most of the burials were accompanied by grave-offerings of tools, utensils, weapons, and ornaments. Red ocher was sometimes placed in the graves, and in one instance a "trophy or ancestral" skull was placed with a burial.

Low circular mounds were erected over the dead, and several might be found in the same site. One such mound was 42 feet in diameter and 3 feet high. In some instances the mound shoulders were reinforced with pebbles and rock slabs. The floors were carefully prepared by removing the humus and burning certain areas.

SOURCES

RITCHIE, 1944.

THE POINT PENINSULA CULTURE
(INTERMEDIATE AND LATE PREHISTORIC PERIODS)
Ca. A.D. 1150–1300

Area.—Western, central, and northern New York State and lower Ontario. Somewhat similar cultures have been discovered in Ohio, Michigan, and Minnesota.

People.—The Point Peninsula Indians show variation in skeletal type, although they seem on the whole to have been a moderately longheaded group. They probably belonged to the Sylvid type.

Villages.—Villages were situated near lakes, rivers, or streams. The cemetery was on the outskirts of the village. Probably dwellings were made of saplings covered with skins, thatch, bark, or mats.

Livelihood.—These Indians obtained their food by hunting, fishing, farming, and the gathering of wild products. They cultivated corn and perhaps other crops.

Pottery.—Unpainted pottery of clay tempered with particles of grit was manufactured by means of the coiling process or the anvil-and-paddle method. The pottery was sun dried, then fired until hard. The natural color was brown or buff. The vessels thus produced were jars with conoidal bottoms and elongated or globular bodies.

Vessel surfaces were coarsely smoothed, brushed, impressed with fabric, or malleated with a cord-wrapped paddle.

Techniques of decoration were incising, punctating, dentate stamping, rocker stamping (roulette), and impressing with a cord-wound stick. The designs were confined to the rim and shoulder area of vessels and consisted of simple geometric patterns involving bands of lines, curvilinear areas, herringbones, triangles, cross-hatching, and all-over patterns.

Tools, utensils, and weapons.—Many varieties of barbed, bone harpoon heads have been found in cemeteries and village sites. Arrows and spears were tipped with chipped-stone points, of which there were numerous styles. Most common were broad, thin, side-notched; broad, triangular points with concave or convex bases; stemmed points; corner-notched points; and leaf-shaped points. There were also conical projectile points of antler with sockets or triangular tangs that were attached to the spear-shafts. Polished stone bar amulets and birdstones might have been used as weights for spear-throwers.

Fish were caught with lines and bone gorges and fishhooks. Probably harpoons and nets, weighted with notched, flat pebbles, also were used.

Grooved stones tied to cords were used as bolas for taking birds and small animals.

Knives and daggers were made of bone and chipped stone.

Tools of general utility, some of which may also have served as weapons, were made of bone, stone, and copper. There were various styles of scrapers and drills of chipped flint; celts; adzes and hoes of chipped sandstone; plano-convex adzes and ungrooved axes of polished stone; chipped-flint strike-a-lights for use with iron pyrites in making fire; hammerstones; anvil stones; pestles and mortars of stone used possibly for pounding corn or nuts into meal; whetstones; sinew stones; and wedges or chisels of antler. There were copper and bone awls; needles, flakers, and scrapers of bone; and copper axes. Beaming tools (drawshave-like implements) made of deer leg bone probably were used as skin scrapers. Sharpened antler tines may have been used as spikes in heads of wooden clubs.

In addition to wedges and chisels of antler, there were chisel-like implements made of porcupine and beaver incisor teeth. A very characteristic Point Peninsula tool consists of one or two beaver incisors with chisel-shaped edge hafted transversely in a deer-antler tine or beam section.

There may have been some slight use of steatite vessels, but pottery was far more popular.

Pipes.—Tubular pipes and right-angled or slightly bent elbow pipes were made of pottery or stone; platform pipes which had either curved or straight bases were made of stone.

Ornaments.—Ornaments consisted of rectanguloid gorgets of polished stone; trianguloid, rectanguloid, and rhomboidal pendants of polished stone; tubular and barrel-shaped beads of copper; tubular bird bones with serrated ends and incised designs; worked teeth of bear, wolf, lynx, and shark; and large decorated combs made of antler. Other ornaments were antler pins with engraved heads, antler beads and armbands, various styles of shell beads, and pieces of uncut sheet mica.

The designs engraved upon ornaments, pipes, and some tools and weapons consisted of zigzag, bands of parallel lines, cross-hatching, line-filled plats, and spurred lines.

Musical instruments.—Bone whistles, turtle-back rattles, and probably drums.

Burials.—The dead were placed in a grave along with tools, weapons, ornaments, and perhaps a dog. In some instances a number of bodies were placed in the same grave. Occasionally, the deceased were cremated. Sometimes the body was disarticulated and arranged in a bundle or placed on a platform to decompose. In the latter case the bones were gathered sometime later, arranged in a bundle, and buried in a grave. Bodies were usually flexed; extended burials were rare.

In some cases considerable attention was focused upon the

preparation of the grave pit. The grave was lined with fragments of sheet mica or with stone slabs or boulders. Some graves were covered with slabs or boulders.

The graves were generally pits dug into the level ground near the village; sometimes natural knolls and hillsides were utilized. Besides the grave-offering with the dead there often was a liberal sprinkling of red ocher.

Conjectures.—In their early stages of development the Point Peninsula Indians seem to have been influenced by the Middlesex and, in their later stages of growth, by Hopewell peoples whom they outlasted. The New York Hopewell culture, in fact, seems to have merged completely with Point Peninsula.

SOURCES

RITCHIE, 1944.

THE OWASCO CULTURE
(LATE PREHISTORIC PERIOD)
Ca. A.D. 1250–1600

Area.—Central New York State, parts of Vermont, northern New Jersey, and eastern Pennsylvania. The influences of this culture extended as far west as Michigan, as far south as Maryland, and as far north as lower Ontario.

People.—Sylvids with long, narrow heads, moderately high vaults, and narrow faces.

Villages.—The camp, village, and workshop sites are indicative of large and semisedentary populations. The villages were built on hilltops some distance from lakes or streams and were surrounded by wooden stockades. Inside the fortification were groups of small, round lodges made of poles covered with bark, skins, or mats. Each lodge had a central fireplace. Numerous cache pits filled with refuse were scattered through the village.

Livelihood.—The Owasco peoples probably obtained most of their food by farming. The principal crops were corn and beans. Hunting and fishing may have supplemented the farming.

Pottery.—Pottery was unpainted and grit-tempered. Cooking jars had elongated bodies, constricted necks, rather broad mouths, and straight or slightly flaring rims. Imitation collars and weak castellations or nodes were sometimes added to the rim. The surfaces of the vessels were smoothed or malleated with a cord-wrapped paddle. The decoration, which was usually confined to the outside of the rim, although sometimes present on the inside rim and lip, consisted of simple geometric patterns produced by a number of different techniques—stamping with a crude dentate stamp, a cord-wrapped stick, or a sharp-edged implement wrapped with cord. The patterns were also produced by punctate impressions and incising.

Tools, utensils, and weapons.—Bows and arrows were made of wood. Characteristic arrowheads of chipped flint were shaped like an equal-sided triangle with a concave base. There were also socketed arrowheads of antler.

Wooden harpoons used for hunting or fishing were tipped with antler harpoon points that had a number of barbs on each side. Fish were also caught with bone hooks or in nets weighted with polished stone sinkers.

Other common tools were chipped-flint drills, polished stone celts, hammerstones, bone needles, bone tools for weaving, bone awls, and antler flakers.

Pipes.—Pipes were unique variants of the obtuse-angled elbow type. Bowls were always bulging and were occasionally decorated with fine-cord or punctate impressions or incising in simple geometric patterns.

Ornaments.—These Indians had few ornaments. They wore necklaces made of bone, marine shell, or rolled sheet-copper beads.

Burials.—The dead apparently were treated with little ceremony. The bodies, usually in a flexed position, were buried in pits. Grave-offerings, when present, consisted of pipes.

Conjectures.—The Owasco Indians were in many respects similar to others who lived at the same time in Wisconsin, Minnesota, Michigan, Ontario, Ohio, and Pennsylvania. These Indians preceded the Iroquois in New York and may be, in part, ancestral to them, although they seem also to have been contemporaries of the early Iroquois. Thus, although Owasco culture may have begun earlier than that of the Iroquois, there is considerable overlapping of the two.

SOURCES

RITCHIE, 1944.

THE OLD IROQUOIS CULTURE
(LATE PREHISTORIC PERIOD)
Ca. A.D. 1350–1600

Area.—The northeastern United States, principally the lower Great Lakes region and New York.

People.—Indians possessing long heads with medium high vaults, Sylvid type.

Villages.—The villages were built on hilltops some distance from navigable waters and sometimes were surrounded by a fortification consisting of a low earthen wall upon or in which was a wooden stockade. The houses were rectangular in shape and probably were made of sapling frames covered with sheets of bark.

Livelihood.—Subsistence was obtained by means of rudimentary agriculture, hunting, fishing, and food-gathering. Cultivated plants were corn and perhaps beans, squash, pumpkins, and sunflowers. The dog was the only domesticated animal.

Pottery.—These Indians manufactured grit-tempered, hard, well-fired cooking and storage jars (Fig. 70) that were buff and gray in color. Iroquois pottery was always unpainted.

Characteristic jars were globular and round-bottomed, with constricted necks and straight rims that were either thickened or topped by collars with circular or rectangular mouths. Frequently rim points in castellations projected upward from the collars. The lips of these jars usually were flattened. Vessel surfaces generally were smooth, but some jars had the imprints of a fabric- or cord-wrapped paddle.

Ornamentation was common and usually confined to the neck and rim or collar. Simple geometric designs were line-filled triangular plats and chevrons. The decoration was achieved by incising while the pottery was still plastic. Generally, the bottom of the collar or the lower border of the thickened rim was enhanced by an encircling row of notches.

Tools, utensils, and weapons.—Probably the principal weapon of the ancient Iroquois was the bow and arrow. Arrows were tipped with small triangular points made of chipped flint. Net or fishline sinkers were made of flat pebbles notched on each side. Other characteristic stone tools were the ungrooved axes; plano-convex adzes; shallow grinding-stones and flattened mullers; small, crude scrapers and chisels; and hammerstones. By and large, the ancient Iroquois used more bone than stone in the manufacture of their tools and ornaments.

Implements made of bone or antler were conical arrow points; various styles of awls, needles, weaving tools, scrapers, and beaming tools; and fishhooks. Rather simple fork-shaped combs were made of four teeth in contrast to the more elaborate forms used by the historic Iroquois.

Pipes.—Pipes were made of pottery or stone (see Fig. 70). The characteristic style was the so-called "trumpet" pipe, although there were also vase-shaped or conoidal pipes with separate stems. Frequently the trumpet-shaped pipes bore decoration similar to that of the pottery jars.

Fig. 70.—Clay tobacco pipes and pottery of the Iroquois culture

Ornaments.—Ornaments were few. Necklaces were made of bird-bone beads, shell beads, or sometimes stone beads. Pendants were made of bone or of animal teeth.

Burial.—The dead were buried in cemeteries and were accompanied by few grave-offerings in contrast to the historic Iroquois, who lavished offerings upon the dead. The bodies were placed in a flexed position or in bundles of disarticulated bones. Sometimes many bodies were placed in one grave. Such a burial is called an *ossuary*.

Conjectures.—We do not know the origin of the old Iroquois culture, which shows relationships with both southern and northern Indian types. We suspect that the Iroquois were an amalgamation—

a mixture of several culture streams. Their immediate ancestors were the proto-Owasco Indians and a somewhat Owasco-like culture in northern Ohio which had been strongly influenced by the Hopewell Indians. At various stages in their genesis the Iroquois seem to have received strong cultural stimuli from the Southeast.

SOURCES

Griffin, 1944b; Ritchie, 1944.

SUMMARY

We have outlined the sequence of prehistoric cultures in New York State, a sequence which in its broadest contours is applicable to the rest of the Northeast. Undoubtedly, there is considerable continuity within this sequence, although we do not yet have the details. We do not know the genetic relationships of these cultures, but, even without these details of cultural growth, aided or retarded by diffusion and culture contact, we can see the trends of culture development in the Northeast.

In the beginning there was a rather simple culture based upon hunting and food-collecting. In many respects this old culture is reminiscent of Cochise in the Southwest and probably represents the same stage of development as Cochise and some of the old cultures of eastern North America. Tools, weapons, and utensils were made of stone, bone, and copper. Later in this same stage a polished stone industry was added and still later pottery was acquired.

The Intermediate period saw the beginnings of agriculture, the climax of the polished stone industry, and a preoccupation with death, manifested by greater attentiveness to details of burial. This stage saw the beginnings and climax of copper ornaments, a possible climax of trade and commerce, and new interest in art and decoration.

The Late Prehistoric stage was the product of intensive agriculture. The emphasis upon the stone, bone, and copper industries of earlier stages is lacking. Less attention was paid to burials. Thus there is a decline in terms of the material remains, but this decline probably is not real. Certainly the improvements in the economy (agriculture), the possible social changes, and the probable lack of need for tools and industries of the past mark a type of climax or florescence that cannot be grasped by archeological techniques.

CHAPTER 18

THE OHIO AREA

INTRODUCTION

THE Ohio area comprised northern Kentucky, Ohio, Indiana, and southern Michigan. In the south it was a region of forested low plateaus, with a growth of oak-hickory and, secondarily, of chestnut and chestnut-oak-yellow-poplar. The vegetation of the lowlands in the north was primarily oak-hickory forest.

The climate was moderate with mild winters. The annual precipitation ranged from 30 to 50 inches, and the annual frostless season prevailed from 150 to 180 days.

The soils and climate were favorable for agriculture, and the forests were filled with wild animals useful as a source of food and raw materials. Numerous lakes and rivers provided waterways for transportation in bark canoes or dugouts.

The Ohio River was an avenue of travel that connected this region and areas farther east with the Mississippi and the rich territory to the south. On the north the Great Lakes and the St. Lawrence River offered opportunities for exploration northwestward and northeastward.

The prehistoric periods of the Ohio area are the Archaic, Burial Mound I, Burial Mound II, and the Late Prehistoric, which corresponds to the Temple Mound period of more southerly regions.

Cultural periods are not uniform throughout the area; for example southern Michigan lacks evidence of the Archaic period, and there are similar cultural gaps elsewhere. The periods and the cultures of each geographical division of the region are given in Chart VI.

THE INDIAN KNOLL CULTURE
(Archaic Period)
Ca. 500 b.c.–*ca.* a.d. 500

Area.—Kentucky. Similar cultures have been found in southern Ohio, in Indiana, and in Illinois.

People.—Sylvids of medium stature, with rather high-vaulted heads, short faces, and medium wide noses.

Villages.—These villages were placed along the riverbanks on top of shell mounds that were accumulations of refuse, something like a city dump. Discarded shells of river clams and other garbage were thrown on the floors of the shelters or on the ground outside. In the course of many years the garbage pile became a huge mound of clam shells, animal and bird bones, and other refuse. As the dump grew, the villagers continued to live on top of it in shelters that probably were crude arbors made of saplings and covered with skins or thatching.

CHART VI

Period	Culture				Probable Date
	Northern Kentucky	Ohio	Indiana	Michigan	
Late Prehistoric	Middle Mississippi	Fort Ancient Whittlesey	Middle Mississippi Late Woodland (not described	Younge	1300–1700
Burial Mound II	Adena	Intrusive Mound Hopewell Glacial Kame	Hopewell	Intrusive Mound Hopewell Glacial Kame	900–1300
Burial Mound I	Adena	Glacial Kame Adena	Adena	Glacial Kame	500–900
Archaic	Indian Knoll	Culture resembling Indian Knoll	Culture resembling Indian Knoll		Probably before 500

Some of the Indian Knoll peoples lived in caves or rock shelters in the hills. The cave sites frequently contain many objects, such as textiles, basketry, and clothing, which are not preserved in the shell-midden sites.

Livelihood.—Agriculture was unknown, and the dog was the only domesticated animal. Food was provided by hunting, fishing, and the gathering of wild plants, nuts, sunflower seeds, berries, and clams.

Tools, utensils, and weapons.—The spear-thrower, the principal weapon, was made of a wooden shaft from fifteen to twenty-two inches long, which was tipped with a socketed antler hook. The hook was glued to the shaft with asphaltum, a tarlike substance, and engaged the butt of the spear, holding it in position and providing a point of propulsion. When greater momentum and force were needed, weights were attached to the shaft. Stone atlatl weights were of various types—prisms, bannerstones, and rectanguloid bars. Other weights were made of perforated sections of antler or segments of conch shell.

Probably the spears were made of cane shafts to which were fastened points of stone, bone, or antler. Several varieties of large-stemmed points were made of chipped stone. Stemmed points of bone and conical points of antler were also fastened to the spear-shafts. Other chipped stone tools were ovate-triangular knives, some of which were stemmed; drills with an expanded base; and side- and end-type and stemmed thumbnail scrapers.

Lapstones, cupstones, mortars, bell-shaped pestles, cylindrical pestles, and manos probably were used for grinding wild foods. Other implements of ground stone were fully grooved axes and several types of hammerstones.

Tools manufactured from bone were fishhooks, small tubes, engraved or notched perforators, several types of awls, forked implements of unknown use, and antler flakers.

Costume.—The principal articles of clothing were woven breech-clouts and cloth or skin robes or possibly shirts with sleeves. These garments were sometimes decorated with beads made from snail shells. Woven sandals and skin moccasins were probably worn.

Ornaments.—Like many other Indians of the Archaic period, the Indian Knoll people were not highly developed aesthetically. They ornamented their clothing with snail-shell beads and wore necklaces of disk-shaped and tubular shell beads, bone beads, stone beads, and perforated teeth of various animals. Pendants were made of animal canine teeth and conch shell. Some bone pins and engraved bone awl-like objects may have been used as hair ornaments.

Burial.—The dead were placed in circular burial pits with the skeletons usually flexed. Sometimes red ocher and other offerings were placed in the graves. The inclusion of dog skeletons with those of humans suggests that the Indian Knoll peoples held this animal in high esteem.

Conjectures.—The Indian Knoll culture probably was the end product of a long tradition of hunting, fishing, and food-gathering. In a broad sense the culture is analogous to Cochise and Folsom, and in its earliest stages, perhaps prior to 500 B.C., there is some suggestion of a relationship to Folsom. Some midden sites of cultures related to

Indian Knoll, but probably earlier, produce several varieties of Folsom-like points and scrapers. The grinding-stones of Indian Knoll, and, for that matter, of almost all Archaic cultures, are like those of Cochise.

By virtue of an abundant supply of river clams, the Indian Knoll midden dwellers were able to lead a sedentary life and probably had developed some of the social structures allowed only by a sedentary life. Agriculture could have been added to their economic pattern without requiring considerable adjustment on the part of the Indians.

The Indian Knoll culture was followed by the Adena. There seems to have been little continuity between the two, but this may be the result of insufficient information about late Indian Knoll and early Adena in the era of possible transition.

SOURCES

HAAG, 1942; MOORE, 1916; WEBB and FUNKHOUSER, 1932; WEBB and HAAG, 1939, 1940.

THE GLACIAL KAME CULTURE
(BURIAL MOUND I PERIOD)
Ca. A.D. 800–1000

The Glacial Kame Indians had the custom of burying their dead in kames—natural hills or knobs composed of gravel and sand deposited by the enfluvial streams of the great glaciers of Pleistocene times.

Area.—Southern Michigan, northwestern Ohio, and northeastern Indiana.

People.—Longheaded, probably Sylvids.

Livelihood.—The meagerness of the archeological remains indicates that the Glacial Kame culture is probably the product of a hunting and food-gathering economy.

Pottery.—Excavations of Glacial Kame sites have been such that there is little likelihood of pottery sherds having been saved, if they were present. A small, undecorated vessel alleged to have come from one of the Ohio sites is grit-tempered, soft, poorly fired, and a dirty gray in color. It is jar-shaped, with straight sides, a semiconoidal bottom, a straight vertical rim, a rounded lip, and a rough surface.

Tools, utensils, and weapons.—Double-pointed awls and trianguloid celts were made of copper. Chipped-stone projectile points were triangular in outline and had rather broad square stems and horizontal shoulders. Birdstones may have been weights for spear-throwers or may have served some ceremonial purpose.

Pipes.—The custom of smoking is manifested by platform and tubular pipes of stone. The Glacial Kame Indians may have cultivated tobacco; in any event, they obtained a vegetal substance suitable for smoking.

Ornaments.—Necklaces were made of copper or shell beads. The copper beads were spheroidal, the largest about an inch in diameter. Other beads were made of disks cut from conch shells or from conch-shell centers.

Other ornaments were circular conch-shell gorgets and sandal-shaped gorgets usually with three perforations. Some specimens were engraved with a simple straight-line design. These gorgets are the most obvious characteristic of the Glacial Kame culture. Another type, made of ground slate, is rectanguloid in shape, usually with three perforations.

Burials.—The dead were buried in pits dug into the natural elevations called kames. The bodies usually were placed in a flexed position and were accompanied by grave-offerings of tools and ornaments. Sometimes red ocher was placed in the graves. A remarkable Glacial Kame burial in Ohio was found in a pit twenty feet deep. If the outlines of the pit had not been observed by the excavators, this burial would have been considered proof of the Indians' contemporaneity with the glaciers. This example should indicate how necessary it is to have such burials excavated under carefully controlled conditions.

Conjectures.—These Indians, probably contemporaries of the late Adena groups, seem to have persisted into Hopewell times and then to have disappeared. They may have been the first settlers of southern Michigan.

SOURCES
GREENMAN, 1931.

THE ADENA CULTURE
(BURIAL MOUND I PERIOD)

Ca. A.D. 500–900

Area.—Ohio, Kentucky, Indiana, West Virginia, and perhaps Pennsylvania.

People.—Centralids, with large, round heads and long faces. They were generally of medium stature, although a few were tall. Some of the skulls are flattened or deformed, probably from having been strapped to a cradle-board.

Villages.—Most of the Adena Indians lived in villages, although some rock shelters have been found. The houses (Fig. 71) were round and about 25 or 30 feet in diameter, with walls made of strong sapling poles placed in the ground in pairs and slanted outward. Willow switches were probably woven among the paired saplings.

Fig. 71.—Construction of Adena house. (After W. S. Webb.)

The roof was supported by central posts and probably was bark-covered. There may have been a smoke hole to carry off the smoke from fires on the central hearths. The doorway could have been between any two pairs of wall posts.

Other interesting features of some sites are earthen walls laid out in large circles or other geometric forms. The most conspicuous architectural features of Adena are large (10–70 feet high) conical burial mounds of earth, usually in groups, although single mounds are not uncommon.

Livelihood.—The Adena Indians raised corn and other crops. They obtained additional subsistence by hunting, fishing, and collecting.

Pottery.—The most common type was a small grit- or limestone-tempered jar with a flat or slightly rounded bottom, constricted neck, and slightly flaring rim. Generally, the rim was thickened and the lip was either round or flat. Some jars had podal supports or feet.

Most of the pottery was smooth-surfaced and undecorated. The exterior of one style, however, was covered with impressions made by a cord-wrapped paddle. The most common decorated variant had incised designs similar to some Tchefuncte decorative styles. The pottery was never painted.

Tools, utensils, and weapons.—The tools and weapons were sandstone hoes, ungrooved axes of polished or chipped stone, leaf-shaped knives and stemmed or notched projectile points of chipped flint, leaf-shaped points of chipped flint with concave bases, flake knives, various types of scrapers, drills, sandstone saws, pitted grindingstones, and boatstone atlatl weights. Although copper was sometimes used for the manufacture of axes and awls, it was used more extensively for ornaments than for tools. Some tools were made of bone and shell. Bone tools in common use were flakers and awls. Dippers or containers made from marine conch shells were rare.

Pipes.—Pipes were tubular and were usually made of ground stone. Sometimes the stem part of the tube was flattened to provide a better mouthpiece. Effigy pipes (Fig. 72) were rare.

Costume.—The men probably wore a breechclout and a robe of skin or fabric. Both skin moccasins and woven sandals may have been worn.

Ornaments.—The Adena Indians manufactured most of their ornaments of copper, mica, and stone. Breastplates, C-shaped bracelets, finger rings, and beads were made of copper. Several styles of polished stone gorgets were made, two of the most representative forms being the reel-shaped and the expanded-center types. Most of the gorgets were perforated for suspension or attachment. Adena perforations are drilled from one side only, a unique type, as usually such perforations are drilled from two sides and meet in the center.

Sandstone or slate tablets engraved with curvilinear designs are associated with some Adena remains.

Mica ornaments consisted of curvilinear designs cut from sheet mica. Large pieces of mica may have been used as mirrors. Bone combs were probably worn as hair ornaments. Necklaces were composed of beads made of shell, pearls, bone, or copper.

Burials.—The large burial mounds usually had a big, central tomb lined with logs. Around this were other log tombs and crematory basins. The dead were usually either extended or flexed, although disarticulated bundles also occur. Cremation, too, was not uncommon; probably most of the "common people" were cremated. A few tools and ornaments and sometimes red ocher were placed with the burials; pottery has rarely been found.

Fig. 72.—Effigy tobacco pipe of stone, Adena culture. Adena Indians of Ohio. (Photograph of cast made from original in Ohio State Museum.)

Conjectures.—The Adena use of such exotic materials as copper, mica, and marine conch shell implies rather widespread trading relationships with other peoples and places. The Adena were also the first Indians in North America to construct tremendous burial mounds the size of which implies a social structure capable of organizing co-operative labor projects on a large scale. It is also possible that the Adena culture contained the seeds of city-state confederacy, a style of government found in later cultures in the Mississippi Valley.

Both in Ohio and in Kentucky the Adena culture was typical of the Burial Mound I period, but in Ohio the Adena seems to have preceded the Hopewell culture of Burial Mound II times, whereas in

Kentucky the Adena culture persisted and was also characteristic of the Burial Mound II period.

SOURCES

BLACK, 1936; FOWKE, 1902; GREENMAN, 1932; GRIFFIN, 1942; MILLS, 1902; WEBB, W., 1940, 1941a, 1941b, 1942, 1943a, 1943b; WEBB and ELLIOT, 1942.

THE HOPEWELL CULTURE
(BURIAL MOUND II PERIOD)
Ca. A.D. 900–1300

Area.—Southern Ohio was the center of the Hopewell culture, although there were subsidiary centers in Michigan, Ohio, Pennsylvania, New York, Tennessee, Indiana, Illinois, Wisconsin, Iowa, and Kansas. The Hopewell culture was largely responsible for the legend of a "mound-builder" race that preceded the Indians in North America. Archeological investigations, however, have shown the error of this myth, and the term "mound-builder" has fallen into disrepute.

People.—Generally longheaded Sylvids, although there may have been some Centralid strain.

Some of the skeletons show bone lesions of a type considered indicative of syphilis. If truly present, syphilis makes its first appearance in eastern North America during the time of the Hopewell culture.

Villages.—Hopewell villages and ceremonial centers were located along rivers and streams. Especially in southern Ohio these villages were markedly conspicuous because of the large burial mounds and great systems of earthen walls arranged in squares, circles, or octagons. Some of the inclosures were hundreds of feet in length; for example, at the Turner site in Hamilton County, Ohio, earthworks and mounds extended along the east bank of the Little Miami River for a mile or more. There was a large oval inclosure, 1,500 feet long, surrounded by an earthen wall 2 feet high and 20 feet broad. At one end of the inclosure was an opening or gate; at the other end a graded road 600 feet long led to an elevated circular platform 500 feet in diameter. Both the road and the platform were surrounded by earthen walls. Within the oval were burial mounds and a small circular inclosure. There were additional burial mounds within this inclosure and scattered around the site.

In Ohio there are other systems of earthworks even more impressive than those at the Turner site, with much higher walls.

Since the Hopewell earthen wall inclosures do not seem adequate as fortifications, they probably had a sacred function. Houses or wigwams of saplings covered with skin or bark may have been arranged in lines along the inside of the walls, but this has not yet been determined by excavation.

Livelihood.—The Indian farmers of the Hopewell culture raised corn and probably squash and beans. Other foods were obtained by hunting and fishing and perhaps by gathering wild nuts, fruits, seeds, and roots.

The women probably tended the crops, while the men hunted or engaged in other pursuits. From the complexities of Hopewell culture one would infer that there were special craftsmen or guilds of craftsmen who worked in pottery or metals or wood; but, despite specialized occupations, each community was capable of great cooperative efforts, such as the building of large earthworks and burial mounds. Trade and commerce were maintained on a broad scale. Raw materials and imported articles were brought to the Hopewell villages, perhaps by a special class of traveling salesmen.

Pottery.—The numerous styles of pottery can be grouped into three major classes: (1) sacred vessels for ceremonial use; (2) ordinary cooking pots; and (3) "Sunday-best" jars, which we guess were used to impress guests but which also had some utilitarian value.

The sacred vessels were exceptionally well made and decorated (Fig. 73) and show no signs of having been used. These small, gray jars were grit- or limestone-tempered with rounded or flattened bottoms.

Vessel surfaces were carefully smoothed before the application of the decoration. The rims of the jars were banded with incised crosshatches bordered at the bottom by a row of punctates. The body of the jar was ornamented with curvilinear zones of fine stamped impressions contrasting with similar zones which were set off with incised lines. Some vessels of this type had bird designs outlined by fine stamping.

The cooking jars were always grit-tempered, buff or gray in color, and covered with the impressions of a cord-wrapped paddle. Although feet were sometimes added, the bottoms of the jars were usually round or conoidal. These vessels were seldom decorated.

A great variety of types comprises the "Sunday-best" pottery (see Fig. 73), all of which was grit-tempered, buff or gray in color, and smoothed before the application of the design. Many of these types were poor copies of the sacred or ceremonial pottery.

Basketry.—Evidence of basketry is rare in Hopewell sites, although these Indians probably had baskets of many kinds. Baskets may have been used to carry the soil used in building earthworks and mounds.

Tools, utensils, and weapons.—We suspect that the Hopewell Indians used the spear and spear-thrower; it is possible that they had also the bow and arrow. The spear-throwers were made of wood,

FIG. 73.—Hopewell pottery. Jar at left from Ohio; jar at right from Michigan. (Latter courtesy of the Museum of Anthropology of the University of Michigan.)

sometimes tipped with a hook having the form of a human effigy and made of antler. Another style of spear-thrower is indicated by a small effigy made of mica. Attached to the handle, there are two rings or loops that probably served as finger grips. For purposes of better balance and greater momentum, stone and antler weights were sometimes attached to the shaft of the spear-thrower. Such weights were stone bars (sometimes called amulets), plain and effigy boatstones, birdstones, and certain types of bannerstones.

It is possible that some of the more elaborate spear-throwers were not used in ordinary hunting activities but were reserved for use in ceremonial warfare and sacrifices or served as symbols of rank.

Hopewell spears were tipped with large points made of various kinds of flint or obsidian (Fig. 74, *c*). Some of these points were broad-ovate or triangular in outline. The former were usually corner-

270   INDIANS BEFORE COLUMBUS

notched, and the latter, often with in-sloping sides, were stemmed. Still other points were leaf-shaped.

Very large, leaf-shaped knives, swords, or spears (Fig. 74, *a* and *f*) were chipped from beautifully colored flints or obsidian. Such weapons were hafted to wooden handles, sometimes by means of notches or stems on the blade. Tools in making chipped-stone weapons were made of deer and elk antler.

Some of the Hopewell Indians were excellent wood-workers. Charred fragments of wooden bowls and other objects show that they

FIG. 74.—Tools and weapons of the Hopewell Indians of Ohio: *a*, obsidian knife, wooden handle reconstructed; *b*, adz of meteoric iron; *c*, obsidian spearhead; *d*, copper adz; *e*, copper ax; *f*, obsidian knife or spearhead.

carved designs on wood with the same skill and care that they exercised on bone artifacts. Tools used in carpentry and wood-carving were rather long and narrow flake knives; drills made of chipped stone, copper, bone, or meteoric iron; long ungrooved axes of polished stone; axes and adzes made of copper or meteoric iron (Fig. 74, *b*, *d*, *e*); chisels made of iron or beaver teeth; and awls made of split deer bone.

Fish were caught with bone hooks, perhaps spears, and by nets, perhaps weighted with plummet-shaped netsinkers.

Dippers or pitchers were made from the shells of the marine conch, *Busycon*.

Pipes.—Pipes were of the platform type and were made of polished

THE OHIO AREA

stone. The bases were either straight or curved, and frequently the bowls were carved in the form of realistic animal (Fig. 75) or human effigies. More rarely platform pipes were made of clay and resembled some of those made by Indians of the Marksville culture in the Lower Mississippi Valley.

Costume.—Clothing was made of woven cloth, fur, and dressed skin. The women wore knee-length skirts that were wrapped around their waists and fastened in back; woven sandals or skin moccasins; and robes of fur, skin, or cloth, to which were fastened copper and

FIG. 75.—Effigy tobacco pipe of stone carved to represent a duck on the back of a fish. The bowl of the pipe is in the back of the duck and the head of the fish is the mouthpiece of the pipe. Hopewell Indians of Ohio.

mica ornaments and pearl beads. The cloth garments, usually of twined weaving, were sometimes painted with curvilinear designs, tan in color and outlined in black on a red background.

Men wore breechclouts of cloth or skin, woven sandals or skin moccasins, and sometimes leggings. Their robes were made of fur, skin, or cloth and sometimes were lavishly decorated with mica and copper ornaments and pearl beadwork.

Ornaments.—The men wore metal headplates, some of which were very elaborate. Most of these were made of beaten copper; silver and meteoric iron were also used. Copper and iron breastplates were suspended over the chest and sometimes worn over the stomach as well.

Both men and women wore copper and silver ear-spools and large polished stone rings in their ears. There were several styles of copper bracelets and armbands (Figs. 76 and 77).

Necklaces were made of pearls; of iron, copper, silver, stone, shell, and bone beads; and of animal teeth. Pendants were made of copper or bone or of bear's teeth inlaid with pearls. Gorgets were carved from polished stone.

Large ornaments attached to clothing were made usually of mica or copper sheets often cut in the forms of animals or humans or in

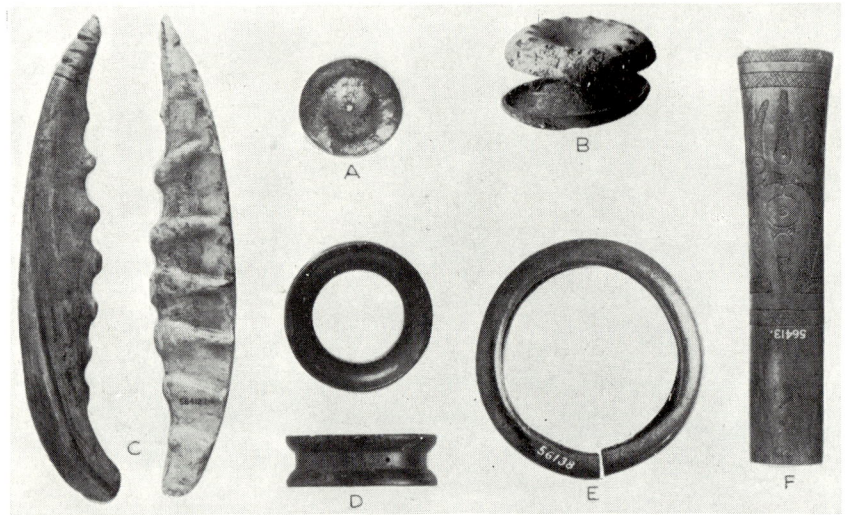

Fig. 76.—Hopewell ornaments: *a*, ear ornament of sheet silver; *b*, ear ornament of sheet copper; *c*, ear ornaments of conch shell; *d*, two views of stone ear ornament; *e*, copper bracelet; *f*, human thigh bone with engraved design.

complex geometric patterns (Figs. 78, 79, 80, and 81). Space does not permit a description of all the metal ornaments that have been found. These Indians, however, were the finest metal-workers in North America before the coming of the White man, and their metalsmithing was employed primarily for the production of ornaments. Copper was used extensively, silver and iron occasionally, and gold rarely. The casting of metals was unknown, but, by beating and annealing metal, they were able to manufacture many different kinds of ornaments of sheet copper, silver, and even meteoric iron.

Other examples of ornamental work are incised handles made of animal or human bone (see Fig. 76, *f*); cut human and animal jaws, some of which were painted; elliptical or rectanguloid slate gorgets; and carved wooden bowls.

Fig. 77.—Hopewell man. The head is enlarged from a clay figurine. The deer-antler headdress of copper, the pearl necklace, and the copper ear ornaments were excavated from a mound in Ohio.

Musical instruments.—The only musical instruments that have been preserved are panpipes made of reed or bone tubes held in place by a metal band corrugated on one side (Fig. 82). These panpipes had three or four and perhaps more tubes of varying length, which were plugged at the bottom and open at the top. The sounds were produced by blowing across the open ends of the tubes, and different notes were obtained by tubes of differing length. Probably these Indians also had drums, rattles, flutes, and whistles.

Art.—The Hopewell Indians were fine artists. Animals carved on stone pipes or spear-thrower weights are exceptionally realistic.

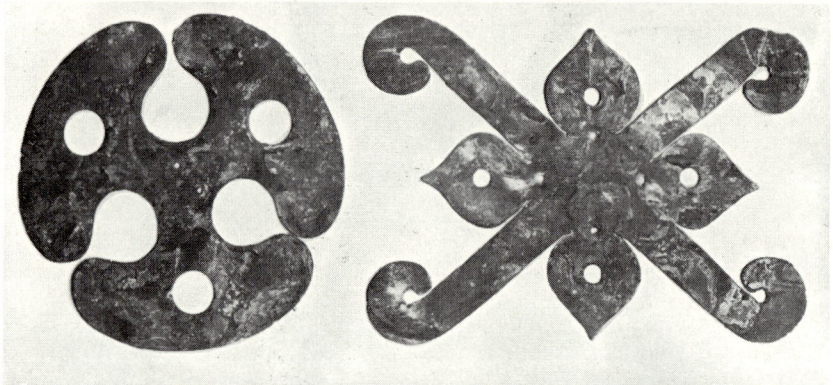

Fig. 78.—Ornaments of sheet copper for attachment to robes. Hopewell Indians of Ohio

Some forms cut from mica or sheet copper also are easily recognizable; other forms, however, are somewhat conventionalized. Some bone engravings, for instance, are more like symbols of animals than attempts at actual representation, whereas other art forms are purely geometric designs which usually were curvilinear and may have had especial meanings.

Burials.—To the archeologist it rather looks as if the most important Hopewell Indians were the dead ones, for these people disposed of their dead more carefully than any other Indian groups in North America.

The deceased, dressed in their best clothing, and accompanied by lavish quantities of fine ornaments, weapons, and tools, were placed in log tombs or on burial platforms. Sometimes the graves were lined with large sheets of mica or stones or woven mats. In some instances the burial platforms were colored with pounded clay or mosaics of

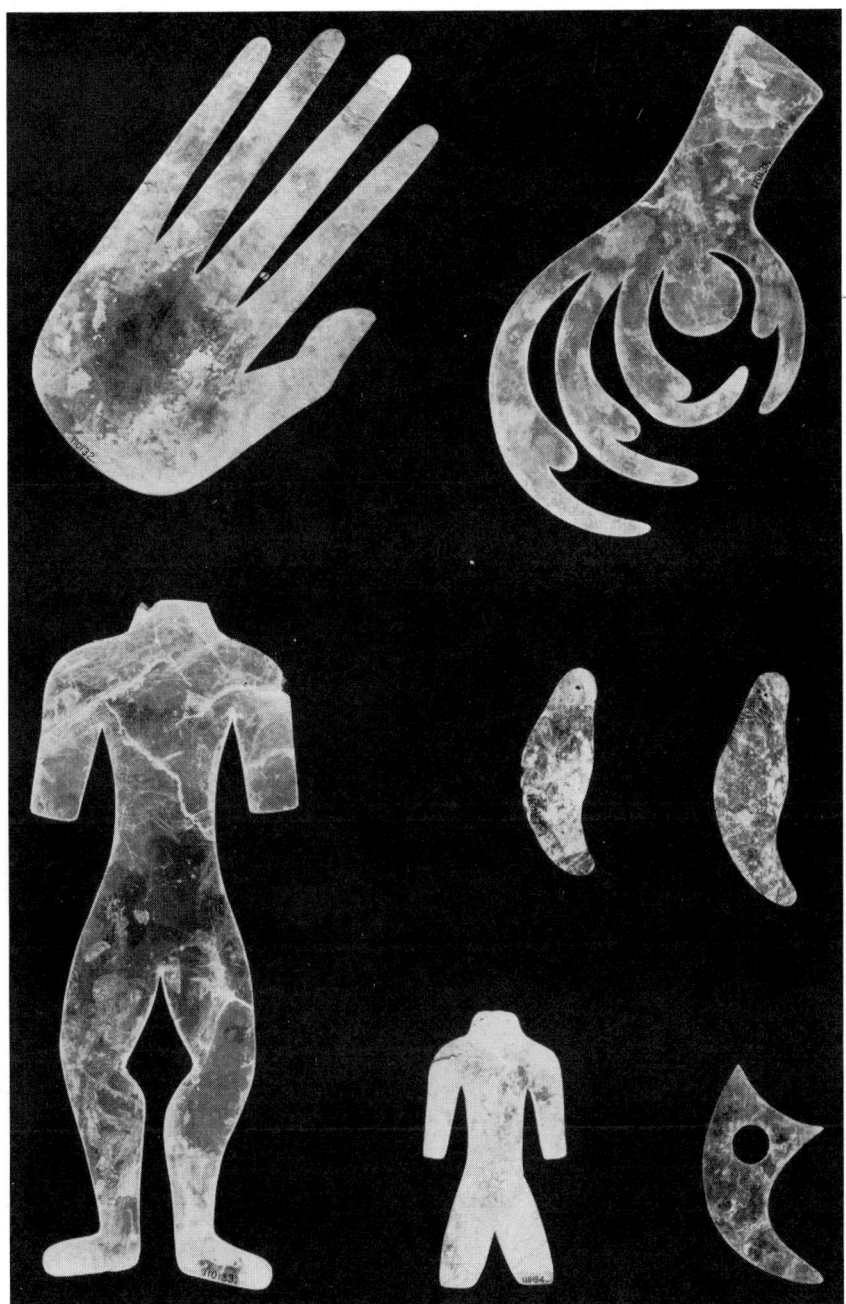

Fig. 79.—Ornaments of sheet mica. *Top row:* left, human hand; right, bird claw. *Middle row:* two ornaments representing the canine teeth of a bear. *Bottom row:* left, large ornament representing headless human; right, representation of a bird talon. Hopewell Indians of Ohio.

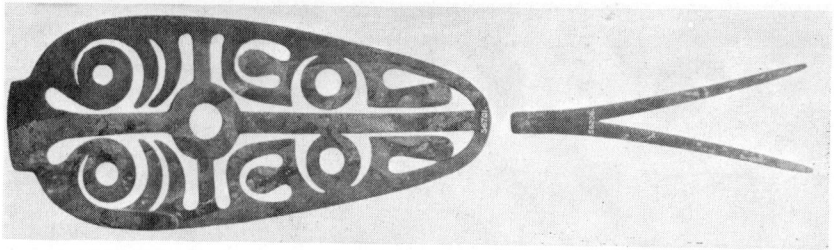

Fig. 80.—Ornament of sheet copper, probably representing the head of a serpent. Hopewell Indians of Ohio.

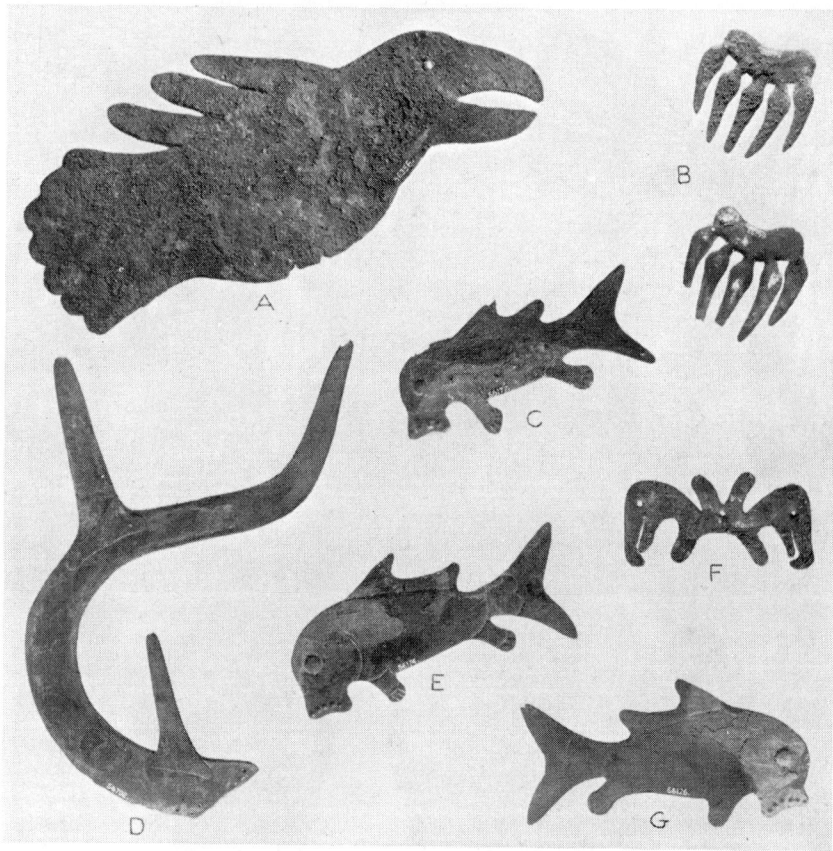

Fig. 81.—Ornaments of sheet copper: *a*, bird with pearl eye; *b*, bear claws; *c, e, g*, fish, probably suckers; *d*, deer antler; *f*, double eagle. Hopewell Indians of Ohio.

mineral paints, and in these burials the bodies were usually extended and linear or conical mounds of earth were placed above them.

Another common burial practice was cremation. In some mounds there were numerous crematory basins made of clay and containing the charred and calcined bones of the dead. Frequently there were vast quantities of melted and finely cracked grave-offerings with or near the cremations.

Sometimes the tools and ornaments placed with the dead were ceremonially "killed" by breaking them. This was done probably to

Fig. 82.—Panpipes of bone and copper. Two views of original and reconstruction. Hopewell Indians of Ohio.

enable the spirit of the dead to use the spirit of the tools or ornaments that had been "killed."

Conjectures.—We surmise that the Hopewell Indians were bound together in a loose confederacy that extended from Kansas to New York and from the Gulf of Mexico to northern Wisconsin. There probably were privileged classes of people, elaborate rituals, special guilds of craftsmen, widespread trade and commerce, and a social organization capable of directing co-operative labor.

The Ohio Hopewell sites seem to represent the center of the culture. Raw materials and exotic objects were brought to Ohio from the Rocky Mountain region, the Atlantic Coast, and the Gulf states. Goods manufactured in Ohio were carried to all the outlying Hopewell groups as well as to other cultures with which trading relations were maintained.

The Marksville culture, although we have described it separately, was probably part of the Hopewell culture. It is not hard to imagine that the agricultural South and the industrial North were not on the most cordial terms even in Burial Mound II times, and it is possible that the farmers of the Marksville culture were "cussing out" (in a friendly way) the "damyankee" Hopewell manufacturers in Ohio. On the other hand, they were probably more than willing to trade seashells, sharks' and alligators' teeth, and perhaps pottery for copper ear-spools, axes, and any other manufactured goods carried by the Hopewell traveling salesmen.

SOURCES
FOWKE, 1902; GRIFFIN, 1944; MILLS, 1907, 1916, 1922; MOOREHEAD,1922; QUIMBY, 1941; SHETRONE, 1930; SHETRONE and GREENMAN, 1931.

THE INTRUSIVE MOUND CULTURE
(BURIAL MOUND II AND LATE PREHISTORIC PERIOD)
Ca. A.D. 1100–1400

Area.—The culture was named "Intrusive Mound" by archeologists who found it to be intrusive into some Hopewell mounds in Ohio. In Ontario and New York a very similar culture is called "Point Peninsula."

People.—Probably Sylvids or mixed Sylvid-Centralid.

Villages.—The Indians probably lived in temporary camps in skin- or bark-covered wigwams.

Livelihood.—Food was obtained by hunting, fishing, gathering, and, possibly, some farming.

Pottery.—Cooking jars were made of unpainted pottery which was tempered with grit and hardened by baking in a fire. After firing, this pottery turned buff or gray in color.

These vessels had conoidal or semiconoidal bottoms and broad mouths, and their surfaces were covered with the imprints of fabric or a cord-wrapped paddle. The jars had constricted necks and slightly flaring rims. Some of the vessels were decorated with encircling rows of crude punctates and impressions were made with a cord-wrapped stick.

Tools, utensils, and weapons.—Arrow or spear points were made of chipped flint, and most of them were notched and triangular. Simple triangular points without stems or notches are also characteristic, although less common. Another representative type of spearhead or arrowhead was made of antler tips, pointed at one end and hollowed at the other. It is possible that these Indians used the spear and spear-thrower. If this assumption is correct, the birdstones and stone bars sometimes associated with this culture were probably used as spear-thrower weights. Large harpoons of bone, usually with barbs on one side only and a line hole near the base, were also characteristic hunting weapons. Plummet-shaped stones may have been net-sinkers or weights for a bolas.

Perhaps the most characteristic tool found in the Intrusive Mound culture was a hafted engraver, consisting of one, sometimes two, beaver incisors hafted transversely in an antler tine. There were also hammers made of antler; polished stone adzes; bone awls and needles; bone and stone scrapers; flint and polished stone celts; and flaking tools, handles, and large combs made of antler. There were occasional copper awls, some of which were hafted in antler handles.

Pipes.—Elbow pipes were made of clay or stone, and straight-based platform pipes were made of stone. The platform type, often with a keeled ridge in the middle of the platform, was the most characteristic.

Costume.—Probably skin moccasins, leggings, breechclouts, and robes of fur or skin were worn.

Ornaments.—Necklaces were made of copper beads, various styles of marine shell beads, and perforated teeth of sharks and other animals. Pendants and gorgets were made of polished stone.

Some of the antler combs may have served as ornaments in addition to any practical function. Similarly, small sheets of mica found at some sites may have been mirrors that served both practical and ornamental purposes.

Burials.—In Michigan and Ontario earth mounds were used as repositories for the dead; in Ohio, the deceased were placed in pits sometimes dug into the tops of Hopewell mounds. The bodies, frequently accompanied by grave-offerings which in several instances included dog skulls, were buried in a flexed position or in bundles of disarticulated bones. Occasionally, they were cremated. Some graves contained a sprinkling of red ocher.

Conjectures.—The Intrusive Mound culture was slightly later than the Hopewell, although the two probably overlapped. A number of Intrusive Mound customs could have been derived directly or indirectly from Hopewell.

SOURCES

HINSDALE, 1929; MILLS, 1922; RITCHIE, 1944.

THE YOUNGE CULTURE
(Late Prehistoric Period)
Ca. a.d. 1400–1700(?)

Area.—Southeastern Michigan

People.—Short-statured and longheaded Sylvids.

Villages.—The camp sites and villages were located along streams and rivers. The dwellings were probably wigwams made of poles and covered with mats, bark, or skin. There were also narrow ceremonial structures, four or five hundred feet long, that were made of upright poles.

Livelihood.—Food was obtained by hunting, fishing, gathering, and probably agriculture.

Pottery.—The unpainted pottery was grit-tempered, the vessels ranging from small jars with globular bodies to large pots with elongated bodies. The bottoms were rounded or semiconoidal, the necks were constricted, and the rims were straight or slightly flaring, often weakly scalloped, and thickened in various ways. Some of these rim thickenings simulated collars. The vessel surfaces were roughly smoothed or were malleated with a cord-wrapped paddle.

The decorative patterns were confined to the rim exteriors, interiors, and lips. The techniques of ornamentation were incising, punctating, and impressing with cord, a stick, a dentate (toothed) stamp, a cord-wrapped stick, or the sharp edge of some other cord-wrapped instrument. The patterns thus produced consisted of simple geometric designs. Undecorated vessels were rare.

Tools, utensils, and weapons.—The principal tools and weapons were angular chipped-flint arrowheads, which were both isosceles and equilateral with straight or slightly concave bases; trianguloid, notched, and stemmed projectile points; retouched flake scrapers; and drills. Awls and flaking tools were manufactured from bone and antler.

Pipes.—Pipes were the clay elbow type, with either an obtuse or a right-angled bowl, and a short, thick stem. Some of the pipe bowls were decorated with incised lines or punctate and cord impressions.

Ornaments.—Ornaments were elliptical and rectanguloid slate gorgets which were perforated. Work in copper was extremely rare, although spheroidal copper beads have been found.

Burials.—The dead were buried in cemeteries. Few artifacts were placed with the burials, but, of all burial offerings, pipes were the most frequent. The bodies were sometimes extended in the flesh or flexed, but often the bones were denuded of flesh and arranged in bundles or in simulation of extended and flexed bodies. There were also separate burials of torsos, long bones, or skulls.

In addition to the interment of rearticulated skeletons, a unique ceremonial practice was the perforation of long bones and the cutting of circular disks from the skulls. This was probably done after death.

A particularly curious burial custom, applicable probably only to married couples, was the placing of the man on top of the woman in the grave, with the man's hands over the woman's pelvis.

Conjectures.—The physical type of the Younge Indians is the same as that of the Hurons. It seems probable that if the Younge Indians themselves are in no way directly ancestral to the Iroquois, they at least are descended from the same type of Hopewell-influenced Woodland Indians who were ancestral to the Iroquois.

SOURCES

GREENMAN, 1937a; GRIFFIN, 1944.

THE WHITTLESEY CULTURE
(LATE PREHISTORIC PERIOD)
Ca. A.D. 1400–1650

Area.—Northwestern Ohio.

People.—Probably Sylvids—longheaded easterners.

Villages.—The villages were situated on bluffs and were protected by a stockade of upright posts or by earthen walls and upright posts combined. The dwellings, made of saplings and covered with bark or thatch, were probably square or rectangular in shape. Throughout the village there were numerous refuse and storage pits as well as ash beds indicative of fireplaces.

Livelihood.—Farming, hunting, fishing, and food-collecting were the principal means of subsistence. The chief crops were corn, squashes, beans, and sunflowers. The dog was the only domesticated animal.

Pottery.—Unpainted pottery jars were used for cooking, storage, and other utilitarian purposes. The pottery was made of clay tempered with grit or shell or both and fired to a color ranging from dark bluish gray to a light brown or, in rare instances, a reddish brown. Probably the pottery was manufactured by the anvil-and-paddle method.

The vessel surfaces usually were marked with the impressions of a cord-wrapped paddle, but some surfaces were smoothed after the cord-marking.

The jars had globular or elongated bodies, constricted necks, and straight or slightly flaring rims. Most of the lips were flat with angular edges, but some were flattened with rounded edges. Bases were rounded. Some jars had loop handles or lugs.

The decoration, always confined to the rim, consisted of geometric patterns composed of punctates, notchlike impressions, impressions made with a cord-wrapped stick, and incised lines. The patterns were linear and extremely simple, consisting of rows, bands, areas, and plats.

Tools, utensils, and weapons.—The bow and arrow was the principal weapon used for hunting and warfare. Arrows were tipped with rather small triangular points of chipped stone or sometimes with larger notched points of chipped stone. Socketed antler points and bone points with concave bases also were used on arrows.

Wooden digging-sticks were probably used for planting, and crops were cultivated with mussel-shell hoes attached to wooden handles. Disks of roughly chipped slate may have been agricultural implements.

Fish were caught with several types of bone hooks and probably also in nets weighted with notched sinkers of stone.

Knives used for hunting, war, or household purposes were elliptical or lanceolate in outline and made of chipped stone. Small flake knives were also used.

Shallow mortars, hammerstones, and rough, bell-shaped pestles of stone may have been used for pounding grains or nuts into meal, but wooden mortars and pestles were probably more common. Ungrooved axes made of ground stone or chipped stone, chipped-stone drills, chisels of stone, bone, and antler, and antler gouges were probably wood-working tools.

For the preparation and sewing of animal skins there were circular, ovoid, rectangular, and triangular scrapers of chipped stone, various styles of bone awls, beaming tools made of deer leg bones (drawshave-like tools), and bone needles.

Tools for the chipping of stone were made of bone and antler.

Pipes.—Tobacco pipes consisted of stone bowls with wooden stems. Some bowls were keel-shaped, and others were in the effigy of stylized birds.

Occasional elbow pipes made of clay were of the obtuse-angled variety, and these probably did not require the use of additional stems.

Ornaments.—The Whittlesey people wore necklaces of beads made of stone, bone, shell disks, and copper. Pendants were made of ground stone, animal teeth and claws, bone, and shell. Gorgets were manufactured of polished stone. Bone combs and various other articles made from bone may have served some ornamental purpose.

Musical instruments.—The musical instruments were flutes made of bird bone, musical rasps, and probably drums and rattles.

Burials.—The deceased were buried in cemeteries near the villages, with bodies flexed or extended. There were also bundle burials and ossuaries (deposits of disarticulated bones and skulls). Grave-offerings were rare and, when present, were scanty.

Conjectures.—One of the four Whittlesey villages that have been excavated contained trade material obtained from White men. The nature of this material suggests that the site where it was found must have been occupied in the first half of the seventeenth century. Other Whittlesey villages were occupied perhaps as early as 1400. The occupants of the seventeenth-century Whittlesey village were probably the Erie tribe of the Iroquois peoples.

The earlier villages probably were ancestral Iroquois: the product of a Hopewellian influence on a Woodland culture. Thus the Whittlesey culture may be very important to our understanding of Iroquois cultural origins. Late Iroquois participated in many Southeastern developments that produced a southern veneer of culture that tends to obscure their basically northern heritage.

SOURCES
GREENMAN, 1937b; GRIFFIN, 1944; MORGAN and ELLIS, 1943.

THE MIDDLE MISSISSIPPI CULTURE IN THE OHIO AREA
(LATE PREHISTORIC PERIOD)
Ca. A.D. 1400–1700

In the Ohio River Valley of Ohio, Indiana, and Kentucky there are remains of old villages of the Middle Mississippi culture. The Angel site in Vanderburgh County, Indiana, is an excellent example of a large Middle Mississippi city-state. This site, covering an area of about a hundred acres, consisted of earthen mounds, houses, and a village square or plaza surrounded by a palisade.

The largest of the eleven or more mounds (44 feet high, 335 feet wide, and 644 feet long) consisted of pyramidal terraces, with ramps leading from one terrace to another. Near one corner of the uppermost terrace was a conical projection possibly used as a watchtower. There may have been a temple upon this terrace, and perhaps there were temples or chiefs' houses on the summits of the smaller mounds.

The houses, rectangular in shape, with steeply pitched roofs, were located around the plaza and were constructed of logs, cane, mud, and grass. The walls were made of small, upright logs, comparable to the studding of our wooden houses, and interlaced among the logs were horizontal strips of split cane plastered inside and out with mud mixed with straw. The plaster was smoothed and sometimes painted with designs or covered with woven mats of cane.

To the steeply pitched log rafters were tied smaller poles running at right angles, and to these poles was fastened the thatching of the roof. The house was windowless, with only a small door and probably a smoke hole in the roof.

Like other Middle Mississippi Indians, those living in the Angel village-state made their living by farming. They hunted with bows and arrows. Small triangular arrowheads were made of chipped flint. Shell or chipped flint was used in the manufacture of hoes, and spades were made of chipped flint.

Both painted and unpainted pottery vessels were made by the villagers, the painted pottery (some of it showing techniques of negative painting) being unusually abundant.

Because Middle Mississippi culture in general has been described elsewhere, we shall not go into further details at this point. Suffice it to say that along the valley of the Ohio River there was an extension of a southern pattern of culture, and the villages representative of this pattern must have been one of the most spectacular sights of the North during this period. Probably it was through these outposts of Middle Mississippi culture that Middle Mississippi influences were spread among northern peoples.

SOURCES

BLACK, 1944.

THE FORT ANCIENT CULTURE
(LATE PREHISTORIC PERIOD)
Ca. A.D. 1400–1650

The Fort Ancient Indians were accidently named after a great system of earthworks which they did not build. The big earthen-walled, hilltop inclosure called Fort Ancient was built by Hopewell

Indians, but at the time of its discovery by archeologists, the Fort Ancient Indians were mistakenly associated with the inclosure and thus named for it. Consequently, the reader must bear the burden of remembering that the Fort Ancient Indians had nothing to do with Fort Ancient.

Area.—Southern Ohio, southern Indiana, northern Kentucky, and western West Virginia.

People.—Longheaded Sylvids, shortheaded Centralids, and a mixture of these two types.

Villages.—The villages were situated near streams or rivers and were composed of rows of circular or rectangular wigwams or huts built of poles and probably covered with thatch and clay, animal skins, bark, or mats. Inside or near the dwellings were basin-shaped fireplaces sometimes made of puddled clay. Larger structures similar to the dwellings were probably chiefs' houses or temples.

Livelihood.—The Fort Ancient Indians were farmers who supplemented their vegetal diets with the products of hunting, fishing, and food-collecting. They raised corn, beans, and probably squash and sunflowers, hunted all the animals and birds of the region, and collected nuts, seeds, berries, and other wild fruits. The elk seems to have been particularly important to them.

Pottery.—Unpainted cooking jars were manufactured from clay tempered with grit or crushed shell. The colors of the pottery after firing were tan, gray to black, and brown to reddish brown.

Most of the jars were squat and globular, with rounded bottoms, broad mouths, a slight constriction of the neck or upper shoulder area, and slightly flaring rims. These jars frequently were equipped with strap handles and less frequently with lugs on the rims.

Vessel surfaces were cord-marked or smooth. Many vessels were decorated on the rim or shoulder, the most common decorative techniques being incising and punctating. Characteristic patterns of design were guilloches, either curvilinear or rectangular; rows or areas of punctates; and line-filled angular plats in bands. Vessel lips were sometimes notched in an ornamental fashion.

Some other types of vessels were colanders and thick basins used for evaporating salt from saline water.

Tools, utensils, and weapons.—The fields were planted with the aid of digging-sticks and were cultivated with shell or battered stone hoes, lashed to a wooden handle. Some hoes were made of elk shoulder blades fastened to wooden handles. Flat stone slabs and small, biscuit-shaped manos were used to pound grain into meal; probably there were wooden mortars and pestles also.

The chief hunting weapon was the bow and arrow. Long, narrow, triangular points of chipped flint were most commonly used, although there were also heavier and cruder notched and stemmed points of chipped flint. Other arrow points were made of antler and the toes of deer.

Shaft-straighteners of antler were used, wrenchlike, to straighten wooden arrow-shafts. Stone smoothers (grooved stones) were utilized for sanding the arrow-shafts.

Knives were made of shell, chipped flint, and long flint flakes. Chipped-flint swords were rare.

Fish were caught with bone hooks and gorges, antler or bone harpoons, and nets weighted with notched stone sinkers. Ungrooved axes of chipped flint or ground stone were more commonly used than grooved axes of ground stone. Other wood-working tools were various styles of chipped-stone drills, adzes of ground stone, many kinds of bone awls, various chipped-stone scrapers, and hammerstones. There were also stone plummets.

Awls, scrapers, needles, and bone beaming tools probably were used in the preparation of animal skins.

In addition to pottery, there were wooden bowls and conch-shell containers. Spoons were made of shell or turtle-back. Picks, hoes, and tools used for chipping and flaking stone were made of antler.

Pipes.—Stone or clay was used in the making of pipes. There was a variety of shapes, most common among which were rectanguloid or conoidal pipes with stone bowls and wooden stems, effigy pipes, equal-armed elbow pipes, short-stemmed elbow pipes, pipes with stems projecting beyond the bowl, and platform pipes.

Ornaments.—Ornaments were fashioned from bone, shell, and other materials. Beads were made of shell, pearl, and decorated bone. Circular and crescent-shaped gorgets were made of shell.

Antler combs, shell hairpins or earpins, and bone hair-spreaders adorned Fort Ancient heads. Pendants were made of animal teeth, shells, and bone. There were also ornaments made of cut jaws of animals.

Some objects, such as masklike gorgets of shell, some engraved shell gorgets, and shell gorgets with cross-designs, were paraphernalia of the Southern Death Cult, described in the chapter on the

Middle Southern area. The flint swords and some other objects probably were also part of the cult regalia.

Musical instruments.—Musical instruments used in Fort Ancient "jam sessions" were drums, musical rasps of bone, rattles of turtle shell and turkey skulls, and bone flutes.

Games.—Chunkeystones (discoidals) and circular engraved stones were used in the playing of games.

Burials.—The dead were buried beneath the houses; others were placed in refuse pits, in especially dug graves in the village, in subfloor pits beneath mounds of earth, or within mounds composed of alternate layers of earth and layers of bodies. Some of the graves in mounds or cemeteries were lined with stone slabs. Bodies generally were fully extended in the graves or extended with the knees bent. Many were flexed and some were secondarily buried as bundles of disarticulated bones. A very few were cremated.

Pottery and other grave-offerings were often placed with the burials, presumably for use in the afterworld.

Conjectures.—The presence of trade goods of European origin shows that at least one Fort Ancient village was in existence in the seventeenth century, but the beginnings of the culture must have been much earlier.

Although no historic tribe or group of tribes can be definitely associated with the Fort Ancient culture, the late Fort Ancient Indians probably belonged to some southern Algonkian-speaking group, perhaps the Shawnee.

The Fort Ancient peoples were in contact with the Iroquois, Oneota, and some Middle Mississippi Indians as well as some northern Woodland groups.

SOURCES

GRIFFIN, 1943.

SUMMARY

The development of cultures within the Ohio area was not uniform. Those in the north were oriented toward northern spheres of influence and those in the south were influenced by cultural developments in the south. During the period of Hopewell predominance this area was the most spectacular culture center in eastern North America.

Our story of culture growth in the area begins with the Archaic Indians, who lived by hunting, fishing, and food-collecting. They hunted with the spear and spear-thrower, lived in caves or rude shelters, made no pottery, and did no farming. Perhaps their ancestors were a combined derivative of the Cochise and Folsom cultures of the West, for Folsom-like points and scrapers and Cochise-like grinding-tools are a part of the culture of the earliest Archaic Indians in the area. The latest Archaic Indians had become sedentary by virtue of their food-collecting and the abundance of river clams, which enabled them to live near the mussel shoals of rivers.

Sometime after 500 the Burial Mound I period began. Some of the Indians of this period buried their dead beneath mounds of earth. This period also saw the beginnings of the custom of smoking, of agriculture, and of pottery and the use of copper for ornaments and tools.

The Burial Mound II period was the classic or golden age. It lasted from about 900 to 1300 or 1400. Typified by the Hopewell culture and late Adena, this period of barbaric splendor was the culmination of all that had gone before. Huge burial mounds and great systems of earthworks were constructed. Beautiful and intricate ornaments were made of copper, silver, mica, meteoric iron, and even, in rare instances, of gold. Materials were imported from all parts of eastern North America, from the Rocky Mountains to the Atlantic Ocean, and from the Gulf of Mexico to the Great Lakes. Sculpture reached its greatest heights at this time.

The Late Prehistoric period was a time of intensive agriculture and village life for many groups of the area. Although the Hopewellian influences of the early period were operative within the cultures of the latest period, the center of achievement had shifted to the south. There were, however, northern extensions of this southern culture typified by city-states, great temple mounds, beautiful pottery, some of which was painted, and intensive agriculture.

The general picture is one of progressive cultural development—changes from nomadic to sedentary life and from family bands to tribal confederacies and city-states. With these changes there must have been considerable development in social structures, customs, and religious beliefs.

CHAPTER 19

THE ILLINOIS AREA

INTRODUCTION

THE Illinois area (the state of Illinois) was for the most part a grass-covered prairie except for river valleys and some border areas of southern hardwood forest. The climate was somewhat variable. Winters were cold in the north and merely cool in the south, but summers were hot throughout the area. There were from 150 to 210 frostless days yearly and precipitation of from 30 to 50 inches. All this land was favorable to agriculture, but the southern part enjoyed the mildest climate and the longest growing period.

Game, fish, and migratory birds were plentiful. The rivers were ideal avenues of travel by canoe and connected the Illinois area with most of the other major areas of the region. Then, as now, it was a central focal point of eastern North America.

The Illinois area was a happy stamping-ground for Indians from earliest to latest times. The earliest inhabitants were seminomadic hunters of the Archaic period; the latest were sedentary farmers of the Late Prehistoric period. The periods and some of the cultures of this area are outlined in Chart VII.

THE FAULKNER CULTURE
(Archaic Period)
Probably before A.D. 500

The Faulkner culture of southern Illinois resembles other Archaic cultures found elsewhere in eastern North America. These Indians probably lived in temporary shelters and obtained their food by hunting, fishing, and gathering of seeds and shellfish. They hunted game with the spear and spear-thrower. They tipped their spears with chipped-flint points, some stemmed, others side-notched with concave bases, and still others lanceolate with concave, thinned bases which suggest Folsom types. Shallow mortars or grinding-stones and various types of manos were probably used for grinding acorns and other nuts or wild seeds.

SOURCES

MacNeish, n.d.

THE BAUMER CULTURE
(Archaic and Intermediate Periods)
Ca. a.d. 700–1000

Area.—Southern Illinois and perhaps northern Kentucky and southwestern Indiana.

Villages.—Villages were usually located on natural ridges. Houses were square in ground plan and made of upright saplings. Nothing is known of the roof shape except that interior supports were necessary. Within the boundaries of the village were narrow, deep, cylindrical trash pits and shallow, jar-shaped refuse pits. There were also clay-lined roasting pits filled with burned animal bone and charcoal.

CHART VII

Probable Date	Period	Culture
a.d. 1300–1700	Late Prehistoric	Middle Mississippi, Tampico, Fisher
a.d. 900–1300	Intermediate	Illinois Hopewell, Lewis
a.d. 500–900	Transitional	Baumer, Red Ocher, Morton
? b.c.–a.d. 500	Archaic	Faulkner

Livelihood.—These Indians apparently were essentially hunters, fishers, and food-gatherers; but they may have practiced a rudimentary form of agriculture in their latest stages.

Pottery.—Baumer pottery consisted of jar forms with flat bottoms, flaring sides, and slightly incurved rims. The paste was tempered with clay pellets or granular particles of limestones which often leached out, leaving small pits. Occasionally, pottery was tempered with small, waterworn pebbles or with sand.

While many vessel surfaces bear the impressions of plain plaited fabrics, others are smooth or bear impressions from a cord-wrapped paddle. Decoration, when present, was confined to the rim and achieved by punctating, impressing single cords, or both. Designs were simple plats of parallel lines, cross-hatching, or rows of punctate impressions. Baumer pottery was never painted.

Tools, utensils, and weapons.—There were several types of chipped-flint projectile points: a large triangular form with a contracted stem, a similar form with a square stem, and a form that was ovate or leaf-shaped with a concave base. Some showed an incipient fluting near the bottom.

Other tools of chipped flint were large flake scrapers double-convex or plano-convex in cross-section, and large knives. Ground-stone tools included small, thick, full-grooved axes; pitted lapstones or grinding-stones; and plummets which may have been netsinkers or fishline sinkers.

Ornaments.—The only ornaments known are ground-stone gorgets, generally made of slate and perforated for suspension. One form was basically rectangular with all sides slightly concave (reel-shaped); another was rectangular; and still another was oval in outline. Objects which may have had an ornamental value were lumps of galena, cannel coal, and hematite (red ocher).

Conjectures and comments.—The Baumer culture is one of the earliest in the area and probably persisted for some time. It is related to the other early cultures of the region as well as to later ones.

SOURCES
BENNETT, 1941; COLE, 1943.

THE RED OCHER CULTURE
(INTERMEDIATE PERIOD)
Ca. A.D. 700–1100

Area.—The Red Ocher Indians lived in central Illinois.

People.—These people were roundheaded Centralids.

Livelihood.—Economic activities probably centered upon hunting, fishing, food-gathering, and possibly rudimentary agriculture.

Pottery.—Thick, coarse, unpainted pottery, tempered with large particles of crushed granite rock, was used occasionally. Rim shapes were outslanting or slightly incurved; lips were flattened, with rounded edges. Colors were tan or yellowish-buff, and vessel surfaces showed the impressions of cords, textiles, or basketry.

Tools, utensils, and weapons.—The stone-chipping techniques of the Red Ocher people were rather well developed. Some of their knives were large and leaf-shaped, with straight, convex, or straight-stemmed bases, or had side notches in the pointed base (turkey tail). Other implements were ovate-triangular stemmed and notched arrow or spear points; drills; stemmed scrapers made of old or broken projectile points; ovate scrapers; flake scrapers; and flint cores. Awls manufactured from copper were square in section and probably pointed at each end. Small, rectanguloid, ungrooved axes were made of ground stone. Bone was utilized for awls and other tools of unknown use but does not seem to have been very important.

Ornaments.—These Indians seem to have been fond of ornaments. From copper they made spherical beads, and tubular beads were rolled from thin sheets. They also made crinoid beads of fossil plant stems and shell beads which included spherical shapes cut from *Marginella* and other large shells. Shell gorgets were circular, concavo-convex with a central perforation; sandal-shaped with perforation at one end; and crescentic, with several perforations. At one site there was a copper breastplate, rectangular in shape, with long, slightly concave sides. A spoon-shaped find of shell may well have been an ornament. Faceted lumps of hematite and cuboids of galena were also used as decorative objects.

Burials.—The dead were placed under small, dome-shaped mounds located upon natural ridges, generally in a flexed position. Some were arranged in disarticulated bundles and others were cremated. Hematite (red ocher) was sprinkled in the graves.

Conjectures and comments.—The Red Ocher culture was coeval with Adena in the Ohio area and probably was coeval with late Baumer in Illinois. It is slightly earlier than the Morton culture.

SOURCES

BENNETT, 1944; COLE, 1943; COLE and DEUEL, 1937.

THE MORTON CULTURE
(INTERMEDIATE PERIOD)
Ca. A.D. 800–1000

Area.—Central Illinois.

People.—Medium longheads, with probably both Sylvid and Centralid populations represented.

Villages.—The Morton Indians lived in small, temporary camps or villages, perhaps changing for summer and winter. They constructed burial mounds, possibly in the vicinity of the summer camps or villages.

Livelihood.—Essentially they were hunters, fishers, and food-gatherers; possibly they practiced rudimentary agriculture.

Pottery.—Poorly fired, soft, grit-tempered pottery was made. Vessel surfaces were covered with the impressions of a cord-wrapped paddle. Decoration, when present, was confined to the rim and was achieved by incising, stamping with a bar or crescent-shaped tool, and punctating with a hollow reed or pointed instrument. Rim bands were generally smoothed before applying the decoration of simple, geometric motifs. Jar shapes with rounded or semiconoidal bottoms were the common form.

Tools, utensils, and weapons.—Various types of flint were utilized for scrapers, drills, knives, and for arrow or spear points that were rather crude, large, and ovate-triangular in form. These points were notched or stemmed for hafting to a shaft. Small flake knives were common. Flint-working tools were made of antler, although hammerstones were probably used also. Awls were made from deer long bones, which were split in half and sharpened at one end. It is likely that grooved stones were used for sharpening bone awls or smoothing wooden spear- and arrow-shafts. Food was ground with crude, flat stones.

Ornaments.—The Morton Indians made pendants of pierced bear canine teeth and necklaces of small, spheroidal copper beads.

Burials.—Low, dome-shaped mounds of earth were piled over the bodies of the deceased. The preferential position seems to have been flexed, although some burials consisted of disarticulated bundles and others of isolated skulls. Dogs were buried in the mounds, but there were few, if any, grave-offerings.

Conjectures and comments.—The Morton culture was simple and unpretentious, but it played an extremely important role in the ancestry of Illinois Hopewell Culture. This role was most obviously expressed in the development of Illinois Hopewell pottery. Many other factors, however, must have contributed also to the building of Illinois Hopewell.

SOURCES
BENNETT, 1944; COLE, 1943; COLE and DEUEL, 1937.

THE HOPEWELL CULTURE OF ILLINOIS
(INTERMEDIATE PERIOD)
Ca. A.D. 900–1300

The Illinois Hopewell culture, the most spectacular of this period, seems to have been born of the fusion of Morton-like cultures and Ohio Hopewell.

The Illinois Hopewell Indians obtained their food by farming, hunting, and fishing. They lived in oblong houses of poles and thatch and buried their dead beneath large mounds of earth. They made tools and weapons of bone, stone, and copper and excellent pottery of many styles for cooking and mortuary usage. Beautiful ornaments were manufactured of copper, mica, and other rare materials. Sculpture and other arts were of a high order. Of all the Hopewell cultures, the Illinois variant most closely paralleled the Ohio Hopewell in achievements.

After a period of florescence, Illinois Hopewell culture disappeared, but several of its traditions were carried on by certain of the late Woodland cultures of the same area.

SOURCES
BENNETT, 1945; COLE and DEUEL, 1937; GRIFFIN, 1941; GRIFFIN and MORGAN, 1941.

THE LEWIS CULTURE
(INTERMEDIATE PERIOD)
Ca. A.D. 900–1300

The Lewis culture preceded the Middle Mississippi culture in southern Illinois. These Indians lived in rectangular houses made of log posts covered with thatch and obtained their food by farming, hunting, and fishing. They manufactured thin-walled jars with rounded bottoms from grit- and clay-tempered pottery and covered them with impressions from cord-wrapped paddles. Decorated vessels had notched rims incised with geometric patterns. Elongated, notched, triangular points of chipped stone were used as spearheads and arrowheads.

SOURCES
BENNETT, 1944; COLE, 1943.

THE MIDDLE MISSISSIPPI CULTURE IN ILLINOIS
(LATE PREHISTORIC PERIOD)
Ca. A.D. 1300–1700

The Middle Mississippi culture has been described in the chapter on the Middle Southern area. In southern Illinois there are large sites illustrative of both early and late Middle Mississippi. Famous sites are Kincaid and Cahokia.

The Middle Mississippi people were Centralids (roundheaded Indians) who made their living by farming. They built large palisaded villages, each containing a plaza and a number of large, pyramidal mounds upon which temples and chiefs' houses were built. Shell-tempered pottery of many styles was plentiful. Arrowheads were small, thin, triangular points of chipped stone.

The village-states of the Middle Mississippi Indians marked the most spectacular cultural development of this period.

THE ILLINOIS AREA

SOURCES

BENNETT, 1944; COLE, 1943; COLE and DEUEL, 1937.

THE TAMPICO CULTURE
(LATE PREHISTORIC PERIOD)
Ca. A.D. 1300–1700

The Tampico Indians of central and southern Illinois were of Sylvid type. They lived by hunting, farming, and fishing. Tools, weapons, utensils, and ornaments were made of stone, bone, shell, and probably wood. Grit-tempered, cord-marked pottery was manufactured in the form of small, coconut-shaped jars with squared mouths raised at the corners, and heavy, utilitarian jars. Characteristic of some of these vessels were notched lips, collars, and lugs. Rims and upper-shoulder areas were decorated by punctating and stamping with cords. Designs were both geometric and pictographic. The dead were placed in a flexed position beneath low burial mounds, often in graves lined with stone slabs.

The Tampico culture had its ancestral roots in Illinois Hopewell but was strongly influenced by Middle Mississippi.

SOURCES

BENNETT, 1944; COLE, 1943; COLE and DEUEL, 1937; TITTERINGTON, 1935.

THE FISHER CULTURE
(LATE PREHISTORIC PERIOD)
Ca. A.D. 1300–1700

The Fisher culture of northeastern Illinois was the product of a Centralid population who obtained their food by farming. This culture is much like the Oneota type described in the chapter dealing with the Wisconsin-Minnesota area. Fisher is also related to the Fort Ancient culture of the Ohio area.

SOURCES

COLE, 1943; LANGFORD, 1927.

SUMMARY

The earliest Indians of the area were hunters and fishers with tools, weapons, and utensils made of stone and bone. They did not have pottery, agriculture, or burial mounds.

In the following period the Indians had pottery of various kinds, and some of them built burial mounds. Possibly agriculture was introduced in this period.

The third period was characterized by agriculture, burial mounds, a florescence of art, and the largest burial mounds. There was widespread commerce, and it is probable that there were elaborations of the social organization of certain Indian groups.

The final period saw the introduction and climax of temple-mound-building groups, the appearance of shell-tempered pottery, and the creation of large village-states. Not all groups in the area participated directly in these innovations, but nearly all were strongly influenced regardless of their participation. This period saw the most intensive cultivation of crops in the history of the area before the arrival of White men. The coming of White settlers, of course, doomed the Indians to cultural extinction.

Probably all the groups of Algonquin-speaking Indians found in the area in historic times were descendants of Indians who participated in the cultural achievements of the Late Prehistoric period.

CHAPTER 20

THE WISCONSIN-MINNESOTA AREA

INTRODUCTION

NORTHEASTERN Minnesota and northern Wisconsin are a part of the Laurentian Upland. The remaining portions of the two states form part of the central lowland. In general, the native vegetation zones tend to be in bands which have a northwest-southeast trend. Southern Minnesota is prairie grassland, which merges into a narrow band of southern hardwoods (oak-hickory) running diagonally from northwestern Minnesota to southeastern Wisconsin. The remaining and greater part of the area is covered with northern coniferous forest (spruce-fir, white, Norway, and jack pine) and northeastern hardwoods (birch, beech, maple, and hemlock).

The Wisconsin-Minnesota area has a Continental forest climate, moist with severe winters. The growing season ranges from 90 to 150 days without frost, and the annual precipitation varies from 20 to 40 inches.

The flora and fauna offered abundant opportunity for exploitation by Indian hunters and food-collectors, and agricultural pursuits were possible in most if not all of the area. The myriad lakes, streams, rivers, and swamps provided an extensive system of waterways for travel by swift birch canoes and dugouts. Much of this country was of the type in which Hiawatha (the hero of Longfellow's poem, not the Iroquois statesman) lived.

Outlined in Chart VIII are the periods and some of the cultures of this area.

The Indians may have reached the Wisconsin-Minnesota area in very early times. Some anthropologists and geologists believe that the famous "Minnesota Man"—actually the remains of a young girl—was an ancient occupant of this region who may have drowned in the icy waters of glacial Lake Pelican as much as twenty thousand years ago. There is, however, considerable controversy over Minnesota Man, and the find is not accepted by all anthropologists and geologists. This find is probably not very old.

The Archaic period may have lasted as noted in Chart VIII from 10,000 B.C. to A.D. 700. During this period the Indians hunted, fished, and collected seeds, nuts, and berries. Late in this period a remarkable copper industry was developed by or introduced to some of the Indians of this area. It is also possible that the beginnings of burial mounds and pottery-making appeared in the Archaic period. One might guess that some of the cultures of the period were rather closely related to certain early, Eskimo-like cultures which perhaps were ancestral to such cultures as Dorset or Pacific Eskimo.

The Intermediate period, perhaps from about 700 to 1300, is characterized by pottery, burial mounds, and ornamental or problematical objects of ground stone. There was a shift from the use of copper for utilitarian objects to its use for ornaments and ritualistic

CHART VIII

Probable Date	Period	Culture
A.D. 1300–1700	Late Prehistoric	Mille Lacs, Keshena, Clam River, Aztalan, Oneota
A.D. 700–1300	Intermediate	Effigy Mound, Wisconsin, Hopewell, Laurel
A.D. 100– 700	Late Archaic	Old Copper
10,000 B.C.—A.D. 100	Early Archaic	Browns Valley

objects. Probably agriculture was introduced into suitable parts of the area during this period.

The Late Prehistoric period seems to represent the time of greatest cultural differentiation. There was an invasion of the area by cultural groups distinctively southern, and there may have been movements out of the Wisconsin-Minnesota area into the Plains. In general, the cultures of the latter part of the Late Prehistoric period do not seem to have been as spectacular as those of earlier periods.

In the following pages we shall describe some of the cultures illustrative of the prehistoric periods of the Wisconsin-Minnesota area.

THE BROWNS VALLEY FIND
(ARCHAIC PERIOD)
Sometime between 10,000 B.C. and perhaps A.D. 100

The Browns Valley find in western Minnesota has been dated geologically in terms of its association with a gravel ridge formed as a bar by water which flowed from glacial Lake Agassiz about twelve thousand years ago. Since Browns Valley remains are intrusive in the gravel ridge, the remains must be younger than the ridge; therefore, the Browns Valley find must be less than twelve thousand years old. But how much less so is a question. Dating these cultural remains is exceedingly difficult. It is not at all impossible that the Browns Valley Indians were "alive and kicking" in A.D. 100. But they might have been present in the area several thousand years earlier.

Area.—The Browns Valley Indian (only one has ever been found) lived in western Minnesota.

People.—This Indian was longheaded with a short face. Physically he belongs to one of the early Sylvid types of American Indian.

Livelihood.—These Indians subsisted by hunting, fishing, and food-collecting.

Tools, utensils, and weapons.—Spear points, perhaps used with spears and spear-throwers, were made of chipped flint. These were long-ovate forms with parallel flaking and straight or slightly concave and thinned bases. A similar but asymmetric blade probably was used as a knife. The six examples of chipped flint of the Browns Valley find are related to the various Yuma styles of the West.

The only tools associated with the Browns Valley find were two small abraders of sandstone and a large, flat, unworked stone which might have been a grinding implement.

Burials.—The Browns Valley Indian was buried in a pit lined with red ocher. His position in the grave is unknown.

Conjectures.—Although this find probably is not twelve thousand years old, it may nevertheless have a respectable antiquity. Because it shows relationships with ancient cultures of the West and probably with later Archaic cultures of the East, the flint work of Browns Valley seems typologically important.

SOURCES

JENKS, 1937.

THE OLD COPPER CULTURE
(ARCHAIC PERIOD)
Probably before A.D. 700

Area.—Minnesota, Wisconsin, Upper Michigan and probably northern Illinois, eastern Iowa, and southern Ontario.

Livelihood.—The Old Copper Indians made their living by hunting, fishing, and collecting wild foods. Probably small bands (family units, perhaps) spent their winters hunting over a given range of territory. In summer, however, there may have been gathering of related bands and the establishment of a summer camp. In summer some of these Indians may have operated the old copper mines on Isle Royale and the Keewenaw Peninsula in Upper Michigan.

Tools, utensils, and weapons.—The Old Copper Indians roamed about the Wisconsin-Minnesota countryside armed with the spear and spear-thrower. Spears probably had points of chipped stone or copper, stemmed and notched. Most typical was a point with a concave base and side notches.

Copper spear points or lance points were of several kinds. One style was leaf-shaped with a long, medium, or short rattail tang (Fig. 83, *a*). Another was leaf-shaped or trianguloid with a spatulate tang (Fig. 83, *f*). Still others had sockets (Fig. 83, *d* and *h*) instead of tangs for attachment to wooden shafts.

These sockets were of several kinds: rectanguloid, trianguloid, and ovoid. The ovoid sockets frequently have rivet holes (Fig. 83, *d*), and in rare instances copper rivets have been found in place, thus indicating how these particular socketed points were fastened to the shafts.

Copper knives were plentiful and varied (Fig. 83, *k*). Some were similar to the socketed spear points but, of course, had longer blades. Others had various kinds of flat tangs for attachment to wooden or perhaps bone handles. A style of notched tang (Fig. 83, *i*) is similar to that used by Dorset Eskimo with slate points. Most of the knives had straight blades, but some were curved.

A rather specialized style of copper knife (Fig. 83, *e*) was like an Eskimo ulu, the blade being crescent-shaped and generally the points of the crescent used as tangs for hafting the knife to a wooden handle. This type of knife resembles a modern food-chopper.

Heavy gouges (Fig. 83, *c*), adzes, and axes were made of copper. A style of adz, the so-called "spud," is unique. These spud-adzes (Fig. 83, *j*) were equipped with large sockets so that they could be hafted to an elbow-shaped wooden handle. Some axes were long, narrow, trianguloid forms. These probably were hafted in split or slotted handles of wood. A broader trianguloid style of ax probably was similarly hafted. Copper gouges probably were lashed to a bent handle of wood.

Copper chisels (Fig. 83, *b*), some of them rather large, were somewhat similar to the narrow trianguloid ax except that the butt of the chisel was flat instead of pointed and often showed the marks of

Fig. 83.—Copper weapons and tools of the Old Copper culture: *a*, knives or spear points with "rat-tail" tangs; *b*, chisels; *c*, gouge; *d*, knives or spearheads with sockets and rivet holes; *e*, crescent-shaped knives; *f*, tanged spearheads; *g*, harpoonhead; *h*, socketed knives or spearheads; *i*, spearheads or knives with notched stems; *j*, adzes or spuds; *k*, knives.

hammering. One type of chisel was T-shaped with a considerably expanded butt.

Copper harpoon heads were barbed on both sides and had a wedge-shaped tang (Fig. 83, *g*).

Projectile points which might have been used on spears or harpoons were conical in shape and hollow, the hollow part being used as a socket for hafting to a wooden shaft.

Gorges of copper were probably used for fishing. The gorge, a short copper pin, pointed at each end, was fastened to a line at its middle. A fish swallowing a baited gorge would have his sides pierced and thus be hooked on the gorge.

Double-pointed copper awls were abundant. The largest of these might well have been hafted in bone or wooden handles for use as stilettos.

Pikes were gigantic awl-like forms in copper. One of these, for example, is forty inches long and weighs five pounds. With a sharp point at each end, it could have done considerable damage if used as a weapon.

Copper bannerstones were extremely rare and may have been used as weights for spear-throwers.

Crude scrapers of chipped stone and manos or hand grinding-stones were also used by the Old Copper Indians.

Pipes.—None.

Ornaments.—Beads of copper.

Burials.—The Old Copper Indians buried their dead in large pits. A number of bodies were placed in the pit along with grave-offerings of copper and stone tools and weapons. The bodies were disarticulated and wrapped in bundles for burial.

Conjectures.—It is amazing to find a well-developed copper industry in an Archaic culture. It seems inconceivable that the forms of copper tools and weapons could have been derived only from work in copper. Instead, the copper tools and weapons were probably copies of similar objects made of stone and bone. For instance, the copper knife blades may have been copies of slate knife blades. The tangs of copper knives were like those of slate knives, and the sockets of some copper knives and spears resembled those of certain styles of bone projectile points and knives. Crescent-like knives of copper may have been copies of similar knives of slate, and the copper spud-adzes may have been adaptations of the two-piece adz heads used by some Eskimos. The conical points of copper were like conical points of bone and antler, while the copper harpoon is an exact replica of a style of bone harpoon.

The source of the bone and stone prototypes of the copper tools and weapons is unknown. One might guess, however, that it was an old Dorset Eskimo–like culture which supplied these prototypes.

The Old Copper culture is still something of a mystery. Some tools indicative of the culture have been found among the Archaic remains of New York State. A small part of the Old Copper industry persisted into the period of Effigy Mound culture, and there is some possibility that a burial mound in northern Wisconsin contained evidence of the Old Copper culture. As a sheer guess, one might reconstruct the history of the Old Copper culture as follows: An ancient hunting and food-collecting group of Indians with a material culture somewhat similar to ancient Dorset Eskimo settled in the Wisconsin-Minnesota area. Using float copper as well as copper mined from the surface pits of Upper Michigan, they gradually replaced their tools and weapons of stone and bone with similar ones of copper. Toward the end of their era, they began to build burial mounds. Then the culture either disappeared or changed gradually into the early Effigy Mound culture.

The Old Copper culture seems to have been related to the Black Sand culture of Illinois as well as to the pre-pottery cultures in Illinois.

SOURCES

McKern, 1942; Ritzenthaler, n.d.; West, 1929; Collections and exhibits in the Chicago Natural History Museum and the Milwaukee Public Museum.

THE EFFIGY MOUND CULTURE
(Intermediate Period)
Ca. a.d. 700–1300

Area.—Wisconsin and bordering sections of Illinois, Minnesota, and Iowa.

People.—Sylvids.

Villages.—The former settlements of these Indians are marked by small camp sites, probably indicative of migratory hunting movements within a given range. Both camp sites and burial mounds were located along rivers or streams or by lakes.

Livelihood.—In their later stages these Indians may have been incipient or marginal farmers, but they were more dependent upon hunting, fishing, and food-gathering than they were upon agriculture.

304   INDIANS BEFORE COLUMBUS

Pottery.—The Effigy Mound people made long, jar-shaped pottery vessels with broad mouths, conoidal bottoms, constricted necks, and slightly flaring or in-slanting rims. The vessel surfaces were covered with impressions from cord-wrapped paddles (Fig. 84). Incised decorations consisted of bands of geometric designs confined to the vessel rims. None of the pottery bore painted designs.

Tools, utensils, and weapons.—Tools were made from copper, stone, and bone. Chisel-shaped celts or axes and double-pointed awls were made from copper, while stone tools in use were small celts, grooved

FIG. 84.—Stone axes and cord-marked pottery jar from Wisconsin

axes, grooved and fluted axes, and large, crude, notched points of chipped flint (see Fig. 84).

Tools made of bone or antler were harpoon-points barbed on one side only, beaming tools, and awls.

Pipes.—These Indians indulged in smoking for pleasure or for ceremonial purposes, or perhaps for both. Their pipes were made of fired clay and were elbow-shaped with a straight, tall bowl, sometimes decorated with incised geometric designs.

Ornaments.—Although Effigy Mound people apparently did not care much for ornamentation, some of them wore necklaces of disk shell beads.

Burials.—Burials were placed in subfloor pits beneath mounds or were deposited within mounds at various stages of construction. There were three major styles of mounds. One was a small, dome-shaped mound, another was linear, and the third was built in the outline of animals and birds. In the effigy mounds the burials show a tendency to be distributed at important focal points such as the head or the heart.

The dead were placed in a flexed position or in disarticulated bundles or were sometimes cremated. Few if any tools and ornaments were placed with the dead, although there were stone fire hearths or cists of clay and pebbles near the burials.

Conjectures.—The early Effigy Mound Indians may have built only linear and conical mounds, and those in the form of effigies belonging to a slightly later period of Effigy Mound culture. These people may have been attacked and their culture destroyed by invading enemies from the South.

SOURCES

McKern, 1942; Collections and exhibits in the Milwaukee Public Museum.

THE WISCONSIN HOPEWELL CULTURE
(Intermediate Period)
Ca. a.d. 900–1300

The Wisconsin Hopewell culture was closely related to the Hopewell culture of Ohio but was not so rich and spectacular as the latter. If southern Ohio was the "New York" of Hopewell times, eastern Wisconsin was the "Milwaukee" of this period.

Area.—The Wisconsin Hopewell Indians occupied the western part of the state.

People.—Probably these Indians were longheaded Sylvids.

Villages.—Villages were located near lakes and streams, generally within sight of their impressive burial-mound cemeteries. Presumably the houses or tents were made of saplings and covered with skins, bark, mats, or thatch.

Livelihood.—Subsistence was gained by hunting, fishing, food-collecting, and perhaps some farming.

Pottery.—The local pottery was grit-tempered and unpainted. Jars, the only form produced, were cord-marked or embellished with stamped decorations. The decoration consisted of linear and curvilinear areas, some plain and others stamped in an arrangement of contrasting patterns to form a unified design. This included dentate, rocked-dentate, and plain-rocked stamping. Incising and punctating were used to outline areas involved in the decoration.

An exceptionally fine variety of jars tempered with limestone found in these sites was probably imported from outside Wisconsin. These were usually flat-bottomed and had four bulges in the body of the vessel. Rims were decorated with a band of finely incised cross-hatching above a row of hemiconical punctates. On the body of these vessels smooth areas were outlined by incising that contrasted with other areas of rocked-dentate stamping. Pottery almost identical to this is found in Iowa, Illinois, and Michigan but seems to be rare in Ohio. The source of this fine imported ware is not known.

Tools, utensils, and weapons.—These Indians used bows and arrows and perhaps also spears and spear-throwers. Arrows and spears were tipped with corner-notched points and stemmed points of chipped flint. Large, leaf-shaped and curved knives were frequently made of locally rare materials such as obsidian, brown chalcedony, and jasper, which must have been traded into Wisconsin. The typical flake knife (a long, straight spawl) also was in use. Drills and scrapers were made of chipped stone, and axes and awls of copper.

Pipes.—Platform pipes of stone and concave bases were smoked by these Indians.

Weaving, bags, and textiles.—There have been found textiles of nettle fiber which show the twined and plain-plaited techniques of weaving.

Ornaments.—Like other Hopewell Indians, those in Wisconsin produced many ornamental objects. There were necklaces of pearl, shell, and copper beads and of perforated canine teeth of bear; copper breastplates and ear-spools; copper- and silver-covered

THE WISCONSIN-MINNESOTA AREA

wooden buttons; copper effigies of animal teeth; copper pendants; and gorgets of polished stone.

Musical instruments.—These Indians had what may have been panpipes made of reed tubes held in place by a metal band. Probably they had drums and rattles also.

Burials.—The Wisconsin Hopewells buried their dead with considerable ceremony. In fact, it rather looks as if more attention was paid to the dead than to the living. Probably as a usual thing bodies were placed upon platforms until decomposition had taken place. The bones were then gathered up and placed in bundles or were cremated. In some cases artistic clay masks were built up over bare skulls before cremation so that the fire turned the clay masks into pottery w hch preserved the skull.

Bodies in a flexed position, bundles of bones, and the remains of cremations were placed in mounds, sometimes on the floor in the central portion, often in oblong, subfloor pits. These pits were lined with bark or logs or were surrounded by low clay walls. Many bodies were placed in the same grave. Tools, weapons, utensils, and ornaments were lavished upon the deceased. The mound, of course, was built up over the burials.

Conjectures.—The rather considerable use of exotic materials and objects indicates that the Wisconsin Hopewell Indians had trade connections with distant places and peoples in North America. It is interesting to note that, with the appearance of Hopewell peoples, the copper industry of the area shifted from utilitarian objects to ornamental and ceremonial ones. The heavy copper tools of earlier times disappeared, and copper became a precious metal instead of a material for the production of ordinary tools and weapons. It is probable but unproved that agriculture entered Wisconsin with the Hopewell culture. In any event, the Hopewell period was the classic or golden age of the North.

SOURCES

COOPER, L. R., 1933; MCKERN, 1931, 1942; COLLECTIONS AND EXHIBITS IN THE MILWAUKEE PUBLIC MUSEUM.

THE LAUREL CULTURE
(INTERMEDIATE PERIOD)
Ca. A.D. 1100–1400

Area.—The Laurel culture is found in northern Minnesota.

People.—Probably these Indians were Sylvids.

Villages.—These Indians had summer villages located near lakes or rivers. Probably they lived in wigwams made of saplings covered by skins or mats.

Livelihood.—They hunted, fished, and gathered wild foods. Perhaps they were part-time farmers, too.

Pottery.—These Indians made unpainted, grit-tempered pottery vessels, which were usually small with round bottoms. Some were shaped like flowerpots, others were bucket-shaped, while still others were bowl-shaped. There were also globular jars with constricted necks and broad mouths (some with long, angular shoulders) and neckless jars with constricted mouths.

Most of the pottery was smooth, although some bore cord or fabric markings.

Rims and upper-shoulder areas were decorated with simple geometric designs, usually stamped into the plastic clay of the vessel before firing. These decorations included rock-dentate stamping, wavy lines, triangles or semicircles, and, rarely, a spiraled cord. Other decorations used were rows of punctate impressions, punched bosses, and bands of short, vertical, incised lines.

Certain other styles of pottery were present but were not common. One rare vessel was shaped like a "rocker-curved tube with a mouth at each end."

Tools, utensils, and weapons.—Probably hunting was done with the bow and arrow, although the spear and spear-thrower is a possibility also. Stemmed projectile points were made of chipped flint.

Harpoons, probably used for spearing sturgeon, were tipped with various styles of barbed heads made of antler or bone. A detachable type of harpoon point was made of antler also; it was pointed and had a socket in the base and a line hole drilled through the side.

Instead of fishhooks these Indians used copper gorges—short pins, pointed at each end. Presumably a baited gorge, swallowed by a fish, stuck in its stomach or throat. The fish was then hauled in by a line tied in the middle of the gorge.

Possibly small animal scapulas found were used as hoes. Knives were made of chipped stone or a copper. Stone knives were leaf-shaped, rectangular, diamond-shaped, or elliptical. There were thin blades of copper and a crescent-shaped copper knife with a wooden handle fastened to the concave side of the blade by means of two copper prongs. These knives look like modern food-choppers.

Side- and end-scrapers were made of chipped stone; awls and chisels or punches were made of cut beaver teeth. There were also chisels made of antler and skin-dressers and gouges made of bone. Flattened cylinders of stone possibly were used as grinding tools.

Pipes.—Bell-shaped tubes of schist and greenstone may have served as pipes. Bone pipes were made of moose or caribou foot bones.

Ornaments.—Grooved centers of large conch shells were used as pendants. There were beads of many kinds, some made from the shells of river clams, perforated bear and lynx teeth, and tubular beads of copper. Ornamental tubes or whistles were made of polished sections of the long bones of water birds. Armbands were made of bone.

Burials.—Dome-shaped mounds of earth were erected over the dead. Each mound contained the remains of about a hundred individuals, usually arranged in successive layers. Bodies of the dead were sometimes cremated, but more often they were buried in a flexed position or arranged in bundles. In some burials the long bones were broken and circular sections cut from the back parts of the skulls. Many of the skulls from one mound had the eye orbits plugged with clay. Burial offerings consisted of pottery, clam shells, beaver teeth, red and yellow ocher, and sometimes ornaments.

SOURCES

WILFORD, 1941.

THE MILLE LACS CULTURE
(LATE PREHISTORIC PERIOD)
Ca. A.D. 1400–1700

Area.—These Indians were probably the ancestors of some of the Dakota tribes and perhaps others. They lived in central Minnesota.

People.—Sylvids.

Villages.—Camp sites and villages were situated beside lakes and streams. Probably the Mille Lacs Indians lived in conical or dome-shaped houses made of saplings covered by mats, bark, or skins. It is likely that the villages were not permanent.

Livelihood.—What little evidence is available suggests that the Mille Lacs were hunters, fishers, and food-gatherers. They may have done some farming.

Pottery.—Unpainted, grit-tempered pottery jars were made with round or semiconoidal bottoms, globular bodies, constricted necks and rather broad mouths. Rims were usually straight, and vessel surfaces were either smooth or covered with cord-wrapped paddle impressions. Decoration was usually confined to the outside rim and consisted of simple geometric designs produced by imprints from cord or cord-wrapped sticks, dentate stamping, rocked-dentate stamping, and incised lines. Also in vogue as a decorative element were rows of nodes or bosses on the outside of the rim.

Tools, utensils, and weapons.—Arrowheads were made of chipped flint and were generally triangular, although some were stemmed or notched. The plain triangular heads seem to have superseded the stemmed or notched styles. There were also leaf-shaped or triangular knives, several styles of scrapers, and drills. Possibly spear-throwers were also in use, because stone objects which may have been spear-thrower weights were found. There were a few small bowls of stone.

Copper gorges were probably used for fishing. Awls and fleshing tools were made of bone.

Pipes.—Evidence of smoking is rare; only two pipes have been found. One was a clay elbow pipe, the other a stone-platform type.

Ornaments.—Bone bracelets.

Burial.—Both linear and circular earthen mounds were erected over the dead. Single- and multiple-bundle burials were placed on the floor of the mounds or shallow, subfloor pits. These burials consisted of disarticulated skeletons. Some bodies were buried in a flexed position and some were cremated. Occasionally, low, circular, cairns of rocks were placed on the mound floor, or a small log structure was placed over the burial before it was covered by the mound. Burial offerings of tools were rare, but sometimes animals were buried in the mound.

Conjectures.—The Mille Lacs Indians seem to have been ancestral to some of the historically known Mdewakanton Dakota.

SOURCES

WILFORD, 1941.

THE KESHENA CULTURE
(LATE PREHISTORIC PERIOD)
Ca. A.D. 1500–1700

Area.—The Keshena peoples formerly lived in Wisconsin and Minnesota. Probably the Algonkian-speaking Menominee tribe was a historic remnant of the Keshena culture.

Villages.—Their small camp sites were located near streams and are suggestive of small populations and perhaps considerable shifting-about within a limited area. In historic times they lived in dome-shaped or conical wigwams made of saplings covered with bark and mats.

Livelihood.—These Indians probably obtained their food by hunting, fishing, collecting, and some farming in the summertime.

Pottery.—The unpainted pottery of the Keshena peoples was made of a rather coarse clay tempered with grit. The vessels were in elongated jar shapes with rounded or semiconoidal bottoms, constricted necks, and relatively broad mouths. Rims were in-slanting, straight-vertical, or slightly flaring. Occasionally, the rims had collar-like thickenings. The vessel surfaces were covered with cord-wrapped paddle impressions.

About half the jars were decorated, the decoration being confined to the outer rim and occasionally to the lip. Punctate, cord-wrapped stick, or cord impressions arranged in simple geometric designs were common. Incised lines forming a similar pattern were also used but generally only after the rim had been roughly smoothed.

Tools, utensils, and weapons.—No copper implements have been found, although stone tools were reasonably well made. From various kinds of flint, ovate and trianguloid arrowheads were made with straight stems or side notches. Another variety of point was distinguished by corner notches and horizontal or receding shoulders. Straight and expanded base drills were also manufactured from flints.

Axes were made of ground stone and were either full-grooved or three-quarter-grooved. Almost any suitable field rock served for hammerstones.

Pipes.—Unlike many of the older pipe forms, the pipes of the Keshena peoples required the addition of a wooden stem. All these pipes were made of ground and polished stone and took the forms of micmac pipes, elbow pipes with short, broad, disk-shaped bowls made of catlanite and other stone, and small, conoidal pipes.

Ornaments.—About the only ornament attributed to the Keshena peoples is an elliptical gorget made of polished stone. This generally had two perforations countersunk from both sides.

Burials.—The dead were buried in shallow, round, or oval pits in groups or cemeteries. Very few if any offerings were placed with the dead. There were three kinds of interments: bundle burials, flexed burials, and cremations.

Conjectures.—The early Menominee and perhaps some Chippewa seen by White explorers of the eighteenth century probably were representative of the last stages of Keshena culture.

SOURCES

McKern, 1942; Collections and exhibits in the Milwaukee Public Museum.

THE CLAM RIVER CULTURE
(Late Prehistoric Period)
Ca. a.d. 1500–1700

Area.—The Clam River Indians lived in northwestern Wisconsin and southern Minnesota. They probably were the ancestors of some of the Santee Dakota Indians seen by White explorers of early times.

Villages.—These Indians probably lived in dome-shaped and conical wigwams of poles covered with skins or mats. They may have had summer villages in which they gathered to farm and to dispose ceremonially of their dead.

Livelihood.—The Clam River Indians made their living by hunting, fishing, collecting wild foods, and probably some farming.

Pottery.—Their pottery was unpainted and grit-tempered. The vessels were jar-shaped with elongated bodies, semiconoidal bottoms, straight or flaring rims, and constricted necks. Vessel surfaces were covered with cord-wrapped tool malleations. Decoration was confined to the outer rim, the inside rim, and the lip and consisted of simple geometric patterns impressed with cord-wrapped sticks.

Tools, utensils, and weapons.—From quartz the Clam River people chipped asymetrical triangular projectile points with concave bases. The only other implements of stone found were retouched flake scrapers, usually triangular in outline.

Large, circular birchbark containers with sewn seams were found in one burial mound used as receptacles for some of the bundle burials. Fragments of simple twined cloth testify to the knowledge of weaving by the Clam River people.

Pipes.—The Clam River Indians smoked right-angle elbow pipes with flared bowls. These were made of pottery, and some were decorated with cords or cord-wrapped sticks to produce simple geometric patterns.

Burials.—When a Clam River Indian died, his body was placed upon a scaffold. After decomposition and disintegration had taken place, the bones were gathered and wrapped in a bundle of skins or placed in birchbark containers. A group of such bundles was then covered with a mound of earth. In some instances an area of the mound or the mound floor was covered with a mosaic of red ocher, yellow ocher, and sand before the bundle burials were deposited. Later, other groups of bundles containing bones were placed upon the top of the old mound and earth was piled upon them. Thus each mound was composed of successive layers of burials and earth coverings and served as community cemeteries. One such mound was twelve feet high and ninety feet in diameter.

A singular feature was the perforating of human long bones by punching with a sharp instrument. This treatment of the long bones is similar to the drilled perforations found in the long bones at some of the sites left by the Younge Indians. Probably these holes were used for rearticulating the skeleton for some ceremonial purpose.

Conjectures.—The discovery by archeologists of a horse skull and a log fragment that showed the marks of an iron ax, both in an undisturbed part of a mound of the Clam River type, shows that these Indians had continued their mound-building activities into the seventeenth century, during which century the Clam River Indians (probably a division of the Santee Dakota) were driven westward by the Chippewa.

SOURCES

MCKERN, 1942.

THE AZTALAN CULTURE
(LATE PREHISTORIC PERIOD)
Ca. A.D. 1300–1650

When the cultures of the great Middle Mississippi Confederacy were expanding and bringing joy and cultural refinement to the barbarians of the wilderness, one group of Middle Mississippi Indians, the Aztalan, fought their way into south-central Wisconsin. Probably the Aztalan Indians came from the vicinity of the gigantic Cahokia mounds near East St. Louis, Illinois.

Area.—A fortified village was established on the Crawfish River in present Jefferson County, Wisconsin.

People.—Roundheaded Centralid type or a mixture of Centralid and longheaded Sylvids.

Villages.—The Aztalan Indians lived in a large village well protected by a palisade of upright logs covered with clay and grass. At frequent intervals along the stockade there were square towers. Within the palisade there were large, flat-topped pyramidal mounds of earth upon which wooden temples or chiefs' houses were built. These pyramids were arranged around a central plaza.

Houses were made of poles and covered with clay and grass. They were either square or round and possibly had dome-shaped or conical roofs. Refuse pits and fireplaces were scattered abundantly throughout the village.

Livelihood.—Squash and probably corn were grown. Fish and available animals and game birds were eaten. There is evidence that the diet of the Aztalan Indians included human flesh. Human bones, many cracked for the marrow, were found in refuse pits along with animal bones similarly cracked and split. It is not known if these Indians had a dietary preference for any particular group, but it seems reasonable to assume that they would have been unpopular with all surrounding tribes.

Pottery.—Aztalan pottery generally was shell-tempered, hard, compact, and smooth. It was probably made by the coiling method and the joints of the coils or rings obliterated and smoothed with pottery anvils. Natural firing colors ranged from light buff to dark gray and black, the latter possibly being the result of a dye. Slips were common and were red or orange.

In addition to the colored slips, there were several methods of decorating pottery. Bowls with incurving rims were painted a solid red or bore a simple geometric design composed of red-and-white painted areas. Painting was relatively rare, but incising was common.

Incised motifs used were spirals, concentric circles, line-filled triangles, and line-filled geometric plats. Usually one of these motifs was repeated in a band around the upper shoulder of the vessel.

The most common style of pottery was a round-bottomed, globular jar with angular shoulders. Less common styles were plates; various styles of bowls; bottles; cups; straight-sided, beaker-like jars with flat bottoms; globular jars with rounded shoulders and loop handles; and many effigy forms of animals, gourds, and seashells.

Most of the shell-tempered pottery was plain and undecorated. It is probable that the decorated ware mostly served some ceremonial or aesthetic purpose, whereas the plain ware was for utilitarian purposes such as cooking and storage.

Another major ware of the Aztalan Indians which was perhaps used for cooking was grit-tempered pottery with cord-impressed surfaces and decoration around the rim. Angular-mouthed jars of this ware seem to have occurred only at Aztalan. The presence of this pottery along with the shell-tempered ware indicates that both were made at the same time and also strongly suggests a northern influence at work on the southern settlers of Aztalan.

Tools, utensils, and weapons.—These Indians tilled their fields with hoes made of clam shells or of chipped flint which were fastened to wooden handles. They hunted with bow and arrow, the arrows being tipped with small, thin, triangular points of chipped flint with side notches or base bones to aid in lashing to the shaft. Other projectile and arrow points were made of antler and carved bone.

Knives were made of chipped stone. Polished perforators (needles without eyes), various kinds of awls, stone-chippers, and fiber-shredders were made of bone. Flat stone mortars and antler pestles were used for grinding or pounding foods. Ungrooved axes (celts) and grooved mauls were of ground stone. Tools possibly used for sharpening bone implements were made of sandstone.

Pipes.—Rather large, biconical, elbow pipes were smoked.

Ornaments.—Copper was never used for tools by these Indians but was wrought into fine ornaments. These were gorgets, beads, and ornaments of copper sheeting on wood or stone, such as stone ear-spools covered with copper. Other ear-spools were made of pottery and some were incised. Beads made from Gulf Coast conch shells were very popular, as were pendants of marine shell.

Burials.—Presumably the Aztalan Indians had a cemetery at a distance from their village, but it has not yet been discovered. The only burial found at Aztalan and definitely attributed to the Middle Mississippi occupancy was that of a young female. Her skeleton lay in an extended position and may have been wrapped in cloth, possibly fastened in place with the three belts of discoidal shell beads that were dug up with her. The body had been placed in a pit covered with a low, dome-shaped mound of earth.

Conjectures.—The Aztalan culture is representative of the Temple Mound period of southern areas and represents a northward extension of a southern culture. It seems doubtful that the Aztalan Indians entered Wisconsin without warfare. They do not seem to have occupied their hard-won territory for any great length of time, and their village was finally burned to the ground never to be rebuilt.

SOURCES

BARRETT, 1933; MCKERN, 1942.

THE ONEOTA CULTURE
(LATE PREHISTORIC PERIOD)
Ca. A.D. 1400–1700

Area.—Northern Illinois, Wisconsin, eastern Minnesota, Iowa, Nebraska and Kansas, and southwestern Missouri.

People.—There were variations in the physical types of Oneota Indians. Some had long heads, rather high vaults, and narrow faces.

Others had shorter, rounder heads and broader faces. Sylvids, Centralids, and Prairids were represented.

Villages.—Villages were usually situated along rivers or streams on level terraces or flat bluffs. Sometimes these Indians occupied rock shelters. They lived in earth lodges in eastern Nebraska and northeastern Kansas. Probably perishable shelters of poles and bark were used in the eastern part of the area. Many cache and refuse pits and sometimes low refuse heaps marked village sites.

Livelihood.—Farming, hunting, some fishing, and probably the gathering of wild foods were important means of livelihood. Corn, beans, squash, and other crops were raised.

Pottery.—Probably unpainted pottery tempered with crushed shell was used for cooking. When fired, it was usually dark gray. Small, globular jars were the usual form, and these had round bottoms, straight or flaring rims, and two or four loop handles in an angle between rim and body. A simple, geometric decoration was usually placed on the upper part of the jar. Incised or trailed and punctate designs composed of rectilinear elements were common. Undecorated surfaces were smooth. Lips were commonly notched, finger-impressed, or otherwise modified.

Tools, utensils, and weapons.—Hoes were made of animal shoulder blades hafted to wooden handles. Probably wooden digging-sticks were used for planting corn. Bun-shaped muller and anvil stones, or perhaps wooden mortars and pestles, were used for grinding corn.

The bow and arrow was the principal weapon. Arrows were tipped with socketed points of antler or small, triangular points of chipped flint. Paired sandstone shaft-smoothers were used for making arrow- or spear-shafts. Antler or bone wrenches were used for straightening arrow-shafts.

Animal skins were worked with small to medium end-scrapers and various knives of chipped flint. Bone awls, bodkins, and eyed needles were used for sewing skins. Probably the Oneota Indians of the eastern part of the area used bone beaming tools for working skins. Large flat needles of bone were most likely used for weaving mats.

Bone fishhooks were used in the eastern and southern parts of the area, and bone gorges (short bone pins) may have been used for fishing also.

It is possible that stone celts, flint drills, and abraders made from pumice fragments were used for working wood. Tapping tools and flakers for shaping flint were made of antler. Spoons made of shell were common.

Pipes.—Pipes were made of polished stone, sometimes of catlinite. Equal-arm, elbow pipes with a long wooden stem were probably used. Platform pipes with disk-shaped bowls were common, but effigy pipes were rare. Small, conoidal pipes, probably with wooden stems, were used frequently.

Ornaments.—Beads were made of shell, bone tubes, and copper. Pendants of copper or shell and bracelets of copper were also worn.

Burials.—The dead were buried in cemeteries or beneath low, dome-shaped mounds, usually in an extended position. Sometimes they were accompanied by grave-offerings of tools, utensils, weapons, ornaments, and the like.

Conjectures.—The presence of European trade material in some Oneota sites indicates a late period for this culture. Early Oneota seems to antedate White contact in certain areas. The Oneota Indians have been identified with the Winnebago in Wisconsin, the Ioway and Oto in Iowa, the Oto in Nebraska, and the Missouris in Missouri. Perhaps the Omah, Ponca, Osage, Kansa, and others should be included as Oneota tribes.

The culture of the Oneota Indians has southern as well as northern affinities. Probably it represents a blending of southern and northern cultures which produced a new hybrid related to both yet distinguishable from either.

SOURCES

McKern, 1942; Mott, 1938; Wedel, 1940.

SUMMARY

The first settlers of this area arrived several thousand years ago after the retreat of the big glaciers. These Indians were hunters, fishers, and food-gatherers. A remarkable feature of the latter part of the Archaic period was the development of the copper industry. Possible cultural contacts of this period seem to have been largely to the northwestward or eastward.

The Intermediate period (A.D. 700–1300?) was a time of transition. Burial mounds, pipe-smoking, pottery-making, and possibly agriculture appeared. There were cultural contacts southward, perhaps especially with Ohio at the time of the Hopewell culture.

The Late Prehistoric period (A.D. 1300–1700?) was a time of great cultural differentiation and invasion from the south. Probably there were closer contacts with Indians of the Plains than heretofore. Intensive agriculture was important in some parts of the area. In general, a degeneration of material culture seems to have been characteristic of the latter part of this period.

CHAPTER 21

THE PLAINS AREA

INTRODUCTION

THE Plains area was the great interior grassland reaching eastward from the Rocky Mountains to the forested areas bordering the Mississippi, and northward from upper Texas into Canada. All this vast region was grassland except for the southern hardwood forests in the river valleys (oak and hickory) or scattered islands of western pine (yellow pine, sugar pine, and Douglas fir). In the western part of the area there was short grass (Plains grassland) and in the eastern part there was tall grass (Prairie grassland).

The climate of most of the area was characterized by hot summers and cold winters, but in the southern part the winters were mild, and in the extreme northern portion the summers were cool. The annual frostless season varied from less than 120 to 210 days. Over most of the area the precipitation ranged from 10 to 30 inches.

Except in the fertile river valleys, the Plains area was not suited for agriculture, but the treeless grasslands supported enormous herds of bison, or American buffalo. Other animals were present, too, but none was so important to the Indians as the buffalo.

The periods and some of the cultures of the Plains area are outlined in Chart IX.

The first Indians of the Plains were Folsom hunters (see chap. 10). A possible Folsom descendant was the Old Signal Butte culture of the Archaic period. Like other hunters of the Archaic period (probably before A.D. 500), those of the Plains used the spear and spearthrower, had no pottery, and lived by means of hunting, fishing, and food-collecting rather than agriculture. Populations of this period probably were small and settlements sparse.

In the Intermediate period, perhaps from A.D. 500 to 1300, groups of Indians from the east penetrated into the Plains area along the river valleys. These Indians had pottery, and some of them, at least, had agriculture. Sometime during this period there existed a Hopewell-like group of Indians in the Plains.

The Late Prehistoric period, probably from about 1300 or before to 1600, is characterized by a somewhat intensive settlement by rather sedentary agricultural groups of Indians. These Indians lived in fairly large villages, farmed, hunted with the bow and arrow, and made pottery.

The Early Historic period (1600–1800) in the Plains lasted longer than in most other areas because settlement by White men lagged considerably. Some Indians of the Early Historic period continued to live much as they had in the Late Prehistoric period; some Indians, because of the arrival of the horse, developed a new way of life.

The White man's horse reached the Plains long before the White settlers. The use of the horse enabled some of the Indians to become

CHART IX

Probable Date	Period	Culture
A.D. 1600–1800	Early Historic	Dismal River
A.D. 1300–1600	Late Prehistoric	Upper Republican, Nebraska
A.D. 500–1300	Intermediate	Sterns Creek, Mira Creek, Kansas Hopewell
? B.C.—A.D. 500	Archaic	Old Signal Butte

nomadic hunters of the bison. Some groups of Indians, however, remained in the river valleys and continued their agricultural pursuits, whereas others divided their time between hunting and farming. During this period displaced peoples from the east entered the Plains and became a part of the "horse culture." Although the nomadic hunting economy of the Plains, observed by White settlers, was historically recent, its roots were probably deep in Plains culture. The hunting tradition was ancient and never was completely discarded, even by the farmers.

THE OLD SIGNAL BUTTE CULTURE
(Archaic Period)
Probably before A.D. 500

Area.—The Old Signal Butte culture has been found at only one site—in western Nebraska. Undoubtedly other sites exist, but they have not yet been located.

Villages.—The villages were located on a windswept plateau elevated above the surrounding flat country. Judged by our standards, this would be an inhospitable place, but for the Indians it may have provided protection against enemies and afforded opportunities to sight distant herds of deer or bison.

The village was marked by many small pot-shaped storage pits, some of which were lined with rock slabs. Also numerous were shallow, round firepits, occasionally lined with small stone slabs.

The dwellings were probably only skin tents, for no evidence of more substantial shelters has been found. Occupancy of the village may have been seasonal. Certainly winters on Signal Butte would have been very rigorous.

Livelihood.—The Old Signal Butte Indians were hunters and food-gatherers. They hunted deer, bison, birds, and other animals, and gathered shellfish and perhaps nuts and wild plants. Agriculture was not practiced. Probably the search for food necessitated a nomadic life.

Pottery.—None.

Tools, utensils, and weapons.—Spearheads were made of flint by means of flaking and chipping. One common type was leaf-shaped with a concave base, often thinned by the removal of flakes from each face. Other popular forms were leaf-shaped with straight or rounded bases. Larger blades, identical in style to the points we have described, were probably knives. It is interesting to note that leaf-shaped points and knives in the Mississippi Valley are associated with the Burial Mound I stage rather than with the Archaic.

Other spear points were stemmed and either long and narrow or short and broad. A few very short points had side notches and concave bases. Probably the spears were thrown with the aid of a wooden spear-thrower.

In addition to the leaf-shaped knives, there was a stemmed variant. There were plano-convex and stemmed end-scrapers, large ovoid and small plano-convex side-scrapers, chipped-flint axes, retouched flake knives, several types of flint drills or awls, and gravers.

Many of these tools could have been used for a variety of purposes—wood-working, preparing skins, and the like. Masses of flint cores and flakes show that the tools were made in the village.

Ground-stone implements consisted of grooved mauls, used for pounding; small grinding-stones and pestle-like objects, used perhaps in food preparation; long, grooved shaft-polishers; rough stone hammers; and a crude, slightly notched or grooved ax made of battered quartzite.

Animal bone (including antler) was utilized for the manufacture of awls, flaking tools, and gouges or scrapers.

Pipes.—None.

Ornaments.—Like many other groups of early hunters, the Old Signal Butte Indians had few ornaments. There was one small shell pendant, notched at the top for suspension. Fragments of bone upon which were incised simple geometric designs may have served a decorative purpose. Tubular beads were manufactured from sections of bird bones.

Both red and yellow mineral paints derived from ochers may have been used to paint on clothing and other objects made of animal skins.

Conjectures and comments.—This culture was followed by later occupancies of the same site and probably the same area. The Old Signal Butte culture seems to show some relationships with archaic cultures in eastern areas as well as with older cultures in the Plains.

Interpretations of the geological evidence provided by the structure of the butte have led a number of geologists and archeologists to suggest that the Old Signal Butte culture is from eight to ten thousand years old. This evidence, however, is only circumstantial. Typological considerations suggest that the culture is much more recent.

SOURCES

STRONG, 1935; WEDEL, 1940a.

THE STERNS CREEK CULTURE
(INTERMEDIATE PERIOD)

Ca. A.D. 500–1300

Area.—Eastern Nebraska.

Villages.—Villages have been found from 2 to 27 feet beneath the present land surface. Probably the remains have been buried by deep alluvial deposits. The Sterns Creek Indians lived a sedentary life, dwelling in villages along streams. They constructed some kind of shelter made of sapling poles set upright and covered with reed thatching. Fireplaces and storage pits were other evidences of their village life.

Livelihood.—Squash and gourds were grown, but not corn or beans, and this diet was supplemented with wild game.

Pottery.—The pottery consisted of unpainted, grit-tempered jars with globular or elongated globular bodies, round or semiconoidal bottoms, constricted necks, and rather small mouths. The rims were slightly flaring, and vessel surfaces were coarsely smoothed or modified by brushing or dragging a straw-wrapped paddle across the plastic clay. The colors were buff or gray.

Decoration, when present, was confined to the upper part of the vessel and consisted of thumbnail and cord impressions arranged in a simple geometric design. The most characteristic design was a narrow rim band of thumbnail impressions arranged in vertical or diagonal rows.

Tools, utensils, and weapons.—From flint the Sterns Creek Indians chipped thick, ovate-triangular projectile points with side notches. From ground stone they manufactured grinding-stones, trianguloid celts, and hammerstones. From bone they made straight needles, curved needles notched along the sides, scrapers made of bison shoulder blades, awls made of leg bones, and antler fleshers and picks.

Pipes.—Fragments of tubular or conical clay pipes have been found.

Ornaments.—The only ornamental objects found in the village were beads made of bird bones.

Conjectures and comments.—The Sterns Creek cultural remains are deeply buried in some parts of the site and shallowly placed in others. This situation aptly illustrates the danger of attempting to assess the antiquity of a site in terms of the amount of natural deposition on top of it. Especially is this true in the Plains area, where wind-blown and alluvial soils accumulate very rapidly. Although the shallow portions of the Sterns Creek village are just as ancient as the deep parts, an archeologist digging only into the deep portion would probably ascribe considerable antiquity to this village.

SOURCES

STRONG, 1935, WEDEL, 1940a.

THE MIRA CREEK CULTURE
(INTERMEDIATE PERIOD)
Ca. A.D. 500–1000

Area.—Surface collections and investigations by amateur archeologists suggest that the Mira Creek culture has a broad distribution in central and west-central Nebraska. Only one site has been excavated.

Villages.—Villages were permanent and were located along streams or rivers. The houses were simple, semisubterranean types, with central fireplaces, and were probably covered by skins or mats supported by light poles.

Livelihood.—Subsistence was gained by hunting, food-gathering, and possibly some agriculture.

Pottery.—Simple, unpainted jars were made having elongated bodies, conoidal bottoms, and direct rims with flat or rounded lips. Some vessels showed an incipient constriction of the upper shoulder and straight vertical rims. Direct rims were either straight or slightly incurved.

Gray or buff pottery was made from a clay paste tempered with sand, grit, or limestone particles. Vessel surfaces were malleated with a cord-wrapped paddle. On decorated vessels the design was applied to the rim and upper shoulder area and sometimes to the inner rim. Decorative techniques employed were cord or cord-wrapped tool stamping, perforating, punctating, and punching from the inside of the vessel to produce external nodes. These techniques were variously combined to produce simple patterns consisting of horizontal rows of punctates, perforations, or nodes, and horizontal, encircling cord impressions.

Tools, utensils, and weapons.—Stone tools were small stemmed, chipped projectile points, simple drills, ovoid end-scrapers, crude ovate knives, and abraders. Bone implements were phalanges with depressed areas that possibly were sockets for bow drills, several types of awls, beaming tools made of split shoulder blades of bison, and serrated fleshers and gouges.

Pipes.—Pipes were not found in the one site excavated, but pipes from surface finds and amateur excavations suggest that clay tubular pipes are representative of this culture.

Ornaments.—The only ornaments found were pendants made of deer crania, mussel-shell pendants, and bone beads.

Burials.—The only known burial was in the village area, probably in a pit. The body was semiflexed and without grave-offerings.

Conjectures and comments.—The Mira Creek culture is a western relative of many Middle Woodland cultures of the northern areas in the eastern United States and Canada. The Mira Creek Indians may have moved into the Plains from the east.

SOURCES

HILL and KIVETT, 1941; WEDEL, 1940a.

THE KANSAS HOPEWELL CULTURE
(Intermediate Period)
Ca. a.d. 900–1300

Area.—Northeastern Kansas, northwestern Missouri, and southeastern Nebraska.

People.—Probably longheaded Sylvids. The heads of infants were possibly artificially deformed by binding them to cradle-boards.

Villages.—These Indians lived in small villages along the river valleys of the Kansas and the Missouri.

Livelihood.—Corn and beans were grown, and this diet was supplemented by hunting and food-gathering. The dog was the only domesticated animal.

Pottery.—Unpainted grit-tempered jars and bowls were the principal types. One style consisted of thick-walled jars with conoidal bases and cord-roughened exteriors. Frequently a row of punched bosses or nodes encircled the upper rim. Another style consisted of thin-walled jars and bowls with rounded bottoms. Some of the jars had four body lobes or bulges. Other typical Hopewell characteristics were the cambered rims, the flat lips, and the ornamentation of these vessels.

Vessel surfaces, usually smoothed, were decorated by dentate stamping, rouletting (or rocker stamping), both plain and notched, stamping with a cord-wrapped stick, incising, and punctating. Rims were decorated with a band of incised cross-hatching or rouletting above a row of hemiconical punctates. Bodies of jars with rims thus ornamented were decorated with zones, areas, or bands of stamping that contrasted in some instances with similar smooth areas. Some vessel exteriors were completely covered by stamped or rouletted decoration alternating with various negative designs in which a pattern of the smooth vessel surface was completely surrounded by stamping.

Some, if not all, of the decorative pottery was used ceremonially, whereas the thick, cord-marked ware was used for cooking and other utilitarian purposes.

Miniature jars and ladles of pottery may have been the toys of children.

Tools, utensils, and weapons.—Spears and arrows were provided with points of conical antler tips, with bone, or with ovate-triangular or chipped-flint points with stems or notches.

Wooden digging-sticks and stone-bladed hoes were probably used in farming. Knives, drills, and a variety of scrapers were made of chipped flint. There were copper adzes and grooved and ungrooved axes of polished stone. Bone awls, needles, and beamers were probably used in dressing animal skins and preparing garments.

Flaking tools were made of antler, and there were strainer-like utensils made of horn.

Ornaments.—Small models of birds made of pottery or bone probably were ornaments. Bone effigies of bear canine teeth were probably pendants. Polished stone gorgets and possibly shell pendants were worn on cords or thongs. The mysterious cone-shaped or mamiform objects of polished stone found generally among Hopewellian peoples were probably ornaments. Fragments of copper likewise may be added to the inventory of decorative objects.

Games.—Disk-shaped flints, balls of stone, and perforated toe bones of deer were probably used in games.

Conjecture.—The Kansas Hopewell Indians presumably were migrants from the east. Why they moved into the Plains is a mystery. These Indians antedate the development of the widespread, intensive Plains cultures such as Upper Republican and Nebraska.

SOURCES

WEDEL, 1938, 1940a, 1943.

THE UPPER REPUBLICAN CULTURE
(LATE PREHISTORIC PERIOD)
Ca. A.D. 1300–1600

Area.—The Great Plains, principally Nebraska and Kansas.

People.—These Indians were probably a mixture of Sylvids and Pacifids and were roundheaded or medium longheaded. The former had relatively high vaults, while the latter were low-vaulted. Both variants had rather large, flat faces.

Villages.—Villages were composed of earthen lodges, generally rectanguloid but sometimes circular in outline, partly underground, and covered by a dome-shaped or semiconical roof of poles, brush, and earth supported by center posts. At the apex of the roof there was a smoke hole; fires were usually placed in a central pit. Entrance to the dwelling was sometimes through a tunnel-like passage.

Within the villages there were underground bell-shaped storage and refuse pits. Near by, in the bottom lands, there were gardens.

On occasion, perhaps during hunting trips, these Indians lived in rock shelters or probably in skin tents.

Livelihood.—Farming was the chief source of subsistence, but the diet of corn, squash, and beans was supplemented by hunting, fishing, and food-gathering. The gardens outside the village were tilled with hoes and digging-sticks. The only domesticated animal was the dog.

Pottery.—Pottery for cooking purposes was made of clay tempered with grit and was unpainted, the buff or gray color being merely the result of firing. These large full-bodied pots had rounded bottoms, constricted necks, and thickened or collared rims. Handles or lugs were occasionally appended to the rims.

Impressions made by a cord-wrapped paddle covered the vessel exteriors generally, but some pots had smoothed surfaces. Incised geometric patterns usually were confined to the thickened or collared rims but also occurred on the neck and lips of these pots. In some cases similar designs were made by impressing cords into the rim while it was still plastic. Sometimes ornamental notches were made along the lip. Another decorative treatment occasionally applied to the bottom of the collar consisted of a row of pinched ridges.

Basketry.—Fragments of coiled basketry have been found at the Ludlow cave in northwestern South Dakota.

Tools, utensils, and weapons.—Agricultural implements were the wooden digging-stick and a hoe made from a bison shoulder blade hafted to a wooden handle. Probably corn was pounded into meal with a wooden pestle and mortar, for stone grinding tools have not been found.

The principal hunting weapon was the wooden bow and the flint-tipped arrow. Chipped-flint arrowheads were triangular in outline, one style being rather large and rough, another style small, delicately chipped, and with side notches. Also made of flint were ovate, triangular, and diamond-shaped knives. Some of the knives had beveled blades.

Fish were caught with bone fishhooks.

Skin-working tools, in addition to the flint knives already described, were small plano-convex end-scrapers and small ovoid side-scrapers of stone; and beamers, awls, bodkins, and needles of bone.

Other tools were antler flakers, punches, perforated arrow-shaft straighteners made of antler or of bison ribs, sandstone arrow-shaft polishers, chipped celts or axes, polished stone celts, and small hammerstones of several shapes.

Pipes.—Pipes, generally of stone but sometimes made of fired clay, were of the elbow type and either equal-armed or with the stem projecting beyond the bowl.

Ornaments.—Red and yellow paints were probably used for adornment. Necklaces were composed of bone or tubular shell beads, and small clawlike pendants of shell were perforated for suspension. There were also bone pendants and gorgets made of bone. Wooden ear ornaments covered with sheet copper may have been obtained from one of the Middle Mississippi cultures, most of which were in the Southeast. Bracelets were manufactured from bone and antler and sometimes bore incised decorations. One bracelet in particular had incised upon it the eye-in-hand design, a symbol of the Southern Death Cult.

Games.—With suitable equipment made of bone these Indians played the cup-and-pin game and a kind of dice.

Burials.—The Upper Republicans practiced secondary burial. The deceased were exposed for some time, perhaps on platforms; then the remains were gathered and buried. Usually a number of individuals were interred in a broad, shallow pit on a hilltop. Some bodies were buried in slab-lined graves. In the graves with the deceased were implements and ornaments, some of which were broken.

Conjectures.—The Upper Republican Indians had trade relations with other groups in different areas. Obsidian was obtained from the Yellowstone Park region and marine conch shells from the Gulf of Mexico.

Judging from the design on an antler bracelet, a symbol of the Southern Death Cult, and the copper-covered wooden ear-spools, there was contact of some kind between the late Upper Republican culture and one of the numerous Middle Mississippi groups that were contemporary. Not to be overlooked is the possibility of contact with some of the southwestern Indians.

The later Upper Republican Indians probably were contemporaries of the Nebraska Indians.

SOURCES

BELL, 1936; STRONG, 1935; WEDEL, 1940a.

THE NEBRASKA CULTURE
(LATE PREHISTORIC PERIOD)
Ca. A.D. 1400–1650

Area.—Along the bluffs of the Missouri River in eastern Nebraska and northeastern Kansas.

People.—Probably short-statured and roundheaded Prairids.

Villages.—The villages were usually single lines of large, partly underground houses strung out along narrow, winding ridges by the river. These houses were generally rectangular pits covered by a roof of poles and earth supported from the interior by large central posts. Entrance to some of the houses was gained through covered passageways; others were entered, by means of a ladder, through a roof opening. Some houses were as large as forty feet long and thirty feet wide, but most of them were smaller. Inside the houses were cylindrical and pot-shaped storage pits and fireplaces. Probably each house was occupied by several families.

Livelihood.—The Nebraska Indians were farmers who raised corn and beans and probably other crops. It is likely that they also gathered wild plants. Their vegetal diet was supplemented by fish and clams from the rivers and the meat of deer, bison, and other animals.

Pottery.—Pots, bowls, and bottles were manufactured in profusion. The pots were globular, with round bottoms, constricted necks, and straight or flaring rims. Some rims were collared, but these were rare. Many pots had loop or strap handles or lugs, some of which had been modeled in the form of birds and animals.

The pottery was tempered with various types of grit particles. It was hardly ever painted, but, when fired, it turned a reddish-brown or gray color. The majority of vessel surfaces were smooth or polished, but many were covered with the imprints of cord- or grass-wrapped paddles. In such instances the cord or twisted-grass impressions were partly obliterated by subsequent smoothing and polishing.

Most of the pottery was not decorated, but sometimes simple geometric designs were incised on the bodies. Some of the rims were scalloped like a pie crust, or blunt diagonal incisions were placed around the outer lip area; some had modeled or incised decorative additions to handles or lugs.

In size the pots ranged from tiny vessels to large jars of six-gallon capacity. Very small vessels and ladles probably were children's toys.

Sometimes found with these vessels are pots of the type made by Upper Republican Indians, Dismal River Indians, and Oneota Indians. Even more significant is the presence of vessels belonging to some of the Middle Mississippi cultures.

Basketry.—No baskets have ever been found. There are, however, impressions of coiled basketry preserved on clay.

Tools, utensils, and weapons.—Probably the bow and arrow was the most important hunting weapon. The majority of chipped-flint arrowheads were triangular, many of them small, with side notches and, in some instances, a basal notch also. Stemmed arrow points were rare.

Arrow-shaft straighteners resembling wrenches were made of antler, with a hole at one end through which a crooked arrow-shaft was inserted; a handle at the other end helped to provide the leverage necessary to straighten the wooden shaft. Several types of ground-stone shaft-smoothers were used in making wooden arrow-shafts. Other characteristic ground-stone tools were celts, discoidal hammerstones, pitted anvil stones (cupstones), and small grinding-stones.

Knives, drills, celts, and scrapers were chipped from stone. Plano-convex end-scrapers and ovoid side-scrapers were common.

Tools used in farming were hoes and spades made of bison shoulder blades and digging-sticks made of antler or wood. Fish were caught with bone hooks, some of which were rather large and marked by notches at the bend of the shank. A rather unusual weapon to find in use among Plains Indians was a bone harpoonhead of a style resembling Eskimo types. The harpoons were probably used for spearing large fish.

Other bone tools were scrapers made of shoulder blades, handles for flint scrapers, some awls and needles, antler flaking tools, gouges, combs, and deer-jaw sinew-stretchers.

Pipes.—Pipes were made of pottery and stone and were platform or obtuse-angled elbow types. Most pipes were plain. Some, however, were modeled in human and animal effigy forms or decorated with geometric or simple, realistic designs.

Costume.—Evidence of clothing has not been preserved, but these Indians are sufficiently close to historic times for us to assume that their clothing was similar to that of Plains Indians at the time of their discovery by White men. The usual dress probably comprised moccasins, breechclouts, and robes made of deer or buffalo skin.

Ornaments.—The numerous ornaments included necklaces of bone and shell beads, bone pendants, clawlike pendants made of shell, and triangular shell gorgets. Some of the shell pendants were decorated with incisions suggesting birds and fish. Bracelets were made of antler, and at least one was decorated with the engraved representation of a hand suggestive of late Middle Mississippi art.

Well-sculptured effigy heads made of pottery or rarely of stone are similar to types characteristic of Middle Mississippi Indians.

Burials.—Burial practices of the Nebraska Indians are not yet well known. There is reason to believe that they dismembered their dead, kept the skeletal remains either in their houses or in a special "temple" house, and eventually buried the bones in natural hillocks or beneath small mounds.

Conjectures and comments.—The Nebraska Culture seems to have been coeval with late Upper Republican and Middle Mississippi cultures of the middle southern area. The Nebraska culture was also coeval with the early period of Dismal River culture.

SOURCES

BELL, 1936; COOPER, PAUL, 1939; STRONG, 1935; WEDEL, 1940a.

THE DISMAL RIVER CULTURE
(EARLY HISTORIC PERIOD)
Ca. A.D. 1600–1700

Area.—River and stream valleys of western Nebraska.

Villages.—The villages, generally small but sometimes large, usually were located on terraces in the stream or river valleys. Some of the houses were circular earth-covered lodges built either above ground or over a shallow circular pit. It is possible that skin-covered tepees and brush-covered shelters were also in use. Some village sites contained shallow refuse pits with round bottoms and bell-shaped roasting pits.

Livelihood.—The Dismal River Indians obtained subsistence primarily by hunting. They raised some corn, squash, and gourds and gathered wild fruits (plum, hackberries, and chokecherries). Animals hunted were bison, elk, deer, antelope, beaver, land turtles, and probably others. Animal bones were broken and split to obtain the marrow. It is possible that dogs, too, were sometimes eaten.

The dog was the only domesticated animal.

Pottery.—The cooking jars were unpainted and were made of clay tempered with fine grit, usually sand. After firing, the color ranged from buff to black, usually a glossy black. Vessel surfaces were smooth or covered with imprints of a grooved paddle and usually were burnished.

Decoration, when present, was very simple and consisted of herringbone or parallel diagonals incised on the lip. Body decoration was rare.

The majority of vessels were small or medium-sized jars with somewhat elongated bodies, conoidal or semiconoidal bottoms, constricted necks, and vertical or out-slanting rims. There were some bowls in use and a number of miniature jars that may have been toys for children.

Tools, utensils, and weapons.—The principal hunting weapon was the bow and arrow. Wooden arrows were tipped with small triangular points made of chipped flint. Some of these points were notched so that they could be more securely fastened to their wooden shafts. A few stemmed points were made of bone and antler.

Arrow-shafts were smoothed with grooved stone-polishers. Rarely present were bone wrenches used for straightening arrow-shafts.

Tools used in agriculture were hoes made of bison shoulder blades and probably wooden digging-sticks.

Diamond-shaped and ovate knives, chipped celts, expanded base drills, straight drills, long flake knives, plano-convex scrapers of various sizes, and plano-convex side-scrapers were made of flint. Abraders and pebble hammerstones were rather common tools, but grinding-stones and manos were infrequent and grooved mauls rare.

Fleshing tools were made of elk or bison leg bones. Punches and awls were made of bone and antler.

Pipes.—Most of the pipes were made of clay and were tubular in shape, with round or sometimes flattened and slightly flared mouthpieces. Some pipes were decorated with incised designs. In occasional use were clay elbow pipes or stone tubular pipes.

Ornaments.—Ornaments were few. Necklaces were usually made of tubular bone beads. Turquoise beads were used rarely, probably because it was difficult to import them from the Southwest. A few pendants and other ornaments were made of shell. Red-ocher paint was available for cosmetic use or for painting articles made of animal skins.

Conjectures.—The Dismal River culture is known to have been contemporaneous in part with the Upper Republican and Nebraska cultures. It may have outlasted the others, for it is found associated with White man's trade materials, and provisional dating by means of tree rings shows that the Dismal River Indians were living in the early eighteenth century. Possibly Dismal River is a descendant of the Sterns Creek culture.

SOURCES

HILL and METCALF, 1941; STRONG, 1935; WEDEL, 1940a, 1940b, 1941.

THE PLAINS AREA

OTHER CULTURES OF THE PLAINS AREA

In the Plains area there were some additional cultures that we have not described. These are the Lower Loupe culture (Pawnee); the Paint Creek culture (Wichita?); and the Arvilla, Mandan, Mill Creek, Antelope Creek, and Oneota. The Oneota Indians, who lived not only in the Plains but in wooded areas of the East, have been described in some detail in the section dealing with the Wisconsin-Minnesota area.

THE PLAINS AND THE SOUTHWEST

Because the Plains are adjacent to the Southwest, it might be expected that there would be contact between cultures of the two areas. But except in latest times there seems to be no concrete evidence of such contact.

The Antelope Creek culture of the Texas Panhandle and periphery is a southern Plains group that may have been influenced by Southwestern Puebloan Indians of the fourteenth, fifteenth, and sixteenth centuries. The compound and single house foundations of stone slabs built by these Indians possibly represent an Antelope Creek adaptation of a Puebloan idea. There were also Upper Republican cultural influences in Antelope Creek, and it is probable that the two cultures were coeval.

The Paint Creek culture of central Kansas showed evidence of actual contact with the Puebloan. In the Paint Creek pottery assemblage there were trade pieces of some of the types used by Pueblo Indians of the Rio Grande during the late seventeenth and early eighteenth centuries.

There seems to have been at least one actual intrusion of Pueblo Indians into the Plains in the late seventeenth or early eighteenth century. In Scott County, Kansas, there was a seven-room pueblo ruin of stone masonry and adobe associated with irrigation ditches. Puebloan pottery, large quantities of charred corn, tools, utensils, and weapons were found at the site. This pueblo may have been the place called Quartelejo, to which a band of Taos Indians fled from the Spaniards in 1650. Possibly the Picuris Indians who left their town in New Mexico were at Quartelejo from 1704 to 1706.

With the probable exception of the pueblo ruin in Scott County, there were no Pueblo Indians settled in the Plains area. Undoubtedly, Pueblo Indians entered the Plains on hunting parties or took temporary refuge there from the Spaniards.

SOURCES

ANONYMOUS, 1910; HODGE, 1900; MARTIN, H. T., 1910; MOOREHEAD, 1931; MULLOY, 1942; STRONG, 1940; WEDEL, 1940a, 1940b, 1941a, 1941b, 1942.

SUMMARY

The development of culture in the Plains area shows a cycle from food-collecting (hunting) in earliest times to food-producing (agriculture) in intermediate times back to food-collecting (hunting) in latest times.

The earliest Indians of the Plains obtained their livelihood by hunting and food-collecting. They probably used the spear and spear-thrower; made their tools and weapons of chipped stone, bone, and wood; and clothed themselves with animal skins. They did not have pottery or agriculture. Probably they were without dogs and perhaps were ignorant of the bow and arrow. It is likely that these ancient Indians of the Plains were seminomadic, living in temporary camps but occupying given locations seasonally. Possibly, bands of these Indians lived in one place part of each year and then separated into smaller units, each of which dwelt elsewhere during the rest of the year.

In the Intermediate period, perhaps from about 500 to 1300, there were in the Plains small groups of Woodland and Hopewellian Indians who probably were migrants from the east. These Indians lived by farming and hunting, made different kinds of pottery, probably had dogs, and manufactured tools, weapons, and ornaments of ground or polished stone, chipped stone, copper, bone, shell, and wood. Probably they wove baskets and textiles, made clothing of animal skins, and lived in semisedentary villages. Agriculture and pottery appear in this period, although not necessarily at the same time. Possibly the raising of squashes and gourds preceded the introduction of corn and beans in the agricultural complex, but of this we cannot be certain.

The Late Prehistoric period, possibly from about 1300 to 1600, saw the development and climax of some typically Plains cultures. These cultures were characterized by sedentary settlement along river valleys, rather intensive agriculture, earth-covered lodges, probable use of the bow and arrow, extensive use of pottery styles indigenous to the area, and trade and commerce with peoples of the Mississippi Valley. Probably this was the golden age of the Plains.

The Early Historic period, from about 1600 to 1800, was basically a continuation of the preceding period, with the addition of consequences arising from the arrival of horses in the area. The horse radically changed the lives of some groups of Indians, as Indians but lately farmers became mounted hunters ranging the Plains in search of bison. Villages became mobile instead of sedentary, and the earth-covered lodge gave way to the Plains tent or tepee previously used only for temporary shelter. Thus, although some groups of Indians remained agriculturists and part-time hunters, other groups rapidly changed to the horse Indian culture of the Plains—the Indians of covered-wagon days, movies, and schoolboys' history books.

Probably in terms of food supply, mobile hunters, preying on tremendous herds of bison, were just as efficient as sedentary hunters—perhaps more so when certain environmental limitations of agriculture (to be discussed later) are considered. But nomadic hunting is a radically different type of life from sedentary farming. The cultural values are quite different. Such hunters behave differently from sedentary farmers, being much more aggressive and warlike and much more efficient killers. Mounted on their swift horses, they could maneuver about the Plains better than any land vehicle except possibly the present-day jeep. In the bow and arrow they had a rapid-fire weapon superior to the muzzle-loading gun of contemporary White men. Not until the repeating gun was invented was the Plains bow and arrow superseded by the firearms of the Whites.

Probably the basic pattern of hunting was always in the tradition of the Plains Indians, even the most intensive farmers. But the mounted hunters of the Early Historic period were a unique phenomenon.

Returning to earlier periods of culture in the Plains, during which farming was undertaken, we find an interesting situation that is analogous to modern conditions of agriculture in the same area. Waldo Wedel (1941) has aptly demonstrated the probability that throughout the history of Plains agriculture farmers have suffered from droughts and ensuing dust storms. A very slight reduction in the yearly rainfall will bring on a drought. During droughts vegetation withers and dies, and the land is blown away by increasing wind activity. Eventually the rainfall increases, and the land again becomes suitable for farming. This long cycle of minimal moisture and drought is known among White farmers of the Plains. Drought causes abandonment of farms, loss of livelihood, and agrarian depression;

but after a very long interval rainfall increases, humus soil is formed, and eventually the farmers return.

The evidence of tree rings and alternate deposits of wind-blown soils and humus layers suggest that the wet-and-dry cycle was in operation long before the White man entered the Plains. The remains of agricultural Indians are found in the humus zones, often buried or separated by sterile zones of wind-blown materials. Thus it looks as if the Indian farmers pushed into the Plains during periods of suitable moisture and abandoned them during periods of drought. It is indeed probable that modern White farmers are victims of the same forces as were the Indian farmers. And thus both Indian and White farmers followed the same pattern of adjustment: pushing into the Plains in favorable periods and abandoning the area in unfavorable time.

SOURCES

WEDEL, 1941a.

CHAPTER 22

THE OZARK PLATEAU AREA

INTRODUCTION

THE Ozark and Ouachita plateaus constitute an interior highland situated in southwestern Missouri, northwestern Arkansas, and eastern Oklahoma. The region was one of low mountains and hills covered by a forest of southern hardwoods (oak-pine and oak-hickory). The climate was moderate, with a frostless season of from 150 to 210 days per year and an annual precipitation which varied from 40 to 50 inches.

In prehistoric times the area was not suited for intensive settlement by large sedentary groups of the kind found near the bottom lands of the Mississippi. Occupancy of the Ozark highlands in early times seems to have been characterized by small groups of Indians who killed animals and birds for food, caught fish in the streams, and collected nuts, seeds, and wild fruits. In later times the area supported an agricultural population who raised corn and other crops but who still found it necessary to maintain their old economy of hunting, fishing, and food-collecting.

The inhabitants of this area did not constitute a single cultural group at any one time. The cultural differences within the area as well as the relationships to outside groups are obscured by the custom of living in rock shelters and by the fact that these dry caves preserved many cultural items which were not preserved in open, lowland sites of the same general culture. In other words, we have peoples of diverse cultural origins classified together because they lived in caves. Moreover, there seems to be a superficial resemblance among all dry cave sites in North America. For instance, the Ozark Bluff cultures superficially resemble Basket Maker cave sites in the Southwest, the Big Bend Basket Maker caves of Texas, and the many different cultures of the Kentucky caves. These resemblances may mean that a Basket Maker–like culture—very broadly defined—was widespread in North America and that vestiges of it persisted for a long time.

Upon the basis of comparatively little investigation of the Ozark area, there seem to be at least three broad periods of culture as outlined in Chart X.

The Archaic period (probably before A.D. 500) was the time of hunters, fishers, and food-collectors who made tools and weapons of chipped stone and hunted with the spear and spear-thrower.

The Intermediate period (*ca.* 500–1300) saw the beginnings of pottery-making and agriculture, although they were not necessarily introduced at the same time. This period corresponds to the Burial Mound I and II periods of the Lower Mississippi Valley.

The Late Prehistoric period, beginning about 1300 is characterized by cultures somewhat akin to Middle Mississippi and most closely resembles the Oneota culture found in the Plains and in the wooded areas of Wisconsin.

CHART X

Probable Date	Period	Culture
A.D. 1300–1700	Late Prehistoric	Top-Layer Culture
A.D. 500–1300	Intermediate	Ozark Bluff Dweller Culture, Proto–Bluff Dweller Culture
Before A.D. 500	Archaic	Proto–Bluff Dweller Culture

THE PROTO–BLUFF DWELLER CULTURE
(Archaic Period)
Probably before A.D. 500

Area.—These Indians lived in the Ozark area of Missouri and Arkansas.

Villages.—The people either lived in the caves or rock shelters or occupied the stream valleys. Camp sites in the stream valleys may have consisted of temporary sapling huts covered with skins or thatch or matting.

Livelihood.—These Indians lived by hunting, fishing, and food-collecting but did not farm. They had no domestic animals except dogs.

Pottery.—None.

Basketry.—Probably these Indians wove baskets of many kinds as well as moccasins, bags, and coarse textiles.

Tools, utensils, and weapons.—The spear and spear-thrower probably was the principal hunting weapon. The spear-throwers were made entirely of wood or consisted of a wooden shaft with a socketed antler hook fastened to the outer end. The spears were tipped with points of chipped flint. There were several styles of such points, some of which were heavy and stemmed or notched for attachment to wooden or cane spear-shafts.

Knives of several styles were made of chipped flint, as were several varieties of drills, scrapers, and axes. Mortars and grinding-stones were probably used for pounding wild seeds and nuts into meal. Awls, flakers, and needles were of bone.

Pipes.—None.

Burials.—The dead were buried in pits within the rock shelters, usually in a flexed position and without grave goods.

SOURCES

HARRINGTON, 1924; PEABODY and MOOREHEAD, 1904; WALKER, W., 1932.

THE OZARK BLUFF DWELLER CULTURE
(INTERMEDIATE PERIOD)
Ca. A.D. 500–1300

Area.—The Ozark Mountains of Arkansas and Missouri were the ancient homeland of the Bluff Dwellers.

Villages.—Caves and rock shelters were the main living-places of the Ozark Bluff Dwellers, although some of these Indians lived in open villages in valleys. Community life in the caves and shelters is manifested by cultural refuse, grass-lined storage pits, and fireplaces.

Livelihood.—Food was obtained by farming, collecting, and hunting. Red and yellow corn, beans, squash, gourds, sunflowers, giant ragweed, pigweed, chenopodium, and canary grass were cultivated. Wild seeds, nuts, and acorns were collected. Animal food consisted of fish, turtle, beaver, wild turkey, raccoon, bear, elk, bison, and deer.

Pottery.—Sometime during this period the Ozark Bluff Dwellers began to use pottery. Some of this is suggestive of that used by the Marksville and Troyville cultures of the Burial Mound II period (chap. 26) and of the Coles Creek culture of the Temple Mound I stage in the Lower Mississippi Valley.

The Ozark pottery, however, frequently had a distinctive base not found in the Lower Mississippi Valley. Such bases have the imprint of basketry. These impressions were of common Bluff Dweller weaves—twilled, plain, plaited, and coiled. In all probability baskets were used as supports during the coiling of the pottery. Basketry shapes, moreover, probably influenced the basilar forms of the pottery. As one example, the squared base with corner extensions found on some pottery jars is probably derived from a basket of similar shape which is a common Bluff Dweller type.

Pottery does not seem to have been extensively used by the Bluff Dwellers. In place of pottery, gourd vessels and buckets of birch bark were used. Food could be cooked in such containers by means of stone-boiling—dropping red-hot stones into the water until it boiled.

Basketry.—The Ozark Bluff Dwellers made and used large quantities of baskets. The usual weave was twilled, but the plain checker weave was also common. A few baskets had intricately woven patterns.

Flat, shallow baskets with open weave were used as meal sieves and large baskets as storage or carrying receptacles. Shallow baskets of several forms served as containers, and pitch-lined basket-bottles of twined weaves for water storage.

Other objects woven were bags, mats, and clothing. Weaving techniques used were twining, netting, and a style of coiling.

Thread, string, and rope were made of bark fibers, grass, and hemp. Some cordage was braided but most was twisted.

Tools, utensils, and weapons.—Farming was carried on with antler or wooden digging-sticks and shell and bone hoes hafted to wooden handles. Corn and other grains were ground or pounded into meal on slab grinding-stones with manos or pestles. In addition to gourd and birch-bark vessels, there were food receptacles made of basketry, turtle shells, and mussel shells. The latter were also made into spoons.

The hunting weapon was the spear and spear-thrower. Bluff Dweller spear-throwers were made entirely of wood. A wooden peg set transversely through the handle served as a finger grip. At the far end was a carved projection for engaging the hollow butt of the cane spears. Some of these cane spears or arrows were equipped with wooden foreshafts and were tipped with fire-hardened cane points or rather crude stemmed and notched points of chipped flint.

Axes were also made of chipped flint and hafted into wooden handles by means of slots cut through the wood. Large rocks were used as hammers. Other tools were crude flint scrapers, bone scrapers, antler flaking tools, various types of bone awls, cane or wooden awls, and cane needles used in making rush mats.

Fish were caught in nets which were perhaps weighted down by pebbles.

Pipes.—Although the Ozark Bluff Dwellers were apparently not habitual pipe-smokers, they did have some tubular and platform pipes of stone.

Costume.—Fragile materials such as cloth, animal skin, basketry, and the like were well preserved in the dry caves. Some robes were made of deerskin with the hair left on. These were held in place by fur belts. Cloth robes were made of woven fibers. Fur robes were fashioned by wrapping rabbit fur around cords which were then woven into a warm robe. Similar coverings were made by wrapping cords with downy feathers and weaving them together to form a robe.

Breechclouts were made of bunches of long grass held together by a knot at one end and were kept in place by a belt.

Woven-grass sandals or deerskin moccasins were worn. Large, thick overshoes of woven grass were worn over the sandals or moccasins in bad weather. Sometimes deerskin leggings were attached to moccasins and wrapped around the wearer's legs.

Cradles.—Baby cradles commonly used were made of basketry, of basketry with wooden frames, of cordage, or of reeds.

Ornaments.—Necklaces of small plant seeds and shell beads cut from the central parts of marine conches were worn. Triangular pendants were made of mussel shell and perforated at their apexes for suspension.

Bundles of feathers tied with strings were probably hair ornaments. White, yellow, and red mineral paints were occasionally used for decorating basketry. They may also have been employed for body painting. Ornamental fans were made of feathers strung together with strips of quill or fiber cords.

Burials.—The dead were buried in pits dug into the dirt floors of the rock shelters. These pits were made in areas between large rocks which had fallen from the cave roof, or along the back wall of the cave.

The burial pits were first lined with a layer of grass and then covered by skin or woven robes. The body was placed on its side in a flexed position and covered first with a layer of old bags, mats, or grass, and then with a layer of wooden poles and sticks. The final covering was composed of dust, ashes, small rocks, and sometimes large rocks.

Sometimes two or three individuals were buried in the same grave. A minor but important burial custom was to deposit bundles of cremated bones in graves.

Conjectures.—Because of the excellent preservation afforded by dry caves, many perishable artifacts of wood, fabric, basketry, and the like have been found. Probably most contemporary Indians possessed similar objects which decayed in the open.

In Kentucky, Texas, and the Southwest, many ordinarily perishable objects similar to those of the Bluff Dwellers have also been preserved in dry caves or rock shelters. In Kentucky and the Ozarks area there are open sites which produce the same kinds of nonperishable artifacts that are found in the caves. It looks, therefore, as if the same peoples lived both in caves and in open villages. In the caves, however, their cultural remains are so much better preserved, and consequently so much more extensive, that some archeologists do not see the connection between the culture of the caves and that of the open village sites.

Except for their agricultural pursuits, the Ozark Bluff Dwellers lived essentially the same life that they had led in the Archaic period. The pre-agricultural Bluff Dwellers and perhaps all the other Indians of the Early Hunting stage were part of a Basket Maker–like pattern of life which was widespread in North America. Such a pattern might well be Asiatic in origin.

It seems possible that the Ozark Bluff Dwellers obtained a knowledge of agriculture and also of plant seeds from certain southwestern Indians who lived during the Basket Maker period (*ca.* 200–500). These Indians were somewhat similar to the Bluff Dwellers and would have been ideal donors of agriculture.

SOURCES

DELLINGER, 1936; DELLINGER and DICKINSON, 1942; GILMORE, 1930; HARRINGTON, 1924.

THE TOP-LAYER CULTURE
(LATE PREHISTORIC PERIOD)
Ca. A.D. 1300–1700

The Top-Layer culture of the Ozarks was so named because the archeologists excavating the Bluff shelters always found a separate and distinct culture in the upper part of the excavations. This was not found in the deeper part, and it was therefore named the Top-Layer culture.

This culture is somewhat similar to the Oneota culture which we have described in chapter 20. The Top-Layer people lived by farming, hunting, fishing, and food-collecting. In physical type they were either Prairids or Centralids.

These Indians hunted with bows and arrows which were tipped with thin, triangular points of chipped flint. With digging-sticks and shell hoes they cultivated their crops of corn, beans, and squash; probably all the crops grown by the Bluff Dwellers and perhaps additional ones besides. They made shell-tempered pottery, often ornamented with incising and punctates arranged in simple geometric patterns.

These Indians were culturally similar to groups in the Plains and in Wisconsin, Illinois, and Ohio.

SOURCES

BERRY and CHAPMAN, 1942; DELLINGER and DICKINSON, 1942; GRIFFIN, 1937; HARRINGTON, 1924.

SUMMARY

The first Indians of the Ozark area lived there from sometime before Christ until about A.D. 500. They were hunters, fishers, and food-collectors. Their principal weapon was the spear and spear-thrower, and their tools, weapons, and utensils were made of chipped stone, bone, shell, and wood. Basketry and finger weaving were well developed. These people frequently lived in caves or rock shelters.

This early culture continued through the Intermediate period, probably from about 500 to 1300, but was modified by the addition of agriculture which may have been introduced from the Southwest. After learning about corn, squashes, and possibly beans, the Bluff Dwellers may have domesticated some plants, the seeds of which they had formerly collected wild. Sometime during this period the Bluff Dwellers began to make a little pottery, but they never seem to have made very much.

In the Late Prehistoric period, probably from about 1300 to 1700, there was a greater use of pottery. The culture of this period seems to have been a regional expression of a cultural type more common to the North. Future investigations of the Ozarks may show that much of the agriculture now associated with the Intermediate period belongs in reality to the Late Prehistoric period. Also the stratigraphy of cultures in the Ozark area does not yet have a sound basis.

CHAPTER 23

THE MIDDLE SOUTHERN AREA

INTRODUCTION

THE Middle Southern area consisted primarily of the states of Arkansas, Mississippi, Alabama, Tennessee, and Kentucky and southern Missouri. This was a forested region primarily of coastal plain and central lowland with some interior low plateaus and mountains.

Southern hardwoods (oak-pine, oak-hickory, and chestnut–chestnut oak–yellow poplar) covered most of the area, but there were vast stretches of southeastern pine forest (long leaf, loblolly, and slash pine) and of river-bottom forest (cypress, tupelo-red gum).

A moderate continental-forest climate with mild winters prevailed throughout the region. Over most of the area the normal temperature in January ranged from 32 to 68 degrees. In exceptional years, however, the winters approximated those normally found farther north. Summers were hot. The frostless season varied from 180 to more than 240 days, and the annual precipitation from 40 to 60 inches.

Climate, soils, and rainfall combined ideally for the intensive agriculture practiced by the latest Indians of the area. The forests supported wild life of all kinds, and berries, roots, nuts, and wild fruits gave sustenance to hunters of earliest times.

Many great rivers and their tributaries drained the Middle Southern area and were conducive to water travel by dugout canoes. These waterways also attracted aquatic animals and provided edible shellfish in tremendous quantities. Almost all the Indians of the area were irrevocably tied to the rivers, whether they were hunters and clam-gatherers of earliest times or farmers of the latest periods. The spread of culture in this area was along the rivers. The periods and some of the cultures are outlined in Chart XI.

The Archaic period we would guess to have lasted from reasonably early postglacial times to perhaps A.D. 500. The cultures of this time were based upon hunting, fishing, and food-collecting. These ancient Indians made tools, weapons, and utensils of stone, bone, and probably wood. They did not have pottery, pipes, or agriculture.

The Intermediate period probably lasted from about 500 to 900. The manufacture of pottery became common during this period, and pipe-smoking and perhaps agriculture were introduced into the area.

The Burial Mound period, probably from about 900 to 1300, was characterized by the use of earthen burial mounds as cemeteries and by rather extensive trade and commerce. Most cultures of this period had some relationship to Hopewell.

The Temple Mound period, perhaps from 1300 to 1700, saw the development and florescence of pyramidal mounds of earth which were used as substructures for wooden temples and the evolution and spread of shell-tempered pottery, polychrome painting on pottery, and intensive hoe agriculture.

CHART XI

Probable Date	Period	Culture
A.D. 1300–1700	Temple Mound	Middle Mississippi
A.D. 900–1300	Burial Mound	Hamilton, Copena
A.D. 500–900	Intermediate	Alexander, Candy Creek
1000 B.C.–A.D. 500	Archaic	Lauderdale

Sometime during the Temple Mound period, probably in the latter half, the Indian groups of the area were swept off their feet by an upsurge of religious fervor—the Southern Death Cult. The Temple Mound culture, although declining, was still in existence when the first White settlers entered the region. Explorations as early as those of Cabeza de Vaca, Hernando de Soto, and Tristan de Luna may have taken place before the cultural culmination or apogee of this period.

In the following pages we shall describe some of the cultures representative of each period. There are, of course, many known cultures which we have not described, and probably many more await discovery by archeologists.

THE LAUDERDALE CULTURE
(Archaic Period)
Probably before A.D. 500

Area.—In the lower levels of shell middens along the Tennessee River in Pickwick, Wilson, and Wheeler basins of northern Alabama and southern Tennessee, the remains of the Lauderdale culture have been found.

People.—Sylvids of medium stature.

Villages.—Some of these Indians lived in rock shelters, but most preferred large shell-mound dumps near rivers. There is no information concerning houses or other shelters, but the presence of hearths of fire-cracked rocks and ash beds suggests that the habitants may have gathered together for purposes of warmth, cooking, and gossip. They probably lived in crude arbors built of saplings covered with thatch or skins.

Livelihood.—Hunting, fishing, and gathering wild foods such as nuts, berries, and shellfish furnished subsistence.

Tools, utensils, and weapons.—Like most Indians of the Archaic period, these people used the spear and spear-thrower. The spear-thrower or atlatl was made of wood tipped with an antler hook for engaging the butt of the spear. Stone weights were fastened to the atlatl shaft for purposes of balance, as were bars, perforated prisms, expanded center bars, and boatstones.

The spears used with the atlatl were probably made of cane and tipped with points made of bone, stone, or antler. There were long, slender, stemmed points of chipped flint, some triangular stemmed points also of chipped flint, simple bone points, and socketed antler points.

For straightening spear-shafts there was a wrenchlike tool of antler with a hole through it.

Drills and long ovate knives were made of chipped flint. Ground-stone axes and fully grooved and spheroidal hammerstones were used for chopping and pounding.

Implements used in the preparation of food were vessels made of steatite or sandstone, mortars, grinding-stones, nutstones, and bell-shaped pestles. Fish were caught with bone hooks and perhaps with nets. There were several types of bone awls in use. Bodkins and needles of bone may have been used in making garments.

Pipes.—Bell-shaped tubular pipes made of stone were present. These are, perhaps, the earliest evidence of smoking in eastern North America.

Ornaments.—Ornaments for the most part consisted of beads and pendants. There were long, tubular beads made either of stone or of the central sections of marine conch shells. There were barrel-shaped stone beads, disk shell beads, and a special type made of snail shells. There were also small triangular pendants of shell, bone hairpins, and polished slate gorgets with two holes in them.

Burials.—Usually burials were made in round pits. Some of the dead were placed in a flexed-sitting position, others were closely flexed with face downward. Occasionally, bodies were beheaded and buried in one place, the head in another. Cremations occurred. Sometimes tools and ornaments were placed with the burial.

Conjectures.—The Lauderdale Indians probably inherited a culture and traditions embodying strong elements of both a Cochise-like and a Folsom-like culture (see chap. 10). The Lauderdale culture was in large part ancestral to the Alexander culture found in the same area.

SOURCES

WEBB and DEJARNETTE, 1942.

THE ALEXANDER CULTURE
(INTERMEDIATE PERIOD)
Ca. A.D. 500–900

Area.—Along the Tennessee River in northern Alabama have been found the remains of the Alexander culture. These Indians for the most part seem to have been a conservative group who lived much like their Lauderdale ancestors. Therefore we shall describe here only the new customs which differentiate the Alexander Indians.

People.—Same as Lauderdale.

Villages.—Same as Lauderdale.

Livelihood.—Same as Lauderdale. There is, however, some possibility that agriculture was introduced during this period in northern Alabama.

Pottery.—Unpainted pottery of several varieties was made. Large, fiber-tempered vessels, either plain or decorated with dentate stamped or punctate impressions all over the vessel exterior, were common. The forms were probably simple bowls and jars. Pottery colors after firing ranged in buffs and grays.

A common kind of pottery consisted of sand- or grit-tempered jars, both plain and decorated. These vessels sometimes had flat bases and tetrapodal supports (four feet). Smoothed surfaces were most frequent, but cord- or fabric-impressed surfaces occasionally occurred. Decoration on the smoothed pottery consisted of several types. One motif was composed of finger-pinched impressions, another consisted of incised lines arranged in rectilinear or triangular plats, and still another involved the use of zones filled with punctate impressions or stamping.

Tools, utensils, and weapons.—Same as Lauderdale.

Pipes.—Same as Lauderdale.

Burials.—The dead were occasionally interred in the midden, but a comparatively small number of skeletons suggests that many were disposed of elsewhere. The skeletons found were closely flexed. Usually there were no artifacts with them.

Conjectures.—The Alexander Indians, although seemingly simple, must have been very influential people. They modified the culture of the Tchefuncte Indians in Louisiana and probably the cultures of some Indian groups in Florida. They were the innovators of the zoned-areal decoration on pottery which was more fully exploited by the Hopewell and Marksville Indians of later times. In short, the Alexander Indians left their mark not only upon their contemporaries in distant places but upon people of later times as well.

SOURCES

WEBB and DeJARNETTE, 1942.

THE CANDY CREEK CULTURE
(INTERMEDIATE PERIOD)
Ca. A.D. 700–1100

Area.—Eastern Tennessee and perhaps adjacent areas.

People.—Indians with heads of medium length who were rather short in stature. They seem to have been hybrids who showed some Centralid characteristics.

Villages.—Camp sites, villages, and cemeteries were located near rivers or streams. Although evidence is scanty, the house type seems to have been circular in outline and constructed of upright poles. Kettle-shaped pits were dug into the ground and used for cooking, storage, and refuse.

Livelihood.—The Candy Creek people made their living by hunting, fishing, and food-gathering. Possibly they practiced some agriculture.

Pottery.—Unpainted pottery was comparatively abundant and diverse. The vessels were granular-tempered, either with grit or limestone. The color of the fired clay was buff, brown, and gray. A common variety of limestone-tempered pottery was a straight-sided jar with a straight, vertical (or occasionally incurved) rim and a fabric-impressed surface. The bases were conoidal or had four small feet (tetrapodal supports). Much less frequent were jar-shaped vessels with constricted necks and straight rims which otherwise conformed to the style of the straight-sided jars. Both types also occurred with fine cord impressions upon their surfaces, although this treatment was most frequent on jars with constricted necks with rims often thickened by the addition of an exterior fold.

Another common style of limestone-tempered vessel was similar except that the surfaces were covered with coarse cord impressions. Other variants had plain surfaces, simple stamped surfaces, check-stamped surfaces, or complicated stamped surfaces, but none of these was particularly abundant and all probably represented late types.

Quartzite-tempered vessels were usually jar-shaped with straight sides and incurved rims, although straight, vertical rims were present. The bases were conoidal and vessel surfaces were covered with fabric or cord impressions. Some minority types found which were probably alien to the Candy Creek culture are suggestive of Deptford or early Swift Creek styles.

Basketry.—Coiled basketry was made.

Tools, utensils, and weapons.—The art of stone-chipping was used for the manufacture of projectile points (arrowheads or spearheads), knives, drills, and scrapers. The projectile points were both long and short and were ovate-triangular in outline with straight stems and straight, horizontal shoulders. Another type was a rather broad shield shape with outcurved sides and either straight or incurved base. Knives were leaf-shaped and usually lopsided. Many were stemmed. Drills were somewhat crude and thick with an expanded base and were either double- or single-tapered. There were thick, ovate, and stemmed scrapers.

Candy Creek Indians also had thick, trianguloid, ungrooved axes, full-grooved axes, hammerstones, whetstones, sinewstones, mortars, conical pestles, notched stone netsinkers, cupstones, and soapstone bowls. Industry in shell and bone was undertaken infrequently, although bone awls and perhaps flaking tools were present.

Pipes.—The occasional presence of tubular, biconical pipes of soapstone suggests that the custom of smoking was known.

Costume.—Probably animal skins and textiles were used for clothing. Impressions of fabrics made by the simple plaiting technique have been found on pottery.

Ornaments.—Ornaments of rectanguloid slate and steatite gorgets with one or two perforations have been found. Occasional gorgets were serrated. There were also plain or engraved pendants, some perforated for suspension, and sometimes necklaces were made of perforated animal teeth.

Burials.—The dead were placed in round or oval pits within the village. Skeletons were generally flexed, and burial accompaniments were exceedingly rare.

Conjectures.—The Candy Creek Indians were probably ancestral to the Hamilton Indians who lived in eastern Tennessee in slightly later times. The Candy Creek Indians may have been the inventors of limestone pottery tempering later used in Adena and Hopewell pottery.

SOURCES

Lewis and Kneberg, 1941.

THE HAMILTON CULTURE
(Burial Mound Period)
Ca. a.d. 1000–1300

Area.—Along the rivers of eastern Tennessee.

People.—Indians of medium stature with long heads or heads of medium length. Both Sylvids and Centralids were represented in the population.

Villages.—Riverbank and island communities probably consisted of scattered households. Refuse heaps and over-the-bank dumps have been found. The type of house is not known but was probably a cabin or wigwam made of saplings and covered by brush, mats, skins, or bark.

Livelihood.—These people made their living by hunting, fishing, food-collecting, and perhaps a little agriculture, although the abundance of clams in the river provided a stable food supply comparable to that provided by farming.

Pottery.—These people made unpainted pottery vessels tempered with particles of limestone. One popular style was a jar with vertical rims, slightly constricted neck, and conoidal or semiconoidal bottom. A related variant lacked the constriction at the neck. Both had smooth surfaces and were undecorated.

Another style was similar to the above, except that the surfaces were malleated with a paddle or other instrument wrapped with fine cord.

Another style bore large cord impressions which were distributed over the exterior vessel surfaces. In addition to the jar forms, there were occasional bowls marked with large cord impressions.

Still another style of pottery consisted of jars with incurved rims, conoidal or semiconoidal bases, and simple-stamped vessel surfaces. The simple-stamped impressions may have been produced by dragging or brushing with a cord-wrapped instrument.

Tools, utensils, and weapons.—The spear and spear-thrower or the bow and arrow or both were probably used. There was a well-developed chipped-stone industry. Some of the common forms made were stemless knives with asymmetrical blades; small triangular projectile points with incurved sides and bases; and ovate-triangular projectile points with straight or flared stems, horizontal shoulders, and short or elongated blades. Less common forms were drills with expanded bases or with stems and shoulders; thick, crude, double-tapered drills; plano-convex end-scrapers, stemmed scrapers, and side-scrapers.

Trianguloid, ungrooved axes, full-grooved axes, hammerstones, whetstones, hones, sinewstones, conical pestles, and steatite vessels were made of ground stone. Short awls, splinter awls, and double-tapered awls were made of bone.

Pipes.—Elbow pipes of clay or steatite indicate the custom of smoking.

Ornaments.—Ornaments were rather meager. Beads and pendants made of river shells and the central whorls of marine shells have been found. The marine shells probably were obtained by trade.

Burials.—Circular burial mounds were erected over the dead, usually two or more at each burial site. The bodies were usually partly flexed, and few if any grave-offerings accompanied them. The mounds were built up by accretions of earth, bodies, and shells.

Conjectures.—The Hamilton culture was an extension of a basically northern culture into the South, but it was, of course, considerably modified along southern lines. The subsequent cultures of the same area were variants of the Middle Mississippi cultures.

SOURCES

LEWIS and KNEBERG, 1941

THE COPENA CULTURE
(BURIAL MOUND PERIOD)
Ca. A.D. 900–1300

Area.—Northern Alabama.

People.—Indians belonging to a physical type characterized by round heads or heads of medium length—a mixed Sylvid-Centralid population. They practiced cradle-board deformation.

Villages.—Villages were located along rivers and streams. Some Copena Indians lived on top of old shell heaps or middens which had been left by Indians of the Archaic and Intermediate periods; others lived in rock shelters. Houses were probably made of saplings covered with thatch or some other material.

Livelihood.—Agriculture, hunting, fishing, and food-gathering were the means of subsistence. Corn, squash, gourds, and beans may have been raised.

Pottery.—These Indians made unpainted, limestone-tempered pottery jars, usually with flat or rounded bottoms, but in a few instances with tetrapodal supports (four short legs). Some vessels were plain; others were tastefully decorated by incising, stamping, or impressing with fabric. Decorations consisted of incised curvilinear zones on the rims and shoulders of jars; check-stamped impressions; simple longitudinal-stamped impressions or complicated stamped impressions covering the entire vessel; and fabric impressions upon the vessel walls.

Tools, utensils, and weapons.—Small trianguloid, ungrooved axes of copper were made. Finely chipped stone projectile points or knives were fashioned in leaf shapes with straight bases and graceful concavities in the lower portion of the blade at each side. These points may have been a late derivative from eastern Folsom types. Large trianguloid celts were manufactured from greenstone by grinding and polishing techniques. Rather large, spadelike implements made of schist were probably used as spades and hoes in agricultural work.

Conch-shell containers made of *Busycon perversum* suggest direct or indirect contact with peoples having access to the Florida Gulf Coast and are indicative of some rudimentary type of commerce. Evidence of weaving has been found in fabric impressions preserved in copper salts.

Pipes.—Large elbow-type pipes of polished steatite were smoked. A less common type of steatite pipe was tubular and was carved in the form of animal effigies.

Ornaments.—Ornaments or ceremonial objects were made of copper, stone, and shell. Reel-shaped gorgets, which seem to be most characteristic of this culture, were made of copper.

Breastplates, double-cymbal type ear-spools, spherical beads, tubular beads, rolled-sheet beads, and C-shaped bracelets were also made of copper.

Other ornamental or ceremonial objects were fragments of cut sheet-mica, lumps of galena, disk-shaped shell beads, and polished-stone gorgets, one the expanded-center type with perforations drilled from one side only.

Burials.—The Copena peoples built large conical burial mounds containing grave pits lined with exotic clays. In the center of some mounds were rectilinear subfloor tombs covered with logs and bark. Burials were both single and compound, and the skeletons were extended in the flesh or deposited in bundles. Infrequent deposits of burned human bone are suggestive of cremation. There were also occasional burials of isolated skulls.

Grave-offerings were placed with the dead, but, surprisingly enough, pottery was never included. Another unusual feature was the breaking or ceremonial "killing" of artifacts which were put in the graves.

Conjectures.—The Copena Indians were closely related to Hopewell, Troyville, and late Adena peoples.

SOURCES

WEBB and DEJARNETTE, 1942.

THE MIDDLE MISSISSIPPI CULTURE
(TEMPLE MOUND PERIOD)
Ca. A.D. 1300–1700

Although there are many varieties of Middle Mississippi culture, each with a respectable history of its own, we have elected to describe the culture in terms broad enough to eliminate regional and temporal variations. It is easy to do this, because all varieties of Middle Mississippi belong to one major period and are largely parallel in their development within this period.

Area.—The river valleys of Arkansas, Mississippi, Alabama, Tennessee, southern Missouri, Kentucky, Illinois, Indiana, and Ohio. There were northward extensions in the Wisconsin-Minnesota area and in the Plains.

People.—Most Middle Mississippi Indians were Centralids. They had short (round) heads artificially flattened on the back or front part or both by the tight binding of infants' heads to their cradle-boards.

It is interesting to note that many individuals seem to have suffered the bone deterioration of syphilis or a similar disease.

Villages.—The Middle Mississippi Indians seem to have been organized into village-states. One large village culturally and politically dominated surrounding satellite villages. The political structure is not known, but there must have been some means of organizing cooperative labor on a large scale.

Middle Mississippi towns and villages were essentially riverine. Each consisted of a plaza or central square, one or more pyramidal mounds, temples, chiefs' houses, and a number of ordinary dwellings. Frequently there was a palisade of upright posts supported by earthen embankments around the town for protection against enemies.

The wooden temples and chiefs' houses were placed on the flat summits of the pyramidal mounds, which were built of earth and clay. In some instances the mound exterior was faced with a smooth covering of clay analogous to the stone or plaster shells over Mexican pyramids. A ramp or stairway of earth or logs led to the summit.

These mounds were built in successive layers over each other. Possibly some ceremony existed in which the temple was destroyed at fixed intervals and a new mound and temple erected over the old one. Whatever the cause, the majority of these pyramidal mounds were constructed in successive levels.

Middle Mississippi mounds were square or rectangular in ground plan. Most of them were about 10 or 20 feet high, although many were larger and were 30–60 feet high. A Middle Mississippi site at East St. Louis, Illinois, has a mound about 100 feet high, 1,080 feet long, and 710 feet wide. It covers an area of about 16 acres.

Temples or chiefs' houses placed on mound summits were rectangular in floor plan and were constructed of poles set into trenches or individual holes. Perhaps the tops of the poles were bent to form different styles of roofs: dome-shaped, arched, conical, etc. Some roofs were constructed of steeply pitched log rafters. In certain cases large central posts were used for support. Walls and roofs were covered by matting or thatch, and frequently walls were plastered with clay over a lath of coarse matting or wicker. It is possible that temples were ornamented with carvings and painted murals and that each temple contained a sacred fire which was kept burning for a year and then extinguished, after which another fire was begun in the "new fire ceremony."

Ordinary dwellings were like the temples and chiefs' houses, but were smaller (10–25 feet long) and less ornate (Fig. 85). Most of them were rectangular. Each house consisted of one room, although mats may have been hung to provide partitions. It is probable that there were no smoke holes, and smoke from the fire seeped through the roof or out of the door. Around the walls were mats and possibly sleeping platforms. There may have been wooden stools, but there was probably no other furniture.

Livelihood.—Bottom-land agriculture was the principal means of support. Corn, squash, gourds, beans, and perhaps other crops were raised and were supplemented by hunting, fishing, and the gathering of wild foods.

Tools, utensils, and weapons.—The Middle Mississippi Indians were hoe-using farmers. Hoes were made of battered or chipped

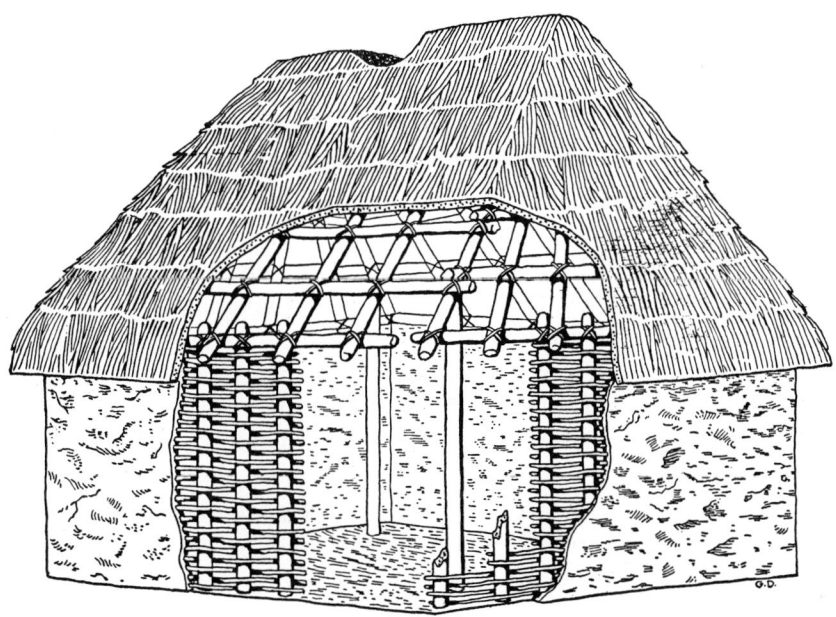

Fig. 85.—Construction of Middle Mississippi house. (After Glenn Black.)

stone, shell, and animal shoulder blades, all fastened to wooden handles. Probably wooden digging-sticks were also employed in planting crops.

It is probable that corn was pounded into meal and flour by wooden mortars and pestles. Occasionally stone mortars and pestles and flat grinding-stones may also have been used.

The principal weapon was the wooden bow and arrow. Arrows were usually tipped with chipped-flint points, but sometimes bone or antler points were used. These points were stemmed or notched in various ways, or were plain, but all were small and thin, nicely executed, and generally triangular in outline. Small grooved sandstone blocks were used for smoothing arrow-shafts. Bone or antler wrenches were used for straightening the arrows.

Some of the Middle Mississippi Indians may have used the spear and spear-thrower, but it must have been unimportant in contrast to the bow and arrow. Possibly the atlatl served as a badge of rank or perhaps its use was ceremonial. Exceptionally well-made boatstones have been found which may have been used as spear-thrower weights attached to the wooden shaft of the atlatl.

Fish were caught with lines and bone hooks. Probably nets were also used.

Celts of ground and polished stone served as axes and hatchets. These were hafted to a wooden handle by means of a hole cut through one end of the handle. Less common celts of copper were similarly hafted.

Various styles of knives, scrapers, and drills were made of chipped flint. There were other occasional objects made of stone, but in general these Indians did not lay much emphasis upon stone work despite the fact that they were superior stone craftsmen.

Needles, awls, and weaving tools were made of bone. Various tools used in stone-working were also made of bone or antler, as were spearheads or arrowheads in some instances.

Spoons, dippers, and other vessels were made of sea and river shells.

Pottery.—In many respects the Middle Mississippi Indians were the best potters in eastern North America. Their pottery, buff, gray, or black in color when fired, was made of clay tempered with particles of broken shell.

There were many different forms: various styles of jars, pots, bowls, bottles, plates, cuplike vessels, effigy forms, and intricate compound forms (Figs. 86, 87, 88).

The bulk of Middle Mississippi pottery was utilitarian and served the everyday needs of cooking and storing food. Usually it was plain and undecorated. One utilitarian type of vessel, however, frequently had a fabric-impressed exterior. This vessel was the saltpan, a thick, shallow, pan-shaped vessel used for obtaining salt by evaporation of saline waters. Many styles of finger weaving are indicated by the fabric impressions on saltpans.

Pottery decorated in various ways was probably used for burial offerings or in religious ceremonies. This decoration was achieved by polishing, incising, modeling, punctating, and, occasionally, engraving. These decorative techniques were used singly or in almost any combination. Both angular and curvilinear motifs were common.

The designs included chevrons, triangles, scrolls, spirals, guilloches, meanders, and a variety of similar forms produced mostly by incising. Rows of punctates and bosses or nodes were also in use. Rather unusual decoration was produced by pinching the plastic clay. Sometimes small animal effigies were added to vessel rims. Other elaborations were festooned rims, various styles of lugs, strap handles, loop handles, three-legged supports, and different kinds of annular bases.

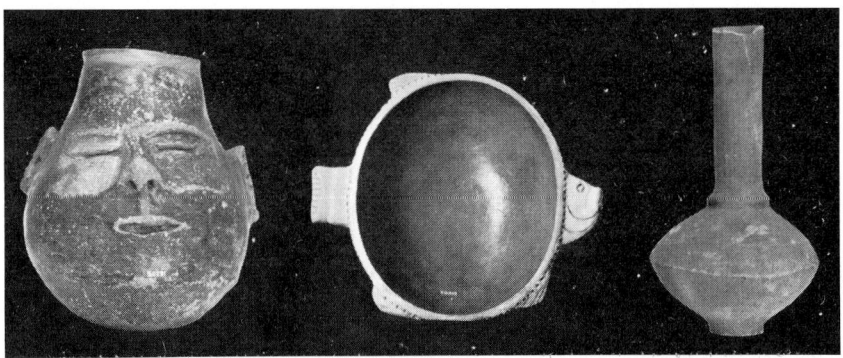

FIG. 86.—Middle Mississippi pottery. *Left*, jar in the form of a human head; *center*, fish-effigy bowl; *right*, bottle.

Other unusual elaborations of vessel forms were spouted jars (something like a teakettle), tripartite, and other compound vessels, shoe-form pots, and stirrup-mouth bottles.

There were different kinds of effigy vessels; pots, jars, and bottles in the form of humans, animals, birds, amphibians, and fishes, some rather elaborate. Certain effigy and other forms exhibit characteristics suggestive of Mexican influence. However, none of these vessels was a common style, even in the more spectacular towns.

Painting as a technique in ceramic decoration reached its culmination among Middle Mississippi Indians. Painted pottery, however, was always one of the minority wares, probably reserved for special functions or ceremonies. Common colors were solid red, red designs on the natural buff color of the pottery, and red, white, and black (or dark brown) on the natural buff. Designs were produced by either direct or negative painting. The negative-painting process was most commonly used in decorating bottles, but painted designs in general

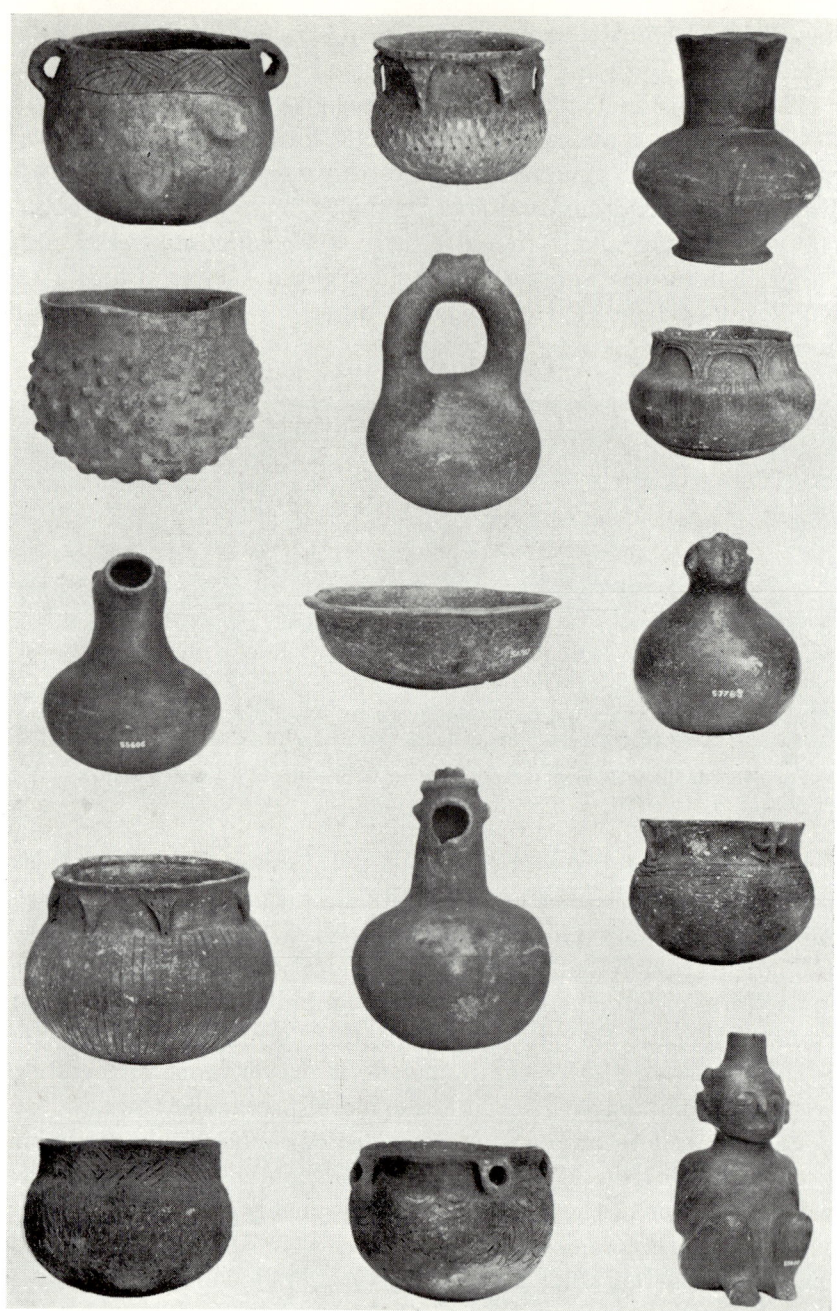

Fig. 87.—Middle Mississippi pottery

THE MIDDLE SOUTHERN AREA   359

were applied to nearly all forms of Middle Mississippi pottery. These designs, like other kinds of ornamentation, ranged from simple geometric motifs to rather complicated symbolic forms.

Not all styles of pottery were to be found in each Middle Mississippi town, but varying combinations of the pottery we have described is representative of the culture as a whole.

Pipes.—Pipes were usually made of pottery, although some were of stone. Most pipes were of the equal-arm elbow-shape variety; that

Fig. 88.—Painted and effigy pottery of the Middle Mississippi culture

is, the stem and bowl were nearly equal in size and were set at right angles to each other. Effigy pipes were also present and were usually in the form of crouching human or animal figures. All required the addition of a wooden stem.

Costume.—The Middle Mississippi Indians wore skin or woven moccasins, breechcloths, and skin or fabric mantles, some decorated with painted designs. Other mantles were probably made of feathers. Most of our knowledge of Middle Mississippi clothing comes from pictorial representations on the sacred paraphernalia of the Southern Death Cult.

Weaving, bags, and textiles.—These Indians wove mats, baskets, and twined textiles of a good quality. Some textiles were probably decorated with either directly painted or resist-painted printed designs.

Ornaments.—Personal ornamentation consisted of shell gorgets and pendants; of ear ornaments made from shell, clay, stone, or copper-covered wood; of hairpins made from wood and copper, bone, bone and copper, or shell; of copper gorgets and pendants; and of beads made from shell, bone, or occasionally copper or stone. Armbands and leg bands were sometimes made from strings of shell beads. Most of the spectacular ornaments were part of the paraphernalia of the Southern Death Cult. In fact, most of the outstanding items of dress and ornament were manifestations of the Death Cult.

Burials.—Usually large quantities of burial offerings were placed in the graves of Middle Mississippi Indians, who were most often buried in cemeteries. The bodies usually were extended, but flexed and bundle burials also occur.

Sometimes burials were made in the village dump or beneath the floors of houses or in the pyramidal temple mounds. These last-mentioned burials may have been beneath the floors of temples.

Sometimes the dead were placed in specially built mounds, usually irregular in shape and consisting of layers of bodies and earth. Occasional mounds of this type were conical in shape.

Various styles of stone-vault graves were used by certain Middle Mississippi Indians. These ranged in style from simple, slab-lined graves to complicated, walled structures of stone and possibly of logs over which earth was piled to form a mound.

Conjectures.—Our survey of Middle Mississippi civilization has not taken account of the many cultural variations within the civilization, nor have we attempted to differentiate the subperiods of Middle Mississippi culture.

Nowhere in North America outside the Southwest was there a civilization which developed so rapidly and expanded so greatly as Middle Mississippi. This culture represents the most intensive Indian occupancy of eastern North America.

In its incipient stages Middle Mississippi partook of Hopewellian influences, but the exact role of Hopewell cultures in the genesis of Middle Mississippi is unknown. There seem also to have been Middle American influences at work.

No single tribe or linguistic group can be given credit. This civilization was rather the product of many different tribes and many different linguistic groups. Indian groups which at the time of their discovery were perhaps members of the Middle Mississippi family were the Cherokee, Chickasaw, Quapaw, Creek, "Muskogean," and others.

SOURCES

BROWN, 1926; COLLINS, 1932; DELLINGER and DICKINSON, 1940; DEUEL, 1935; FOWKE, 1910; HARRINGTON, 1922; JENNINGS, 1941; LEWIS and KNEBERG, 1941; MOORE, 1899, 1901, 1905, 1907, 1908, 1910; MYER, 1928; PHILLIPS, P., 1940; THRUSTON, 1897; WEBB, 1938, 1939; WEBB and DEJARNETTE, 1942; WEBB and FUNKHOUSER, 1932.

THE SOUTHERN DEATH CULT

The Southern Death Cult (also called Buzzard Cult) flourished sometime during the latter part of the Temple Mound period, or about 1450–1650. This was a new religion that seems to have spread relatively rapidly among some of the cultures in the Mississippi Valley and the Southeast. The existence of this cult is inferred from the form and distribution of certain implements, ornaments, and art styles found in the eastern United States.

It is presumed that not all of the Death Cult elements are of the same age. Some, perhaps, were early introductions into the Caddo area from the Huastec region of eastern Mexico. Other elements may have been developed in the Southeast at a later time or perhaps were the result of stimulus from Mexico at a later time.

In any event, there seems to be the possibility of a religious revival in connection with the Death Cult. This revival probably occurred late in the period of the cult, perhaps after 1500. Some of the reasons for this hypothetical revival are as follows. By the year 1550 the Indians of eastern America must have experienced a premonition of impending doom. Wild rumors and stories about the Spanish conquest of the Aztec empire by treachery and the consequent rapacious pillaging and plundering had probably reached their ears. They had perhaps also learned of the barbarous treatment accorded the Southwestern Indians by the Spaniards. Then, too, the De Soto expedition, which started from Florida and wandered through many of the southern states, had certainly made a most unpleasant impression on the terrified Indians and had probably given them some inkling as to how their wives, children, property, and their own lives would be ravaged. The Indians sensed the fact that they had "two strikes" on them. The Whites were unconquerable because they had guns, crossbows, armor, and horses.

It is also probable that, in addition to the coming of the White man, the Indians may have been experiencing other serious setbacks, such as crop failures and new and strange diseases that swept the country in epidemic form.

Apparently, then, about 1550, the Indians of the Southeast realized that they were in danger. It was a time of chaos, fear, and widespread tension. The general psychological symptoms typical of such a period are an uncertain feeling of dissatisfaction, unhappiness, unrest, and perhaps despair. Consequently, conditions were meet for the acceptance of a religious revival.

Presumably, the paraphernalia of the Southern Death Cult somewhat resembled that of Middle American religions. There were, however, no objects of Mexican manufacture in the Southeast. Nevertheless, it appears the Southeastern Indians had copied Mexican objects or had worked from verbal descriptions of Mexican (probably Huastecan) religious paraphernalia.

These assumptions imply that a contact existed between Mexican Indians and Indians of the Southeast. This contact perhaps occurred during the expedition of Tristan de Luna (1559–61), for the exploring party of Spanish soldiers contained, in addition, a great number of Mexican Indians. For two years these Mexican Indians wandered about the middle part of the South, an area which has produced considerable evidence of the Death Cult. It is not known how many Mexican Indians were left in the South when the De Luna expedition departed, but, even if none were left, the two years of contact between Mexicans and southerners seem to have been sufficient for the introduction of the Death Cult.

The Southern Death Cult was not only a crystallization of recently introduced ideas; it was also part of a religious tradition going back to Hopewell times (Burial Mound period). Certain aspects of Hopewellian burial practices are suggestive of a death cult, and it seems likely that Hopewell tradition, in diluted form, persisted into Temple Mound times. Thus many groups of Indians already possessed the basic pattern of a death cult. Possessing this pattern and beset by troublesome times, they would have been eager to accept imported ideas. Consequently, a number of new customs, probably Mexican, combined at different times with an old tradition (Hopewellian) to produce the Southern Death Cult.

As a religious revival, the Death Cult materially changed the lives of the southern Indians. Born in a period of chaos and despair, the cult probably was responsible for the inauguration of a "boom time" in the South. During these years there was a short-lived flowering of southern Indian civilization. It was especially the time of the culmination of Middle Mississippi culture as well as that of the Etowa and some Caddo cultures. In short, this was an American renaissance. But this resurgence of Indian culture did not last long, for by 1680 the Death Cult had largely disappeared, and once again the Indian cultures seem to have been on the decline.

The following objects and symbols are supposed to be representative of the Death Cult, especially in its Mexicanized aspects.

1. Monolithic axes: both head and handle made of a single piece of stone.
2. Ceremonial clubs or batons of stone.
3. Shell pendants with background cut out to form crosses (Fig. 89).
4. Copper pendants with circles or weeping-eye symbol formed by *repoussé* or cut-out background, or both.
5. Conch-shell masks marked with winged or weeping-eye symbol (Figs. 89 and 91).
6. Shell gorgets showing fighting cocks, woodpeckers, rattlesnakes, or spiders (Fig. 89).
7. Pottery jars or bottles painted, modeled, or engraved with circles, crosses, hands, skulls, rattlesnakes, flying horned serpents, and feathered serpents (Fig. 90).
8. Rectangular or circular paint palettes of stone, frequently with scalloped rims, either plain or engraved with cult symbols such as skulls or horned and winged rattlesnakes (Fig. 91, d and e).
9. Large stone figures with Negroid faces and a special arrangement of the hair across the top of the forehead (Fig. 92).
10. Copper plates on which were depicted dancing eagle warriors sometimes carrying a human trophy head in one hand and a baton in the other.
11. Shell gorgets with engraved or cut and engraved figures of eagle warriors similar to those on the copper plates, or of fighting warriors, or of chunkey players (Fig. 89).
12. The vestments of the Death Cult warrior, as observed on copper plates and shell gorgets, consisted of a cloak of eagle feathers; a beaded belt to which was attached a fringed, heart-shaped pouch; a cloth breechclout with a fringed sash which hung down in front; beaded bands for the arms and legs; a beaded neckband; a necklace from which hung a pendant; and moccasins. Sometimes representations of large animal or bird claws were worn at the heel.

The headdresses of the Death Cult warriors were lavish. These consisted of a beaded forelock, a copper roach, feathers or feather representation in copper, a hair ornament made in the shape of a bilobed arrow (examples of these have been found), a tasseled head tablet, and an occipital hair knot. Simpler headdresses consisted of antlers and only a few of the characteristics of the more elaborate style.

Ear ornaments were generally worn. These were ear-plugs or ear-spools to which were fastened beads or pendants or other ornaments.

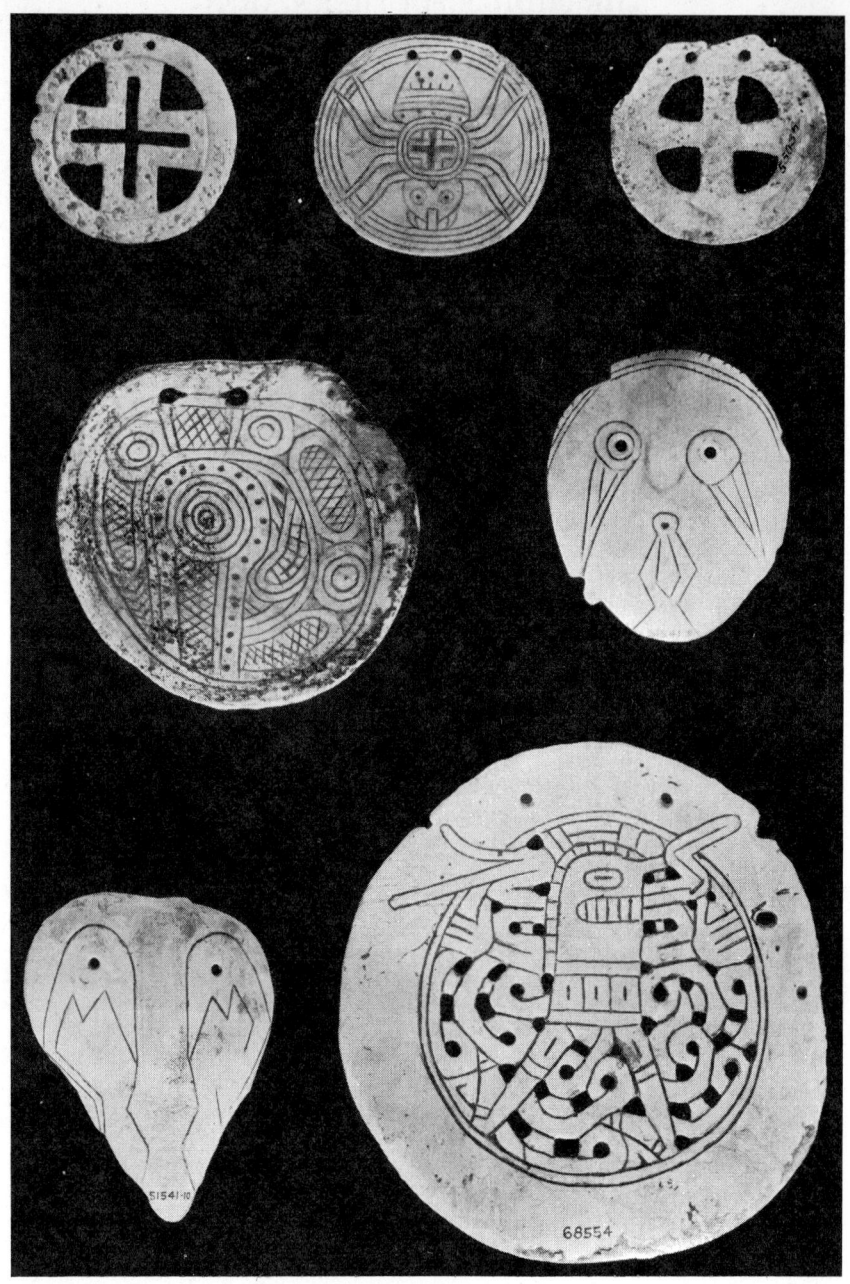

Fig. 89.—Shell gorgets of the Southern Death Cult. *Top row:* left, cross motif; center, spider motif; right, cross motif. *Middle row:* left, snake motif; right, masklike gorget with "weeping-eye" motif. *Bottom row:* left, masklike gorget with "weeping-eye" motif; right, human figure motif.

Fig. 90.—Pottery of the Southern Death Cult. *Left*, jar with hands and arm bones in low relief; *center*, effigy jar with "weeping-eye" motif; *right*, effigy jar representing hunchback.

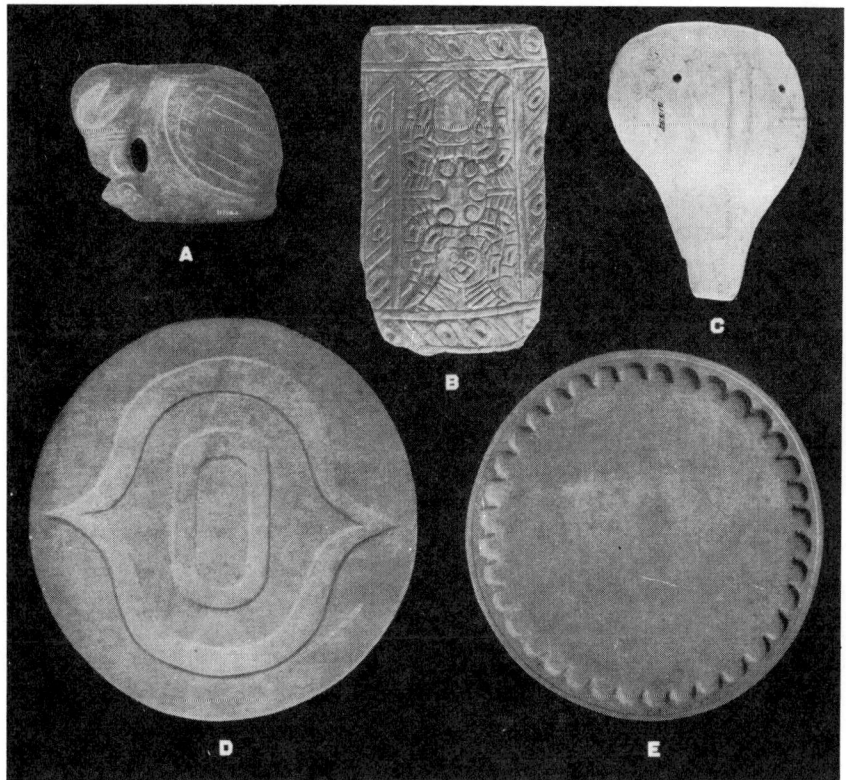

Fig. 91.—Sacred paraphernalia of the Southern Death Cult: *a*, tobacco pipe of stone in the form of a bird with weeping eyes; *b*, wooden plaque with engraved spider motif; *c*, masklike ornament of shell; *d, e*, stone pallettes.

The spatulate celt is probably a ceremonial object associated with the Death Cult and is generally made of soft stone and never shows signs of use. Other spatulate objects of stone may have been used as ceremonial clubs.

Certain paraphernalia were regional expressions of the Death Cult and did not have so broad a distribution as some of the objects and symbols previously mentioned. Examples of such objects are: copper masks perhaps representing a long-nosed god; effigy trophy heads made of pottery; effigy vessels of pottery which may have represented a hunchback or a partly desiccated mummy; and circular, embossed plaques of copper or even gold in rare instances.

The preceding lists contain most of the objects and symbols of the Southern Death Cult. Some of these are obviously the result of Mexi-

FIG. 92.—Stone idol of the Southern Death Cult. This figure, carved of fluorite, stands 12 inches high.

can Indian influences in the Southeast. There are a number of towns and villages of the Middle Mississippi culture which have yielded evidences of the cult. The most famous of these sites is Moundville in Alabama; Etowah in Georgia, a town occupied by Indians of the Lamar culture; and Spiro (the Temple Mound) in Oklahoma, a ceremonial center of the Indians of the Caddo culture. However, the Death Cult seems to have been more common east of the Mississippi than it was west of the river.

SOURCES

FORD and WILLEY, 1941; GRIFFIN, 1944a; KRIEGER, A., 1945; PHILLIPS, P., 1940.

THE MIDDLE SOUTHERN AREA

SUMMARY

In the Middle South we have the story of a sequence of cultural development which began with nomadic hunters and ended with hoe agriculturists. In this area, as well as in most southern areas, the hoe-wielding farmers were tending to become urbanized.

The earliest of the Archaic cultures in the Middle South may be represented by the eastern Folsom points found on the surface. In presumably somewhat later Archaic cultures there was still present a Folsom-like tradition along with a Cochise-like complex of grinding implements. Some of these late Archaic cultures had become sedentary by virtue of an abundant supply of river clams, which enabled the Indians to obtain food from a stable and unfailing source. These Archaic Indians did not possess pottery or practice agriculture, but they did have dogs. They hunted with the spear and spear-thrower.

The Intermediate period was characterized by pottery, tobacco pipes, burial mounds, and the beginnings of agriculture. Probably not all these arrived or were developed at the same time. This period seems to have witnessed the merging of northern and southern traditions in varying proportions. There appears also to have been greater cultural diversity than was exhibited by the Archaic period. This was a time of transition.

If agriculture was not practiced in the Intermediate period, it almost certainly was by Burial Mound times. The Burial Mound period shows both cultural diversity and a crystallization of tendencies or trends exhibited in the Intermediate period. Probably trade and commerce flourished and cultural isolation broke down.

The Indians of the Burial Mound period made their living by hunting, fishing, farming, and food-collecting. They used pottery, made tools and weapons of chipped stone, ground stone, shell and other materials, and were fond of ornaments. The earliest use of copper in the Middle South appears to have been in this period.

The great Temple Mound period was a time of village-states and hoe agriculture. If one could have seen the Indian women in corn fields, hoeing up the little hills and ridges of dirt or chopping out the weeds, one would have been reminded of cotton-chopping time in the same area today. The Temple Mound period was one of urbanization, village-states, intensive agriculture, religious cults, and shifting populations. This was the period interrupted by the arrival of White men. But the basic pattern of the period is with us even to this day in the rural South.

In the southern rural regions today there are small villages with a central square or plaza surrounded by dwellings and usually by a church (corresponding to a temple) and a courthouse (corresponding to a chiefs' house). Stretched around the village are farms on which corn, squash, beans, and tobacco, as well as other crops, are grown. Hunting, fishing, food-gathering, and dogs are still important cultural items. There are yet harvest festivals and quests for blood revenge. In some areas the arrival of spring is marked by drinking of the "black draught," a patent medicine. In former times the Indians of the Middle South used ceremonially the "black drink," compounded of the leaves of the dahoon holly (*Ilex cassine*).

We are not attempting to suggest that the rural South is unchanged since the Temple Mound period. We merely wish to point out that a basic pattern of living, persistent from early times and from other cultures, is even today to be found in the region.

CHAPTER 24

GEORGIA

INTRODUCTION

THE state of Georgia is about equally divided between coastal plain and the piedmont province of the Appalachian Highlands. The coastal plain area in southern and eastern Georgia was covered with southeastern pine forest (longleaf, loblolly, and slash pine) except for river valleys and marshy islands of river-bottom forest (cypress, tupelo, and red gum). The piedmont province of northern and western Georgia was forested with southern hardwoods (oak and pine).

The climate was relatively mild, with hot summers and cool or mild winters. The yearly frostless season varied by area from 190 to 240 days, and the annual rainfall ranged from 40 to 60 inches.

The climate, soils, and rainfall were suited to the agricultural activities of Indians living in later times, whereas the animals and birds of the forests and the fish and clams of the rivers supplied the basic diet for Indians of earliest times.

The rivers and streams, although not so plentiful as in some other areas of the East, offered opportunity for travel by canoe, and undoubtedly there were numerous trails for travel on foot.

The periods of culture in Georgia were the Archaic, Burial Mound I, Burial Mound II, and Temple Mound. These periods and cultures are outlined in Chart XII. In the following pages we shall describe most of the cultures of Georgia by period.

THE EARLY MACON CULTURE
(Archaic Period)
Probably before A.D. 500

The early Macon culture is known only from scattered finds of old flint tools and weapons. These finds are believed to be old because they underlay the flints and pottery of recent cultures and because they exhibit a degree of patination or decomposition greater than that of flints belonging to other cultures of the same area which are in the same soil. Thus the physical conditions of these flint tools and weapons and their stratigraphic position show that Early Macon culture is older than any other known culture in central Georgia.

Area.—Central Georgia in the vicinity of Macon.

Livelihood.—Probably these Indians obtained their living by hunting, fishing, and collecting wild foods.

Pottery.—None.

Tools, utensils, and weapons.—The early Macon Indians probably did not have the bow and arrow but used the spear and spear-thrower or atlatl. Spears were probably equipped with points of chipped flint. These points were generally rather crude notched and stemmed

CHART XII

Period and Probable Date	Cultures of Interior Georgia	Cultures of Coastal Georgia
Temple Mound II (A.D. 1500–1700)	Ocmulgee Fields, Etowah, Lamar	Irene
Temple Mound I (A.D. 1300–1700)	Macon Plateau	Savannah
Burial Mound II (A.D. 900–1300)	Swift Creek	Wilmington
Burial Mound I (A.D. 700–900)		Deptford
Archaic (1000 B.C.–A.D. 700)	Early Macon	Savannah River

forms. One point was of the Eastern Folsom type: a long, leaf-shaped form with a concave base, earlike projections on each side of the concavity, and longitudinal flutes on each face in the basilar third of the point.

There were crude knives of several styles, flint drills, large, turtle-back scrapers, rough flake knives or scrapers, and snub-nosed, plano-convex scrapers with shelflike hafts.

Pipes.—None.

Conjectures.—Perhaps the early Macon culture is a later, eastern counterpart of the hunting horizons of the West which are best exemplified by the Folsom culture. The Early Macon culture would thus be but one variation of the generalized eastern Folsom culture.

SOURCES

KELLY, 1938.

THE SAVANNAH RIVER CULTURE
(ARCHAIC PERIOD)
Probably before A.D. 700

Area.—Mostly on the coastal plain of Georgia, but there were also settlements along the coasts of southern Carolina and perhaps along the Atlantic side of northern Florida.

People.—Longheaded Sylvids.

Villages.—These Indians lived in rude shelters on top of large shell-mound dumps located along streams or rivers where there was an abundant supply of shellfish.

Livelihood.—Food was obtained by hunting, fishing, and gathering wild plants, seeds, nuts, and clams. There were no domestic animals except dogs.

Pottery.—In the early stages of their culture the Savannah River Indians did not make pottery. There must have been untold centuries of pottery-less Savannah River Indians until one day (perhaps 9:30 A.M., October 13, A.D. 500) some enterprising Indian (probably a woman) began to make pottery bowls instead of stone bowls. Whether our hypothetical lady thought of making pottery all by herself or heard about it from neighboring Indians is a question we cannot answer. But Savannah River Pottery is among the earliest, if not actually the earliest, in eastern North America.

At first the pottery was without ornamentation; but somewhat later (perhaps a hundred years or less) some was embellished with very simple designs (Fig. 93). None of the pottery was painted. Thick bowls with straight or incurved rims were made of sandy clay tempered with plant fibers. When the pottery was baked in a fire, the clay turned buff, gray, or brown, and the plant fiber burned out, leaving tiny holes.

Bowls were usually decorated, but some had plain, smooth surfaces. Ornamentation was generally produced by punctating, incising, and linear punctating arranged in zones, or in bands, or in overall patterns. These designs, both angular and curvilinear, were simple and geometric, consisting of cross-hatches, meanders, vertical lines or bands, and diamonds and triangles.

Some bowls had simple stamped impressions which gave them a grooved and ridged appearance. A few were brushed- or fabric-worked.

Tools, utensils, and weapons.—The primary hunting weapon was the spear and spear-thrower. This weapon consisted of a wooden shaft about fifteen to twenty-four inches long. At one end was a handle or grip, and glued to the other end was a socketed antler hook for engaging the butt of the spear.

For purposes of greater momentum and force, stone weights were attached to the atlatl shaft. These weights were prism- and wing-shaped bannerstones, rectanguloid bars, and boat-shaped stones.

Fig. 93.—Pottery of the Savannah River culture

Spears were made of wood or cane and tipped with large lopsided triangular points chipped from flint or hard slate. These points had stems which were used in hafting the point to the wood or cane spear-shaft. Other types of spear points, conical and socketed for hafting, were made of bone and antler.

Fish were caught with bone hooks or nets weighted down with small perforated soapstone slabs or notched soapstone pebbles.

Large ovate and triangular knives and cross-shaped and expanded-base drills were made of chipped stone. Fully grooved or three-quarter-grooved axes were made of stone by grinding and polishing techniques. Whetstones may have been used for shaping bone tools. Large and small spherical stones were used as hammers.

Stone mortars and disk-shaped mullers or grinders were probably used in the preparation of collected foods such as nuts, roots, and wild seeds.

There were a number of styles of bone awls, antler flakers, antler handles, cylindrical tubes, spatulas, and chisels.

Pipes.—None.

Ornaments.—Necklaces were made of small, disk-shaped stone beads, or spherical and tubular shell beads. Another style of bead was obtained by cutting the spires from olivella shells.

Rectangular pendants with single holes used for suspension were made of bone or shell, and two-hole bar gorgets were made of ground stone.

Long and short bone pins of various styles found may have been ornaments. Some of these were decorated with painted or incised designs. At one of the sites (Bilbo) the decorated bone pins were found only with the late Savannah River culture and were not present in the early levels. These pins were decorated with engraved designs, cross-hatches, rectangular frets, and other simple geometric patterns, somewhat reminiscent of certain designs in Hopewell bone ornaments and pottery, and especially Alexander pottery.

Burials.—The dead were deposited in graves dug into the midden. Bodies were flexed, extended, or disarticulated and buried in bundles. Probably the bundle burials represent a secondary deposition of the dead: burial of the bones of individuals who had been buried elsewhere and disinterred or who had been allowed partly to decompose before burial. Burial accompaniments were not abundant, although there were grave-offerings of tools, weapons, and ornaments with some of the burials.

Conjectures.—The Savannah River culture was coeval with other Archaic cultures of the southeastern United States and was among the first of these cultures to have pottery. The Savannah River culture was followed by the Deptford Culture.

SOURCES

CLAFLIN, 1931; FAIRBANKS, 1942; WARING, n.d.

THE DEPTFORD CULTURE
(BURIAL MOUND I PERIOD)
Ca. A.D. 700–900

Area.—The coast of Georgia and of northwest Florida was the prehistoric homeland of the Indians responsible for the Deptford culture.

Villages.—Villages were located along the seashore or a short distance inland along the rivers and streams. Some were built on shell middens.

Livelihood.—Hunting, fishing, and food-gathering furnished subsistence. The abundance of sea food and game offered by the environment made possible a rather sedentary life.

Pottery.—Deptford pottery was never painted and consisted of several varieties which were sand- or grit-tempered. The usual forms were jars or hemispherical bowls made by the coiling technique. Some jars had conoidal or rounded bottoms, others had squared bottoms and tetrapodal supports added to the base. Exterior surfaces were covered with bold check-stamped impressions, linear check-stamped impressions, or simple stamped impressions consisting of grooves. Pottery colors were buffs and gray and were merely the result of baking in a fire.

In the latest stage of the Deptford culture in Georgia some of the vessels were decorated with complicated stamped impressions.

Tools, utensils, and weapons.—Very little is known about the tools of the Deptford Indians. For one thing, they lived in areas where stone was not abundant and had to be used sparingly. The only implements considered characteristic of this culture were large chipped-flint projectile points, triangular in outline, stemmed, and having horizontal or barbed shoulders; whetstones; bone splinter awls; and awls made of animal ulnae.

Conjectures.—Despite the meager information, the Deptford culture is important because of its strategic position. In coastal Georgia it is slightly later than the Savannah River culture but earlier than the Wilmington, which belongs to the Burial Mound II period.

SOURCES

CALDWELL, n.d.; CALDWELL and McCANN, 1941; WILLEY and WOODBURY, 1942.

THE WILMINGTON CULTURE
(Burial Mound II Period)
Ca. a.d. 1000–1300 or 1400

Area.—Coastal Georgia.

Villages.—The Wilmington Indians lived in villages. Probably their houses were made of thatch-covered saplings.

Livelihood.—Hunting, fishing, the gathering of wild foods, and probably farming were the means of subsistence.

Pottery.—Unpainted pottery is most abundant. Broad-mouthed pots with rather straight sides and round or conoidal bottoms were made, tempered with particles of grit or previously fired clay (probably broken pottery). Firing produced colors in buff and gray.

The entire exterior of these pots was covered with various types of stamped impressions or brush marks such as could have been produced by dragging a wad of grass or something similar over the vessel walls while the clay was still plastic.

The stamped impressions were produced with a grooved or complicated stamp or by the use of heavy cord, fabric, or netting as a stamp.

Probably all Wilmington pottery was used for cooking.

Tools, utensils, and weapons.—Unfortunately there is little information, but we would guess that the Wilmington Indians hunted with the spear-thrower. Spear points were made of bone, antler, and perhaps rarely of stone. They had thick, stubby celts of ground stone which were probably set in wooden handles and used as axes. They also had bone awls or pins and punchlike implements made of antler.

Pipes.—These Indians probably smoked platform pipes of fired clay somewhat similar to the clay pipes of the Marksville and Troyville Indians.

Ornaments.—Central whorls of conch shells, two-hole gorgets, and small fragments of mica were probably used as ornaments.

Burials.—The Wilmington Indians erected dome-shaped mounds of earth over their dead. These mounds were small (about five feet high and thirty or forty feet in diameter). Burials were probably made in pits beneath the mound or on prepared floors at various levels of mound construction. Bodies were usually buried in a flexed position, although sometimes a number were cremated and the burned bone and ash placed in a single deposit within the mound.

Conjectures.—The Wilmington culture, which is not really so easy to separate from the Deptford culture as we have made it appear, is a coastal Georgian counterpart of Hopewell. The development from Deptford to Wilmington was interrupted by Hopewellian influences. These influences (not necessarily from Ohio) were incorporated into the already existing cultural stream, and the resultant mixture came to be the fully developed Wilmington culture.

SOURCES

CALDWELL, n.d.; CALDWELL and McCANN, 1941; FORD and WILLEY, 1941.

THE SWIFT CREEK CULTURE
(BURIAL MOUND II PERIOD)
Ca. A.D. 900–1300

Area.—The prehistoric Indian bearers of the Swift Creek culture seem to have fixed central Georgia as their homeland, although they extended their influences over a greater area, particularly northwestern Florida.

People.—Sylvids and Centralids.

Villages.—Swift Creek villages were situated in the bottom lands along rivers or streams. Rounded pits at these sites may have been used for storage. There were fire basins also. Conspicuous features of these villages were low, irregularly shaped mounds with flattened summits, which seem to have been erected haphazardly by gradual additions of bottom-land dirt separated by layers of sand. At different stages of construction rectangular houses were erected on top of these mounds. These houses were made of saplings, probably covered with thatch and cane mats.

The Swift Creek mounds do not appear to have been built as substructures for temples, a custom common in later times. Rather, they seem to be attempts to duplicate, in a small way, the large shell middens found in various parts of the Southeast. We would guess that these Indians, at least in their early stages, had a shell-mound-village tradition, but, having become farmers rather than shellfish gatherers, they improved their lowland living conditions by raising part of their villages on synthetic middens made of earth and sand instead of shells.

Livelihood.—The Swift Creek Indians obtained their food by agriculture, hunting, fishing, and perhaps some gathering of wild foods. They definitely had corn and probably grew squash and beans.

Pottery.—Unpainted cooking jars were made of clay tempered with particles of sand or grit. The color of this pottery—brown, buff, or occasionally orange—was merely the result of firing.

These jars were made with the coiling technique, usually having conoidal bottoms, slightly constricted necks, slightly flaring rims, and rather broad mouths. Some had smooth surfaces, and others were covered with stamped impressions produced by a carved paddle applied while the pottery was still plastic.

These paddles were made either of wood or of clay and were carved to produce a checkered pattern. The majority of paddle stamps were made to produce a complicated design composed of curvilinear or angular motifs. Angular designs were more popular with the early Swift Creek Indians; the later Swift Creek potters preferred curvilinear patterns.

The designs were cut deeply into the paddle, and the stamping of the plastic pottery was done very carefully; thus the patterns show up clearly. In cases where the impressions overlap one another, it is readily apparent, because of the otherwise careful application of the stamp. Usually the decorated jars were completely covered with stamped impressions, but some had stamped decoration only on the rim, whereas others had it only on the body.

Tools, utensils, and weapons.—Probably the spear and spear-thrower was in use among the Swift Creek Indians. The spear-thrower was probably made of wood, the remains of which have not been preserved. There have been found, however, several types of stone weights which may have been attached to spear-thrower shafts to obtain better balance and greater momentum in throwing the spear. The types of weights used were bannerstones (some of the winged variety) and boatstones.

Projectile points (spearheads or arrowheads) were chipped from flint. Most of these were large, slightly lopsided, and stemmed or notched for fastening to wooden shafts. Some points were large and triangular and did not have stems or notches.

There were notched knives with beveled blades (these may have been spearheads); large, stemmed knives, also of chipped flint; and small flake knives. Large or medium-sized ovate and triangular flint blades may have been used as knives or scrapers.

Many small end-scrapers (thumbnail type) and a few stemmed scrapers were used. Flint drills had three styles of bases—an unmodified base, a cross-shaped butt, and an expanded base.

Double-notched, crudely chipped choppers seem to have been the principal chopping implement, although the Swift Creek Indians also had grooved axes of ground stone and long polished-stone celts (ungrooved axes).

Implements for grinding corn and perhaps other foods were irregularly shaped, flat grinding-stones with small depressions and rectangular, oval, or round mullers (grinders).

Small perforated slabs of soapstone were used as sinkers on fishnets. It seems probable that fish were also caught with spears or bone hooks, but we have no evidence of this. Whetstones and rocks used as hammers complete the list of Swift Creek stone tools. Since no bone implements were found, it is possible that the Swift Creek Indians did not utilize bone. However, such a supposition seems unreasonable to us. Perhaps soil conditions were not suitable for the preservation of bone.

Pipes.—None.

Burials.—Burial customs of the Swift Creek Indians are known incompletely because the main burial centers have not yet been discovered. A few burials made in the peripheries of Swift Creek mounds were in intrusive pits. The bodies were in a flexed position and not accompanied by grave-offerings.

Conjectures and comments.—The Swift Creek culture probably lasted for a long time, and its influences were felt over a considerable area. In the region of central Georgia the Swift Creek culture was followed by the Macon Plateau culture.

SOURCES

FAIRBANKS, n.d.; JENNINGS, 1939; KELLY, 1938; WILLEY, 1939.

THE SAVANNAH CULTURE
(TEMPLE MOUND I PERIOD)
Ca. A.D. 1300–1500

In coastal Georgia the Wilmington culture was followed by the Savannah culture, which was partly contemporaneous with the late Swift Creek culture of central Georgia.

Area.—The coastal plain of Georgia.

People.—The Savannah Indians, of rather small stature, had heads which were broad or medium broad in proportion to length, and they belonged to the Centralid variety of American Indian.

Villages.—The dwellings of these Indians probably were placed outside the periphery of a palisaded ceremonial center. This center was dominated by a large, flat-topped mound in the form of an elongated pentagon. This mound was of sand and shells and was built up in successive stages (one over another). On the summit, which was reached by a ramp topped with log steps, was a square temple or sacred building surrounded by a small palisade of closely set posts. The temple was made of poles interwoven with reeds and plastered with clay. Probably the roof was thatched. In the center of the floor was a fire basin surrounded by gutters.

The mound and buildings similar to the temple in construction were surrounded by a great palisade in the form of a broken circle. Buildings were set both within and outside the great palisade.

Livelihood.—Probably the Savannah Indians were farmers, fishermen, hunters, and food-collectors.

Pottery.—Pottery vessels of grit-tempered clay were made by the coiling technique. This pottery was sun-dried and then fired to colors in buff, red, and dark gray. Surfaces were smoothed, polished, or stamped.

Decoration was achieved by stamping or impressing with a paddle wrapped with fine cord, a gridded paddle, and a wooden paddle into which were carved complex designs based upon concentric circles, figure eights, squares, and diamonds.

Jars or bowls of various sizes and shapes were made, all with round bottoms. Much of the pottery was used for cooking and possibly storage, but some vessels were used only for burial purposes.

Tools, utensils, and weapons.—Probably these Indians used bows and arrows. Arrow points of chipped stone were exceedingly rare, but there were triangular points with concave bases, as well as narrow, trianguloid points with flat bases. Possibly hardened wood or cane points were used on arrows.

Perforated conch shells may have served as blades for hoes. Unfortunately, we do not have any concrete information on other tools, weapons, and utensils of this culture. Perhaps they used various types of chipped-stone scrapers, bone awls, and ungrooved axes of stone. They had bowls made of conch shells.

Pipes.—The Savannah Indians smoked elbow pipes made of baked clay.

Ornaments.—These Indians had small, circular gorgets of shell, knob-headed pins of conch-shell centers for ear ornaments, and probably necklaces of shell beads. There were also a few ornaments made from sheet copper and decorated with a *repoussé* design.

Burials.—The Savannah Indians usually buried their dead under mounds of sand and shell, although there were rare burials in the village area. Cremations were frequent. Some cremations, infant burials, and burials of bones were placed in pottery urns (jars with tops) for interment. Pottery, ornaments, and tools were sometimes placed in the graves in small quantities.

Conjectures and comments.—The Savannah Indians seem to have been somewhat isolated from the Indians of central Georgia. They preceded and were ancestral to the Irene Indians of the Georgia coast.

SOURCES

CALDWELL and MCCANN, 1941.

THE IRENE CULTURE
(TEMPLE MOUND II PERIOD)
Ca. A.D. 1500–1650

Area.—The Irene Indians were descendants of the Savannah Indians and lived in coastal Georgia.

People.—These Indians, of rather small stature and with broad heads, were Centralids. Some may have practiced cradle-board deformation.

Villages.—Probably dwellings were outside the double palisade of posts that surrounded a large pentagonal plaza. The posts of the palisade may have been interlaced with reeds and plastered with clay, but it was probably ceremonial rather than defensive in purpose.

Inside the palisade and at one end of the plaza was a large circular rotunda or winter council chamber, 120 feet in diameter. This was built with six concentric circular walls made of vertical posts, probably interwoven with reeds and plastered with clay. The different chambers must have had connecting doorways. The flat roof was probably thatched with palmetto fronds, except for the round courtyard in the center.

At the other end of the plaza and outside the palisade there was a large circular mound of sand, clay, and shell about 160 feet in diameter and 16 feet high, rounded on top. Adjoining this mound was a small dome-shaped burial mound of sand and shell.

Some distance from the large mound and the council chamber was a mortuary house. This building, square with rounded corners and partly underground, was made of posts interlaced with cane or reed lathing covered on the inside with a plaster of clay and Spanish moss and on the outside with cane or palmetto matting. It had a projecting entrance passage, and the roof consisted of poles and palmetto thatching upheld by four central posts. This mortuary may have been used for the preparation of bodies for burial. In time, however, it was burned and the area made into a cemetery surrounded by a circular double palisade. The ruins of the burned building and the rest of the cemetery area were covered with sand.

Dwellings were square or rectangular and were constructed in much the same fashion as the sacred ceremonial buildings.

Livelihood.—Probably farming, hunting, fishing, and the gathering of wild plants, nuts, fruits, and shellfish furnished food. There is no direct evidence of agriculture, but probably corn and other crops were raised.

Pottery.—Several styles of grit-tempered pottery were made by the coiling process and were decorated or undecorated. The pottery was in the forms of jars and bowls and was sun dried before firing. The natural (unpainted) colors after firing ranged from buff through red to dark gray.

All the jars and bowls had round or semiconoidal bottoms. Ornamented vessels were decorated by incising or stamping. Stamped decoration covered the entire vessel exterior and was produced by a paddle stamp into which had been carved many variations of the peculiarly shaped fylfot cross. Incised decoration was confined to the rim or shoulder area of vessels otherwise plain and consisted of horizontal bands of repeating or alternating motifs of linear or curvilinear designs. Appliqué pellets or nodes were sometimes added to the design.

Pottery was used for cooking and other utilitarian purposes as well as for ceremonial occasions.

Tools, utensils, and weapons.—Probably fields were cultivated with digging-sticks and hoes of wood or of perforated conch shells attached to wooden handles. There were narrow triangular arrow points and small stemmed points of chipped flint. Possibly there were also points of wood or cane. Boatstones may have been used as weights for spear-throwers or they may have been ornaments. Fire drills were used for making fire, and the drill sockets were of stone. Hones made of pottery sherds were plentiful. Awls were made of bone, and ungrooved axes of ground stone. Probably there were a number of tools, weapons, and utensils of which we are yet ignorant, or perhaps perishable materials such as wood were used for the manufacture of implements.

Pipes.—Elbow pipes of stone and probably fired clay were used.

Ornaments.—Necklaces of shell beads were probably worn. The women wore knob-headed pins of shell in their ears. Large circular gorgets of conch shell were probably worn as ornaments on the chest.

Games.—Numerous disks of pottery and some of stone may have been used in games.

Burials.—Most of the dead were buried in the cemetery, although some were interred in the burial mounds and others in the center of the rotunda. Bodies were usually flexed, although some were cremated. The remains of infants and children were placed in pottery urns, and burials of individual skulls occurred. Some of the burial pits were sealed with clay plugs. When present at all, grave-offerings were scanty. In one instance a burial was accompanied by red ocher, and in another case fragments of mica were present.

Conjectures and comments.—The Irene culture was contemporary with the Lamar culture of central Georgia. Probably the Irene Indians were Guale (Yamassee) or Cusabo, and most likely they spoke a Muskhogean language. The Irene culture was related to those of various Muskhogean-speaking and proto-Creek groups in Georgia.

SOURCES

CALDWELL and MCCANN, 1941.

THE MACON PLATEAU CULTURE
(TEMPLE MOUND I PERIOD)
Ca. A.D. 1300–1600

Returning from the Georgia coast to the central regions, and going back in time to Temple Mound I period, we have the Macon Plateau culture, which followed Swift Creek.

Area.—Central Georgia.

People.—The Macon Plateau Indians were Centralids. Their heads were broad in proportion to length.

Villages.—Villages consisted of dwellings and temple mounds arranged around a central plaza. These villages were surrounded by a double-ditch system of moats, perhaps for defense.

Dwellings were rectangular houses built of upright posts intertwined with cane and plastered with clay. Roofs were probably thatched.

Temples or chief's houses similar to ordinary dwellings were built on the flat summits of large pyramidal mounds of earth faced with clay. Steps led upward to the summits.

Large circular lodges, made of logs and saplings and covered with earth, were used as council chambers. Entrance was through a covered passage. Inside the chamber and around the wall were raised seats of clay. In front of each there was a basin-like depression in the floor—possibly a vomitorium used in the black-drink ceremony. In the center of the chamber was a raised platform or an eagle effigy made of clay. This is the only instance of earthen lodges in eastern United States outside the Plains area.

Livelihood.—Food was obtained by farming, hunting, and gathering. Corn was planted and cultivated in rows rather than in hills. Deer, bear, and small animals were hunted, and river clams (mussels) were collected.

Pottery.—These Indians made unpainted pottery, fired to a reddish or reddish-buff color, tempered with fine grit or grit mixed with shell. Probably the coiling method was used. Most vessels had undecorated, smooth, plain surfaces.

Large globular jars with wide mouths were the most common form. Some of these had plain or noded loop handles. Bowls often had erect animal effigies modeled on their rims, and water bottles were usually modeled to represent animals. Salt pans (shallow vessels used for evaporating salt from saline waters) were present. Some of these were basin-shaped and either plain or fabric impressed. Another style was a small, thick-walled, cylindrical jar, plain or decorated with cord-roughening, stamping, incising, or punctating. There were also some pottery jars impressed with plain-plaited fabric.

Tools, utensils, and weapons.—Probably the bow and arrow and the spear and spear-thrower were used. Arrow and spear points of several kinds were made of chipped flint. There were asymetric stemmed points, notched points, triangular points, and notched points with beveled edges.

Pick-shaped bannerstones may have been used as weights for spear-throwers. Probably wooden digging-sticks and hoes for planting and cultivating corn were in use. Other tools were large ungrooved axes of polished stone, long, slender bone awls, hammerstones, thumbnail type scrapers of chipped flint, small flat adzes of polished stone, and several types of flint drills.

There were conch-shell dippers and probably mussel-shell spoons.

Pipes.—Pipes of several kinds were smoked—stone elbow pipes with flattened stems and large equal-armed elbow pipes of pottery. These also had flattened stems which projected slightly beyond the bowl.

Ornaments.—These Indians wore necklaces of cut, tubular, disk, or Marginella shells, although circular gorgets of conch shell were used occasionally. Copper ornaments were rare, but there were cut animal jaws covered with sheet copper and sheet-copper ornaments with raised designs.

It is possible that some of the Macon Plateau Indians painted their bodies red and their faces white. One figurine was thus decorated. Except for the shell beads described, ornaments were not plentiful.

Games.—Biconcave discoidals of ground stone were probably used for playing a game which in historic times was called chunkey. Pottery disks may also have been used in some game.

Burials.—The dead were sometimes buried in the village, but more often they were placed in pits dug into the summits of the pyramidal mounds. In some instances there were submound pits containing log tombs. Flexed and bundle burials were common. There were a few cremations. Some bodies were extended, and in a few instances there were rearticulated, extended burials in which skeletons or dismembered bodies were rearticulated to look like untouched bodies in extended positions. In a few cases the burials were accompanied by shell beads, pottery, conch-shell dippers, pipes, bone awls, and tools of stone.

Conjectures and comments.—The Macon Plateau culture followed the Swift Creek culture in central Georgia. Macon Plateau was strongly influenced by certain early groups of Middle Mississippi Indians who may even have entered central Georgia and mixed with indigenous populations. The Macon Plateau culture evinces vestiges of a Hopewell tradition which may also have entered with the Middle Mississippi influences or could have already been in the area.

SOURCES

FAIRBANKS, n.d.; JENNINGS, 1939; KELLY, 1938; WILLEY, 1939.

GEORGIA

THE LAMAR CULTURE
(TEMPLE MOUND II PERIOD)
Ca. A.D. 1450–1700

Area.—Central and western Georgia.

People.—Broadheaded Centralids.

Villages.—Villages consisted of large flat-topped mounds at each end of a plaza surrounded by the dwellings of the villagers.

At the type site of the Lamar culture, the village was on an island surrounded by river or river and swamp. Around the village was a palisade. Inside was a plaza separating the two mounds, which were built of earth in successive levels and capped or plated with a smooth layer of clay. Upon the flat summits of the mounds, and reached by spiral ramps, were temples or ceremonial buildings made of posts, poles, thatching, and clay plaster.

Between the mounds near the center of the plaza was a court where chunkey probably was played.

The houses of the village were rectangular in plan and made of vertical posts set into the ground. Reed or cane was interwoven through the uprights to serve as lathing upon which clay was plastered. Roofs were probably made of poles and thatched with grass.

Livelihood.—The Lamar Indians obtained their food by farming, hunting, and gathering. They raised corn and beans and gathered acorns and wild peas.

Pottery.—Pottery of several styles was made by the coiling method. Plain and decorated jars and bowls were made of clay tempered with sand, grit, or shell. Natural colors of the pottery resulting from firing were buffs, browns, and grays. None of the pottery was painted.

Large jars with straight or flaring rims and conoidal bottoms and bowls with angular shoulders (carinated bowls) and round bottoms were common.

Undecorated jars usually were shell-tempered and had smooth surfaces. When decorated, jars usually bore a paddle-stamped design of fylfot crosses, concentric circles, paired concentric circles, loops, and other curvilinear motifs.

Incised decoration was usually placed on the rims of bowls and consisted of a band of clockwise scrolls often accompanied by other motifs.

Tools, utensils, and weapons.—Arrow points were made of chipped flint or antler. Those of flint were stemmed and thick and of medium size. Less common were small, thin, triangular points of chipped flint.

No agricultural tools have been found, but digging-sticks and hoes of wood were probably used for planting and tilling.

Other tools used were small ungrooved axes of polished stone, several styles of bone awls, triangular and ovate knives of chipped flint, shallow mortars of various sizes, bun-shaped or oval manos, smoothing-stones, and hammerstones.

Pipes.—Clay pipes of a rather flamboyant style were smoked. These were right-angle, elbow pipes with projecting stems and flaring bowls, often decorated with numerous pyramidal points or nodes.

Ornaments.—The Lamar Indians adorned themselves with such ornaments as necklaces of beads made from the central portions of conch shells, knobbed pins of shell which were worn in the hair or perhaps the ear, and circular shell gorgets that were engraved and pierced. Unperforated bear canine teeth and worked beaver incisors may also have been ornaments.

Games.—Possibly biplane disks of polished stone and pottery disks of various sizes were used in games.

Burials.—The dead, usually in a flexed position, were interred in grave pits. Sometimes burials were accompanied by grave-offerings such as pottery vessels, pipes, shell ornaments, and smoothing-stones.

Conjectures and comments.—The Lamar culture in its earliest stages may have been coeval with late Savannah. Lamar certainly was coeval with the Irene culture of the Georgia coast and with the Macon Plateau. Lamar, for the most part, preceded the historic Ocmulgee Fields culture of central Georgia and probably was proto-Creek.

SOURCES

FAIRBANKS, n.d.; JENNINGS, 1939; KELLY, 1938; WILLEY, 1939.

THE ETOWAH CULTURE
(TEMPLE MOUND II PERIOD)
Ca. A.D. 1400–1700

The great mound site of Etowah belonged to the Lamar Indians who had mixed with or had been influenced by Middle Mississippi Indians. Moreover, Etowah was one of the ceremonial centers of the Southern Death Cult. Consequently, the Etowah variant of the Lamar culture is extremely spectacular.

The Etowah site was situated on the north bank of the Etowah River near Carterville in Bartow County, Georgia. The village extended 3,000 feet along the river and 1,500 feet inland. A moat or ditch completely surrounded the landward parts of the village. Near the center there were three pyramidal mounds of earth, the largest of these being 60 or 70 feet high and about 380 feet square at the base. Probably this mound contained some 4,300,000 cubic feet of earth. The other mounds were considerably smaller.

All three mounds probably had temples or chief's houses upon their summits which were reached by means of earthern ramps. One of the smaller mounds contained a number of burials, some of them in graves lined with stone slabs. In these graves and elsewhere within the mound were tremendous quantities of elaborate ornaments and paraphernalia of the Southern Death Cult, as well as the ordinary tools, weapons, and utensils of the Lamar type.

SOURCES

MOOREHEAD, 1932.

THE OCMULGEE FIELDS CULTURE
(TEMPLE MOUND II PERIOD)
Ca. A.D. 1650–1700

Area.—The Ocmulgee Fields culture followed the Lamar culture in central Georgia and represents the historic Creeks and perhaps other tribes.

People.—Broadheaded Centralids.

Villages.—Villages consisted of small round or oval houses made of posts, probably covered by thatching of grass or by woven mats.

Livelihood.—Corn and probably other crops were raised. Additional food was obtained by hunting and gathering.

Pottery.—Jars and bowls were made of clay either untempered or tempered with fragments of shell. The natural color of the pottery after being fired was buff or light gray. Some of the jars had strap handles. Vessel surfaces were smoothed or roughened by brushing or stippling. Some vessels were plain; others were decorated by incising or painting.

Incised decoration was confined to the rim areas of bowls and consisted of bands of chevrons, diagonals, guilloches, loops, and pine-tree-like herringbones. Stamped decorations were no longer used.

Painted pottery was in solid red or natural colors decorated with red scrolls and other curvilinear designs.

Tools, utensils, and weapons.—Arrows were tipped with small triangular points of chipped flint. Besides bow and arrow, these Indians used guns, swords, knives, and axes obtained from White traders.

Iron hoes, ungrooved axes of polished stone, small, thumbnail-type scrapers of chipped flint, hammerstones, and mussel-shell spoons were used.

Pipes.—The Ocmulgee Fields Indians smoked small clay elbow pipes of their own manufacture, or white clay church-warden pipes obtained from White traders.

Ornaments.—Conch-shell beads, Venetian glass beads, armbands of European copper, small bells of brass or bronze, and pendants of copper were used as items of adornment.

Burials.—The dead, forced into a flexed posture, were buried in shallow graves. Tools, weapons, and ornaments were usually placed with them.

SOURCES

FAIRBANKS, n.d.; JENNINGS, 1939; KELLY, 1938; WILLEY, 1939.

SUMMARY

The earliest Indians of Georgia obtained their food by hunting, fishing, and collecting or gathering. They made their tools, weapons, and utensils of stone, bone, and wood. They did not have pottery, agriculture, or burial mounds. Toward the end of the Archaic period some undecorated pottery was made, and somewhat later decorated pottery was manufactured.

The Burial Mound I period was characterized by the beginning of the use of mounds, the start of agriculture, and the use of pottery decorated by stamping. The culture of this period was still oriented toward the Archaic.

In Burial Mount II times agriculture, mounds, and stamped pottery were characteristic. Tobacco pipes appeared, possibly for the first time. Houses were rectangular and perhaps more substantially constructed than in previous periods.

The Temple Mound I and II periods were the climax of the prehistoric development of Georgian culture. There were great ceremonial centers of different kinds, hoe agriculture was practiced intensively, and aesthetic pursuits were cultivated. Some Indians of the late Temple Mound period participated in the activities of the Southern Death Cult. The culture of the latest Indians of Georgia showed the disintegration brought about by the inroads of White settlement.

As in many other areas, the prehistory of Georgia is the story of the Indians' development from a nomadic hunting culture to a sedentary life based upon agriculture.

CHAPTER 25

THE FLORIDA AREA

INTRODUCTION

THE Florida area was a forested coastal plain. Southeastern pine forest (longleaf, loblolly, and slash pine) covered most of the region, but in the southern part there were areas of marsh and prairie grassland and of subtropical forest.

The climate was moderate, having mild winters and hot summers. There was a yearly frostless season of more than 240 days, and the annual rainfall ranged from 50 to 60 inches.

CHART XIII

Probable Date	Period	Culture
A.D. 1400–1700	Late Prehistoric	Late Weeden Island, Fort Walton, Key Marco
A.D. 900–1400	Late Transitional	Crystal River, Santa Rosa–Swift Creek, Early Weeden Island
A.D. 500–900	Early Transitional	Late Tick Island, Deptford
Before A.D. 500	Archaic	Tick Island

Animal life was abundant, and agriculture was feasible. Thus the environment afforded opportunities to obtain food by hunting and fishing or by farming.

The ocean and the rivers offered fine waterways for travel by dugout canoe, and the Indians of Florida probably should be considered a maritime people.

The earliest inhabitants of this region were Sylvids, some of whom may have been contemporaries of animals that are now extinct, such as the mammoth, mastodon, ancient horse, and tapir. This association need not imply great antiquity, for it is probable that many of the animals now extinct were living in Florida only a few thousand years ago. However, the problem of the association of man with extinct animals in Florida is by no means settled.

THE FLORIDA AREA

Whether or not the earliest Indians of Florida hunted animals now extinct, it is certain that they lived by hunting and fishing. They did not have pottery, agriculture, mounds, pipes, or certain other characteristics of later inhabitants in the same area.

In the Early Transitional period that followed the Archaic, fiber-tempered pottery was made. It is possible that agriculture was introduced sometime during the Early Transitional stage.

The Late Transitional period was characterized by earthen mounds, new kinds of pottery, agriculture, and trade relationships with distant peoples.

The Late Prehistoric period saw the development of intensive hoe agriculture, temple mounds, and many styles of pottery.

Briefly outlined in Chart XIII are the periods and some of the cultures of the Florida area.

THE TICK ISLAND CULTURE
(ARCHAIC AND EARLY TRANSITIONAL PERIODS)
Ca. 500 B.C.—A.D. 900

The Tick Island culture somewhat resembled the Savannah River culture of the Georgia area. It was the product of Indians who lived by hunting, fishing, and food-collecting. Their villages were on top of middens or garbage dumps containing discarded clam shells and other refuse.

Tools, weapons, and utensils were made of stone, bone, shell, and probably wood. There were no pipes. Fiber-tempered pottery was manufactured by the late Tick Island peoples, but pottery of any kind was unknown to the Early Transitional inhabitants.

SOURCES
GRIFFIN, 1946; MOORE, 1894 (Part I); WYMAN, 1874.

THE DEPTFORD CULTURE
(EARLY TRANSITIONAL PERIOD)
Ca. A.D. 500–900

The Deptford culture, described in the chapter on Georgia, appeared also in northwestern Florida during the Early Transitional period. It was coeval in part with the Late Tick Island culture.

SOURCES
WILLEY and WOODBURY, 1942.

THE SANTA ROSA–SWIFT CREEK CULTURE
(Late Transitional Period)
Ca. A.D. 900–1300

The Santa Rosa–Swift Creek culture of northwestern Florida seems to have been the product of a mixture of Marksville-Troyville with Swift Creek elements. Although there was probably some knowledge of agriculture, the unsuitable soils of the area and the abundant supply of shellfish made food-collecting the most feasible means of subsistence. Stone tools were not abundant, although rather large chipped-stone projectile points and ground-stone ungrooved axes were in use.

Characteristic pottery was sand-tempered and consisted of jars and bowls decorated with stamped and incised designs. Complicated stamped designs covered the entire vessel or a band around the upper part on some. Rocked-stamp designs were used but were usually confined to zones outlined by incising, although some vessels were completely covered with rocked-stamp impressions.

Flexed and bundle burials have been found in conical sand mounds.

SOURCES
Willey and Woodbury, 1942

THE CRYSTAL RIVER CULTURE
(Late Transitional Period)
Ca. A.D. 1200–1400

The Crystal River culture was in part the result of a mixture of Early Weeden Island with traits from Ohio Hopewell and Lower Mississippi Valley Marksville-Troyville.

The Crystal River people obtained food by gathering shellfish, by hunting and fishing, and probably by some farming. They fashioned tools and weapons from bone, stone, shell, and wood. Pottery was made in various styles and included a negative painted ware. Elbow and platform pipes were of stone and fired clay.

These Indians wore Hopewell-like ornaments such as antler effigies made of wood covered with sheet copper, copper-covered wooden ear-spools, solid copper ear-spools that were sometimes covered with sheets of silver or meteoric iron, *repoussé* and stencil-like copper ornaments, beads and breastplates of copper, effigies of sheet mica, pierced bear teeth, and shell effigies of bear teeth.

The dead were buried under conical mounds of sand.

SOURCES
Willey and Phillips, 1944.

THE WEEDEN ISLAND CULTURE
(Late Prehistoric Period)
Ca. A.D. 900–1600

Area.—A four-hundred mile stretch of the Florida Gulf Coast southward from Mobile Bay.

People.—Roundheaded Centralids who practiced head deformation.

Villages.—Small villages, probably with religious and political autonomy, were situated along the coast and rivers up to fifty (sometimes a hundred) miles inland. Sites were characterized by shallow middens of shell and other refuse. Houses were probably made of poles covered with thatching.

Flat-topped domiciliary mounds and conical burial mounds of sand were associated with some villages.

Livelihood.—Food was obtained by gathering shellfish and other collectible items, by hunting and fishing, and by some farming.

Pottery.—Weeden Island pottery exhibited tremendous variations in form and was made of sand-tempered clay, as a rule, by the coiling (annular ring) technique. When fired, the pottery was buff in color.

Basic shapes were bowls, beakers, jars, plates, effigy vessels, and other forms so elaborated that they defy definition. Some of these unusual forms were square bowls and beakers with flat bottoms, double bowls, V-shaped vessels with two openings, multiple bowls (many joined together), bowls and jars with multiple lobes, trays with multiple compartments, double-globed jars, and still other eccentric forms.

More or less conservative styles frequently were embellished with handles, effigies, and holes and "windows" punched in the vessel walls during construction.

Pottery was plain or decorated with painting, incising, punctating, pinching, and stamping with checked or complicated stamps. There were many different designs—simple and complicated geometric patterns, pictographic ornamentation, and elaborate combinations of various curvilinear motifs.

Tools, utensils, and weapons.—Notched and stemmed projectile points, knives, lance points, and scrapers were all made of chipped stone.

Hammers, hones, sinkers, and ungrooved axes were manufactured of ground stone. Bone awls were in common use.

Drinking cups, hoes, and unidentified tools were made of shell. Probably there were also many tools of wood which have not been preserved.

Pipes.—Elbow pipes were made of fired clay or of ground stone.

Ornaments.—Stone gorgets, stone and shell pendants, effigies of spear points, lumps of galena, red ocher, fragments of sheet mica and copper, perforated animal and fish teeth, and cut animal jaws—all were used as ornaments.

Burials.—Flexed or bundle burials were placed within or beneath conical mounds of sand. Single and multiple graves occurred in the same mound. During the burial ceremonies fires were made at various stages in the mound under construction. Mortuary offerings were placed with the dead. Pottery in the graves was "killed," sometimes by being broken but more frequently by having holes punched through vessel bottoms.

Weeden Island culture was the climax of the Gulf Coast and was related to cultures in the Lower Mississippi Valley and Georgia. It was somewhat influenced by developments in the Middle Southern area but maintained itself as a typically Floridian culture.

SOURCES

WILLEY, 1945.

THE FORT WALTON CULTURE
(LATE PREHISTORIC PERIOD)
Ca. A.D. 1500–1700

The Fort Walton culture of northwestern Florida was a mixture of Late Weeden Island and Middle Mississippi. The broadheaded Fort Walton Indians obtained their food by collecting shellfish, hunting, fishing, and farming. They made several styles of pottery tempered with quartzite and other grit, sand, or occasionally shell.

Decoration was achieved by incising and punctating designs upon the upper parts of bowls and jars and the upper surfaces of triangular rim projections on dishes. Designs included animal and human figures highly conventionalized, curvilinear and rectilinear meanders, hachures, scrolls, loops, and diamonds.

Flat-topped pyramidal mounds with ramps were built of sand. Probably there were temples or chiefs' houses on the summits of these mounds.

SOURCES

WILLEY, 1942.

THE FLORIDA AREA

THE KEY MARCO CULTURE
(LATE PREHISTORIC PERIOD)
Ca. A.D. 1400–1700

Area.—Southern Gulf Coast of Florida.

People.—Roundheaded Centralids.

Villages.—Thatch-covered houses of wood built on piles along the shores of artificial lagoons or bayous. Shell middens marked the sites of the village dumps, and flat-topped pyramidal mounds (sometimes faced with whole conch shells) served as substructures for sacred buildings.

Livelihood.—Food was obtained by collecting shellfish, by hunting and fishing, and perhaps by some agriculture.

Pottery.—Untempered (muck ware) pottery bowls and jars, either plain or decorated, were made and used for cooking.

Basketry and weaving.—Nets, mats, and baskets were woven of various materials.

Tools, utensils, and weapons.—Wooden weapons used were beautifully carved spear-throwers (Fig. 94, *b* and *c*) of several kinds, and spears, clubs, and swords made with blades of closely spaced sharks' teeth glued into a slot (Fig. 94, *f*).

Fish were caught with nets weighted with shell sinkers or with compound fishhooks (wooden shanks and bone hooks).

Other tools were adzes with wooden handles, blade sockets of antler, sometimes carved in the form of animals, and blades of shell (Fig. 94, *d*); scrapers of clam shell; clam-shell hoes; picks (Fig. 94, *a*), hammers, gouges, and adzes of conch shell with wooden handles; ungrooved shell axes, also with wooden handles; shark-tooth knives; bone knives; fish-jaw saws; rasps of coral-sandstone; and various styles of bone awls.

Four-footed stools (Fig. 94, *e*) were fashioned of wood, cylindrical pillows were made of matting, and mats and rugs were woven of rushes and shredded bark.

Spoons, ladles, and dippers were manufactured from clam and conch shells, and cups, bowls, trays, and mortars from wood.

Travel and transportation.—Dugout canoes (Fig. 94, *h*) of various sizes and wooden paddles (Fig. 94, *g*) were in use. Perhaps double canoes with a platform between them were equipped with sails of bark matting.

Ornaments.—Beads of shell and deer antler, shell pendants and gorgets, wooden brooches inlaid with tortoise shell, wooden labrets,

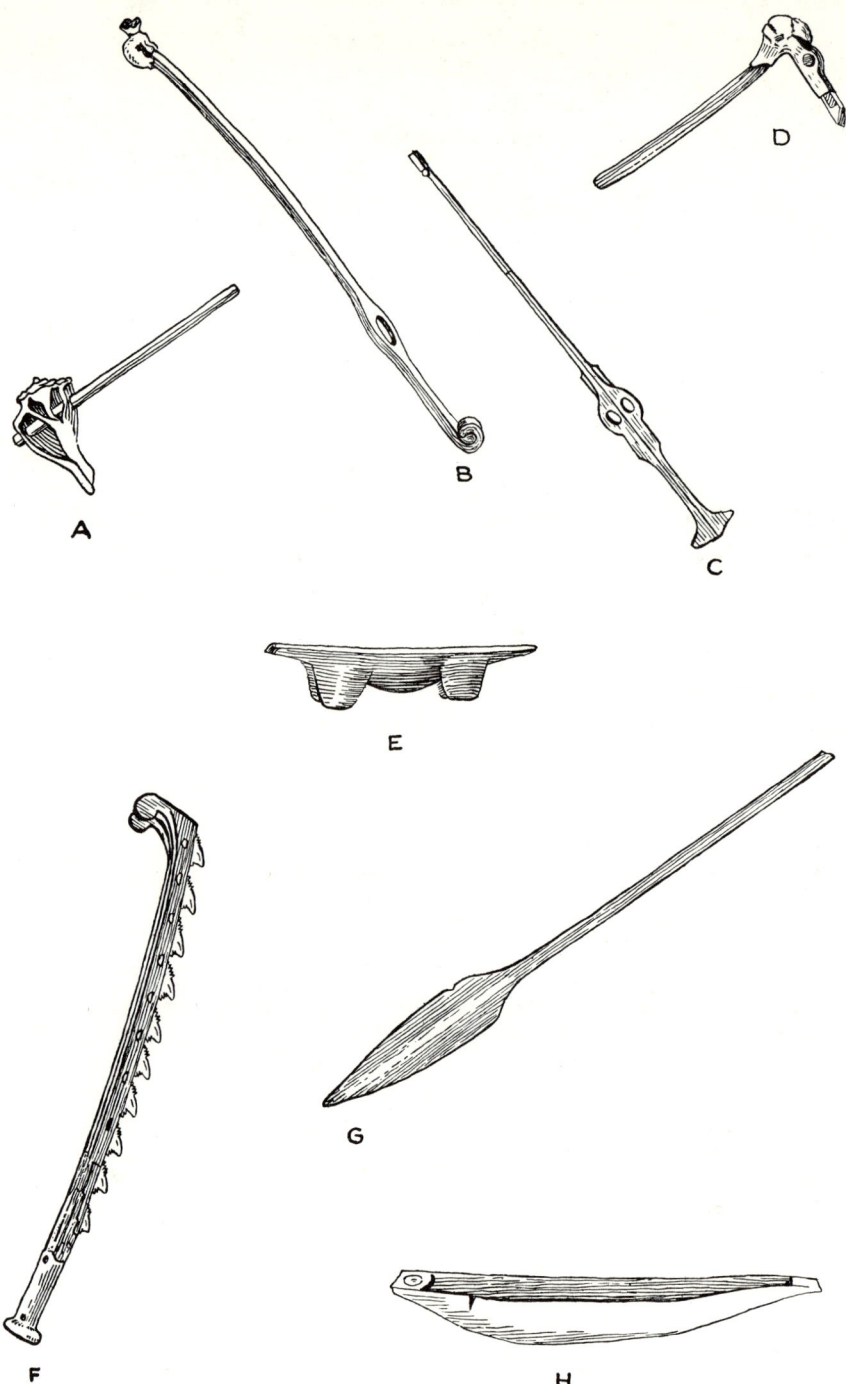

FIG. 94.—Tools, utensils, and weapons of the Key Marco culture: *a*, conch-shell pick with wooden handle; *b, c*, wooden spear-throwers; *d*, adz with wooden handle, socket of antler, and blade of shell; *e*, wooden stool; *f*, club or sword of wood with inset sharks' teeth; *g*, canoe paddle of wood; *h*, model of dugout canoe. (After F. H. Cushing.)

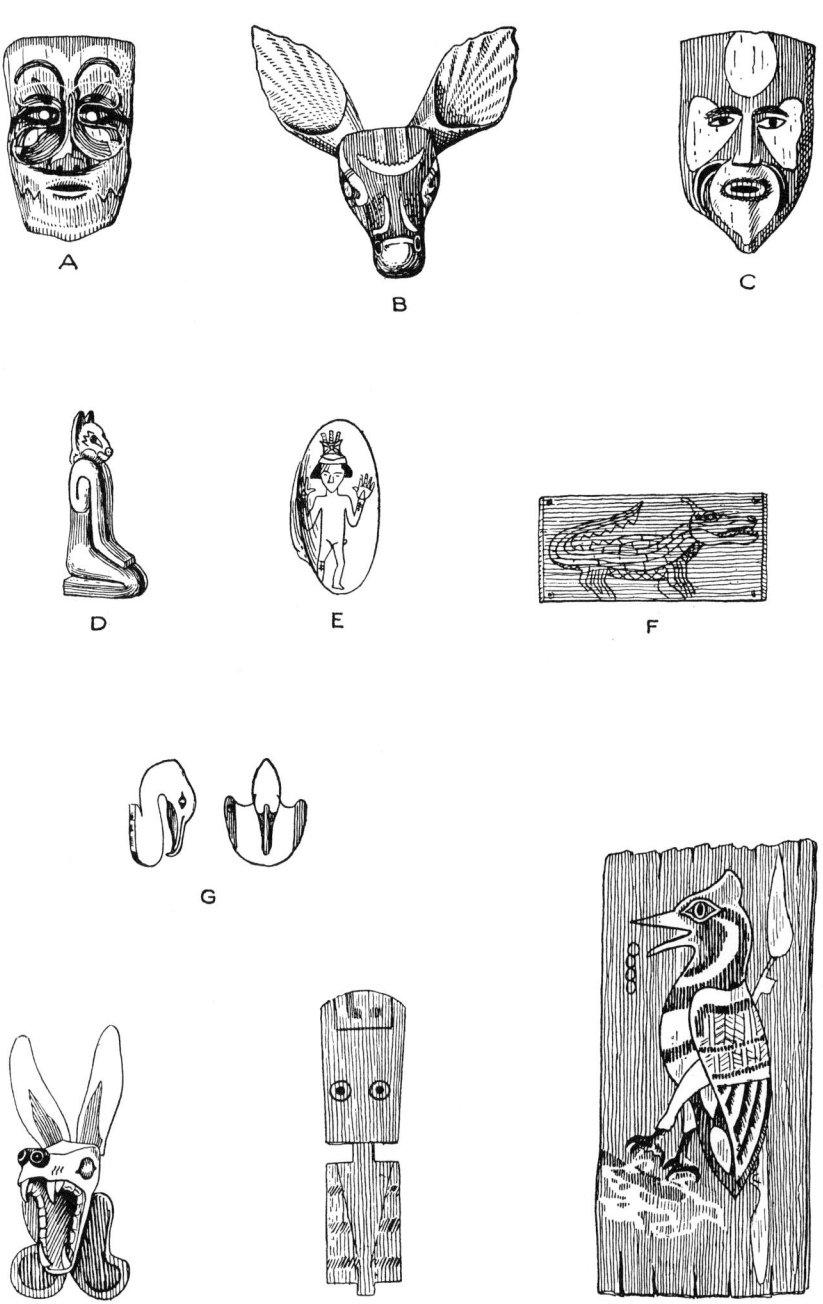

Fig. 95.—Key Marco art: *a*, painted mask of carved wood; *b*, painted deer head of carved wood; *c*, painted mask of carved wood; *d*, wooden figurine representing god-animal; *e*, ornament of painted shell; *f*, horned alligator painted on wooden box top; *g*, painted wood carving representing the head of a pelican; *h*, painted wood carving representing the head of a wolf; *i*, painted and carved wooden object; *j*, wooden tablet with painted bird. (After F. H. Cushing.)

and various styles of ear ornaments, often inlaid with shell or decorated with blue-and-white painted designs, served as objects of personal adornment.

Ornate flat wooden disks bearing various curvilinear designs and hachures found may also have been ear ornaments. Nicely made plummets of coral stone with cords attached seem to have had a decorative function. There were also tortoise-shell plates with incised dolphin-like figures; large wooden tablet-like objects with carved and painted decoration; wooden boards upon which were painted woodpeckers (Fig. 95, *j*), horned alligators (Fig. 95, *f*), and deer; and shells painted with effigies of outspread hands or human figures (Fig. 95, *e*).

Beautiful wooden sculptures represented human figures, some painted in various colors. Effigies of gods, part human and part animal (Fig. 95, *d*), deer heads, one with ears attached by leather hinges (Fig. 95, *b*), wolf heads (Fig. 95, *h*), and masks with human features (Fig. 95, *a* and *c*) were also part of the ornamental art.

Conjectures and comments.—Probably the Calusa Indians and their ancestors were responsible for the Key Marco culture. It seems to have been influenced by the Southern Death Cult.

SOURCES

Cushing, 1896.

SUMMARY

The earliest inhabitants of the Florida area were hunters, fishers, and food-collectors who did not have pottery or agriculture. They seem to have had permanent villages marked by shell middens.

The intermediate periods were characterized by the appearance of pottery, burial mounds, agriculture, and smoking-pipes, by the development of trade, and by an increasing diversity of cultures.

The latest inhabitants practiced agriculture, but hunting, fishing, and food-collecting were still far more important means of subsistence in some parts of Florida. Burial and temple mounds, many kinds of pottery, smoking pipes, and objects indicative of a high regard for aesthetic pursuits were characteristic of the last period.

CHAPTER 26

THE LOWER MISSISSIPPI VALLEY

INTRODUCTION

THE Mississippi Valley of Louisiana and Mississippi is a forested coastal plain with a mild climate. The native vegetation consists of river-bottom forest (cypress, tupelo, and red gum), southeastern pine forest (longleaf, loblolly, and slash), southern hardwood forest (oak-pine), prairie grassland (tall grass), and marsh grassland (marsh grass) along the coast.

CHART XIV

Date	Period	Culture
A.D. 1500–1700	Temple Mound II	Plaquemine, Natchezan
A.D. 1300–1500	Temple Mound I	Coles Creek
A.D. 900–1300	Burial Mound II	Marksville, Troyville
A.D. 500–900	Burial Mound I	Tchefuncte, Poverty Point
500 B.C.–A.D. 500	Archaic	Copell

The annual rainfall ranges from 50 to 80 inches, and the average frostless season lasts more than 240 days.

This area is dissected by a broad network of rivers, streams, bayous, and swamps, all of which were navigable by the dugout canoes of the Indians. The fauna furnished ample food for prehistoric hunters and food-collectors. The alluvial soils of the bottom lands were suited to the food-producing activities of the prehistoric farmers.

The cultural periods in the Lower Mississippi Valley are the Archaic, Burial Mound I, Burial Mound II, Temple Mound I, and Temple Mound II. The Archaic stage is characterized by Indians who were hunters and food-collectors. The Burial Mound I stage saw the addition of tobacco pipes, pottery, burial mounds, and possibly farming to the old hunting and food-collecting mode of life.

In the Burial Mound II stage there was construction of large burial mounds, greater emphasis on aesthetic ends, establishment of commercial contacts with distant regions, and some use of imported metal. The Temple Mound stage was marked by the use of pyramidal mounds of earth as substructures or platforms for temples of wood and thatch. It was also a time of intensive agriculture. The first half of this stage is called Temple Mound I; the second half, Temple Mound II. The cultures and periods are outlined in Chart XIV.

THE COPELL CULTURE
(ARCHAIC PERIOD)
Probably before A.D. 500

Area.—Coastal Louisiana.

People.—Indians of medium stature with large, broad faces and high heads. They were Sylvids.

Livelihood.—Hunting, fishing, and food-collecting furnished subsistence. Deer, raccoon, otter, muskrat, and other animals supplied food, clothing, and bone for tools. Clams, other shellfish, and wild plants supplied additional food. The dog was the only domesticated animal.

Pottery.—None.

Tools, utensils, and weapons.—The spear and spear-thrower was the principal weapon used in hunting.

The spear-thrower consisted of a wooden shaft perhaps sixteen inches long with an antler hook fastened to the outer end. This hook served to engage the notched or hollow butt of the spear. Boat-shaped or rectangular stones were attached to the shaft of the spear-thrower, probably to give better balance or increased momentum when the spear-thrower was swung.

The spears were equipped with clumsy stemmed points of chipped stone or with socketed (hollow) points of bone or antler that were glued to the cane or wood shafts with asphaltum.

Leaf-shaped knives with a flat base were made of chipped stone. Small tools used for scraping were made of flint flakes with retouched edges. Bone awls were used for drilling or punching holes. Containers or vessels were made of seashells or turtle shells.

Pipes.—None.

Ornaments.—Beads for necklaces were made of shell or of perforated dogs' teeth. Pendants were made of the perforated penis bones of otter and raccoon.

Burials.—The deceased were buried in cemeteries, placed upon layers of red and yellow pigment. Burial offerings consisted of tools, weapons, utensils, ornaments, and some additional items such as clam shells filled with asphaltum, inner whorls of conch shells, jaws of muskrats, worked sections of jaws and teeth of dogs, and teeth of drumfish.

SOURCES

COLLINS, 1941; FORD and QUIMBY, 1945.

THE TCHEFUNCTE CULTURE
(BURIAL MOUND I PERIOD)
Ca. A.D. 500–900

Area.—The Tchefuncte Indians lived in southern Louisiana, some in the coastal areas, others inland. The coastal variant of the culture is believed to be somewhat earlier than the inland variant and probably lasted longer.

People.—Sylvid and Centralid Indians of medium stature, with large, broad faces, and high heads. The men had medium-long heads; the women had short or round heads.

Villages.—Villages were placed on top of large shell heaps or middens composed of cultural refuse and clam shells. Just as a city dump grows by the accretion of refuse, so grew Tchefuncte shell heaps, only in this case the people were living on top of their dump. Scattered postholes suggest that their dwellings were crude shelters or windbreaks, probably constructed of sapling frames covered by thatch, for these materials were most easily obtainable, and the environs contain little else of which a house could be built. Numerous ash beds are found throughout the middens.

The inland tribes lived in small villages along the rivers and bayous. A conspicuous feature of the inland sites were the dome-shaped burial mounds of earth ranging in height from a few feet to fifteen feet and in diameter from about fifty feet to more than a hundred.

Livelihood.—The Indians living along the coast hunted, fished, and gathered food. The inland tribes probably were farmers who supplemented their vegetal foods by hunting and gathering. There is no direct evidence of agriculture, but the lack of large deposits of food refuse such as animal bones and shells implies its existence.

Pottery.—The pottery is rather distinctive (Fig. 96). The most characteristic form was a vessel shaped like a flowerpot with either a flat bottom or four short legs. Less common were shallow bowls with rounded bottoms. The pottery was tempered with sand or clay and poorly fired. The colors were buffs and grays.

Some of the vessels were decorated by means of incising, punctating, pinching, and various kinds of stamping. Plain rocker stamping or rocked dentate stamping were the most common techniques.

The designs were composed of rectilinear elements arranged in simple geometric patterns that covered the exterior. The designs were simple vertical or horizontal rows, or nested squares or diamonds, interlocking L's, or line-filled triangles. In a very few instances the vessels were covered with a red slip both inside and out, but most pottery was unpainted.

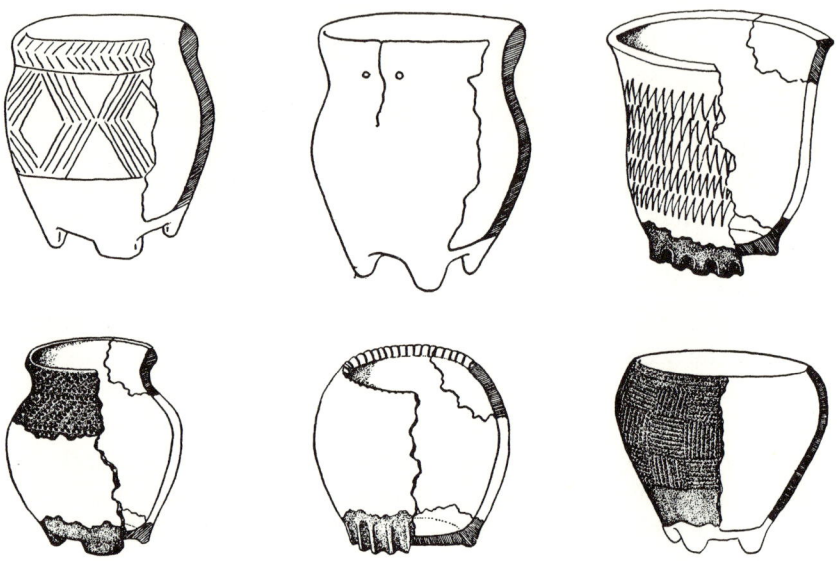

FIG. 96.—Tchefuncte pottery. (After Ford and Quimby.)

The pottery of the Tchefuncte was similar to that of other early Southeastern cultures and foreshadowed the later Marksville ceramic complex.

Tools, utensils, and weapons.—Small hammerstones, flaking implements of bone and antler, sandstone hones for sharpening bone tools, and sandstone saws were used for cutting bone and shell. With these basic tools, other implements, weapons, and ornaments were produced. Awls (Fig. 97, *k*) and other perforating tools were made from conch shell, bone, or antler. Chisels, celts, and adzes (Fig. 97, *l*) were made from thick conch shell. Spear points were made of antler, bone, or stone. Bone points (Fig. 97, *b, g, i*) were large, hollow, and generally glued to their shafts with bitumen. Chipped-stone points (Figs. 97, *e* and *f*) made from river pebbles were long and narrow

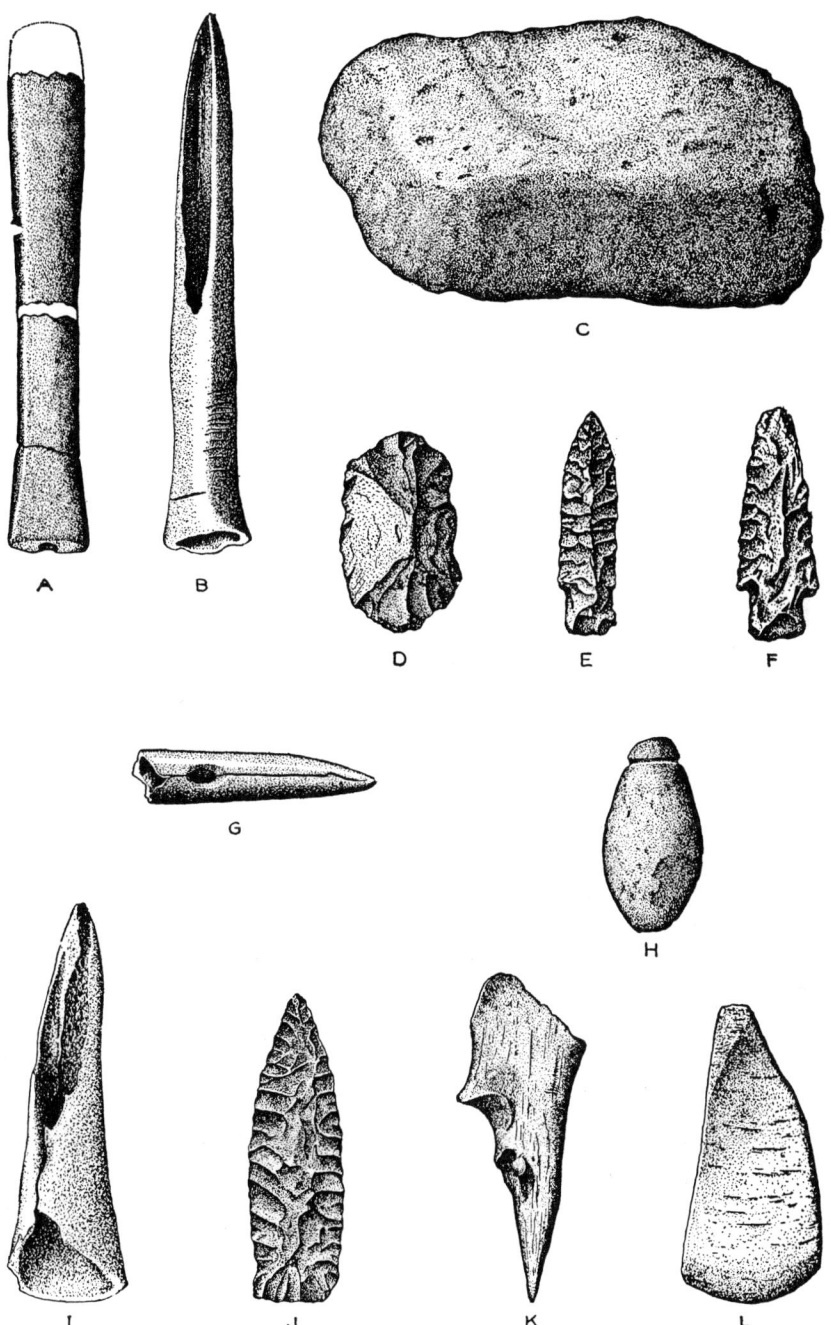

Fig. 97.—Tchefuncte tools, utensils, and weapons; *a*, tubular pipe of clay; *b*, bone spear point; *c*, grinding-stone; *d*, scraper of chipped flint; *e, f*, spear points of chipped flint; *g*, detachable spear point of bone; *h*, stone fishline sinker; *i*, bone spear point; *j*, knife of chipped flint; *k*, bone awl; *l*, adz blade of conch shell. (After Ford and Quimby.)

with a squared stem for hafting to a shaft. Knives (Fig. 97, *j*) and scrapers (Fig. 97, *d*) were also made of chipped flint. Fishline sinkers (Fig. 97, *h*) and food-grinders (Fig. 97, *c*) were made of stone.

The principal hunting weapon was probably the spear and spear-thrower made of wood and antler. Curiously shaped objects of fired clay (Poverty Point objects) that probably served some unknown utilitarian purpose were found at many sites.

Pipes.—Pipes were made of clay and resembled an elongated cigar-holder (Fig. 97, *a*). Most of them were plain, but some were decorated with incised or punctate designs.

Ornaments.—Ornaments were made of stone, bone, shell, and animal teeth. Pendants were made of tortoise shell, cut animal jaws, bone, conch shell, crystal, and perforated bear canines or alligator teeth. Beads were made of shell or animal teeth. In comparison with that of later cultures in Louisiana, the ornamentation was crude.

Burials.—The coastal Tchefuncte buried their dead in small pits dug in the midden, with the bodies usually flexed. The inland tribes buried their dead in mounds. Cremation was sometimes practiced, but more often bodies were placed in a flexed or extended position and earth piled over them to form a mound. Tchefuncte mounds were not large—never more than ten or fifteen feet high, generally smaller—but they foreshadow a tremendous development in mound-building which did not reach its climax until several hundred years later.

SOURCES

FORD and QUIMBY, 1945.

THE POVERTY POINT CULTURE
(BURIAL MOUND I PERIOD)
Ca. A.D. 500–900

Many miles north of the Tchefuncte culture but still within the area of the Lower Mississippi Valley there have been found the remains of the Poverty Point culture. This culture is so imperfectly known that most of our statements concerning it are merely guesses.

Area.—Northern Louisiana.

Villages.—Aside from the fact that there were large cache pits, perhaps of a ceremonial nature, we have no information about villages or dwellings.

Livelihood.—Probably these tribes were hunters and food-collectors, but they may also have been farmers.

Pottery.—None.

Tools, utensils, and weapons.—The spear and spear-thrower was probably the principal weapon. Projectile points of chipped stone were large and heavy, with stems that were used for hafting the points to their shafts. Knives of chipped stone were leaf-shaped or triangular. Other tools were large crude scrapers and small flake drills.

Plummet-shaped stones of steatite or hematite may have had a utilitarian use, possibly as bird-bolas stones; or they may have been ornaments. All were perforated or grooved at the narrow end.

Other objects of unknown use were various types of baked-clay balls like those found in Tchefuncte sites. These crude objects were cylindrical, sometimes with spiral, horizontal, or vertical grooves, or were biconoidal.

Grooved and ungrooved axes were made of stone. Stone vessels were used so extensively that they may be considered the most characteristic item of Poverty Point material culture. Deep bowls with outslanting walls and rounded or flattened bottoms were made of steatite. Most vessels showed gouge marks where the bowl had been carved, and some of them had lugs near the rim. Some lugs and rims were either notched or engraved with simple geometric designs such as zigzags or transverse or horizontal lines. A few of the bowls were decorated with animal figures in low relief. One figure, the representation of an eagle, is very realistic and graceful; another represents a combination of a mountain goat and a wildcat.

Because many fragments of bowls intentionally "killed" or broken have been found in a cache pit, stone bowls seem to have played some part in the ceremonial life of the Poverty Point Indians.

Pipes.—Tubular pipes were made of stone and pottery.

Ornaments.—Beads were carved from stone, many of jasper. Some were tubular or barrel-shaped, while others were exquisite carvings of birds; one bead was in the form of a miniature bannerstone.

Jasper and shale gorgets were rectanguloid with convex sides, triangular with convex sides, or leaf-shaped. Usually they had two perforations.

Conjectures.—The Poverty Point tribes may have been foreigners in the Lower Mississippi Valley, since their cultural orientation seems to have been northern except for their connections with Tchefuncte. Furthermore, the closest source of the steatite that was used in their stone bowls was northern Alabama. A less probable source was the Lake Superior region.

Considering all the available evidence, our best guess is that the Poverty Point Indians moved into the northern part of the Lower Mississippi Valley during the time in which the Tchefuncte culture was developing in the southern part. Why the Poverty Point Indians used pottery for the construction of clay balls and occasional pipes but preferred stone for the construction of their bowls is a puzzle that may never be solved.

Like the Tchefuncte culture, the Poverty Point culture was followed by the Marksville and Troyville cultures of the Burial Mound II period. But whereas Tchefuncte contributed much to the ancestry of Marksville, Poverty Point seems to have contributed little, if anything. Probably the descendants of the Poverty Point Indians were absorbed by the Marksville people.

SOURCES

WEBB, C., 1944.

THE MARKSVILLE CULTURE
(BURIAL MOUND II PERIOD)
Ca. A.D. 900–1100

Area.—The southern half of the Lower Mississippi Valley was the center of the Marksville culture, although its influence spread over a much broader area.

People.—Longheaded Sylvids.

Villages.—The villages and ceremonial centers were along rivers. Houses were probably made of saplings covered with thatch.

Livelihood.—Subsistence was gained by farming, hunting, fishing, and food-gathering. It is interesting to note that some White Louisianians living near Marksville sites lead a similar life today.

Pottery.—Excellent bowls and jars were made by means of the coiling process (Fig. 98). To keep vessels from cracking when fired, the Marksville Indians added particles of fired clay to the paste. All vessels were flat and generally square. Jars varied from straight-walled types to styles with constricted necks and slightly flaring chambered rims. Some were constructed with quadrilobate bodies. Both interiors and exteriors were always smooth. The color of the fired pottery ranged from gray to buff.

The principal techniques of decoration used were punctating, broad-line incising, fine-line incising, cord-wrapped-stick stamping, plain rocker stamping, and rocker stamping with a denticulated instrument or the edge of a pectin shell. A few of the vessels had a red slip.

The most common decorative motif was a conventionalized serpent or bird that was either outlined in broad incised lines or by zones bounded by broad incised lines. These zones were filled with stamped impressions or else left plain. The bird or serpent motif was always confined to the body of the vessel. Other body decorations were curvilinear or rectilinear; scattered stamped impressions; rectilinear zones bounded by broad incised lines and either left plain or filled with stamped impressions; and geometric plats composed of straight or of curvilinear, broad incised lines.

FIG. 98.—Pottery of the Marksville culture. (Courtesy of Louisiana State University.)

Regardless of body decoration, the rims were usually ornamented with a band of finely incised cross-hatched lines, in some cases arranged in geometric plats. Often the band was bordered by a row of semiconical punctate impressions. In some cases the band or rim decoration was composed entirely of rows of these.

Tools, utensils, and weapons.—Projectile points, knives (Fig. 99, *g*), drills, and scrapers were made of chipped stone. The projectile points were ovate-triangular in outline, with considerable variation in the treatment of the stem shapes. Grooved and ungrooved boatstones might have been used as spear-thrower weights.

Long flint flakes were used as knives, and ungrooved axes (Fig. 99, *f*) were made of ground stone. Large rocks were used as hammers. Conch shells from the Gulf Coast were used as containers. Awls and fishhooks were made from animal bone.

Pipes.—Clay platform pipes were made with curved bases and spool—or nozzle-shaped bowls. Some pipes were made with animal effigy bowls (Fig. 99, *a*).

Ornaments.—Small round solid-copper beads and tubular rolled sheet-copper beads were used in necklaces or were attached to cloth-

Fig. 99.—Marksville tools and ornaments: *a*, platform pipe of clay in the form of a bear; *b*, ornament of bituminous shale; *c*, stone sculpture; *d*, fragment of clay figurine; *e*, half of copper ear ornament; *f*, stone ax; *g*, knife of chipped flint. (Courtesy of Louisiana State University.)

ing. Columellas of the conch were also used as beads. Both men and women wore copper ear-spools of the double-cymbal type (Fig. 99, *e*). Barrel-shaped stone beads and large quartz crystals were occasionally grooved at the top. Ornaments were also made of bituminous shale (Fig. 99, *b*). Occasional grooved or perforated plummets of hematite and galena may have been used as ornaments. Sculptures of clay (Fig. 99, *d*) and of stone (Fig. 99, *c*) were rare.

Burials.—The dead were interred in large conical mounds of earth, some of which were 25 feet high and 150 feet in diameter at the base. At one site there was a semicircular earthen wall or embankment 10 feet high, which served as an inclosure for the mounds and the plaza. The mounds were built in mantles or layers. Bodies were placed on top of one layer and covered with another. Sometimes a rectanguloid log tomb was constructed just beneath the top of a primary mound. After the dead had been placed in the tomb, another mantle of earth was added to the mound, thereby covering the tomb and adding to the height.

Marksvillians were buried singly or in groups, with the skeletons flexed or extended. Occasionally an isolated skull was placed in some part of the mound or perhaps an extra skull would be placed with a more conventional burial. Very rarely were grave-goods placed with the burials; on occasion, however, lumps of red ocher were placed in the graves.

SOURCES

COLLINS, 1941; FORD and WILLEY, 1940; SETZLER, 1933a, 1933b.

THE TROYVILLE CULTURE
(BURIAL MOUND II PERIOD)
Ca. A.D. 1100–1300

Area.—In Louisiana the Marksville culture developed into the Troyville culture. The two were very similar but can be differentiated by the stratigraphic position and typology. The Troyville Indians were descendants of the Marksville tribes.

Troyville sites are generally larger and more numerous than are Marksville. Troyville influences are found in Texas, Arkansas, Mississippi, Alabama, and Florida.

Villages.—Villages were built along the rivers and bayous. In some of the coastal areas the settlements were placed on top of ancient shell middens. The inland peoples built large villages and ceremonial centers.

A conspicuous feature of late villages were the flat-topped earthen pyramids, usually oriented around a central plaza, each with a wooden temple on the summit. These temples had circular bases and walls made of upright saplings placed in postholes or set in trenches. Walls and roofs were probably covered with thatch or woven cane mats.

Pottery.—The pottery, made by coiling, with surfaces generally smoothed, is rather similar to that of the Marksville culture. The vessels were tempered with clay or particles of volcanic tuff which looks like limestone and were in the form of bowls and jars of various shapes. Bottoms were usually flat and squared, although round or semiconoidal ones were not rare. The characteristic Troyville rim had a broad, flat lip and was so thick at the top that it looks like a wedge when viewed in cross-section.

Decorative techniques consisted of punctating, incising, stamping, and malleating with a cord-wrapped paddle. Many of the designs were very Marksvillian, but there were striking differences. The common Marksville bird design was absent in Troyville, and the cross-hatched rim and quadrilobate jar forms were rare. A characteristic Troyville design consisted of positive and negative curvilinear or angular bands or zones in which some areas were filled with notched or plain rocked-stamp impressions or punctate impressions. Another ornamentation consists of curvilinear or angular patterns made of closely spaced, broad, shallow, incised lines. In the execution of all these patterns, the individual motifs were repeated or alternately repeated until the entire vessel exterior was decorated.

Another style consisted of rather large jars covered with cord-wrapped-paddle impressions. These vessels were straight-walled, barrel-shaped, or broad-mouthed with constricted necks. This type is somewhat similar to varieties found in northern Hopewellian sites.

Tools, utensils, and weapons.—Several types of projectile points and occasional large blades were made of chipped stone. The points were stemmed types, usually with horizontal or receding shoulders, although barbed shoulders have been found. The outlines of the points were triangular or ovate and closely resembled those commonly found in the sites of the Marksville culture. Bone was used for implements somewhat sporadically. There were awls or perforators made of arm bones, socketed bone, and antler points; atlatl hooks (one example), splinter awls, antler flakers, and problematical forms.

Pipes.—Pipes were made of fired clay and were usually straight-based platform types. Occasionally, large equal-armed elbow pipes were found, some of them highly ornamented with modeled effigies or incised decoration.

Ornaments.—Copper from the Upper Great Lakes region was utilized in making ear-spools. These were the solid, double-cymbal type, or were slate, covered with copper. Other ornaments were occasional clay figurines, imitation bear teeth made of shell, perforated bear teeth, worked animal jaws, tubular shell beads, and clay ear ornaments.

Burials.—Some of the dead were buried within small or medium-sized, dome-shaped earthen mounds, and such burials were generally accompanied by tools and ornaments. In the late phases of Troyville culture, when pyramidal mounds and temples were coming into use, burials were made in cemeteries. A very few burials were placed in pyramidal mounds.

Conjectures.—The Troyville culture is especially significant because it represents a transition from Marksville-Hopewell to Coles Creek–Middle Mississippi. In short, it is a link between the Burial Mound II stage and the Temple Mound stage in the prehistory of the Lower Mississippi Valley.

SOURCES

FORD and WILLEY, 1941; WALKER, W., 1936; UNPUBLISHED DATA IN THE FILES OF THE LOUISIANA STATE ARCHEOLOGICAL SURVEY, GEOLOGY BUILDING, BATON ROUGE.

THE COLES CREEK CULTURE
(TEMPLE MOUND I PERIOD)
Ca. A.D. 1300–1500

There is a cultural continuum from Marksville through Troyville to Coles Creek. The Coles Creek culture, representative of the fully developed Temple Mound stage, was foreshadowed by the late Troyville culture that preceded it.

Area.—Principally in the Lower Mississippi Valley area of Louisiana and Mississippi, although there seem to have been outposts in eastern Texas and southern Arkansas.

People.—Roundheaded Centralids who practiced head deformation. Probably this head deformation resulted from the binding of infants to a cradle-board.

Villages.—The villages were large (Fig. 100) and usually contained ceremonial centers consisting of groups of flat-topped pyramidal mounds which were crowned with temples. The mounds, some of which had ramps leading to the summit, were arranged about a large central plaza. Some mounds were as much as 40 feet high and 200 feet square at the base, and in very late Coles Creek times there were a few mounds as high as 70 or 80 feet.

Villages and mounds were usually placed along rivers and streams. In some instances the Coles Creek tribes occupied Troyville sites.

There is no available evidence concerning the types of dwellings, but remains of temple foundations in the form of post molds indicate that the structures on the mound summits were rectangular in outline and that only single rows of posts were used in their construction. The walls of the temples were plastered with clay and covered with woven mats.

Livelihood.—Coles Creek people were farmers who supplemented their vegetal diet by hunting, fishing, and food-gathering. Marginal

Fig. 100.—Reconstruction of a Coles Creek village. (Diorama created by A. L. Rowell, Chicago Natural History Museum.)

groups living in the swamps of coastal Louisiana probably practiced little agriculture.

Pottery.—These Indians made excellent plain and ornamented clay-tempered pottery (Fig. 101) of a rather fine and compact texture. Colors of unpainted pottery usually ranged in buffs and grays, and vessel surfaces were always carefully smoothed or polished. The principal forms were plates, bowls, and jars. Some jars were somewhat similar to modern flower pots, others were barrel-shaped, and still others had slightly constricted necks and straight-vertical or slightly flaring rims. The bottoms were usually flat and sometimes squared.

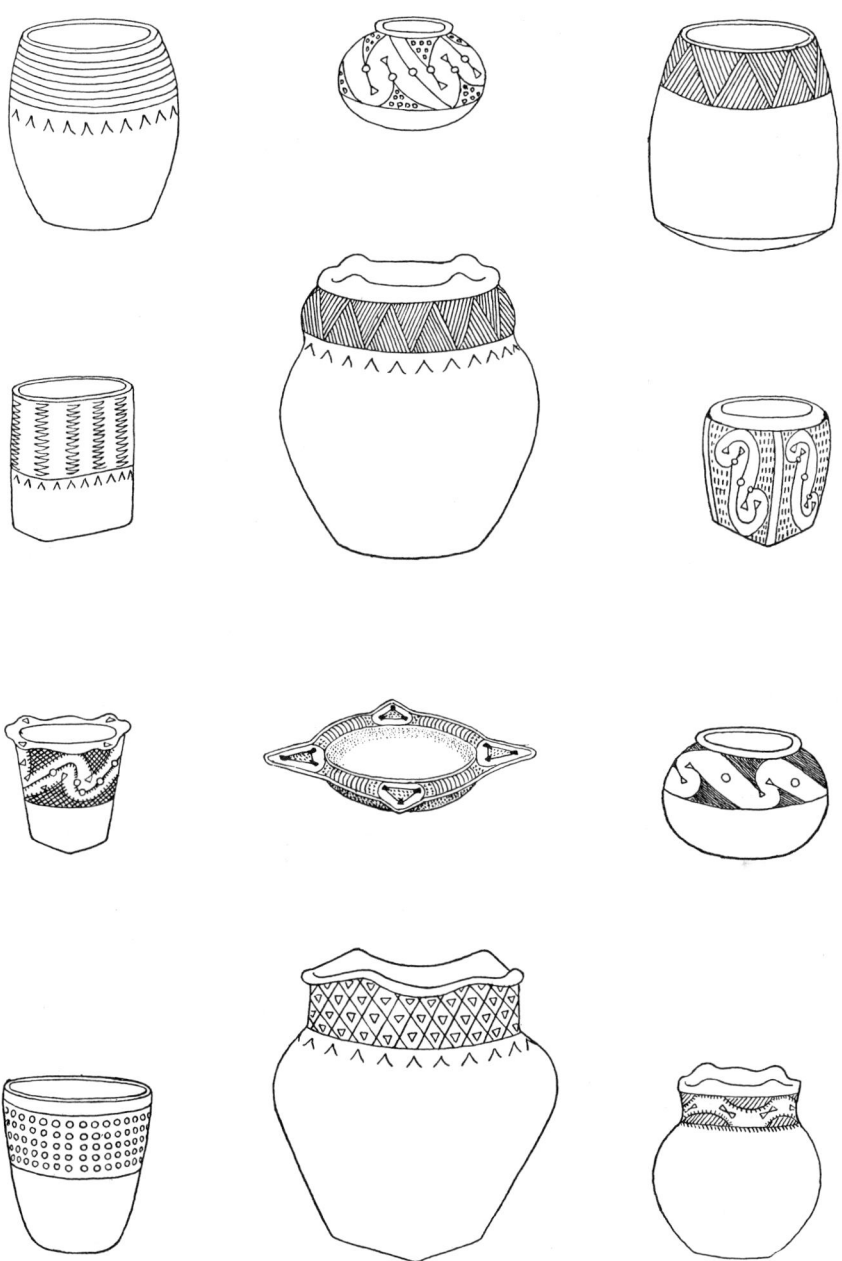

Fig. 101.—Coles Creek pottery. (After J. A. Ford.)

Polychrome pottery was rare. The colors used were red and white or red, white, and black. Monochrome pottery was much more common. Red, the preferred color, was applied to the entire vessel or perhaps to only the interior or exterior.

Decorative stamping, punctating, and incising were sometimes combined with painting but more often were applied to unpainted vessels. One type of vessel had small check-stamped impressions over all the exterior except the base. The upper parts of other types of jars were variously decorated with closely spaced, horizontal, incised lines; line-filled triangles; diamond cross-hatching with a punctation in the center of each diamond; bands or zones of punctate impressions; and closely spaced, vertical rows of plain rocked-stamp impressions. A style of decoration which appeared upon the body as well as the rim consisted of curvilinear or meandering zones outlined by incised lines. These zones were plain or filled with closely spaced punctate impressions. Frequently some of the incised lines were terminated by a triangular punctate impression. This decoration was often placed on the interior rim of plates.

Tools, utensils, and weapons.—There were four styles of projectile points: (1) large, wide, triangular points with broad, short, rounded, or convex stems and horizontal shoulders; (2) small, wide, triangular points with narrow, long, rounded, or convex stems and receding shoulders; (3) small, wide, triangular points with broad, round, or convex stems and barbed shoulders; and (4) small, medium-wide, fir-tree-shaped points with barbed shoulders and broad, square stems contracted slightly toward the tip. Other objects of chipped flint were expanded base drills and ovate scrapers. Flint implements were manufactured from river pebbles, the only abundant source of stone in the region.

Other stone tools consisted of hammerstones; crude mortar-like forms with very small and shallow depressions; abraders; and smoothing-stones. Occasionally present were ungrooved axes and delicately executed boatstones.

Antler punches, flakers, awls, and socketed tine projectile points were used. Various kinds of awls and weaving tools were made of animal bone.

Pipes.—The pipes were large and were made of clay. Usually they were equal-armed elbow types, and some of them were elaborately shaped and decorated with incised designs. There were other sculptured pipes with bowls in the form of crouching animals or human figures. It is probable that a wooden stem was added to these pipes, as their size and shape would make smoking very difficult without such an addition.

Ornaments.—Rather crude statuettes of humans or animals were modeled in clay.

The only important articles of personal adornment were cylindrical ear-spools of clay.

Burials.—Burials were occasionally made in the temple mounds or village midden, but more often they were made in cemeteries near the village. The bodies were flexed or extended. Mass burials seem to have been common. Few burial offerings were placed in the graves.

Conjectures.—The Coles Creek Indians were probably contemporaries of the tribes which were developing the Middle Mississippi city-states. Coles Creek culture, as such, seems to have disappeared before the time of the flowering of the Middle-Mississippi states (A.D. 1550–1650).

Probably the Coles Creek culture can be considered as essentially a development from the preceding Troyville. There are, however, contributing influences from other areas. The check-stamped pottery as well as some of the decoration composed of punctated and plain zones probably came from Florida.

In the Lower Mississippi Valley the Coles Creek culture developed into the Plaquemine culture, which is representative of the Temple Mound II stage.

SOURCES
FORD and WILLEY, n.d.

THE PLAQUEMINE CULTURE
(TEMPLE MOUND II PERIOD)
Ca. A.D. 1500–1600

Area.—Louisiana and Mississippi.

Villages.—Villages were usually located along the bayous and rivers, probably because dugout canoes were the common method of transportation.

The ceremonial centers or perhaps formal gathering places usually consisted of single pyramidal mounds with flat summits. That these mounds served as substructures for buildings is manifested by the patterns of post molds on the various levels of accretion. In some instances there was a ramp from the ground level to the mound summit.

In some cases Plaquemine Indians lived on sites whose history went back to Marksville times. They did not hestitate to use a pyramidal mound built by late Troyville or Coles Creek tribes. They also made additions to old mounds.

As indicated by the post-mold patterns, the temples on the mound summits were rectanguloid in outline with either square or rounded corners. Average dimensions were 15 by 20 feet. In most cases single rows of posts were used, although there is one example of a double row. Another type of sacred structure was circular in outline, from 40 to 60 feet in diameter, and was indicated by deep wall trenches. The roof of the structure was supported by large center posts of which there may have been any number from one to six. Other related and conspicuous features were hearths, pits (cruciform in one instance), and slightly raised circular platforms that may have been altars. The structures with circular foundations were always at the ground level and in one instance **the structure** was beneath the mound.

Livelihood.—Subsistence was gained by farming supplemented by hunting, fishing, and food-gathering. Bones of deer, small mammals, birds, and fish have been found in the sites.

Pottery.—Most of the pottery was plain, and all shapes found in the undecorated wares have also been recorded in ornamented varieties. Bowls, plates, cups, and jars were made with direct rims or constricted necks and straight or slightly flaring rims. Decoration on the bowls and plates consisted of incising or, in a few cases, of engraving simple and complicated geometric patterns. Many of the low bowls and plates had interior decoration. Some of the cup forms had incised plats, and the jars were brushed, incised, punctated, or check-stamped. The incised and punctated decorations were confined to the upper vessel, whereas the check-stamping and brushing covered the vessel exteriors in much the same way that cord or fabric impressions covered some northern pottery. Some pottery was decorated with red paint, which covered the exterior or the interior or both.

The paste was rather fine and was clay- or shell-tempered. Numerous coil fractures indicate that coiling was the method of manufacture.

Tools, utensils, and weapons.—Possible evidence of the spear-thrower consists of beautifully made boatstones which probably were attached to the shaft of the spear-thrower for the purpose of obtaining better balance and momentum. Projectile points of chipped flint were of several kinds and could have been used on arrows or spears.

The large projectile points were rather broad and were ovate-triangular in outline, with squared stems and horizontal shoulders. Small, delicate points were triangular or leaf-shaped. The former style had a rectangular stem and the latter had a stem shaped something like a fish tail. Crudely chipped scrapers probably were used in a number of ways.

In addition to boatstones, celts and discoidals were manufactured by the stone-grinding technique.

Pipes.—Pipes were made of fired clay and were usually the elbow type. One style was small, while others were similar to those of the Coles Creek Indians. All probably had wooden stems.

Ornaments.—Articles of personal adornment were scarce. Shell pins and ear ornaments of fired clay were cylindrical in shape with flat ends which sometimes were decorated with incised or engraved patterns consisting of curvilinear elements.

Burials.—A few burials were made in the temple mounds. Few burial offerings were placed with the deceased. Bodies were in an extended position or were merely redeposited bundles of bones.

Conjectures.—The Plaquemine Indians were contemporaries of the Caddo and the Middle Mississippi groups. Plaquemine culture, at least in part, was ancestral to the historic Natchezan culture.

SOURCES

FORD and WILLEY, 1941; QUIMBY, 1942.

THE NATCHEZAN CULTURE
(TEMPLE MOUND II PERIOD)
Ca. A.D. 1600–1750

The Natchezan culture flourished in the latter part of the Temple Mound II period from about 1600 to 1750 and was shared by such tribes of the Lower Mississippi Valley as the Natchez, Tiou, Grigra, Taensa, Bayougoula, Mugulasha, and some Houma and Tunica, all of whom were observed by early French explorers and missionaries in the first half of the eighteenth century.

Area.—The Lower Mississippi Valley in Louisiana and Mississippi.

People.—Indians with short, broad heads. Skull deformation was produced by the binding of infants' heads to cradle-boards.

Villages.—Villages were situated near creeks or rivers and consisted of a large central plaza surrounded by huts. At either or both ends of the plaza were small (about ten feet high) pyramidal mounds of earth upon which were placed temples or the houses of chiefs.

Typical houses had rectangular ground plans and were made of poles set into the ground and lashed together at the top to provide dome-shaped roofs. The pole frames were covered with a plaster of mud and Spanish moss, over which were mats of cane. These mats in turn were covered by grass thatch and more woven mats of cane. Each village might possess a hundred or more such houses.

The temples and chiefs' houses were larger than the ordinary dwellings but were otherwise similar.

Each village had a large granary or corncrib, a boxlike structure supported on four posts and having an opening in the top reached by a ladder. In some instances villages were surrounded by palisades of wooden posts or closely spaced canes.

Livelihood.—Food was obtained by farming, hunting, fishing, and food-collecting. The principal crop was corn, of which there were several varieties. There were also other grains, either cultivated or collected, vegetables, and wild fruits. Many animals and birds were hunted. There were even organized buffalo hunts outside the Natchezan territory. Dogs and perhaps turkeys were domesticated.

Pottery.—Vessels were made of clay tempered with fine particles of shell, grit, or organic matter. The vessels were coiled by hand, sun dried, and then fired. Pottery was in the form of bowls, jars, or bottles and was either plain or decorated. Vessels had hollow platform bases extended in the form of an inverted cone.

Some vessels were covered with a film of red paint and embellished with incised designs. The most characteristic motifs were meanders, scrolls, triangles, and volutes arranged in a symmetrical, repetitive pattern on the exterior surfaces. Similar designs were produced by means of combs. Other patterns were triangular plats of punctate impressions, bands of horizontal, incised lines, curvilinear zones of engraved or incised cross-hatching, bands or large areas scored by brushing with wadded fiber, and bands of line-filled triangular plats. Most Natchezan pottery, however, was not decorated.

Basketry and weaving.—Baskets and mats were used extensively. Cloth was spun of buffalo hair, opossum fur, and bast fiber.

Tools, utensils, and weapons.—Bows and arrows were made of wood. Arrows were tipped with points of cane splinters, fire-hardened wood, garfish scales, bone, or chipped stone. The stone points were trianguloid, with stems for attachment to the wooden shaft. Most of these points were thin and nicely chipped. Knives were made of cane splinters. Ungrooved axes were made of ground stone. Household utensils used were bison-horn spoons, wooden mortars and pestles for grinding food, skin-scrapers of flint, bone awls, and fire drills. Agricultural implements used were wooden digging-sticks and digging tools and perhaps hoes made of bison bone.

Fish were caught in nets. Ball-headed clubs with curved blades were made of wood.

Pipes.—Small elbow pipes were made of clay or perhaps of stone.

Travel and transportation.—Common travel was by water in a dugout canoe or a raft made of bundles of cane. For the ceremonial transportation of chiefs or sacred personages there were litters or palanquins made of four posts crossed to form a square with a seat in the center and with handles for carrying.

Costume.—Winter clothing consisted of moccasins, leggings, skirts, and shirts of skin. Robes of bison skin sometimes were decorated with dyed porcupine quills or were painted with various designs. In summer the women wore only skirts and the men wore breechclouts. Both sexes tattooed and painted their bodies and faces, wore feathers in their hair, and blackened their teeth. The Natchezan peoples had elaborate feather mantles, probably for use only on special occasions. These mantles were woven by a netting technique of bast fiber and covered with the feathers.

Musical instruments.—Rattles and drums were made by stretching a membrane over the mouth of a pottery vessel.

Ornaments.—Small circular gorgets of shell, bone bracelets, pearl necklaces, earpins of shell, large shell beads, quartz crystals, sheet mica, lumps of galena, and figurines of pottery or stone have been found.

Burials.—The dead were placed upon raised platforms with appropriate ritual. After decomposition had taken place, the bones were placed in chests of wood or cane inside the temple. Burials consisted of bundles of bones, probably from the temples, or of flexed or extended bodies. In some graves there was an abundance of burial offerings. Graves were made in pits near the village, were intrusive into pyramidal mounds, or were beneath low circular burial mounds.

SOURCES

QUIMBY, 1942

SUMMARY

The preceding outline of the archeology of the Lower Mississippi Valley enables us to view in perspective the growth of indigenous cultures from earliest times to the arrival of the White settlers in 1700. This growth seems to have been an orderly process which at times was interrrupted or accelerated by cultural contact with other areas and peoples; but, by and large, there seems to have been a developmental trend from cultures based upon hunting and food-collecting to cultures based upon intensive agriculture. Strangely enough, the richest material remains are found neither with the intensive agriculturalists nor with the hunters and food-collectors but with intermediate peoples. The climax of the archeological cultures of the Lower Mississippi Valley came with Marksville–Troyville–Coles Creek. Plaquemine and Natchezan seem to represent a material degeneration, although this picture might be reversed if we knew more about the perishable content of the material culture and had some knowledge of the social structures of these extinct peoples. But even without such knowledge the reader can sense something of the long fluctuating climb from a hunting way of life to a sedentary agricultural existence.

In the same region today it is possible to see White farmers who obtain their food by raising corn and vegetables and by hunting and fishing. These White men travel through bayous in pirogues—small boats on the model of the Indian dugout. They smoke tobacco in elbow pipes and stuff their mattresses with feathers or Spanish moss. Thus, in some degree at least, the culture of the Indians has become a part of the culture of the White man.

CHAPTER 27

THE CADDO AREA

INTRODUCTION

THE Caddo area of northeastern Texas, southeastern Oklahoma, northwestern Louisiana, and southwestern Arkansas was largely a forested coastal plain. The predominant vegetation was southern hardwood forest (oak-pine and oak-hickory) except for areas of prairie grassland in northeastern Texas, a river-bottom forest (cypress-tupelo-red gum), and some areas of southeastern pine forest (longleaf, loblolly, and slash pine) in northwestern Louisiana.

The climate was relatively mild, with the annual frostless season ranging from 210 to more than 240 days and the rainfall from 40 to 60 inches. The climate and soils made agriculture possible, and the flora and fauna offered excellent opportunities for hunters and food-collectors.

The Caddo area may have been inhabited during the Archaic and the late Burial Mound periods (from before A.D. 500 to about 1300), but the first extensive settlements were probably made by the Indian bearers of the Caddo culture during the Temple Mound period (*ca.* 1300–1700). Researches not yet published show that the Caddo culture has considerable historical depth and can be separated into periods (Temple Mound I and II) as well as into taxonomic units (Gibson Aspect and Fulton Aspect). For our purposes we shall describe the various periods as a single culture that was in existence in the entire area from about 1300 to 1700+.

THE CADDO CULTURE
(TEMPLE MOUND PERIOD)
Ca. A.D. 1300–1700

The Caddo culture is named for the Caddoan-speaking Indians who were occupying parts of Texas and Louisiana when the White explorers arrived.

Area.—Eastern Texas, eastern Oklahoma, southern Arkansas, and northern Louisiana.

People.—Roundheaded Centralids with artificially deformed skulls. The tops of some Caddo skulls excavated in Louisiana were flattened both in front and in back.

Villages.—Villages usually were located by rivers or bayous and consisted of clusters of round or rectanguloid houses. The walls were made of upright saplings set in wall trenches or postholes and were covered with grass thatch or woven mats. Some walls were reinforced with woven strips of cane plastered with clay. The dome-shaped roofs probably were made of saplings covered with thatch and/or mats.

Most villages had a central square or plaza that was usually flanked at each end by a pyramidal mound of earth from 5 to 30 feet high. In some cases an earthen ramp led to the temples or other sacred buildings on top of the mound. The temples were similar to dwellings but were probably more ornate and perhaps larger.

Livelihood.—Farming, hunting, fishing, and the gathering of wild food were the means of livelihood. Corn and probably other crops were cultivated. Shellfish and probably nuts, roots, and berries were gathered for food.

Pottery.—There were several styles of pottery primarily differentiated by design or surface treatment rather than by shape. These are:

1. Plain
2. Polished plain
3. Brush-roughened: vessel surfaces roughened by brushing with wads of grass or similar substance while the clay was still plastic
4. Incised: linear, angular, and curvilinear designs incised on vessels while the clay was still plastic
5. Engraved: linear, angular, and curvilinear designs engraved or scratched on the vessels after firing; sometimes combinations of plain and cross-hatched areas, meanders, scrolls, spurred lines and circles, fringed lines and circles, festoons (Fig. 102)
6. Punctated: simple geometric decoration produced by punchlike implement or fingernail while clay was still plastic
7. Pinched: design produced by pinching plastic clay between the fingers to produce a ridge
8. Painted: usually a red film either plain or relieved by engraving; polychrome decoration, rare; black or buff engraved vessels, sometimes with red pigment in engraved lines, rarely with white pigment

Alone or in varying combinations, the above decorations appear on bottles, jars, plates, bowls, and cups. Effigy forms are relatively rare.

Pottery generally was well made and was tempered with grit, sand, limestone, crushed sherd, shell, and perhaps bone.

Basketry and weaving.—Matting was woven of strips of cane and twined and twilled cloth of spun vegetal fiber.

Tools, utensils, and weapons.—Shell and stone hoes, probably hafted to wooden handles, were used for tillage, as in all probability were wooden digging-sticks. Stone mortars, pestles, grinding-stones, and manos were used for preparing corn or other vegetal foods.

The bow and arrow was the principal weapon of the hunters. Arrowheads were rather delicate and made of chipped flint. The arrows were tipped with plain triangular points, triangular points with

Fig. 102.—Caddo pottery. (After C. B. Moore.)

stems or notches, points with eared shoulders and concave bases, and points shaped like the silhouette of a fir tree. Some points had serrated edges. Larger, cruder points of chipped flint or antler could have been used as arrowheads or spearheads. Various types of boatstones and allied forms of ground stone possibly were used as spearthrower weights.

Knives of different sizes and quality as well as scrapers and drills were also made of chipped flint. Grooved axes and different styles of celts were used for chopping. Notched stone netsinkers, bone awls, flaking tools, weaving implements, and beamers were found in some sites.

These Indians wore moccasins, breechclouts or skirts, and robes, all of which were made of skin, bark cloth, or woven cloth.

Pipes.—Pottery pipes were common, but stone pipes were also used occasionally. There were many shapes and sizes: equal-armed elbow pipes, long-stemmed elbow pipes, and pseudo-platform pipes in which the stem projects beyond the bowl. A variant of the last type has an upward curl to the stem projection. Effigy pipes were rare but were present at some sites.

Ornaments.—Necklaces were made of stone, copper, or marine shell beads. Ear ornaments were made of clay, copper, or copper over a wooden core. Pendants were made of quartz crystals, copper, or shell.

Some Caddo ornaments were religious in nature. Occasional finds such as copper masks, perhaps representative of a long-nosed god, and antler effigy headdresses of copper should be considered as variants of the art of the Southern Death Cult, which was (in its broadest sense) a part of Caddo culture. Ornaments and objects characteristic of the cult are described in the chapter on the Middle Southern area, although not necessarily all these would be associated with the Caddo divisions of the cult.

Burials.—Generally burial was in cemeteries. The bodies, usually extended but sometimes flexed, were placed in rectangular pits. Occasionally they were cremated. Pottery vessels, tools, weapons, and ornaments were usually placed with the dead. Probably special pottery vessels were made for burial purposes, although ordinary pottery was used also. In a few instances the bodies were buried in the temple mounds.

Conjectures.—The Indian carriers of the Caddo culture probably had trade relations with Indians of the Mississippi Valley, the Gulf Coast, and Florida. In historic times the Caddo culture was contemporary with Natchezan and groups of late Middle Mississippi Indians; early Caddo was contemporaneous with Coles Creek, Plaquemine, and Middle Mississippi. In its earliest stages it might have been coeval with Marksville-Troyville. It seems to have been a link between the Lower Mississippi Valley and the Plains. The Caddo area, as a whole, is closely linked with the Lower Mississippi Valley.

SOURCES

DICKINSON, 1936; HARRINGTON, 1920; LEMLEY, 1936; KRIEGER, A., n.d.; ORR, 1939, 1941; WALKER, W., 1935; WEBB and DODD, 1939.

PART VI
THE PACIFIC SLOPE

CHAPTER 28

CALIFORNIA

INTRODUCTION

CALIFORNIA comprises three archeological areas: northern, central, and southern. Northern California is a peripheral region. The western portion affiliates primarily with the coasts of Oregon and Washington, and the eastern portion with Nevada and southeastern Oregon. Central California includes the great central valley and the adjacent coast. It was typically Californian in culture and showed only slight evidence of outside influences from the Northwest Coast and the Southwest. Southern California possessed many Californian characteristics, particularly with regard to the basic mode of subsistence, but was strongly affected by cultural influences from the Southwest.

Central California and the coast of southern California consist mainly of broad valleys covered with bunch grass and groves of oaks, bordered by chaparral-covered hills and pine-forested mountains. The rainfall is moderate and comes in winter. In northern California the valleys are narrower, the rainfall is greater, and the pine forests (including redwoods on the coast) are denser and more extensive. Southern California east of the Coast Range is a desert with less than 10 inches of rainfall annually.

Agriculture was never practiced in California except along the Colorado River. In central California and along the southern California coast the basis of subsistence was the acorn, but other wild seeds were gathered, and hunting and fishing were practiced wherever possible. Fishing and gathering shellfish were more important along the coast. In northwestern California the acorn was augmented by fish and shellfish on the coast and salmon in the interior. In the Santa Barbara region fishing and the hunting of sea mammals were important. The desert dwellers lived by hunting small game and gathering a variety of wild seeds.

Pottery-making was confined largely to the desert region. In late prehistoric times pottery was made also on the southern California coast and to a limited extent in the upper San Joaquin Valley. Instead of pottery a variety of well-made twined and coiled baskets were used for storage, for carrying water, for transporting food, for eating-utensils, and for cooking by the stone-boiling method.

NORTHERN CALIFORNIA

Archeological knowledge of northwestern California is limited to evidence from the excavation of a single prehistoric site on an island in Humboldt Bay, a region occupied in historic times by the Wiyot Indians. The finds at this site included large ceremonial blades of red and black obsidian, curved adz handles and hand mauls of stone, splitting-wedges of bone and horn, one-piece and composite harpoon heads of horn, flat grease dishes of steatite, beads ma defrom dentalium and pine-nut shells, and long tubular pipes of steatite (Fig. 103). All these traits were typical of the historic Wiyot, Yurok, and Hupa Indians of northwestern California. The site also yielded cremations, animal-shaped clubs of stone ("slave-killers"), short, tubular pipes of clay, and clay balls. These traits did not exist in the historic culture of the region. The stone clubs were typical of the Northwest Coast, whereas the pipes and balls of clay and the cremations were characteristic of the late prehistoric period in central California. This evidence indicates that in prehistoric times northwestern California as far south as Humboldt Bay was affiliated primarily with the Northwest Coast but that there were cultural connections with central California as well.

Northeastern California is little known archeologically. Prehistoric camp sites occur around springs, lakes, and streams, and cave habitations are common. Burials are found in rock crevices and in thermal springs. Distinctive traits include the high development of flint and obsidian chipping, a cross-shaped type of charmstone, flat metates, and stone mortars with deep, conical cavities. The region seems to be culturally affiliated with Nevada and southeastern Oregon.

CENTRAL CALIFORNIA

Area.—The area consists of the great interior valley (actually, the valleys of the Sacramento and San Joaquin) stretching from Red Bluff in the north to Bakersfield in the south; the flanking Sierra Nevada and Coast ranges; and the adjacent coast. Included also are the Santa Barbara region (Point Sal to Los Angeles) and the Channel Islands, inhabited in historic times by the Chumash Indians. Ethnological classifications place the Chumash in the southern California area, but archeologically the Santa Barbara region passed through the same general stages of cultural development as did central California, and strong influences from the Southwest were lacking.

The archeological remains in the area fall into four main chronological and developmental periods which we shall call Archaic, Early, Middle, and Late. With the exception of the finds at Borax Lake,

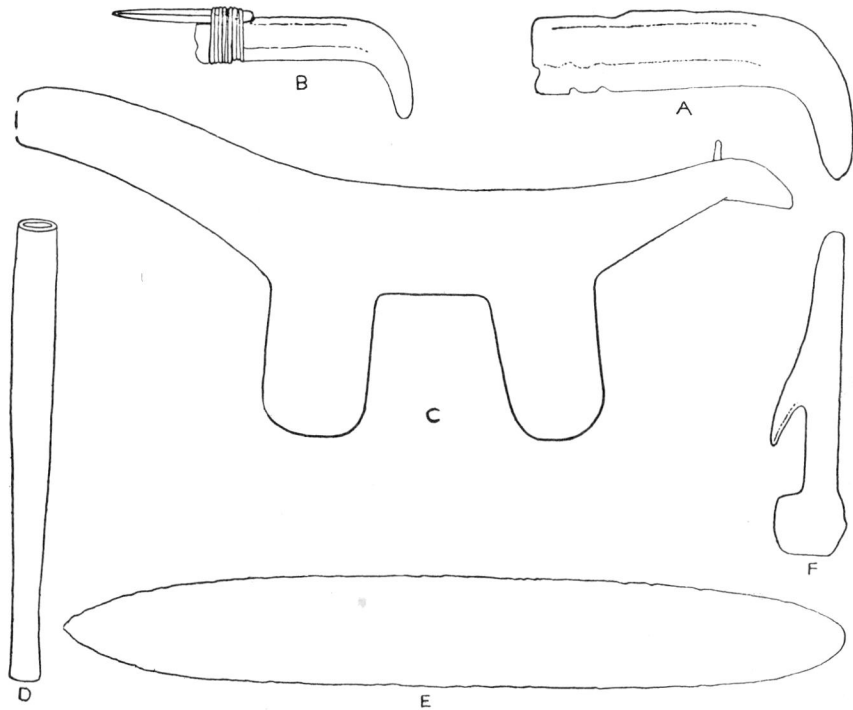

FIG. 103.—Implements from Humboldt Bay, California: *a* and *b*, stone adz handle and sketch showing method of hafting adz blade; *c*, animal-shaped club ("slave-killer") of steatite; *d*, steatite pipe; *e*, large ceremonial blade of obsidian; *f*, antler harpoon point. Scale 1:4. (After Loud.)

which we shall describe later, the Archaic culture is the earliest known for the area. It is probably at least two thousand years old, and its beginnings are much older. The Late culture ends with the historic period, which began in most of the area about A.D. 1825. In some regions it is possible to identify the last phase of the Late culture with the cultures of historic Indian groups.

Archaic period.—Remains of this period have been found at only two places, and very little is known about the culture. On the shore of Buena Vista Lake (Upper San Joaquin River) the earliest cultural level (called Early Buena Vista) contained extended burials in shallow graves near camping places. These burials were not sufficiently preserved to determine the physical appearance of the people. The only other cultural items found were manos and metates.

In the Santa Barbara region the remains of the earliest period (called Oak Grove) consisted of longheaded people; circular semi-underground houses; manos and metates (mortars and pestles rare); heavy chipped projectile points, leaf-shaped or with square bases; crudely chipped flake scrapers; bone bodkins; and extended burials containing red ocher and marked by piles of beach boulders and inverted metates.

Early period.—Remains of this period have been found in deep shell middens in the Lower Sacramento and Santa Barbara regions. The most characteristic traits were longheaded people; extended burials; manos and metates; large, roughly chipped, leaf-shaped or stemmed projectile points; and perforated charmstones. Charmstones are plummet-shaped amulets, probably used to bring luck in hunting and fishing.

In the Lower Sacramento region, the Early period (called Early Sacramento) contained the following traits: longheaded people; metates (mortars present but rare); large, roughly chipped projectile points of flint or slate, either leaf-shaped or with stems and shoulders (Fig. 104, *m*); notched prongs of bone or antler for fishgigs (Fig. 104, *n* and *o*); one-piece, curved fishhooks of bone (Fig. 104, *q*); straight fishhooks (gorges) of bone; short, thick-walled, conically drilled pipes of stone (Fig. 104, *p*); quartz crystal ornaments; rectangular shell beads (olivella and abalone); circular ornaments of abalone with two perforations; perforated charmstones and charmstones with phallus form (Fig. 104, *r*); asphaltum used for adhesive purposes, including appliqué of shell beads; and extended burials accompanied by implements.

In the Santa Barbara region the Early period (called Early Mainland and Point Sal I) included these features: longheaded people; possibly basketry; manos and metates (mortars and pestles rare); large stemmed projectile points; chipped-flint scrapers and knives; straight fishhooks (gorges) of bone; bone awls; beads of shell and steatite; red ocher; charmstones (common); and extended burials accompanied by tools and ornaments.

Middle period.—Cultural remains belonging to this period have been found on the Lower Sacramento River, around San Francisco

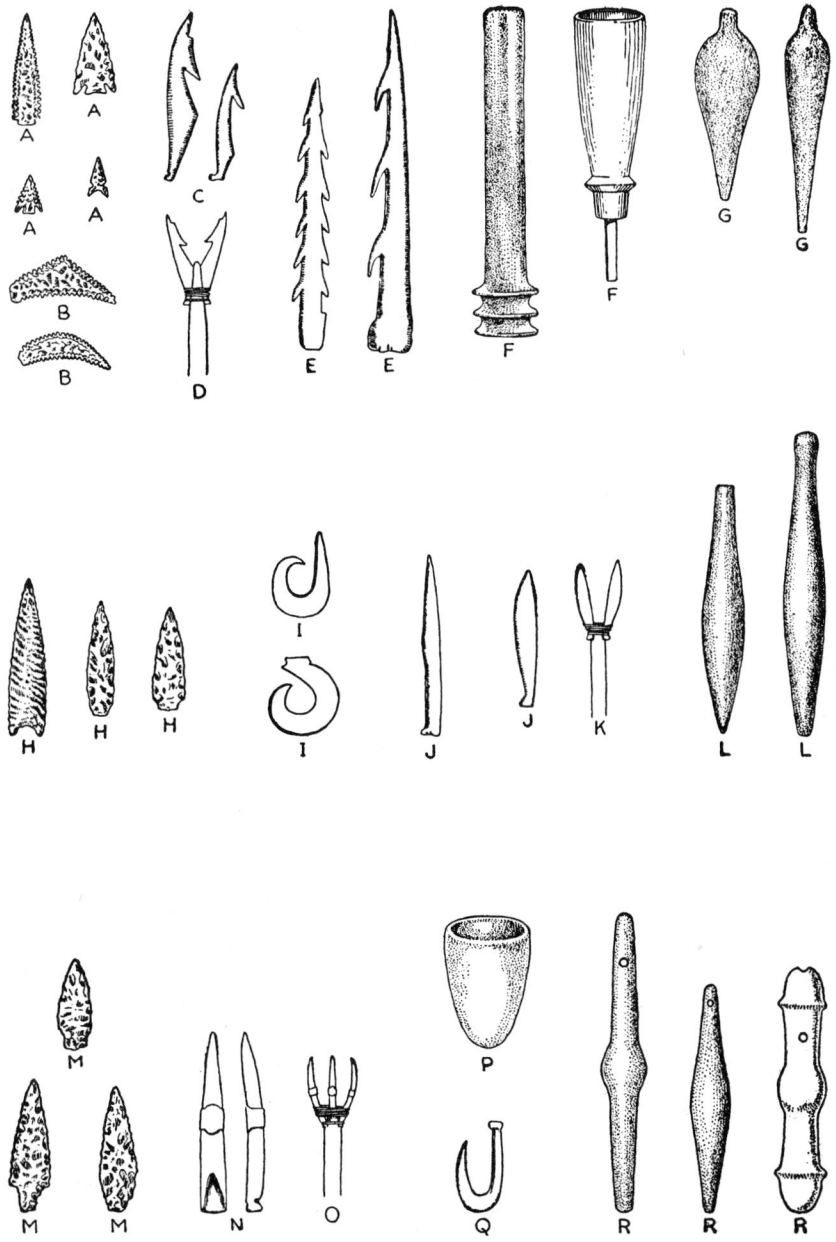

Fig. 104.—Succession of implement types in central California. *Top row:* Late period; *center row:* Middle period; *bottom row:* Early period. *a*, arrow points of obsidian; *b*, obsidian crescents; *c*, fishgig prongs of antler (the smaller points of this type may have served as barbs for composite fishhooks); *d*, reconstruction of fishgig; *e*, points of antler for harpoon or fish spears; *f*, stone pipes, one with bone stem; *g*, charmstones; *h*, projectile points of obsidian and slate; *i*, shell fishhooks from Santa Barbara region; *j*, prongs for fishgig; *k*, reconstruction of fishgig; *l*, charmstones, fishtail type; *m*, projectile points of flint and slate; *n*, prong for fishgig, front and side views; *o*, reconstruction of fishgig; *p*, stone pipe; *q*, bone fishhook; *r*, perforated charmstones. Scale 1:5. (After Heizer; Lillard, Heizer, and Fenenga; Olson; Schenck and Dawson.)

Bay, at Buena Vista Lake, and in the Santa Barbara region. This horizon, although possessing certain unique features, was a transitional period during which certain Early period traits became less important or disappeared and new traits appeared which became fully developed in the Late period. Thus there was a shift toward a roundheaded physical type (typical of the Late period); manos and metates became less numerous and mortars and pestles more important; flexed burials and cremations occurred along with extended burials; the chipping on projectile points became finer; and charmstones changed in form and decreased in number.

In the Lower Sacramento region the Middle period (called Transitional Sacramento) was characterized by the following features: mediumheaded people; coiled basketry; stone pestles and probably wooden mortars (manos and metates still used); large, finely chipped projectile points of obsidian or slate, either leaf-shaped or stemmed (Fig. 104, h); flat prongs of bone with basal flange for fishgigs (Fig. 104, j and k); straight fishhooks (gorges) of bone; circular beads of steatite and shell (olivella and abalone); circular oranments of abalone with two perforations and serrated edges; ear-plugs of steatite or baked clay; asphaltum used for adhesive purposes; and unperforated charmstones (fishtail type) (Fig. 104, l).

The Middle period at Buena Vista Lake (called Intermediate Buena Vista) contained the following: medium- or roundheaded people; circular, dome-shaped houses made of poles thatched with tule, occasionally having central posts; roasting pits; coiled and twined basketry; mortars and pestles (manos and metates still used); leaf-shaped and stemmed projectile points; bone awls; straight fishhooks (gorges) of bone; possibly compound fishhooks with bone barbs; bowls and jars of steatite; circular shell beads; use of asphaltum; unperforated charmstones; red ocher; and flexed burials.

The Middle period in the Santa Barbara region (called Intermediate Mainland and Point Sal II) included the earliest occupation on the Channel Islands (called Early Island). It was characterized by wickerwork basketry (coiled and twined baskets present); mortars and pestles (manos and metates less common); straight fishhooks (gorges) of bone; circular shell fishhooks (present) (Fig. 104, i); steatite bowls; possibly tubular pipes of steatite; beads of steatite and shell (common); asphaltum used for inlay of shell beads; bone pendants; and charmstones (rare).

Late period.—Remains of the late period have been found on the

Lower Sacramento, in the San Francisco Bay region, at Buena Vista Lake, and in the Santa Barbara region. In this period longheaded people, extended burials, manos and metates, and charmstones were rare or absent; whereas roundheaded people, extended burials and cremation, small triangular notched points, and tubular steatite pipes were characteristic. The crude pottery made at this time in the Buena Vista Lake region was probably derived from the east (Nevada) rather than from southern California.

On the Lower Sacramento the Late period culture (called Late Sacramento) developed ultimately into the culture of the historic Plains Miwok Indians. It was characterized by the following: roundheaded people; semiunderground round or elliptical houses with thatched and earth-covered roofs supported by central posts; coiled basketry; mortars and pestles (manos and metates rare); small, finely chipped, triangular notched projectile points of obsidian, often with serrated edges (Fig. 104, *a*); straight fishhooks (gorges) of bone; straight fishhook barbs of wood with a basal perforation for the attachment of a leader; barbed prongs of bone for fishgigs (Fig. 104, *c* and *d*); bone fishspear points with unilateral or bilateral barbs (Fig. 104, *e*); perforated arrow-straighteners of antler; baked clay balls; perforated, flat stone disks (spindle whorls?); biconically drilled, long tubular pipes of steatite with enlarged base rings and bone stems (Fig. 104, *f*); short tubular pipes of clay; disk beads of clamshell; ovoid and banjo-shaped ornaments of abalone with small perforations near the edge and incised decoration; incised geometric designs on birdbone tubes; curved or crescent-shaped blades of obsidian with serrated edges (Fig. 104, *b*); asphaltum used as adhesive; rarity or absence of charmstones (Fig. 104, *g*); and flexed burials and cremations.

At Buena Vista Lake the Late period culture (called Late Buena Vista) probably merged into that of the historic Yokuts Indians. Strong influences from the Santa Barbara region are indicated by the well-developed and varied steatite industry and the abundance of shell ornaments of the coastal type. The crude pottery suggests influences from Nevada, and the soft twined textiles indicate influences from southern California. The following features are characteristic: roundheaded people; flimsy, circular, dome-shaped houses made of poles and tule, perhaps daubed with mud; thick, coarse, buff to gray pottery vessels with gravel and some shell temper, probably in the forms of bowls and jars; coiled and twined baskets; soft twined textiles; mortars and pestles (metates rare); small triangular projectile points; straight fishhooks (gorges) of bone; compound fishhooks with bone barbs; bowls and jars of steatite (common); abundance of several types of bone awls; baked clay balls; large numbers of shell and steatite ornaments; use of asphaltum for adhesive purposes; red ocher (common); charmstones (rare); and flexed burials.

The culture of the Late period in the Santa Barbara region (called Late Mainland and Point Sal III) included the Late occupation of the Channel Islands (called Late Island). It merged into the culture of the historic Chumash Indians. The following features were characteristic: medium- or roundheaded people; circular, dome-shaped houses of poles with roofs thatched with grass and tule and supported by central posts; twined and coiled baskets; twined tule mats; mortars and pestles (manos and metates rare or absent); small notched projectile points; straight fishhooks (gorges) of bone; compound fishhooks of bone; circular shell fishhooks (common); bone harpoon-heads with one to six unilateral barbs; profusion of bone awls; abundance of jars, bowls, and pans of steatite (Fig. 105, *d*); multiplank wooden canoes; tubular pipes of steatite, sometimes with bone stems (Fig. 105, *a*); profusion of beads, pendants, and ornaments of shell; steatite carvings representing sea mammals and fish (Fig. 105, *b* and *c*); asphaltum used for shell inlay on stone vessels and bone tubes; and flexed burials with inverted mortars over the bodies.

Borax Lake site.—Folsom-like fluted projectile points have recently been found on the edge of Borax Lake in Lake County, about a hundred miles north of San Francisco. They were discovered in a thick cultural deposit lying in an alluvial fan possibly of late Pleistocene or pluvial age. Along with the few fluted points were found leaf-shaped points and square-shouldered points with straight stems, as well as chipped scrapers, flake knives, gravers, and drills. Also present were types of projectile points already known from Gypsum Cave in Nevada and from Pinto Basin in the California desert. Most of these implements were made of chipped obsidian. There were also crude manos, metates, and hammerstones. No skeletal material was found.

It is thought that the Borax Lake site was a camp ground used by visiting Indians who had come to secure obsidian from quarries in the vicinity. It is evident that the fluted points found at various levels of the deposit were generally contemporaneous with the other types of points found there; but it is not clear whether these diverse types were used by one people or by different peoples who camped there at various times. The age of the Borax Lake site is uncertain. It has been suggested that the alluvial fan was laid down during the last pluvial period, which ended about ten thousand years ago; but the possibility has not been eliminated that it was formed during the later wet period of about 1000 B.C. This later date is more reasonable on archeological grounds. Thus the Borax Lake finds are at least as old as the Archaic period in central California and may be older.

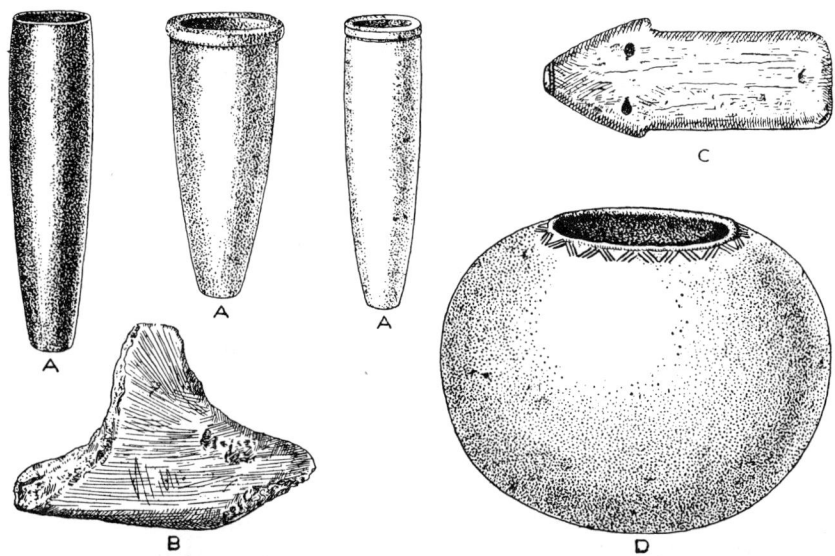

FIG. 105.—Steatite objects from the Santa Barbara Region and San Nicolas Island: a, pipes; b, carving representing killer whale; c, carving possibly representing seal or sea otter; d, jar with incised decoration. Scale: a and b, 1:3; c and d, 1:6. (Chicago Natural History Museum specimens.)

Summary.—With the exception of the Borax Lake finds, the historical position of which is not clear, the archeological remains in central California fall into a reasonably coherent, although far from complete, developmental sequence. The longheaded physical type, the manos and metates, and the extended burials of the Archaic period were carried over into the subsequent Early period. During this time the mortar and pestle was first generally used, although it probably first occurred at an earlier time. The relatively specialized Early culture was characterized by large stemmed projectile points, charmstones, the extensive use of shell for ornaments, and the use of asphaltum. During the transitional Middle period there was a shift toward a roundheaded population. Flexed burials and cremations occasionally occurred, mortars and pestles became more important; charmstones changed in form; and small triangular notched projectile points came into use along with the larger points. In the Late period the population was predominantly roundheaded; flexed burials and cremation were typical; the mortar and pestle largely replaced the mano and metate; charmstones grew rare; small triangular points predominated; and steatite was used extensively for ornaments, tubular pipes, and utensils. It is possible that the large projectile points of the Early period were used only on spears or spear-thrower darts and that the introduction of small triangular points in the Middle period marked the first appearance of the bow and arrow in central California.

SOUTHERN CALIFORNIA

In terms of environment and prehistoric culture, southern California is composed of a desert region lying between the Coast Range and the Colorado River and a coastal region extending from Los Angeles southward into Lower California.

Coastal region.—On the coast the earliest culture, called San Dieguito, has been found on the plateau bearing that name in San Diego County. The camp sites of the San Dieguito people were located on mesa and ridge tops. They made crudely chipped stone knives and scrapers but not projectile points of stone. Nothing is known of their physical appearance or of their burials. Their culture was probably earlier than the Oak Grove culture in the Santa Barbara region.

The next cultural period has been found in middens along the coast near San Diego. This culture, called La Jolla, has been divided into two phases. The people of the earlier phase used basined metates, unshaped manos, crude flake scrapers, and beach-cobble choppers, but no stone projectile points. Burials were made at random and contained no grave-offerings.

In the later phase metates were more common, and there was an increase in the quantity and types of chipped-stone tools. Burials were segregated in cemeteries and included offerings such as shell beads, perforated stone disks, and metates inverted over the bodies. The La Jolla people were long- or mediumheaded, with the long-headed type becoming rarer in the later phase. This phase of La Jolla culture spread southward along the Pacific Coast of Lower California.

The final prehistoric culture, called Diegueño, appeared on the coast probably in the fifteenth century and eventually developed into the cultures of the historic Diegueño and Luiseño Indians. The Diegueño people used mortars and metates, including bedrock types; made reddish pottery cooking pots and water jars tempered with crushed rock; used chipped-stone arrow points, flake scrapers, and bone awls; and practiced cremation. It is evident that the distinctive traits of the Diegueño culture spread to the California coast from the desert or were brought there by a migration of desert people.

Desert region.—In the California desert the earliest evidence of human occupation consists of camp sites and stone tools occurring along the shores and terraces of dry lakes and river beds. These were left by peoples with simple hunting and plant-gathering cultures. Typical examples are the Lake Mohave and Pinto Basin complexes. Along the beaches of ancient Lake Mohave, which is at present a dry basin or playa, there have been found hammerstones, abraders, crudely flaked choppers, scrapers, flake and oval knives, drills, leaf-shaped blades, and projectile points of two distinctive types. In arid Pinto Basin, some sixty-five miles south of Lake Mohave, hearths and stone tools have been found in terraces which were formerly the banks of a broad, sluggish river. These people used manos, metates, pestles, hammerstones, flaked choppers, scrapers, knives, and several distinctive types of projectile points.

The age of the Lake Mohave and Pinto Basin cultures is debatable. Geological studies have shown that the lake and river existed during a period of moist climate. This probably occurred during the last pluvial period ten thousand or more years ago rather than during the moist period of shorter duration and magnitude that prevailed about three thousand years ago. Thus the Lake Mohave and Pinto Basin remains, found on the pluvial terraces, may have an age of at least ten thousand years, but there is considerable doubt that the remains are contemporaneous with the terraces. A large camp of the Lake Mohave people has been found on a bar extending across the outlet channel of Lake Mohave, a site that would have been uninhabitable during the period of lake overflow. Furthermore, remains of the camps of the Pinto Basin people have been found in sand dunes resting on top of playa or alluvial deposits probably of postpluvial origin. It is therefore more likely that the Lake Mohave and Pinto Basin cultures flourished during the last wet period three to four thousand years ago rather than at a much earlier time. Pinto Basin culture appears to have been later than Lake Mohave.

After the Pinto Basin culture there existed a related desert culture called Amargosa. The Amargosa people possessed a stone industry similar to that of Pinto Basin, but their knives were of different forms, their stone drills were more elaborate and numerous, and they made little use of chopping and scraping tools. The Amargosa culture lasted until A.D. 500 or later.

Probably about A.D. 800, a people with a culture similar to the La Jolla culture of the southern California coast began pushing across the California desert to the Colorado, where they were subjected to strong Southwestern influences. As a result, they adopted farming and pottery-making. The exact source of the pottery is not clear, since the earliest Colorado River pottery possessed both Early Anasazi traits (in vessel forms and lug handles) and Hohokam traits (in vessel forms and the use of red-on-buff decoration and paddle-and-anvil technique). This new culture has been given two names: Prehistoric Yuman and Patayan. Once established on the Colorado River, Prehistoric Yuman culture went through three phases of development, leading, finally, to the culture of the historic Yuman-speaking tribes of the region, such as the Mohave and Yuma. The center of this development was on the Lower Colorado. During the second and third phases this culture spread up the Colorado as far as Black Canyon, Nevada, westward into the Mohave Desert, eastward into Arizona, and southward into Lower California. The Prehistoric Yuman people were great traders, as were their historic descendants. They acted as middlemen in the shell trade from the Pacific Coast to the Southwest, and it was through them that some Southwestern traits such as pottery-making reached the coast of southern California.

CONJECTURES

The determination of the age of the prehistoric culture sequence in California is of primary importance for understanding the nature of cultural developments in this area and for placing the sequence into a wider continental perspective. But a reliable chronology for California is at present lacking.

The difficulties are twofold. First, the broad sequence of California cultures is in part conjectural. Although reasonably sound relative chronologies based on stratigraphic sequences have been established for some regions, the correlation of one region with another rests on typological comparisons rather than on stratigraphic cross-ties. For this reason possible time lags from one region to another cannot be discerned.

Second, there is no reliable basis for assigning an age in years to the various cultural periods. Geological studies of the climatic and other conditions under which various cultural deposits were laid down and of the length of time required for their accumulation have failed as yet to yield reliable results. There is hope that this approach will eventually produce useful conclusions.

A more immediate possibility is that of tying the California sequence to the absolute chronology of the Southwest. This correlation is feasible because of the extensive prehistoric trade relations between the two areas. A careful study of numerous California shell ornaments and other artifacts discovered in dated Southwestern sites and of dated Southwestern potsherds and other artifacts in California sites should yield dates for the later periods in California. Such a study has not yet been made.

Despite these difficulties, we have arranged the California cultures in a chronological sequence, which is shown in Chart XV. This chronology is based on two pivotal dates: A.D. 1000 for the beginning of the Late period and a minimum date of 2000 B.C. for the Lake Mohave culture.

The date for the inception of the Late period was arrived at on the following basis. Circular shell fishhook blanks of the Santa Barbara type have been found in a Pueblo ruin near Flagstaff dating from the twelfth century. Shell fishhooks first appeared in the Santa Barbara region during the Middle period but did not become common until the Late period. In the vicinity of Los Angeles two Hohokam sherds dating from 900–1100 have been found in one site, and fragments of a Hohokam vessel of the period 700–900 in another. The former site probably belongs to the Late period, and the latter is probably Middle and/or Late. These facts suggest 1000 as a conservative date for the beginning of the Late period.

The basis for the Lake Mohave date has already been discussed. The prehistoric Yuman chronology is based in part on intrusive Southwestern sherds of known date.

The chronology presented is conservative with respect to the age assigned to the various periods. New research may well lengthen the time spans suggested, particularly for the earlier horizons.

CHART XV
CHRONOLOGY IN THE CALIFORNIA AREA

Date	Central California					Southern California	
	Sacramento Valley	San Francisco Bay	Buena Vista Lake	Point Sal	Santa Barbara and Channel Islands	Coast	Desert
Late —1800—	Late Sacramento	Late San Francisco Bay	Late Buena Vista	Point Sal III	Late Mainland and Late Island	Prehistoric Diegueño	Yuman III
—1000—	Transitional Sacramento	Transitional San Francisco Bay	Intermediate Buena Vista	Point Sal II	Intermediate Mainland and Early Island	La Jolla II	Yuman II
Middle —500—							Yuman I
Early A.D./B.C.	Early Sacramento		Early Buena Vista	Point Sal I	Early Mainland	La Jolla I	
—1000—					Oak Grove		Amargosa
Archaic	? Borax Lake					San Dieguito	Pinto Basin
—2000—							Lake Mohave

SOURCES

CAMPBELL and CAMPBELL, 1935; CAMPBELL *et al.*, 1937; CARTER, 1941; COLTON, 1939, 1941; GIFFORD, 1940; GIFFORD and SCHENCK, 1926; HARRINGTON, 1938a, 1938b, 1939, 1945; HAURY, 1943a; HEIZER, 1939a, 1939b, 1941a, 1941b, 1945; HEIZER and FENENGA, 1939; KROEBER, 1925, 1936, 1938, 1939; LILLARD, HEIZER, and FENENGA, 1939; LILLARD and PURVES, 1936; LOUD, 1918; MCGREGOR, 1941; OLSON, 1930, 1934; ROBERTS, 1940b; ROGERS, D. B., 1929; ROGERS, M. J., 1929b, 1939, 1945; SCHENCK and DAWSON, 1929; WALKER, E. F., 1945, WEDEL, 1941c.

CHAPTER 29

THE PLATEAU AREA

INTRODUCTION

THE region in northwestern America that lies between the Cascade and the Rocky Mountains and stretches from the great bend of the Fraser River southward into Oregon is known as the Plateau. This interior plateau is drained by two great rivers, the Columbia and the Fraser.

In historic times this area was occupied by about twenty-five Indian tribes which shared a common culture, called Plateau culture. In modified form this culture was distributed over most of the geographical plateau, while the territories of two tribes of Plateau type, the Kutenai and the Flathead, extended eastward in the intermountain valleys of the Rockies. The Plateau area included tribes belonging to four different linguistic stocks. In the extreme north were Athabascan tribes, and in the north and central regions were Salish-speaking peoples. The south was occupied by tribes of Sahaptin speech, while in the east were the linguistically isolated **Kutenai**.

Within the plateau there is variation in topography, climate, vegetation, and animal life. It is convenient to divide the area into a number of regions in terms of drainage. (1) The Middle Columbia region is an arid plateau through which the river has cut a deep gorge. The sparse vegetation consists of sagebrush and bunch grass. Trees and game are scarce. (2) The Lower Snake country is very similar, although above the confluence with the Clearwater River the land is higher, the bunch-grass tracts are interspersed with pine, and deer and other game are more abundant. (3) The region of the Upper Columbia is mountainous and forested, with grassland along the river valleys and with more rain than the plateau to the south. Game and wild edible plants are abundant. Although from the mouth of the Spokane River to the confluence with the Okanogan River the Columbia flows through an arid, treeless plateau similar in environment to the Middle Columbia region, the hinterland immediately to the north is wooded and like the rest of the Upper Columbia region. (4) The Fraser-Thompson drainage, although mountainous and wooded, is drier than the Upper Columbia and less heavily forested, and there are stretches of dry steppe.

People.—The Indians of the Plateau were roundheaded and of medium stature. The meager information on skeletal material that is available from archeological sites indicates that there has been no significant change in physical type in the past few centuries. Skull deformation was not practiced in prehistoric or historic times, except to a limited extent in the middle Columbia region, where the custom was undoubtedly intrusive from the coast.

Livelihood.—No agriculture was practiced by the Indians of the Plateau area. Subsistence was based on salmon fishing, hunting, and gathering of wild plant products. Without the salmon the surprisingly dense Indian population of the arid Middle Columbia region would have been impossible. Salmon and other fish were speared and caught along all the larger rivers. Certain rapids and falls were fishing centers where thousands of Indians camped during the salmon run. The collecting of roots, seeds, and wild fruits was also important, particularly in the higher, better-watered regions. The most important wild plant product was the bulb of the camass lily. Hunting was practiced everywhere but was less important in arid, treeless regions. River clams were eaten in times of famine but were of little importance when other foods were available.

Villages.—Most of the historic Indian groups lived in politically independent, permanent villages located on waterways. A group of such villages, bound together by cultural and linguistic similarity but lacking political unity, constituted the tribe as that term is used in preceding paragraphs. This political anarchy was undoubtedly characteristic of the prehistoric Plateau also. The nineteenth-century tribal political organization of the southeastern and eastern Plateau developed as a result of the adoption of the horse and of influence from the Plains. The independent villages usually contained from fifty to a hundred persons, although some were much larger. In summer these villages were largely abandoned for camps at fishing sites and berrying and root-digging grounds.

Early history and archeological knowledge.—The Plateau was first explored by Whites between 1793 and 1811. Although by 1793 a few European trade objects had reached the Plateau from the Pacific Coast, these were not common until the area was opened to trade between 1805 and 1820. For archeological purposes, Indian sites containing trade objects in any abundance may be dated post-1805, and those containing very large amounts of trade goods as post-1815.

Just before and at the beginning of the historic period, extensive cultural changes occurred among the southern and eastern Plateau tribes as a result of the adoption of the horse, which reached the Plateau about 1730. The horse increased enormously the contact of these tribes with the Plains, and there followed a striking overlay of Plains culture traits, such as the tepee, styles of clothing, and patterns of warfare. This Plains influence affected only slightly the peoples of the Upper Columbia and Thompson River regions.

Archeological research in the Plateau has not yet developed a prehistoric chronology. It is possible on the basis of presence or absence of White trade objects to distinguish historic from prehistoric sites, but at present the prehistoric sites cannot be chronologically differentiated. On the basis of available evidence archeological remains in the Plateau do not appear to be very old, nor is there evidence of much cultural change in the prehistoric period. It is therefore necessary to present a description of Plateau archeology in terms of regions rather than in terms of time periods. In the following sections, in order to enrich the picture of prehistoric Plateau culture, certain information on the historic culture has been added to the strictly archeological data in cases where there is good reason to believe that there has been no significant change from prehistoric times.

THE UPPER COLUMBIA REGION

Archeological investigation has been carried out in the region only along the Columbia from the mouth of the Sanpoil to the Canadian border. In historic times the region was inhabited by Salish-speaking tribes which shared a generally similar culture. This similarity of culture in the region existed in prehistoric times as well.

Houses.—Two principal types of dwelling were used, the semisubterranean earth lodge or pit-house and the mat-covered surface house. Probably the earth lodge was the exclusive form of winter house in prehistoric times, but in the early nineteenth century it was displaced by the mat-covered house. Remains of house pits have been reported for the region, but archeological information on prehistoric pit-houses is lacking. Ethnological evidence indicates that the earth lodge consisted of a circular pit four to six feet deep and ten to sixteen feet in diameter, covered with a conical roof or sometimes a flat roof. The conical roof was supported by radiating poles fastened to one or more center posts. On this framework were placed cedar planks, a layer of grass and brush, and, finally, earth. A single hole in the top near the center post served as entrance and smoke hole. The floor of the house was reached by means of a ladder made by lashing crosssticks to two vertical poles. Notched pole ladders have been reported also.

The mat-covered house was rectangular in plan with rounded ends and an inverted-V roof covered with tule mats. It was sixteen feet wide and twenty to sixty feet long, accommodating two to eight families. Each family occupied a section on one side of this long, narrow structure and shared a hearth with the family on the other side. The hearth was in the center under the smoke opening which ran the length of the roof peak.

In summer, when the people moved about gathering roots and berries or camped at the fishing grounds, the large mat lodges were dismantled, and single families lived in circular or rectangular matcovered windbreaks or in small conical mat lodges.

Hemispherical sweat lodges were constructed of willow branches and covered with grass and earth. Food was stored in circular cache pits or on elevated wooden platforms.

Pottery.—In historic times some tribes in the Upper Columbia region are reported to have used clay to a limited extent to make rings for the hoop-and-pole game and for unfired pots. No pottery or other clay objects have been found in archeological sites.

Basketry.—In the whole of the Plateau area basketry was used for a great variety of purposes, serving as household utensils and cooking vessels which in other areas of the continent were often made of pottery, wood, or bark. On the Upper Columbia coiled baskets made of spruce or cedar root were used for water carriers, berry containers, cooking utensils, and drinking cups. Cooking was performed in baskets by placing hot stones in the liquid to be boiled. Most coiled baskets were plain, but some were decorated with geometric designs by sewing the coils alternately with cedar root and the lighter-colored spruce-root fibers, or with dyed spruce root. Occasionally, imbricated decoration was made with bear grass or dyed spruce root.

Soft baskets and bags were made by a plain twined technique from Indian hemp or the bark of willow or sagebrush. Twined basket hats were sometimes worn by women. The bags and sometimes the baskets were decorated with false embroidery. This was done by wrapping the weft with tule, red bark, or dyed grasses. The designs, in one or several colors, were triangular figures arranged in various combinations.

Matted bags made by sewing strips of rush or twisted cedar bark were in use in early historic times but were displaced by the twined bag.

Mats used to cover the roofs and floors of dwellings and to dry food were made by sewing strips of tule with cord of Indian hemp. Bedding mats and mats used to hold food at meals were made of slough grass twined with Indian hemp cord.

Containers of cottonwood or pine bark were used for storage of food, for cooking, and as buckets.

Tools, utensils, and weapons.—The bow and arrow was the principal hunting weapon of the region. The spear was used to a limited extent for hunting and warfare, and there was some use of armor made of rawhide or wooden slats. Arrow and spear points were chipped largely from flint or argillite, and a few points made of obsidian from southeastern Oregon have been found. Only about one-third of the points had stems. Of the nonstemmed forms, the most common was a large leaf-shaped blade with slightly convex base. Also common were small triangular points with side notches and concave bases. Stemmed points had a variety of forms, the most common being barbed, with stem expanding toward a straight base. Nonstemmed points tended to be larger than stemmed points (Fig. 106, *a* and *b*).

Arrow and spear points of bone had tapering points and wedge-shaped bases which were inserted into the arrow-or spear-shaft and bound with sinew (Fig. 107, *e* and *f*).

Arrow-shafts were smoothed with paired smoothers of sandstone which were long, hemispherical in section, slightly tapering toward the ends, and with a groove down the center of the flat face. The shafts were straightened with a wrench made by drilling a hole in an elk rib.

Fish were caught by spearing and netting and with weirs and traps. Three forms of wooden fish spear were used: (1) the commonest form had one or two prongs with detachable heads attached to the shaft by a line (Fig. 108, *a*); (2) spears with one, two, or three prongs with nondetachable heads, of which the trident form was most common (Fig. 108, *b*); (3) a spear with a large, detachable antler point with one or two barbs on one side, the line from the shaft being fastened to the base of the point by means of a hole in or flange on the point base (Fig. 107, *g*), and the point attached to the shaft with a two-piece

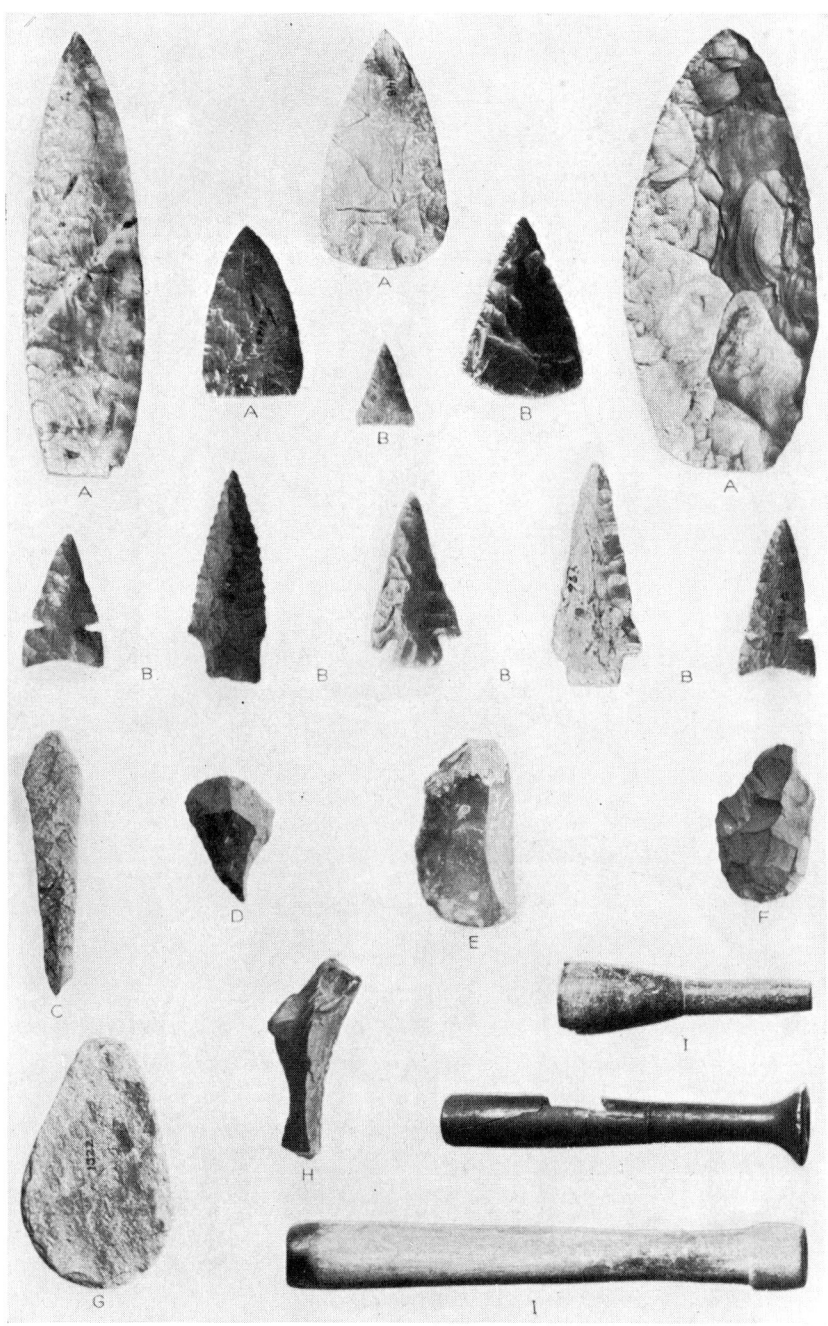

FIG. 106.—Stone projectile points, tools, and pipes from the Upper Columbia Region: *a*, spear points; *b*, arrow points; *c*, drill; *d*, graver; *e*, side-scraper; *f*, end-scraper; *g*, hide-scraper; *h*, flake knife; *i*, pipes. Scale: *a* and *g*, 1:3; *b–f*, *h*, and *i*, 1:2. (Courtesy Eastern Washington State Historical Society.)

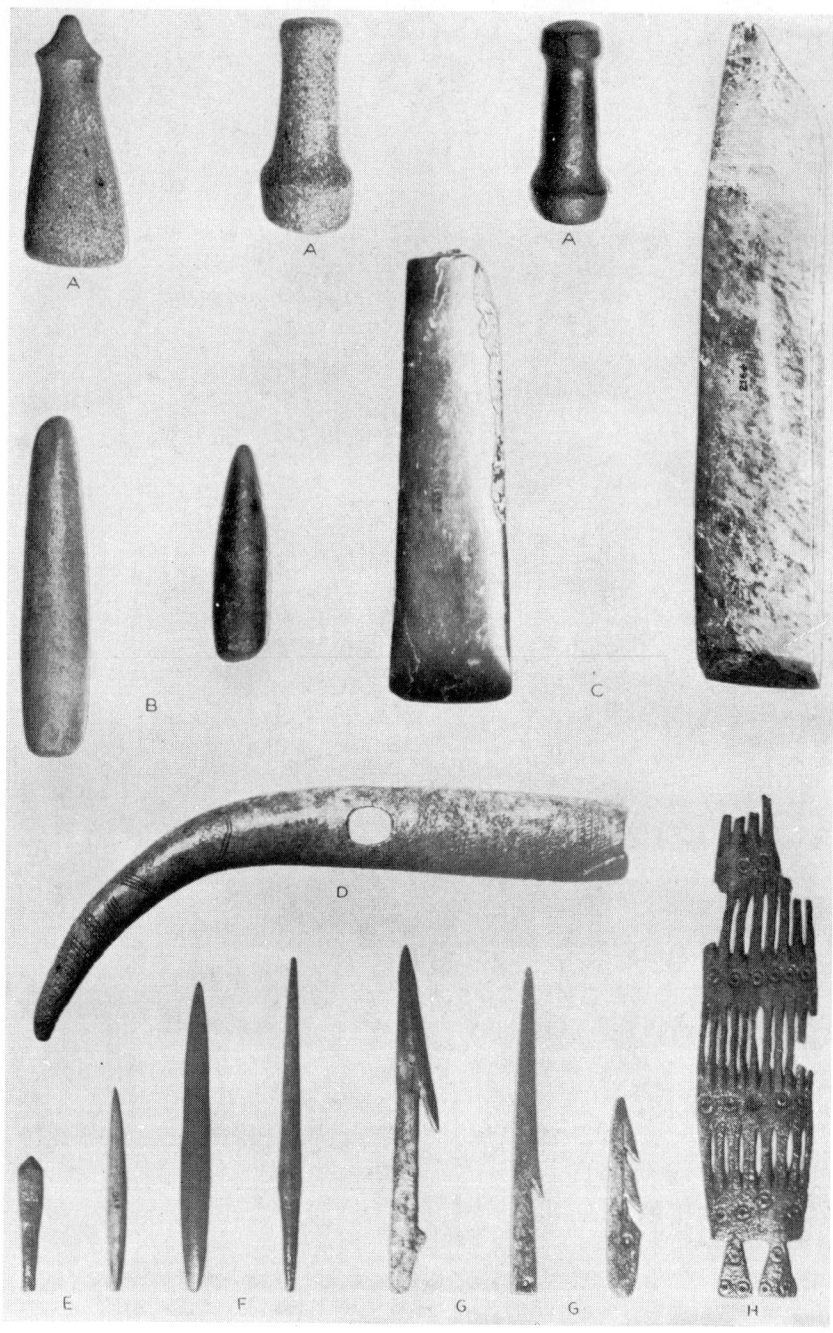

Fig. 107.—Tools, projectile points, and ornament from the Upper Columbia region: *a*, hand mauls of stone; *b*, stone pestles; *c*, adz blades of stone; *d*, digging-stick handle of antler with incised decoration; *e*, bone arrow points; *f*, bone spear points; *g*, harpoon points of antler; *h*, bone ornament. Scale: *a* and *b*, 1:6; *c–g*, 1:3; *h*, 1:2. (Courtesy Eastern Washington State Historical Society.)

bone coupling with deep sockets for both shaft and point, or merely inserted into a socket in the end of the shaft. This third type did not survive into recent times, although the other types are still in use.

Nets were made of Indian hemp cord. The dip net was most common, although larger nets were used also. Probably the numerous notched or grooved river pebbles found in the region served as net-sinkers. Occasionally, small fish were caught with hook and line. Hooks were made by lashing together crossed splinters of bone.

Camass bulbs and roots were dug with a slightly curved digging-stick about three feet long, onto which was fitted a perforated cross-

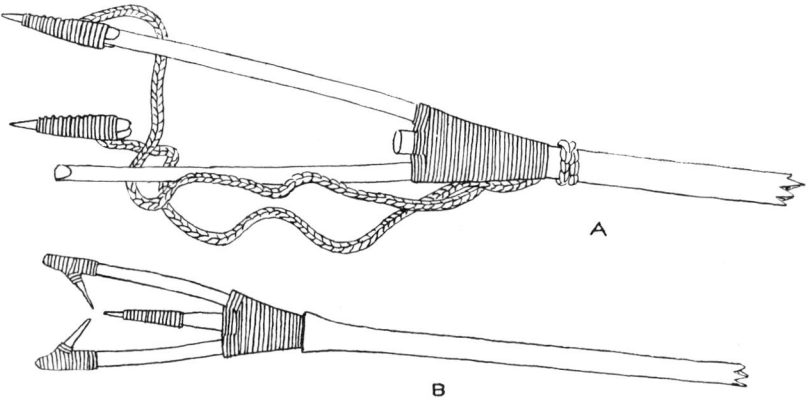

FIG. 108.—Fish spears from the Plateau: *a*, salmon spear with detachable barbed heads of bone; *b*, trident fish spear with bone point on center prong and fixed barbs of bone on lateral prongs. Scale 1:5. (After Teit.)

handle of antler or wood. Sometimes the sticks were tipped with antler. The antler handles were decorated with incised designs, of which simple hatched triangles or parallel bands were most common (Fig. 107, *d*). Camass bulbs were usually cooked in earth ovens heated by hot stones. Many of these cooking pits have been found in prehistoric and early historic sites.

Drills, gravers, side- and end-scrapers, and flake knives were chipped from flint and occasionally from argillite (Fig. 106, *c–f, h*). A special type of flat scraper, generally round or oval in shape, was made of quartzite (Fig. 106, *g*). This tool was hafted in the end of a straight handle two to three feet long and was used for scraping hides. Fleshers were made from split deer bones.

Well-made and polished hand mauls were ground from basalt. They had a distinct handle, a flaring base, and a smaller but also flaring top, the upper surface of which was flat or occasionally hat-shaped (Fig. 107, *a*). They were used to pound antler wedges in splitting wood and for driving stakes. Roughly shaped hammerstones were used for heavier pounding. Pestles ground from basalt or diorite were generally round in section and larger at the bottom, with flat base and rounded top (Fig. 107, *b*). Mortars were of wood or rawhide.

Highly polished adzes (Fig. 107, *c*) and chisels were ground from green nephrite or anthophylite. These materials came either from the Fraser or the Skagit River in western Washington. Since the tools have the same form as those found along the Thompson and Fraser rivers, it is possible that not only the material but the implements themselves reached the Upper Columbia by trade.

Awls were ground from deer scapulas or from split and unsplit long bones of mammals. Slender pointed needles with eyes and blunter bodkins with eyes were made from bone. Spoons were of mountain-sheep horn, and swan-wing bones were used for whistles.

The upper incisors of beaver were used for dice. A set consisted of four teeth, one decorated with incised dots, the others with incised parallel lines. The incisions were filled with red pigment.

Pipes.—The prehistoric pipe of the region was tubular (Fig. 106, *i*) and made of talc schist (similar to steatite). The typical form was straight, with the stem flaring at the end to form a flange. Some pipes had a flaring bowl and a straight stem without flange. A tubular pipe of catlinite has been found in a prehistoric or possibly early historic site, indicating that some trade connection with the Plains area existed at this time. In a later, fully historic site was found a catlinite pipe of typical Plains form. In the nineteenth century the tubular pipe was largely displaced by elbow forms, undoubtedly under influence from the Plains.

Costume.—Except for the presence of deer and elk hides and an occasional fragment of buffalo hide in nineteenth-century graves, there is no archeological evidence relating to clothing. According to ethnological evidence, prehistoric dress for both men and women consisted of a bark breechcloth or apron and a simple twined poncho-like garment of bark falling a little below the waist. In winter men wrapped their legs with fur, and women had hemp leggings. Presumably fur robes were used in cold weather. Apparently moccasins were not worn.

Probably during the eighteenth century untailored skin garments, moccasins, and fur caps came into use. Finally, in the early nineteenth century, tailored skin garments of Plains type were adopted in the region.

Travel and transportation.—Two kinds of dugout canoe were used, a shovel-nosed type with flat, projecting bow and stern, and a sharp-nosed type with pointed bow and stern. Some groups in the region used bark canoes also. Snowshoes were long and narrow, with rounded front and tapering tail, or oval.

Ornaments.—The principal ornaments were necklaces, pendants, and earrings. Two types of marine shell from the Pacific Coast—olivella and dentalium—were used most frequently in making necklaces. The spires of olivella shells were ground off in order to string them. The long tubular and slightly curved dentalium shells were strung whole or in segments. Disk beads ground from river clams or marine shells were less common. Bone beads, teeth of elk, bear, and lynx, claws of bear and cougar, and bird beaks were also strung on necklaces. Possibly native copper was used to a limited extent in prehistoric times for tubular beads and pendants. This copper probably came from the Pacific Coast or the interior of British Columbia. In historic times the fur-traders furnished the Indians with large quantities of sheet copper and brass which were made into tubular beads, pendants, and bracelets.

Pendants of river clam and abalone shell were common, and pendants of stone rare. A single pendant of turquoise has come from the region. The nearest known turquoise deposits are in Nevada.

Earrings were made of shell or bone and suspended from a hole in the ear by sinew. Carved bone ornaments decorated with rows of filigree and rows of incised dots within circles (Fig. 107, *h*) were probably worn in the hair or fastened to garments.

Burials.—Two forms of burial were practiced in both prehistoric and historic times. Most frequently the dead were buried in pits dug in sand or gravel near river banks. In the southern part of the region, from the mouth of the Spokane River westward, these pit burials were usually marked with circular piles of river boulders placed on the surface above the grave. Most of the graves so marked had placed over the body a circular or oval inclosure of cedar planks charred at the upper ends. Evidently, when making the burial, the body was covered with sand to a depth of about two feet and the planks driven into this fill to a depth of about a foot. They were then set afire and allowed to burn down to the level of the fill. Later, the filling of the burial pit was completed and the fill covered with the circle of stones. The body remained unburned, since it was protected by the sand fill. Cremation burial was not practiced.

Less frequently burials were placed in rock slides at the foot of cliffs bordering the river flats. The body was placed in a hole excavated in the rocks, covered with stones, and a cedar stake was left projecting above the rocks as a marker.

In nearly all sand-pit and rock-slide burials the body was flexed, reclining, and with head pointing downstream. A few extended burials were made. It was customary to bury ornaments, tools, and pipes with the dead, often in large quantities.

THE THOMPSON RIVER REGION

Archeological investigation in this region has been carried out only in the vicinity of Lytton at the mouth of the Thompson River, and up the Thompson River at Spence's Bridge, in the Nicola Valley, and at Kamloops. With the exception of Kamloops, which was Shushwap territory, these places were in the historic range of the Upper Thompson Indians, who spoke a Salish language.

Houses.—The winter dwelling was a circular pit-house with pyramidal earth-covered roof supported by four center posts and with a square hatchway at the center provided with a notched-log ladder (Fig. 109). These houses were twenty to forty feet in diameter and accommodated fifteen to thirty people. The pit-house was in use by the Thompson Indians until about 1890, when it was replaced by the log house of the Whites. The mat-covered long house used in winter in the Upper Columbia region was not found here.

The summer dwelling was a gabled, pyramidal, or conical surface lodge covered with mats. Sweat lodges were constructed as in the Upper Columbia region. Circular cache pits for food storage were roofed with poles, pine needles, and earth. Food was also kept on elevated wooden platforms.

Pottery.—The use of clay for utensils has not been reported for the region.

Basketry.—Basketry forms and techniques were generally similar to those of the Upper Columbia region. Geometric designs made by imbrication were much more common in the Thompson region, the general practice being to imbricate the whole outer surface of coiled baskets. Storage baskets often had lids. Twined baskets and bags were made, but the technique was less well developed than in the

Plateau to the south. Possibly false embroidery, used to a limited extent, was a recent introduction from the central or southern Plateau. Bark containers of birch or of spruce were also used.

Mats for covering summer houses were made by sewing tule with Indian hemp cord. Mats used to cover floors and to hold food at meals were twined, the warp being made of rushes or grass.

Tools, utensils, and weapons.—The bow and arrow was the chief hunting weapon. The bow and arrow, short spears, clubs of stone, bone, or wood, daggers of bone, and wooden slat armor were used in warfare. Arrow and spear points were chipped from flint or glassy basalt and occasionally argillite. Large leaf-shaped blades and small

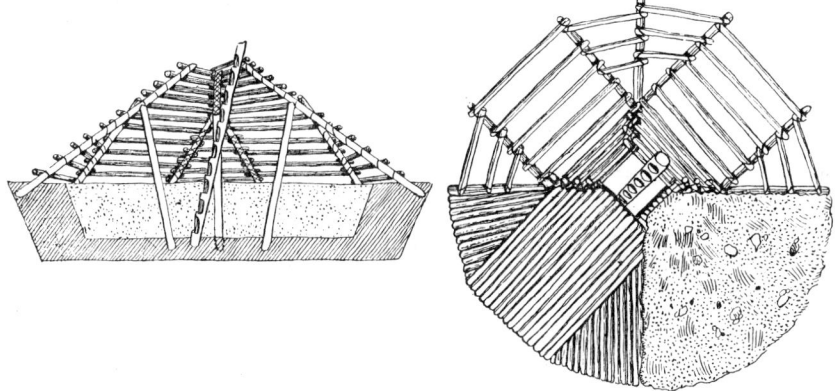

Fig. 109.—Pit-house of Thompson River type. *Left,* cross-section showing pit, center posts, roof framework, and notched log ladder. *Right,* view of roof from above, showing hatchway, rafter construction, sheathing of poles, and covering of earth. (After Teit.)

triangular points with side notches were common. Stemmed forms with or without barbs appear to have been much less frequent. Bone arrow and spear points similar in form to those from the Upper Columbia region were also used. Barbed arrow points of bone, some of which were detachable, were apparently used for small game. Sandstone arrow-shaft smoothers were of the Upper Columbia type.

Fish were caught by spearing, netting, and hook and line, or by means of weirs and traps. The three types of fish spear described for the Upper Columbia region were employed here. The third type, with large detachable barbed point of antler with a hole at the base for line attachment, apparently did not survive into historic times. Dipnets and dragnets were employed. Two types of fishhook were used: (1) a wooden shank to the bottom of which was lashed a bone barb and (2) two bone points lashed together to form a shallow V, the line being attached to the bottom of the V with points facing upward. Lines were of Indian hemp, weighted with stone sinkers.

Digging-sticks with cross-handles of antler or wood, sometimes with incised decorations, were of the same type as those of the Upper Columbia region.

Drills and end- and side-scrapers chipped from flint were similar in form to the types reported for the Upper Columbia, as were the flat, hafted scrapers of quartzite used for working hides. Hand mauls, hammerstones, and pestles are also similar in form. Unlike the region to the south, mortars were of stone.

Well-polished adzes and chisels were ground from nephrite. These were of the same form as the cutting implements of greenstone from the Upper Columbia.

Wedges for wood-splitting and flakers for stone-chipping were of antler. Awls and eyed needles were of bone. Dice in sets of four decorated in the manner described for the Upper Columbia region were of beaver or woodchuck teeth.

Pipes.—Tubular pipes of steatite were identical in form with those of the Upper Columbia. As in that region, the elbow pipe displaced the tubular pipe in historic times.

Travel and transportation.—Both bark and dugout canoes were used. Snowshoes were long and tapering toward the tail or were oval.

Costume.—As in the Upper Columbia region, the nineteenth-century costume consisted of tailored skin garments of Plains type. The prehistoric costume probably consisted of bark breechcloths, twined bark ponchos or cloaks, bark skirts, and fur robes.

Ornaments.—Necklaces of dentalium and other marine shells, bone, and animal teeth were common. It is believed that dentalium shells (of marine origin) reached the Thompson region by trade from the north of Vancouver Island, across the mountains, and thence down the Fraser River. Possibly the Indians of the Upper Columbia depended on this same source for dentalium shells. Pendants and ear ornaments were made of bone and shell, including abalone.

In historic times the Thompson Indians made tubular beads, pendants, and bracelets from trade copper and brass. It has not been determined to what extent native copper was used in prehistoric times.

Burials.—Prehistoric burials consisted of inhumations in sand or gravel benches along rivers or in rock slides. The rock-slide burials were marked with upright branches or stakes, while the sand-pit burials were marked with wooden posts or slabs of wood or stone. Bodies were flexed, and ornaments and tools were placed with them. In recent times, probably as a result of coastal influence, the dead were disposed of above ground in wooden boxes or structures, and some cremation was practiced.

THE MIDDLE COLUMBIA REGION

There exist published data on archeological sites in the Yakima Valley, along the Columbia River at Vantage, Wahluke, and the mouth of the Snake, at Blalock Island, and on both sides of the Columbia from the mouth of the Deschutes River to the Dalles. All these sites fall within the historic and probably also the prehistoric range of Sahaptin-speaking tribes. At the Dalles, which was at the upper end of the passage of the Columbia through the Cascade Range and which marked the western boundary of the Plateau type of culture at this point, the Sahaptin people were in contact with the Wishram, who spoke Chinookan, the language of the Lower Columbia. The Middle Columbia region, particularly the eastern and southeastern parts, was very strongly affected by Plains influence in the early nineteenth century.

Houses.—As in the Upper Columbia region, the prehistoric winter dwelling was the circular pit-house with conical earth-covered roof. Here also the pit-house was displaced, probably at the end of the eighteenth century, by the surface mat-covered house. When Lewis and Clark passed down the Columbia from the Snake in 1805, they saw only mat-covered houses in use, although the abandoned remains of pit-houses were still visible.

Pottery.—Pottery was not made in the region.

Basketry.—Coiled and twined baskets were made, their forms and uses being generally similar to those of the Upper Columbia. Coiled baskets were decorated with imbricated designs, and false embroidery was placed on twined baskets. Bark containers were also used.

Tools, utensils, and weapons.—The bow and arrow was the principal hunting weapon, and the spear was probably used to some extent for hunting and warfare. Stone clubs, probably used in war, were common. Arrow and spear points were chipped from flint and occasionally from obsidian and basalt. In contrast to the Upper Columbia region, stemmed forms predominated. In the Dalles-Deschutes locality, the only one of the region for which there is adequate information, 81 per cent of chipped points had stems. The common nonstemmed forms were leaf-shaped with convex base and triangular without side notches. The commonest form of stemmed point had a parallel-sided stem with straight base and was more frequently barbed than shouldered. Stemmed points generally were small; leaf-shaped blades were larger.

Bone arrow and spear points, similar in form to those of the Upper Columbia, were also used. In addition, a shouldered arrow point of bone with tapering stem was used in the Dalles-Deschutes locality.

Paired arrow-shaft smoothers similar to the Upper Columbia type were made of basalt rather than of sandstone.

Spears, nets, and weirs were used in fishing, and there probably were single and multiple pronged spears with and without detachable heads. The large detachable harpoon point of antler (Type 3 of Upper Columbia and Thompson regions) is apparently absent, but bone couplings like those of the Upper Columbia have been found in prehistoric sites. In the Dalles-Deschutes locality the fishhook was the compound type, with a wood or bone shank to which was lashed at an acute angle a barbed bone point. It was thus similar in form to the Aleut fishhook. Large numbers of notched or grooved pebbles found in the region were possibly line sinkers but more likely were net-sinkers.

Cross-handles for digging-sticks were made of antler, mountain-sheep horn, or wood.

Stone drills, scrapers, and knives were generally similar to those described for the Upper Columbia region. The special flat scraper of quartzite hafted for working hides used to the north is replaced by a hafted, thicker flint scraper with straight or rounded edge and tapering top.

Hand mauls and pestles were ground from basalt and granite. In form the mauls were generally similar to those of the Upper Columbia, although they sometimes lacked the flaring top or had more bulbous bases. Roughly shaped hammerstones made from convenient river pebbles were used for heavier pounding. Pestles similar in form to the Upper Columbia type were common. In addition, there was a more carefully ground type which was longer and more slender, round in section, and usually with a flaring top which was decorated with incised lines or circles or carved in the form of an animal head. Mortars were of stone, and flat stone slabs were also used for grinding.

The highly polished nephrite adzes characteristic of the Thompson and Upper Columbia regions were not made, although a few of these implements reached the Middle Columbia through trade.

Wedges for wood-splitting and flakers for stone-chipping were of antler. Awls and needles were of bone.

Beaver-tooth dice were absent, flat, oblong bone dice decorated with incised dots or parallel lines in the manner of the Upper Columbia being used instead.

Pipes.—In prehistoric times tubular pipes similar to those used to the north were made of steatite or sandstone, but in historic times these were replaced by the Plains type of elbow pipe. Some of the elbow pipes were imported from the Plains and others were made locally. Another type, a disk-bowl pipe, occurs in late prehistoric sites in the Yakima Valley. The bowl opening is in the rim of a stone disk about three-fourths of an inch thick and two inches in diameter, and the stem hole penetrates the disk rim at right angles to the bowl. This type occurs also on the Lower Snake and has been reported ethnologically for the Middle and the Upper Columbia and the Klamath Indians. Present evidence indicates that the type developed on the Middle Columbia in late prehistoric times and spread outward from there.

Travel and transportation.—Both shovel-nosed and sharp-nosed dugout canoes were used. Snowshoes were elongated, with pointed tails, or were oval.

Costume.—Little evidence of clothing has been preserved in archeological sites, and earlier types of dress had been displaced by tailored skin garments of Plains type before the Whites reached the region early in the nineteenth century. Probably earlier types of clothing were very similar to those described for the Upper Columbia region. One feature which survived into recent times was the twined basket hat worn by women.

Ornaments.—Necklaces, pendants, and earrings of bone, teeth, and land and marine shells were very similar to ornaments in the Plateau to the north. In historic sites copper and brass beads and ornaments are also common.

Art.—Although occasional examples of sculptured or incised representations of human or animal figures have been found along the Upper Columbia and the Thompson rivers, the prevailing art style of these regions was geometric. Implements and ornaments were decorated with incised lines, circle-and-dot designs, and geometric hatched areas. In the Middle Columbia region there existed, in addition, another art style which apparently was the result of a blending of the geometric art of the Plateau with the naturalistic art of the coast. Chief elements of this style were conventionalized human and animal figures, often with accentuated, carved ribs, sculptured on stone pipes and mortars or incised on mortars or bone ornaments (Fig. 110). These figures were decorated with bands or geometric arrangements of incised lines or filigree. Some of the figures strongly suggest the art style of the coast of southern British Columbia. This coastal influence must have come up the Columbia from its mouth. Although the exact age of this style is not known, it probably developed and flourished in the eighteenth century but did not survive far into the nineteenth.

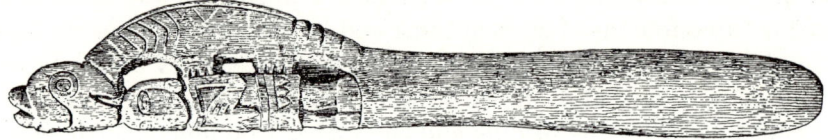

Fig. 110.—Carved bone implement from the Dalles, Columbia River. Note delineation of ribs on the animal surmounting the human figure. Scale: 1:3. (Chicago Natural History Museum specimen.)

Burials.—Rock-slide and pit burials are found throughout the region and were made in both prehistoric and historic times. Rock-slide burials were often marked with projecting stakes, as along the Upper Columbia. Pit burials were dug in sand or gravel banks and flats along rivers and, in the Yakima Valley, in domes of volcanic ash. Pit burials were often lined with split cedar planks, sometimes with stone slabs, and frequently these graves were marked on the surface with rings or piles of stones. The cedar inclosures were not charred at the top as on the Upper Columbia. Bodies were flexed, and tools and ornaments were often placed with them.

Cremation burials have been found in the Yakima Valley, at Wahluke, and in the Dalles-Deschutes locality. Apparently the body was placed in the burial pit in a flexed position, and a pyre of driftwood logs built over the pit. Many of the skeletons were only charred or partially burned. The grave was often protected by a ring of stones on the surface. Sometimes several individuals were cremated in the same burial, and usually considerable numbers of tools and ornaments were placed with the bodies. Cremation burial was practiced in prehistoric times and seems to have survived into the period of White contact in the Dalles-Deschutes locality, but not farther north in the Yakima Valley and at Wahluke. In the latter places it is not clear whether rock-slide and pit burials were used contemporaneously with cremations, there being a gradual abandonment of cremation, or whether there was a sudden shift from cremation as the exclusive form to the other types of burial. The former was the case in the Dalles-Deschutes locality, and therefore probably in the north also, although in the north the complete shift occurred earlier.

Another method of disposing of the dead, used along the Columbia from the Dalles as far up as Blalock Island, consisted of placing bodies in surface sheds of wood, a practice characteristic of the Lower Columbia. It seems to have been followed in the region above the Dalles only in late prehistoric times and was already being abandoned by 1805. Its presence in the Plateau was undoubtedly the result of influence from the downriver Chinookan tribes.

THE SNAKE-CLEARWATER REGION

When more is known of the archeology of the Snake-Clearwater region, which was the territory of the Sahaptin-speaking Nez Percé, it will probably be possible to include it culturally with the Middle Columbia. The region is treated separately here because its archeology is so little known and because, on the one hand, it lacked the coastal influence which affected the Middle Columbia and, on the other, was more strongly influenced by Plains culture.

Houses.—The circular pit-house with flat roof was the prehistoric winter dwelling of the region. At the time of the visit of Lewis and Clark in 1805 the pit-house had already been displaced by the multifamily, rectangular mat-covered house. Skin tepees were already in use at this time and were soon to replace the mat house.

Pottery and basketry.—No pottery was made, but coiled and twined baskets were manufactured. Surviving into recent times were women's hats of twined basketry.

Tools, utensils, and weapons.—Chipped-flint arrow points and other tools were generally similar in form to those of the Middle Columbia. Stemmed points probably outnumbered nonstemmed points and tended to be small. Three-pronged fish spears with nondetachable heads barbed with bone were used, as were single-pronged spears with detachable bone heads like those of the Upper Columbia. Large detachable barbed antler points were absent. Gorges for catching fish were made by lashing together two hardened thorns, or two points of bone, the line being attached in the middle.

Paired arrow-shaft smoothers of volcanic tufa were rectangular rather than hemispherical in section.

Hand mauls, pestles, and hammerstones were very similar to those of the Middle Columbia region, although the heads of pestles were rarely incised or sculptured to represent animals. Apparently the specialized Middle Columbia art style did not extend up the Snake. Wooden mortars and basket mortars placed over flat stones were common; stone mortars were rare. A few nephrite adzes reached the region by trade.

In place of digging-stick cross-handles of antler, used elsewhere in the plateau, cylindrical stones grooved on one side were lashed across digging-sticks. Probably wooden handles were used also.

Antler was used for wedges and flakers and bone for awls and needles. Dice were made of bone, not beaver teeth.

Pipes.—Pipes were of the familiar tubular type with straight or flaring stem forming a flange at the mouth. Also used was the discoidal type found in the Yakima Valley. Both forms were displaced by Plains elbow forms.

Travel and transportation.—Dugout canoes were of the shovel-nosed type, and snowshoes were oval.

Costume.—There is no archeological information regarding clothing. By the early nineteenth century earlier forms of clothing, with the exception of basketry hats for women, had been completely replaced by garments of the Plains type.

Burials.—Burials were made in rock slides and in pits dug in sand or earth. Pit burials were usually marked with surface piles of stones and projecting wooden stakes. Bodies were flexed or extended, and artifacts and ornaments were buried with the dead.

CONJECTURES

The foregoing archeological synthesis gives a picture of the material aspects of Plateau culture before the period of recent and strong influences from the Plains and the coast and reveals a culture that was distinct from the cultures of the two flanking areas. The archeological evidence confirms the same conclusion reached on the basis of ethnological studies (see especially Ray, 1939).

House forms, types of implements, methods of hunting and fishing, and other traits link the Plateau to the north with the interior Indian tribes of northern British Columbia and Alaska and the Aleut and southward to a lesser extent with California. Plateau culture appears as a local specialization of a basic type of culture extending in the interior from California to Alaska.

A comparison of the four archeological regions which have been discussed indicates that the prehistoric cultures of the Upper Columbia and the Thompson regions fall together and that there are minor contrasts between them and the cultures of the Middle Columbia and the Snake regions. Thus in prehistoric times there seem to have been at least two cultural subtypes, one in the north and one in the south, although fundamentally one can speak of a single culture type for the whole area. This picture is obviously incomplete because of the many geographical gaps in our archeological knowledge of the area.

Time perspective in prehistoric Plateau culture is almost completely lacking. At present it is clear that this relatively simple culture had existed largely unchanged for two or three centuries, or even longer, before the coming of the Whites. Its more primitive antecedents, or earlier local cultures of other types, remain to be discovered.

SOURCES

Archeology: COLLIER, HUDSON, and FORD, 1942; KRIEGER, H. W., 1928; PERRY, 1939; SMITH, H. I., 1899, 1900, 1910; SPINDEN, 1908; STRONG, SCHENCK, and STEWARD, 1930. *Ethnology:* CLINE et al., 1938; KROEBER, 1939; RAY, 1932a, 1932b, 1936, 1939, 1942; RAY et al., 1938; SPIER, 1930; SPINDEN, 1908; TEIT, 1900. *Early history:* FRASER, 1889; HAINES, 1938; LEWIS and CLARK, 1893; MACKENZIE, 1902; THOMPSON, 1916.

CHAPTER 30

THE NORTHWEST COAST

INTRODUCTION

THE cultural area known as the Northwest Coast formerly extended along the Pacific Coast from Yakutat Bay in southern Alaska to Humboldt Bay in northern California. At the time of discovery by Europeans, the Indian tribes of this long, narrow coastal strip shared these characteristics: a basically similar fishing and hunting economy; the extensive utilization of wood for utensils, houses, and canoes and as a medium for decorative art; a preference for bone, horn, and shell rather than stone for the manufacture of cutting implements and projectile points; a high development of basketry; the absence of pottery and agriculture; a lack of extensive political organization; and the importance of the local village as opposed to the tribe.

Because archeological information for the Oregon and northern California coasts is so meager (see chap. 28), only the northern part of the area, as far south as Puget Sound, will be treated here. This northern section was inhabited in historic times by the Tlingit, Haida, and Tsimshian in the north, by the Bella Coola and Kwakiutl in the central part, and by the Nootka and Coast Salish tribes in the south.

Early history.—Although the Northwest Coast was first reached by Juan de Fuca in 1592 and again by Bering and Chirikov in the "St. Peter" and the "St. Paul" in 1741, significant European contacts with the natives did not take place until the arrival of seafaring traders in search of sea-otter furs a few years after Captain Cook's visit in 1778. This trade supplied the Indians with quantities of goods, such as steel knives, copper kettles, and cloth, but otherwise it affected their lives little. From the explorations of Vancouver (1792–94) and of others it is evident that tribal locations on the Northwest Coast have remained virtually unchanged since the end of the eighteenth century.

Archeological knowledge.—The numerous old village sites, cemeteries, and shell middens of great extent and thickness found along the coast from Washington to Alaska are evidence of the intensive occupation of the area by prehistoric Indians. But, because so few systematic investigations have been made in the area, we know little about the prehistoric culture. Excavations in a few of these remains have indicated that the prehistoric inhabitants, like the historic Indians, were a maritime people who built their villages of wooden houses close to the shores, traveled by canoe, and subsisted primarily on the products of the sea. There appears to be only slight difference between the archeological culture and the culture of the historic Indians.

Some of the ancient middens, which were formed by the gradual accumulation of shells and other refuse, were abandoned before A.D. 1500, as indicated by the age of the trees growing on top of them. The bottom layers of these shell heaps are much older. Thus a time span of five hundred years or more for the prehistoric culture is possible. Despite this chronological depth, as yet we are unable to discern any significant changes in the prehistoric culture, and the origins of the Northwest Coast culture pattern remain obscure.

In the following pages we give a summary of the prehistoric culture based on archeological remains and on inferences from the historic Indian culture.

THE PREHISTORIC CULTURE

Natural environment.—The coast line of this area, as a result of the subsidence of the land and the flooding of valleys by the sea, is cut by a network of channels and fiords, and there are many large and small islands. The warm Japan Current, which flows along the coast southward from Alaska, gives the region a moderate climate and a heavy rainfall. In many places mountain ranges rise abruptly from the shore, and everywhere dense forests of hemlock, Douglas fir, spruce, and cedar grow to the water's edge. Beneath the trees there is a dense undergrowth of bushes, many of which produce edible berries, such as wild currants, blueberries, huckleberries, and salmon berries. Ferns grow lushly, and thick moss carpets the ground.

People.—In historic times the Indians of the Northwest Coast were roundheaded and of medium stature. Head deformation was practiced by the Coast Salish and the Kwakiutl. Among the former the forehead was flattened, and among the latter the top of the head was bound so as to elongate it upward and backward. It is not clear whether these practices were also prehistoric.

In prehistoric times there were two types of Indian—a round-headed type very similar to the historic people and a longheaded type. Skulls of both types have been found in ancient shell heaps at the mouth of the Fraser River and on the southeastern tip of Vancouver Island. In one midden longheaded skulls were found in the lower levels and roundheaded skulls in the upper levels; at another midden both types were found together; and in other middens only roundheaded skulls occurred. This evidence indicates that the earliest inhabitants of the region were longheaded and that they mixed with and were absorbed by a later, roundheaded people. During the transitional period when these two peoples were intermingling, there was some practice of the trephining of skulls of living persons, a custom not followed in later times. The early longheaded Indian type has not been found as yet in other regions of the Northwest Coast.

Livelihood.—Agriculture was never practiced by the Indians of the Northwest Coast. Subsistence was based primarily on fishing and secondarily on the hunting of sea and land mammals and the gathering of wild plant products. The staple of the area was salmon, although halibut, cod, eulachon (candlefish), smelt, and herring were also important. The seal, sea lion, and porpoise were hunted for their meat, and the sea otter was trapped for its fur. The diet was supplemented with shellfish (clams, oysters, mussels, crabs), edible seaweeds, roots and berries, and the flesh of deer, elk, and bear.

Food was cooked over open fires, boiled in baskets and wooden boxes in which hot stones were placed, and roasted or steamed in earth ovens heated by hot stones.

Houses and villages.—The houses of the area were large rectangular structures of split planks fastened to upright posts. There were two general types of house. The northern type, built by the Kwakiutl and all the peoples to the north of them, was nearly square, 30–60 feet across, with corner posts, vertical side planking, and a gabled roof (Fig. 111, *a* and *b*). Sometimes the house contained a central pit with stepped or terraced sides, the fire being on the lowest level and sleeping compartments on the upper levels. The southern type, built by the Coast Salish and Nootka and formerly by the Kwakiutl, was long and narrow, with horizontal planking fastened to side posts and a shed roof sloping from front to back across the short axis of the house (Fig. 111, *c*). Houses of this type tended to be very large and were occupied by many families, each with its own fire. One of the largest of these houses was 520 feet long and 60 feet wide. These two types of house were prehistoric also, although it is not clear how ancient.

Villages were invariably located at the water's edge on a beach convenient for landing canoes. In winter the people congregated in large permanent villages for a season of feasting and ceremony. During the rest of the year the villagers, often in clan or lineage groups, occupied a series of smaller settlements at places convenient for the various types of fishing, for sea-mammal hunting, or for the gathering of shellfish.

Pottery.—No pottery was ever made. Its place was taken by bowls of wood and stone, by baskets, and by wooden boxes.

Basketry.—Although little basketry has been found in prehistoric sites, probably baskets were as important as they were in the historic culture. Twined baskets, usually decorated with false embroi-

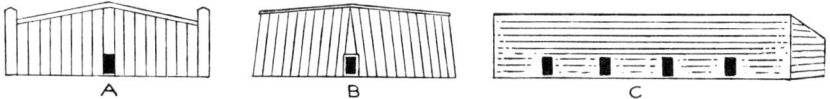

FIG. 111.—Northwest Coast house forms: *a* and *b*, northern type with gabled roof; *c*, southern type with shed roof.

dery, and checkerwork baskets and mats were made in a variety of forms and for many purposes, including cooking by the stone-boiling method.

Wood-working.—The high development of wood-working was an outstanding trend in the historic culture. The existence in prehistoric sites of some carved wood and an abundance of wood-working tools indicates that this emphasis was characteristic of earlier times as well. Wood was used for houses, canoes (Fig. 112), bowls and spoons, boxes for cooking and storage, drums and rattles, masks, and for a variety of ornaments, including carved house posts and panels.

Tools, utensils, and weapons.—The principal weapons were bows and arrows, spears, and harpoons. In addition, traps and deadfalls were used for catching land animals, and hooks, nets, traps, and weirs for fish. Spear-throwers were used in recent times, at least, in the northernmost part of the area, no doubt as a result of contact with the Eskimo. Arrow and spear points of chipped stone were rare throughout the area. They were used most frequently in the region about the mouth of the Fraser River, probably as the result of influence or trade from the Plateau coming down the river; a few have been found in the north in Tlingit territory. Commonly, arrow and spear points were of bone (Fig. 113, *i*). For special purposes, such as shooting birds and sea otter, arrow points were barbed, as were the spear points used for spearing salmon (Fig. 113, *j*). Spear points of ground slate were also common (Fig. 113, *h*).

A variety of clubs of stone, whale bone, or wood were used for killing sea mammals and fish, in warfare, and for ceremonial purposes. Many of these clubs were elaborately carved.

Harpoons were used for catching sea mammals and fish. Bone harpoon points were of two types—one piece and composite. One-piece points had one or more barbs and a hole, slot, or flange at the base for

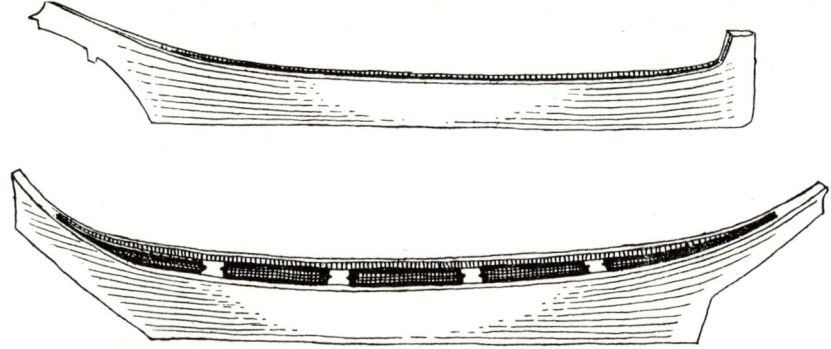

FIG. 112.—Canoes of the Northwest Coast Indians. These dugout canoes were 25 to 70 feet long. Prehistoric canoes were probably similar but smaller. *Top*, southern type (bow to left); *bottom*, northern type (bow to right). (After Niblack.)

attaching a line (Fig. 113, *l*). The composite point consisted of two barbs fitted and lashed together to form a basal socket for insertion of the harpoon shaft, the outer ends forming a socket or slot to hold a bone or slate point (Figs. 113, *k;* 108, *b*). A special form of this composite harpoon with a broad triangular point of shell was used in recent times by the Nootka and their neighbors for harpooning whales. Whaling was not practiced elsewhere on the Northwest Coast in historic times. Whether the earlier peoples hunted whales is not known.

Wood-working was done with hand-held or hafted stone mauls used for driving wooden or whale-bone splitting wedges; with hafted adzes and chisels of stone, bone, or shell; and with bone drills. Finer smoothing was accomplished by rubbing the wood with sandstone and shark's skin, which served as sandpaper.

Hafted mauls or hammers were three-quarter-grooved with one to three grooves (Fig. 113, *c*); another type was perforated for hafting.

Fig. 113.—Tools and weapons of the Northwest Coast: *a*, stone blade of splitting-adz; *b*, hand maul of stone; *c*, stone maul grooved for hafting, top and side views; *d*, stone blade of trimming- or planing-adz, front and side views; *e*, hafting for planing-adz; *f*, hafting for trimming-adz; *g*, stone chisel with antler haft; *h*, spear point of slate; *i*, bone arrow point, front and side views; *j*, bone point for fish spear; *k*, composite harpoon point of bone with bone or slate tip; *l*, bone harpoon points. Scale: *a–g*, 1:4; *h–l*, 3:8. (After Drucker; Chicago Natural History Museum specimens.)

The commonest hand maul was cylindrical with expanded or flanged ends (Fig. 113, *b*) and often with a hat-shaped top. Another type had a T-shaped or stirrup-shaped handle.

Two types of adz blade, usually of stone but sometimes of bone or shell, were employed. A heavy blade, used for chopping and splitting, was grooved or notched on one face and hafted to a T-shaped handle (Fig. 113, *a*). A thinner blade without notch or groove (Fig. 113, *d*) was hafted to a V-shaped handle and used for trimming (Fig. 113, *f*) or lashed to a rectangular handle like that of a carpenter's saw and used for planing (Fig. 113, *e*). Similar slender blades were hafted in socketed antler handles for use as chisels (Fig. 113, *g*) or were sometimes struck directly with a hammer without a haft to absorb the blow. The thin adz and chisel blades were usually made of serpentine or nephrite.

Knives were made of bone and shell or ground from slate. Drills, awls, scrapers, and gouges were also made of bone. Whorls on spindles for spinning twine and thread were made of stone or bone and were often decorated with carved geometric or animal designs.

Pipes.—In prehistoric times only the Indians of the Straits of Georgia region, particularly at the mouth of the Fraser River, used pipes. These tubular pipes were made of steatite. They had flaring bowls and slender stems. The material and the form are typical of the prehistoric pipes of the interior (see Fig. 106, *i*). The presence of this type of pipe on the coast is attributable to Plateau influence coming down the Fraser.

Costume.—Little is known of the prehistoric costume, but from historical data we can infer that dress consisted of woven robes and capes, furs, and basketry hats. Apparently no moccasins or other footgear were worn. Blankets and capes of shredded cedar bark were woven by the twining technique on a warp suspended from an upright weaving frame. More elaborate blankets of mixed cedar bark and mountain-goat wool woven by the same technique also may have been made, as they were by the historic Tlingit. It is not clear whether the dog-wool blankets of the recent Coast Salish, twined on a more elaborate weaving frame, were also prehistoric.

Ornaments.—Beads were made of bone and shell, the most common being dentalium shells and disks ground from clam shells. There was some prehistoric use of copper for crescent-shaped ornaments and possibly for tubular beads and pendants. Pendants were commonly made of bone and horn, animal teeth and claws, deer hoofs, shell, and stone. Labrets of stone, bone, or wood were worn in perforations in the lower lips.

Burials.—Several different methods of burial were followed by the prehistoric Indians. Interment in middens was practiced throughout the area. In the northern and central regions bodies were buried in boxes placed in caves or rock shelters, whereas to the south about the Straits of Georgia and Puget Sound they were buried in cairns of stone. Cremation was occasionally practiced in the southern region and possibly in the north also.

CONJECTURES

On the basis of the geographical occurrence of types of prehistoric tools and other traits it is possible to divide that portion of the Northwest Coast treated in this chapter into three regions: (1) northern, including the territories of the Tlingit, Haida, and Tsimshian; (2) central, including Kwakiutl and possibly Bella Coola territories; and (3) southern, including Coast Salish territory around the Straits of Georgia and Puget Sound. These three archeological regions correspond to the three geographical divisions of the historic culture of the area.

The presence or abundance in the northern and southern regions, but not in the central region, of such traits as chipped-stone projectile points, ground-stone points, slate blades, one-piece barbed harpoon points, and extensive use of nephrite for adzes, suggests a connection between the northern and southern regions and sets them off from the central region. Probably many of the traits common to the northern and the southern regions were the result of cultural influences from the interior which did not affect the central region. The southern region was apparently most strongly influenced by the Plateau culture, for the greatest abundance of chipped-stone tools occurs there, as well as such additional traits, typical of the interior, as tubular stone pipes and extensive use of geometric decorations. On the other hand, the northern region possessed a number of traits, such as hafted mauls, grooved splitting adzes, and a great variety of one-piece, barbed harpoons that suggest cultural connections with the Eskimos of southern Alaska.

What is known of Northwest Coast prehistory can be summarized in a few words. The archeological remains indicate an age of at least five or six centuries for the Northwest Coast pattern of culture. The earliest inhabitants, who were longheaded, mixed with and were absorbed by a later roundheaded people who may have come from the interior. As yet it has not been possible to correlate significant cultural changes with this meeting of races. At some time during the prehistoric period the people of the southern region were strongly affected by cultural influences from the Plateau, and the people of the northern region received influences both from the interior and from the Eskimo peoples of southern Alaska.

A prehistoric sequence of culture changes on the Northwest Coast cannot be demonstrated at present, but the available evidence of considerable time depth and of outside cultural influences from the east and north suggests that such a sequence can be established upon adequate investigation. The deep midden deposits of the area are ideal repositories for evidence of cultural change. It is probable that, when these archeological records have been read, Northwest Coast culture will be revealed as a specialization from the same ancient cultural base from which developed the cultures of the Plateau Indians and the interior Indians of northern British Columbia.

SOURCES

DRUCKER, 1943; GODDARD, 1934; JENNESS, 1932; KROEBER, 1939; NIBLACK, 1890; SMITH, H. I., 1903, 1907, 1924, 1929; SMITH and FOWKE, 1900.

PART VII
THE FAR NORTH

CHAPTER 31

THE NORTHWESTERN ESKIMO AREA

INTRODUCTION

THE Northwestern Eskimo area, comprising a small part of northeastern Siberia and most of northwestern Alaska, is a high-latitude desert with a cold climate. Tundra and alpine vegetation are characteristic. The rainfall ranges from less than 10 to 20 inches a year. Winters are long, dark, and cold; summers are short, bright, and cool. Some of the periods and cultures of this area are outlined in Chart XVI.

CHART XVI

Probable Date	Period and Culture
A.D. 1000–1800+	Post-Punuk
A.D. 500 or 600–1000	Punuk, Birnirk
100 B.C.–A.D. 500 or 600	Okvik, Old Bering Sea, Ipiutak
1000–100 B.C.	Original Eskimo

THE ORIGINAL ESKIMO CULTURE
Ca. 1000–100 B.C.

No archeologist has yet found a site of the Original Eskimo culture, but, by eliminating culture traits which do not appear early in the Eskimo sequence and by reversing trends of development, we can make some guesses about this culture. Future excavations will show whether or not our guesses are correct.

Area.—Probably Siberia and Alaska.

People.—Probably longheaded Asiatics little different from ancient Indian types.

Villages.—Temporary shelters such as tents and underground or partly underground houses.

Livelihood.—Hunting, fishing, and food-collecting.

Pottery.—None.

Tools, utensils, and weapons.—Harpoons of various kinds were used for hunting sea mammals. The harpoon heads were pointed or beveled for the addition of a stone blade by lashing or equipped with a bed into which the blade was lashed. Various kinds of spears were cast by means of spear-throwers. They may or may not have had bows and arrows. Knives, scrapers, and other tools were made of chipped stone or bone. Bow drills were lacking, but hand drills with chipped-stone points probably were used. Oil lamps of bone or stone probably were in use.

Pipes.—None.

Travel and transportation.—Probably these hypothetical Eskimos had skin-covered boats, small hand-drawn sleds, and snowshoes.

Costume.—Probably fur and skin garments carefully sewn.

Art.—The engraving of bone, wood, and perhaps ivory was not well executed. Designs were simple, geometric, and linear; no curvilinear motifs were used.

Comments.—Compared with historic Eskimos, our hypothetical Eskimos would have been relatively unspecialized, with potentialities for adaptation to inland or sea-coast environments. They were, however, specialized to the extent of being at home only in circumboreal or circumpolar areas and were subjected to indirect pressures from higher cultures of Asia. Probably throughout the history of the western Eskimos they were influenced by Asiatic developments. These influences seem to have been especially strong during the time of the Old Bering Sea and Ipiutak cultures.

THE OKVIK CULTURE
Ca. 100 B.C.—A.D. 100

Area.—Northern Alaska and northeastern Siberia.

People.—Probably longheaded, high vaulted, with relatively narrow faces.

Villages.—Sedentary villages along the seashore consisted of round houses which were underground or partly underground. These had paved stone floors and central open hearths.

Livelihood.—Food was obtained by hunting, fishing, and collecting. Sea mammals, fish, birds, and probably eggs were easily obtainable.

Pottery.—Simple round or oval cooking pots, some with simple stamped decoration, were made of clay tempered with grit. This pottery resembled that of the Old Bering Sea culture.

Tools, utensils, and weapons.—The Okvik Eskimos hunted sea mammals with harpoon and lance. Among their remains were such harpoon parts as socket pieces, foreshafts, finger rests, ice picks, and toggle heads of ivory, the latter of a unique type characterized by multipronged spurs and a peculiar style of decoration. Ivory float plugs and kayak rests indicate that the harpoons were used in hunting at sea with inflated bladders attached to the harpoon lines. Small, toggle-type harpoon heads were used for seals and walrus, large heads for whales. Stone blades were fastened in the slots of harpoonheads and lanceheads.

Birds were taken with bows and arrows or by special bird darts cast from spear-throwers. Probably snares and nets were also used.

Fish were caught with multibarbed hooks and lines weighted with slender sinkers of ivory. Also in use were trident-like fish spears with a sharp central prong and side prongs, each of which was tipped with an inward projecting barb of ivory.

Wooden bows and long barbed arrows were used in warfare. Knives were made of ground slate or of chipped chert and jasper or possibly of metal. The woman's knife consisted of a semilunar blade of slate and an ivory or bone handle (Fig. 114, *a*); the man's, of a bone or ivory handle with a side or end blade of ground slate or chipped stone (Fig. 114, *f*).

Bow drills, hand drills, awls, reamers, and marlin spikes were extensively used in working ivory, bone, wood, baleen (a kind of whalebone), and skin. The chopping adz consisted of a handle, an ivory head, and a stone blade. Heavy picks with bone or ivory heads on wooden handles were employed for cutting sod blocks, for digging, or for breaking holes in the ice.

Stone flaking tools were made of bone or ivory. Some were composite, with slotted handles for attachment of points.

Tools for the working of skins were side- and end-scrapers of chipped stone; ivory scrapers, some of them spoon-shaped; very fine needles of bone or ivory; and crude needles. There were needle cases of bone or ivory.

Small and large bone shovels were used for clearing house floors of refuse. Buckets, trays, and bowls were made of wood and baleen.

The type of seal-oil lamp used by the Okvik Eskimos is not known, but the tools used for trimming the moss wicks of oil lamps were made of bone.

Pipes.—None.

Travel and transportation.—Probably skin-covered boats with wooden frames such as the kayak and the larger umiak were used.

Small low sleds of ivory and bone were pulled by hand or possibly by dogs. Baleen toboggans were also in use.

Ice-creepers (cleats or crampons) tied to boot soles aided the traveler walking on ice. Snow goggles (Fig. 114, *c*) usually with round eyeholes, helped to protect the traveler's eyes from the glare of sun on ice and snow. These were not so efficient as later styles of goggles.

Costume.—Probably skin garments similar to those of modern Eskimos.

Ornaments.—Ivory pendants and ear or hair ornaments were worn. Ivory figurines (Fig. 114, *e*) suggest that Okvik Eskimos tat-

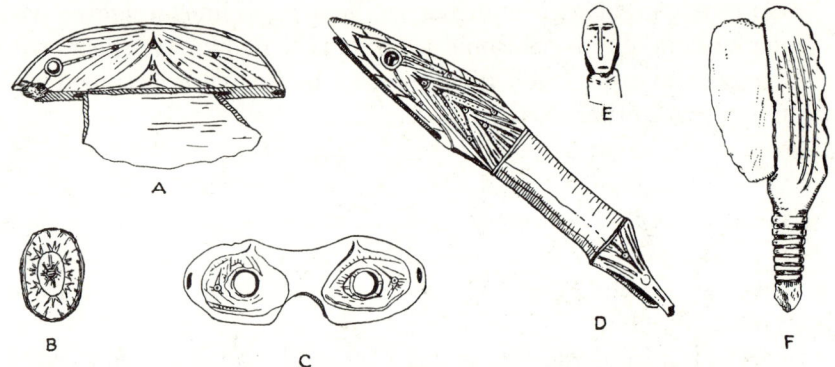

Fig. 114.—Decorated objects of the Okvik Eskimo: *a*, crescent-shaped knife of slate with decorated handle of ivory; *b*, decorated button of ivory; *c*, decorated snow goggles; *d*, decorated lancehead of ivory; *e*, ivory representation of human head; *f*, slate knife with decorated handle of ivory. (After F. G. Rainey.)

tooed their faces. The use of ivory chain-link ornaments and wing-shaped objects of ivory was unknown.

Musical instruments.—The tambourine type of drum with ivory or bone handle was probably used for singing and dancing ceremonies.

Art.—Okvik art consisted of sculpture and engraving of bone and ivory. The sculpture was somewhat realistic. Carved human figures were characterized by long, narrow, pointed heads and long noses of a curious type.

Engraved designs were geometric. The motifs such as spurred lines, Y-figures, nucleated circles, parallel lines, and ladder-like figures were also used in later periods, but the arrangement of these motifs was typically Okvik. This Okvik style is the same as Old Bering Sea Style 1.

The designs were engraved upon some tools, weapons, utensils, and ornaments and upon objects of unknown function typical of which were wing-shaped figures of ivory with sockets for the insertion of shafts.

Conjecture and comment.—The Okvik culture preceded Old Bering Sea. Some authorities consider Okvik as an early stage of Old Bering Sea rather than a separate culture. Either way, Okvik is probably the oldest known culture in the northwestern Eskimo area and, in our opinion, is closest to the proto-Eskimo cultures which await discovery.

Okvik is closely related to Old Bering Sea, which, for example, had the Okvik style of art (Old Bering Sea Style 1) plus some other art styles. Similarly, Okvik is related to Ipiutak. But in our opinion all three cultures, but especially Old Bering Sea and Ipiutak, were partaking of Asiatic influences which were increasing in strength and frequency, although the nature of these influences was changing from time to time.

SOURCES

COLLINS, 1937, 1940, 1941, 1943; RAINEY, 1941a.

THE OLD BERING SEA CULTURE
Ca. A.D. 100–500

Area.—Northern Alaska and northeastern Siberia.

People.—These ancient Eskimos were somewhat similar to their modern descendants, except that they were markedly longheaded.

Villages.—The Old Bering Sea Eskimos lived the year round in villages along the seashore. Houses were small, partly underground, square or rectangular, and about nine to thirteen feet long. The walls were made of horizontal timbers and sometimes whale jaws, held in place by upright stakes of bone or wood. The exact method of roof construction is unknown, but, when complete, it was covered with earth. The floor was made of stone, but there were no sleeping platforms such as are present in later Eskimo dwellings. The house entrance was a long, narrow tunnel with stone walls and floor and a timbered roof.

Livelihood.—Food and raw materials were obtained by hunting sea mammals such as seals and walrus. Dead whales probably were utilized when they drifted ashore. Many kinds of sea birds and fishes were additional important sources of food. Domesticated dogs of small breed were kept, possibly for food.

Pottery.—Saucer-shaped lamps of pottery provided heat and light for the household. These lamps, thick and made of poorly fired clay coarsely tempered with sand, small particles of stone, or grass, burned oil and fat from sea mammals by means of a wick made of grass or moss.

Pottery cooking pots were deep, round, and thin-walled and were probably round-bottomed. These pots were tempered much the same as the lamps. Some method of coiling seems to have been known but rarely used. Generally, both lamps and pots were modeled directly from the clay paste.

Pottery was usually undecorated and had a roughly smoothed exterior, but some vessels had corrugated exteriors produced by patting with a grooved paddle. Such simple stamping or paddling may be connected with the method of manufacture of this pottery.

Tools, utensils, and weapons.—Seals, walrus, and, rarely, whales were hunted with harpoons. These were composed of a detachable bone or ivory head (Fig. 115, *d*) with a stone blade and a loose foreshaft of ivory with one end supporting the harpoonhead and the other fitting into an ivory socket fastened to the end of a long wooden shaft. To the butt of the harpoon shaft was fastened an ice pick of bone or ivory. Although there were several styles of harpoonheads, they were, as a class, very distinctive and different from those of other Eskimo cultures.

Wooden plugs may have been placed in the wounds of freshly killed animals to preserve the valuable blood. Ice scoops of netted baleen were used to clear small pieces of floating ice from seals' breathing-holes.

Birds were killed with bows and arrows or with bird spears launched from a wooden spear-thrower. Bird spears generally were tipped with a barbed central prong of ivory or bone and three somewhat similar side prongs at the middle of the shaft. The side prongs were arranged radially around the wooden spear-shaft and projected outward at an acute angle. Birds also were captured in snares and perhaps with long-handled nets.

Fish, principally cod, were probably caught with hooks of wood and bone. Plummet-shaped sinkers of ivory were attached to the fishlines. Probably very light fish spears were also in use.

Knives and projectile points were made of chipped or rubbed stone. Other stone tools were adzes, gravers, whetstones, side- and end-scrapers, drills, reamers, and wedges. Snow shovels were made of walrus shoulder blades; picks were made of walrus tusks; mattocks were made of whale ribs.

THE NORTHWESTERN ESKIMO AREA

With the exception of pottery, described elsewhere, household utensils consisted of bone or ivory needles and needle cases (Fig. 115, *f*); ladles and spoons of ivory, bone, and wood; wooden trays and bowls; and pails with round or oval wooden bottoms and sides of baleen.

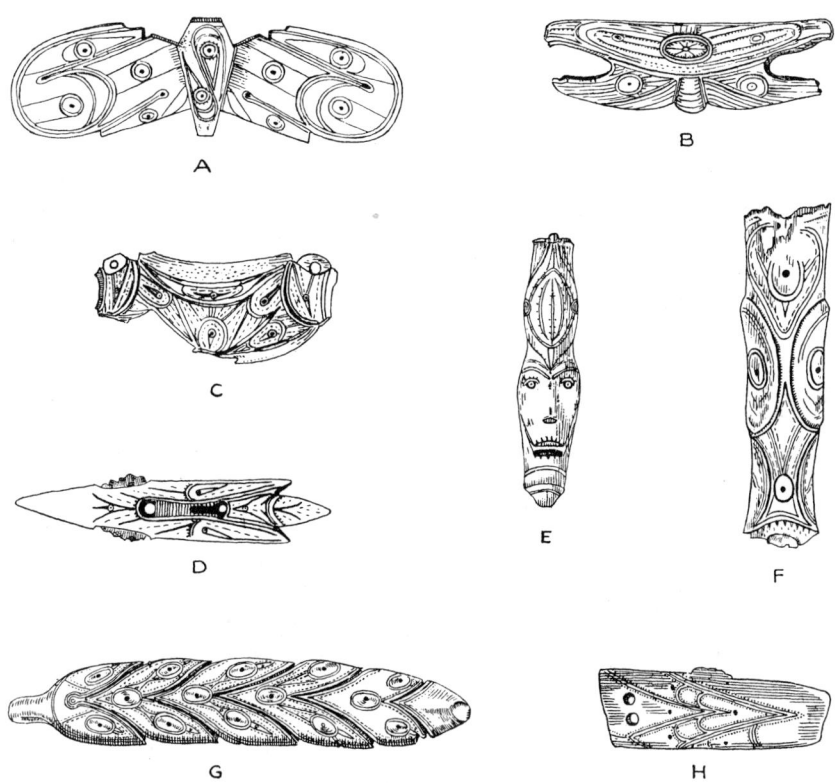

FIG. 115.—Art of the Old Bering Sea Eskimo: *a*, winged object of ivory; *b, c, e, g*, decorated objects of ivory; *d*, decorated harpoonhead of ivory with side blades of chipped stone; *f*, decorated needle case of ivory; *h*, decorated adz handle of ivory. (After H. B. Collins.)

Pipes.—None.

Travel and transportation.—The Old Bering Sea Eskimos did not have dog traction; their small sledges and toboggans were pulled by hand. The small breed of dogs kept by Old Bering Sea Eskimos seem to have been used for food.

Toboggans were made of long strips of baleen and probably were used for hauling meat over the ice. The small, low hand-sledge was provided with ivory or whalebone runners or with wooden runners in protective shoes of ivory. Old Bering Sea Eskimos did not travel much on the ice. Instead, they seem to have been seafarers who made extensive voyages in the summer months. For travel at sea there were skin-covered kayaks and umiaks. Kayaks were one-seated boats of sealskin-covered wooden framework and decked with sealskin except for a round hatch amidship. Umiaks were large open boats about thirty feet long. Double-bladed paddles of wood were probably used for kayaks, and perhaps single-bladed oars were used to propel the umiaks.

Ice-creepers of bone or ivory (like hobnails) were attached to the soles of boots to keep a person from slipping on the smooth ice. Snow goggles, masklike objects with narrow slits, were worn to protect the eyes from the glare of the spring sun on ice and snow.

Costume.—Clothing was made of sealskins or of bird skins. There were fur or bird-skin shirtlike garments, probably with hoods to cover the head. Waterproof coats were made of walrus and seal intestines. Boots were of heavy sealskin.

Ornaments.—Ornaments, for the most part, consisted of browbands, gorgets, and buttons. Ornaments as such were not abundant, but many utilitarian objects were tastefully decorated.

Art.—There are three discernible styles of Old Bering Sea art. The first style (Fig. 115, *b, c, d, e, h*), probably the earliest, was distinctly linear and somewhat "scratchy." Decorated surfaces were covered with radiating lines, long spurs, short detached lines, and intermittent lines. Some use also was made of freehand concentric circles and ellipses with central dots or inlays and of other motifs.

Another, perhaps more typical, style of Old Bering Sea art (Fig. 115, *a*), especially adapted to rounded ivory surfaces, consisted of closely spaced, parallel lines, broken lines, small circles between converging lines, and small independent design units of various kinds placed in panels.

The third style of Old Bering Sea art (Fig. 115, *f* and *g*) is principally identified by its use of elevated concentric circles and ellipses which are larger and more important in designs than are the smaller circles of the other art styles. Frequently the raised circles and ellipses are arranged in pairs as if to suggest the eyes of some animal.

All three styles of Old Bering Sea art may appear upon the same kinds of objects—additional evidence of their contemporaneity in Old Bering Sea times. But the first style, which is essentially linear, is a holdover from Okvik.

Conjectures and comment.—The Old Bering Sea culture probably is coeval with Ipiutak and is, in part at least, an outgrowth of Okvik. Old Bering Sea, however, may have received Asiatic stimuli lacking in Okvik times. As with Ipiutak, it may have developed from an Okvik-like culture; but its origins are obscured by flamboyant aspects that probably were importations from Asia. Old Bering Sea was followed by the Punuk culture.

SOURCES

COLLINS, 1937, 1940, 1941, 1943; RAINEY, 1941a.

THE IPIUTAK CULTURE
Ca. A.D. 100–600

Area.—The remarkable Eskimo culture called Ipiutak is known at only one place—on the shore of the Arctic Ocean near Point Hope, Alaska, two hundred miles north of Bering Strait.

Villages.—The Ipiutak lived in a large village on the shore of the Arctic Ocean. There were about eight hundred dwellings arranged in five long avenues. Their partly underground houses were about 10–16 feet square. At the west side of each house stood a covered entrance passage or tunnel about 7–16 feet long.

The houses were built either of logs or of blocks of sod, moss, or skin supported by a wooden frame. The floors were of planks or poles except for a central hearth, which was open.

From the size of this village it has been estimated that there were several thousand inhabitants—more, perhaps, than in the modern city of Fairbanks.

Livelihood.—The Ipiutak made their living by hunting, fishing, and gathering. Their most common food consisted of hair seal, walrus, bearded seal, and caribou, although fishes and birds were also probably important in the diet. Hunting must have been exceptionally good to sustain the large population indicated by the size of the village. Since this population must have included every Eskimo for miles around, it seems unlikely that there were any other villages near by. And the food necessities of a settlement the size of Ipiutak must have utilized all the available animal resources of the region. It is, of course, possible that the Ipiutakers occupied their village only in summer. In such a case, they would have spent their winters hunting and fishing inland along the rivers.

Tools, utensils, and weapons.—Hunting weapons were the harpoon, bow and arrow, lance, spear, and probably spear-thrower. Of all the weapons, the bow and arrow seems to have been the most popular, which suggests that land animals were extensively hunted. Bows were made of wood and may have had a sinew-spring backing. Arrows were tipped with many different kinds of heads made of bone. There were blunt-headed arrows for killing birds. Some arrowheads had a sharp point and many barbs along one or both sides. A somewhat similar type of arrowhead had a chipped-stone blade in a slot at the end. Another style of bone arrowhead was pointed and had inset blades of chipped stone along each side.

Sea mammals were killed with harpoon and lance. Wooden lances had bone heads equipped with inset blades of chipped stone along the sides.

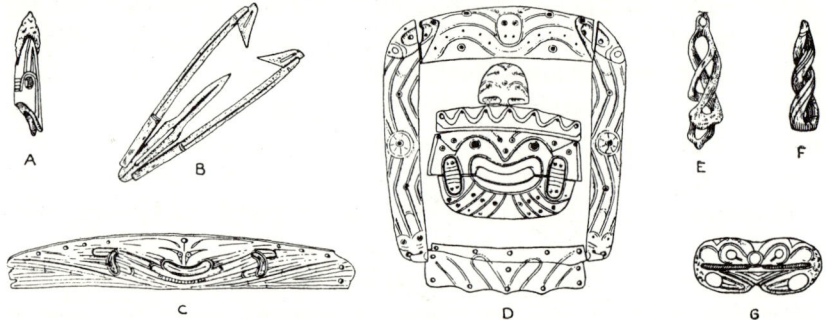

Fig. 116.—Ipiutak weapons and ornaments: *a*, harpoonhead of ivory with blade of chipped stone; *b*, trident-shaped head of bone for salmon spear; *c*, ivory ornament; *d*, set of ivory carvings from grave; *e*, *f*, spiral ornaments of ivory; *g*, snow goggles of ivory. (After F. G. Rainey.)

The harpoons were equipped with wooden shafts, bone or ivory socket pieces, ivory foreshafts, and toggle-type harpoonheads with chipped-stone blades in a slot at the point (Fig. 116, *a*) or in grooves along the sides. Some of these harpoonheads had engraved designs.

The absence of certain harpoon gear suggests that the methods of hunting on ice or in open water were different from those of other northern Eskimo.

Birds were hunted with blunt arrows, were caught in nets, or were taken with a special bird spear with multiple prongs—one at the end of the spear-shaft, the others projecting obliquely from the shaft somewhat beneath the center prong. Probably these spears were cast with the aid of spear-throwers.

Fish were taken with special spears. These consisted of wooden shafts with a compound head of trident form, a central point of bone, on each side of which was a side prong of bone to which was lashed a pointed bone barb (Fig. 116, b).

Projectile points, knives, and scrapers were made of chipped stone. Weapons and tools of ground stone were not used by the Ipiutak Eskimos.

Among the common tools of these Eskimos were many kinds of scrapers made of chipped stone; various knives of chipped stone, some of which had bone handles; stone and possibly iron graving tools; engraving tools with rodent-teeth blades; flaking hammers, chipping tools and awls and wedges of bone; some ground adz blades of stone; bone adz heads; whetstones; paint-grinding stones; scrapers made of caribou leg bones; mattock blades; and boat-skin stretchers.

The women sewed with bone needles which had small eyes; possibly small bone tubes served as needle cases. Spoons were made of bone. For alleviating the discomfort of an itching back, there were long-handled back-scratchers resembling those of the Chinese.

Pipes.—None.

Travel and transportation.—Dog traction and sleds seem to have been lacking among the Ipiutak Eskimo. They had skin-covered boats, probably both the kayak and the umiak. Ivory goggles (Fig. 116, g) with narrow slits for the eyes protected the traveler from snow blindness caused by glare.

Costume.—Information about Ipiutak clothing is lacking, but undoubtedly they wore fur garments. Pendants and other ornaments were made of bone and ivory.

Art.—One of the most distinctive characteristics of the Ipiutak is their art, which consisted primarily of carvings and engravings in bone and ivory. The style of engraving is similar to that of the Old Bering Sea Eskimos. The design elements consisted of circles, curvilinear lines, straight lines, spurs, nucleated circles, and other motifs often arranged in patterns which were largely curvilinear and very graceful. Although Ipiutak styles of engraving have not been completely described or analyzed, they seem to belong to the same tradition which produced the Old Bering Sea styles of engraving.

Ipiutak carvings consisted of strange animal forms nicely executed, various complicated masklike forms of ivory, which were decorated with engraved designs (Fig. 116, d), and unique spiral objects of unknown use (Fig. 116, e and f). These spiral objects of ivory are suggestive of Asiatic forms.

As a whole, Ipiutak art is rather spectacular and similar to Old Bering Sea art. It seems to represent the florescence of ancient Eskimo carving and engraving.

Burials.—The Ipiutak dead were buried in cemeteries not far from the village. Some of the graves were shallow deposits of artifacts and skeletons apparently buried in groups. Other graves consisted of log tombs sunk a few feet beneath the surface of the beach gravel. Each tomb contained one (more in several instances) skeleton lying at full length, generally on the back with hands over the pelvic area. Some of those skeletons were equipped with carved and inlaid eyeballs of ivory, cup-shaped mouth covers of ivory, and, in one instance, carved nose plugs of ivory. There were elaborately carved and engraved masklike objects of ivory. These were of eight or more plates, presumably joined by thongs through drilled holes. The total appearance is that of a mask in a rectangular frame. Such composite carvings were placed with the dead in Ipiutak graves.

Unique spiral objects of ivory were also placed in graves, but possible uses of such objects are unknown. Equally strange are carved animal figures, some as parts of linked chains of ivory. These, too, were placed in the graves.

Ipiutak Eskimos had one custom in common with the Hopewell Indians of Ohio: they provided their dead with spectacular equipment.

Conjectures.—Probably the Ipiutak were contemporaries of the Old Bering Sea Eskimos. Some of their art styles were closely related to the latter; and there were other similarities which would argue for close relationship. It is not impossible to see in both Ipiutak and Old Bering Sea cultures the results of Asiatic influences upon an older, somewhat undifferentiated, culture intrenched in western Alaska. Okvik would be closer to, but still not representative of, such a culture.

SOURCES

COLLINS, 1943; RAINEY, 1941b.

THE PUNUK CULTURE
Ca. A.D. 500–1000

Area.—Northeastern Siberia and northwestern Alaska.

Villages.—Villages were similar to those of the Old Bering Sea type except that Punuk houses were larger.

Livelihood.—Same as Old Bering Sea, but whales were added to the list of sea mammals hunted with harpoons.

Pottery.—Grit-tempered pottery lamps and cooking pots were somewhat similar to those of the Old Bering Sea Eskimos. Some Punuk pottery, however, was covered with the impressions of various kinds of curvilinear stamps.

Tools, utensils, and weapons.—The Punuk Eskimos had many tools, weapons, and utensils which were similar to, or stylistic variations of, those used by the Old Bering Sea people. There were, however, a number of new tools, weapons, and utensils which appeared for the first time in the Punuk culture, probably as importations from Siberia. These new elements were whaling harpoonheads of bone and ivory; some later types of smaller harpoonheads; stone, bone, or ivory bird bolas; the sinew-backed bow; bow braces and sinew-twist-

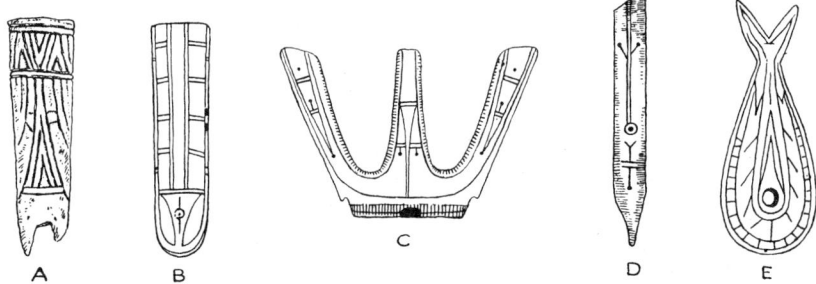

FIG. 117.—Art of the Punuk Eskimo: *a*, decorated ivory object; *b*, decorated wrist guard of ivory; *c*, decorated trident of ivory; *d*, decorated reamer of ivory; *e*, ivory ornament. (After H. B. Collins.)

ers; bone or ivory wrist guards (Fig. 117, *d*); plate armor of ivory or bone; daggers of bone and ivory; and iron-pointed engraving tools. Implements of chipped stone, very common in the Old Bering Sea culture, were largely replaced in Punuk times by similar forms made of rubbed slate.

Pipes.—None.

Travel and transportation.—Same as Old Bering Sea, with some stylistic modifications.

Ornaments.—Beads and pendants were made of bone and ivory. Ornaments of unknown use were trident-shaped (Fig. 117, *c*) or wing-shaped objects with basal sockets for the insertion of a shaft. These objects were either plain or decorated with engraved designs. Many otherwise utilitarian objects were decorative in that they bore engraved designs.

Art.—Punuk engraving was in part a development from Old Bering Sea styles to which were added Siberian concepts. The fine incising, freehand circles and ellipses, curving lines, and general gracefulness were now replaced by rigid, formal, mechanical motifs such as dots and circles, straight spurred lines, and others—all engraved with metal tools. The designs are stiff and create the impression of machine-made decoration undertaken in a hurry.

Carving in the round or in bas-relief in bone and ivory was tastefully done and comparable to that of Old Bering Sea.

Conjecture and comments.—The Punuk culture was derived from Old Bering Sea and modified by Asiatic additions and local developments.

SOURCES
COLLINS, 1937, 1940; RAINEY, 1941.

THE BIRNIRK CULTURE
Ca. A.D. 600–1000

Area.—Northeastern Siberia and northwestern Alaska, especially Point Barrow.

People.—Relatively longheaded Eskimos.

Villages.—Villages near the seashore consisted of rectangular houses made of driftwood and covered with blocks of sod. The walls were composed of pieces of wood placed vertically, and roofs were of parallel logs which reached from the tops of the walls to the ridgepole. Each house had a skylight—a covering of translucent gut over a wooden frame.

Livelihood.—Food was obtained by hunting, fishing, and gathering. Land mammals, sea mammals, and birds were hunted. Shellfish, roots, berries, and birds' eggs were gathered, and fish were taken from the sea and the rivers.

Pottery.—Lamps and cooking pots were similar to those of the Punuk culture. The pottery was of clay tempered with grit, and vessel surfaces were covered with the impressions of curvilinear stamps, the dies for which were carved in paddles of wood, bone, or ivory.

Tools, utensils, and weapons.—Toggle heads for harpoons were of a characteristic Birnirk style. Other weapons were the sinew-backed bow, arrows with points of stone or bone, lances, bird spears with side prongs, and spear-throwers. Wrist guards and sinew-twisters of bone or ivory, seal-scratchers, wound plugs, meat hooks, ice scoops, and bird bolas were additional equipment useful in hunting. Fish were caught with trident-like spears.

The woman's knife of ground slate, the man's knife of flint or slate, bow drills, scrapers of flint, adz heads of antler with blades of slate or jade and snow shovels were tools in common use.

Needles, semiwinged needle cases, awls, and thimble holders were made of bone and ivory. Oval bowls of wood, baleen, horn, and antler, wooden spoons and dippers, and round, flat lamps of baked clay were ordinary household equipment.

Travel and transportation.—Skin-covered boats were the kayak and the larger umiak, both of which were propelled with single-bladed paddles. Snow goggles with narrow eye slits were worn by travelers as protection against the glare of the sun on snow and ice. Small sleds probably were pulled by hand.

Costume.—Hooded shirtlike garments were made of bird or animal skins. Skin boots had inner soles of layers of thin wood shavings.

Ornaments.—Many styles of bone or ivory pendants were worn as ornaments, and various utilitarian objects were decorated, thus functioning as ornaments as well as tools.

Burials.—The dead were placed in sod-covered houses of wood. Many bodies, dressed in fur clothing and accompanied by tools, weapons, utensils, and ornaments, were placed in a given gravehouse. Some bodies covered with fur robes lay upon beds of moss and ground-willow surrounded by split logs of wood. Others were resting on hewn planks of wood. Many of the bodies were deposited in layers. The corpses were preserved by the Arctic cold.

Conjectures and comment.—The Birnirk culture is related to both Punuk and Thule (of the eastern Eskimo area). Birnirk may have been ancestral to Thule.

SOURCES

COLLINS, 1937, 1940; DE LAGUNA, 1940; MASON, J. A., 1928; MATHIASSEN, 1927.

THE POST-PUNUK CULTURE
Ca. A.D. 1000–1800+

The Post-Punuk culture of northwestern Alaska and northeastern Siberia is not well known. The last stages of this culture were in existence at the time of the arrival of White men in the area.

People.—Relatively broadheaded Eskimos.

Villages.—These Eskimos lived in villages near the seashore. Many different kinds of dwellings were used. There were rectangular houses built of wooden planks, some of which were partly underground with the projecting portions covered with turf. There were large communal houses in some places, and in a few instances snow-houses were used; but these were never so important as they were in the eastern area. Skin-covered tents for summer use were dome-shaped, conical, or double-domed.

Livelihood.—Hunting, fishing, and food-gathering were highly developed. There were special and elaborate techniques for hunting sea mammals at sea or from the ice.

Pottery.—Crude, thick pottery vessels were made of clay tempered with grit, fiber, feathers, or sand.

Tools, utensils, and weapons.—Toggle-headed harpoons and lances were used in hunting whale, walrus, and seal. Bird-spears, thrown from spear-throwers, and bolas and nets were employed in hunting birds. Fish were taken with nets, weirs, lines and hooks, or spears. Sinewback bows and arrows tipped with stone or bone were used for war and the hunting of land animals.

Plate armor of bone, wood, ivory, or skin was worn in warfare.

Practically all the tools of earlier periods existed in modified form during this time. There were snow shovels, snow knives, and crescent-shaped ulo, the man's knife, the crooked knife, many kinds of scrapers, bow drills, fire drills, wooden vessels, stone lamps, spoons, needles, needle cases, stone adzes, pounders, meat hooks, seal scrapers, wound plugs, and a host of other very useful tools and utensils.

Pipes.—Tobacco pipes, absent in prehistoric times, were finally introduced into the area from Asia. Pipes, of course, were originally introduced into southern Asia from America by way of Europe. Thus an American invention traveled completely around the world to reach some Arctic Americans who were without it.

Travel and transportation.—Large sledges of wood with runner shoes of bone, ivory, frozen muck, or ice were pulled by teams of large dogs harnessed tandem fashion. The toboggan and small hand-drawn sled were also used. The skin-covered kayak and the larger umiak were used for water travel. Snow goggles and ice-creepers were also common. Snowshoes were worn by some Eskimos.

Costume.—Tailored fur garments, parkas, trousers, boots, and mittens were made of animal furs, bird skins, fish skins, and sea mammal guts.

Ornaments.—Pendants, beads, and other ornaments were worn.

Art.—Sometime, probably early in this stage, pictographic art developed. Objects of bone and ivory were engraved with simple pictograph pictures representing hunting and fishing activities. Other engraved motifs were the compass-drawn dot and circle, spurred lines, and Thule-like border designs. Sculpture in the round was simply stylized. With the exception of the new pictographic art, all the engraving was simplified and exceedingly rigid in contrast with that of earlier periods.

SOURCES

BIRKET-SMITH, 1936; WEYER, 1932.

SUMMARY

The earliest Eskimos possessed a relatively simple culture. Their hunting techniques were adaptable to land or sea. Their art was simple, geometric, and linear. After a period of adjustment to their northern Alaskan environment, they were subjected to some exotic influences from Asia. Under this stimulation, the Eskimo cultures became elaborate and spectacular, despite the increasing specialization imposed by their environment. Their art reached its apogee. Designs were elaborate, geometric, and curvilinear. After a while this art became more simplified, but other aspects of the culture became elaborate under Asiatic influence.

The last stage of Eskimo culture saw the simplification of all the earlier customs and traits plus the addition of new ways. The culture became even better adapted to the northern environment. Transportation reached its highest development as did probably all the hunting techniques.

What especially appears to be a degeneration of culture was actually an elaborate adjustment to an arctic environment. Although the art appears to have been poorer, there were vast improvements in tools, techniques, and transportation.

CHAPTER 32

THE SOUTHWESTERN ESKIMO AREA

INTRODUCTION

THE Southwestern Eskimo area, comprising the Aleutian Islands, part of the Alaska peninsula, Kodiak Island, and Cook Inlet is a land of tundra and alpine vegetation with some pine forest. Of all the Eskimo areas, this had the mildest but wettest climate. The annual rainfall ranged from 40 to over 80 inches. It was damp, cool, generally treeless, foggy, and stormy. The ice and snow conditions of other Eskimo areas were lacking; consequently, the people never developed the dogsledge method of transportation or the techniques for hunting on ice.

In historic times these southern Eskimos were quite different from their northern relatives for a number of reasons. These historic cultures were descended from a very old cultural stratum, probably the Original Eskimo culture. Their environment did not necessitate the type of adjustment that was required of the northern Eskimos. Also southern Eskimos were relatively independent of those around Bering Strait. Moreover, the late cultures of the area were receiving Asiatic influences via Kamchatka and Indian influences from the northwest coast area of America.

The cultures and periods of the Southwestern Eskimo area are outlined in Chart XVII.

THE EARLY ALEUT CULTURE
Ca. 100 B.C.—A.D. 500

Area.—The Aleutian Islands and part of the Alaska peninsula.

People.—Longheaded, high-vaulted people resembling certain types of Indians.

Villages.—Rectanguloid pit-houses with sod-covered roofs supported by driftwood timbers were built in exposed places near the seashore.

Livelihood.—Food was obtained by hunting sea mammals, fishing, and gathering shellfish.

Tools, utensils, and weapons.—Most commonly harpoons had barbed bone heads of many styles with various arrangements and

THE SOUTHWESTERN ESKIMO AREA

shapes of barbs and with differences in the base shapes (Fig. 118, *b*). Less common was the harpoon with a toggle head of bone, equipped with a scoop-shaped bed into which was lashed a blade of chipped stone (Fig. 118, *e*). Lanceheads of bone with blades of chipped stone somewhat resembled the barbed harpoonheads but were longer and more spectacular in shape and arrangement of barbs (Fig. 118, *a* and *d*). Some lanceheads (Fig. 118, *a*) were decorated, and on the ends of many were scoop-shaped beds into which were fastened blades of chipped stone (Fig. 118, *d*).

Projectile points, several kinds of knives (Fig. 118, *h* and *i*), and various styles of side- and end-scrapers (Fig. 118, *f* and *g*) were also made of chipped stone. Fragments of stone oil-burning lamps have been found. Ovoid or crescentic knives of stone were also used (Fig. 118, *j*).

CHART XVII

Probable Date	Culture		
	Aleutians	Kodiak	Cook Inlet
A.D. 1000–1750	Late Aleut	Koniag	Late Kachemak Bay
A.D. 500–1100	Middle Aleut	Pre-Koniag	Middle Kachemak Bay
100 B.C.—A.D. 500	Early Aleut		Early Kachemak Bay

Bone clubs, flaking tools, awls, and wedges for splitting logs were in use, and the splitting-wedges were sometimes converted into sockets for bow or strap drills. Bone fishhooks consisted of a barbed hook lashed to a knobbed shank (Fig. 118, *c*). Bone needles with fine grooves rather than eyes were used for sewing.

Travel and transportation.—Boats with wooden frames covered with sea-mammal skins were the only means of transportation.

Ornaments.—Cylindrical ivory objects engraved on the ends with encircling lines and rows of dots have been found. They were probably used as ear ornaments.

Art.—Except for the curvilinear designs found on ear ornaments, Early Aleut art was linear and very simple. Designs engraved upon bone lanceheads (Fig. 118, *a*) consisted of *X*'s, groups of straight lines, short detached lines somewhat like spurs, and other straight-line motifs. Representations of human faces were sometimes carved on the sides of lanceheads.

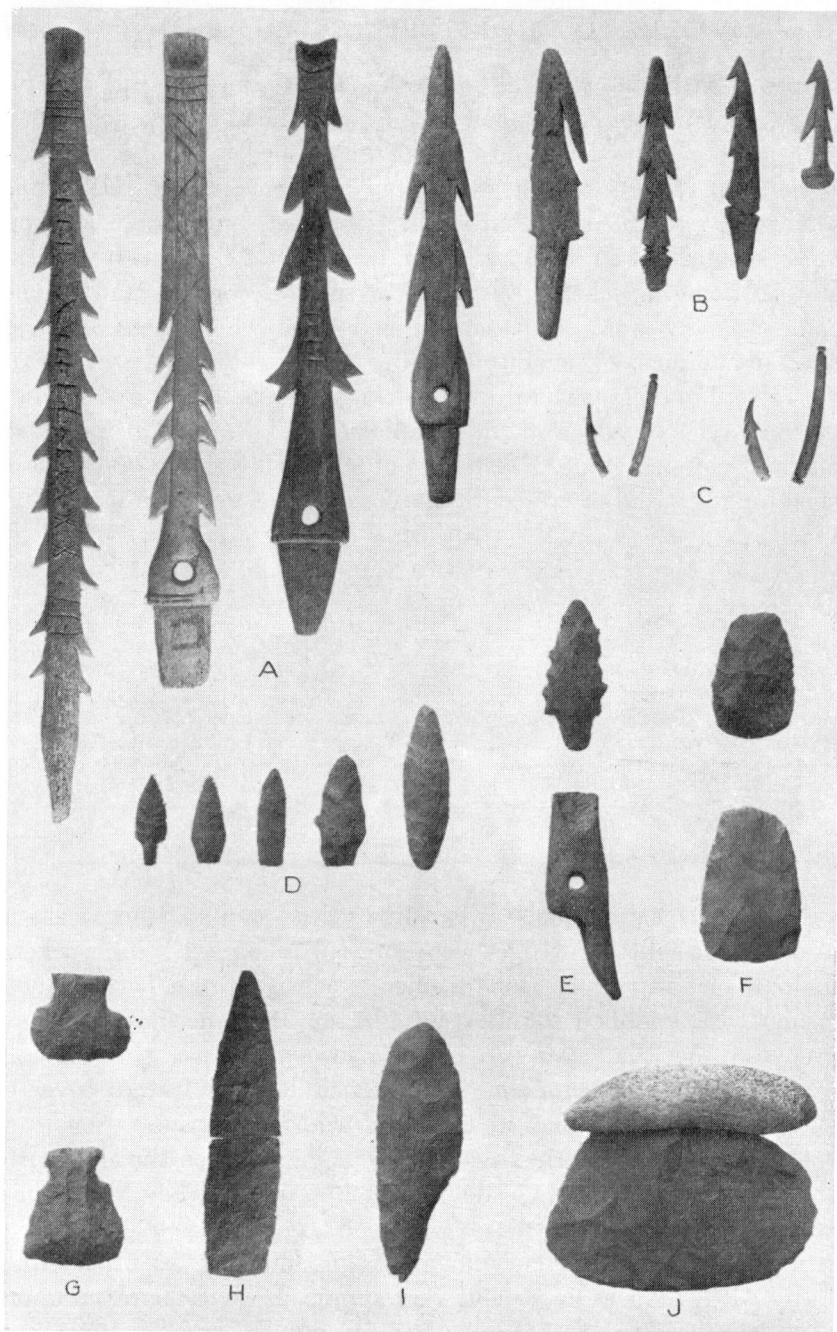

FIG. 118.—Tools and weapons of the Early Aleut: *a*, lanceheads of bone; *b*, harpoonheads of bone; *c*, compound fishhooks of bone; *d*, projectile points of chipped stone; *e*, toggle harpoonhead of bone and harpoon blade of chipped stone; *f*, scrapers of chipped stone; *g*, chipped-stone blades for hafted scrapers; *h*, *i*, chipped-stone knives; *j*, chipped-stone knife with bone handle.

THE SOUTHWESTERN ESKIMO AREA

Conjectures and comments.—The Early Aleut peoples probably were an offshoot of the Original Eskimo strain. They entered the Aleutian Islands from the American mainland, adapted themselves to the unique environment, and remained somewhat isolated.

SOURCES
COLLINS, 1940; HRDLIČKA, 1945; JOCHELSON, 1925; QUIMBY, 1945a.

THE MIDDLE ALEUT CULTURE
Ca. A.D. 500–1100

Area.—Same as Early Aleut.

People.—Longheaded and medium longheaded people with relatively high vaults; shortheaded people with low vaults and broad faces.

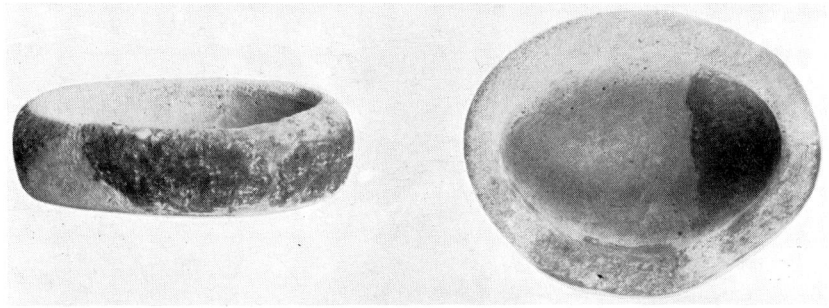

FIG. 119.—Middle Aleut pottery bowl

Villages.—Same as Early Aleut.

Livelihood.—Same as Early Aleut.

Pottery.—Thick, crude, shallow pottery bowls (Fig. 119), oval in outline, with straight or slanting walls, were made of clay heavily tempered with fragments of volcanic rock.

Tools, utensils, and weapons.—Same as Early Aleut with the addition of stone netsinkers; bone net-spacers for making nets; bird-bone awls made by inserting a small pointed bone into a larger, hollow bird bone; paint-grinding stones and manos; stone bowls like those of fired clay; toggle harpoons and lanceheads with slots instead of beds for the attachment of stone blades; and crescentic and ovoid knives of rubbed slate.

Certain lamps of ground stone were exceptionally well made and were oval, round, square, **or** triangular in shape (Fig. 120). Many were crude, boulder-like objects with oval reservoirs pecked into the top of the stone.

Probably bows and arrows and slat or rod armor were typical of Middle Aleut culture. Copper and perhaps iron engraving tools and compasses were used in making a common style of design motif.

Travel and transportation.—Skin-covered boats—the small kayak and the large umiak—were used for travel at sea.

Ornaments.—Bone, ivory, and stone labrets of several shapes were inserted through holes in the wearer's upper or lower lips. Pendants of bone and ivory and ear ornaments similar to those of the Early period were also worn, as were ivory chain-link ornaments.

Art.—Masks and small animal effigies were carved of bone, wood, and ivory. Remnants of the engraved art of the early period persisted on lanceheads which were engraved with straight lines in groups of three. New motifs were the compass-drawn dot and circle, the dot and concentric circles, and the diamond cross-hatch.

Conjectures and comments.—The Middle Aleut culture seems to have been influenced by Punuk and Asiatic cultures, possibly through Kamchatka. Our Middle and Early periods of Aleut culture are comparable to what Hrdlicka calls "Pre-Aleut."

SOURCES

COLLINS, 1940; HRDLIČKA, 1945; JOCHELSON, 1925; QUIMBY, 1945a, 1945b; WEYER, 1929.

THE LATE ALEUT CULTURE
Ca. A.D. 1100–1750

Area.—Aleutian Islands and Alaska peninsula.

People.—Shortheaded people with low vaults and broad faces. Pacifids.

Villages.—Large and small underground houses with sod-covered, driftwood roofs were used communally. Entrance was through an opening in the roof and down a notched log ladder.

Livelihood.—Same as Middle Aleut culture. Whales were killed by smearing aconite poison on lance blades, a method of unknown age in this area.

Basketry.—Baskets and mats were woven of dried grasses, usually with a twining technique.

Tools, utensils, and weapons.—Essentially the same as Middle Aleut with some modifications. Bone lancehead and barbed harpoonheads were not so elaborate. The beautiful stone lamps were lacking, but the crude oval ones were common. With some exceptions, the tools, utensils, and weapons were simpler than in earlier periods, although most of the same kinds were still in use.

Travel and transportation.—Of all seafaring Eskimos, the Aleuts were outstanding. Kayaks and umiaks were in constant use. During this period, or perhaps after contact with White men, the two-seated and three-seated kayaks were developed.

Costume.—Long shirtlike garments, sometimes with hoods, were of fur, bird skin, and sewn strips of sea-mammal intestine. Boots were of skin; hats of fur, feathers, or wood. When hats and visors were made of wood, thin boards were bent into shape and elaborately painted.

Ornaments.—Bone and ivory labrets or lip-plugs were inserted through holes in the upper lips or beneath the lower lips. Bone nose pins were sometimes inserted through the nasal septum. Pendants were made of bone and ivory.

Art.—Grotesque and elaborate masks were carved of wood and painted in several colors. Graceful, multicolored, curvilinear designs and pictographic representations of animals, people, and objects were painted on wooden hats. Nicely carved and engraved ivory ornaments and somewhat realistic animal figures were attached to these hats.

Burials.—The dead, sometimes prepared by removal of the viscera and the substitution of dried grass, were often placed in caves. They were dressed in fine clothing and accompanied by ornaments, tools, weapons, utensils, and even kayaks and paddles. Sometimes one or more bodies were placed in a log tomb or crypt with lavish graveofferings. Some bodies were buried in pits. A few were cremated.

SOURCES

COLLINS, CLARK, and WALKER, 1945; HEIZER, 1938; HRDLIČKA, 1945; JOCHELSON, 1925, 1933; QUIMBY, 1944.

THE PRE-KONIAG CULTURE
Ca. A.D. 500–1100

Area.—Kodiak Island.

People.—Relatively longheaded, high-vaulted people with narrow faces.

Villages.—Villages, situated near the sea, consisted of rectangular houses, partly underground (two or three feet) with central, oblong fireplaces made of rock slabs. Walls and roofs may have been constructed of poles covered with skins or brush.

Livelihood.—Hunting, fishing, and food-gathering were the means of sustenance. Whales, seals, sea otters, and bears were the most important animals hunted.

Domesticated animals were dogs and foxes.

Pottery.—Crude unfired oval clay pots with thick straight walls and flat bottoms were used.

Basketry.—Mats and baskets were woven of dried grasses by a twining technique.

Tools, utensils, and weapons.—Toggle-headed harpoons were used for hunting small sea mammals. Some bone toggle heads were slotted for the attachment of bone, ivory, or rubbed-slate blades; others were merely pointed or barbed. Many were decorated with engraved designs.

Fish were caught with lines and two-piece hooks of bone or with nets weighted with notched stones. Stone or bone fish clubs were used and probably spears. Notched stone bolas and possibly spears were used in hunting birds.

General utility stone tools were scrapers of several kinds; ungrooved axes, adzes, chisels, and fleshers; grooved clubs and mauls; digging-tools; whetstones; hammerstones; and flaking tools. Several kinds of knives were made of chipped or polished stone, such as oval (women's knives); double-edged and side-bladed (men's knives); and bayonet-shaped knives. Large spear points and many types of projectile blades were also made of chipped stone.

Bone tools included long harpoon- or spearheads with multiple barbs, several sizes of unbarbed harpoon- or lanceheads with two-piece bases that were lashed together, barbed arrowheads, adzes, tool handles, splitting wedges, parts for bow drills, root-diggers, knives, poniards, shovels, net gauges, awls, pins, needles with eyes, and hollow-bone needle cases. Spoons, ladles, dishes, cups, and other household objects were also made of bone and perhaps of wood.

Oil-burning lamps were manufactured of both stone and bone. Oval stone lamps were especially well made and rather elaborately decorated by engraving or carving. Some had projecting knobs or realistic animal figures projecting from their reservoirs. Crude ovoid lamps of stone were also in common use.

Travel and transportation.—Skin boats (probably kayaks and perhaps umiaks) were used for travel.

Ornaments.—Several styles of stone, ivory, and bone labrets were worn in holes in the skin of the chin or upper lip. Stone, shell, and bone beads, bone finger rings and nose pins, as well as shell pendants were in use.

Art.—The Pre-Koniags were excellent sculptors, and their human portraits in bone and ivory rank with the best of ancient Eskimo sculpture. They carved figurines, animal effigies, portrait plaques, and chain-link ornaments from bone, stone, and ivory. Engraved art consisted of motifs, such as the compass-drawn dot and circle; dot and concentric circles; diamond cross-hatching; short detached lines in pairs; spurred lines; and other elements, usually grouped to form an over-all pattern. In many respects the engraved art resembles that of the Punuk Eskimos.

Burials.—The dead were buried in a flexed position in pits. Dismembered bodies with bones broken as if to remove the marrow are perhaps evidence of cannibalism. These were dumped into graves. Finds of isolated skulls drilled for suspension indicate the custom of collecting heads as trophies. One such skull was equipped with carved ivory eyes.

SOURCES

HRDLIČKA, 1944.

THE KONIAG CULTURE
Ca. A.D. 1100–1750

Area.—Kodiak Island.

People.—Shortheaded, low-vaulted, broad-faced Pacifids.

Villages.—Houses were rectangular, partly underground, and made of wooden beams or whale ribs covered with sod. A doorway led into the combination living-room and kitchen, in the top of which

Fig. 121.—Koniag hat of wood with ivory ornaments

was a skylight and smoke hole. Adjoining were the sleeping-rooms or compartments. Each village also had a meeting-house built much like ordinary dwellings but considerably larger.

Livelihood.—Food was obtained by hunting, fishing, and gathering shellfish, berries, and other edibles. Whales were killed with lances smeared with aconite poisoning.

The only domestic animals were dogs.

Pottery.—Some groups of Koniags made crude, undecorated baked pottery jars shaped somewhat like flowerpots.

Basketry.—Hats, baskets, and mats were woven with twining techniques from grasses and roots.

Tools, utensils, and weapons.—Harpoons, lances, spears, spearthrowers, clubs, and sinew-backed bows and arrows were the weapons of hunting. Harpoonheads were toggle heads of bone with a blade of rubbed slate or long multibarbed heads of bone. Various kinds of lanceheads and projectiles were made of rubbed slate and sometimes of chipped stone.

Slat or rod armor of wood, lances, and bows and arrows were used in warfare.

Most tools, weapons, and utensils were similar to those of Pre-Koniag culture, but simpler. Some lamps, for instance, were well made but lacked the embellishments of the Pre-Koniag types.

Travel and transportation.—Kayaks and umiaks were used.

Costume.—Long shirtlike garments were made of animal skins, bird skins, or sea-mammal gut. Skin boots and hats of fur, wood (Fig. 121), feathers, or woven matting completed the wardrobe.

Ornaments.—Labrets and nose pins were in common use, as were other ornaments of bone and perhaps of wood.

Art.—Designs engraved upon ornaments and certain weapons included old elements such as the compass-drawn dot and circle, but the designs were more formal and stiff. Geometric designs were painted upon some of the wooden or basketry hats. Various kinds of masks were carved of wood and painted.

Burials.—The deceased, dressed in their best garments and accompanied by mortuary offerings, were buried in log tombs, placed in caves, or put upon small islands of rock. Some were prepared for the grave by removal of the viscera and the substitution of dried moss.

SOURCES

HRDLIČKA, 1944.

THE EARLY KACHEMAK BAY CULTURE
Ca. A.D. 100–500

Area.—Cook Inlet, Alaska.

Livelihood.—Hunting, fishing, and food-gathering.

The only domestic animals were dogs.

Tools, utensils, and weapons.—Harpoons for hunting sea mammals were equipped with a pointed toggle head of bone and used without the addition of a stone blade or were tipped with a barbed point of bone. Dartheads of bone were barbed and either pointed or tipped with stone. Fish were caught with lines and compound fishhooks (barbed hook of bone lashed to a wooden shank) or with fish spears.

Projectile points were of chipped stone, leaf-shaped with pointed, rounded, or straight bases. Chipped-stone knives were oval or leaf-shaped, whereas those of rubbed slate were leaf-shaped, ovoid, or crescentic. Other stone tools were planing adzes, whetstones, and hammerstones. Oil-burning lamps, too, were of stone and were round or oval in shape.

Tools of bone were drills, pins, awls, splitting-wedges, flaking tools, needles, and needle cases.

Ornaments.—Bone or ivory pendants and labrets.

Art.—Crude representations of human heads were carved on stone. Engraved decorations consisted of longitudinal lines.

SOURCES

DE LAGUNA, 1934.

THE MIDDLE KACHEMAK BAY CULTURE
Ca. A.D. 500–1000

Area.—Same as Early Kachemak Bay.

Villages.—Villages were always situated near the shore and consisted of partly underground houses built of stone and whale bones or of wood and with central hearths. Probably these houses were rectangular in outline.

Livelihood.—Same as Early Kachemak Bay.

Tools, utensils, and weapons.—Much the same as those of Early Kachemak Bay, though some had dropped from use as new forms were added to the culture, such as the harpoon foreshaft with central hole, polished-slate blades with barbs, notched-stone netsinkers, pierced-stone sinkers, semicircular stone lamps, stone saws, and slate awls.

Ornaments.—Ornaments were labrets, ear plugs, beads, and pendants of bone, stone, or ivory.

Art.—There were realistic carvings in stone and ivory. Engraved designs consisted of longitudinal lines and groups of transverse lines, lines with paired spurs on both sides, and dots and circles. The engraving was done with metal tools—probably copper gravers.

Burials.—The dead were buried in a flexed position. Sometimes artificial eyes carved of ivory, wood or clay masks, and labrets were placed with the bodies.

Conjectures and comments.—Middle Kachemak Bay culture seems to have been coeval (at least in part) with the Pre-Koniag culture and the Middle Aleut culture.

SOURCES
DE LAGUNA, 1934.

THE LATE KACHEMAK BAY CULTURE
Ca. A.D. 1000–1750

Area.—Same as Middle Kachemak Bay.

Villages.—Villages were located near the sea and consisted of rectangular wooden houses, partly underground. A partly underground wooden passage served as an entrance. There were stone hearths inside and outside the houses.

Livelihood.—Same as Middle Kachemak Bay.

Pottery.—Sometimes thick vessels, and perhaps lamps, were made of baked clay.

Tools, utensils, and weapons.—Harpoons, lances, darts, spears, fishhooks, netsinkers, bows and arrows, knives, projectile points, and other weapons or parts of weapons were similar to those of the preceding periods, although there were some stylistic changes and minor additions like copper knives, a Thule-like style of toggle head for harpoons, barbed lanceheads, and others.

Stone tools were splitting adzes, planing adzes, grinding-stones and manos, saws, hammers, whetstones, drills, awls, and various styles of knives and scrapers. Stone lamps were oval in outline, plain, or decorated with human figures in low relief. Slate mirrors came into use.

Bone tools were pins, antler pins with transverse knobs, various styles of awls, needles, needle cases, scrapers, flaking tools, shovels, picks, wedges, daggers, clubs, spoons, buckles, toggles, and dippers.

Ornaments.—There were labrets of stone, bone, or ivory; beads of bone, stone, shell, and copper; bone nose pins and finger rings; copper bracelets; and ivory pendants.

Art.—Engraving was done with metal tools, probably copper gravers. Decorations included some like those of earlier periods plus such elements as encircling, spurred, and dotted lines; V's, X's, and Y's, with hatching between the prongs; the double-ended Y; double concentric circles; dot and circle; and the spurred circle and dot. There was some realistic sculpture in stone and ivory.

Conjectures and comments.—The Late Kachemak Bay culture seems to have been closely related to and coeval with Late Pre-Koniag and Koniag.

SOURCES
DE LAGUNA, 1934.

SUMMARY

The earliest people of this area were longheaded with medium-high vaults and narrow faces. They lived by hunting and fishing. They made their tools, weapons, and utensils of bone, stone, and wood. Chipped-stone tools, knives, and weapon points were predominant. Engraved designs were simple and linear.

In the intermediate period, both medium longheaded and shortheaded people occupied the area. Tools and weapon points of polished stone became more popular. Beautiful stone lamps were manufactured, and there were stylistic changes of various kinds. The dot-and-circle motif became popular in the creation of engraved designs. The most spectacular manufactures were produced either late in the Intermediate period or early in the Late period.

In the Late period the people were shortheaded with rather low vaults and broad faces. Tools and weapon points of polished slate became popular in the Aleutians and predominant at Kodiak Island and Cook Inlet. The compass-drawn dot-and-circle design was firmly intrenched in the art traditions.

The changes in culture from one period to another were not particularly radical. The livelihood and basic categories of tools and weapons remained the same, although there were some stylistic changes and minor innovations.

There probably were contacts with Asia by way of the Aleutian Islands and with groups of Indians and northern Eskimos. The material remains available for archeological interpretation do not fully indicate the richness of this Pacific Eskimo culture as revealed by ethnology. When first discovered by White men, the Southwestern Eskimo area was one of the most densely populated regions in North America.

CHAPTER 33

THE EASTERN ESKIMO AREA

INTRODUCTION

THE Eastern Eskimo area includes the Hudson's Bay region and the arctic islands of Canada, Greenland, Labrador, and northern Newfoundland. Most of the region is tundra, but there are areas of northern subarctic forest (without fir) and southern subarctic forest (spruce and fir).

In most of the region there were cold winters and cool summers. The climate of Newfoundland and southern Labrador, however, was more moderate, with mild summers and cold winters. Annual rain-

CHART XVIII

Probable Date	Culture
A.D. 900–1800	Thule, Inugsuk
A.D. 100–1000	Dorset

fall varied from less than 10 inches in the northern part of the area to 60 inches in the extreme southern part.

There were many land animals (caribou, musk oxen, deer, bear, and others), sea mammals (whales, narwhales, walrus, and seals), migratory birds, and fishes. The fauna of the region provided the inhabitants with food and raw materials for their manufactures.

The cultures in the Eastern Eskimo area and their estimated dates are outlined in Chart XVIII.

THE DORSET CULTURE
Ca. A.D. 100–900 or 1000

Area.—The Dorset culture centered around Hudson's Bay but also existed in Baffin Island, Ellesmere Island, northern Greenland, Labrador, and Newfoundland.

Villages.—The Dorset Eskimos lived near the seashore in small circular, partly underground houses which may have been made of stone or of driftwood or of bone and sod blocks. Some houses had paved floors of stone and raised sleeping platforms. Short entrance passages were observed in certain instances. Some Dorset people probably used snow-houses. In several cases long rows of stones (jumping-stones) were associated with Dorset villages.

Livelihood.—The Dorset people lived by hunting, fishing, and food-collecting. They hunted small sea mammals, land animals, and birds. They fished and probably collected shellfish, birds' eggs, and berries.

Pottery.—Pottery probably was unknown.

Tools, utensils, and weapons.—Harpoons and lances were used for hunting sea mammals. Harpoonheads were of a unique type, with rectangular sockets, and gouged line holes, and were either pointed or had a slot for inserting a stone blade. Lances were equipped with leaf-shaped blades of ground slate which had notched tangs for attachment to wooden shafts.

Arrowheads were of bone or of chipped stone, typical of which was a triangular style with a concave base. Bird spears were cast by means of spear-throwers. If the bow and arrow were lacking in the early stages of Dorset, stone-pointed spears and spear-throwers must have been in use. Fish spears were of several types. One style was unique, consisting of a trident type of barbed head made in one piece.

Hand drills may have been equipped with stone blades, but bow drills were lacking; the Dorset characteristically gouged holes instead of drilling. The semilunar blade for the woman's knife was also lacking in some sites. Dorset knives consisted of ground- or chipped-stone blades fastened in slots at the sides or ends of bone and ivory handles and of ground-stone, double-edged knives with tangs. Knife blades of meteoric iron were used occasionally. Some small double-bladed knives had bone handles with blades set in slots on each side. Flake knives were in use in Newfoundland.

Stone adzes were of several types. Other tools were scrapers of bone, chipped stone, and polished stone; snow knives of bone or ivory; flaking tools of bone; hammerstones; and rubbing-stones.

Cooking pots and seal-oil lamps were made of stone. Lamps were ovoid and rather crude.

Bone needles with gouged eyes and awls were used for sewing. The needles were kept in tubular cases of bone.

Possibly graving points and wire for binding were made of raw copper.

Travel and transportation.—Skin-covered boats, both kayak and umiak, were used. There were small hand-drawn sleds with sled-shoes of bone or of ivory. For walking on ice there were ice-creepers (crampons) of bone which were attached to the soles of the travelers' boots. Snow goggles with narrow-slit eyeholes were used for protection against the glare of the sun on ice and snow.

Ornaments.—Pendants of bone, ivory, or wood were sometimes decorated with engraved designs. Beads for necklaces were made of animal teeth or small disks of stone. Stone lamps were sometimes painted with red ocher.

Art.—Ornaments and utilitarian objects were occasionally sculptured or engraved. Bone, ivory, or wooden figures were sculptured in the round. While some of these carvings were realistic, others were stylized.

Human heads in relief were carved upon the sides of some ornaments and tools, the Dorset carvers generally portraying a short, chunky human figure with a broad face and a broad nose.

Engraved designs, simple and geometric, consisted of straight-line motifs combined to form crosses, *X*'s, spurred lines, and other forms. The design was generally symmetrical and covered the whole surface of the object to which it was applied. The engraving gives the impression of gashes in the ivory, bone, or wood.

Conjectures and comment.—The Dorset culture was the earliest in the Eastern Eskimo area. In its latest stages it was coeval with the Thule culture. We guess that the Dorset culture was an offshoot of the Original Eskimo culture and that the ancestral homeland of Dorset was Alaska and Siberia. The Dorset culture influenced some of the early cultures in the New York area (Frontenac and Laurentian) and perhaps some early cultures in the Wisconsin-Minnesota area.

SOURCES

COLLINS, 1940; JENNESS, 1925; LEECHMAN, 1943; LETHBRIDGE, 1939; MATHIASSEN, 1927; QUIMBY, 1945a; ROWLEY, 1940; WINTEMBERG, 1939–40.

THE THULE CULTURE
Ca. A.D. 900–1800

Area.—Most of arctic Canada, the Hudson's Bay region, the arctic islands, Greenland, and Labrador.

People.—Several varieties of longheaded or medium longheaded Eskimos.

Villages.—Villages were situated along the seashore and consisted of circular, partly underground houses with walls built of whale bones, stones, and turf and with roofs supported by whale jawbones and ribs. The house was entered through a covered passage built of stones. Inside each house at the rear there was an elevated platform.

Some temporary houses were built of stone and turf and roofed with skin; others were dome-shaped dwellings made of blocks of snow. In somewhat later times snow-houses were the only winter residences in certain areas. In the summer the Thule people lived in skin tents.

Livelihood.—Food was obtained by hunting, fishing, and food-collecting. The whale, walrus, seal, bear, musk ox, and caribou were the most important animals hunted. Foxes were trapped. Many kinds of birds and fishes were caught in various ways, and roots, berries, eggs, and shellfish were gathered.

Pottery.—occasionally some of the Thule Eskimos made thick, crude vessels of grit-tempered clay which was unbaked or poorly fired.

Tools, utensils, and weapons.—Harpoons consisted of a toggle head with a thin blade of bone or ground slate; a movable foreshaft of ivory; a wooden shaft; a bone, ivory, or wooden finger rest; and a long harpoon line of rawhide fastened to an inflated sealskin float. Sometimes a bone or ivory ice pick was attached at the butt. The various types of harpoonheads were basically similar to those of other Eskimo cultures but were stylistically diagnostic of Thule. Harpoons were used for hunting sea mammals. Other hunting weapons used were lances with stone points and bows and arrows. Arrows were tipped with points of bone, ivory, and chipped or ground stone. Bladder darts were spears with barbed heads of bone fastened to wooden shafts equipped with inflated bladders of sealskin that hindered the progress of a wounded animal. Wound plugs, box traps, tower traps, baleen-spring wolf-killers, and ice scoops were also employed in hunting.

For bird hunting there were special bird spears and spear-throwers, gull hooks, bird bolas, and blunt arrows.

Fish were most frequently speared, but sometimes they were caught in traps or with composite hooks. The fish spear consisted of a wooden shaft with a sharp central prong of bone and side prongs to which were attached small bone barbs pointing inward.

Snow-knives for cutting blocks of snow used in the construction of snow-houses were of bone, wood, or ivory. Snow shovels were of bone or wood, sometimes with an ivory edging. Many kinds of men's knives were made of chipped and rubbed stone. Women's knives were generally crescent-shaped and made of rubbed slate. Stone adzes were hafted to handles of bone or wood. Bone wedges were used in splitting pieces of bone and wood. Mattocks with heavy bone blades and wooden or bone handles were employed for the cutting of grassy turf used in the building of houses.

Bow drills, hand drills, hammers, clubs, mauls, flint flakers, scrapers, and whalebone shavers were tools in common use.

Bone needles, a winged-type needle case of bone or ivory, sealskin thimbles, thimble holders of bone or ivory, and bodkins were used by women in the manufacture and repair of garments.

Oval or crescent-shaped oil-burning lamps of stone were equipped with ledges against which rested moss wicks. Bone trimmers were used to adjust the wicks.

Stone cooking pots were of several styles. Bowls and cups were made of wood and baleen.

Pipes.—None.

Travel and transportation.—Skin-covered boats with wooden frames were the kayak and umiak. The dog sledge was in common use. The dogs were fastened fanwise to the sleds rather than in the tandem fashion of the Northwestern area. Snow goggles were used to protect the travelers' eyes from the painful glare of sun on ice and snow.

Costume.—Hooded, shirtlike garments of skin and fur were worn. Trousers and boots were likewise made of skin or fur. Buttons and buckles were made of ivory and bone.

Ornaments.—Combs, often decorated, were made of bone and ivory. Pendants were made of animal teeth, ivory, and stone. Beads were of bone and amber.

Art.—Sculpture was represented by stylized bird figures of ivory and human figurines of ivory and wood. The human figure was conventionalized and was represented as being naked, without arms, and flat-faced. Engraving on bone or ivory was much more common than sculpture and usually consisted of geometric design, although in some instances it was pictographic. Common geometric-design motifs were double lines with alternating cross-lines, lines with short spurs at right angles, ladders, Y-shaped elements, V-shaped elements, and double lines. Geometric engraving was usually employed to decorate the borders of various objects.

Burials.—The dead, fully clothed and accompanied by tools, weapons, utensils, and ornaments were placed beneath cairns of boulders.

Conjectures and comments.—The Thule culture spread to all parts of the Eastern Eskimo area and to northern Alaska. Thule, however, is most characteristic of the central regions of the Eastern area. It probably was in these central regions that Thule, as such, developed its unique characteristics. The ancestry of Thule lies in the Alaskan region and probably is connected with Birnirk (see chap. 31). In the east, Thule encountered Dorset, and mixed Thule-Dorset sites are indicative of the period of this meeting. Thule, in fact, may have driven Dorset southward, and the Newfoundland Dorset may represent a vestigial Dorset coeval with Thule but not intermixed with it.

The Thule culture in Greenland assumed a local stamp and was diverging considerably from Central Thule at the time of the second Norse colonization of Greenland about A.D. 1350.

SOURCES

COLLINS, 1940; MATHIASSEN, 1927.

THE INUGSUK CULTURE
Ca. A.D. 1200–1400

Area.—Greenland.

People.—Longheaded Eskimos.

Villages.—Villages situated along the sea coast consisted of small round, partly underground houses with stone walls, driftwood-supported roofs, paved stone floors, and deep sunken doorways. This type of house was derived from the Thule whalebone dwelling.

Livelihood.—Food was obtained by hunting sea mammals and birds, by fishing, and by gathering eggs, shellfish, and berries.

Pottery.—None.

Tools, utensils, and weapons.—Although similar to Thule for the most part, certain types were stylized to the point where they were diagnostic of Inugsuk. Some tools and utensils were indicative of contact with Norse settlers; for example, hammers made of church-bell metal; coopered, tub-shaped vessels of wood with baleen hoops; spindle whorls; cloth; bone spoons; and runic inscriptions.

Pipes.—None.

Travel and transportation.—Same as Thule.

Ornaments.—Ornaments generally were like those of the Thule people, but with such additions as Norse chessmen carved of bone and wooden sculptures representing Norsemen in medieval costume.

Conjecture and comment.—The Inugsuk culture affords us the first concrete example of culture contact between Europeans and American aborigines. Historical documentation tells us that the Norsemen and Eskimos did not live together peacefully and that some of the Norse settlements in Greenland were destroyed.

This period of Norse settlement in Greenland probably corresponds to this hypothetical period of Norse exploration in the southwestern Hudson's Bay region of Canada and the upper Great Lakes of the United States. If the Norsemen entered this area, they came from Greenland.

SOURCES

MATHIASSEN and HOLTVED, 1936.

SUMMARY

The earliest inhabitants of the Eastern Eskimo area were the Dorset people. Dorset culture seems to have been an early offshoot of the hypothetical original Eskimo culture of Siberia and Alaska.

Next in the area were the Thule Eskimos, whose ancestry is connected with the Birnirk culture of Alaska. Thule culture emphasized sea-mammal hunting and specialized hunting techniques and implements to a much greater degree than did Dorset. Moreover, the Thule peoples with their dog sleds were much more mobile than the Dorset. There was some cultural intermixing between Dorset and Thule, and probably the Dorset Eskimos were assimilated or driven away by the Thule. Probably Dorset lasted the longest in Newfoundland.

Thule culture was spread over a tremendous area and varied somewhat from one locality to another. The Inugsuk culture was a mixture of Greenland Thule and medieval Norse. The modern Eskimo cultures of the Eastern area are all descendants of Thule.

PART VIII
CONCLUSION

CHAPTER 34

CHRONOLOGY AND CORRELATION OF SEQUENCES OF CULTURES

IN THE preceding chapters we have described in chronological sequence the major cultures and cultural periods or phases in the different parts of North America during the last fifteen thousand years. In order to bring these various historical sequences into temporal relation to one another, we have placed them together in a chronological chart (Fig. 122). The four major divisions on the chart correspond to the four parts into which we have divided the continent; the separate columns, to the archeological areas or divisions, to each of which we have devoted a chapter.

We have already discussed the basis of the dates given for each area, but a further caution is necessary here concerning the conjectural nature of the majority of the dates in the chart. The only absolute ones are those for the Southwest based on tree-ring dating. These include the Anasazi sequence, the Mogollon sequence (in part), and indirectly the Hohokam sequence back to, but not including, the Pioneer period. All the other dates are conservative estimates based on the available evidence. As these guess-dates are pushed backward in time, they become less and less certain. The more recent dates are probably correct within a century or less; the earliest ones may be wrong by as much as two thousand years.

In addition to showing what Indian cultures were flourishing in different parts of North America at any given period, the chart serves to demonstrate objectively the unevenness of our archeological knowledge of the continent as a whole. Indian history in the Southwest and in eastern North America is most complete; in the area of the Pacific Slope the course of prehistoric cultural development is just beginning to be known. Omitted entirely from the chart is the vast, archeologically unknown forested area of Canada stretching from the Yukon to the St. Lawrence. The chart also shows plainly the progressively greater incompleteness of the archeological record as earlier and earlier horizons are reached.

Two very important events in Indian history were the appearance

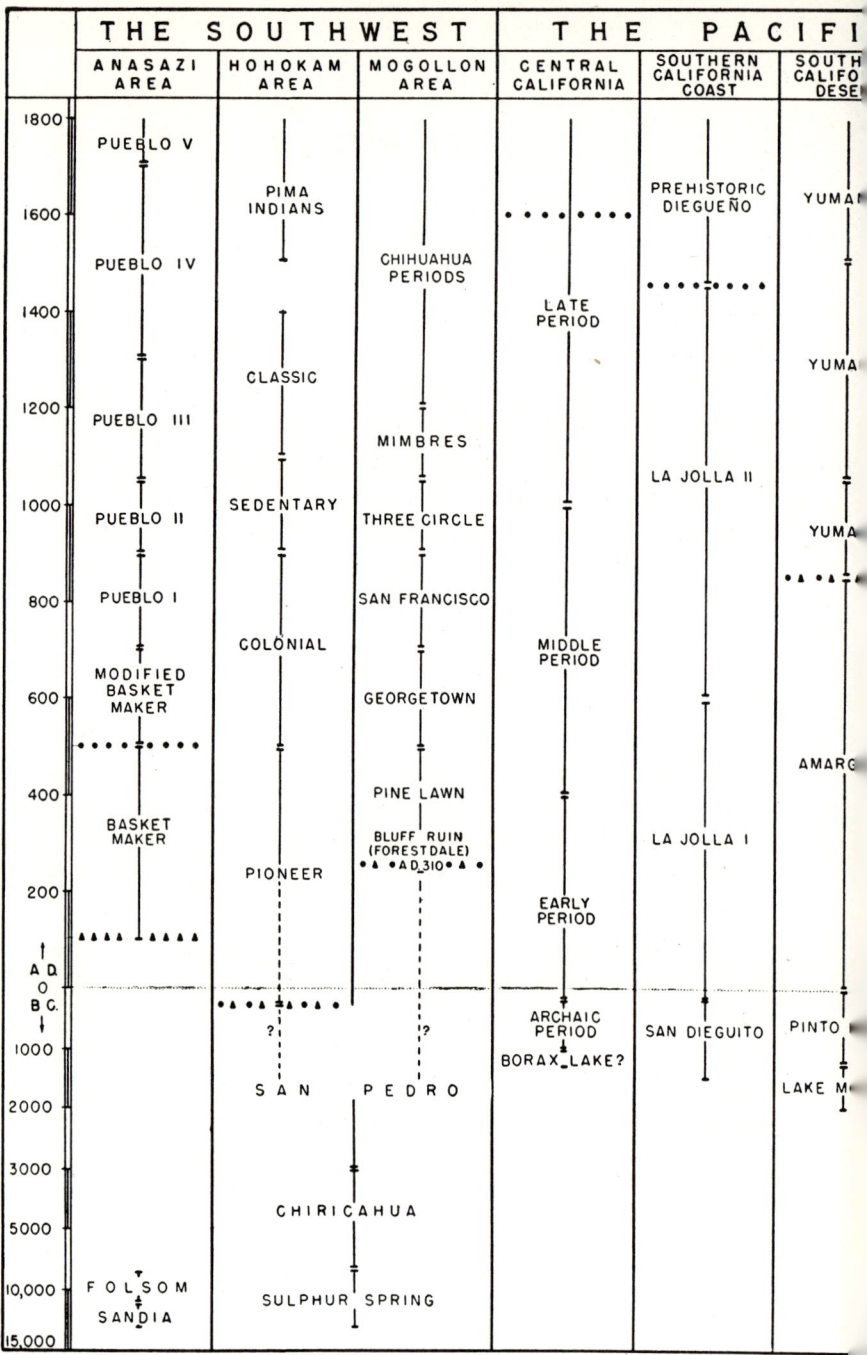

Fig. 122

F NORTH AMERICA

SLOPE		THE FAR NORTH		
ATEAU AREA	NORTHWEST COAST AREA	NORTHWESTERN ESKIMO AREA	SOUTHWESTERN ESKIMO AREA	EASTERN ESKIMO AREA

(chronological chart spanning 15,000 BC to 1800 AD)

- HISTORIC ATEAU / PREHISTORIC NORTHWEST COAST / POST-PUNUK
- LATE ALEUT — KONIAG — LATE KACHEMAK BAY
- THULE — INUGSUK
- PUNUK — BIRNIRK
- MIDDLE ALEUT — PRE-KONIAG — MIDDLE KACHEMAK BAY
- DORSET
- OLD BERING SEA — IPIUTAK
- EARLY ALEUT — EARLY KACHEMAK BAY
- OKVIK
- ORIGINAL ESKIMO CULTURE

▲▲▲ First appearance of farming
•• First appearance of pottery-making

FIG. 122.—*Continued*

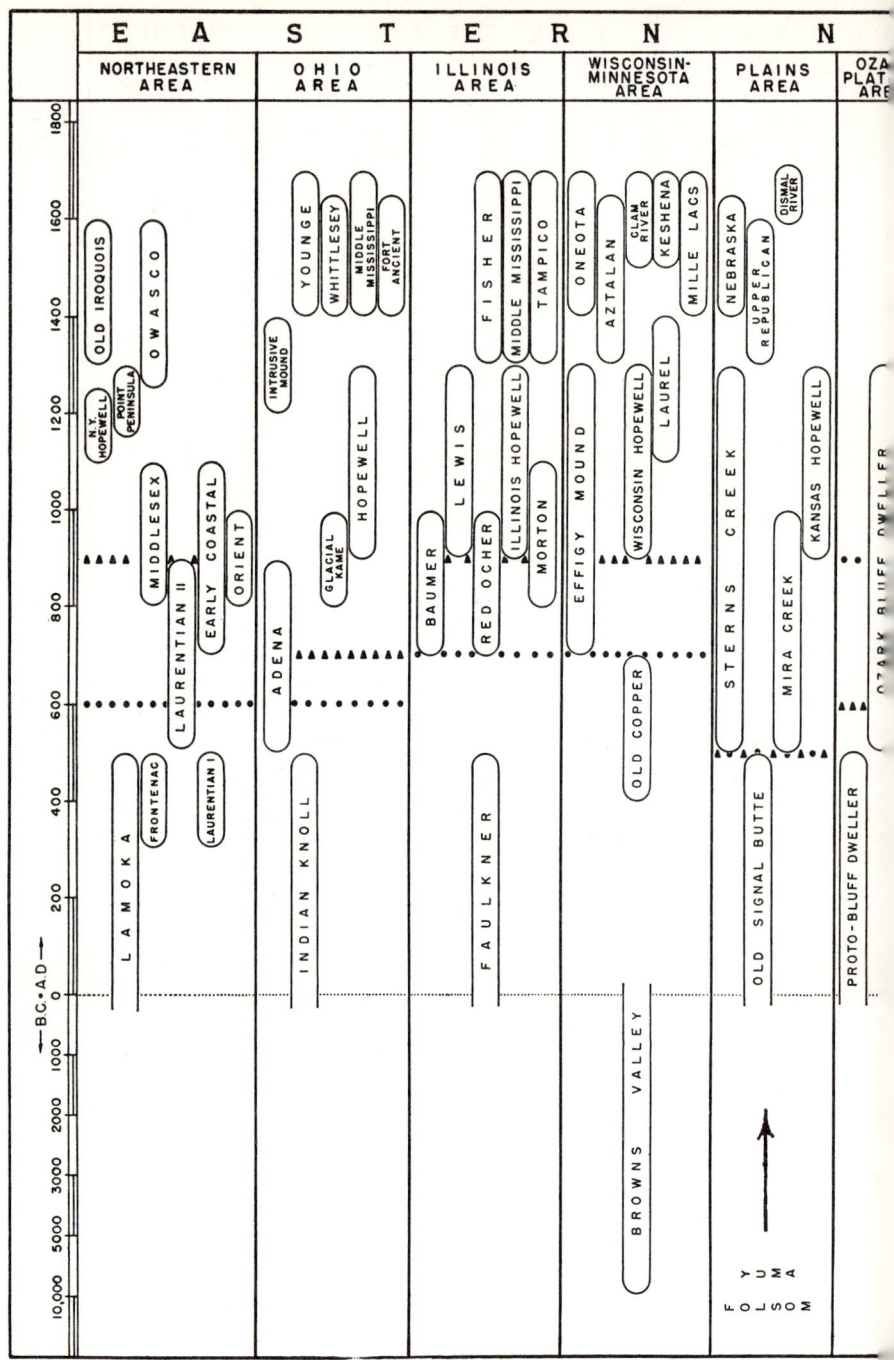

Fig. 122.—Continued

FIG. 122.—*Continued*

of farming and the beginning of pottery-making. The former revolutionized Indian economy by increasing and stabilizing the food supply, thereby making possible the development of large towns, a richer social and ceremonial life, and a more elaborate art. The latter introduced a new handicraft of great practical value and an artistic medium of great potentialities.

We have indicated on the chart the time of first occurrence of farming and pottery-making in each area. This task has been easy for pottery because potsherds are virtually indestructible and furnish reliable evidence of the presence of the art of pottery-making. But it is often difficult to secure proof of the presence of agriculture. The remains of Indian crops were perishable, and farming implements were often made of wood. For this reason it has been necessary to infer from indirect evidence the time of the first appearance of agriculture in many areas, particularly those of eastern United States, where conditions of preservation are poor. We have followed the principle that the conjunction within a given culture of a pattern of concentrated settlement in permanent villages with evidence of little dependence on hunting and food-gathering is presumptive proof of the presence of farming. This presumption becomes highly probable if, in addition, the economic patterns contrast with those of the preceding, patently nonagricultural period but are quite similar to those of near-by contemporaneous cultures or immediately succeeding cultures known to possess agriculture.

The two great farming areas in America north of Mexico were the southwestern and the eastern United States. As indicated on the chart, the practice of farming was at least five hundred years earlier in the Southwest than in the East. In both areas corn was one of the first crops grown. The history of corn and the other cultivated plants of the Indians is complex and as yet imperfectly known. It is clear, however, that the idea of farming and most of the cultivated plants were introduced to the United States from Mexico.

The two earliest known strains of corn in the Southwest—those of the Basket Maker and the Hohokam peoples—were similar but not identical and may have come to the area by a like route up the west coast of Mexico. During the early Pueblo periods Basket Maker corn was modified by the introduction of varieties coming apparently from highland Mexico. Hohokam corn has persisted with only slight modifications until the present and is still grown by the Pima and Papago Indians of southern Arizona.

The earliest known corn in eastern United States was of the Basket Maker type, introduced from the Southwest or possibly directly from the same source in Mexico from which the Basket Makers derived their corn. At a later time, another strain of corn similar to that from Guatemala made its way into the area, probably via the east coast of Mexico. In the thirteenth century this later eastern type of corn spread to the Southwest and strongly influenced the corn of the Pueblopeoples of that time (late Pueblo III period). Several cultivated plants, such as the sunflower, giant ragweed, canary grass, and pigweed, were apparently domesticated independently in eastern United States, although probably not before the introduction of corn.

As was the case with farming, pottery-making was earlier in the Southwest than elsewhere in America north of Mexico. Here the idea, at least, of making pottery was probably derived from Mexico. Once established, the three quite different pottery traditions of the Southwest—Anasazi, Hohokam, and Mogollon—followed each its own line of development, although they did influence one another and were probably affected by occasional Mexican influences as well.

In eastern North America there were two pottery complexes of diverse origin. The earliest pottery in the South, which was fiber-tempered, appears to have been an indigenous development, although the idea of making pottery may have come from outside the area. At about the same time there appeared to the north another pottery tradition which emphasized vessels with conoidal bases and stamped decoration. This northern pottery complex was probably derived from Asia via Bering Strait. The technique of stamped decoration was soon incorporated into the southern pottery complex. The northern pottery tradition apparently spread also to the northeastern periphery of the Southwest and has survived in that area in the conoidal-base cooking pots of the Navahos.

The pottery of southern California was derived from the Southwest by way of the prehistoric Yuman farmers living along the Colorado River.

Eskimo pottery, which appeared at an earlier time than in any other area except the Southwest, was derived from Asia. Aleut pottery appears to be unrelated to Eskimo pottery types and to those of northeastern Asia. The shapes of vessels seem to have been derived from the forms of Aleut stone lamps, and pottery-making may have been independently invented by the Aleuts.

The histories of pottery and of agriculture in North America—histories which were even more complex than our summary has indicated—serve to illustrate some of the basic trends of cultural development in the continent. From the time of arrival of the first Asiatic immigrants, with their simple hunting and food-gathering cultures, there existed a continuous process of adaptation to local environments, of specialization, and of independent invention. This process led to the development of a series of regional Indian cultures, different from one another, but all bearing a distinctive American stamp which set them off from the cultures of the Old World. But this development in North America did not take place in complete isolation. From time to time, new stimuli and influences arrived from Asia, and influences of basic importance came from the Indian cultures of Mexico and Central America.

BIBLIOGRAPHY

BIBLIOGRAPHY

AMSDEN, CHARLES A. 1932. "Some Popular Misconceptions about Primitive Peoples and Their Study," *Masterkey* (Los Angeles), VI, No. 2, 56–57.

———. 1934. *Navaho Weaving*. Santa Ana, Calif.

ANDERSON, EDGAR. 1945. "The Maize Collections from Painted Cave," in E. W. HAURY, *Painted Cave, Northeastern Arizona*, pp. 77–85. Amerind Foundation, Inc., Pub. No. 3. Dragoon, Ariz.

ANONYMOUS. 1910. "Quartelejo," p. 337 in *Handbook of American Indians*, ed. F. W. HODGE. Bureau of American Ethnology, Bull. 30, Part II. Washington, D.C.

ANTEVS, ERNST. 1935a. "The Occurrence of Flints and Extinct Animals in Pluvial Deposits near Clovis, New Mexico, Part II: Age of the Clovis Lake Clays," *Proceedings of the Academy of Natural Sciences of Philadelphia*, LXXXVII, 304–12.

———. 1935b. "Spread of Aboriginal Man to North America," *Geographical Review*, XXV, 302–9.

———. 1937. "Climate and Early Man in North America," chap. xiii in *Early Man*, ed. G. G. MACCURDY. Philadelphia and New York.

———. 1945. "Correlation of Wisconsin Glacial Maxima," *American Journal of Science*, CCXLIII-A (Daly vol.), 1–39.

BAER, J. L. 1921. "A Preliminary Report on the So-called 'Bannerstones,'" *American Anthropologist*, XXIII, 445–59.

BANDELIER, A. F. 1892. *Final Report of Investigations among the Indians of the Southwest United States, Carried on Mainly in the Years from 1880–1885.* "Papers of the Archaeological Institute of America, American Series," No. 4, Part II. Cambridge, Mass.

BARRETT, S. A. 1933. *Ancient Aztalan*. "Bulletin of the Public Museum of the City of Milwaukee," Vol. XIII.

BEALS, RALPH; BRAINERD, GEORGE W.; and SMITH, WATSON. 1945. *Archaeological Studies in Northeast Arizona*. "University of California Publications in American Archaeology and Ethnology," Vol. XLIV, No. 1. Berkeley and Los Angeles.

BELL, E. H. (ed.). 1936. *Chapters in Nebraska Archaeology*, Vol. I, Nos. 1–6. Lincoln: University of Nebraska.

BENNETT, J. W. 1941. "Excavations at Kincaid," *Southeastern Archaeological Conference Newsletter*, II, No. 4, 13–17.

———. 1944. "Archaeological Horizons in the Southern Illinois Region," *American Antiquity*, X, No. 1, 12–22.

———. 1945. *Archaeological Explorations in Jo Daviess County, Illinois.* "University of Chicago Publications in Anthropology: Archeological Series." Chicago.

BERRY, BREWTON, and CHAPMAN, CARL. 1942. "An Oneota Site in Missouri," *American Antiquity*, VII, No. 3, 290–305.

BIRKET-SMITH, KAJ. 1936. *The Eskimos*. Translated from the Danish by W. E. CALVERT; revised by C. DARYLL FORDE. London.

BLACK, G. A. 1936. *Excavation of the Nowlin Mound*. Indiana Historical Society Bull., Vol. XIII, No. 7. Indianapolis.

———. 1944. *Angel Site, Vanderburgh County, Indiana*. "Indiana Historical Society, Prehistory Research Series," Vol. II, No. 5. Indianapolis.

BRADFIELD, WESLEY. 1931. *Cameron Creek Village*. Santa Fe, N.M.: School of American Research.

BRAND, D. D. 1938. "Aboriginal Trade Routes for Sea Shells in the Southwest," *Year Book of the Association of Pacific Coast Geographers*, IV, 3–10.

BROWN, C. S. 1926. *The Archaeology of Mississippi*. University, Miss.: Mississippi Geological Survey.

BRYAN, KIRK. 1937. "Geology of the Folsom Deposits," chap. xv in *Early Man*, ed. G. G. MACCURDY. Philadelphia and New York.

BRYAN, KIRK, and RAY, LOUIS L. 1940. *Geologic Antiquity of the Lindenmeier Site in Colorado*. "Smithsonian Miscellaneous Collections," Vol. XCIX, No. 2. Washington, D.C.

BRYAN, W. A. 1929. "The Recent Bone-Cavern Find at Bishop's Cap, New Mexico," *Science*, LXX, 39–41.

CALDWELL, JOSEPH, n.d. "Cultural Relationships of Four Indian Sites of the Georgia Coast." Master's thesis, Department of Anthropology, University of Chicago.

CALDWELL, JOSEPH, and MCCANN, CATHERINE. 1941. *Irene Mound Site, Chatham County, Georgia*. Athens, Ga.: University of Georgia.

CAMPBELL, E. W. C., et al. 1937. *The Archeology of Pleistocene Lake Mohave*. "Southwest Museum Papers," No. 11. Los Angeles.

CAMPBELL, WILLIAM H. and ELIZABETH W. 1935. *The Pinto Basin Site*. "Southwest Museum Papers," No. 9. Los Angeles.

CARTER, G. F. 1941. "Archaeological Notes on a Midden at Point Sal," *American Antiquity*, VI, 214–26.

CARTER, G. F., and ANDERSON, EDGAR. 1945. "A Preliminary Survey of Maize in the Southwestern United States," *Annals of the Missouri Botanical Garden*, XXXII, 297–322.

CHAMBERLAIN, A. F. 1907. "Chinook Jargon," in *Handbook of American Indians*, ed. F. W. Hodge, pp. 274–75. Bureau of American Ethnology, Bull. 30, Part I. Washington, D.C.

CHARD, CHESTER S. 1940. *Distribution and Significance of Ball Courts in the Southwest*. "Papers of the Excavators' Club," Vol. I, No. 2. Cambridge, Mass.

CLAFLIN, W. H. 1931. *The Stallings Island Mound, Columbia County, Georgia*. "Papers of the Peabody Museum of American Archaeology and Ethnology," Vol. XIV, No. 1. Cambridge, Mass.

CLINE, WALTER, et al. 1938. *The Sinkaietk or Southern Okanagon of Washington*. "General Series in Anthropology," No. 6, ed. LESLIE SPIER. Menasha, Wis.

COFFIN, E. F. 1932. *Archaeological Exploration of a Rock Shelter in Brewster County, Texas*. "Museum of the American Indian, Heye Foundation, Indian Notes and Monographs," No. 48. New York.

COLE, FAY-COOPER. 1943. "Chronology in the Middle West," *Proceedings of the American Philosophical Society*, LXXXVI, No. 2, 299–303.

COLE, FAY-COOPER, and DEUEL, THORNE. 1937. *Rediscovering Illinois*. "University of Chicago Publications in Anthropology: Archeological Series." Chicago.

COLLIER, DONALD; HUDSON, A. E.; and FORD, ARLO. 1942. *Archaeology of the Upper Columbia Region*. "University of Washington Publications in Anthropology," Vol. IX, No. 1. Seattle.

COLLINS, H. B., JR. 1932. "Excavations at a Prehistoric Indian Village Site in Mississippi," *Smithsonian Institution, United States National Museum, Proceedings*, Vol. LXXIX, Art. 32. Washington, D.C.

———. 1937. *Archeology of St. Lawrence Island, Alaska.* "Smithsonian Miscellaneous Collections," Vol. XCVI, No. 1. Washington, D.C.

———. 1940. "Outline of Eskimo Prehistory," in *Essays in Historical Anthropology of North America*, pp. 533–92. "Smithsonian Miscellaneous Collections," Vol. C. Washington, D.C.

———. 1941. "Relationships of an Early Indian Cranial Series from Louisiana." *Journal of the Washington Academy of Sciences*, XXXI, No. 4, 145–55.

———. 1943. "Eskimo Archaeology and Its Bearing on the Problem of Man's Antiquity in America," *Proceedings of the American Philosophical Society*, LXXXVI, No. 2, 220–35.

COLLINS, H. B., JR.; CLARK, A. H.; and WALKER, E. H. 1945. *The Aleutian Islands: Their People and Natural History.* "Smithsonian Institution War Background Studies," No. 21. Washington, D.C.

COLTON, H. S. 1939. *Prehistoric Culture Units and Their Relationships in Northern Arizona.* Museum of Northern Arizona, Bull. 17. Flagstaff, Ariz.

———. 1941. "Prehistoric Trade in the Southwest," *Scientific Monthly*, LII, 308–19.

———. 1945. "The Patayan Problem in the Colorado River Valley," *Southwestern Journal of Anthropology*, I, No. 1, 114–21.

COLTON, H. S., and BAXTER, F. C. 1932. *Days in the Painted Desert.* Museum of Northern Arizona, Bull. 2. Flagstaff, Ariz.

COLTON, H. S., and HARGRAVE, L. L. 1933. *Pueblo II in the San Francisco Mountains, Arizona; and Pueblo II Houses of the San Francisco Mountains, Arizona.* Museum of Northern Arizona, Bull. 4. Flagstaff, Ariz.

———. 1937. *Handbook of Northern Arizona Pottery Wares.* Museum of Northern Arizona, Bull. 11. Flagstaff, Ariz.

COLTON, H. S., and McGREGOR, JOHN C. 1941 *Winona and Ridge Ruin*, Parts I and II. Museum of Northern Arizona, Bulls. 18 and 19. Flagstaff, Ariz.

COOPER, L. R. 1933. *The Red Cedar Variant of the Wisconsin Hopewell Culture.* "Bulletin of the Public Museum of the City of Milwaukee," Vol. XVI, No. 2.

COOPER, PAUL. 1939. *Report of Explorations: The Archeological Exploration of 1938 by the Nebraska State Historical Society.* "Nebraska History," Vol. XX, No. 2. Lincoln, Nebr.

COSGROVE, H. S. and C. B. 1932. *The Swarts Ruin, a Typical Mimbres Site of Southwestern New Mexico.* "Papers of the Peabody Museum of American Archaeology and Ethnology," Vol. XV, No. 1. Cambridge, Mass.

CRESSMAN, L. S. 1942. *Archaeological Researches in the Northern Great Basin.* Carnegie Institution of Washington, Pub. 538. Washington, D.C.

———. 1943. "Results of Recent Archaeological Research in Northern Great Basin of South Central Oregon," *Proceedings of the American Philosophical Society*, LXXXVI, No. 2, 236–46.

CURTIS, EDWARD S. 1926. *The North American Indian*, Vols. XVI and XVII. Norwood, Mass.

CUSHING, F. H. 1894a. "Primitive Copper Working: An Experimental Study," *American Anthropologist*, VII, 93–117.

———. 1894b. "The Germ of Shore-Land Pottery," *Memoirs of the International Congress of Anthropology*, pp. 217–34. Chicago.

———. 1895. "The Arrow," *American Anthropologist*, VIII, 307–49.

———. 1896. "Exploration of Ancient Key Dwellers' Remains on the Gulf Coast of

Florida," *Proceedings of the American Philosophical Society*, XXXV, No. 150, 329–432.

DELLINGER, S. C. 1936. "Baby Cradles of the Ozark Bluff Dwellers," *American Antiquity*, I, No. 3, 197–214.

DELLINGER, S. C., and DICKINSON, S. D. 1940. "Possible Antecedents of the Middle Mississippi Ceramic Complex in Northeastern Arkansas," *American Antiquity*, VI, No. 2, 133–47.

———. 1942. "Pottery from the Ozark Bluff Shelters," *ibid.*, VII, No. 3, 276–89.

DEUEL, THORNE. 1935. "Basic Cultures of the Mississippi Valley," *American Anthropologist*, XXXVII, No. 3, 429–46.

DICKINSON, S. D. 1936. "The Ceramic Relationships of the Pre-Caddo Pottery from the Crenshaw Site," *Texas Archaeological and Paleontological Society Bulletin*, VIII, 56–69.

DIXON, R. B. 1913. "Some Aspects of North American Archeology," *American Anthropologist*, XV, No. 4, 549–66.

———. 1928. *The Building of Cultures*. New York.

DONALDSON, THOMAS. 1893. "Moqui Pueblo Indians of Arizona," *Extra Census Bulletin, Eleventh Census of the United States*. Washington, D.C.

DOUGLASS, A. E. 1935. "Dating Pueblo Bonito and Other Ruins of the Southwest," *National Geographic Society, Pueblo Bonito Series*, No. 1, pp. 48–49.

———. 1942. "Checking the Date of Bluff Ruin, Forestdale: A Study in Technique," *Tree Ring Bulletin*, IX, No. 2, 2–7.

DRUCKER, PHILIP. 1943. "Archeological Survey of the Northern Northwest Coast." in *Anthropological Papers, Nos. 19–26*, pp. 17–132. Bureau of American Ethnology, Bull. 133. Washington, D.C.

ELLIS, H. HOLMES. 1940. *Flint-working Techniques of the American Indians: An Experimental Study*. Columbus, Ohio: Lithic Laboratory, Department of Archaeology, Ohio State Museum.

FAIRBANKS, C. H. n.d. "Lamar Trait List." Macon, Ga.: National Park Service, Ocmulgee National Monument. (MS.)

———. n.d. "Ocmulgee Trait List." Macon, Ga.: National Park Service, Ocmulgee National Monument. (MS.)

———. n.d. "Swift Creek Trait List." Macon, Ga.: National Park Service, Ocmulgee National Monument. (MS.)

———. n.d. "Trait List for Macon Plateau Culture." Macon, Ga.: National Park Service, Ocmulgee National Monument. (MS.)

———. 1942. "The Taxonomic Position of Stallings Island, Georgia," *American Antiquity*, VII, No. 3, 223–31.

FEWKES, J. W. 1911. *Antiquities of the Mesa Verde National Park: Cliff Palace*. Bureau of American Ethnology, Bull. 51. Washington, D.C.

———. 1919. "Designs on Prehistoric Hopi Pottery," *Bureau of American Ethnology, Thirty-third Annual Report*, pp. 207–84. Washington, D.C.

FIGGINS, J. D. 1927. "The Antiquity of Man in America," *Natural History*, XXVII, No. 3, 229–39.

FORD, J. A., and QUIMBY, G. I. 1945. *The Tchefuncte Culture, an Early Occupation of the Lower Mississippi Valley*. "Memoirs of the Society for American Archaeology," supplement to *American Antiquity*, Vol. X, No. 3.

FORD, J. A., and WILLEY, G. R. n.d. "The Greenhouse Site." Baton Rouge: Department of Anthropology, Louisiana State University. (MS.)

———. 1940. *Crooks Site, a Marksville Period Burial Mound in La Salle Parish, Louisiana.* "Louisiana Department of Conservation, Anthropological Study," No. 3. New Orleans.

———. 1941. "An Interpretation of the Prehistory of the Eastern United States," *American Anthropologist*, XLIII, No. 3, 325–63.

FORREST, EARLE R. 1929. *Missions and Pueblos of the Old Southwest.* Cleveland.

FOWKE, GERARD. 1894. "Material for Aboriginal Stone Implements," *Archaeologist*, II, No. 10, 328–35.

———. 1896. "Stone Art," *Bureau of American Ethnology, Thirteenth Annual Report*, pp. 47–178. Washington, D.C.

———. 1902. *Archaeological History of Ohio.* Columbus, Ohio: Ohio State Archaeological and Historical Society.

———. 1910. *Antiquities of Central and Southeastern Missouri.* Bureau of American Ethnology, Bull. 37. Washington, D.C.

FRASER, SIMON. 1889. "Journal of a Voyage from the Rocky Mountains to the Pacific Coast," in *Le Bourgeois de la Compagnie Nord-Ouest*, I, 156–221, ed. L. F. R. MASSON. Quebec.

GARDNER, MAJOR FLETCHER, and MARTIN, GEORGE C. 1933. *A New Type of Atlatl from a Cave Shelter on the Rio Grande near Shumla, Valverde County, Texas.* "Big Bend Basket Maker Papers," No. 2. Southwest Texas Archaeological Society of the Witte Memorial Museum, Bull. 2. San Antonio.

GATSCHET, A. D., and THOMAS, CYRUS. 1907. "Mobile," p. 916 in *Handbook of American Indians*, ed. F. W. HODGE. Bureau of American Ethnology, Bull. 30, Part I. Washington, D.C.

GIFFORD, E. W. 1928. *Pottery Making in the Southwest.* "University of California Publications in American Archaeology and Ethnology," Vol. XXIII, No. 8. Berkeley and Los Angeles.

———. 1940. *Californian Bone Artifacts.* "University of California, Anthropological Records," Vol. III, No. 2. Berkeley and Los Angeles.

GIFFORD, E. W., and SCHENCK, W. E. 1926. *Archaeology of the Southern San Joaquin Valley.* "University of California Publications in American Archaeology and Ethnology," Vol. XXIII, No. 1. Berkeley and Los Angeles.

GILLIN, JOHN. 1938. "Archaeological Investigation in Nine Mile Canyon, Utah," *Bulletin of the University of Utah*, Vol. XXVIII, No. 11.

———. 1941. *Archaeological Investigations in Central Utah.* "Papers of the Peabody Museum of American Archaeology and Ethnology," Vol. XVII, No. 2. Cambridge, Mass.

GILMORE, M. R. 1925. *Arikara Uses of Clay and of Other Earth Products.* "Museum of the American Indian, Heye Foundation, Indian Notes and Monographs," Vol. II, No. 4. New York.

———. 1930. *Vegetal Remains of the Ozark Bluff-Dweller Culture.* "Papers of the Michigan Academy of Science, Arts, and Letters," Vol. XIV. Ann Arbor, Mich.

GLADWIN, HAROLD S. 1928. *Excavations at Casa Grande, Arizona.* "Southwest Museum Papers," No. 2. Los Angeles.

GLADWIN, HAROLD S. and WINIFRED. 1930. *Some Southwestern Pottery Types.* Series I. "Gila Pueblo, Medallion Papers," No. 8. Globe, Ariz.

GLADWIN, HAROLD S.; HAURY, E. W.; SAYLES, E. B.; and GLADWIN, NORA. 1937. *Excavations at Snaketown: Material Culture.* "Gila Pueblo, Medallion Papers," No. 25. Globe, Ariz.

GLADWIN, WINIFRED and HAROLD S. 1934. *A Method for Designation of Cultures and Their Variations.* "Gila Pueblo, Medallion Papers," No. 15. Globe, Ariz.

GODDARD, P. E. 1934. *Indians of the Northwest Coast.* 2d ed. "American Museum of Natural History Handbook Series," No. 10. New York.

GREENMAN, E. F. 1931. "Department of Archaeology," *Museum Echoes,* IV, No. 8, 55. Columbus, Ohio: Ohio State Archaeological and Historical Society.

———. 1932. "Excavation of the Coon Mound and an Analysis of the Adena Culture," *Ohio State Archaeological and Historical Quarterly,* XLI, 369–423.

———. 1937a. *The Younge Site, an Archaeological Record from Michigan.* "University of Michigan Museum of Anthropology, Occasional Contributions," Vol. VI. Ann Arbor, Mich.

———. 1937b. "Two Prehistoric Villages near Cleveland, Ohio," *Ohio State Archaeological and Historical Quarterly,* XLVI, No. 4, 305–66.

———. 1943. "An Early Industry on a Raised Beach near Killarney, Ontario," *American Antiquity,* VIII, No. 3, 260–65.

GREENMAN, E. F., and STANLEY, G. M. 1943. *The Archaeology and Geology of Two Early Sites near Killarney, Ontario.* "Papers of the Michigan Academy of Science, Arts, and Letters," Vol. XXVIII. Ann Arbor, Mich.

GRIFFIN, J. B. 1937. "Culture Identity of the Ozark 'Top Layer,'" *American Antiquity,* II, No. 4, 296–97.

———. 1941. *Additional Hopewell Material from Illinois.* "Indiana Historical Society, Prehistoric Research Series," Vol. XI, No. 3. Indianapolis.

———. 1942. "Adena Pottery," *American Antiquity,* VII, No. 4, 344–58.

———. 1943. *The Fort Ancient Aspect.* Ann Arbor, Mich.

———. 1944a. "The De Luna Expedition and the Buzzard Cult in the Southeast," *Journal of the Washington Academy of Sciences,* XXXIV, 299–303.

——— 1944b. *The Iroquois in American Prehistory.* "Papers of the Michigan Academy of Science, Arts, and Letters," Vol. XXIX. Ann Arbor, Mich.

———. 1946. *Cultural Change and Continuity in Eastern United States Archaeology.* "Papers of the Robert S. Peabody Foundation for Archaeology," Vol. III. Andover, Mass.

GRIFFIN, J. B., and MORGAN, R. G. (eds.). 1941. "Contributions to the Archaeology of the Illinois River Valley," *American Philosophical Society Transactions,* XXXII, No. 1, 1–209.

GUERNSEY, S. J. 1931. *Explorations in Northeastern Arizona.* "Papers of the Peabody Museum of American Archaeology and Ethnology," Vol. XII, No. 1. Cambridge, Mass.

GUERNSEY, S. J., and KIDDER, A. V. 1921. *Basket Maker Caves in Northeastern Arizona.* "Papers of the Peabody Museum of American Archaeology and Ethnology," Vol. VIII, No. 2. Cambridge, Mass.

GUTHE, CARL E. 1925. *Pueblo Pottery Making: A Study at the Village of San Ildefonso.* "Papers of the Phillips Academy, Southwestern Expedition," No. 2. New Haven, Conn.

HAAG, W. G. 1942. "Early Horizons in the Southeast," *American Antiquity,* VII, No. 3, 209–22.

HACK, JOHN T. 1942. *The Changing Physical Environment of the Hopi Indians of Arizona.* "Papers of the Peabody Museum of American Archaeology and Ethnology," Vol. XXXV, No. 1. Cambridge, Mass.

HACKETT, CHARLES WILSON. 1942. *Revolt of the Pueblo Indians of New Mexico and*

Otermin's Attempted Reconquest, 1680–1682. "Coronado Cuarto Centennial Publications," Vol. VIII. Albuquerque, N.M.

HAILE, FATHER BERARD. 1943. *Origin Legend of the Navaho Flintway.* "University of Chicago Publications in Anthropology: Linguistic Series." Chicago.

HAINES, FRANCIS. 1938. "The Northward Spread of Horses among the Plains Indians," *American Anthropologist*, XL, No. 3, 429–37.

HALL, E. T., JR. 1944a. *Early Stockaded Settlements in the Governador, New Mexico.* "Columbia Studies in Archaeology and Ethnology," Vol. II, Part I. New York.

———. 1944b. "Recent Clues to Athapascan (Navaho) Prehistory in the Southwest," *American Anthropologist*, XLVI, No. 1, Part I, 98–105.

HARGRAVE, L. L. 1932a. *Guide to Forty Pottery Types from the Hopi Country and the San Francisco Mountains.* Museum of Northern Arizona, Bull. 1. Flagstaff, Ariz.

———. 1932b. *Oraibi: A Brief History of the Oldest Inhabited Town in the United States.* "Museum of Northern Arizona, Museum Notes," Vol. IV, No. 7. Flagstaff, Ariz.

HARRINGTON, M. R. 1908. "Catawba Potters and Their Work," *American Anthropologist*, N.S., X, No. 3, 399–407.

———. 1920. *Certain Caddo Sites in Arkansas.* "Museum of the American Indian, Heye Foundation, Indian Notes and Monographs, Miscellaneous Series," Vol. X. New York.

———. 1922. *Cherokee and Earlier Remains on the Upper Tennessee River.* "Museum of the American Indian, Heye Foundation, Indian Notes and Monographs, Miscellaneous Series," Vol. XXIV. New York.

———. 1924. "The Ozark Bluff Dwellers," *American Anthropologist*, XXVI, No. 1, 1–21.

———. 1933. *Gypsum Cave, Nevada.* "Southwest Museum Papers," No. 8. Los Angeles.

———. 1934. "A Camel-Hunter's Camp in Nevada." *Masterkey*, VIII, No. 1, 22–24.

———. 1938a. "Folsom Man in California," *ibid.*, XII, No. 4, 133–37.

———. 1938b. "Pre-Folsom Man in California," *ibid.*, No. 5, pp. 173–75.

———. 1939. "The Age of the Borax Lake Finds," *ibid.*, XIII, No. 6, 208–9.

———. 1945. "Farewell to Borax Lake," *ibid.*, XIX, No. 6, 181–84.

HAURY, E. W. 1932. *Roosevelt: 9 : 6, a Hohokam Site of the Colonial Period.* "Gila Pueblo, Medallion Papers," No. 11. Globe, Ariz.

———. 1934. *The Canyon Creek Ruin and the Cliff Dwellings of the Sierra Ancha.* "Gila Pueblo, Medallion Papers," No. 14. Globe, Ariz.

———. 1936a. *The Mogollon Culture of Southwestern New Mexico.* "Gila Pueblo, Medallion Papers," No. 20. Globe, Ariz.

———. 1936b. *Some Southwestern Pottery Types*, Series IV. "Gila Pueblo, Medallion Papers," No. 19. Globe, Ariz. (A description of Mogollon-Mimbres pottery.)

———. 1940. *Excavations in the Forestdale Valley, East-Central Arizona.* "University of Arizona Bulletin," Vol. XI, No. 4. Tucson, Ariz.

———. 1942. "Some Implications of the Bluff Ruin Dates," *Tree-Ring Bulletin*, IX, No. 2, 7–8.

———. 1943a. "The Stratigraphy of Ventana Cave, Arizona," *American Antiquity*, VIII, No. 3, 218–33.

———. 1943b. "A Possible Cochise-Mogollon-Hohokam Sequence," *Proceedings of the American Philosophical Society*, LXXXVI, No. 2, 260–63.

———. 1945a. *Painted Cave, Northeastern Arizona.* Amerind Foundation, Inc., Pub. No. 3. Dragoon, Ariz.

HAURY, E. W. 1945b. *The Excavation of Los Muertos and Neighboring Ruins in the Salt River Valley, Southern Arizona.* "Papers of the Peabody Museum of American Archeology and Ethnology," Vol. XXIV, No. 1. Cambridge, Mass.

HAURY, E. W., and HARGRAVE, L. L. 1931. *Recently Dated Pueblo Ruins in Arizona.* "Smithsonian Miscellaneous Collections," Vol. LXXXII, No. 11. Washington, D.C.

HAWLEY, F. M. 1929. "Prehistoric Pottery Pigments in the Southwest," *American Anthropologist*, XXXI, No. 4, 731–54.

———. 1936. *Field Manual of Prehistoric Southwestern Pottery Types.*"Bulletin, University of New Mexico, Anthropological Series," Vol. I, No. 4. Albuquerque, N.M.

HAYDEN, IRWIN. 1930. "Mesa House, Nevada," in *Archeological Explorations in Southern Nevada.* "Southwest Museum Papers," No. 4. Los Angeles.

HEIZER, R. F. 1938. "Aconite Arrow Poison in the Old and New World," *Journal of the Washington Academy of Sciences*, XXVIII, 358–64.

———. 1939a. Personal communication.

———. 1939b. "Some Sacramento Valley–Santa Barbara Archeological Relationships," *Masterkey*, XIII, No. 1, 31–35.

———. 1941a. "Aboriginal Trade between the Southwest and California," *ibid.*, XV, No. 5, 185–88.

———. 1941b. "The Direct-Historical Approach in California Archaeology," *American Antiquity*, VII, No. 2, 98–122.

———. 1945. Personal communication.

HEIZER, R. F., and FENENGA, FRANKLIN. 1939. "Archaeological Horizons in Central California," *American Anthropoloigst*, XLI, No. 3, 378–99.

HENDRON, J. W. 1940. *Prehistory of El Rito de los Frijoles, Bandelier National Monument.* "Southwestern Monuments Association, Technical Series," No. 1. Coolidge, Ariz.

HENSHAW, H. W. 1883. "Animal Carvings from the Mounds of the Mississippi Valley," *Bureau of American Ethnology, Second Annual Report*, pp. 123–66. Washington, D.C.

HEWITT, J. B. N. 1910. "Wampum," pp. 904–9, in *Handbook of American Indians*, ed. F. W. HODGE. Bureau of American Ethnology, Bull. 30, Part II. Washington, D.C.

HIBBEN, FRANK C. 1941. *Evidences of Early Occupation in Sandia Cave, New Mexico, and Other Sites in the Sandia-Manzano Region. With Appendix on Correlation of the Deposits of Sandia Cave, New Mexico, with the Glacial Chronology, by Kirk Bryan.* "Smithsonian Miscellaneous Collections," Vol. XCIX, No. 23. Washington, D.C.

HILL, A. T., and KIVETT, MARVIN. 1941. "Woodland-like Manifestations in Nebraska," *Nebraska History Magazine*, Vol. XXI, No. 3.

HILL, A. T., and METCALF, GEORGE. 1941. "A Site of the Dismal River Aspect in Chase County, Nebraska," *Nebraska History Magazine*, Vol. XXII, No. 2.

HINSDALE, W. B. 1929. *Indian Mounds, West Twin Lake, Montmorency County, Michigan.* "Papers of the Michigan Academy of Science, Arts, and Letters," Vol. X. Ann Arbor, Mich.

HODGE, F. W. 1900. "Pueblo Ruins in Kansas," *American Anthropologist*, N.S., II, No. 4, 778–79.

———. 1923. *Circular Kivas near Hawikuh, New Mexico.* "Museum of the American Indian, Heye Foundation, Contributions," Vol. VII, No. 1. New York.

———. 1937. *History of Hawikuh.* "Frederick Webb Hodge Anniversary Publication Fund, Southwest Museum," Vol. I. Los Angeles.
HOLAND, HJALMAR R. 1940. *Westward from Vinland.* New York.
HOLMES, W. H. 1883. "Art in Shell of the Ancient Americans," *Bureau of American Ethnology, Second Annual Report,* pp. 185–305. Washington, D.C.
———. 1901. "Aboriginal Copper Mines of Isle Royale, Lake Superior," *American Anthropologist,* N.S., III, No. 4, 684–96.
———. 1903. "Aboriginal Pottery of the Eastern United States," *Bureau of American Ethnology, Twentieth Annual Report, Accompanying Paper,* pp. 1–237. Washington, D.C.
———. 1919. *Handbook of Aboriginal American Antiquities,* Part I: *Introduction: The Lithic Industries.* Bureau of American Ethnology, Bull. 60. Washington, D.C.
HOOTON, E. A. 1930. *Indians of Pecos Pueblo.* "Papers of the Phillips Academy, Southwestern Expedition," No. 4. New Haven, Conn.
———. 1933. "Racial Types in America," in *American Aborigines,* ed. DIAMOND JENNESS. Toronto.
HOUGHTON, J. J. 1879. "Ancient Copper Mines of Lake Superior," *Wisconsin Historical Collections,* VIII, 140–51.
HOWARD, EDGAR B. 1935. "Evidence of Early Man in North America," *Museum Journal,* Vol. XXIV, Nos. 2 and 3. Philadelphia.
HOWELLS, WILLIAM. 1944. *Mankind So Far.* Garden City, N.Y.
HRDLIČKA, ALEŠ. 1944. *The Anthropology of Kodiak Island.* Philadelphia.
———. 1945. *The Aleutian and Commander Islands and Their Inhabitants.* Philadelphia.
JEANÇON, J. A. 1923. *Excavations in the Chama Valley, New Mexico.* Bureau of American Ethnology, Bull. 81. Washington, D.C.
JENKS, A. E. 1937. *Minnesota's Browns Valley Man and Associated Burial Artifacts.* "Memoirs of the American Anthropological Association," No. 49. Menasha, Wis.
JENNESS, DIAMOND. 1925. "A New Eskimo Culture in Hudson Bay," *Geographical Review,* XV, No. 3, 428–37.
———. 1932. *The Indians of Canada.* Ottawa.
JENNINGS, J. D. 1939. "Recent Excavations at the Lamar Site, Ocmulgee National Monument, Macon, Georgia," *Proceedings of the Society for Georgia Archaeology,* Vol. II, No. 2. Macon.
———. 1941. "Chickasaw and Earlier Indian Cultures of Northeast Mississippi," *Journal of Mississippi History,* III, No. 3, 155–266.
JOCHELSON, WALDEMAR. 1925. *Archaeological Investigations in the Aleutian Islands.* Carnegie Institution Pub. 367. Washington, D.C.
———. 1933. *History, Ethnology and Anthropology of the Aleut.* Carnegie Institution Pub. 432. Washington, D.C.
JOHNSON, FREDERICK. 1942. *The Boylston Street Fishweir.* "Papers of the Robert S. Peabody Foundation for Archaeology, Phillips Academy," Vol. II. Andover, Mass.
KELLEY, J. CHARLES; CAMPBELL, T. N.; and LEHMER, D. J. 1940. "The Association of Archaeological Materials with Geological Deposits in the Big Bend Region of Texas," *Sul Ross State Teachers College Bulletin,* Vol. XXI, No. 3. Alpine, Tex.
KELLY, A. R. 1938. *A Preliminary Report on Archeological Explorations at Macon, Georgia.* "Anthropological Papers," No. 1, in Bureau of American Ethnology, Bull. 119. Washington, D.C.
KEUR, DOROTHY L. 1941. *Big Bead Mesa: An Archaeological Study of Navaho Ac-*

culturation. "Memoirs of the Society for American Archaeology," supplement to *American Antiquity*, Vol. VII, No. 2, Part II.

KEUR, DOROTHY L. 1944. "A Chapter in Navaho-Pueblo Relations," *American Antiquity*, X, No. 1, 75–86.

KIDDER, A. V. 1924. *An Introduction to the Study of Southwestern Archaeology*. New Haven, Conn.

———. 1931. *Pottery of Pecos*, Vol. I: *The Dull-Paint Wares*, "Papers of the Phillips Academy Southwestern Expedition," No. 5. New Haven, Conn.

———. 1932. *Artifacts of Pecos*. "Papers of the Phillips Academy Southwestern Expedition," No. 6. New Haven, Conn.

KIDDER, A. V., and GUERNSEY, S. J. 1919. *Archeological Explorations in Northeastern Arizona*. Bureau of American Ethnology, Bull. 65. Washington, D.C.

KIDDER, A. V., and SHEPARD, ANNA O. 1936. *Pottery of Pecos*, Vol. II: *The Glaze-Paint, Culinary, and Other Wares*. "Papers of the Phillips Academy Southwestern Expedition," No. 7. New Haven, Conn.

KRIEGER, A. D. n.d. "Caddo Archaeology." Department of Anthropology, University of Texas. (MS.)

———. 1945. "An Inquiry into Supposed Mexican Influence on a Prehistoric 'Cult' in the Southern United States," *American Anthropologist*, XLVII, No. 4. 483–515.

KRIEGER, H. W. 1928. "A Prehistoric Pit House Village Site on the Columbia River at Wahluke, Grant County, Washington," *Proceedings of the United States National Museum*, Vol. LXXIII, Art. 11. Washington, D.C.

KROEBER, A. L. 1923. *Anthropology*. New York.

———. 1925. *Handbook of the Indians of California*. Bureau of American Ethnology, Bull. 78. Washington, D.C.

———. 1927. "Arrow Release Distributions," pp. 283–96 in "University of California Publications in American Archaeology and Ethnology," Vol. XXIII. Berkeley and Los Angeles.

———. 1928. "Native Culture of the Southwest," *ibid.*, pp. 375–98.

———. 1936. "Prospects in California Prehistory," *American Antiquity*, II, No. 2, 108–16.

———. 1938. "Lodi Man," *Science*, LXXXVII, 137–38.

———. 1939. *Cultural and Natural Areas in Native North America*. "University of California Publications in American Archaeology and Ethnology," Vol. XXXVIII. Berkeley and Los Angeles.

LAGUNA, FREDERICA DE. 1934. *The Archaeology of Cook Inlet, Alaska*. Philadelphia.

———. 1940. "Eskimo Lamps and Pots," *Journal of the Royal Anthropological Institute of Great Britain and Ireland*, LXX, Part I, 53–76.

LANGFORD, GEORGE. 1927. "The Fisher Mound Group, Successive Aboriginal Occupations near the Mouth of the Illinois River," *American Anthropologist*, XXIX, No. 3, 153x–205x.

LAUFER, BERTHOLD. 1929. "The American Plant Migration," *Scientific Monthly*, XXVIII, 239–51.

———. 1931. "Columbus and Cathay, and the Meaning of America to the Orientalist," *Journal of American Oriental Society*, LI, No. 2, 87–103.

LEECHMAN, DOUGLAS. 1943. "Two New Cape Dorset Sites," *American Antiquity*, VIII, No. 4, 363–75.

LEMLEY, H. J. 1936. "Discoveries Indicating a Pre-Caddo Culture on the Red River in Arkansas," *Texas Archaeological and Paleontological Society Bulletin*, VIII, 25–55.

LETHBRIDGE, T. C. 1939. "Archaeological Data from the Canadian Arctic," *Journal of the Royal Anthropological Institute of Great Britain and Ireland*, LXIX, 187–233.

LEWIS, MERIWETHER, and CLARK, WILLIAM. 1893. *History of the Expedition under the Command of Lewis and Clark to the Sources of the Missouri River, Thence across the Rocky Mountains and down the Columbia River to the Pacific Ocean Performed during the Years 1804–05–06*, ed. ELLIOT COUES. 4 vols. New York.

LEWIS, T. M. N., and KNEBERG, MADELINE. 1941. *The Prehistory of the Chicamauga Basin in Tennessee.* "Tennessee Anthropology Papers, University of Tennessee," No. 1. Knoxville, Tenn.

LILLARD, J. B.; HEIZER, R. F.; and FENENGA, FRANKLIN. 1939. *An Introduction to the Archaeology of Central California.* Sacramento Junior College, Department of Anthropology, Bull. 2.

LILLARD, J. B., and PURVES, W. K. 1936. *The Archaeology of the Deer Creek–Cosumnes Area, Sacramento County, California.* Sacramento Junior College, Department of Anthropology, Bull. 1.

LOUD, L. L. 1918. *Ethnography and Archaeology of the Wiyot Territory.* "University of California Publications in American Archaeology and Ethnology," Vol. XIV, No. 3. Berkeley and Los Angeles.

MACCURDY, GEORGE GRANT (ed.). 1937. *Early Man: An International Symposium.* Philadelphia.

McGREGOR, JOHN C. 1941. *Southwestern Archaeology.* New York.

McGUIRE, J. D. 1892. "Material, Apparatus, and Processes of the Aboriginal Lapidary," *American Anthropologist*, V, No. 2, 165–76.

———. 1896. "A Study of the Primitive Methods of Drilling," *Annual Report of the United States National Museum for 1894*, pp. 623–756. Washington, D.C.

———. 1899. "Pipes and Smoking Customs of the American Aborigines, Based on Material in the United States National Museum," *Annual Report of the United States National Museum for 1897*, pp. 351–645. Washington, D.C.

MACKENZIE, ALEXANDER. 1902. *Voyages from Montreal through the Continent of North America to the Frozen and Pacific Oceans in 1789 and 1793.* 2 vols. New York.

McKERN, W. C. 1931. *A Wisconsin Variant of the Hopewell Culture.* "Bulletin of the Public Museum of the City of Milwaukee," Vol. X, No. 2.

———. 1937. "An Hypothesis for the Asiatic Origin of the Woodland Culture Pattern," *American Antiquity*, III, No. 2, 138–43.

———. 1942. "First Settlers of Wisconsin," *Wisconsin Magazine of History*, XXVI, No. 2, 153–69.

McLEOD, B. H. 1937. "An Examination of the Structure of Cast Copper Bells," Appendix III in *Excavations at Snaketown: Material Culture*, pp. 278–81. "Gila Pueblo, Medallion Papers," No. 25. Globe, Ariz.

MACNEISH, R. S. n.d. "The Faulkner Site." Department of Anthropology, University of Chicago. (MS.)

MALCOLM, ROY L. 1939. "Archaeological Remains, Supposedly Navaho, from Chaco Canyon, New Mexico," *American Antiquity*, V, No. 1, 4–20.

MANGELSDORF, P. C., and REEVES, R. G. 1939. *The Origin of Indian Corn and Its Relatives.* Texas Agricultural Experiment Station, Bull. 574. College Station, Tex.

MARTIN, GEORGE C. 1933. "The Big Bend Basket Maker," in *Big Bend Basket Makers Papers*, No. 1. Southwest Texas Archaeological Society of the Witte Memorial Museum, Bull. 1. San Antonio.

MARTIN, H. T. 1910. "Further Notes on the Pueblo Ruins of Scott County," *Kansas University Science Bulletin*, V, No. 2, 11–12.

MARTIN, PAUL S. 1936. *Lowry Ruin in Southwestern Colorado.* "Field Museum of Natural History, Anthropological Series," Vol. XXIII, No. 1. Chicago.

———. 1938. *Archaeological Work in the Ackmen-Lowry Area, Southwestern Colorado, 1937.* "Field Museum of Natural History, Anthropological Series," Vol. XXIII, No. 2. Chicago.

———. 1939. *Modified Basket Maker Sites in the Ackmen-Lowry Area, Southwestern Colorado.* "Field Museum of Natural History, Anthropological Series," Vol. XXIII, No. 3. Chicago.

———. 1940. *The SU Site: Excavations at a Mogollon Village, Western New Mexico, 1939.* "Field Museum of Natural History, Anthropological Series," Vol. XXXI, No. 1. Chicago.

———. 1943. *SU Site: Excavations at a Mogollon Village, Western New Mexico, Second Season, 1941.* "Field Museum of Natural History, Anthropological Series," Vol. XXXII, No. 2. Chicago.

MARTIN, PAUL S., and WILLIS, ELIZABETH S. 1940. *Anasazi Painted Pottery.* "Field Museum of Natural History, Anthropology Memoirs," Vol. V.

MASON, J. A. 1930. "Excavations of Eskimo Thule Culture Sites at Point Barrow, Alaska," *Proceedings of the Twenty-third International Congress of Americanists*, pp. 383–94. New York.

MASON, O. T. 1891. "Arrows and Arrow-makers: A Symposium," *American Anthropologist*, IV, No. 1, 45–74.

———. 1894. "North American Bows, Arrows, and Quivers," *Annual Report of the Smithsonian Institution for 1893*, pp. 631–79. Washington, D.C.

———. 1895. "Overlaying with Copper by the American Aborigines," *Proceedings of the United States National Museum*, XVII, 475–77.

———. 1904. "Aboriginal American Basketry," *Annual Report of the Smithsonian Institution for 1902*, Part II. Washington, D.C.

———. 1907. "Commerce," pp. 330–32 in *Handbook of American Indians*, ed. F. W. HODGE. Bureau of American Ethnology, Bull. 30, Part I. Washington, D.C.

MATHIASSEN, THERKEL. 1927. *Report of the Fifth Thule Expedition, 1921–24*, Vol. IV: *Archaeology of the Central Eskimos.* Copenhagen.

MATHIASSEN, THERKEL, and HOLTVED, ERIK. 1936. "The Eskimo Archaeology of Julianehaab District with a Brief Summary of the Prehistory of the Greenlanders," *Meddelelser om Grønland Kommissionen for Videnskabelige Undersøgelser 1 Grønland*, Bd. 118, No. 1. Copenhagen.

MERA, H. P. 1933. *A Proposed Revision of the Rio Grande Glaze-Paint Sequence.* "Laboratory of Anthropology, Technical Series, Archaeological Survey," Bull. 5. Sante Fe, N.M.

———. 1935. *Ceramic Clues to the Prehistory of North Central New Mexico.* "Laboratory of Anthropology, Technical Series, Archaeological Survey," Bull. 8. Santa Fe, N.M.

———. 1939. *Style Trends of Pueblo Pottery in the Rio Grande and Little Colorado Cultural Areas from the Sixteenth to the Nineteenth Century.* "Laboratory of Anthropology, Memoirs," Vol. III. Santa Fe, N.M.

———. 1940. *Population Changes in the Rio Grande Glaze-Paint Area.* "Laboratory of Anthropology, Technical Series, Archaeological Survey," Bull. 9. Santa Fe, N.M.

MILLS, W. C. 1902. "Excavations of the Adena Mound," *Ohio Archaeological and Historical Quarterly*, X, No. 4, 452–79.

———. 1907. "The Explorations of the Edwin Harness Mound," *Ohio Archaeological and Historical Quarterly*, XVI, No. 2, 113–93.

———. 1916. "Exploration of the Tremper Mound," *ibid.*, XXV, No. 3, 262–398.

———. 1922. "Exploration of the Mound City Group," *ibid.*, XXXI, No. 3, 423–584.

MOONEY, JAMES. 1928. "The Aboriginal Population of America North of Mexico," *Smithsonian Miscellaneous Collections*, LXXX, No. 7, 1–40.

MOORE, C. B. 1894–96. "Certain Sand Mounds of the St. Johns River, Florida," *Journal of the Academy of Natural Science of Philadelphia*, Vol. X, 5–103, 129–246. (For copper analysis, see pp. 213–41.)

———. 1899. "Certain Aboriginal Remains of the Alabama River," *Journal of the Academy of Natural Science of Philadelphia*, XI, No. 3, 289–348.

———. 1901. "Certain Aboriginal Remains of the Tombigbee River," *ibid.*, XI, No. 4, 497–514.

———. 1903. "Sheet-Copper from the Mounds Is Not Necessarily of European Origin," *American Anthropologist*, N.S., V, No. 1, 27–49.

———. 1905. "Certain Aboriginal Remains of the Black Warrior River," *Journal of the Academy of Natural Science of Philadelphia*, XIII, 125–244.

———. 1907. "Moundville Revisited," *ibid.*, pp. 337–405.

———. 1908. "Certain Mounds of Arkansas and Mississippi," *ibid.*, Part I, pp. 481–605.

———. 1910. "Antiquities of the St. Francis, White, and Black Rivers, Arkansas," *ibid.*, XIV, Parts I and II, 254–364.

———. 1916. "Some Aboriginal Sites on Green River, Kentucky," *ibid.*, XVI, 440–87.

MOOREHEAD, W. K. 1910. *The Stone Age in North America*. 2 vols. Boston and New York.

———. 1917. *Stone Ornaments of the American Indians*. Andover, Mass.

———. 1922. *The Hopewell Mound Group of Ohio*. "Field Museum of Natural History, Anthropological Series," Vol. VI, No. 5. Chicago.

———. 1931. *Archaeology of the Arkansas River Valley*. Department of Archaeology, Phillips Academy, Andover, Massachusetts. New Haven, Conn.

———. 1932. *Etowa Papers*. Department of Archaeology, Phillips Academy, Andover, Massachusetts. New Haven, Conn.

MORGAN, R. G., and ELLIS, H. H. 1943. "The Fairport Harbor Village Site," *Ohio Archaeological and Historical Quarterly*, LII, No. 1, 1–62.

MORRIS, EARL H. 1928. *The Aztec Ruin*. "American Museum of Natural History, Anthropological Papers," Vol. XXVI. New York.

———. 1939. *Archaeological Studies in the La Plata District*. Carnegie Institution of Washington Pub. 519. Washington, D.C.

———. 1941. "Annual Report of the Chairman of the Division of Historical Research," *Fortieth Yearbook of the Carnegie Institution of Washington*, pp. 304–6. Washington, D.C.

MORRIS, EARL H., and BURGH, ROBERT F. 1941. *Anasazi Basketry: Basket Maker II through Pueblo III*. Carnegie Institution of Washington Pub. 533. Washington, D.C.

MORSS, NOEL. 1931. *The Ancient Culture of the Fremont River in Utah*. "Papers of the Peabody Museum of American Archaeology and Ethnology," Vol. XII, No. 3. Cambridge, Mass.

MOTT, MILDRED. 1938. "Relation of Historic Indian Tribes to Archaeological Manifestations in Iowa," *Iowa Journal of History and Politics*, XXXVI, No. 3, 227–314.

MULLOY, WILLIAM. 1942. *The Hagen Site: A Prehistoric Village on the Lower Yellowstone.* "University of Montana Publications in Social Sciences," Vol. I. Missoula.

MYER, W. E. 1928. "Two Prehistoric Villages in Middle Tennessee," *Bureau of American Ethnology, Forty-first Annual Report*, pp. 485–614. Washington, D.C.

NESBITT, PAUL H. 1931. *The Ancient Mimbreños, New Mexico*, "Logan Museum Bulletin," No. 4. Beloit, Wis.

———. 1938. *The Starkweather Ruin, New Mexico.* "Logan Museum Publications in Anthropology," Bull. 6. Beloit, Wis.

NEUMANN, GEORGE. 1943. "The Varieties of Prehistoric Indians of Eastern United States," in *El Norte de Mexico y el sur de Estados Unidos: tercera reuinon de mesa redonda sobre problemas antropologicos de Mexico y Centro America, 25 de Agosto a 2 de Septiembre de 1943*, pp. 171–79. Castillo de Chapultepec, Mexico, D.F.: Sociedad Mexican de Antropologia.

NIBLACK, A. P. 1890. "The Coast Indians of Southern Alaska and Northern British Columbia," *Annual Report of the United States National Museum for 1888*, pp. 225–386. Washington, D.C.

NORDENSKÏOLD, G. 1893. *The Cliff Dwellers of the Mesa Verde, Southwestern Colorado.* English trans. by D. LLOYD MORGAN. Stockholm.

NUSBAUM, J. L. 1922. *Basket Maker Cave in Kane County, Utah.* "Museum of the American Indian, Heye Foundation, Indian Notes and Monographs, Miscellaneous," No. 29. New York.

OLSON, R. L. 1930. *Chumash Prehistory.* "University of California Publications in American Archaeology and Ethnology," Vol. XXVIII, No. 1. Berkeley and Los Angeles.

———. 1934. "Recent Archaeological Work on the Pacific Coast," *Proceedings of the Fifth Pacific Science Congress*, pp. 2841–46.

O'NEALE, LILA M. 1937. *Archaeological Explorations in Peru: Textiles of Early Nazca Period.* Part III. "Field Museum of Natural History, Anthropology Memoirs," Vol. II, No. 3. Chicago.

ORR, KENNETH G. 1939. "Field Report on Excavation of Indian Villages in the Vicinity of the Spiro Mound," *Oklahoma Prehistorian*, II, No. 11, 8–15.

———. 1941. "The Eufaula Mound: Contributions to the Spiro Focus," *ibid.*, IV, No. 1, 2–15.

PACKARD, R. L. 1893. "Pre-Columbian Copper-mining in North America," *Annual Report of the Smithsonian Institution for 1892*, pp. 175–98. Washington, D.C.

PARSONS, ELSIE CLEWS. 1939. *Pueblo Indian Religion.* 2 vols. "University of Chicago Publications in Anthropology, Ethnological Series." Chicago.

PATTERSON, J. T. 1937. *Boat-shaped Artifacts of the Gulf Southwest States.* "Bulletin of the University of Texas, Anthropological Papers," Vol. I, No. 2, 3732.

PEABODY, CHARLES, and MOOREHEAD, W. K. 1904. *Explorations of Jacobs Cavern, McDonald County, Missouri.* Phillips Academy, Department of Archaeology, Bull. 1. Andover, Mass.

PEPPER, GEORGE H. 1920. *Pueblo Bonito.* "American Museum of Natural History, Anthropological Papers," Vol. XXVII. New York.

PERRY, JAY. 1939. "Notes on a Type of Indian Burial in the Mid-Columbia River District of Central Washington," *New Mexico Anthropologist*, III, No. 5, 80–83.

PHILLIPS, G. B. 1925. "The Primitive Copper Industry of America," *American Anthropologist*, XXVII, No. 2, 284–89.

PHILLIPS, PHILIP. 1940. "Middle American Influences on the Archaeology of the Southeastern United States," in *The Maya and Their Neighbors*, pp. 349–67. New York.

POND, A. W. 1930. *Primitive Methods of Working Stone Based on Experiments of Halvor L. Skavlem.* "Logan Museum Bulletin," No. 2, Part I. Beloit, Wis.

POPE, S. T. 1922. *A Study of Bows and Arrows.* "University of California Publications in American Archaeology and Ethnology," Vol. XIII, No. 9. Berkeley and Los Angeles.

PUTNAM, F. W. 1881. "Notes on the Copper Objects from North and South America Contained in the Collections of the Peabody Museum," *Peabody Museum of American Archaeology and Ethnology, Fifteenth Annual Report*, III, No. 2, 83–148.

———. 1887. "The Way Bone Fish-Hooks Were Made in the Little Miami Valley," *Peabody Museum of American Archaeology and Ethnology, Twentieth Annual Report*, III, No. 7, 581–86.

QUIMBY, G. I. 1941. *The Goodall Focus, an Analysis of Ten Hopewellian Components in Michigan and Indiana.* "Indian Historical Society, Prehistory Research Series," Vol. IX, No. 1. Indianapolis.

———. 1942. "The Natchezan Culture Type," *American Antiquity*, VII, No. 3, 255–75.

———. 1944. *Aleutian Islanders, Eskimos of the North Pacific.* "Chicago Natural History Museum, Anthropology Leaflet," No. 35. Chicago.

———. 1945a. "Periods of Prehistoric Art in the Aleutian Islands," *American Antiquity*, XI, No. 2, 76–79.

———. 1945b. "Pottery from the Aleutian Islands," *Fieldiana, Anthropology*, XXXVI, No. 1, 1–13. Chicago: Chicago Natural History Museum.

RAINEY, F. G. 1941a. *Eskimo Prehistory: The Okvik Site on the Punuk Islands.* "American Museum of Natural History, Anthropological Papers," Vol. XXXVII, Part IV. New York.

———. 1941b. "The Ipiutak Culture at Point Hope, Alaska," *American Anthropologist*, XLIII, No. 3, 364–75.

RAY, V. F. 1932a. "Pottery on the Middle Columbia," *American Anthropologist*, XXXIV, No. 1, 127–33.

———. 1932b. *The Sanpoil and Nespelem: Salishan People of Northwestern Washington.* "University of Washington Publications in Anthropology," Vol. V. Seattle.

———. 1936. "Native Villages and Groupings of the Columbia Basin," *Pacific Northwest Quarterly*, XXVII, 99–152.

———. 1939. *Cultural Relations in the Plateau of Northwestern America.* "Frederick Webb Hodge Anniversary Publication Fund, Southwest Museum," Vol. III. Los Angeles.

———. 1942. *Cultural Element Distributions: XXII–Plateau.* "University of California, Anthropological Records," Vol. VIII, No. 2. Berkeley and Los Angeles.

RAY, V. F., et al. 1938. "Tribal Distribution in Eastern Oregon and Adjacent Regions," *American Anthropologist*, XL, No. 3, 384–415.

REITER, PAUL. 1938. *The Jemez Pueblo of Unshagi, New Mexico*, Parts I and II. "University of New Mexico and the School of American Research Monographs," Vol. I, Nos. 4 and 5. Santa Fe, N.M.

RINALDO, JOHN B. 1941. "An Analysis of Prehistoric Anasazi Culture Change." Unpublished dissertation, University of Chicago Libraries.

RITCHIE, W. A. 1938. "A Perspective of Northeastern Archaeology," *American Antiquity*, IV, No. 2, 94–112.

———. 1944. *The Pre-Iroquoian Occupations of New York State.* "Rochester Museum Memoir," No. 1. Rochester, N.Y.

RITZENTHALER, ROBERT. n.d. "Excavations of an Old Copper Site in Wisconsin." (MS.)

ROBERTS, FRANK H. H., JR. 1929. *Shabik'eshchee Village: A Late Basket Maker Site in Chaco Canyon, New Mexico.* Bureau of American Ethnology, Bull. 92. Washington, D.C.

———. 1930. *Early Pueblo Ruins in the Piedra District, Southwestern Colorado.* Bureau of American Ethnology, Bull. 96. Washington, D.C.

———. 1931. *The Ruins at Kiatuthlanna, Eastern Arizona.* Bureau of American Ethnology, Bull. 100. Washington, D.C.

———. 1932. *The Village of the Great Kivas on the Zuñi Reservation, New Mexico.* Bureau of American Ethnology, Bull. 111. Washington, D.C.

———. 1939a. *Archaeological Remains in the Whitewater District, Eastern Arizona,* Part I: *House Types.* Bureau of American Ethnology, Bull. 121. Washington, D.C.

———. 1939b. "The Folsom Problem in American Archaeology," *Annual Report of the Smithsonian Institution for 1938*, pp. 531–46. Washington, D.C. (Reprint of revised article from *Early Man*.)

———. 1940a. *Archaeological Remains in the Whitewater District, Eastern Arizona,* Part II: *Artifacts and Burials.* Bureau of American Ethnology, Bull. 126. Washington, D.C.

———. 1940b. "Developments in the Problem of the North American Paleo-Indian," in *Essays in Historical Anthropology of North America*, pp. 51–116. "Smithsonian Miscellaneous Collections," Vol. C. Washington, D.C.

———. 1941. "Latest Excavations at Lindenmeier Site Add Information on the Folsom Complex," *Explorations and Field Work of the Smithsonian Institution in 1940*, pp. 79–82. Washington, D.C.

ROGERS, D. B. 1929. *Prehistoric Man of the Santa Barbara Coast.* Santa Barbara, Calif.

ROGERS, M. J. 1929a. *Report of an Archaeological Reconnaissance in the Mohave Sink Region.* "San Diego Museum, Archaeology Series," Vol. I, No. 1. San Diego.

———. 1929b. "The Stone Art of the San Diegnito Plateau," *American Anthropologist*, XXXI, No. 3, 454–67.

———. 1939. *Early Lithic Industries of the Lower Basin of the Colorado River and Adjacent Desert Areas.* "San Diego Museum Papers," No. 3.

———. 1941. "Aboriginal Cultural Relations between Southern California and the Southwest," *San Diego Museum Bulletin*, V, No. 3, 1–6.

———. 1945. "An Outline of Yuman Prehistory," *Southwestern Journal of Anthropology*, I, No. 2, 167–98.

ROWLEY, GRAHAM. 1940. "The Dorset Culture of the Eastern Arctic," *American Anthropologist*, XLII, No. 3, 490–99.

SAFFORD, W. E. 1927. "Our Heritage from the American Indian," *Annual Report of the Smithsonian Institution for 1926*, pp. 405–11. Washington, D.C.

SAPIR, EDWARD. 1916. *Time Perspective in Aboriginal American Culture: A Study in Method.* "Geological Survey of Canada, Anthropological Series," No. 13. Ottawa.

SAYLES, E. B. 1935. *An Archaeological Survey of Texas.* "Gila Pueblo, Medallion Papers," No. 17. Globe, Ariz.

———. 1936a. *An Archaeological Survey of Chihuahua, Mexico.* "Gila Pueblo, Medallion Papers," No. 22. Globe, Ariz.

———. 1936b. *Some Southwestern Pottery Types*, Series V. "Gila Pueblo, Medallion Papers," No. 21. Globe, Ariz. (A description of Chihuahua pottery.)

SAYLES, E. B., and ANTEVS, ERNST. 1941. *The Cochise Culture.* "Gila Pueblo, Medallion Papers," No. 29. Globe, Ariz.

SCHENCK, W. E., and DAWSON, E. J. 1929. *Archaeology of Northern San Joaquin Valley.* "University of California Publications in American Archaeology and Ethnology," Vol. XXV, No. 4. Berkeley and Los Angeles.

SCHMIDT, KARL P. 1931. "On the Zoogeography of the Holarctic Region," *Lingnan Science Journal* (Canton, China), X, No. 4, 441–49.

SELTZER, CARL C. 1944. *Racial Prehistory in the Southwest and the Hawikuh Zunis.* "Papers of the Peabody Museum of American Archaeology and Ethnology," Vol. XXIII, No. 1. Cambridge, Mass.

SETZLER, F. M. 1933a. "Hopewell Type Pottery from Louisiana," *Journal of the Washington Academy of Sciences*, XXIII, No. 3. 149–53.

———. 1933b. "Pottery of the Hopewell Type from Louisiana," *United States National Museum, Proceedings*, Vol. LXXXII, No. 2693, Art. 22, pp. 1–21.

———. 1935. "A Prehistoric Cave Culture in Southwestern Texas," *American Anthropologist*, XXXVII, No. 1, 104–10.

SHETRONE, H. C. 1930. *The Mound Builders.* New York.

SHETRONE, H. C., and GREENMAN, E. F. 1931. "Exploration of the Seip Group of Prehistoric Earthworks," *Ohio Archaeological and Historical Quarterly*, XL, No. 3, 349–509.

SMITH, ELMER R. 1941. Archaeology of Deadman Cave, Utah. "Bulletin of the University of Utah," Vol. XXXII, No. 4. Salt Lake City.

SMITH, G. V. 1893. "The Use of Flint Blades To Work Pine Wood," *Annual Report of the Smithsonian Institution for 1891*, pp. 601–5. Washington, D.C.

SMITH, H. I. 1899. *Archaeology of Lytton, British Columbia.* "American Museum of Natural History, Memoirs," Vol. II, Part III. New York.

———. 1900. *Archaeology of the Thompson River Region, British Columbia.* "American Museum of Natural History, Memoirs," Vol. II, Part VI. New York.

———. 1903. *Shell-Heaps of the Lower Fraser River.* "American Museum of Natural History, Memoirs," Vol. IV, Part IV. New York.

———. 1907. *Archaeology of the Gulf of Georgia and Puget Sound.* "American Museum of Natural History, Memoirs," Vol. IV. Part VI. New York.

———. 1910. *Archaeology of the Yakima Valley.* "American Museum of Natural History, Anthropological Papers," Vol. VI, Part I. New York.

———. 1924. "Trephined Indian Skulls from British Columbia and Washington," *American Journal of Physical Anthropology*, VII, No. 4, 447–52.

———. 1929. "Kitchen-Middens of the Pacific Coast of Canada," *National Museum of Canada, Anthropological Report for 1927*, Bull. 56, pp. 42–46. Ottawa.

SMITH, H. I., and FOWKE, GEORGE. 1900. *Cairns of British Columbia and Washington.* "American Museum of Natural History, Memoirs," Vol. IV, No. 2. New York.

SPIER, LESLIE. 1917. *An Outline for a Chronology of Zuñi Ruins.* "American Museum of Natural History, Anthropological Papers," Vol. XVIII, Part III. New York.

SPIER, LESLIE. 1918. *Notes on Some Little Colorado Ruins.* "American Museum of Natural History, Anthropological Papers," Vol. XVIII, Part IV. New York.

———. 1919. *Ruins in the White Mountains, Arizona.* "American Museum of Natural History, Anthropological Papers," Vol. XVIII, Part V. New York.

———. 1930. *Klamath Ethnography.* "University of California Publications in American Archaeology and Ethnology," Vol. XXX. Berkeley and Los Angeles.

SPINDEN, H. J. 1908. "The Nez Percé Indians," *American Anthropological Association, Memoirs,* II, 165–274.

———. 1930. "The Population of Ancient America," *Annual Report of the Smithsonian Institution for 1929,* pp. 451–71. Washington, D.C.

STALLINGS, W. S., JR. 1939. *Dating Prehistoric Ruins by Tree-Rings.* "Laboratory of Anthropology, General Series," Bull. 8. Santa Fe, N.M.

———. 1941. "A Basket Maker II Date from Cave du Pont, Utah," *Tree-Ring Bulletin,* VIII, No. 1, 3–6.

STEARNS, R. E. C. 1889. "Ethno-conchology: A Study of Primitive Money," *Report of the United States National Museum for 1887,* pp. 297–334. Washington, D.C.

STEWARD, JULIAN H. 1933. *Early Inhabitants of Western Utah,* Part I: *Mounds and House Types.* "Bulletin of the University of Utah," Vol. XXIII, No. 7. Salt Lake City.

———. 1936. *Pueblo Material Culture in Western Utah.* "University of New Mexico Bulletin, Anthropological Series," Vol. I, No. 3. Albuquerque, N.M.

———. 1937. *Ancient Caves of the Great Salt Lake Region.* Bureau of American Ethnology, Bull. 116. Washington, D.C.

———. 1940. "Native Cultures of the Intermontane (Great Basin) Area," in *Essays in Historical Anthropology of North America,* pp. 445–502. "Smithsonian Miscellaneous Collections," Vol. C. Washington, D.C.

STIRLING, M. W. 1942. *Origin Myth of Acoma and Other Records.* Bureau of American Ethnology, Bull. 135. Washington, D.C.

STRONG, W. D. 1935. *An Introduction to Nebraska Archaeology.* "Smithsonian Miscellaneous Collections," Vol. XCIII, No. 10. Washington, D.C.

———. 1940. "From History to Prehistory in the Northern Great Plains," in *Essays in Historical Anthropology of North America,* pp. 353–94. "Smithsonian Miscellaneous Collections," Vol. C. Washington, D.C.

STRONG, W. D.; SCHENCK, W. E.; and STEWARD, H. H. 1930. Archaeology of the Dalles-Deschutes Region. "University of California Publications in American Archaeology and Ethnology," Vol. XXIX, No. 1. Berkeley and Los Angeles.

SWANTON, J. R. 1907. "Media of Exchange," pp. 446–48 in *Handbook of American Indians,* ed. F. W. HODGE. Bureau of American Ethnology, Bull. 30, Part I. Washington, D.C.

TEIT, J. H. 1900. *The Thompson Indians of British Columbia.* "American Museum of Natural History, Memoirs," ed. FRANZ BOAS. Vol. II, Part IV, New York.

THOMPSON, DAVID. 1916. *David Thompson's Narrative of His Explorations in Western America, 1784–1812,* ed. J. B. TYRRELL. Toronto.

THRUSTON, G. P. 1897. *The Antiquities of Tennessee.* Cincinnati, Ohio.

TITIEV, MISCHA. 1944. *Old Oraibi: A Study of the Hopi Indians of Third Mesa.* "Papers of the Peabody Museum of American Archaeology and Ethnology," Vol. XXII, No. 1. Cambridge, Mass.

TITTERINGTON, P. F. 1935. "Certain Bluff Mounds of Western Jersey County, Illinois," *American Antiquity,* I, No. 1, 6–46.

UNDERHILL, RUTH. 1945. *Pueblo Crafts*. "Publication of the Education Division, United States Indian Service, Indian Handcrafts," No. 7. Phoenix, Ariz.

WALKER, E. F. 1945. "The Dig at Big Tujunga Wash," *Masterkey*, XIX, 188–93.

WALKER, W. M. 1932. "The Cave Culture of Arkansas," *Explorations and Field Work of the Smithsonian Institution in 1931*, pp. 159–68. Washington, D.C.

———. 1935. *A Caddo Burial Site at Natchitoches, Louisiana*. "Smithsonian Institution, Miscellaneous Collections," Vol. XCIV, No. 14. Washington, D.C.

———. 1936. *The Troyville Mounds, Catahoula Parish, Louisiana*. Bureau of American Ethnology, Bull. 113. Washington, D.C.

WARING, ANTONIO, JR. n.d. "The Bilbo Site." (MS.)

WARING, ANTONIO, JR., and HOLDER, PRESTON. 1945. "A Prehistoric Ceremonial Complex in the Southeastern United States," *American Anthropologist*, XLVII, No. 1, 1–34.

WATSON, DON. 1940. *Cliff Palace: The Story of an Ancient City*. Ann Arbor, Mich.

WEBB, C. H. 1944. "Stone Vessels from a Northeast Louisiana Site," *American Antiquity*, IX, No. 4, 386–94.

WEBB, C. H., and DODD, MONROE. 1939. "Further Excavations of the Gehagan Mound: Connections with a Florida Culture," *Texas Archaeological and Paleontological Society Bulletin*, XI, 92–127.

———. 1941. "Pottery Types from the Belcher Mound Site," *ibid.*, XIII, 88–116.

WEBB, W. S. 1938. *An Archaeological Survey of Norris Basin in Eastern Tennessee*. Bureau of American Ethnology, Bull. 118. Washington, D.C.

———. 1939. *An Archaeological Survey of Wheeler Basin on the Tennessee River in Northern Alabama*. Bureau of American Ethnology, Bull. 122. Washington, D.C.

———. 1940. *The Wright Mounds, Montgomery County, Kentucky*. "University of Kentucky Reports in Anthropology and Archaeology," Vol. V, No. 1. Lexington.

———. 1941a. *Mount Horeb Earthworks and Drake Mound, Fayette County, Kentucky*. "University of Kentucky Reports in Anthropology and Archaeology," Vol. V, No. 2. Lexington.

———. 1941b. *The Morgan Stone Mound, Bath County, Kentucky*. "University of Kentucky Reports in Anthropology and Archaeology," Vol. V, No. 3. Lexington.

———. 1942. *The C. and O. Mounds at Paintsville (Johnson County, Kentucky)*. "University of Kentucky Reports in Anthropology and Archaeology," Vol. V, No. 4. Lexington.

———. 1943a. *The Crigler Mounds and the Hartman Mound, Boone County, Kentucky*. "University of Kentucky Reports in Anthropology and Archaeology," Vol. V, No. 6. Lexington.

———. 1943b. *The Riley Mound and the Landing Mound*. "University of Kentucky Reports in Anthropology and Archaeology," Vol. V, No. 7. Lexington.

WEBB, W. S., and DEJARNETTE, DAVID L. 1942. *Archeological Survey of Pickwick Basin in the Adjacent Portions of the States of Alabama, Mississippi, and Tennessee*. Bureau of American Ethnology, Bull. 129. Washington, D.C.

WEBB, W. S., and ELLIOT, J. B. 1942. *The Robbins Mounds, Boone County, Kentucky*. "University of Kentucky Reports in Anthropology and Archaeology," Vol. V, No. 5. Lexington.

WEBB, W. S., and FUNKHOUSER, W. D. 1932. *Archaeological Survey of Kentucky*. "University of Kentucky Reports in Anthropology and Archaeology," Vol. II. Lexington.

WEBB, W. S., and HAAG, W. G. 1939. *The Chiggerville Site, Site 1; Ohio County,*

Kentucky. "University of Kentucky Reports in Anthropology and Archaeology," Vol. IV, No. 1. Lexington.

WEBB, W. S., and HOAG, W. G. 1940. *Cypress Creek Villages, Sites 11 and 12, McLean County, Kentucky.* "University of Kentucky Reports in Anthropology and Archaeology," Vol. IV. No. 2. Lexington.

WEDEL, W. R. 1938. "Hopewellian Remains near Kansas City, Missouri," *Proceedings of the United States National Museum,* LXXXVI, 99–106. Washington, D.C.

———. 1940a. "Culture Sequences in the Central Great Plains," in *Essays in Historical Anthropology of North America,* pp. 291–352. "Smithsonian Miscellaneous Collections," Vol. C. Washington, D.C.

———. 1940b. "Archaeological Exploration in Western Kansas," *Smithsonian Institution Explorations and Field Work in 1939,* pp. 83–86. Washington, D.C.

———. 1941a. *Environment and Native Subsistence Economies in the Central Great Plains.* "Smithsonian Miscellaneous Collections," Vol. CI, No. 3. Washington, D.C.

———. 1941b. "In Search of Coronado's Province of Quivira," *Smithsonian Institution Explorations and Field Work in 1940,* pp. 71–74. Washington, D.C.

———. 1941c. *Archeological Investigations at Buena Vista Lake, Kern County, California.* Bureau of American Ethnology, Bull. 130. Washington, D.C.

———. 1942. *Archeological Remains in Central Kansas and Their Possible Bearing on the Location of Quivira.* "Smithsonian Miscellaneous Collections," Vol. CI, No. 7. Washington, D.C.

———. 1943. *Archeological Investigations in Platte and Clay Counties, Missouri.* United States National Museum, Bull. 183. Washington, D.C.

WELTFISH, GENE. 1930. "Prehistoric North American Basketry Techniques and Modern Distributions," *American Anthropologist,* XXXII, No. 3, 454–95.

WEST, G. A. 1927. "Exploration in Navajo Canyon, Arizona," *Year Book of the Public Museum of the City of Milwaukee, Report for 1925,* V, 7–39.

———. 1929. *Copper: Its Mining and Use by the Aborigines of the Lake Superior Region.* "Bulletin of the Public Museum of the City of Milwaukee," Vol. X, No. 1.

———. 1932. *Exceptional Prehistoric Copper Implements.* "Bulletin of the Public Museum of the City of Milwaukee," Vol. X, No. 4.

WEYER, E. M., JR. 1929. *An Aleutian Burial.* "American Museum of Natural History, Anthropological Papers," Vol. XXXI, Part III. Washington, D.C.

———. 1930. *Archaeological Material from the Village Site at Hot Springs, Port Möller, Alaska.* "American Museum of Natural History, Anthropological Papers," Vol. XXXI, Part IV. Washington, D.C.

———. 1932. *The Eskimos, Their Environment and Folkways.* New Haven, Conn.

WHITE, LESLIE A. 1932a. "The Acoma Indians," *Bureau of American Ethnology, Forty-seventh Annual Report,* pp. 31, 49, 73. Washington, D.C.

———. 1932b. *Pueblo of San Felipe.* "Memoirs of the American Anthropological Association," No. 38. Menasha, Wis.

———. 1935. *Pueblo of Santo Domingo, New Mexico.* "Memoirs of the American Anthropological Association," No. 43. Menasha, Wis.

———. 1942. *Pueblo of Santa Ana, New Mexico.* "Memoirs of the American Anthropological Association," No. 60. (*American Anthropologist,* Vol. XLIV, No. 4, Part II.)

WHITTLESEY, CHARLES. 1863. *Ancient Mining on the Shores of Lake Superior.* "Smithsonian Contributions to Knowledge," Vol. XIII, No. 155. Washington, D.C.

WILFORD, L. A. 1941. "A Tentative Classification of the Prehistoric Cultures of Minnesota," *American Antiquity*, VI, No. 3, 231–49.

WILLEY, G. R. 1939. "Ceramic Stratigraphy in a Georgia Village Site," *American Antiquity*, V, No. 2, 140–47.

———. 1945. "The Weeden Island Culture: A Preliminary Definition," *ibid.*, X, No. 3, 225–54.

WILLEY, G. R., and PHILLIPS, PHILIP. 1944. "Negative-painted Pottery from Crystal River, Florida," *American Antiquity*, X, No. 2, 173–85.

WILLEY, G. R., and WOODBURY, R. G. 1942. "A Chronological Outline for the Northwest Florida Coast," *American Antiquity*, VII, No. 3, 232–54.

WILLOUGHBY, C. C. 1903. "Primitive Metal Working," *American Anthropologist*, V, No. 1, 55–57.

WILSON, CURTIS L., and SAYRE, M. 1935. "A Brief Metallographic Study of Primitive Copper Work," *American Antiquity*, I, No. 2, 109–12.

WILSON, THOMAS. 1899. "Arrowpoints, Spearheads, and Knives of Prehistoric Times," *Annual Report of the United States National Museum for 1897*, pp. 811–988. Washington, D.C.

WINSHIP, GEORGE PARKER. 1896. "The Coronado Expedition," *Bureau of American Ethnology, Fourteenth Annual Report*, Part I, pp. 329–613. Washington, D.C.

WINTEMBERG, W. J. 1939–40. "Eskimo Sites of the Dorset Culture in Newfoundland," *American Antiquity*, V, No. 2, 83–102, and No. 4, pp. 309–33.

WISSLER, CLARK. 1938. *The American Indian*. 3d ed. New York.

WOODWARD, ARTHUR. 1931. *The Grew Site (Arizona)*. "Los Angeles Museum of History, Science, and Art, Occasional Papers," No. 1. Los Angeles.

WYMAN, JEFFRIES. 1875. *Fresh-Water Shell Mounds of the St. John's River, Florida*. Salem, Mass.: Peabody Academy of Science.

INDEX

INDEX

Abajo Red-on-Orange pottery, 115–16
Abalone (haliotis): Central California, 430; trade in, 70, 73, 74
Abraders (abrading stones), 414; Browns Valley, 299; Coles Creek, 414; Dismal River, 322; Frontenac, 242; Mira Creek. 324; New York Hopewell, 250
Abrading stones; *see* Abraders
Acculturation, definition of, 159
Acoma, 146, 159, 160; kivas, 136
Aconite poison: Koniag, 498; Late Aleut, 495
Acorns, 25; California. 427; Faulkner, 289; Lamar, 385; Laurentian I, 244; trade in, 74
Adamsville site, 192
Adena culture, 262, 263–67
Adobe wall; *see* Walls
Adzes: Birnirk, 487; Dorset, 504; Early Coastal, 274; Early Kachemak Bay, 500; Fort Ancient, 286; Frontenac, 242; Hohokam, Classic, 193; Hopewell, 270 (and Fig. 74); Intrusive Mound, Ohio, 279; Ipiutak, 483; Kansas Hopewell, 326; Key Marco, 395, 396 (Fig. 94); Lamoka, 241; Late Kachemak Bay, 501; Laurentian I, 244, 245 (Fig. 69); Macon Plateau, 384; manufacture of, 31; Middle Columbia region, 456; New York Hopewell, 250; Northwest Coast area, 466, 468, 469; Okvik, 475; Old Bering Sea, 478; Old Copper, 300, 301 (Fig. 83); Old Iroquois, 256; Orient, 248; Point Peninsula, 252; Post-Punuk, 488; Pre-Koniag, 497; Snake-Clearwater Region, 460; Tchefuncte, 402 (and Fig. 97); Thompson River region, 454; Upper Columbia region, 448 (Fig. 107), 450
Agriculture: advantages of, 234; antiquity, eastern North America, 234; appearance of, 518, 519; areas, 518; Baumer, 290; beginnings of, 80, 234; California area, 427; Coles Creek, farmers, 412; Crystal Island, 392; culture changes by, 234–35; eastern North America, second stage, 233; Florida area, 391; Fort Walton, farming, 394; Georgia area, 388; Illinois Hopewell, 293; invented in North America, 21; Irene, 381; Lamar, 385; Lewis, 294; Lower Mississippi Valley area, 399; Macon Plateau area, 383; Marksville, farming, 406; Middle Mississippi, 294; Mogollon-Mimbres, Pine Lawn, 201; Natchezan, 418; Northwest Coast area, 464; Ocmulgee Fields, 387; Ohio area, 288; Plaquemine, farming, 416; Red Ocher, 291; Santa Rosa–Swift Creek, 392; southeastern Nevada, 227; southeastern Oregon, 228; Swift Creek, 377; Tchefuncte, 401; Weeden Island, 393; Wilmington, 375; Younge, 280
Alabama, 41, 345, 347, 353, 366, 405, 409
Alaska, 20, 463, 470, 473, 474, 477, 484, 486, 487, 490, 495, 499, 505, 508
Aleut cultures, 490–96; *see also* Early Aleut culture; Late Aleut culture; Middle Aleut culture
Aleut pottery, independent origin, 519
Aleut stone lamps, 519
Aleutian Islands, 490, 495
Alexander culture, 347–48
Algonkian Indians, 287
Alligator teeth, trade in, 72, 278
Alloying copper, 42
Alma Neck-banded pottery, 206, 209
Alma Plain pottery, 116, 208, 212
Alma Punched pottery, 207, 208
Alma Rough pottery, 202
Alma Scored pottery, 206
Altars, Navaho, 158
Amargosa culture, 438
Amazonian region, 80
America, 15
American Indian, origin of, 16–22
Amerind, 15
Amsden, Charles, 25
Amulets: Central California, 430; Point Peninsula, 252
Anasazi: areas, 215; chronology, 513, 514 (Fig. 122); culture, 101–67, 198; decline, 146; influences on: Big Bend Cave, 221; Hohokam, 170; Mogollon-Mimbres, 208, 210, 211; Puebloid, 224; southeastern Nevada, 228; southeastern Oregon, 227; meaning of name, 101; periods: Basket Maker, 103–11; Modified Basket Maker, 111–20; Pueblo I, 120–24; Pueblo II, 124–29; Pueblo III, 129–49; Pueblo IV, 149–59; Pueblo V, 159–67; pottery, 51, 193, 202, 212, 519 (*see also* Pottery, Anasazi culture); sandals, 216; shell trade, 69; skulls, 98; *see also* Houses; Livelihood; Ornaments; Tools, utensils, and weapons; Villages
Angel site, 283, 284
Animal bones; *see* Bones, animal

Animals: domesticated, 226; extinct, 82, 83; southeastern Nevada, extinct, 227; *see also* Bison; Dire wolf; Domesticated animals; Mammoth; Sloth; Tapir
Annealing, copper, 43; Hopewell, 272
Antelope Creek culture, 333
Anthropoid apes, 20
Anthropology: definition of, 3; significance of, 4
Antimony, 45
Antiquity of Indians, 79
Antler tool, chipping with, 30–31
Anvils, pottery, 53; Hohokam, 173; Nebraska, 330; Oneota, 316; Point Peninsula, 253
Apache Indians, 196
Apes; *see* Anthropoid apes
Apima, Browns Valley, 299
Appalachian Mountains, 42
Aprons: Anasazi, Modified Basket Maker, 119; Pueblo III, 140
Arbors, Indian Knoll, 260
Archaic Indians, Ohio area, 287
Archaic period, 67; Central California, 429–30; eastern North America, dates, 92; Florida area, 391; Georgia area, 369–73, 388; Illinois area, 289–91; Lower Mississippi Valley area, 399, 400–401; Middle Southern area, 344, 345–47, 367; Northeastern area, 239–46; Ohio area, 259–62; Ozark Plateau area, 338–39; Plains area, 319, 320–22; Wisconsin-Minnesota area, 298–303
Archeology, work of, 3
Architecture: invention, 21; Mogollon-Mimbres, Three Circle, 208; *see also* Houses; Temples; Villages
Area: Adena, 263; Alexander, 347; Anasazi, Basket Maker, 103; Anasazi, Modified Basket Maker, 111; Anasazi, Pueblo I, 121; Anasazi, Pueblo II, 124; Anasazi, Pueblo III, 129; Anasazi, Pueblo IV, 149; Aztalan, 313; Baumer, 290; Birnirk, 486; Browns Valley site, 299; Caddo, 421–24; California, 427–41; California, chronology, 440 (Chart XV); Candy Creek, 348; central California, 428; Clam River, 312; Cochise, 85; Coles Creek, 411; Copell, 400; Copena, 351; Deptford, 374; Dismal River, 331; Dorset, 503; Early Aleut, 490; Early Coastal, 247; Early Kachemak Bay, 499; Early Macon, 370; Eastern Eskimo, 503–9; Effigy Mound, 303; Florida, 390–98; Folsom, 83; Fort Ancient, 285; Frontenac, 241; Georgia, 369–89; Glacial Kame, 262; Hamilton, 350; Hohokam, 168–69; Hohokam, Classic, 188; Hohokam, Colonial, 174; Hohokam, Sedentary, 182; Hopewell, 267; Illinois, 289–96; Indian Knoll, 259; Intrusive Mound, 278; Inugsuk, 508; Ipiutak, 481; Irene, 380; Kansas Hopewell, 325; Keshena, 310; Key Marco, 395; Koniag, 498; Lamar, 385; Lamoka, 240; Late Aleut, 495; Late Kachemak Bay, 501; Lauderdale, 345; Laurel, 307; Laurentian I, 243; Laurentian II, 246; Lower Mississippi Valley, 399–418; Macon Plateau, 382; Marksville, 406; Middle Aleut, 493; Middle Kachemak Bay, 500; Middle Mississippi, 353; Middlesex, 248; Mille Lacs, 309; Mira Creek, 323; Mogollon-Mimbres, Chihuahua, 214; Mogollon-Mimbres, Georgetown, 206; Mogollon-Mimbres, San Francisco, 206; Mogollon-Mimbres, Three Circle, 207; Morton, 292; Natchezan, 417; Nebraska, 328; New York Hopewell, 250; northern Utah, 223; Northwestern Eskimo, 473–89; Ocmulgee Fields, 387; Okvik, 474; Old Bering Sea, 477; Old Copper, 299; Old Iroquois, 255; Old Signal Butte, 320; Oneota, 315; Orient, 248; Original Eskimo, 473; Owasco, 254; Ozark Bluff Dweller, 339; Plaquemine, 415; Point Peninsula, 251; Post-Punuk, 487; Poverty Point, 404; Pre-Koniag, 496; Proto–Bluff Dweller, 338; Punuk, 484; Red Ocher, 291; Savannah, 378; Savannah River, 371; southeastern Nevada, 227; Southwestern (U.S.), 97–228; Southwestern Eskimo, 490–502; southwestern Texas, 218–23; Sterns Creek 322; Swift Creek, 376; Tchefuncte, 401; Thule, 505; Troyville, 409; Upper Republican, 326; Weeden Island, 393; Whittlesey, 281; Wilmington, 375; Wisconsin Hopewell, 305; Younge, 280
Argillite, trade in, 71
Arikara pottery, method, 53
Arizona, 189, 192, 197, 198
Arkansas, 337, 338, 339, 343, 353, 409, 411
Armbands: Hopewell, 272; Laurel, 309; Middle Mississippi, 360; Ocmulgee Fields, 388; Point Peninsula, 253
Armor: Koniag, slat, 499; Middle Aleut, slat, 494; Post-Punuk, plate, 485, 488; Thompson River, 453
Arrow: Anasazi, Pueblo II, 127; Anasazi, Pueblo III, 139; Anasazi, Pueblo IV, 155; Aztalan, 314; Birnirk, 486; Dismal River, 332; Dorset, 504; eastern North America, fourth stage, 237; flight of, 34; Hamilton, 351; Hopewell, 269; Ipiutak, 481, 482; Kansas Hopewell, 325; Koniag, 499; Late Kachemak Bay, 501; Laurel, 308; Laurentian I, 244; Macon Plateau, 383;

Middle Aleut, 494; Middle Columbia region, 455; Middle Mississippi, 284, 356; Natchezan, 418; Nebraska, 330; Northwest Coast area, 465; Ocmulgee Fields, 388; Okvik, 475; Old Bering Sea, 478; Old Iroquois, 256; Oneota, 316; Original Eskimo, 474; Owasco, 255; Point Peninsula, 252; Post-Punuk, 488; Puebloid, 224; Savannah, 379; Southern Death Cult, 363; Thompson River region, 452; Thule, 506; Top-Layer, 342; Upper Columbia region, 446; Upper Republican, 327; Whittlesey, 282; Wisconsin Hopewell, 306

Arrow-shaft polishers: Old Signal Butte, 321; Upper Republican, 327

Arrow-shaft rubbers, 37

Arrow-shaft smoothers: Mogollon-Mimbres, Chihuahua, 216; Nebraska, 330; Oneota, 316; Snake-Clearwater region, 460

Arrow-shaft straighteners, 37; Anasazi, Pueblo IV, 155; Fort Ancient, 286; Hohokam, Classic, 193; Nebraska, 330; Upper Republican, 327; *see also* Wrenches

Arrowheads; *see* Projectile points

Arsenic, impurity in copper, 45

Art: Dorset, 505; Early Aleut, 491; Early Kachemak Bay, 500; Hopewell, 274; Ipiutak, 482 (Fig. 116), 483–84; Key Marco, 397 (Fig. 95); Koniag, 499; Late Aleut, 495–96; Late Kachemak Bay, 501; Middle Aleut, 494; Middle Columbia region, 457; Middle Kachemak Bay, 500; Okvik, 476, 477 (and Fig. 114); Old Bering Sea, 479 (Fig. 115), 480; Original Eskimo, 474; Post-Punuk, 488–89; Pre-Koniag, 497; Punuk, 485 (and Fig. 117), 486; Thule, 507

Arvilla, 333

Asia (Asiatic), 22; antiquity of man, 79; culture traits, 21; migrants, 19; origin of corn, 80; people, 22; pottery, 50, 519

Asphaltum: Buena Vista Lake site, 434; Lower Sacramento region, 432, 433

Athabascan: language, 157; Promontory, 227; tribes, 442

Atlantic Coast, Hopewell trade, 277

Atlantis, 16, 22

Atlatl; *see* Spear-throwers

Atlatl weights; *see* Weights, spear-thrower

Awatobi, pueblo, 150

Awls: Adena, 265; Aztalan, 315; Buena Vista Lake region, 432; Caddo, 423; Candy Creek, 349; Coles Creek, 414; Copell, 400; Dismal River, 332; Dorset, 504; Early Aleut, 491; Early Coastal, 247; Early Kachemak Bay, 500; Effigy Mound, 304; Fort Ancient, 286; Frontenac, 242; Glacial Kame, 262; Hamilton, 351; Hohokam, Classic, 194; Hohokam, Sedentary, 185; Indian Knoll, 261; Intrusive Mound, 279; Ipiutak, 483; Irene, 381; Kansas Hopewell, 326; Key Marco, 395; Lamar, 386; Lamoka, 241; Late Kachemak Bay, 501; Lauderdale, 346; Laurentian I, 244; Macon Plateau, 384; Marksville, 407, 410; Middle Aleut, 493; Middle Columbia region, 457; Middle Kachemak Bay, 500; Middle Mississippi, 356; Middlesex, 249; Mille Lacs, 310; Mira Creek, 324; Mogollon-Mimbres, Chihuahua, 216; Mogollon-Mimbres, Mimbres, 213; Mogollon-Mimbres, Pine Lawn, 204; Mogollon-Mimbres, Three Circle, 209; Morton, 293; Natchezan, 419; Nebraska, 330; New York Hopewell, 250; Okvik, 475; Old Signal Butte, 321, 322; Old Copper, 302; Old Iroquois, 256; Oneota, 316; Owasco, 255; Ozark Bluff Dweller, 340; Point Peninsula, 253; Pre-Koniag, 497; Promontory, 226; Proto–Bluff Dweller, 339; Puebloid, 225; Red Ocher, 291, 292; Santa Barbara region, 430; Savannah River, 373, 374; southeastern Nevada, 227; southeastern Oregon, 228; Sterns Creek, 323; Tchefuncte, 402, 403 (Fig. 97); Upper Columbia region, 450; Weeden Island, 393; Whittlesey, 282; Wilmington, 375; Wisconsin Hopewell, 306; Younge, 280

Axes, 31; Adena, 265; Anasazi, Modified Basket Maker, 118; Anasazi, Pueblo I, 123; Anasazi, Pueblo II, 128; Anasazi, Pueblo III, 140; Anasazi, Pueblo IV, 155; Aztalan, 315; Baumer, 291; Big Bend Cave, 220; Bravo Valley, 222; Caddo, 423; Candy Creek, 349; Cochise, 203; Cochise, Chiricahua, 88; Coles Creek, 414; Copena, 352; Early Coastal, 247; Effigy Mound, 304 (and Fig. 84), 305; fluted, 36; Fort Ancient, 286; Frontenac, 242; full-grooved, 36; Hamilton, 351; Hohokam, Classic, 193; Hohokam, Colonial, 179; Hohokam, Pioneer, 173; Hohokam, Sedentary, 185; Hopewell, 270 (Fig. 74), 278; Indian Knoll, 261; Irene, 381; Kansas Hopewell, 326; Keshena, 311; Key Marco, 395; Lamar, 386; Lauderdale, 346; Laurentian I, 244; Macon Plateau, 384; Marksville, 407; Middlesex; 249; Mogollon-Mimbres, Chihuahua, 216; Mogollon-Mimbres, Pine Lawn, 203; Mogollon-Mimbres, Three Circle, 209; Natchezan, 418; New York Hopewell, 250; Norse, 15; Ocmulgee Fields, 388; Old Copper, 300; Old Iroquois, 256;

Old Signal Butte, 321; Orient, 248; Ozark Bluff Dweller, 340; Point Peninsula, 252, 253; Poverty Point, 405; Pre-Koniag, 496–97; Proto–Bluff Dweller, 339; Puebloid, 226; Red Ocher, 291; Santa Rosa–Swift Creek, 392; Savannah River, 373; stone, 35; Swift Creek, 378; three-quarter-grooved, 36; time to make, 37; Upper Republican, 327; Whittlesey, 282; Wisconsin Hopewell, 306

Aztalan culture, 313–15
Aztec civilization, 79
Aztec language, 99

Babicora pottery, 215
Back-scratchers, Ipiutak, 483
Baffin Island, 503
Bags (basketry), 61; *see also* Weaving, bags, and textiles
Bakavi settlements, 163
Balcony House, 12, 13
Ball courts: Hohokam, Classic, 192, 195; Hohokam, Colonial, 174, 175; Hohokam, Sedentary, 182; Mogollon-Mimbres, Pine Lawn, 201
Balls: Buena Vista Lake, 434; Hohokam, Classic, 195
Band-built pottery, 53
Bandelier National Monument, 151
Bangs, 140
Bannerstones, 37, 38; Early Coastal, 247; Frontenac, 241, Hopewell, 269, Laurentian I, 244, 245 (Fig. 69); Macon Plateau, 383; Northeastern area, 240; Old Copper, 302; Savannah River, 372; Swift Creek, 377; *see also* Weights, spear-thrower
Bark, inner, 61
Barracuda jaws, trade in, 72
Bars: Intrusive Mound, 279; Middlesex, 249
Barter, 68; *see also* Trade and commerce
Basket Maker Periods, Anasazi culture, 103–11, 225, 337; corn, 518; Indians, 88; racial origin, 97; skulls, 98; *see also* Anasazi
Basketry (baskets, basketry and weaving), 61–65; Anasazi, Basket Maker, 105; Anasazi, Modified Basket Maker, 117, 144; Anasazi, Pueblo I, 122; Anasazi, Pueblo II, 127; Anasazi, Pueblo III, 139, 144; Big Bend Cave, 219; Black Rock Cave, 223; Caddo, 422; California area, 428; Candy Creek, 349; coiled method, 63; decoration of, 61, 64; Hohokam, Classic, 193, 194; Hohokam, Colonial, 179; Hohokam, Sedentary, 187; Hopewell, 269; Key Marco, 395; Koniag, 499; Late Aleut, 495; Lower Sacramento region, 432, 433; materials for, 61; Middle Columbia region, 455; Mogollon-Mimbres, Chihuahua, 215; Mogollon-Mimbres, Mimbres, 213; Mogollon-Mimbres, Three Circle, 209; Natchezan, 418; Northwest Coast area, 465; Ozark Bluff Dweller, 340; Pre-Koniag, 496; preservation of, 65; Promontory, 226; Proto–Bluff Dweller, 338; Puebloid, 224, 226; Santa Barbara region, 432, 434; Snake-Clearwater region, 459; southeastern Oregon, 228; storage, 61; techniques of, 63–65; Thompson River region, 452; trade in, 68, 73, 74; Upper Columbia region, 445; Upper Republican, 327; *see also* Anasazi; Weaving, bags, and textiles

Batik method, painting, 57–58
Batten, 62; Anasazi, Pueblo III, 143
Baumer, 290–91, 292
Bayougoula tribe, 417
Beads: Adena, 265; Anasazi, Basket Maker, 110; Anasazi, Modified Basket Maker, 119; Anasazi, Pueblo I, 124; Anasazi, Pueblo III, 142; Anasazi, Pueblo IV, 156; Aztalan, 315; Big Bend Cave, 220; Bravo Valley, 222; Caddo, 424; Copell, 400; Copena, 352; Crystal River, 392; Dismal River, 332; Dorset, 505; Effigy Mound, 305, Fort Ancient, 286; Glacial Kame, 263; Hamilton, 351; Hohokam, Classic, 194; Hohokam, Colonial, 181; Hohokam, Pioneer, 173; Hohokam, Sedentary, 187; Hopewell, 272; Indian Knoll, 261; Intrusive Mound, 279; Irene, 382; Key Marco, 395; Lamar, 386; Lamoka, 241; Late Kachemak Bay, 501; Lauderdale, 346; Laurel, 309; Macon Plateau, 384; Marksville, 408; Middle Kachemak Bay, 500; Middlesex, 249; Mira Creek, 324; Mogollon-Mimbres, Chihuahua, 216; Mogollon-Mimbres, Mimbres, 213; Mogollon-Mimbres, Pine Lawn, 205; Morton, 293; Natchezan, 419; Nebraska, 330; New York Hopewell, 251; Ocmulgee Fields, 388; Old Copper, 302; Old Iroquois, 257, Old Signal Butte, 322; Owasco, 255; Ozark Bluff Dweller, 341; pearl, 49; Point Peninsula, 253; Post-Punuk, 488; Poverty Point, 405; Pre-Koniag, 497; Punuk, 485; Red Ocher, 292; Santa Barbara region, 430; Savannah, 380; Savannah River, 373; shell, 48; Sterns Creek, 323; Tchefuncte, 404; Thule, 507; trade in, 68; Troyville, 411; Upper Republican, 328; Whittlesey, 283; Wisconsin Hopewell, 306; Younge, 280
Beaks, bird, use of, 47
Beaming tools (beamers): Caddo, 423; Fort Ancient, 286; Kansas Hopewell, 326; Mira Creek, 324; Old Iroquois, 256;

Oneota, 316; Point Peninsula, 253; Upper Republican, 327; Whittlesey, 282
Beans: Anasazi, Pueblo I, 121; Anasazi, Pueblo III, 137; Big Bend Cave, 219; Bravo Valley, 222; Copena, 352; eastern North America, 233-34, 237; Fort Ancient, 285; Hohokam, Classic, 192; Hohokam, Colonial, 175; Hohokam, Pioneer, 170; Hopewell, 268; Kansas Hopewell, 325; Lamar, 385; Middle Mississippi, 355; Nebraska, 329; Old Iroquois, 256; Oneota, 316; Owasco, 254; Ozark Bluff Dweller, 339; Puebloid, 224; Swift Creek, 376; Top-Layer, 343; Upper Republican, 327; Whittlesey, 281
Bear Ruin, 189
Beast of burden, 66; *see also* Travel and transport
Beaver teeth: Promontory, 226; saw, 34
Bee plant, as source of paint, 57
Bella Coola Indians, 462, 469
Bella Coola Mountains, 74
Bells: Anasazi, Pueblo III, 143; copper, 42, 70; Hohokam, Classic, 193; Hohokam, Sedentary, 184; Mogollon-Mimbres, Chihuahua, 216; Ocmulgee Fields, 388
Belts: Ozark Bluff Dweller, 341; Southern Death Cult, warriors, 363; weaving of, 63
Bering, Vitus, 462
Bering Strait, 19, 20, 22, 81, 481, 490, 519
Berries, 25; *see also* Livelihood
Big Bend Cave, 218, 219-21, 337; sites, 93
Bilbo site, 373
Birchbark: Clam River, 312; trade in, 73
Birdstones, 39; Glacial Kame, 263; Hopewell, 269; Intrusive Mound, 279; Middlesex, 249; Northeastern area, 240; Point Peninsula, 252
Birnirk culture, 486-87, 508
Biscuit ware, trade in, 71
Bismuth, 45
Bison, 82, 87, 319, 320
Black Canyon, Nevada, 438
Black Mesa Black-on-White pottery, 126, 127 (Fig. 23), 187
Black Rock Cave, 223-24
Black Sand, 303
Black-on-white pottery, method, 59
Bladders, Okvik, 475
Blades, 34, 35, 37; Frontenac, 242; Laurentian II, 246 (Fig. 69); Marksville, 410; northern California, 428, 429 (Fig. 103); *see also* Projectile points
Blalock Island, 455
Blankets: Chilkat, 74; Northwest Coast area, 468; weaving, 63, 159
Blanks (stone) for arrowheads, 30; "fresh," 35; use of, 34, 35

Boats: Early Aleut, 491; migration by, 20; Original Eskimo, 474; *see also* Canoes; Kayak; Travel and transport; Umiak
Boatstones, 37; Adena, 265; Caddo, 423; Coles Creek, 414; Hopewell, 269; Irene, 381; Lauderdale, 346; Marksville, 407; Middlesex, 249; Northeastern area, 240; Plaquemine, 416; Swift Creek, 377
Bodkins: Lauderdale, 346; Oneota, 316; Santa Barbara region, 430; Thule, 507; Upper Columbia region, 450; Upper Republican, 327
Bolas: Birnirk, 486; Early Coastal, 247; Intrusive Mound, 279; Middlesex, 249; New York Hopewell, 250; Point Peninsula, 252; Post-Punuk, 488; Pre-Koniag, 496; Punuk, 485; Thule, 506
Bone: polished, 47; Promontory, 226
Bone tools; *see* Awls; Bodkins; Hooks; Projectile points; Tools, utensils, and weapons
Bone work, 31, 47-49
Bones, animal: Mogollon-Mimbres, Georgetown, 206; Mogollon-Mimbres, Mimbres, 211; Mogollon-Mimbres, San Francisco, 207; Promontory, 226; Younges, 281
Boots: Birnirk, 487; Koniag, 499; Late Aleut, 595; Old Bering Sea, 480; Post-Punuk, 488; Thule, 507
Borax Lake site, 434-35
Bow: Anasazi, Modified Basket Maker, 117; Anasazi, Pueblo II, 127; Anasazi, Pueblo III, 139; Anasazi, Pueblo IV, 155; Aztalan, 314; Birnirk, 486; Caddo, 423; composite, 21; Dismal River, 332; Dorset, 504; eastern North America, 237; Fort Ancient, 286; Hamilton, 351; Hopewell, 269; Ipiutak, 481, 482; Koniag, 499; Late Kachemak Bay, 501; Laurel, 308; Laurentian I, 244; Macon Plateau, 383; Middle Aleut, 494; Middle Columbia region, 455; Middle Mississippi, 355, 356; Middle Mississippi in Ohio, 284; Natchezan, 418; Nebraska, 330; Northwest Coast area, 465; Ocmulgee Fields, 388; Okvik, 475; Old Bering Sea, 478; Old Iroquois, 256; Oneota, 316; Original Eskimo, 474; Owasco, 255; Post-Punuk, 488; Promontory, 226; Puebloid, 224; Punuk, 485; Savannah, 379; Upper Columbia region, 446; Upper Republican, 327; Thompson River region, 452; Thule, 506; Top-Layer, 342; Whittlesey, 282; Wisconsin Hopewell, 306
Bow braces, Punuk, 485
Bow drills; *see* Drills
Bowls: Birnirk, 487; Candy Creek, 349; Fort Ancient, 286; Frontenac, 242;

Hohokam, Colonial, 179; Hohokam, Sedentary, 185, 186; Key Marco, 395; Middle Aleut, 493; Mille Lacs, 310; Mogollon-Mimbres, Mimbres, 212; New York Hopewell, 250; Okvik, 475; Old Bering Sea, 479; Orient, 248; Savannah, 379; Thule, 507; time to make, 59

Boylston fish-weir site, 93

Bracelets: Adena, 265; Copena, 352; Hohokam, Classic, 194; Hopewell, 272 (Fig. 76); Late Kachemak Bay, 501; Mille Lacs, 310; Natchezan, 419; Nebraska, 330; shell, 49; *see also* Ornaments

Braiding, 63

Brass implements, 40

Bravo Valley culture, 219, 221–23

Breaking, stone manufacture, 29–30, 34

Breastplates: Adena, 265; Crystal River, 392; Hopewell, 271; Red Ocher, 292; Wisconsin Hopewell, 306

Breechclout: Adena, 265; Anasazi, Pueblo III, 140; Caddo, 424; Hopewell, 271; Indian Knoll, 261; Intrusive Mound, 279; Middle Mississippi, 359; Natchezan, 419; Nebraska, 330; Ozark Bluff Dweller, 341; Southern Death Cult, warrior's, 363; *see also* Costume

Brew, J. O., 116

British Columbia, 470

Brooches, Key Marco, 395; *see also* Ornaments

Browbands, Old Bering Sea, 480

Browns Valley find, 298–99

Brushes, paint, 57

Buckets (pails): Okvik, 475; Old Bering Sea, 479; Ozark Bluff Dweller 340

Buckles: Late Kachemak Bay, 501; Thule, 507

Buena Vista Lake, 429, 432, 433

Bulbs, Mogollon-Mimbres, Pine Lawn, 202

Bundle burials: Adena, 266; Clam River, 312; Copena, 353; Frontenac, 243; Intrusive Mound, 279; Keshena, 311; Laurel, 309; Macon Plateau, 384; Mille Lacs, 310; Natchezan, 419; Old Copper, 302; Old Iroquois, 257; Plaquemine, 417; Red Ocher, 292; Santa Rosa–Swift Creek, 392; Savannah River, 373; Weeden Island, 394; Whittlesey, 283; Wisconsin Hopewell, 307; Younge, 281; *see also* Burials

Bureau of Ethnology, 43

Burial cairns: Northwest Coast area, 469; Thule, 508

Burial caves: Koniag, 499; Late Aleut, 496

Burial goods; *see* Burial offerings

Burial Mound Period, Middle Southern area, 345, 350, 353, 367

Burial Mound I period: Georgia area, 369, 388; Lower Mississippi Valley area, 399, 401–6; Ohio area, 259, 262–67, 288

Burial Mound II period: Georgia area, 369, 375–78, 388; Lower Mississippi Valley area, 399, 406–11; Ohio area, 259, 267–79, 287, 288

Burial mounds: Copena, 353; eastern North America, 234–36, 237; Effigy Mound, 303; Hamilton, 351; Hopewell, 267; Irene, 382; Lower Mississippi Valley area, 399; Marksville, 409; Natchezan, 419; Old Copper, 303; Tchefuncte, 401; Troyville, 411; Weeden Island, 393; Wisconsin Hopewell, 306

Burial offerings (grave-offerings, burial goods, mortuary offerings), 60; Coles Creek, 415; Copell, 400–401; Copena, 353; Fort Ancient, 287; Frontenac, 243; Glacial Kame, 263; Hopewell, 277; Intrusive Mound, 279; Irene, 382; Ipiutak, 484; Lamar, 386; Late Aleut, 496; Laurentian I, 244; Marksville, 409; Middlesex, 249; Mille Lacs, 310; Mogollon-Mimbres, Mimbres, 213; New York Hopewell, 251; Ocmulgee Fields, 388; Orient, 248; Owasco, 255; Savannah River, 373; Weeden Island, 394; Whittlesey, 283; Younge, 280

Burial pits, Indian Knoll, 261

Burial platforms, 274

Burials: Adena, 266; Alexander, 348; Anasazi, Basket Maker, 110; Anasazi, Modified Basket Maker, 119, 145; Anasazi, Pueblo I, 124; Anasazi, Pueblo II, 128; Anasazi, Pueblo III, 142, 145; Anasazi, Pueblo IV, 156; Aztalan, 315; Big Bend Cave, 220; Birnirk, 487; Bravo Valley, 222; Browns Valley site, 299; Buena Vista Lake, 430; Candy Creek, 350; Central California, 432, 433; Clam River, 312–13; Cochise, Sulphur Spring, 88; Coles Creek, 415; Copell, 400; Copena, 353; Early Coastal, 247; Effigy Mound, 305; Fort Ancient, 287; Frontenac, 242; Glacial Kame, 263; Hamilton, 351; Hohokam, Classic, 195; Hohokam, Colonial, 181; Hohokam, Pioneer, 173; Hohokam, Sedentary, 188; Hopewell, 274–77; Indian Knoll, 261; Intrusive Mound, 279; Irene, 382; Ipiutak, 484; Keshena, 311; Koniag, 499; La Jolla, 437; Lamar, 386; Lamoka, 241; Late Aleut, 496; Lauderdale, 347; Laurel, 309; Laurentian I, 244; Laurentian II, 246; Lower Sacramento region, 430; Macon Plateau, 384; Marksville, 409; Middle Columbia region, 458; Middle Kachemak Bay, 500; Middle Mississippi, 360; Middlesex, 249; Mille Lacs, 310; Mira Creek, 324; Mogollon-

INDEX

Mimbres, Chihuahua, 216; Mogollon-Mimbres, Georgetown, 206; Mogollon-Mimbres, Mimbres, 213; Mogollon-Mimbres, Pine Lawn, 205; Mogollon-Mimbres, Three Circle, 209; Mogollon-Mimbres, San Francisco, 207; Morton, 293; Natchezan, 419; Nebraska, 331; New York Hopewell, 250; northern California, 428; Northwest Coast area, 469; Ocmulgee Fields, 388; Old Copper, 302; Old Iroquois, 257; Oneota, 317; Orient, 248; Owasco, 255; Ozark Bluff Dweller, 341; Plaquemine, 417; Point Peninsula, 253; Pre-Koniag, 497; Proto–Bluff Dweller, 339; Red Ocher, 292; Santa Barbara region, 430; Santa Rosa–Swift Creek, 392; Savannah, 380; Savannah River, 373; Snake-Clearwater region, 460; Swift Creek, 378; Tampico, 295; Tchefuncte, 404; Thompson River region, 454; Thule, 508; Troyville, 411; Upper Columbia region, 451; Upper Republican, 328; Weeden Island, 394; Whittlesey, 283; Wilmington, 375; Wisconsin Hopewell, 307; Younge, 280
Burnet Cave, 93
Butterfly-stones, 37
Button: Okvik, 476 (Fig. 114); Old Bering Sea, 480; Thule, 507; Wisconsin Hopewell, 307
Buzzard Cult; *see* Southern Death Cult

Cabeza de Vaca (Álvar Núñez), 345
Caches of stone, 29, 35
Caddo area, 421–24; chronology of, 517 (Fig. 122)
Caddo culture, 363, 366, 421–24
Caddo Indians, 417
Caddo pottery, 423 (Fig. 102)
Cahokia mounds, 313
Cahokia site, 294
Cahuilla pottery, 53
Cairns, burial: Northwest Coast area, 469; Thule, 508
California areas, 427–41; bone work, 48; Central area, 428–36; chronology of, 440 (Chart XV), 514 (Fig. 122); Northern area, 428; pottery origin, 519; Southern area, 436–38; trade, 73–74
Calusa Indians, 398
Camel, 82, 87
Canada, 157, 444, 503
Canals (irrigation): Hohokam, 168; Hohokam, Classic, 192; Hohokam, Colonial, 175; Hohokam, Pioneer, 170; Hohokam, Sedentary, 182; *see also* Irrigation
Canary grass: domestication of, 519; Ozark Bluff Dweller, 339

Candy Creek culture, 348
Cane, 61
Cannel coal, Baumer, 291
Cannibalism, Pre-Koniag, 497
Canoes: Key Marco, 395, 396 (Fig. 94); Middle Columbia region, 457; Natchezan, 419; Northwest Coast, 466 (Fig. 112); outrigger, 15; Santa Barbara region, 434; Snake-Clearwater region, 460; Thompson River region, 454; trade in, 68, 73, 74; Upper Columbia region, 451
Cape Cod (Mass.), 15
Carrying-bands, Anasazi, Pueblo III, 142
Carving, ivory, 21; *see also* Art
Casa Blanca site, 192
Casa Grande Red-on-Buff pottery, 192
Casa Grande site, 192, 215
Cascade Range, 455
Cast, copper, 42, 70
Casting metals, Hohokam, Sedentary, 185
"Catch our archeology alive" (Lummis), 159
Catlinite, trade in, 67, 73
Cattails, 61
Cave deposits, 91
Caves: Anasazi, Basket Maker, 143; Anasazi, Modified Basket Maker, 112; Anasazi, Pueblo III, 143; Indian Knoll, 260; Koniag, 499; Late Aleut, 496; Oregon, 93; Promontory, 226; Proto–Bluff Dweller, 338; Salt Lake City, 93; southeastern Oregon, 228; Texas, 219; Utah, 223; *see also* Big Bend Cave; Burnet Cave; Gypsum Cave; Obelisk Cave; Ventana Cave
Celts: 36; Caddo, 423; Copena, 352; Dismal River, 332; Early Coastal, 247; Effigy Mound, 304; Glacial Kame, 262; Intrusive Mound, 279; Lamoka, 241; Middle Mississippi, 356; Nebraska, 330; New York Hopewell, 250; Oneota, 316; Orient, 248; Owasco, 255; Plaquemine, 417; Point Peninsula, 252; Sterns Creek, 323; Swift Creek, 378; Tchefuncte, 402; Upper Republican, 327; Wilmington, 375
Central America, 92; culture source, 520
Centralids: Adena, 263; Aztalan, 313; Caddo, 421; Coles Creek, 411; eastern North America, 231–32; Fort Ancient, 285; Hamilton, 350; Hopewell, 267; Irene, 380; Key Marco, 395; Lamar, 385; Macon Plateau, 382; Marksville, 278; Middle Mississippi, 353; Middle Mississippi in Illinois, 294; Morton, 292; Ocmulgee Fields, 387; Oneota, 316; Red Ocher, 291; Savannah, 378; Swift Creek, 387; Tchefuncte, 401; Top-Layer, 342; Weeden Island, 393
Cerrillos Mountain, 71
Chaco area, 131

Chaco Black-on-White pottery, 137, 138
Chaco Canyon, 70, 126, 129, 167
Chalcedony, 29
Chamita River, 165
Channel Islands, 48, 432, 434; trade with, 74
Charcoal, 86, 219
Charmstones (central California): defined, 430; Early period, 430, 435; Late period, 433, 436; Middle period, 432, 436; northeastern California area, 428
Charts: I, Cochise Culture, 86; II, Development of the Anasazi Civilization, 103; III, Development of the Hohokam Civilization, 169; IV, Development of the Mogollon-Mimbres Civilization, 200; V, Periods and Cultures of the Northeastern Area, 239; VI, Periods and Cultures of the Ohio Area, 260; VII, Periods and Cultures of the Illinois Area, 290; VIII, Periods and Cultures of the Wisconsin-Minnesota Area, 298; IX, Periods and Cultures of the Plains Area, 320; X, Periods and Cultures of the Ozark Plateau Area, 338; XI, Periods and Cultures of the Middle Southern Area, 345; XII, Periods and Cultures of the Georgia Area, 370; XIII, Periods and Cultures of the Florida Area, 390; XIV, Periods and Cultures of the Lower Mississippi Valley Area, 399; XV, Chronology in the California Area, 440; XVI, Periods and Cultures of the Northwestern Eskimo Area, 473; XVII, Cultures and Periods of the Southwestern Eskimo Area, 491; XVIII, Cultures and Dates, Eastern Eskimo Area, 503; Chronological Chart of North America, 514–17 (Fig. 122)
Chavin culture, Peru, 79
Checked-stamp, pottery impressions, 55, 56
Checkerwork weave, 63
Cheekbones, 17; see also Physical traits
Chenopodium, Ozark Bluff Dweller, 339
Cherokee Indians, 361
Chert, 29
Chessmen, Norse, Inugsuk, 508
Chevlon, 150
Chicago, University of, vi
Chickasaw Indians, 361
Chihuahua area, 149
Chihuahua periods, 214–17; see also Mogollon-Mimbres culture
Chihuahua pottery, 51, 71, 222
Chilkat blankets, trade in, 74
Chimneys, Anasazi, Pueblo IV, 150
China (Chinese): development of pottery in, 50; people of, related to Indians, 19
Chinook, 68, 455
Chippewa, 311, 313

Chipping, stone, methods and techniques, 29–34; see also Tools, utensils, and weapons
Chiricahua periods, 88–89; see also Cochise culture
Chirikov, Alexei, 462
Chisels, 31; Early Coastal, 247; Frontenac, 242; Hopewell, 270; Laurel, 309; Laurentian I, 244; Northwest Coast area, 466; Old Copper, 300, 301 (Fig. 83); Old Iroquois, 256; Point Peninsula, 253; Pre-Koniag, 497; Savannah River, 373; Tchefuncte, 402; Thompson River region, 454; Upper Columbia region, 450; Whittlesey, 282
Choctaw jargon, distribution, 68
Choppers, 34; Anasazi, Modified Basket Maker, 118; Frontenac, 242; La Jolla, 437; Lamoka, 240; Laurentian I, 244; Maravillas, 219; Mogollon-Mimbres, Pine Lawn, 203, 204; Mogollon-Mimbres, San Francisco, 207; Swift Creek, 378
Chronology (chronological stages): California area, 438, 440 (Chart XV); correlation of cultures, 513; definition of, 9; eastern North America, 232–38; methods of dating, 9–13; of periods and cultures (see Charts); tree-ring dating, 11–12; Yuman, 439
Chucovi, 150
Chunkey (chunkeystones), 39, 58; Fort Ancient, 287; Lamar, 385; Macon Plateau, 374; Southern Death Cult, 363
Chupadero Black-on-White pottery, 221
Cibola: derivation of, 156; Seven Cities of, 156
Cibola area: Anasazi, Pueblo IV, 152
Cigarettes, cane, Hohokam, Colonial, 181
Cinnebar, trade in, 71
Circle motif, Southern Death Cult, 363
Cists, slab-lined, New York Hopewell, 251
Civilization: development of, 79; overlapping, 195, 196; see also Culture
Clam River culture, 312
Clams: Copell, 400; Macon Plateau, 383; Savannah River, 371
Clark, George Rogers, 455
Classic Hohokam Period, 188–95; see also Hohokam
"Classic Period," Anasazi, Pueblo III, 29
Clays: ferruginous, 57; pottery, 51
Clearwater River, 442
Cliff-houses, 129, 130, 131, 150, 170
Cliff Palace, Mesa Verde National Park, 113, 158
Climate: Bravo Valley, 221; Caddo area, 421; California, 427; desert region, 437; early, 81; Eastern Eskimo area, 390; Florida area, 390; Georgia area, 369; Hohokam

area, 168; Illinois area, 289; Lower Mississippi Valley area, 399; Maravillas, 219; Middle Southern area, 344; Mogollon-Mimbres, Chihuahua, 215; Northeastern area, 239; northern Utah, 223; Northwest Coast area, 463; Northwestern Eskimo area, 473; Ohio area, 259; Ozark Plateau area, 337; Plains area, 319; Plateau area, 442; southeastern Nevada, 227; southeastern Oregon, 228; Southwestern area, 97, 147; Southwestern Eskimo area, 490; Wisconsin-Minnesota area, 297

Cloth, 61-65; Anasazi, Modified Basket Maker, fur, 119; Anasazi, Pueblo I, 124; Anasazi, Pueblo III, 142; cotton, 70; Hohokam, Sedentary, cotton, 186; Hopewell, 271; Inugsuk, 508; preservation of, 65; Promontory, 226; Puebloid, 225; *see also* Cotton

Clothing, tailored, 21; *see also* Costume

Clovis (N.M.), 83

Clubs: Early Aleut, 491; Early Coastal, 247; Key Marco, 396 (Fig. 94); Koniag, 499; Late Kachemak Bay, 501; Middle Columbia region, 455; Natchezan, 419; northern California, 428; Northwest Coast area, 466; Point Peninsula, 253; Pre-Koniag, 496, 497; Puebloid, 224; Southern Death Cult, 363; Thompson River region, 453; Thule, 507

Coal, Anasazi, Pueblo IV, 150; *see also* Cannel coal

Coast Salish, 463, 464, 469

Coastal region cultures, Southern California, 436-37

Cochise culture, 82, 85-91, 92; dating of, 11; parent of Mogollon, Hohokam, 198; periods: Chiricahua, 88-89; San Pedro, 89-90; Sulphur Spring, 86, 87-88; *see also* Ventana Cave

Cochiti, 161

Cocopa pottery, 53

"Coffee-bean"-eye motif, Hohokam, Colonial, 179

Coiled basketry; *see* Basketry

Cole, Fay-Cooper, vi

Coles Creek culture, 339, 411-15, 416, 424

Collier, Mrs. Donald, vi

Colonial period, Hohokam, 174-181; *see also* Hohokam

Colorado, 146; Balcony House, 13

Colorado River, 427, 436, 519

Columbia River, 74, 442, 455

Columbus, Christopher 15, 21, 97

Combs, 47; Adena, 265; Fort Ancient, 286; Frontenac, 242; Intrusive Mount, 279; Nebraska, 330; Old Iroquois, 256; Point Peninsula, 253; Thule, 507; weaving, 62; Whittlesey, 283

Commerce, 66-75; *see also* Trade and commerce

Compound: Hohokam, Classic, 190; Hohokam, Sedentary, 182; *see also* Villages

Cones, stone objects, 39

Contact, European, 156

Containers: Copena, 352; Copell, 400; Fort Ancient, 286; Marksville, 407; New York Hopewell, 250; *see also* Pottery; Tools, utensils, and weapons

Cook, Captain, 462

Cook Inlet, 490, 499, 502

Cooking, 61; California, 428; Mogollon-Mimbres, Pine Lawn, 201; Northwest Coast area, 464, 465; Upper Columbia region, 445

Coolidge Dam, 168

Copell culture, 400-401

Copena culture, 351-53

Copenhagen, 36

Copper, 40-46, 57; Adena, 265, 266; beating, 43; Caddo, 424; Copena, 352; Crystal River, 392; drift, 40; European, 45; float, 40; Frontenac, 242; Glacial Kame, 262, 263; Hopewell, 270, 274; Hopewell in Illinois, 293, 294; Intrusive Mound, 279; Kansas Hopewell, 326; Late Kachemak Bay, 501; Laurentian I, 244; Macon Plateau, 384; Marksville, 408; Middle Aleut, 494; Middle Kachemak Bay, 500; Middle Mississippi, 356, 360; Middlesex, 249; native, 40, 43, 44, 45; New York Hopewell, 250, 251; Northwest Coast area, 468; Point Peninsula, 252, 253; Red Ocher, 291, 292; Savannah, 380; tempering of, 24; trade in, 66, 72, 73, 74, 75; Troyville, 410; Weeden Island, 394; Whittlesey, 283; Wisconsin Hopewell, 306, Younge, 280

Copper River, 74

Coppermine River, 40, 75

Core-implements, Folsom, 84

Corn, 79-80, 233, 234, 237, 518; Adena, 264; Anasazi, Basket Maker, 104; Anasazi, Modified Basket Maker, 113; Anasazi, Pueblo I, 121; Anasazi, Pueblo III, 137; Aztalan, 314; Big Bend Cave, 219; Bravo Valley, 222; Caddo, 422; Copena, 352; development of, 80, 91; Dismal River, 331; evolution of, 80; Fort Ancient, 285; Hohokam, 518; Hohokam, Classic, 192; Hohokam, Colonial, 175; Hohokam, Pioneer, 170; Hohokam, Sedentary, 182; Hopewell, 268; Indian strains, 519; Irene, 381; Iroquois, 256; Kansas Hopewell, 325; Lamar, 385; Macon Plateau, 383; Middle Mississippi, 355; Middlesex, 249; Mogollon-Mimbres, Chihuahua, 215; Mogollon-Mimbres,

Georgetown, 206; Mogollon-Mimbres, Mimbres, 211; naked-seeded, 80; Natchezan, 418; Nebraska, 329; Ocmulgee Fields, 387; Oneota, 316; origin of, 80; Owasco, 254; Ozark Bluff Dweller, 339; Point Peninsula, 252; Puebloid, 224; Swift Creek, 376; Top-Layer, 343; Upper Republican, 327; Whittlesey, 281

Corncrib, Natchezan, 418

Coronado, Francisco Vásquez, 156, 157

Coronation Gulf, 75

Corridors, glacial, 81

Cortez, Hernando, 156

Costume: Adena, 265; Anasazi, Basket Maker, 108; Anasazi, Modified Basket Maker, 119, 145; Anasazi, Pueblo I, 124; Anasazi, Pueblo III, 140, 145; Anasazi, Pueblo IV, 156; Big Bend Cave, 220; Birnirk, 487; Candy Creek, 349; Hohokam, Classic, 194; Hohokam, Colonial, 181; Hopewell, 271; Indian Knoll, 261; Intrusive Mound, 279; Ipiutak, 483; Koniag, 499; Late Aleut, 495; Middle Columbia region, 457; Middle Mississippi, 359; Mogollon-Mimbres, Chihuahua, 216; Mogollon-Mimbres, Mimbres, 213; Natchezan, 419; Nebraska, 330; Northwest Coast area, 468; Okvik, 476; Old Bering Sea, 480; Original Eskimo, 474; Ozark Bluff Dweller, 341; Post-Punuk, 488; Puebloid, 226; Snake-Clearwater region, 460; Thompson River region, 454; Thule, 507; Upper Columbia region, 450

Cotton: Anasazi, Pueblo I, 121; Anasazi, Pueblo III, 137; Hohokam, Classic, 194; Hohokam, Colonial, 175; Hohokam, Sedentary, 182; *see also* Cloth

Cotton textiles; *see* Cloth; Cotton

Cottonwood Ruin ("city"), 150

Cottonwood trees, 86

"Crack-lacing holes," 60

Cradles: Anasazi, Basket Maker, 108, 145; Anasazi, Modified Basket Maker, 119; Anasazi, Pueblo III, 141, 145; Big Bend Cave, 220; Mogollon-Mimbres, Mimbres, 213; Ozark Bluff Dweller, 341; Puebloid, 225

Crawfish River, 313

Creek Indians, 361, 382, 386, 387

Cremation: Adena, 266; Anasazi, Pueblo III, 142; Big Bend Cave, 220; central California, 432, 433; Copena, 353; Effigy Mound, 305; Fort Ancient, 287; Frontenac, 243; Hohokam, Classic, 190, 195; Hohokam, Colonial, 181; Hohokam, Pioneer, 173; Hohokam, Sedentary, 188; Intrusive Mound, 279; Irene, 382; Keshena, 311; Late Aleut, 496; Lauderdale, 347; Laurel, 309; Laurentian I, 244; Macon Plateau, 384; Middlesex, 249; Mogollon-Mimbres, Pine Lawn, 205; New York Hopewell, 251; northern California, 428; Northwest Coast area, 462, 469; Orient, 248; Ozark Bluff Dweller, 341; Point Peninsula, 253; Red Ocher, 292; Savannah, 380; Tchefuncte, 404; Wilmington, 375; Wisconsin Hopewell, 307

Crematory basins, Hopewell, 277

Crete, island of, 16

Cross-dating, 9–10, 11, 178; *see also* Chronology; Dating

Cross-designs: motif, Fort Ancient, 286; Southern Death Cult, 363, 364 (Fig. 89)

Crutches, Anasazi, Pueblo III, 143

Crystal River culture, 392

Cuba, 42

Cultivated plants, 519; *see also* Agriculture; Beans; Canary grass; Corn; etc.

Culture, 5; Adena, 263–66; Alexander, 347–48; Amargosa, 438; Anasazi, 101–67, 198; Antelope Creek, 333; Arvilla, 333; Baumer, 290–91; Big Bend Cave, 219–21; Birnirk, 486–87; Black Rock Cave, 223–24; Bravo Valley, 221–23; Caddo, 421–24; Candy Creek, 348–50; Clam River, 312–15; Cochise, 82–83, 85–91; Coles Creek, 411; Copell, 400–401; Copena, 351–53; Crystal River, 392; Deptford, 374; Deptford in Florida area, 391; Diegueño, 436–37; Dismal River, 331; Dorset, 503–6; Early Aleut, 490–93; Early Buena Vista, 429–30; Early Coastal, 247; Early Island, 432; Early Macon, 369–70; Early Mainland, 430; Early Sacramento, 430; Effigy Mound, 303–5; Etowah, 386; Faulkner, 289; Fisher, 295; Folsom, 82, 83–85; Fort Ancient, 284–87; Fort Walton, 394; Frontenac, 241–43; Glacial Kame, 262–63; Hamilton, 350–51; Hohokam, 168–97; Hopewell, 267–78; Hopewell in Illinois area, 293–94; Indian Knoll, 259–62; Intermediate Buena Vista, 432; Intermediate Mainland, 432; Intrusive Mound, 278–79; Inugsuk, 508–9; Ipiutak, 481–84; Irene, 380–82; Kansas Hopewell, 325–26; Keshena, 310–11; Key Marco, 395–98; Koniag, 498–99; La Jolla, 436, 438; Lake Mohave, 83, 437–38; Lamar, 385; Lamoka, 240–41; Late Aleut, 495–96; Late Buena Vista, 433–34; Late Island, 434; Late Kachemak Bay, 501; Late Mainland, 434; Late Sacramento, 433; Lauderdale, 345–47; Laurel, 307–9; Laurentian I, 243–44; Laurentian II, 246; Lewis, 294; Lower Loupe, 333; Macon Plateau, 382–84; Mandan, 333; Maravillas, 219; Marksville, 406; Middle Aleut, 493, 495; Middle Kachemak Bay,

500–501; Middle Mississippi, 353–61; Middle Mississippi in Illinois, 294–95; Middle Mississippi in Ohio, 283–84; Middlesex, 248–49; Mill Creek, 333; Mille Lacs, 309–10; Mira Creek, 323–24; Mogollon-Mimbres, 198–217; Morton, 292–93; Natchezan, 417; Nebraska, 329–31; New York Hopewell, 250–61; Oak Grove, 436; Ocmulgee Fields, 387; Okvik, 474–77; Old Bering Sea, 477–81; Old Copper, 299–303; Old Iroquois, 255–58; Old Signal Butte, 320–22; Oneota, 315–17, 333; Orient, 248; Original Eskimo, 473–74; Ozark Bluff Dweller, 339–42; Owasco, 254–55; Paint Creek, 333; Patayan, 438; Pinto Basin, 83, 92, 437–38; Plaquemine, 415; Point Peninsula, 251–54; Point Sal I, 430; Point Sal II, 432; Point Sal III, 434; Post-Punuk, 487–89; Poverty Point, 404–6; Prehistoric Yuma, 438; Promontory, 226–27; Proto-Bluff Dweller, 338–39; Puebloid, 224–26; Punuk, 484–86; Red Ocher, 291–92; San Dieguito, 436; Sandia, 82, 92; Santa Rosa-Swift Creek, 392; Savannah, 378–80; Savannah River, 371–73; southern California, 436–41; Sterns Creek, 322–23; Swift Creek, 376; Tampico, 295; Tchefuncte, 401–4; Thule, 505–8; Tick Island, 391; Top-Layer, 342–43; Transitional Sacramento, 432; Troyville, 409–11; Upper Republican, 326–28; Weeden Island, 393–94; Whittlesey, 281–83; Wilmington, 375; Wisconsin Hopewell, 305–7; Younge, 280–81

Culture areas, chronology of, 514–17 (Fig. 122)

Culture lag, 102

Cultures, chronology and correlation of, 513

Cups: Frontenac, 242; Key Marco, 395; Pre-Koniag, 497; Thule, 507; Weeden Island, 394; *see also* Tools, utensils, and weapons

Cupstones: Candy Creek, 349; Indian Knoll, 261

Currency, 68

Cusabo Indians, 382

Cushing, Frank Hamilton, 43–44

Cutting disks from skulls; *see* Trephining

Daggers: Frontenac, 242; Late Kachemak Bay, 501; Point Peninsula, 252; Punuk, 485; Thompson River region, 453

Dakota tribes, 309

Dalles River, 455, 456, 457, 458, 459

Dalstrom, Gustaf, vi

Darts: bladder, Thule, 506; Late Kachemak Bay, 501; Okvik, 475; *see also* Spears

Dating (dates): Black Rock Cave, 224; cross-, 178; by dendrochronology (*see* Tree-ring dating); early finds, 92; eastern North America, 238; geological, 82; Hohokam, Colonial, 178; methods of, 9–13; North American cultures, 513; southern California cultures, 439; tree-ring, earliest, 80; use of pottery types, 155; *see also* Chronology

De Soto, Hernando, 345, 361

Dead Man's Black-on-Red pottery, 178, 184

Death Cult, Southern; *see* Southern Death Cult

Decorated objects, Okvik, 476 (Fig. 114)

Decoration: basketry, 61, 63–65; pottery, 54–58

Deerskins, trade in, 74

Deformation, head, 23, 150; Anasazi, Pueblo I, 121; Anasazi, Pueblo IV, 150; Copena, 351; Middle Mississippi, 353; Mogollon-Mimbres, Pine Lawn, 200; Northwest Coast, 463

Dendrochronology; *see* Tree-ring dating

Denmark, 36

Dentalium shells, trade in, 73, 74

Deptford culture, 374; in Florida area, 391

Deschutes River, 455

Desert culture, 103

Desert region, southern California, 437–38

Dice, 47; Anasazi, Pueblo III, 143; Middle Columbia region, 457; Promontory, beaver teeth, 226; Snake-Clearwater region, 460; Thompson River region, 454; Upper Columbia region, 450; *see also* Games

Diegueño culture, 437–38

Diegueño pottery, 53

Digging-sticks: Anasazi, Basket Maker, 106; Anasazi, Modified Basket Maker, 114, 117; Anasazi, Pueblo II, 127; Anasazi, Pueblo III, 137, 139; Anasazi, Pueblo IV, 155; Caddo, 423; Dismal River, 332; Fort Ancient, 285; Hohokam, Pioneer, 170; Irene, 381; Kansas Hopewell, 325; Lamar, 386; Macon Plateau, 383; Middle Mississippi, 355; Natchezan, 419; Nebraska, 330; Oneota, 316; Ozark Bluff Dweller, 340; Thompson River region, 454; Top-Layer, 342; Upper Republican, 327; Whittlesey, 282

Digging-tools, Pre-Koniag, 497

Diorite, trade in, 71

Dippers: Adena, 265; Birnirk, 487; Hopewell, 270; Key Marco, 395; Late Kachemak Bay, 501; Macon Plateau, 384; Middle Mississippi, 356

Dire wolf, 87

Disarticulated bundles, Effigy Mound, 305

Disarticulation burial: Mille Lacs, 310; Old Copper, 302; *see also* Burials

Discoidals, 38; Macon Plateau, 384; Plaquemine, 417
Disease, 25; epidemic of, Anasazi, Pueblo III, 147
Dishes, Pre-Koniag, 497; *see also* Tools, utensils, and weapons
Disks, 35; Key Marco, 398; Lower Sacramento region, 433
Dismal River culture, 331-32
Dog, 66; Anasazi, Basket Maker, 105; Anasazi, Modified Basket Maker, 114; Anasazi, Pueblo I, 121; Anasazi, Pueblo III, 137; Big Bend Cave, 219; Bravo Valley, 222; Copell, 400; Dismal River, 331; Early Kachemak Bay, 499; Frontenac, 241, 243; Hohokam, Classic, 192; Hohokam, Pioneer, 171; Indian Knoll, 260, 261; Intrusive Mound, 279; Kansas Hopewell, 325; Koniag, 498; Laurentian I, 243; Mogollon-Mimbres, Chihuahua, 215; Mogollon-Mimbres, Mimbres, 212; Mogollon-Mimbres, Pine Lawn, 202; Morton, 293; Natchezan, 418; Old Bering Sea, 477, 479; Old Iroquois, 256; Point Peninsula, 253; Post-Punuk, 488; Pre-Koniag, 496; Promontory, 226; Proto-Bluff Dweller, 338; Puebloid, 225, 226; Savannah River, 371; southeastern Oregon, 228; Thule, 507; Upper Republican, 327; Whittlesey, 281
Dog sledge; *see* Sled
Dolls, 47
Domesticated animals: Anasazi, Modified Basket Maker, 114; Anasazi, Pueblo I, 121; Anasazi, Pueblo III, 137; Hohokam, Pioneer, 171; *see also* Dog; Fox; Horse; Turkey
Domesticated plants, 519
Doorways, Anasazi, Pueblo III, 131
Dorset culture, 298, 300, 303, 503-5, 508
Douglass, A. E., 11, 147
Draw knives, 84, 89; *see also* Knives
Dresses, weaving of, 63; *see also* Costume
Drills (types and parts), 29, 32, 33; Adena, 265; Anasazi, Modified Basket Maker, 118; Anasazi, Pueblo I, 123; Anasazi, Pueblo II, 128; Birnirk, bow, 487; Borax Lake region, 434; bow, 33; Bravo Valley, 222; Caddo, 423; Candy Creek, 349; Coles Creek, 414; conical, 33; copper, 32; Dismal River, 332; Dorset, hand, 504; Early Aleut, 491; Early Coastal, 247; Early Kachemak Bay, 500; Early Macon, 370; Fort Ancient, 286; Frontenac, 242; Hamilton, 351; Hohokam, Classic, 194; Hohokam, Colonial, 179; Hohokam, Pioneer, 173; Hopewell, 270; Indian Knoll, 261; Irene, 381; Kansas Hopewell, 326; Keshena, 311; Lamoka, 240; Late Kachemak Bay, 501; Lauderdale, 346; Laurentian I, 244; Macon Plateau, 384; manufacture, 34; Marksville, 407; Middle Columbia region, 456; Middle Mississippi, 356; Middlesex, 249; Mille Lacs, 310; Mira Creek, 324; Mogollon-Mimbres, Pine Lawn, 204; Morton, 293; Natchezan, fire, 419; Nebraska, 330; New York Hopewell, 250; Northwest Coast, 466, 468; Old Bering Sea, 478; Old Signal Butte, 321; Okvik, 475; Oneota, 316; Original Eskimo, 474; Owasco, 255; Point Peninsula, 252; Post-Punuk, 488; Poverty Point, 405; Pre-Koniag, bow, 497; Proto-Bluff Dweller, 338; pump, 33; Red Ocher, 291; Savannah River, 373; strap, 33; Swift Creek, 377; Thompson River region, 454; Thule, 507; Upper Columbia region, 449; Whittlesey, 282; Wisconsin Hopewell, 306; Younge, 280; *see also* Tools, utensils, and weapons
Drought, Anasazi, Pueblo III, 147
Drucker, Philip, vi
Drums: Anasazi, Pueblo III, 136; Fort Ancient, 287; Frontenac, 242; Hopewell, 274; Lamoka, 241; Natchezan, 419; Okvik, 476; Point Peninsula, 253; Whittlesey, 283; Wisconsin Hopewell, 307; *see also* Musical instruments
Dublan pottery, 215
Dwellings: Coles Creek, 412; Fort Ancient, 285; Irene, 380, 381; Lamar, 385; Macon Plateau, 382-83; Middle Mississippi, 354; Middlesex, 249; Old Signal Butte, 321; Point Peninsula, 252; Savannah, 378-79; Tchefuncte, 401; Whittlesey, 281; Younge, 280; *see also* Houses; Villages

Ear ornaments (earrings, ear-plugs, -pins, -spools), 39, 49; abalone shell, 70; Aztalan, 315; Caddo, 424; Coles Creek, 415; Copena, 352; copper, 44; Crystal River, 392; Fort Ancient, 286; Hopewell, 272 (and Fig. 76), 273 (Fig. 77), 278; Key Marco, 398; Lower Sacramento region, 432; Marksville, 408; Middle Kachemak Bay, 500; Middle Mississippi, 360; Natchezan, 419; New York Hopewell, 251; Plaquemine, 417; Savannah, 379; Southern Death Cult, 363; Troyville, 410, 411; Upper Columbia region, 451; Upper Republican, 328; Wisconsin Hopewell, 306; *see also* Ornaments
Early Aleut culture, 490-93
Early Anasazi, 438
Early Coastal culture, 247
Early Historic period, Plains area, 320, 331
Early Island, 432
Early Kachemak Bay culture, 499-500

Early Macon culture, 369-70
Early Mainland culture, 430
Early period, central California, 430
Early Sacramento culture, 430
Early Transitional period, Florida area, 391
Earth lodge, Upper Columbia region, 444; *see also* Pit-houses
Earthworks: eastern North America, third stage, 236; Ohio area, 288
East St. Louis (Ill.), 313
Eastern Eskimo area, 503-9
Eastern Folsom; *see* Folsom, Eastern
Eastern North America, chronology of, 516-17 (Fig. 122)
Effigies: Crystal River, antler, 392; Kansas Hopewell, 326; Key Marco, 398; Middle Aleut, 494; Pre-Koniag, 497; Weeden Island, 394; Wisconsin Hopewell, 307; *see also* Figurines
Effigy headdresses, Caddo, 424
Effigy Mound culture, 303-5
Effigy tobacco pipe: Adena, 266 (Fig. 72); Hopewell, 271 (Fig. 75)
Effigy vessels, Hohokam, 179, 186
Egyptians, 16, 79
El Paso Polychrome pottery, 221, 222
Elk, Fort Ancient, 285
Ellesmere Island, 503
Embossing, pottery, 56
Embroidery, false, 63
Emerson, Mrs. J. N., vi
Emigration, Asiatic, 21
Engraving, pottery, 56
Engraving tools (engravers, gravers): Anasazi, Pueblo I, 123; Borax Lake region, 434; Frontenac, 242; Intrusive Mound, 279; Ipiutak, 483; Middle Aleut, 494; Old Bering Sea, 478; Old Signal Butte, 321; Point Peninsula, 253; Punuk, 485; Upper Columbia region, 449; *see also* Tools, utensils, and weapons
Environment, adaptation to, 520
Epicanthic fold, 17
Epidemic, Anasazi, Pueblo III, 147
Erie Indians, Whittlesey, 283
Eskimo: areas, 473-509; chronology of, 473 (Chart XVI), 491 (Chart XVII), 503 (Chart XVIII), 515 (Fig. 122); cultures, 473-509; pottery, 54, 519 (*see also* Pottery); trade, 75
Estrella Red-on-Gray pottery, 171
Etching, pottery, 56; *see also* Art
Etowah culture, 366, 386; site, 387
Etowah River, 387
Europeans, 40
Excavation, 7
Extinct animals; *see* Animals, extinct
Eyes, 17

Face size, 17
Fairbanks, Charles, vi
Fans, Ozark Bluff Dweller, 341
Farming, 293, 294; *see also* Agriculture
Faulkner culture, 289
Fauna, Eastern Eskimo area, 503
Feather-cloth: Anasazi, Pueblo I, 124; Anasazi, Pueblo III, 140
Feathered serpents, Southern Death Cult, 363
Feathering arrows, 34
Feathers: Ozark Bluff Dweller, 341; trade in, 67
Ferns, 61
Fiber-shredders, Aztalan, 315
Fiber-tempered pottery, 519
Fiber textile, Hohokam, Classic, 194; *see also* Cloth
Fibers, shredded, 61
Field, Stanley, vi
Fighting-cocks motif, Southern Death Cult, 363
Figurines (figures): Hohokam, Classic, 193; Hohokam, Colonial, 178; Hohokam, Pioneer, 172; Hohokam, Sedentary, 184, 185; Hopewell, 273 (Fig. 77); Key Marco, 397 (Fig. 95); Macon Plateau, 384; Natchezan, 419; Okvik, 476 (Fig. 114); Pre-Koniag, 497; Puebloid, 225; Southern Death Cult, 363; Thule, 507; Troyville, 410; *see also* Art; Effigies
Finger technique, articles made with, 63
Finger weaving, 61
Finishing, pottery, 54-56
Fire-and-water, chipping method, 30
Firepits: Mogollon-Mimbres, Mimbres, 211; Mogollon-Mimbres, Pine Lawn, 201; Mogollon-Mimbres, Three Circle, 208
Firing, pottery, 58
Fish, 25; *see also* Livelihood
Fish gorges: Fort Ancient, 286; Frontenac, 242; Lamoka, 240; Laurel, 308; Laurentian I, 244; Lower Sacramento region, 432, 433; Mille Lacs, 310; Old Copper, 302; Oneota, 316; Point Peninsula, 252; Santa Barbara region, 430, 434; Snake-Clearwater region, 459
Fish spear, 482; *see also* Spears
Fish-weir site, Boylston, 93; *see also* Weirs
Fishgigs, Lower Sacramento region, 430, 432
Fishhooks: Early Aleut, 491; Early Kachemak Bay, 500; Fort Ancient, 286; Frontenac, 242; Hopewell, 270; Indian Knoll, 261; Key Marco, 395; Lamoka, 240; Late Kachemak Bay, 501; Lower Sacramento region, 432, 433; Marksville, 407; Middle Columbia region, 456; Middle Mississippi, 356; Nebraska, 330; New York Hopewell,

250; Northwest Coast area, 465; Okvik, 475; Old Bering Sea, 478; Old Iroquois, 256; Oneota, 316; Owasco, 255; Point Peninsula, 252; Post-Punuk, 488; Pre-Koniag, 496; Santa Barbara region, 430, 434, 439; Savannah River, 372; Thompson River region, 453; Thule, 506; trade in, 70; Upper Columbia region, 449; Upper Republican, 327; Whittlesey, 282

Fishing, 464; *see also* Livelihood

Fishtail sandals, Big Bend Cave, 220

Flaking technique, 29, 30, 34

Flaking tools (flakers): Adena, 265; Caddo, 423; Candy Creek, 349; Coles Creek, 414; Dorset, 504; Early Aleut, 491; Early Coastal, 247; Folsom, 85; Frontenac, 242; Indian Knoll, 261; Intrusive Mound, 279; Ipiutak, 483; Kansas Hopewell, 326; Lamoka, 241; Late Kachemak Bay, 501; Laurentian I, 244; Mogollon-Mimbres, Pine Lawn, 204; Nebraska, 330; Okvik, 475; Old Signal Butte, 322; Oneota, 317; Owasco, 255; Ozark Bluff Dweller, 340; Point Peninsula, 253; Pre-Koniag, 497; Proto–Bluff Dweller, 339; Savannah River, 373; Thule, 507; Upper Republican, 327; Younge, 289; *see also* Tools, utensils, and weapons

Flathead tribe, 442

Fleshing tools: Dismal River, 332; Mille Lacs, 310; Mira Creek, 324; Pre-Koniag, 497; Sterns Creek, 323

Flint, 29; trade in, 67; weathered, 35

Float: plugs, Okvik, 475; sealskin, Thule, 506

Floated surface, pottery, 57

Flood-water irrigation, Hohokam, Pioneer, 171; *see also* Canals; Irrigation

Floods, action of, 86

Florida, 371, 374, 376, 392, 393, 395, 409, 415

Florida area, 390–98; chronology of, 517 (Fig. 122); periods and cultures, 390 (Chart XIII); trade with, 72

Flutes: Fort Ancient, 287; Frontenac, 242; Hopewell, 274; Lamoka, 241; Whittlesey, 283; *see also* Musical instruments

Folk tales, 21

Folsom culture, 11, 82, 83–85, 89, 91, 92, 261, 262, 289, 319, 367; Eastern type, 370; "fluted" point, 84; in Ohio, 288; migration eastward, 94

Food-collecting; *see* Livelihood

Foods: Amazonian region, 80; effect of agriculture, 518; trade in, 67; *see also* Livelihood

Ford, James A., vi

Forestdale Smudged pottery, 116, 178, 184, 189

Fort Ancient culture, 284–87

Fort Collins (Colo.), 83

Fort Walton culture, 394

Fossil shark teeth; *see* Shark teeth

Four-Mile Polychrome pottery, 152, 153, 193

Fox, domesticated, Pre-Koniag, 496

Fracturing, stone work, 29, 30, 34

Fraser River, 74, 442, 450, 464, 465, 468

Frijoles Canyon; *see* Rito de los Frijoles Canyon

Frontenac culture, 241–43, 505

Fulton Aspect, Caddo area, 421

Fur: robes, 220; trade in, 67, 73, 74; *see also* Cloth, fur

Gabbro, 32

Galena, 72, 291, 292, 353, 394, 408, 419

Games: Fort Ancient, 287; Irene, 381; Kansas Hopewell, 326; Lamar, 386; Macon Plateau, 384; Upper Republican, 328

Gaming bones, Promontory, 226

Gaming-sticks, 47; *see also* Games

Garters, weaving of, 63

Geology, 81; dating, 79, 82, 91

Georgia Lake industry, 83

Georgetown period culture; *see* Mogollon-Mimbres culture

Georgia, 366, 369, 371, 374, 375, 376, 378, 380, 382, 385, 387, 394

Georgia area, 369–89; chronology, 370 (Chart XII), 517 (Fig. 122)

Gibson Aspect, Caddo area, 421

Gila Basin, 197

Gila Butte Red-on-Buff pottery, 176, 178

Gila Plain pottery, 171, 176, 182, 192

Gila Polychrome pottery, 152, 153, 192, 195, 215

Gila Red pottery, 192

Gila River, 85, 168, 171, 174, 182, 188

Gila shoulder, 182, 183

Gila Smudged pottery, 192

Gila Valley, 70

Gilmore, M. R., 53–54

Glacial Kame culture, 262–64

Glaciers (glaciation, glacial): continental, 81 corridors, 81; deposits, 91; in Europe, 20

Glaze paint, pottery, 57, 154

Glaze ware pottery, trade in, 71

Glazed ware, 154

Gneiss, tools from, 32

Goggles, snow: Birnirk, 487; Dorset, 505; Ipiutak, 482 (Fig. 116), 483; Okvik, 476 (Fig. 114); Old Bering Sea, 480; Post-Punuk, 488; Thule, 507

Gold, Hopewell, 272

Gorges; *see* Fish gorges

Gorgets, 39; Adena, 265; Aztalan, 315; Baumer, 291; Candy Creek, 349; Copena, 352, 353; Early Coastal, 247; Fort Ancient, 286; Frontenac, 242; Glacial Kame, 263; Hopewell, 272; Irene, 382; Intrusive Mound,

INDEX 561

279; Kansas Hopewell, 326; Keshena, 311; Key Marco, 395; Lamar, 386; Lauderdale, 346; Macon Plateau, 384; Middle Mississippi, 360; Middlesex, 249; Natchezan, 419; New York Hopewell, 251; Old Bering Sea, 480; Point Peninsula, 253; Poverty Point, 405; Red Ocher, 292; Savannah, 379; Savannah River, 373; Southern Death Cult, 363, 364 (Fig. 89); Upper Republican, 328; Weeden Island, 394; Whittlesey, 283; Wilmington, 375; Wisconsin Hopewell, 307; Younge, 280

Gouges: Frontenac, 242; Key Marco, 395; Laurel, 309; Laurentian I, 244 (Fig. 69); Middlesex, 249; Mira Creek, 324; Nebraska, 330; Old Copper, 300, 301 (Fig. 83); Old Signal Butte, 322; Orient, 248; Whittlesey, 282

Gourds, 233–34, 331, 339, 340, 352, 355

Grand Canyon, 71

Grass, 61; canary, 234

Grave-goods; *see* Burial offerings

Grave-house, Birnirk, 487

Grave-offerings; *see* Burial offerings

Gravers; *see* Engraving tools

Graves, slab-lined: Point Peninsula, 254; Upper Republican, 328; *see also* Burials

Great House, Casa Grande, Arizona, 191, 215

Great Kiva, 134, 136, 137

Great Lakes, 40, 255, 259

"Green" blanks, stone work, 35

Greenland, 15, 503, 508, 509

Gregg, Clifford C., vi

Griffin, James B., vi

Griga tribe, 417

Grinding-stones, 29, 31, 35; Adena, 265; Baumer, 291; Caddo, 423; Dismal River, 332; Faulkner, 289; Lamoka, 240; Late Kachemak Bay, 501; Lauderdale, 346; Middle Aleut, 493; Nebraska, 330; Old Iroquois, 256; Old Signal Butte, 321; Proto-Bluff Dweller, 339; Sterns Creek, 323; Swift Creek, 378; Tchefuncte, 403 (Fig. 97); *see also* Manos

Grinding tools: Cochise, 91; Laurel, 309

Ground sloth, giant, 82

Guaco; *see* Rocky Mountain bee plant

Guale tribe, 382

Guatemala, 79, 519

Gulf of California, 69

Gulf Coast, 393, 394

Gulf of Mexico, 69, 70, 72, 231, 277, 288, 328

Guns, 40, 387

Gypsum Cave, Nevada, 82, 219, 227, 434

Haida, 462, 469
Hair, 17

Hair brushes, Anasazi, Pueblo III, 143

Hair ornaments: Anasazi, Basket Maker, 110; Indian Knoll, 261; Okvik, 476; shell, 49; Southern Death Cult, 363; *see also* Ornaments

Hair-spreaders, Fort Ancient, 286

Hairdress: Anasazi, Basket Maker, 100; Anasazi, Pueblo III, 140; Anasazi, Pueblo IV, 156

Hairpins, 47; Fort Ancient, 286; Lauderdale, 346; Middle Mississippi, 360

Haliotis shells, trade in, 73, 74; *see also* Abalone

Hamilton County, Ohio, 267

Hamilton culture, 350–51

Hammers (hammerstones), 30, 31, 37, 57; Anasazi, Pueblo II, 128; Borax Lake site, 434; Candy Creek, 349; Coles Creek, 414; copper mining, 41; Dismal River, 332; Dorset, 504; Early Kachemak Bay, 500; Fort Ancient, 286; Frontenac, 242; Hamilton, 351; Hohokam, Classic, 194; Hohokam, Pioneer, 173; Hohokam, Sedentary 185; Indian Knoll, 261, Intrusive Mound, 279; Inugsuk, 508; Keshena, 311; Key Marco, 395; Lamar, 386; Lamoka, 241; Late Kachemak Bay, 501; Macon Plateau, 384; Marksville, 407; Middle Columbia Region, 456; Mogollon-Mimbres, Mimbres, 212; Mogollon-Mimbres, Pine Lawn, 203; Morton, 293; Nebraska, 330; New York Hopewell, 250; Ocmulgee Fields, 388; Old Iroquois, 256; Old Signal Butte, 321; Owasco, 255; Ozark Bluff Dweller, 340; Point Peninsula, 253; Savannah River, 373; Snake-Clearwater region, 460; Sterns Creek, 323; Tchefuncte, 402; Thule, 507; Upper Columbia region, 450; Weeden Island, 393; Whittlesey, 282

Handbook of the American Indians, 39

Handles: Hopewell, 272; Intrusive Mound, 279

Handstones: Anasazi, Basket Maker, 106; Cochise, Chiricahua, 88, 89; Cochise, San Pedro, 90; Cochise, Sulphur Springs, 87; Mogollon-Mimbres, Pine Lawn, 203

Hano town, 100

Harpoons (harpoon parts): Birnirk, 486; Dorset, 504; Early Aleut, 491, 492 (and Fig. 118); Early Kachemak Bay, 499; Fort Ancient, 286; Frontenac, 242; Intrusive Mound, 279; Ipiutak, 481, 482 (and Fig. 116); Koniag, 499; Late Aleut, 495; Late Kachemak Bay, 501; Laurel, 308; Middle Aleut, 493; Middle Kachemak Bay, 500; Nebraska, 330; northern California, 428, 429 (Fig. 103); Northwest Coast area, 465, 466, 469; Okvik, 474, 475; Old Bering Sea,

478, 479 (Fig. 115); Old Copper, 301 (Fig. 83), 302; Original Eskimo, 473; Owasco, 255; Point Peninsula, 252; Post-Punuk, 488; Pre-Koniag, 496, 497; Punuk, 485; Santa Barbara region, 434; Thule, 506
Harris, Alfred, vi
Harvard University, 44
Hats: basketry, Northwest Coast area, 468; Koniag, 499; Late Aleut, 495, 496; see also Costume
Havasupai Indians: pottery, 53; trade in red ocher, 71
Hawikuh Glaze-on-White pottery, 153
Head shapes, 17
Headplates, Hopewell, 271
Heads, deformed; see Deformation
Hearing, sense of, 24
Hearths, Cochise, 86; see also Firepits
Hearthstones: Cochise, 86; Maravillas, 219
Heddle, weaving, 62
Height: physical trait, 17; of Southwest Indians, 98
Heizer, Robert F., vi
Hematite; see Red ocher
Hemp, 61
Heshotauthla Polychrome pottery, 153
Hiawatha, 297
Hickory trees, 86
Hidatsa pottery, 54
Hides, trade in, 68, 70, 73
Historic period, Northeastern area, 240
Hoes: Adena, 265; Anasazi, Pueblo II, 128; Anasazi, Pueblo III, 139; Aztalan, 314; Caddo, 422; Copena, 352; definition of, 194; Dismal River, 332; eastern North America, 237; Fort Ancient, 285; Hohokam, Classic, 194; Hohokam, Colonial, 194; Irene, 381; Kansas Hopewell, 325; Key Marco, 395; Lamar, 386; Laurel, 308; Macon Plateau, 383; Middle Mississippi, 355; Middle Mississippi in Ohio, 284; Mogollon-Mimbres, Mimbres, 213; Mogollon-Mimbres, Pine Lawn, 204; Natchezan, 419; Nebraska, 330; Ocmulgee Fields, 388; Oneota, 316; Ozark Bluff Dweller, 340; Point Peninsula, 252; Savannah, 379; Top-Layer, 343; Upper Republican, 327; Weeden Island, 394; Whittlesey, 282
Hogan, Navaho, 158
Hohokam, 9, 42, 198, 212, 213, 215, 217, 438; chronology of, 514 (Fig. 122); culture, 168–97, 198, 210; periods: Classic, 188–94; Colonial, 174–81; Pioneer, 169–74; Sedentary, 182–88; physical type, 98; pottery, 93, 202, 519; trade, 69–70; villages, 193
Hohokam Red-on-Buff pottery, 188
Homolobi pueblo, 150
Hones; see Whetstones

Hoods, Late Aleut, 495
Hooks: fish (see Fishhooks); gull, Thule, 506; meat, Birnirk, 486; meat, Post-Punuk, 488; spear-thrower, 38
Hooton, E. A., 17
Hopewell, 249, 258, 263, 266, 278, 281, 284, 287, 348, 350, 353, 373, 376, 384, 392; culture, 267–78; mounds, 279; trade, 72
Hopewell culture in Illinois, 293–94
Hopi area, 149
Hopi language, 99
Hopi pottery, 151
Hopi pueblos, 161–64
Hopi trade, 67, 70, 71
Horn, 47
Hornstone, 29
Horse, 73, 82, 87, 313, 320, 390, 444
Hotevilla pueblo, 162, 163
Houma tribe, Natchezan culture, 417
Houses, 5, 92; Adena, 264 (Fig. 71); Anasazi, Basket Maker, 104; Anasazi, Modified Basket Maker, 112; Aztalan, 313; Baumer, 290; Birnirk, 486; Buena Vista Lake region, 432, 433; Caddo, 422; Candy Creek, 348; Clam River, 312; Copena, 352; Dismal River, 331; Dorset, 503–4; Early Aleut, 490; Early Coastal, 247; Hamilton, 350; Hohokam, Classic, 191; Hopewell, 268; Hopewell in Illinois, 293; Intrusive Mound, 278; Inugsuk, 508; Keshena, 310; Key Marco, 359; Koniag, 498; Lamar, 385; Lamoka, 240; Late Aleut, 495; Late Kachemak Bay, 501; Lauderdale, 346; Laurel, 308; Laurentian I, 243; Lewis, 294; Lower Sacramento Region, 433; Middle Columbia Region, 455; Middle Kachemak Bay, 500; Middle Mississippi, 355 (Fig. 85); Middle Mississippi in Ohio, 283, 284; Mille Lacs, 309; Mira Creek, 323; Mogollon-Mimbres, Chihuahua, 215; Mogollon-Mimbres, Georgetown, 206; Mogollon-Mimbres, Mimbres, 210; Mogollon-Mimbres, Pine Lawn, 201; Natchezan, 418; Nebraska, 329; Northwest Coast area, 464, 465 (and Fig. 111); Ocmulgee Fields, 387; Okvik, 474; Old Bering Sea, 477; Old Iroquois, 256; Original Eskimo, 473; Owasco, 254; Pre-Koniag, 496; Post-Punuk, 487–88; Puebloid, 225; Punuk, 484; Santa Barbara region, 430, 434; Snake-Clearwater region, 459; Swift Creek, 376; terraced, 159; Thompson River region, 452; Thule, 505–6; Upper Columbia region, 444; Weeden Island, 393; Wilmington, 375; Wisconsin Hopewell, 306; see also Villages
Hrdlička, Aleš, 495
Hudson's Bay, 503, 505
Humboldt Bay, 428, 462

INDEX

Hunting, 21, 34, 84, 87, 518, 520; *see also* Livelihood
Hupa Indians, 428
Huron Indians, 281

Ice-creepers: Dorset, 505; Okvik, 476; Old Bering Sea, 480; Post-Punuk, 488
Ice picks: Okvik, 475; Old Bering Sea, 478
Ice-scoops: Birnirk, 486; Old Bering Sea, 478; Thule, 506
Ice sheets, geological, 21
Idol, Southern Death Cult, 366 (Fig. 92)
Illinois, 259, 261, 289, 290, 291, 292, 294, 299, 303, 315, 353
Illinois area, 289–96; chronology of, 516 (Fig. 122)
Illinois Hopewell culture; *see* Hopewell culture in Illinois
Imbrication, weaving, 64, 445
Immigration from Asia, 19, 21
Implements; *see* Tools, utensils, and weapons
Impressing, pottery, 56
Incising, pottery, 56
Inclosure, village: Hohokam, Classic, 190; Hopewell, 267; *see also* Villages
Indented Corrugated pottery, 127, 138, 139, 152, 155
Indian Knoll culture, 259–62
Indiana, 259, 262, 263, 283, 285, 290, 353
Indians: "Amerind," 15; fallacies about, 23–25; origin of, 15–21; personality traits of, 23, 24; physical traits of, 17–19, 23, 24; race, 19; role of, in United States history, 23
Inhumation; *see* Burials
Intermediate Buena Vista culture, 432
Intermediate Mainland culture, 432
Intermediate period: Middle Southern area, 345, 347–50, 367; Northeastern area, 240, 247–54, 258; Ozark Plateau area, 338, 339–42, 343; Plains area, 319, 322–26; Wisconsin-Minnesota area, 298, 303–9
Intrusive Mound culture, 278–79
Inugsuk, Eastern Eskimo area, 508–9
Invention, independent, 520
Iowa, 267, 299, 303, 315, 317
Ipiutak culture, 474, 477, 481–84
Irene culture, 380, 386
Iron, 45, 272, 393, 504; implements, 40; *see also* Tools, utensils, and weapons
Iroquois, 255, 281, 283; confederacy, 240
Irrigation: Hohokam, 168, 192, 194; Hohokam, Colonial, 175; Hohokam, Pioneer, 170, 171; Hohokam, Sedentary, 182; Mogollon-Mimbres, Mimbres, 212; Mogollon-Mimbres, Pine Lawn, 202; *see also* Canals
Inscriptions, runic, Inugsuk, 508
Insects, Mogollon-Mimbres, Pine Lawn, 202

Isle Royale, 40, 300
Isleta pueblo, 164
Israel, Ten Lost Tribes of, 16, 22
Ivory, 21, 47, 75

Jadeite, 67, 74, 216
Japan current, 463
Jasper, 29, 32
Jeddito Black-on-Orange pottery, 139
Jeddito Black-on-Yellow pottery, 70, 151, 193
Jeddito Corrugated pottery, 151
Jeddito Plain pottery, 151
Jeddito Tooled pottery, 151
Jefferson County, Wisconsin, 313
Jemez Indians, 146, 159, 164
Jemez River, 166

Kachemak Bay culture; *see* Early Kachemak Bay culture; Late Kachemak Bay culture; Middle Kachemak Bay culture
Kamchatka, Alaska, 495
Kamloops, Thompson River region, 452
Kana-a Black-on-White pottery, 121, 178, 184
Kana-a Gray pottery, 114, 121
Kansa tribe, 317
Kansas, 267, 277, 316, 325, 326, 328
Kansas Hopewell culture, 325–26
Kayak, Birnirk, 487; Dorset, 504; Ipiutak, 483; Koniag, 499; Late Aleut, 495; Middle Aleut, 494; Okvik, 475; Old Bering Sea, 480; Post-Punuk, 488; Pre-Koniag, 497; Thule, 507; *see also* Umiak
Kayenta (Anasazi, Pueblo III), 129; kivas, 137; masonry, 131; trade, 222
Kayenta Black-on-White pottery, 138
Kayenta Polychrome pottery, 139
Keewenaw Peninsula, 300
Kentucky, 259, 263, 266, 267, 283, 285, 290, 342, 344, 353
Keres language, 165, 166
Kersantite, 32
Keshena culture, 310–11
Key Marco culture, 395–98
Kiatuthlanna Black-on-White pottery, 122
Kiet Siel Polychrome pottery, 139
"Killed" bowls: Mogollon-Mimbres, Mimbres, 214; Poverty Point, 405
Kiln pottery, Mogollon-Mimbres, Pine Lawn, 202
Kilts, Anasazi, Pueblo IV, 156; *see also* Costume
Kincaid site, 294
Kivas, 126, 159, 211; Anasazi, 208; Anasazi, Modified Basket Maker, 113; Anasazi, Pueblo II, 125; Anasazi, Pueblo III, 131, 132, 145, Acoma, 136, Chaco, 134, Kayenta, 137, Mesa Verde, 132, 135 (Fig. 29);

Anasazi, Pueblo IV, 150; Puebloid, 224, 225
Knitting, 64, 109
Knives, 30, 31, 34, 37, 84; Adena, 265; Anasazi, Basket Maker, 106; Anasazi, Modified Basket Maker, 117; Anasazi, Pueblo II, 127; Anasazi, Pueblo III, 140; Aztalan, 315; Baumer, 291; Birnirk, 486; Black Rock Cave, 223; Borax Lake region, 434; Bravo Valley, 222; Browns Valley, 299; Caddo, 423; Candy Creek, 349; Copell, 400; Copena, 352; desert region, 437; Dismal River, 332; Dorset, 504; Early Aleut, 491, 492 (Fig. 118); Early Kachemak Bay, 500; Early Macon, 370; Folsom, 84; Fort Ancient, 286; Frontenac, 242; Hamilton, 351; Hohokam, Classic, 194; Hohokam, Colonial, 179; Hohokam, Sedentary, 185; Hopewell, 270 (and Fig. 74); Indian Knoll, 261; Kansas Hopewell, 326; Key Marco, 395; Lamar, 386; Lamoka, 240; Late Kachemak Bay, 501; Lauderdale, 346; Laurel, 308; Laurentian I, 244; Laurentian II, 246 (Fig. 69); Maravillas, 219; Marksville, 407; Middle Aleut, 493; Middle Columbia region, 456; Middle Mississippi, 356; Middlesex, 249; Mille Lacs, 310; Mira Creek, 324; Mogollon-Mimbres, Pine Lawn, 203, 204; Morton, 293; Natchezan, 418; Nebraska, 330; New York Hopewell, 250; Northwest Coast area, 468; Ocmulgee Fields, 388; Okvik, 475, 476 (Fig. 114); Old Bering Sea, 478; Old Copper, 300, 301 (Fig. 83); Old Signal Butte, 321; Orient, 248; Original Eskimo, 474; Point Peninsula, 252; Poverty Point, 405; Pre-Koniag, 497; Proto–Bluff Dweller, 339; Puebloid, 225; Red Ocher, 291; San Dieguito region, 436; Savannah River, 372; Swift Creek, 377; Tchefuncte, 403 (Fig. 97), 404; Thule, 507; time to make, 31–32; Upper Colombia region, 449; Upper Republican, 327; Weeden Island, 393; Whittlesey, 282; Wisconsin Hopewell, 306; see also Draw knives; Snow knives
Kobuk River, 75
Kodiak Island, 490, 496, 498, 502
Kokopnyama, 150
Koniag culture, 498–99, 501
Kutenai Indians, 442
Kwakiutl Indians, 462, 463, 464, 469

La Ciudad site, 192
La Jolla culture, 436
La Plata Black-on-Red pottery, 122
La Plata Black-on-White pottery, 115
Labrador, 503, 505
Labrets: Key Marco, 395; Koniag, 499; Late Aleut, 495; Late Kachemak Bay, 501; Middle Aleut, 494; Middle Kachemak Bay, 500; Northwest Coast area, 469; Pre-Koniag, 497
Ladles; see Spoons; Tools, utensils, and weapons
Laguna, 165
Lake Agassiz, 298
Lake Mohave, 83; complex, 437
Lake Pelican, 297
Lake Superior, 66, 67, 405; region, 40, 44
Lakes, dried-up, 91
Lamar culture, 366, 382, 385, 387
Lamoka culture, 240–41, 243
Lamps, 519; Birnirk, 487; Dorset, 504; Early Aleut, 491; Early Kachemak Bay, 500; Koniag, 499; Late Aleut, 495; Late Kachemak Bay, 501; Middle Aleut, 493–94; Middle Kachemak Bay, 500; Okvik, 475; Old Bering Sea, 477–78; Original Eskimo, 474; Pre-Koniag, 497; Post-Punuk, 488; Thule, 507; trade in, 75
Lances; see Projectile points; Spears
Language, 99; Anasazi, Basket Maker, 104; Athapascan, 157; Aztec, 99; Keres, 165, 166; Mobilian, 68; Muskhogean, 361, 382; prehistoric, 232; Salish, 452; sign, 68; Southwest, 99; Tewa, 165, 166, 167; Tigua, 165, 166
Lapstones: Baumer, 291; Indian Knoll, 261
Late Aleut culture, 495–96
Late Buena Vista culture, 433
Late Coastal culture, 247
Late Island culture, 434
Late Kachemak Bay culture, 501
Late Mainland culture, 434
Late period: Central California, 429, 432; southern California, 439
Late Prehistoric period: Florida area, 391, 394–98; Illinois area, 294–96; Northeastern area, 240, 247, 254–58; Ohio area, 259, 278–88; Ozark Plateau area, 338, 342–43; Plains area, 319, 326–31; Wisconsin-Minnesota area, 309–16
Late Sacramento culture, 433
Late Transitional period, Florida, 391, 392
Lauderdale culture, 345–47
Laurel culture, 307–09
Laurentian I culture, 243–45, 505
Laurentian II culture, 246
Lead, 45, 57, 154
Leggings: Anasazi, Pueblo III, 140; Hopewell, 271; Intrusive Mound, 279; Natchezan, 419; Ozark Bluff Dweller, 341; Upper Columbia region, 450; see also Costume
Lewis, Meriwether, 455
Lewis culture, 294

INDEX

Lignite, trade in, 71
Lindenmeier site, 83
Lino Black-on-Gray pottery, 115, 178
Lino Gray pottery, 114, 121
Lip ornaments, 39; *see also* Labrets; Ornaments
Litters, Natchezan, 419
Little Colorado River, 149; Indians of, 189
Little Miami River, 267
Livelihood: Adena, 264–65; Anasazi, Basket Maker, 104; Anasazi, Modified Basket Maker, 113, 144; Anasazi, Pueblo I, 121; Anasazi, Pueblo II, 126; Anasazi, Pueblo III, 137, 144; Anasazi, Pueblo IV, 151; Aztalan, 314; Baumer, 290; Big Bend Cave, 219; Birnirk, 486; Bravo Valley, 222; Browns Valley site, 299; Caddo, 422; Candy Creek, 348; Clam River, 312; Cochise, Chiricahua, 88; Cochise, San Pedro, 89; Cochise, Sulphur Spring, 87; Coles Creek, 412; Copell, 400; Deptford, 374; Dismal River, 331; Dorset, 504; Early Aleut, 490; Early Coastal, 247; Early Kachemak Bay, 499; Early Macon, 370; Effigy Mound, 303; Folsom, 84; Fort Ancient, 285; Frontenac, 241; Glacial Kame, 262; Hamilton, 350; Hohokam, Classic, 192; Hohokam, Colonial, 174; Hohokam, Pioneer, 170; Hohokam, Sedentary, 182; Hopewell, 268; Indian Knoll, 260; Intrusive Mound, 278; Inugsuk, 508; Ipiutak, 481; Irene, 381; Kansas Hopewell, 325; Keshena, 310; Key Marco, 395; Koniag, 498; Lamar, 385; Lamoka, 240; Late Aleut, 495; Late Kachemak Bay, 501; Lauderdale, 346, 347; Laurel, 308; Laurentian I, 243; Laurentian II, 246; Macon Plateau, 383; Maravillas, 219; Marksville, 406; Middle Aleut, 493; Middle Kachemak Bay, 500; Middle Mississippi, 355; Middlesex, 249; Mille Lacs, 309; Mira Creek, 323; Mogollon-Mimbres, Chihuahua, 215; Mogollon-Mimbres, Georgetown, 206; Mogollon-Mimbres, Mimbres, 211; Mogollon-Mimbres, Pine Lawn, 201; Mogollon-Mimbres, San Francisco, 207; Mogollon-Mimbres, Three Circle, 208; Morton, 292; Natchezan, 418; Nebraska, 329; New York Hopewell, 250; Northwest Coast area, 464; Ocmulgee Fields, 387; Okvik, 474; Old Bering Sea, 477; Old Copper, 299–300; Old Iroquois, 256; Old Signal Butte, 321; Oneota, 316; Orient, 248; Original Eskimo, 473; Owasco, 254; Ozark Bluff Dweller, 339; Plaquemine, 416; Plateau area, 443; Point Peninsula, 252; Post-Punuk, 488; Poverty Point, 404; Pre-Koniag, 496; Puebloid, 224; Punuk, 484; Red Ocher, 291; Savannah, 379; Savannah River, 371; Sterns Creek, 322; Swift Creek, 376; Tchefuncte, 401; Thule, 506; Upper Republican, 327; Weeden Island, 393; Whittlesey, 281; Wilmington, 375; Wisconsin Hopewell, 306; Younge, 280
Lodges, earthen, Macon Plateau, 383
Loincloths; *see* Breechclouts; Costume
Long Island, 248
Long-nosed god, Southern Death Cult, 366
Longheads, 98; *see also* People; Physical traits; Skulls
Loom: Puebloid, 226; true, 62, 63, 124; weights, 155
Looping, weaving technique, 64, 109
Los Muertos site, 192, 195, 215
"Lost color" method, 57
"Lost continent"; *see* Atlantis
Lost wax method, 58, 184
Louisiana, 40, 399, 400, 401, 404, 409, 411, 415, 417, 421
Lower Loupe culture, 333
Lower Mississippi Valley area, 270, 399–418
Lower Sacramento region, 430, 432, 433
Luiseño Indians, 437
Luiseño pottery, 53
Lummis, C. F., 159
Luna, Tristan de, 345, 362

Macaws, trade in, 71
McGregor, John C., 116
McGuire, J. O., 31, 32
Mackenzie River, 81
Mackenzie Valley, 81
McKern, W. C., vi
McNary, Agnes, vi
MacNeish, Richard, vi
Macon Plateau culture, 378, 382–84, 386
Madera Black-on-Red pottery, 215
Maine, 248
Maize; *see* Corn
Malachite, trade in, 71
Malleations, pottery finish, 54
Mammoth, 87, 390; *see also* Animals, extinct
Man, antiquity of, in Europe, 79; *see also* Indians
Mancos Black-on-White pottery, 126, 128
Mandan culture, 333; pottery, 54
Manganese, 57
Manioc, 80
Manos: Anasazi, Basket Maker, 106; Anasazi, Modified Basket Maker, 117; Anasazi, Pueblo I, 122; Anasazi, Pueblo II, 127; Anasazi, Pueblo III, 140; Anasazi, Pueblo IV, 155; Big Bend Cave, 220; Borax Lake region, 434; Bravo Valley, 222; Caddo, 423; central California, 432, 433; Cochise, Chiricahua, 88; Dismal River, 332; Faulkner,

289; Fort Ancient, 286; Hohokam, Classic, 193; Hohokam, Colonial, 179; Hohokam, Pioneer, 173; Hohokam, Sedentary, 185; Indian Knoll, 261; La Jolla, 436; Lamar, 386; Late Kachemak Bay, 501; Maravillas, 219; Mogollon-Mimbres, Georgetown, 206; Mogollon-Mimbres, Mimbres, 212; Mogollon-Mimbres, San Francisco, 207; Mogollon-Mimbres, Three Circle, 209; Old Copper, 302; Santa Barbara region, 430

Mantles, feather, Natchezan, 419; *see also* Costume

Manufacture, primitive methods, 30–39, 42, 43

Maravillas culture, 219

Marksville culture, 270, 278, 339, 348, 375, 392, 406–9, 411, 416

Marksville pottery, 407 (Fig. 98)

Marlin spikes, 475

Marsh elder, 234

Martin, Paul S., 116

Maryland, 254

Masks: Caddo, 424; Key Marco, 398, 397 (Fig. 95); Middle Aleut, 494; Middle Kachemak Bay, 500; Southern Death Cult, conch shell, 363; Wisconsin Hopewell, 307

Masonry: Anasazi, Pueblo III, 131; Mogollon-Mimbres, Mimbres, 210; Mogollon-Mimbres, Three Circle, 208; Puebloid, 225; southeastern Nevada, 227

Massachusetts, 15

Mastodon, 390

Mats (matting), 61; Anasazi, Pueblo III, 142; Caddo, 422; Coles Creek, 412; Fort Ancient, 285; Hohokam, Classic, 194; Hohokam, Sedentary, 186; Irene, 381; Key Marco, 395; Koniag, 499; Middle Mississippi, 284; Mogollon-Mimbres, Three Circle, 209; Natchezan, 418; Ocmulgee Fields, 387; Point Peninsula, 252; Santa Barbara region, 434; Swift Creek, 376; Ozark Bluff Dweller, 340; Younge, 280

Mattocks: Old Bering Sea, 478; Ipiutak, 483; Thule, 507

Mauls, 31, 37, 40; Anasazi, Modified Basket Maker, 118; Anasazi, Pueblo I, 123; Anasazi, Pueblo II, 128; Anasazi, Pueblo IV, 155; Dismal River, grooved, 332; Middle Columbia region, 456; Mogollon-Mimbres, Mimbres, 212; Mogollon-Mimbres, Pine Lawn, 203; Mogollon-Mimbres, San Francisco, 207; Mogollon-Mimbres, Three Circle, 209; northern California, 428; Northwest Coast area, 466, 468, 469; Old Signal Butte, 321; Pre-Koniag, 497; Snake-Clearwater region, 460; Thompson River region, 454; Thule, 507; Upper Columbia region, 449

Mayas, 10, 16, 79, 92; ball courts, 174

Mdewakanton tribe, 310

Meat, trade in, 74

Medicines, 48

Mediterranean race, 19

Medium of exchange, 68

Melons, 233

Menominee Indians, 311

Mesa: First, 161; Second and Third, 162

Mesa Verde, 113, 128, 129; area, 131

Mesa Verde Black-on-White pottery, 138

Mesa Verde National Park, 13, 113, 129, 146, 166

Mesquite, 170; *see also* Vegetation

Metals, casting, 185; *see also* Copper; Iron

Metates (milling-stones), 37, 106; Anasazi, Basket Maker, 106; Anasazi, Modified Basket Maker, 117; Anasazi, Pueblo I, 122; Anasazi, Pueblo II, 127; Anasazi, Pueblo III, 140; Anasazi, Pueblo IV, 155; Big Bend Cave, 220; Black Rock Cave, 223; Borax Lake region, 434; Bravo Valley, oval, 222; central California, 430, 432, 433; Cochise, 92; Cochise, Chiricahua, 88; Cochise, San Pedro, 89; Cochise, Sulphur Spring, 88; Diegueño, 437; Hohokam, Classic, 193; Hohokam, Colonial, 179; Hohokam, Pioneer, 172; Hohokam, Sedentary, 185; La Jolla, 437; Maravillas, 219; Mogollon-Mimbres, Chihuahua, 216; Mogollon-Mimbres, Georgetown, 206; Mogollon-Mimbres, Mimbres, 212; Mogollon-Mimbres, Pine Lawn, 203; Mogollon-Mimbres, San Francisco, 207; Mogollon-Mimbres, Three Circle, 209; northern California, 428; Promontory, 226; Puebloid, 224, 226; southeastern Nevada, 227; southeastern Oregon, 228

Mexico, 156, 221, 520

Mica: Adena, 265, 266; Cochise, San Pedro, 90; Copena, 353; Hohokam, Classic, 192; Hopewell, 269, 272, 274; Hopewell in Illinois, 294; Intrusive Mound, 279; Natchezan, 419; New York Hopewell, 251; Point Peninsula, 253; trade in, 67, 72; Weeden Island, 394; Wilmington, 375

Michigan, 251, 254, 255, 259, 262, 263, 267, 279, 280, 299, 300, 303

Middens, 5; Copena, 352; Deptford, shell, 374; Indian Knoll, shell, 260; Key Marco, 395; Lauderdale, shell, 345, 346; Laurentian II, 246; Northwest Coast area, 462, 463, 464, 469, 470; Savannah River, 371; Swift Creek, 376; Tchefuncte, 401; Tick Island, 391; Troyville, 409; Weeden Island, 393

Middle Aleut culture, 493–95, 501
Middle Columbia region, 442, 455–59
Middle Kachemak Bay culture, 500–501
Middle Mississippi culture, 284, 287, 295, 313, 315, 328, 330, 331, 338, 351, 353–61, 366, 384, 386, 394, 415, 417; in Illinois, 294–95; in Ohio, 283–84
Middle period, central California, 429, 430–32
Middle Southern area, 294, 344–68, 394; chronology, 345 (Chart XI), 517 (Fig. 122)
Middlemen, 69, 70
Middlesex culture, 248–50
Migration: from Asia, 81; of Folsom Indians, 94
Mill, grinding, 37; *see also* Metates; Mortars
Mill Creek culture, 333
Mille Lacs culture, 309–10
Milling-stones; *see* Metates
Mimbres Black-on-White pottery, 45, 212
Mimbres Boldface Black-on-White pottery, 184, 208
Mimbres Corrugated pottery, 212
Mimbres period, 164, 200, 210–14; *see also* Mogollon-Mimbres culture
Mimbres River, 210
Mining, methods of, 40
Minnesota, 251, 255, 299, 303, 353
"Minnesota Man," 297
Mira Creek culture, 323–24
Mirrors: Adena, 265; Intrusive Mound, 279; Late Kachemak Bay, 501
Mishongnovi pueblo, 146, 162
Mississippi, 266, 344, 353, 399, 409, 411, 415, 417
Mississippi River, 259
Missouri, 315, 317, 325, 337, 338, 339, 344, 353
Mittens: Post-Punuk, 488; Promontory, 226; *see also* Costume
Moats: Etowah, 387; Macon Plateau, 382, *see also* Earthworks; Villages
Mobile Bay, 393
Mobilian language, 68
Moccasins, 21; Adena, 265; Caddo, 424; Hopewell, 271; Indian Knoll, 261; Intrusive Mound, 279; Middle Mississippi, 359; Natchezan, 419; Nebraska, 330; Ozark Bluff Dweller, 341; Promontory, 226; Puebloid, 226; Southern Death Cult, 363; *see also* Costume
Modified Basket Maker period, 111–20, 144; *see also* Anasazi
Moenkopi pueblo, 163
Mogollon-Mimbres culture, 93, 98, 198–217; chronology, 200 (Chart IV), 514 (Fig. 122); culture elements, 199 (Fig. 60); periods: Chihuahua, 214–17; Georgetown, 206;

Mimbres, 210–14; Pine Lawn, 200–205; San Francisco, 206–7; Three Circle, 207–10
Mogollon Red-on-Brown pottery, 178, 207, 215
Mohave Desert, 70, 438
Mohave Indians, 67, 70
Mohave pottery, 53
Mold, metal-work, 44
Mongoloid, 17, 19, 22, 97, 100
Moore, Clarence B., 45
Morris, Earl H., 116
Mortars, 37; Anasazi, Pueblo I, 122; Anasazi, Pueblo II, 127; Aztalan, 315; Bravo Valley, paint, 222; Caddo, 423; Candy Creek, 349; Cochise, San Pedro, 90; Diegueño, 437; Early Coastal, 247; Faulkner, 289; Fort Ancient, 286; Frontenac, 242; Hohokam, Pioneer, 173; Hohokam, Sedentary, 185; Indian Knoll, 261; Key Marco, 395; Lamar, 386; Lamoka, 240; Lauderdale, 346; Laurentian I, 244; Lower Sacramento region, 432, 433, 434; Middle Columbia region, 456; Middle Mississippi, 355; Mogollon-Mimbres, Mimbres, 212; Mogollon-Mimbres, Pine Lawn, 203, 204; Mogollon-Mimbres, Three Circle, 209; Natchezan, 419; northern California, 428; Oneota, 316; Point Peninsula, 253; Proto–Bluff Dweller, 339; Santa Barbara region, 430; Savannah River, 373; Snake-Clearwater region, 460; Upper Columbia region, 450; Upper Republican, 327; Whittlesey, 282; *see also* Metates
Morton culture, 292–93
Mortuary offerings; *see* Burial offerings
Mosaics: Hohokam, Colonial, 181; Hopewell, 274
Mounds, 5; Caddo, pyramidal, 422; Clam River, 312–13; Coles Creek, pyramidal, 411; Crystal River, 392; eastern North America, 237; Effigy Mound, 305; Etowah, pyramidal, 387; Fort Ancient, 287; Fort Walton, flat-topped, 394; Hohokam, Classic, 191; Hopewell, 267, 277; Hopewell in Illinois, 293; Intrusive Mound, 279; Irene, 380; Key Marco, flat-topped, 395; Lamar, 385; Laurel, 309; Lower Mississippi Valley area, pyramidal, 400; Macon Plateau, 382–83, 384; Marksville, 409; Middle Mississippi, 360; Middle Mississippi in Illinois, 294; Middle Mississippi in Ohio, 283, 284; Mille Lacs, 310; Morton, 292, 293; Natchezan, 417, 419; Nebraska, 331; New York Hopewell, 251; Ohio area, 288; Oneota, 317; Plaquemine, 415–16; Santa Rosa–Swift Creek, 392; Savannah, 379, 380; Swift Creek, 376, 378; Tampico, 295; Tchefuncte, 401, 404; Troyville, 409, 411;

Weeden Island, 393, 394; Wilmington, 375; Wisconsin Hopewell, 307
Moundville, 366
"Mountain culture," 103
Mouth, 17; *see also* Physical traits
Mu, hypothetical continent of, 16, 22
Mugulasha tribe, 417
Mullers, 37; Lamoka, 240; Laurentian I, 244; Old Iroquois, 256; Oneota, 316; Savannah River, 373; Swift Creek, 378
Mummies, 17, 129, 142
Musical instruments: Fort Ancient, 287; Frontenac, 242; Hopewell, 274; Key Marco, 395; Lamoka, 241; Natchezan, 419; Okvik, 476; Point Peninsula, 253; Whittlesey, 283; Wisconsin Hopewell, 307
Muskhogean language, 361, 382
Mussels, trade in, 74

Nambé pueblo, 165
Natchez tribe, 417
Natchezan culture, 417, 424
Natural environment, Northwest Coast area, 463
Navaho Indians, 157-59
Near East pottery, 50
Nebraska, 315, 316, 317, 322, 325, 326, 328; culture, 326, 328-31, 332; Indians, 328
Necklaces, 49; Southern Death Cult, 363; *see also* Ornaments
Needle cases: Birnirk, 487; Dorset, 504; Early Kachemak Bay, 500; Ipiutak, 483; Late Kachemak Bay, 501; Okvik, 475; Old Bering Sea, 479 (and Fig. 115); Post-Punuk, 488; Pre-Koniag, 497; Thule, 507
Needles: Birnirk, 487; Dorset, 504; Early Aleut, 491; Early Coastal, 247; Early Kachemak Bay, 500; Folsom, 85; Fort Ancient, 286; Frontenac, 242; Intrusive Mound, 279; Ipiutak, 483; Kansas Hopewell, 326; Late Kachemak Bay, 501; Lauderdale, 346; Laurentian I, 244; Middle Columbia region, 457; Middle Mississippi, 356; Mogollon-Mimbres, Pine Lawn, 204; Nebraska, 330; Okvik, 475; Old Bering Sea, 478; Old Iroquois, 256; Oneota, 316; Owasco, 255; Ozark Bluff Dweller, 340; Point Peninsula, 253; Post-Punuk, 488; Pre-Koniag, 497; Proto-Bluff Dweller, 339; Snake-Clearwater region, 460; Sterns Creek, 323; Thule, 507; Upper Columbia, 450; Whittlesey, 282
Negative painting, 57, 58; *see also* Pottery
Negroid, 17; *see also* Physical traits
Nephrite, 31, 74, 75
Net gauges, Pre-Koniag, 497
Net-spacers, Middle Aleut, 493
Nets (netting), 64; Anasazi Basket Maker, 104; Fort Ancient, 286; Frontenac, 242; Hopewell, 270; Ipuitak, 482; Key Marco, 395; Lamoka, 240; Laurentian I, 244; Middle Columbia region, 456; Middle Mississippi, 356; Natchezan, 419; New York Hopewell, 250; Northwest Coast area, 465; Okvik, 475; Old Bering Sea, 478; Owasco, 255; Ozark Bluff Dweller, 340; Point Peninsula, 252; Post-Punuk, 488; Savannah River, 372; trade in, 73; Upper Columbia region, 449; Whittlesey, 282
Netsinkers; *see* Sinkers
Nevada, Southeastern area; *see* Southeastern Nevada area
New England, 239, 243, 246
New Jersey, 247, 254
New Mexico, 198
New Oraibi pueblo, 163
New York Hopewell culture, 250-51
New York State 239, 243, 246, 247, 248, 251 254, 255, 267, 277, 278, 303
Newfoundland, 503, 504, 508
Nickel, 45
Nicola Valley, 452
Noding, 56
Nomadic groups, 20
Nomads, Folsom, 84
Nootka, 462, 464
Norse (Norsemen), 15, 508, 509
Northeastern area, 239-58; chronology, 239 (Chart V), 516-17 (Fig. 122); definition of, 239; vegetation, 239
Northern Fort Apache Reservation, 189
Northern pottery complex, 519
Northern Utah area, 223-27; Black Rock Cave culture, 223-24; Promontory culture, 226-27; Puebloid culture, 224-26
Northwest Coast area, 428, 462-70; archeological knowledge, 462-63; chronology of, 517 (Fig. 122); pattern, 469; trade, 74-75
Northwest Eskimo area, 473-89; chronology, 473 (Chart XVI), 517 (Fig. 122)
Nose form; *see* Physical traits
Nose pins: Koniag, 499; Late Aleut, 495; Late Kachemak Bay, 501; Pre-Koniag, 497; *see also* Ornaments
Notched pebbles, Savannah River, 372; *see also* Sinkers
Nuggets, copper, 41
Nuts: parching of, 61; pine, trade in, 74
Nutstones, Lauderdale, 346

Oars, Old Bering Sea, 480
Oak Grove culture, 430, 436
Obelisk Cave, 116
Obsidian: chipping, 428; trade in, 67, 71, 72, 73
Oceanic Negroid, 19

INDEX

Ocmulgee Fields culture, 386, 387–88
Ohio, 249, 251, 255, 259, 262, 263, 266, 267, 278, 279, 281, 283, 285, 292, 353, 376
Ohio Area, 259–88; chronology of, 260 (Chart VI), 516 (Fig. 122)
Ohio Hopewell culture; *see* Hopewell culture in Ohio
Ohio River, 259, 283
Oil, trade in, 74
Okanogan River, 442
Oklahoma, 366, 421
Okvik culture, 474–77, 480, 481, 484
Old Bering Sea culture, 474, 476, 477–81, 483, 484, 485, 486
Old Copper culture, 299–303
Old Iroquois culture, 255–58
Old Signal Butte culture, 319, 320–22
Olivella shells, 430; trade in, 73, 74
Omah Indians, 317
Oñate, Juan de, 157
Oneota culture, 287, 315–17, 333, 338
Ontario, 243, 246, 251, 254, 255, 278, 279, 299
Oraibi pueblo, 150, 159, 163, 164
Oregon, 442; caves, 93, 221; Southeastern area (*see* Southeastern Oregon)
Orient culture, 248
Original Eskimo culture, 473–74, 493, 505
Ornaments: Adena, 265; Anasazi, Basket Maker, 110; Anasazi, Modified Basket Maker, 119, 145; Anasazi, Pueblo I, 124; Anasazi, Pueblo II, 128; Anasazi, Pueblo III, 142, 145; Anasazi, Pueblo IV, 156; Aztalan, 315; Baumer, 291; Big Bend Cave, 220; Birnirk, 487; bone, 47; Bravo Valley, 222; Caddo, 424; Candy Creek, 349; Cochise, San Pedro, 90; Coles Creek, 415; Copell, 400; Copena, 352; copper, 40, 42, 45; Crystal River, 392; Dismal River, 332; Dorset, 505; ear and lip, 39; Early Aleut, 491; Early Coastal, 247; Early Kachemak Bay, 500; Effigy Mound, 305; Folsom, 85; Fort Ancient, 286; Frontenac, 242; Glacial Kame, 263; Hamilton, 351; Hohokam, Classic, 194; Hohokam, Colonial, 181; Hohokam, Pioneer, 173; Hohokam, Sedentary, 186, 196; Hopewell, 271–73, 274 (Fig. 78), 275 (Fig. 79), 276 (Fig. 81); Hopewell culture in Illinois, 293–94; Indian Knoll, 261; Intrusive Mound, 279; Inugsuk, 508; Ipiutak, 482 (Fig. 116); Irene, 382; Kansas Hopewell, 326; Keshena, 311; Key Marco, 395–98; Koniag, 499; Lamar, 386; Lamoka, 241, Late Aleut, 495, Late Kachemak Bay, 501; Lauderdale, 346; Laurel, 309; Laurentian I, 244; Laurentian II, 246; Lower Sacramento region, 430; Macon Plateau, 384; Marksville, 408, 410; Middle Aleut, 494; Middle Columbia region, 457; Middle Kachemak Bay, 500; Middle Mississippi, 360; Middlesex, 249; Mille Lacs, 310; Mira Creek, 324; Mogollon-Mimbres, Chihuahua, 216; Mogollon-Mimbres, Georgetown, 206; Mogollon-Mimbres, Mimbres, 213; Mogollon-Mimbres, Pine Lawn, 205; Mogollon-Mimbres, San Francisco, 207; Mogollon-Mimbres, Three Circle, 209; Morton, 293; Natchezan, 419; Nebraska, 330–31; New York Hopewell, 251; Northwest Coast area, 468–69; Ocmulgee Fields, 388; Okvik, 476; Old Bering Sea, 480; Old Copper, 302; Old Iroquois, 257; Old Signal Butte, 322; Oneota, 317; Owasco, 255; Ozark Bluff Dweller, 341; Plaquemine, 417; Point Peninsula, 253; Post-Punuk, 488; Poverty Point, 405; Pre-Koniag, 497; Puebloid, 225; Punuk, 485; Red Ocher, 292; Santa Barbara region, 430; Savannah, 379; Savannah River, 373; shell, 48; southwestern California, 439; Sterns Creek, 323; Tchefuncte, 404; Thompson River region, 454; Thule, 507; Upper Columbia region, 451; Upper Republican, 328; Weeden Island, 394; Wilmington, 375; Wisconsin Hopewell, 306; Younge, 280
Osage, 317
Ossuary: Old Iroquois, 257; Whittlesey, 283
Oto Indians, 317
Ouachita Plateau, 337
Outrigger canoe, 15; *see also* Canoes
Overshoes, Ozark Bluff Dweller, 341; *see also* Costume
Owasco culture, 254–55
Ozark Bluff Dweller culture, 339–42
Ozark Mountains, caves, 221
Ozark Plateau area, 337–43; chronology, 338 (Chart X), 516 (Fig. 122)

Pacific Coast, 462
Pacific Eskimo, 298
Pacific Islands, 15
Pacific Ocean, 16
Pacific Slope areas: California area, 427–41; chronology, 514–15 (Fig. 122); Northwest Coast area, 462–70; Plateau area, 442–61
Pacifids, 231, 232; Koniag, 498; Late Aleut, 495; Upper Republican, 326; *see also* Physical traits
Paddle, cord-wrapped, for pottery, 55
Paddle-and-anvil, pottery method, 52, 53, 172, 192, 438
Paddles: Birnirk, 487; Key Marco, 395; Old Bering Sea, 480
Pails; *see* Buckets; Tools, utensils, and weapons
Paint, glaze, 57

Paint brushes, 57
Paint Creek, 333
Paint cups, 37, 212
Paint-grinding stones: Middle Aleut, 493; Ipiutak, 483
Painting: negative, 57, 58; pottery, 57
Paints: Hopewell, 277; trade in, 67, 71
Paleobotany, 81
Paleontology, 81
Palettes: Hohokam, Classic, 194; Hohokam, Colonial, 179; Hohokam, Pioneer, 173; Hohokam, Sedentary, 185; Mogollon-Mimbres, Mimbres, 213; Southern Death Cult, 363, 365 (Fig. 91)
Palisades: Aztalan, 313; Irene, 380, 381; Lamar, 385; Middle Mississippi in Illinois, 294; Middle Mississippi in Ohio, 283; Natchezan, 418; Savannah, 379
Panpipes: Hopewell, 274, 277 (Fig. 82); Wisconsin Hopewell, 307; *see also* Musical instruments
Papago Indians, 518
Papago pottery, 53
Papoose, 25
Parching seeds, 61
Parkas, Post-Punuk, 488
Patayan, 438
Payupki village, 165
Pawnee Indians, 333
Peabody Museum, 44
Pearls: Adena, 265; Fort Ancient, 286; Hopewell, 271, 272, 273 (Fig. 77); New York Hopewell, 251
Peas, wild, Lamar, 385
Pebbles, notched: Laurentian I, 241; Point Peninsula, 252; *see also* Sinkers
Pebbles, painted, Big Bend Cave, 220
Pecking, 29, 31, 35
Pecos, 70, 71, 150
Pecos River, 149, 218
Pemmican, 37
Pendants: Anasazi, Basket Maker, 110; Aztalan, 315; Birnirk, 487; Caddo, 424; Candy Creek, 349; Copell, 400; Dismal River, 332; Dorset, 505; Early Kachemak Bay, 500; Fort Ancient, 286; Frontenac, 242; Hamilton, 351; Hohokam, Classic, 194; Indian Knoll, 261; Intrusive Mound, 279; Ipiutak, 483; Kansas Hopewell, 326; Key Marco, 395; Lamoka, 241; Late Aleut, 495; Late Kachemak Bay, 501; Lauderdale, 346; Laurel, 309; Middle Aleut, 494; Middle Kachemak Bay, 500; Middle Mississippi, 360; Middlesex, 249; Mira Creek, 324; Morton, 293; Nebraska, 330; Northwest Coast area, 468–69; Ocmulgee Fields, 388; Old Iroquois, 257; Old Signal Butte, 322; Ozark Bluff Dweller, 341; Point Peninsula, 253; Post-Punuk, 488; Pre-Koniag, 497; Punuk, 485; Savannah River, 373; Southern Death Cult, 363; Tchefuncte, 404; Thule, 507; trade in, 68; Upper Columbia region, 451; Upper Republican, 328; Weeden Island, 394; Whittlesey, 283; Wisconsin Hopewell, 307; *see also* Ornaments
Pennsylvania, 247, 254, 255, 263, 267
People (physical types, traits), 16–20, 22, 97, 98, 231–32; Adena, 263; Anasazi, Basket Maker, 103, 146; Anasazi, Modified Basket Maker, 111, 114; Anasazi, Pueblo I, 121; Anasazi, Pueblo II, 124; Anasazi, Pueblo III, 130, 144, 145; Anasazi, Pueblo IV, 149; Aztalan, 313; Big Bend Cave, 219; Birnirk, 486; Browns Valley, 299; Buena Vista Lake region, 432; Caddo, 421; Candy Creek, 348; Centralids, 231, 232; Cochise, Sulphur Spring, 87; Coles Creek, 411; Copell, 400; Copena, 351; desert region, southern California, 439; Early Aleut, 490; Early Coastal, 247; Folsom, 83; Fort Ancient, 285; Fort Walton, 394; Frontenac, 241; Glacial Kame, 262; Hamilton, 350; Hohokam, Classic, 190; Hohokam, Pioneer, 169; Hopewell, 267; Indian Knoll, 259; Intrusive Mound, 278; Inugsuk, 508; Irene, 380; Kansas Hopewell, 325; Key Marco, 395; Koniag, 498; La Jolla, 436; Lamar, 385; Lamoka, 240; Late Aleut, 495; Lauderdale, 346, 347; Laurel, 307; Lower Sacramento region, 433; Macon Plateau, 382; Marksville, 406; Middle Aleut, 493; Middle Mississippi, 353; Middlesex, 248; Mille Lacs, 309; Mogollon-Mimbres, Georgetown, 206; Mogollon-Mimbres, Mimbres, 210; Mogollon-Mimbres, Pine Lawn, 200; Mogollon-Mimbres, San Francisco, 206; Mogollon-Mimbres, Three Circle, 207; Morton, 292; Natchezan, 417; Nebraska, 328; New York Hopewell, 250; Northwest Coast area, 463–64; Ocmulgee Fields, 387; Old Bering Sea, 477; Okvik, 474; Old Iroquois, 256; Oneota, 315–16; Original Eskimo, 473; Owasco, 254; Pacifids, 231–32; Plateau area, 443; Point Peninsula, 251; Post-Punuk, 487; Prairids, 231–32; Pre-Koniag, 496; Red Ocher, 291; San Dieguito region, 436; Santa Barbara, 430; Savannah, 378; Savannah River, 371; Swift Creek, 376; Sylvids, 231–32, 240, 247, 248, 250; Tchefuncte, 401; Thule, 505; Upper Republican, 326, Weeden Island, 393; Whittlesey, 281; Wisconsin Hopewell, 306; Youngse, 280.
Percussion chipping and flaking, 84–89, 204, 209
Perforation of long bones, Youngse, 281

Periods; *see* Anasazi; Areas; Charts; Chronology; Cochise; Hohokam; Mogollon-Mimbres
Peru, 92, 156; civilization in, 79, 92; "mummies" of, 17
Pestles, 37; Aztalan, 315; Bravo Valley, 222; Buena Vista Lake region, 434; Caddo, 423; Candy Creek, 349; Cochise, San Pedro, 88; Early Coastal, 247; Fort Ancient, 286; Frontenac, 242; Hamilton, 351; Hohokam, Pioneer, 173; Hohokam, Sedentary, 185; Indian Knoll, 261; Lamoka, 240; Lauderdale, 346; Laurentian I, 244; Lower Sacramento region, 432, 433; Mogollon-Mimbres, Mimbres, 212; Mogollon-Mimbres, Pine Lawn, 203, 204; Natchezan, 419; Old Signal Butte, 321; Point Peninsula, 253; Santa Barbara region, 430, 432; Whittlesey, 282; *see also* Metates; Mortars
Phase, definition, 168
Physical traits, "types," general discussions, 16–20, 231–32; *see also* People
Physiography: Caddo area, 421; California region, 427; Eastern Eskimo area, 503; Florida area, 390; Georgia area, 369; Glacial Kame, 262; Illinois area, 289; Lower Mississippi Valley area, 399; northeastern United States area, 239 northern Utah, 223; Northwest Coast area, 463; Northwestern Eskimo area, 473; Ohio area, 259; Plains area, 319; Plateau area, 442–43; southeastern Nevada, 227; southeastern Oregon, 228; southwestern area, 97; Southwestern Eskimo area, 490; southwestern Texas, 218; Wisconsin-Minnesota area, 297; *see also* Topography
Pick, 37; Fort Ancient, 286; Hohokam, Classic, 193; Late Kachemak Bay, 501; Key Marco, 395; Okvik, 475; Old Bering Sea, 478; Sterns Creek, 323
Pickwick Basin, 345
Pictographs, Puebloid, 226
Picuris Indians, 165, 333
Pigmies, 25
Pigweed, 234, 339, 519
Pikes, Old Copper, 302
Pillows, Key Marco, 395
Pima Indians, 197, 518
Pima pottery, 53
Pine Lawn periods; *see* Mogollon-Mimbres
Pine nuts, trade in, 74
Pinto Basin, 83, 434, 437
Pinto Polychrome pottery, 139
Pins: Early Kachemak Bay, 500; Indian Knoll, 261; Irene, 382; Lamar, 386; Late Kachemak Bay, 501; Plaquemine, 417; Point Peninsula, 253; Pre-Koniag, 497; Savannah, 379; Savannah River, 373; Wilmington, 375
Pioneer Period, Hohokam; *see* Hohokam
Pipes, 31, Adena, 265; Alexander, 348; Anasazi, Basket Maker, 106; Anasazi, Modified Basket Maker, 119, 144; Anasazi, Pueblo I, 123; Anasazi, Pueblo II, 128; Anasazi, Pueblo IV, 155; Aztalan, 315; Big Bend Cave, 220; Caddo, 424; Candy Creek, 349; central California, 433; Clam River, 312; Coles Creek, 414–15; Copell, 400; Copena, 352; Crystal Island, 392; Dismal River, 332; Early Coastal, 247; Early Macon, 370; eastern North America, 235; Effigy Mound, 305; Fort Ancient, 286; Frontenac, 242; Glacial Kame, 263; Hamilton, 351; Hohokam, Classic, 194; Hohokam, Colonial, 181; Hohokam, Sedentary, 186; Hopewell, 270–71, 274; Intrusive Mound, 279; Inugsuk, 508; Ipiutak, 483; Irene, 382; Keshena, 311; Lamar, 386; Lamoka, 241; Lauderdale, 346; Laurel, 309; Laurentian I, 244; Laurentian II, 246; Lower Mississippi Valley area, 399; Lower Sacramento region, 430, 433; Macon Plateau, 384; Marksville, 408, 410; Middle Columbia region, 457; Middle Mississippi, 359; Middlesex, 249; Mille Lacs, 310; Mira Creek, 324; Mogollon-Mimbres, Chihuahua, 216; Mogollon-Mimbres, Georgetown, 206; Mogollon-Mimbres, Mimbres, 213; Mogollon-Mimbres, Pine Lawn, 205; Mogollon-Mimbres, San Francisco, 207; Mogollon-Mimbres, Three Circle, 209; Natchezan, 419; Nebraska, 330; New York Hopewell, 251; northern California, 428; Northwest Coast area, 468, 469; Ocmulgee Fields, 388; Okvik, 475; Old Bering Sea, 479; Old Copper, 302; Old Iroquois, 257 (Fig. 70); Old Signal Butte, 322; Oneota, 317; Original Eskimo, 474; Owasco, 255; Ozark Bluff Dweller, 340; Plaquemine, 417; Point Peninsula, 253; Post-Punuk, 488; Poverty Point, 405; Promontory, 225, 226; Proto-Bluff Dweller, 339; Punuk, 485; Santa Barbara region, 432, 434; Savannah, 379; Savannah River, 373; Snake-Clearwater region, 460; southeastern Nevada, 227; Southern Death Cult, 365 (Fig. 91); Sterns Creek, 323; Swift Creek, 378; Tchefuncte, 403 (Fig. 97), 404; Thompson River region, 454; Thule, 507; Trade in, 68; Upper Columbia region, 450; Upper Republican, 327–28; Weeden Island, 394; Whittlesey, 282–83; Wilmington, 375; Wisconsin Hopewell, 306; Younge, 280
Pipestone, trade in, 67
Pit-houses, 196; Anasazi, Modified Basket

Maker, 111; Anasazi, Pueblo I, 121; Anasazi, Pueblo III, 145; Bravo Valley, 222; depressions, 8; Early Aleut, 490; Hohokam, Classic, 190; Hohokam, Colonial, 174; Hohokam, Pioneer, 169; Mogollon-Mimbres, Mimbres, 210; Mogollon-Mimbres, Pine Lawn, 200; Mogollon-Mimbres, San Francisco, 206; Mogollon-Mimbres, Three Circle, 207, 208; Puebloid, 224, 225; southeastern Nevada, 227; square, 224; Upper Columbia region, 444

Pits, storage; *see* Storage pits

Pizarro, Francisco, 156

Plains area, 298, 319–36, 383, 444, 455; chronology of, 320 (Chart IX), 516 (Fig. 122); Indians of, 73; pottery of, 54; trade in, 73

Plains Miwok Indians, 433

Plaiting, weaving, 65

Planting-sticks; *see* Digging-sticks

Plaquemine culture, 415–17, 424

Plaques, portrait, Pre-Koniag, 497

Plateau area, 103, 442–59, 465, 469, 470; chronology, 515 (Fig. 122); trade in, 74–75

Plato, 16

Plaza: Aztalan, 313; Caddo, 422; Coles Creek, 411; Irene, 380; Lamar, 385; Marksville, 409; Macon Plateau, 382; Middle Mississippi, 354; Middle Mississippi in Illinois, 294; Middle Mississippi in Ohio, 283, 284; Natchezan, 417; Troyville, 409

Pleistocene, 11, 79, 81

Plugs: lip (*see* Labrets); wound (*see* Wound plugs)

Plummets, 39; Baumer, 291; Early Coastal, 247; Fort Ancient, 286; Frontenac, 242; Key Marco, 398; Laurentian I, II, 244 (Fig. 69); Marksville, 408; Middlesex, 249; Poverty Point, 405

Pluvial period, 86

Pod corn, 80

Point Barrow (Ala.), 486

Point Hope (Ala.), 481

Point Peninsula culture, 251–54, 278

Point Sal I, 430

Point Sal II, 432

Point Sal III, 434

Points; *see* Projectile points

Poison, aconite; *See* Aconite poison

Polishing stones (polishers), 29, 31, 35; Dismal River, 332; Hohokam, Colonial, 181; Hohokam, Pioneer, 173; Mogollon-Mimbres, Pine Lawn, 203

Polychrome, definition of, 154

Ponco Indians, 317

Population of Indians, ca. 1492, 21

Portales (N.M.), 83

Post-Punuk culture, 487–89

Potatoes, sweet, 80

Pottery, 21, 50–60, 518, 519; band-built, 53; basket impression on, 179; coiled method, 52, 53; cord-marked, 21; dating by, 155; decoration, 51, 54, 55; distribution, 50; engraving of, 56; etching of, 56; fiber-tempered, 519; finishing, 54; firing, 58; importance of, 50; impression of, 56; incising, 56; ingredients, 51; "killed," 394; mending, 60; naming system, 51; northern complex, 519; production time, 59; punctated, 56; ring-built, 53; rocked-dentate stamping, 56; rouletting, 56; shapes of, 54; sherds, 51; stamping of, 56; temper, 51; trade in, 68, 70, 116, 177, 178, 184, 193, 222; trailing, 56

Pottery, by cultures and types:

Adena, 265

Anasazi, Basket Maker, 105

Anasazi, Modified Basket Maker, 114, 116, 144; types: Abajo Red-on-Orange, 115; Alma Plain, 116; Forestdale Smudged, 116; La Plata Black-on-White, 115; Lino Black-on-Gray, 115; Lino Gray, 114; San Francisco Red, 116

Anasazi, Pueblo I, types: Kana-a Black-on-White, 121; Kana-a Gray, 121; Kiatuthlanna Black-on-White, 122; La Plata Black-on-Red, 122; Lino Gray, 121

Anasazi, Pueblo II, types: Black Mesa Black-on-White, 126; Mancos Black-on-White, 126, 128; Red Mesa Black-on-White, 126; Reserve Black-on-White 126

Anasazi, Pueblo III, 129, 137–39, 144; types: Chaco Black-on-White, 137, 138; Indented Corrugated, 138, 139; Jeddito Black-on-Orange, 139; Kayenta Polychrome, 139; Kiet Siel Polychrome, 139; Mesa Verde Black-on-White, 138; Pinedale Polychrome, 139; Pinto Polychrome, 139; Roosevelt Black-on-White, 139; Sagi Black-on-White, 138; St. John's Polychrome, 138, 139; Tularosa Black-on-White, 139; Tusayan Black-on-Red, 139; Tusayan Black-on-White, 138; Tusayan Polychrome, 139; Zuñi glazes, 139

Anasazi, Pueblo IV, types: Four-Mile Polychrome, 153; Gila Polychrome, 152, 153; Hawikuh Glaze-on-White, 153; Heshotauthla Polychrome, 153; Indented Corrugated, 152, 155; Jeddito Black-on-Yellow, 151; Jeddito Corrugated, 151; Jeddito Plain, 151; Jeddito Tooled, 151; Sikyatki Polychrome, 151; Tonto Polychrome, 152, 153

INDEX

Armagosa, 438
Aztalan, 314
Baumer, 290; Birnirk, 486; Big Bend Cave, 219; Bravo Valley, 222; Buena Vista Lake, 433
Caddo, 422, 423 (Fig. 102); California area, 427; Candy Creek, 348; Clam River, 312; Coles Creek, 412–14, 413 (Fig. 101); Colorado River, 438; Copell, 400; Copena, 352
Deptford, 374; Diegueño, 437; Dismal River, 331; Dorset, 504
Early Coastal, 247; Early Macon, 370; eastern North America, 233, 237; Effigy Mound, 304 (and Fig. 84)
Fort Ancient, 285; Fort Walton, 394; Frontenac, 241
Glacial Kame, 262
Hamilton, 350
Hohokam, Classic: Casa Grande Red-on-Buff, 192; types: Four-Mile Polychrome, 193; Gila Plain, 192; Gila Polychrome, 192, 193, 195; Gila Red, 192; Gila Smudged, 192; Jeddito Black-on-Yellow 193; Tonto Polychrome, 192, 195
Hohokam, Colonial, types: Deadman's Black-on-Red, 178; Forestdale Smudged, 178; Gila Butte Red-on-Buff, 176; Gila Plain, 176; Kana-a Black-on-White, 178; Lino Black-on-Gray, 178; Mogollon Red-on-Brown, 178; San Francisco Red, 178; Santa Cruz Buff, 176; Santa Cruz Red-on-Buff, 176, 177
Hohokam, Pioneer, types: Estrella Red-on-Gray, 171; Gila Plain, 171; San Francisco Red, 172; Snaketown Red-on-Buff, 171; Sweetwater Polychrome, 171; Sweetwater Red-on-Gray, 171; Vahki Plain, 171; Vahki Red, 171
Hohokam, Sedentary, types: Black Mesa Black-on-White, 184; Deadman's Black-on-Red, 184; Forestdale Smudged, 184; Gila Plain, 182; Kana-a Black-on-White, 184; Mimbres Boldface Black-on-White, 184; Sacaton Buff, 182; Sacaton Red, 182; Sacaton Red-on-Buff, 182, 183; San Francisco Red, 184; Santan Red, 182
Hopewell, 268, 269 (and Fig. 73); Hopewell in Illinois, 293
Intrusive Mound, 278; Inugsuk, 508; Irene, 381
Kansas Hopewell, 325; Keshena, 311; Key Marco, 395; Koniag, 498
Lamar, 385; Lamoka, 240; Late Kachemak Bay, 501; Lauderdale, 347; Laurel, 308; Laurentian I, 243; Laurentian II, 246; Lewis, 294; Lower Mississippi Valley area, 399

Macon Plateau, 383; Marksville, 278, 406, 407 (Fig. 98); Middle Aleut, 493; Middle Columbia region, 455; Middle Mississippi, 356, 357 (and Fig. 86), 358 (and Fig. 87), 359 (Fig. 88); Middle Mississippi in Illinois, 294; Middle Mississippi in Ohio, 284; Middlesex, 249; Mille Lacs, 309–10; Mira Creek, 324
Mogollon-Mimbres, Chihuahua, 51, 215, 217; types: Babicora, 215; Dublan, 215; Gila Polychrome, 215; Madera Black-on-Red, 215; Ramos polychromes, 215; Salado, 215; Tonto Polychrome, 215; Villa Ahumada, 215
Mogollon-Mimbres, Georgetown, types: Alma Neck-banded, 206; Alma Plain, 206; Alma Scored, 206; San Francisco Red, 206
Mogollon-Mimbres, Mimbres, types: Alma Plain, 212; Mimbres Black-on-White, 212; Mimbres Corrugated, 212; San Francisco Red, 212
Mogollon-Mimbres, Pine Lawn, types: Alma Plain, 202; Alma Rough, 202; San Francisco Red, 202
Mogollon-Mimbres, San Francisco, types: Alma Neck-banded, 207; Alma Plain, 207; Alma Punched, 207; Alma Scored, 207; Mogollon Red-on-Brown, 207; San Francisco Red, 207; Three Circle Red-on-White, 207
Mogollon-Mimbres, Three Circle, types: Alma Plain, 208; Alma Punched, 208; Mimbres Boldface Black-on-White, 208; San Francisco Red, 208; Three Circle Neck Corrugated, 208–9; Three Circle Red-on-White, 208
Morton, 292–93
Natchezan, 418; Navaho, 158; Nebraska, 329; New York Hopewell, 250; Northwest Coast area, 465
Ocmulgee Fields, 387–88; Okvik, 474; Old Bering Sea, 477–78; Old Iroquois, 256, 257 (Fig. 70); Old Signal Butte, 321; Oneota, 316; Orient, 248; Original Eskimo, 473; Owasco, 254–55; Ozark Bluff Dweller, 339
Plaquemine, 416; Point Peninsula, 252; Post-Punuk, 488; Poverty Point, 404; Pre-Koniag, 496; Proto–Bluff Dweller, 338; Puebloid, 224, 225, 226; Punuk, 484
Red Ocher, 291
Santa Rosa–Swift Creek, 392; Savannah, 379; Savannah River, 371 (and Fig. 93); Snake-Clearwater region, 459; southeastern Nevada, 227; southern California, 519; Southern Death Cult.

Pottery, by culture and types—*continued*
363, 365 (Fig. 90); Sterns Creek, 322–23; Swift Creek, 377
Tchefuncte, 401, 402 (Fig. 96); Thompson River region, 452; Thule, 506; Tick Island, 391; Top-Layer, 343; Troyville, 409–10
Upper Columbia region, 445; Upper Republican, 327
Weeden Island, 393; Whittlesey, 281–82; Wilmington, 375; Wisconsin Hopewell, 306
Younge, 280

Pounders, Post-Punuk, 488; *see also* Hammers; Handstones
Poverty Point culture, 404–6
Prairids, 231–32, 316, 328, 342; *see also* People; Physical traits
"Pre-Aleut" (Hrdlička), 495
Pre-Koniag culture, 496–97, 501
Prehistoric culture: New York, 258; Northwest Coast area, 463
Prehistoric period: Illinois area, 289; Late, Florida area, 391, 393–98
Prehistoric Yuman culture, 438
Pressure chipping, flaking, 31, 89, 204
Problematical objects, 38
Prognathism, 17; *see also* Physical traits
Projectile points (arrowheads, blades, spear points, spearheads), 30, 31, 34, 194, 223; Adena, 265; Anasazi, Basket Maker, 106; Anasazi, Modified Basket Maker, 117; Anasazi, Pueblo I, 123; Anasazi, Pueblo II, 127; Anasazi, Pueblo III, 140; Anasazi, Pueblo IV, 145; Aztalan, 315; Baumer, 290–91; Black Rock Cave, 223; Borax Lake region, 434; Bravo Valley, 222; Browns Valley, 299; Caddo, 423; Candy Creek, 349; Clam River, 312; Coles Creek, 414; Copena, 352; Copell, 400; Deptford, 374; Dismal River, 332; Dorset, 504; Early Aleut, 491, 493 (Fig. 118); Early Coastal, 247; Early Kachemak Bay, 499, 500; Early Macon, 370; Effigy Mound, 305; Faulkner, 289; Folsom, 84; Fort Ancient, 286; Frontenac, 241; Glacial Kame, 262; Hamilton, 351; Hohokam, Classic, 194; Hohokam, Colonial, 179; Hohokam, Pioneer, 173; Hohokam, Sedentary, 185; Hopewell, 269, 270 (and Fig. 74); Indian Knoll, 261; Intrusive Mound, 278; Ipiutak, 482, 483; Irene, 381; Kansas Hopewell, 325; Koniag, 499; Koshena, 311; Lamar, 385–86; Lamoka, 240; Late Kachemak Bay, 501; Lauderdale, 346; Laurel, 308; Laurentian I, 244 (and Fig. 69); Laurentian II, 246; Lewis, 294; Lower Sacramento region, 433; Macon Plateau, 383; Maravillas, 219; Marksville, 407, 410; Middle Mississippi, 355, 356; Middle Mississippi in Illinois, 294; Middle Mississippi in Ohio, 284; Middlesex, 249; Mille Lacs, 310; Mira Creek, 324; Mogollon-Mimbres, Pine Lawn, 202, 204; Mogollon-Mimbres, San Francisco, 207; Morton, 293; Natchezan, 418; Nebraska, 330; New York Hopewell, 250; Northwest Coast area, 465, 469; Okvik, 475, 476 (Fig. 114); Old Bering Sea, 478; Old Copper, 300, 301 (Fig. 83), 302; Old Iroquois, 256; Old Signal Butte, 321; Oneota, 316; Orient, 248; Owasco, 255; Ozark Bluff Dweller, 340; Plaquemine, 416, 417; Point Peninsula, 250, 252; Poverty Point, 405; Pre-Koniag, 497; Proto–Bluff Dweller, 338; Red Ocher, 291; Santa Barbara region, 430, 433, 434; Santa Rosa–Swift Creek, 392; Savannah, 379; Savannah River, 372; Snake-Clearwater region, 459; southeastern Nevada, 227; Sterns Creek, 323; Swift Creek, 377; Tchefuncte, 402, 403 (Fig. 97); Thompson River region, 453; Top-Layer, 342; Upper Columbia region, 446; Upper Republican, 327; Weeden Island, 393; Whittlesey, 282; Wilmington, 375; Wisconsin Hopewell, 306; Younge, 280; Yuma, 84

Promontory culture, 226–27
Proto–Bluff Dweller culture, 338
Proto-Owasco Indians, 258
"Pseudo-slip," pottery, 57
Pueblo: civilization, 160; Indians, 97, 98, 333; meaning of term, 210; revolt, 157; social organization, 147, 163; *see also* Anasazi
Pueblo Grande, 192
Pueblo Periods I–V; *see* Anasazi culture
Puebloid culture, 224–26; Phase I, 224–25; Phase II, 225–26
Puerco River, 149
Puget Sound, 462, 469
"Pulley-stones," 39
Pump drill; *see* Drills
Pumpkins, 104, 113, 121, 137, 233, 256
Punches: Coles Creek, 414; Dismal River, 332; Frontenac, 242; *see also* Awls; Tools, utensils, and weapons
Punctating pottery, 56
Punuk culture, 481, 484–86, 494
Pyramids, 409; *see also* Mounds
Pyrites: Frontenac, 242; Point Peninsula, 252

Quapaw Indians, 361
Quarry, 35
Quartelejo, 333
Quebec, 243, 246

Rabbit-skin blankets, Big Bend Cave, 220
"Rabbit" stick, Big Bend Cave, 220

Race (racial types), 16, 97; *see also* People; Physical traits
Raft, Natchezan, 419
Ragweed, giant, 234, 339, 519
Rainfall; *see* Climate
Ramos polychromes, pottery, 215
Ramps: Caddo, 422; Coles Creek, 411; Etowah, 387; Fort Walton, 394; Lamar, 385; Middle Mississippi, 354; Middle Mississippi in Ohio, 283; Plaquemine, 415; Savannah, 379; *see also* Villages
Rasps, musical: Fort Ancient, 287; Key Marco, 395; Whittlesey, 283; *see also* Musical instruments
Rattles: Fort Ancient, 287; Frontenac, 242; Hopewell, 274; Natchezan, 419; Point Peninsula, 253; Whittlesey, 283; Wisconsin Hopewell, 307
Rattlesnake motif, Southern Death Cult, 363
Raw materials, trade in, 67, 71
Reamers: Hohokam, Classic, 194; Hohokam, Colonial, 179; Hohokam, Pioneer, 173; Hohokam, Sedentary, 185; Old Bering Sea, 478; Okvik, 475; Punuk, 485 (Fig. 117); *see also* Awls; Drills; Gouges; Tools, utensils, and weapons
Rearticulated skeletons, Younge, 281; *see also* Burials
Recent period, geology, 81
Reconstruction, village, Anasazi, Pueblo III, 131
Red Mesa Black-on-White pottery, 126
Red ocher (hematite): Adena, 266; Baumer, 291; Browns Valley site, 299; Clam River, 312; Dismal River, 332; Dorset, 505; Frontenac, 243; Glacial Kame, 263; Indian Knoll, 261; Irene, 382; Intrusive Mound, 279; Laurel, 309; Laurentian I, 244; Marksville, 408, 409; Middlesex, 249; New York Hopewell, 251; Old Signal Butte, 322; Orient, 248; Point Peninsula, 254; Red Ocher, 292; trade in, 71; Weeden Island, 394
Red Ocher culture, 291–92
"Renaissance" period, Anasazi, Pueblo IV, 149
Reserve Black-on-White pottery, 126
"Resist" method, 58
Reverse painting, 57
Revolt of Pueblo Indians, 157
Ring-built pottery, 53
Rings: Adena, 265; Late Kachemak Bay, 501; Pre-Koniag, 497; *see also* Ornaments
Rio Grande area, 149, 153
Rio Grande River, 149, 165, 166, 218
Rio Grande Valley, 154
Rito de los Frijoles Canyon, 151, 161, 165, 166

Robes: Adena, 265; Caddo, 424; Hopewell, 271; Indian Knoll, 261; Intrusive Mound, 279; Natchezan, 419; Nebraska, 330; Ozark Bluff Dweller, 341; *see also* Costume
Rock shelters: Adena, 264; Bravo Valley, 222; Copena, 352; Indian Knoll, 260; Lauderdale, 346; Oneota, 316; Ozark Bluff Dweller, 339, 341; Ozark Plateau area, 337; Proto–Bluff Dweller, 338, 339; Texas, 219; Upper Republican, 326
Rocked dentate, pottery stamp, 56
Rocky Mountain bee plant (guaco), 57
Rocky Mountains, 231, 277, 288, 442
Roosevelt Black-on-White pottery, 139
Roosevelt Lake, 215
Root crops, 80
Root-diggers, Pre-Koniag, 497
Roots, 25, 61, 192
Rope, Ozark Bluff Dweller, 340
Ross, Lillian, vi
Rotunda, Irene, 380, 382
Roundheads, 463; *see also* People; Physical traits; Skulls
Rubber ball, Hohokam, Colonial, 174
Rubbing-stones: Dorset, 504; Mogollon-Mimbres, Mimbres, 212; Mogollon-Mimbres, Pine Lawn, 203; *see also* Grinding-stones; Polishers; Tools, utensils, and weapons
Rugs, Key Marco, 395; *see also* Blankets
Runic inscriptions, 15
Rushes, 61

Sacaton Buff, 182
Sacaton Red, 182
Sacaton Red-on-Buff, 182, 183
Sacramento Valley, 428
Sagi Black-on-White, 138
St. John's Polychrome pottery, 138, 139
St. Lawrence River, v, 40, 248, 259, 513
Sahaptin tribes, 442, 455
Salado area, 149, 152; civilization, 198; Indians, 190, 192; people, 197, 216, 217; pottery, 215; tribes, 188
Salish, 442, 462
Salmon, 464; Northwest Coast area, 464
Salt, trade in, 67, 71
Salt Lake City, 93
Salt pans, Macon Plateau, 383
Salt River, 70, 149, 168, 174, 182, 188
San Dieguito, 436
San Felipe, 165
San Francisco, 434
San Francisco Bay, 430, 431, 433
San Francisco period; *see* Mogollon-Mimbres culture
San Francisco Red pottery, 116, 172, 184, 202, 206, 208, 212

San Francisco River, 149
San Ildefonso, 165
San Joaquin Valley, 427, 428
San Juan, 165
San Juan River Basin, 129, 189
San Juan River Pueblo Indians, 189
San Pedro; *see* Cochise culture
Sand Paintings, Navaho, 159
Sandals: Adena, 265; Anasazi, Basket Maker, 108; Anasazi, Pueblo I, 124; Anasazi, Pueblo III, 140; Anasazi, Pueblo IV, 156; Big Bend Cave, 220; Hohokam, Classic, 194; Hohokam, Colonial, 181; Hopewell, 271; Indian Knoll, 261; Mogollon-Mimbres, Chihuahua, 216; Mogollon-Mimbres, Mimbres, 213; Ozark Bluff Dweller, 341; Puebloid, 226; southeastern Oregon, 228
Sandia culture, 82, 92, 165
Sanpoil River, 444
Santa Ana, Pueblo V, 166
Santa Barbara region, 429, 430, 434
Santa Catalina Island, trade with, 74
Santa Clara, 166
Santa Cruz Buff, 176
Santa Cruz Red-on-Buff, 176
Santa Cruz River, 85
Santa Rosa-Swift Creek culture, Florida area, 392
Santan Red, 182
Santee Dakota Indians, 312, 313
Santo Domingo, Pueblo V, 166
Sashes, 63; Anasazi, Modified Basket Maker, 119; Anasazi, Pueblo IV, 156; *see also* Costume
Savannah culture, Georgia area, 378–80, 386
Savannah River culture, Georgia area, 371–73, 391
Sawing tools (saws), 29, 34; Hohokam, Classic, 193; Key Marco, 395; Late Kachemak Bay, 501; Middle Kachemak Bay, 500; *see also* Tools, utensils, and weapons
Scott County, Kansas, 333
Scrapers, 30, 60; Adena, 265; Anasazi, Pueblo I, 123; Anasazi, Pueblo II, 128; Baumer, 291; Birnirk, 487; Black Rock Cave, 223; Borax Lake region, 434; Caddo, 423; Candy Creek, 349; Clam River, 312; Cochise, Chiricahua, 88; Cochise, San Pedro, 88; Coles Creek, 414; Dismal River, 332; Dorset, 504; Early Aleut, 491, 492 (Fig. 118); Early Coastal, 247; Early Macon, 370; Fort Ancient, 286; Frontenac, 242; Hamilton, 351; Hohokam, Colonial, 179; Hohokam, Pioneer, 173; Kansas Hopewell, 326; Key Marco, 395; Indian Knoll, 261; Intrusive Mound, 279; La Jolla, 437; Lamoka, 241; Late Kachemak Bay, 501; Laurel, 308; Laurentian I, 244; Macon Plateau area, 384; Maravillas, 219; Marksville, 407; Middle Columbia, 456; Middle Mississippi, 356; Middlesex, 249; Mille Lacs, 310; Mira Creek, 324; Mogollon-Mimbres, Pine Lawn, 203, 204; Morton, 293; Natchezan, 419; Nebraska, 330; New York Hopewell, 250; Ocmulgee Fields, 388; Okvik, 475; Old Bering Sea, 478; Old Copper, 302; Old Iroquois, 256; Old Signal Butte, 321, 322; Original Eskimo, 474; Ozark Bluff Dweller, 340; Plaquemine, 417; Point Peninsula, 252, 253; Post-Punuk, 488; Poverty Point, 405; Pre-Koniag, 496; Proto–Bluff Dweller, 339; Red Ocher, 291; San Dieguito region, 436; Santa Barbara region, 430; Sterns Creek, 323; Swift Creek, 377; Tchefuncte, 403 (Fig. 97), 404; Thule, 507; time to make, 31; Upper Columbia region, 449; Upper Republican, 327; Weeden Island, 393; Whittlesey, 282; Wisconsin Hopewell, 306; Younge, 280
Screw beans, 170, 175
Sculptures, 57; Hopewell, in Illinois, 294; Key Marco, 398; Marksville, 408; Norsemen, Inugsuk, 508; *see also* Art; Effigies; Figurines
Sea foods, trade in, 73
Seal-scratchers (scrapers): Birnirk, 486; Post-Punuk, 488
Seals, trade in, 74
Seaweed, trade in, 74
Sedentary economy, 87, 88
Sedentary period, Hohokam; *see* Hohokam
Seeds, 61, 192, 202
"Self-slip," 57
Seltzer, Carl C., 145
Seven Cities of Cibola, 156
Shark teeth, 72, 278
Shark's skin, as sandpaper, Northwest Coast area, 466
Shavers, Thule, 507
Shawnee Indians, 287
"Shed," definition, 62
Shellfish, California, 427
Shells: beads (*see* Beads); bracelets (*see* Bracelets); middens (*see* Middens); money, 68; ornaments (*see* Ornaments); trade in, 67, 69, 73, 74; worked, 48–49
Shelters: Faulkner, 289; Indian Knoll, 260; Oneota, 316; Savannah River, 371; Sterns Creek, 322; *see also* Houses; Rock shelters; Villages
Sherds, pottery, 51, 439
Shipaulovi, 162
Shirts (shirtlike garments): Birnirk, 487; Koniag, 499; Late Aleut, 495; Natchezan,

419; Old Bering Sea, 480; Thule, 507; *see also* Costume
Shoshoni, 99, 227
Shoshoni-Ute complex, 223
Shovels, snow: Birnirk, 487; Late Kachemak Bay, 501; Okvik, 475; Old Bering Sea, 478; Post-Punuk, 488; Pre-Koniag, 497; Thule, 506–7
Shungopovi, 162
Shushwap Indians, 452
Sia, 166
Siberia, 20, 473, 474, 477, 484, 486, 487, 505
Sichomovi, 161
Sieve, Ozark Bluff Dweller, 340
Sign language, 68
Sikyatki Polychrome pottery, 151
Silver, 45; Crystal River, 392; Hopewell, 271; Navaho, 159; New York Hopewell, 251
Sinew stones: Candy Creek, 349; Early Coastal, 247; Hamilton, 351; Point Peninsula, 253
Sinew-stretchers, Nebraska, 330
Sinew-twisters: Birnirk, 486; Punuk, 485
Sinkers (net, fishline), 39; Baumer, 291; Caddo, 423; Candy Creek, 349; Early Coastal, 247; Fort Ancient, 286; Frontenac, 242; Hopewell, 270; Intrusive Mound, 279; Key Marco, 395; Lamoka, 240; Middle Aleut, 493; Middle Kachemak Bay, 500; Middlesex, 249; Okvik, 475; Old Bering Sea, 478; Old Iroquois, 256; Owasco, 255; Pre-Koniag, 496; Savannah River, 372; Swift Creek, 378; Tchefuncte, 403 (Fig. 97), 404; Weeden Island, 393; Whittlesey, 282
Sites, selection of, 5
Skagit River, 450
Skavlem, H. L., 36, 37
Skeena River, 74
Skeleton, 16, 91; Younge, 281; *see also* Burials
Skin, color of, 17; *see also* Physical traits
Skins, trade in, 74
Skirts: Caddo, 424; Hopewell, 271; Natchezan, 419; *see also* Costume
Skulls: Anasazi, Basket Maker, 98; Anasazi, Pueblo I, 121; Anasazi, Pueblo II, 124; deformed (*see* Deformation); longheaded, 98; Marksville, 409, Morton, 293; Pre-Koniag, 497; roundheaded, 98, 150; trophy, New York Hopewell, 251; *see also* People; Physical traits
Skylight, Birnirk, 486
Slabs: Etowah, 387; Fort Ancient, 287; Savannah River, 372; Tampico, 295
"Slave-killer" clubs, northern California, 428, 429 (Fig. 103)
Sledges; *see* Sleds
Sleds (sledges): Birnirk, 487; Dorset, 505; Okvik, 476; Old Bering Sea, 479–80; Original Eskimo, 474; Post-Punuk, 488; Thule, 507
Sleeping platforms, Middle Mississippi, 355
Slip, pottery, 57
Sloth, giant ground, 82
Smith, G. V., 36
Smoking, eastern North America, 235
Smoothing-stones (smoothers): Coles Creek, 414; Fort Ancient, 286; *see also* Polishing stones; Rubbing-stones
Snake-Clearwater Region, 459–61
Snake Dance, 161
Snake River, 455
Snaketown, 9, 10, 168
Snaketown Red-on-Buff pottery, 171
Snares: Anasazi, Basket Maker, 104; Okvik, 475; Old Bering Sea, 478
Snow knives: Dorset, 504; Post-Punuk, 488; Thule, 506; *see also* Knives
Snowshoes: Middle Columbia region, 457; Original Eskimo, 474; Post-Punuk, 488; Snake-Clearwater region, 460; Thompson River region, 454; Upper Columbia region, 451
Soapstone; *see* Steatite
Soto, Hernando de; *see* De Soto, Hernando
Southeastern Nevada area, 227
Southern California area, 436–41
Southern Death Cult, 238, 286, 328, 345, 359, 360, 361–66, 386, 387, 389, 398, 424
Southwestern area, 17, 97–228, 342; chronology of, 514 (Fig. 122); trade in, 69–71
Southwestern Eskimo area, 499–502; chronology, 491 (Chart XVII), 515 (Fig. 122)
Southwestern Texas area, 218–23; Big Bend, 219; Bravo Valley, 221, Maravillas, 219
Spades: Copena, 352; Middle Mississippi in Ohio, 284; Nebraska, 330
Spain (Spaniards, Spanish), 21, 156, 197
Spatulas, Savannah River, 373
Spear points; *see* Projectile points
Spear-throwers (atlatl, throwing-stick): Birnirk, 486; Browns Valley, 299; Copell, 400; Dorset, 504; Early Macon, 369; Faulkner, 289; Frontenac, 241; Hamilton, 351; Hopewell, 269; Indian Knoll, 260; Intrusive Mound, 279; Ipiutak, 481; Key Marco, 395, 396 (Fig. 94); Koniag, 499; Lamoka, 240; Lauderdale, 346; Laurel, 308; Laurentian I, 243, 244 (Fig. 69); Macon Plateau, 383; Middle Mississippi, 356; Mille Lacs, 310; Northwest Coast area, 465; Okvik, 475; Old Bering Sea, 478; Old Copper, 300; Old Signal Butte, 321; Original Eskimo, 474; Ozark Bluff Dweller, 340; Plaquemine, 416; Point Peninsula, 252; Post-Punuk, 488; Poverty Point, 405;

578   INDIANS BEFORE COLUMBUS

Proto-Bluff Dweller, 338; Puebloid, 224; Savannah River, 371-72; southeastern Oregon, 228; Swift Creek, 377; Tchefuncte, 404; Thule, 506; Wilmington, 375; Wisconsin-Hopewell, 306; *see also* Weights, spear-thrower

Spearheads; *see* Projectile points

Spears (darts, lances): Birnirk, 486; Copell, 400; Dorset, 504; Early Kachemak Bay, 500; Early Macon, 370; Faulkner, 289; Frontenac, 241; Hamilton area, 351; Hopewell, 269, 270; Indian Knoll, 261; Intrusive Mound, 279; Ipiutak, 481; Kansas Hopewell, 325; Key Marco, 395; Koniag, 499; Lamoka, 240; Late Kachemak Bay, 501; Lauderdale, 346; Laurel, 308; Laurentian I, 243, 244; Macon Plateau, 383; Middle Columbia region, 456; Middle Mississippi, 356; Northwest Coast area, 465; Okvik, 474; Old Bering Sea, 478; Old Copper, 300; Old Signal Butte, 321; Ozark Bluff Dweller, 340; Point Peninsula, 252; Post-Punuk, 488; Poverty Point, 405; Pre-Koniag, 496; Proto-Bluff Dweller, 338; Orient, 248; Original Eskimo, 474; Savannah River, 371, 372; Snake-Clearwater region, 459; Swift Creek, 377; Tchefuncte, 404; Thule, 506; Upper Columbia region, 446; Wisconsin Hopewell, 306

Spiro Mound, 366;

Spokane River, 442, 451

"Spools," 39

Spoons (ladles): Birnirk, 487; Fort Ancient, 286; Inugsuk, 508; Ipiutak, 483; Key Marco, 395; Late Kachemak Bay, 501; Macon Plateau, 384; Middle Mississippi, 356; Natchezan, 419; Ocmulgee Fields, 419; Old Bering Sea, 479; Oneota, 317; Post-Punuk, 488; Pre-Koniag, 497

Spuds (adzes): Old Copper, 300, 301 (Fig. 83)

Squash, 233-34, 237; Aztalan, 314; Big Bend Cave, 219; Bravo Valley, 222; Copena, 352; Dismal River, 331; Fort Ancient, 285; Hohokam, Classic, 192; Hohokam, Pioneer, 170; Hopewell, 268; Middle Mississippi, 355; Old Iroquois, 256; Oneota, 316; Ozark Bluff Dweller, 339; Puebloid, 224; Swift Creek, 376; Top-Layer, 343; Upper Republican, 327; Whittlesey, 281

"Squash blossom" hairdress, Anasazi, Pueblo III, 141

Squaw, 25

Stalling's Island, 374

Statuettes, Coles Creek, 415; *see also* Effigies; Figures

Steatite: central California, 433; Poverty Point, 405; Santa Barbara region, 434; trade in, 71, 74, 75

Stern's Creek culture, 322-23, 332

Stikine River, 74

Stiletto, Old Copper, 302

Stockades: Old Iroquois, 256, Whittlesey, 281; *see also* Palisades; Villages

Stone: bars of, Hopewell, 269; kinds of, 29; objects of, 34-39; primitive working methods, 29-34

Stone-chippers, Aztalan, 315

Stools: Key Marco, 395, 396 (Fig. 94); Middle Mississippi, 356

Storage pits (bins): Anasazi, Basket Maker, 104; Anasazi, Modified Basket Maker, 111; Mogollon-Mimbres, Pine Lawn, 201; *see also* Houses

Straighteners, arrow-shaft; *see* Arrow-shaft straighteners

Straits of Georgia, Northwest Coast area, 469

Stratigraphy, 9

Strike-a-lights, Point Peninsula, 252

String, Ozark Bluff Dweller, 340

"SU" site, 198

Sulphur Spring period, 87-89; *see also* Cochise culture

Sunflowers, 234, 519; Anasazi, Pueblo III, 137; Fort Ancient, 285; Old Iroquois, 256; Ozark Bluff Dweller, 339, Whittlesey, 281

Survey, archeological, 5

Swarts Village, New Mexico, 211

Sweat lodges, Upper Columbia, 445

Sweet potatoes, 80

Sweetwater Polychrome pottery, 171

Sweetwater Red-on-Gray pottery, 171

Swift Creek Culture, 376, 382, 384

Sword (batten), weaving, 62; *see also* Weaving

Swords: Fort Ancient, 286; Hopewell, 270; Key Marco, 395; Ocmulgee Fields, 388

Sylvid-centralid, Copena, 351

Sylvids, 231-32, 254, 256, 259, 262, 267, 278; Aztalan, 313; Browns Valley, 299; Copell, 400; Effigy Mound, 303; Florida area, 390; Fort Ancient, 285; Hamilton, 350; Kansas Hopewell, 325; Lauderdale, 346; Laurel, 307; Marksville, 406; Mille Lacs, 309; Morton, 292; Oneota, 316; Savannah River, 371; Swift Creek, 376; Tchefuncte, 401; Upper Republican, 326; Whittlesey, 281; Wisconsin Hopewell, 306; Younge, 280; *see also* People; Physical traits

Syphilis: Hopewell, 267; Middle Mississippi, 353

Tablets, 39; Adena, 265; Key Marco, 398

Tampico culture, 295

Taos, 159, 165, 166, 333

Taos River, 167
Tapir, 390
Tarahumara civilization, 217
Tchamahia, 139
Tchefuncte culture, 348, 401-4, 405, 406
Teeth: animal, 47; human incisor, 17; *see also* Alligator teeth; Beaver teeth; Shark teeth
Temper: metal, 24; pottery, 51, 60
Temple Mound period: Caddo area, 421-24; Middle Southern area, 345, 353-61, 367
Temple Mound I period: Georgia area, 378-80, 382-84, 388, 389; Lower Mississippi Valley area, 399, 411-15
Temple Mound II period: Georgia area, 385-88, 389; Lower Mississippi Valley area, 399, 415-19
Temples: Aztalan, 313; Caddo, 422; Coles Creek, 411, 412; Etowah, 387; Fort Ancient, 285; Fort Walton, 394; Lamar, 385; Lower Mississippi Valley area, 400; Middle Mississippi, 354; Middle Mississippi in Illinois, 294; Middle Mississippi in Ohio, 284; Plaquemine, 416; Savannah, 379; Swift Creek, 376; Troyville, 409, 411
Ten Lost Tribes of Israel; *see* Israel, Ten Lost Tribes of
Tennessee, 221, 267, 344, 345, 347, 353
Tennessee River, Lauderdale, 345
Tents: Original Eskimo, 473; Post-Punuk, 488; Thule, 506; Upper Republican, 326; *see also* Houses; Villages
Terraces, 159, 200, 283; *see also* Villages
Tesuque, 167
Tewa language, 100, 165, 166, 167
Texas, 219, 342, 409, 411, 421; *see also* Southwestern Texas area
Textiles; *see* Cloth; Weaving, bags, and textiles
Thimbles: Birnirk, 487; Thule, 507
Thompson River region, 444, 452-55
Thread, Ozark Bluff Dweller, 340
Three Circle Neck Corrugated pottery, 208
Three Circle period; *see* Mogollon-Mimbres culture
Three Circle Red-on-White pottery, 207, 208
Throwing-stick; *see* Spear-thrower
Thule culture, 487, 501, 505-8
Tick Island culture, 391
Time sequences; *see* Charts; Chronology; Dating; Tree-ring dating
Tiou tribe, 417
Tlingit Indians, 462, 466, 469
Tlingit River, 74
Tobacco, Glacial Kame, 263
Toboggans: Okvik, 476; Old Bering Sea, 479; Post-Punuk, 488
Toggles: Late Kachemak Bay, 501; Okvik, heads, 475

Tombs, log: Adena, 266; Hopewell, 274; Ipiutak, 484; Koniag, 499; Late Aleut, 496; Macon Plateau, 384; Marksville, 409; *see also* Burials
Tonto cliff-dwellings, 215
Tonto Polychrome pottery, 152, 153, 192, 195, 215
Tools, utensils, and weapons: Adena, 265; Alexander, 348; Anasazi, Basket Maker, 105-6; Anasazi, Modified Basket Maker, 117-19, 144; Anasazi, Pueblo I, 122-23; Anasazi, Pueblo II, 127-28; Anasazi, Pueblo III, 139-40, 144; Anasazi, Pueblo IV, 155; Aztalan, 314-15; Baumer, 290-91; Big Bend Cave, 219, 220; Birnirk, 486; Black Rock Cave, 223; Bravo Valley, 222; Browns Valley, 299; Caddo, 422-23; Candy Creek, 349; Clam River, 312; Cochise, 86, 198; Cochise, Chiricahua, 88; 89; Cochise, San Pedro, 89; Cochise, Sulphur Spring, 87; Coles Creek, 414; Copell, 400; Copena, 352; Deptford, 374; Dismal River, 332; Dorset, 504; Early Aleut, 490-91, 492 (Fig. 118); Early Coastal, 247; Early Kachemak Bay, 499; Early Macon, 370; Effigy Mound, 304; Folsom, 84, 85; Fort Ancient, 285; Frontenac, 241; Glacial Kame, 262-63; Hamilton, 351; Hohokam, Classic, 193-94; Hohokam, Colonial, 179-81; Hohokam, Pioneer, 172-73; Hohokam, Sedentary, 185; Hopewell, 269; Indian Knoll, 260-61; Intrusive Mound, 278-79; Inugsuk, 508; Ipiutak, 481-82; Irene, 381; Kansas Hopewell, 325-26; Keshena, 311; Key Marco, 395, 396 (Fig. 94); Koniag, 499; Lamar, 385-86; Lamoka, 240; Late Aleut, 495; Late Kachemak Bay, 501; Lauderdale, 346; Laurel, 308-9; Laurentian I, 243; Laurentian II, 246; Lower Sacramento region, 432; Macon Plateau, 383-84; Maravillas, 219; Marksville, 407, 410; Middle Aleut, 493; Middle Columbia region, 455; Middle Kachemak Bay, 500; Middle Mississippi, 355; Middlesex, 249; Mille Lacs, 310; Mira Creek, 324; Mogollon-Mimbres, Chihuahua, 216; Mogollon-Mimbres, Georgetown, 206; Mogollon-Mimbres, Mimbres, 212-13; Mogollon-Mimbres, Pine Lawn, 203-4; Mogollon-Mimbres, San Francisco, 207; Mogollon-Mimbres, Three Circle, 209; Morton, 293; Natchezan, 418-19; Nebraska, 330; New York Hopewell, 250; Northwest Coast area, 465-66, 467 (Fig. 113); Ocmulgee Fields, 388; Okvik, 474-75; Old Bering Sea, 478-79; Old Copper, 300-302; Old Iroquois, 256; Old Signal Butte, 321-22; Oneota, 316-17; Orient, 248; Original

Eskimo, 473–74; Owasco, 255; Ozark Bluff Dweller, 340; Plaquemine, 416; Point Peninsula, 252; Post-Punuk, 488; Poverty Point, 405; Pre-Koniag, 496; Promontory, 226; Proto-Bluff Dweller, 338; Puebloid, 225; Punuk, 485; Red Ocher, 291–92; Savannah, 379; Savannah River, 371; Snake-Clearwater Region, 459; southeastern Nevada, 227; southeastern Oregon, 228; Sterns Creek, 323; Swift Creek, 377–78; Tchefuncte, 402, 403 (Fig. 99); Thompson River region, 452; Thule, 506; Tick Island, 391; time to make, 31, 32; Upper Columbia region, 446; Upper Republican, 327; Weeden Island, 393–94; Whittlesey, 282; Wilmington, 375; Wisconsin Hopewell, 306; Younge, 280

Top-Layer culture, 342–43

Topography: Middle Southern area, 344; Ozark Plateau area, 337; *see also* Physiography

Towers, Aztalan, 313

Towns: Anasazi, Pueblo III, abandoned, 146; Anasazi, Pueblo IV, open, 150; Mogollon-Mimbres, Mimbres, abandoned, 164; *see also* Villages

Toys, 47

Trade and commerce, 40, 45, 48, 66–75; Arctic, 75; California, 73; eastern United States, 72–73; expeditions, 67, 72; Hopewell, 268; manufactured goods, 67; medium of exchange, 68; middlemen, 69, 70; Northwest Coast, 74; Plateau, 74; pottery, 116, 175, 177, 178, 193, 222; Prehistoric Yuma, 438; raw materials, 67, 71; routes, 69, 70; Southwest, 69–71

Trailing, pottery finish, 56

Traits, physical, 16–19; *see also* People

Transitional Sacramento, 432

Transportation, 20; *see also* Travel and transport

Traps: Northwest Coast area, 465; Thompson River region, 453; Thule, 506; Upper Columbia region, 446

Travel and transport: Birnirk, 487; Dorset, 504–5; Early Aleut, 491; glacial period, 81; Inugsuk, 508; Ipiutak, 483; Key Marco, 395; Koniag, 499; Late Aleut, 495; Middle Aleut, 494; Middle Columbia region, 457; Natchezan, 419; Okvik, 475–76; Original Eskimo, 474; Post-Punuk, 488; Pre-Koniag, 497; Punuk, 485; Snake-Clearwater region, 460; Thompson River region, 454; Thule, 507; Upper Columbia region, 451

Trays: Key Marco, 395; Mogollon-Mimbres, Chihuahua, 215; Okvik, 475; Old Bering Sea, 479; *see also* Tools, utensils, and weapons

Treasure, sought by Coronado, 157

Tree-ring dating (dendrochronology), 11, 12 (and Fig. 3), 13, 79, 80, 177, 178, 238, 513

Trees; *see* Vegetation

Trephining: Northwest Coast area, 464; Younge, 281

Trident, Punuk, 485 (Fig. 117)

Trimmers, wick, Thule, 507

Tropical agricultural complex, eastern North America, 234

Tropical forests, 80

Troughed metates; *see* Metates

Trousers: Post-Punuk, 488; Thule, 507; *see also* Costume

Troyville culture, 339, 353, 375, 392, 409–11, 415, 416

Tsimshian Indians, 462, 469

Tularosa Black-on-White pottery, 139

Tunica tribe, 417

Tunnel, house: Ipiutak, 481; Old Bering Sea, 477

Turkey, 105, 114, 121, 137, 171, 192, 202, 418

Turner site, 267

Turquoise, 67, 71, 216

Turquoise Mountains, 71

Turtle shell, 47

Tusayan Black-on-White pottery, 138, 139

Tusayan Polychrome pottery, 139

Twilled basketry, 139

Twilled plaiting, 65

Twining (twined), 65, 109, 119, 219; *see also* Weaving

Tyuonyi, 151, 165

Uaxactun, 79

Ulus, 31, 37; Post-Punuk, 246 (Fig. 69), 488; *see also* Knives

Umiak: Birnirk, 487; Dorset, 504; Ipiutak, 483; Koniag, 499; Late Aleut, 495; Middle Aleut, 494; Okvik, 475; Old Bering Sea, 480; Post-Punuk, 488; Pre-Koniag, 497; Thule, 507; *see also* Kayak

Unfired pottery, 116

United States, Indians in history of, 23

Upper Columbia region, 442, 444–46

Upper Gila River, 149

Upper Little Colorado area, 154

Upper Republican culture, 326–28, 331, 332, 333

Ural Mountains, 20

Utah, northern; *see* Northern Utah area

Ute language, 99

Utensils; *see* Tools, utensils, and weapons

Utility pottery, 151, 152

Vahki Plain pottery, 171
Vahki Red pottery, 171
Vancouver Island, 454, 462, 464
Vanderburgh County, Indiana, 283
Vantage, Canada, 455
Vargas, Diego de, 157
Vegetation: Caddo Area, 421; California, 427; East Eskimo area, 503; Florida area, 390; Georgia area, 369; Illinois area, 289; Lower Mississippi Valley area, 399; Middle Southern area, 344; Northeastern area, 239; northern Utah, 223; Northwest Coast area, 463; Northwest Eskimo area, 473; Ohio area, 259; Plains area, 319; Plateau area, 442–43; southeastern Nevada, 227; southeastern Oregon, 278; Southwest Eskimo area, 490; southwestern Texas, 218; Wisconsin-Minnesota area, 297
Ventana Cave, 83, 93, 198
Ventilator shaft, 211
Verde River, 149
Verde Valley, 70
Vermont, 248, 254
Vessels: Hamilton, Steatite, 351; Hohokam, Pioneer, 171, 173; Inugsuk, coopered, 508; Lauderdale, stone, 346; Point Peninsula, steatite, 253; Post-Punuk, wood, 488; Poverty Point, stone, 405; *see also* Buckets; Tools, utensils, and weapons
Victoria Island, 75
Villa Ahumada pottery, 215
Villages: Adena, 264; Anasazi, Modified Basket Maker, 111–12, 144; Anasazi, Pueblo I, 121; Anasazi, Pueblo II, 125–26; Anasazi, Pueblo III, 130–37; Anasazi, Pueblo IV, 150–51; Anasazi, Pueblo V, 160–67; Aztalan, 313; Baumer, 290; Big Bend Cave, 219; Birnirk, 486; Bravo Valley, 222; Caddo, 422; Candy Creek, 348; Clam River, 312; Coles Creek, 411; Copena, 352; Deptford, 374; Dismal River, 331; Dorset, 503–4; Early Aleut, 490; Early Coastal, 247; Effigy Mound, 303; Folsom, 83; Fort Ancient, 285; Frontenac, 241; Hamilton, 350; Hohokam, Classic; 190, 191; Hohokam, Colonial, 174; Hohokam, Pioneer, 169; Hohokam, Sedentary; 182; Hopewell, 267–68; Indian Knoll, 260; Intrusive Mound, 278; Inugsuk, 508, Ipiutak, 481; Irene, 380; Kansas Hopewell, 325; Keshena, 310; Key Marco, 395; Koniag, 498; Lamar, 385; Lamoka, 240; Late Aleut, 495; Late Kachemak Bay, 501; Lauderdale, 347; Laurel, 307–8; Laurentian I, 243; Laurentian II, 246; Macon Plateau, 383–84; Marksville, 406; Middle Aleut, 493; Middle Kachemak Bay, 500; Middle Mississippi, 353–55; Middle Mississippi in Illinois, 294; Middlesex, 249; Mille Lacs, 309; Mira Creek, 323–24; Mogollon-Mimbres, Chihuahua, 215; Mogollon-Mimbres, Georgetown, 206; Mogollon-Mimbres, Mimbres, 210; Mogollon-Mimbres, Pine Lawn, 200; Mogollon-Mimbres, San Francisco, 206; Mogollon-Mimbres, Three Circle, 207; Morton, 292; Natchezan, 417; Nebraska, 329; Northwest Coast area, 462, 464–65; Ocmulgee Fields, 387; Okvik, 474; Old Bering Sea, 477; Old Iroquois, 256; Old Signal Butte, 320–21; Oneota, 316; Orient, 248; Original Eskimo, 473; Owasco, 254; Ozark Bluff Dweller, 339; Plaquemine, 415; Plateau, 443; Point Peninsula, 252; Post-Punuk, 487–88; Poverty Point, 404; Pre-Koniag 496; Proto-Bluff Dweller, 338; Puebloid, 225; Punuk, 484; Savannah, 378–79; Savannah River, 371; southeastern Nevada, 227; Sterns Creek, 322; Swift Creek, 376; Tchefuncte, 401; Thule, 505–6; Troyville, 409; Upper Republican, 326; Weeden Island, 393; Whittlesey, 281; Wilmington, 375; Wisconsin Hopewell, 306; Younge, 280
"Vinland," 15
Vision, 24
Visors, Late Aleut, 495
Vomitorium, Macon Plateau, 383

Wahluke, 455
Wall poles, 191
"Walled-house" mound, 191
Walls: adobe, 190; earthen, 267, 409
Walpi, 146, 161
Wampum, 68
Warp, 62, 65; *see also* Weaving
Washington, state of, 463
Watchtower, Middle Mississippi culture in Ohio area, 284
Waterproof coats, 480
Weapons; *see* Tools, utensils, and weapons
Weaving, bags, and textiles (textiles, weaving tools, implements, weaves), 61–65, 194; Anasazi, Basket Maker, 109; Anasazi, Modified Basket Maker, 119, 145; Anasazi Pueblo I, 124; Anasazi, Pueblo III, 141, 143, 145; Anasazi, Pueblo IV, 156; batten, 62; Big Bend Cave, 220; Black Rock Cave, 223; Caddo, 423; Clam River, 312; comb, 62; Copena, 352; finger method, 61, 63; heddle, 62; Hohokam, Classic, 193–94; Hohokam, Colonial, 181; Hohokam, Sedentary, 186; loom, 62; loom weights, 155; Middle Mississippi, 356, 360; Mogollon-

Mimbres, Chihuahua, 213, 215; Mogollon-Mimbres, Mimbres, 213; Mogollon-Mimbres, Three Circle, 209; Navaho, 158; Old Iroquois, 256; Ozark Bluff Dweller, 340; Puebloid, 225, 226; shed, 62; southeastern Oregon, 228; techniques of, 63, 64 (and Fig. 11), 65; trade in, 68, 73; warp, 62; weft, 62; Wisconsin Hopewell, 306; *see also* Cloth

Wedel, Waldo, 335

Wedges: Early Aleut, 491; Early Coastal, 247; Early Kachemak Bay, 500; Ipiutak, 483; Late Kachemak Bay, 501; Middle Columbia region, 457; Old Bering Sea, 478; Point Peninsula, 253; Pre-Koniag, 497; Snake-Clearwater region, 460; Thompson River region, 454; Thule, 507

Weeden Island culture, 392, 393–94

"Weeping-eye" motif, Southern Death Cult, 363, 364 (Fig. 89), 365 (Fig. 91)

Weft, 62, 65

Weft-warp openwork technique," Hohokam, Sedentary, 186

Weights, spear-thrower (atlatl, throwing-stick weights), 29, 31, 38; Adena, 265; Anasazi, Basket Maker, 106; Caddo, 423; Early Coastal, 247; Hopewell, 269; Intrusive Mound, 279; Lauderdale, 346; Laurentian I, 243; Marksville, 407; Middlesex, 249; Mille Lacs, 310; Point Peninsula, 252; Savannah River, 372; Swift Creek, 377

Weirs: Boylston fish-weir site, 93; Middle Columbia region, 456; Northwest Coast area, 465; Post-Punuk, 488; Thompson River region, 453; Upper Columbia region, 446

West Virginia, 263, 285

Whalebone, 47

Whaling, Northwest Coast area, 466

Wheeler Basin, 345

Whetstones: Candy Creek, 349; Deptford, 374; Early Kachemak Bay, 500; Hamilton, 351; Hohokam, Colonial, 179; Hohokam, Pioneer, 173; Hohokam, Sedentary, 185; Ipiutak, 483; Irene, 381; Lamoka, 241; Late Kachemak Bay, 501; Laurentian I, 244; Old Bering Sea, 478; Point Peninsula, 253; Pre-Koniag, 497; Savannah River, 373; Swift Creek, 378; Tchefuncte, 402; Weeden Island, 393

Whistles: Frontenac, 242; Hopewell, 274; Point Peninsula, 253

White people, 17, 23

Whitewater Creek, 85

Whittlesey culture, 281–83

Whorls: Anasazi, Pueblo IV, 156; Inugsuk, 508; Northwest Coast area, 468

Wichita Indians, 333

Wickerwork, 65

Wigwams: Early Coastal, 247; Fort Ancient, 285; Middlesex, 249; Younge, 280

Willoughby, C. C., 44

Wilmington culture, 375, 378

Wilson Basin, 345

Winnebago Indians, 317

Wisconsin, 255, 267, 277, 299, 305, 353

Wisconsin-Minnesota area, 298–318, 505; chronology, 298 (Chart VIII), 516 (Fig. 122)

Wiyot Indians, 428

Wolf-killers, Thule, 506

Wood, trade in, 75

Wood-working, 193, 465, 466; *see also* Tools, utensils, and weapons

Woodland cultures, 294

Wound plugs: Birnirk, 486; Old Bering Sea, 478; Post-Punuk, 488; Thule, 506

Wrenches: Dismal River, 332; Oneota, 316; Upper Columbia region, 446; *see also* Arrow-shaft straighteners

Wrist guards: Birnirk, 486; Punuk, 485 (and Fig. 117)

Writing, 21, 79; *see also* Pictographs, Puebloid; Runic inscriptions

Yakima Valley, 455, 457, 458, 459, 460

Yakutat Bay, 462

Yamassee Indians, 382

Yankton Dakota pottery, 54

Yellow ocher: Clam River, 312; Laurel, 309; Old Signal Butte, 322

Yellowstone Park, 72, 328

Yokut Indians, 433

Younge culture, 280–81, 313

Yucca, 61

Yukon River, v, 513

Yuma farmers, 519

Yuma points, 84

Yurok Indians, 428

Zoögeography, 20

Zuñi, 70, 146, 154, 167; area, 149, 152, 197; Indians, 166; Spanish conquest of, 156

Zuñi glazes pottery, 139